www.wadsworth.com

wadsworth.com is the World Wide Web site for Wadsworth and is your direct source to dozens of online resources.

At *wadsworth.com* you can find out about supplements, demonstration software, and student resources. You can also send email to many of our authors and preview new publications and exciting new technologies.

wadsworth.com
Changing the way the world learns®

The Research Process in the Human Services

Behind the Scenes

LESLIE B. ALEXANDER
Bryn Mawr College

PHYLLIS SOLOMON
University of Pennsylvania

THOMSON

BROOKS/COLE

Australia • Brazil • Canada • Mexico • Singapore • Spain • United Kingdom • United States

THOMSON
™
BROOKS/COLE

The Research Process in the Human Services: Behind the Scenes
Leslie B. Alexander/Phyllis Solomon

Executive Editor: *Lisa Gebo*
Assistant Editor: *Alma Dea Michelena*
Editorial Assistant: *Sheila Walsh*
Marketing Manager: *Caroline Concilla*
Marketing Assistant: *Rebecca Weisman*
Editorial Production Manager: *Michael Burggren*
Senior Print Buyer: *Mary Beth Hennebury*

Advertising Project Manager: *Tami Strang*
Permissions Editor: *Kiely Sisk*
Production Service/Compositor:
   Interactive Composition Corporation
Cover Designer: *Brenda Duke Design*
Cover Printer: *Transcontinental*
Printer: *Transcontinental*
Cover Image: © *Jean Louis Batt/Getty Images*

Printed in Canada
1 2 3 4 5 6 7 09 08 07 06 05

For more information about our products, contact us at:
Thomson Learning Academic Resource Center
1-800-423-0563

For permission to use material from this text or product, submit a request online at
http://www.thomsonrights.com
Any additional questions about permissions can be submitted by email to
thomsonrights@thomson.com

Library of Congress Control Number:
2005922303

ISBN 0-534-62610-6

Thomson Higher Education
10 Davis Drive
Belmont, CA 94002-3098
USA

Asia (including India)
Thomson Learning
5 Shenton Way
#01-01 UIC Building
Singapore 068808

Australia/New Zealand
Thomson Learning Australia
102 Dodds Street
Southbank, Victoria 3006
Australia

Canada
Thomson Nelson
1120 Birchmount Road
Toronto, Ontario M1K 5G4
Canada

UK/Europe/Middle East/Africa
Thomson Learning
High Holborn House
50-51 Bedford Road
London WC1R 4LR
United Kingdom

Latin America
Thomson Learning
Seneca, 53
Colonia Polanco
11560 Mexico
D.F. Mexico

Spain (including Portugal)
Thomson Paraninfo
Calle Magallanes, 25
28015 Madrid, Spain

Contents

ACKNOWLEDGMENTS   X

FOREWORD   XII

CONTRIBUTORS   XV

INTRODUCTION   XXI

SECTION I—HUMAN SERVICE EXPERIMENTS, QUASI-EXPERIMENTS, AND META-ANALYSIS   1

Brief Overview of Section by Editors

Randomized Experiments

CHAPTER 1   3

McKay, M. M., Stoewe, J., McCadam, K., & Gonzales, J. (1998). Increasing access to child mental health services for urban children and their caregivers. *Health & Social Work, 23,* 9–15.

Commentary by Mary M. McKay

CHAPTER 2   20

Zanis, D. A., Coviello, D., Alterman, A. I., & Appling, S. E. (2001). A community-based trial of vocational problem-solving to increase employment among methadone patients. *Journal of Substance Abuse Treatment, 21,* 19–26.

Commentary by David A. Zanis

Quasi-experiments

CHAPTER 3   41

Phillips, E., Barrio, C., & Brekke, J. S. (2001). The impact of ethnicity on prospective functional outcomes from community-based psychosocial rehabilitation for persons with schizophrenia. *Journal of Community Psychology, 29,* 657–673.

Commentary by John S. Brekke

CHAPTER 4   66

Glisson, C., & Hemmelgarn, A. (1998). The effects of organizational climate and interorganizational coordination on the quality and outcomes of children's service systems. *Child Abuse & Neglect, 22,* 401–421.

Commentary by Charles Glisson

CHAPTER 5   98

Marshall, T., & Solomon, P. (2004). Confidentiality intervention: Effects on provider-consumer-family collaboration. *Research on Social Work Practice, 14,* 3–13.

Commentary by Tina Marshall

Meta-analysis

CHAPTER 6   122

Wilson, S. J., Lipsey, M. W., & Soydan, H. (2003). Are mainstream programs for juvenile delinquency less effective with minority youth than majority youth? A meta-analysis of outcomes research. *Research on Social Work Practice, 13,* 3–26.

Commentary by Sandra Jo Wilson

SECTION II—CORRELATIONAL/OBSERVATIONAL DESIGNS 149

Brief Overview of Section by Editors

Cross-Sectional

CHAPTER 7   151

Smith, B. D., & Marsh, J. C. (2002). Client-service matching in substance abuse treatment for women with children. *Journal of Substance Abuse Treatment, 22,* 161–168.

Commentary by Jeanne C. Marsh and Brenda D. Smith

Longitudinal/Cohort

CHAPTER 8   171

Morrow-Howell, N. L., Proctor, E. K., & Rozario, P. A. (2001). How much is enough? Perspectives of care recipients and professionals on the sufficiency of in-home care. *The Gerontologist, 41,* 723–732.

Commentary by Nancy L. Morrow-Howell, Enola K. Proctor, and Philip A. Rozario

CHAPTER 9   194

Solomon, P., Draine, J., & Marcus, S. (2002). Predicting incarceration of clients of a psychiatric probation and parole service. *Psychiatric Services, 53,* 50–56.

Commentary by Phyllis Solomon and Jeffrey Draine

Case Control Designs

CHAPTER 10   214

Herman, D. B., Susser, E. S., Struening, E. L., & Link, B. L. (1997). Adverse Childhood experiences: Are they risk factors for adult homelessness? *American Journal of Public Health, 87,* 249–255.

Commentary by Dan Herman

CHAPTER 11   234

Wolfe, S., Toro, P., & McCaskill, P. (1999). A comparison of homeless and matched housed adolescents on family environment variables. *Journal of Research on Adolescence, 9,* 53–66.

Commentary by Paul A. Toro, Susan Wolfe, and Pamela McCaskill

SECTION III—QUALITATIVE METHODS   253
Brief Overview of Section by Editors

Intensive Interviews

CHAPTER 12   255
Parks, C. (1999). Lesbian identity development: An examination of differences across generations. *American Journal of Orthopsychiatry, 69,* 347–361.
Commentary by Cheryl A. Parks

CHAPTER 13   281
Zippay, A. (2001). Dynamics of income packaging: A 10-year longitudinal study. *Social Work, 47,* 291–300.
Commentary by Allison Zippay

Focus Groups

CHAPTER 14   302
Kruzich, J., Friesen, B., Williams-Murphy, T., & Longley, M. (2002). Voices of African American families: Perspectives on residential treatment. *Social Work, 47,* 461–470.
Commentary by Jean M. Kruzich and Barbara J. Friesen

Ethnographic Methods

CHAPTER 15   326
Alverson, H., Alverson, M., & Drake, R. E. (2001). Social patterns of substance-use among people with dual diagnoses. *Mental Health Services Research, 3,* 3–14.
Commentary by Hoyt Alverson, Marianne Alverson, and Robert E. Drake

SECTION IV—MIXED METHODS   353
Brief Overview of Section by Editors

CHAPTER 16   354
Campbell, K., Baumohl, J., & Hunt, S. R. (2003). The bottom line: Employment and barriers to work among former SSI DA&A beneficiaries. *Journal of Contemporary Drug Problems, 30,* 195–240.
Commentary by Jim Baumohl

CHAPTER 17   387

Korbin, J. E., Coulton, C. J., Chard, S., Platt-Houston, C., & Su, M. (1998). Impoverishment and child maltreatment in African American and European American neighborhoods. *Development and Psychopathology, 10,* 215–233.

Commentary by Claudia Coulton and Jill Korbin

SECTION V—USE OF AVAILABLE DATA   417

Brief Overview of Section by Editors

CHAPTER 18   418

DePanfilis, D., & Zuravin, S. J. (2002). The effect of services on the recurrence of child maltreatment. *Child Abuse & Neglect, 26,* 187–205.

Commentary by Diane DePanfilis

CHAPTER 19   443

Hollingsworth, L. D. (2002). Transracial adoptees in the media: 1986–1996. *American Journal of Orthopsychiatry, 72,* 289–293.

Commentary by Leslie Doty Hollingsworth

CHAPTER 20   459

Snowden, L. R. (2001). Social embeddedness and psychological well-being among African Americans and Whites. *American Journal of Community Psychology, 29,* 519–536.

Commentary by Lonnie R. Snowden

INDEX   481

Acknowledgments

Our major thanks go to the authors of the research articles and commentaries, who made this book possible. We deeply appreciate their interest, their responsiveness to our requests and suggestions, and their willingness to take us backstage to better understand what was involved when they planned and conducted their research.

We also thank Alma Dea Michelena, our editor at Brooks/Cole, who encouraged us from the very beginning, providing prompt answers to our myriad questions and making the whole process as easy as possible for us. We also wish to thank the reviewers, who read the draft with speed, thoroughness, and thoughtful commentary. We are delighted that the format of the book resonated with them, making us feel more confident that our approach might be useful to students and professional researchers in the human services. The reviewers were Carol Gagliano, Florida State University; Allen Rubin, University of Texas, Austin; James D. Stafford, University of Mississippi; and Marian Swindell, Mississippi State University. We also thank Allen Rubin for his generous foreword.

We both thank John Alexander for helping us obtain permissions, for superb editorial work, and for some wonderful dinners.

LESLIE'S ADDITIONAL THANKS

I want to thank the late M. Patricia Golden, whose 1976 volume, *The Research Experience,* inspired the format of this book. I benefited from the knowledge, wit, and charm of Richard Welna, an editor at F. E. Peacock (the publisher of Golden's book), who accepted an early draft for Peacock before the book was sold to Wadsworth/Thomson Learning. Julia Littell, Associate Professor in the Graduate School of Social Work and Social Research at Bryn Mawr was also involved during the incubation period of this book. I very much appreciate her contribution to the conceptual organization of the book, and articles that are included in this text.

I thank my coeditor, Phyllis Solomon, for making the collaborative process so fruitful and pleasant. We also had a lot of fun.

My thanks also to William W. Vosburgh, now an Emeritus Professor at Bryn Mawr, who first brought the Golden volume to my attention, and with whom I taught research design in the 1970s and '80s. Bill deemed the Golden text a "winner," and taught me a large part of what I currently know about research and other topics. I am grateful to the many students to whom I have taught research design over the years. They have always made me want to communicate the excitement that actually doing research can provide. I hope that this volume will be helpful in that regard. I also thank Marcia Martin and Raymond Albert for making the School a pleasant and productive place to work, and Peggy Robinson for her excellent technical assistance on this project.

And finally, to my family, I owe continuing gratitude. I thank my three children, John, Emily, and Caroline, and my daughter-in-law, Roberta. They have always been a source of great pride and delight to me. While they were pleased that their mother (and mother-in-law) was writing a book, they didn't want too many details. And, finally, to my husband John, my constant and best supporter and marvelous companion, my thanks for his care, and for making me feel every day as if I deserved all of those awards that Meryl Streep, Bette Midler, and Whoopi Goldberg keep winning.

PHYLLIS'S ADDITIONAL THANKS

I would like to thank Leslie for the wonderful opportunity to collaborate with her on this book. It was an intellectually stimulating experience, and one that provided me with confirmation that other researchers have shared similar trials and tribulations in the research process. It was enjoyable working with Leslie, due to her easygoing style and her choices of work venues that best suited my vices.

I would also like to thank the many graduate students in my research classes, who have provided me with an understanding of what they needed to learn in order to become true researchers and not mere technicians. They have taught me the importance of providing real-life examples of the conduct of research, which give a clearer picture of what is truly required.

And finally, I would like to thank my sister, Barbara, who only wanted to know when she would receive her copy of the book!

Foreword

S tudents and practitioners seeking to learn how to conduct research in the human services need to learn a lot more than is typically taught in classroom courses and texts on research methods. No matter how well they may understand such topics as avoiding measurement and sampling error, constructing rigorous experimental and quasi-experimental designs, qualitative methods, and data analysis, that understanding alone won't adequately prepare them for the pragmatic obstacles and conundrums they will encounter when they attempt to implement their pristine (or not-so-pristine) research protocols in real service settings. Traditionally, researchers have to learn from the school of hard knocks about the many practical pitfalls that they inevitably will encounter.

Most human service agencies are overburdened, and research is a relatively low priority for most agencies and their employees. This can be frustrating, since research is an extremely high priority for the researcher—perhaps it is their *raison d'être*. Researchers must strike a delicate balance in trying to get agency staff to follow through (in supporting and complying with the research protocol to which they agreed), and yet not alienating them (and, perhaps, thus losing their willingness to participate in any future research). Finding this balance is a challenge, one that entails additional work and constant follow-up on the part of the researcher.

Moreover, some administrators and practitioners who request honest evaluations will later try to influence program evaluators to slant their methods or findings, to yield implications that make the agencies look good (and perhaps enhance funding prospects). The same administrators and practitioners might find fault with every trivial flaw in a study if it yields findings that they don't like, while praising the merits of seriously flawed studies that make them or their agencies look good.

I have encountered practitioners who, no matter how well I have explained my study and no matter how emphatically they have agreed to comply with the research procedures, will violate those procedures. For example, practitioners have provided an experimental group's intervention to clients in the control group. Some practitioners in this circumstance just forget; others feel bad for the client and decide (without telling the researcher) that their concern for the client takes precedence over the research design. Still others, despite saying that they understand the research design, really do not understand it—and thus do not even realize that they are violating it.

I've heard of practitioners who, in administering posttests to experimental group clients, introduce the tests with biasing comments like, "When you complete this instrument you can show how much this program helped you and how you have improved more than the other treatment (or control) group."

Researchers who rely on practitioners to complete their research instruments—even if the study has been adequately explained, and the practitioners have promised their compliance—should not be surprised if some practitioners eventually become resistant, and either refuse to complete the instruments, or rush through them haphazardly when the time comes to actually provide the data. Researchers who rely on administrators or other practitioners to implement their case assignment protocol (through random assignment or an overflow design, for example) often learn after the fact that the practitioners deviated from the research protocol, and rigged the assignment by putting cases in treatment groups according to their administrative or clinical agenda and vested interests. (For example, they might put clients who appear most motivated to improve in the group that receives their services, and less motivated clients in the control group.)

If you rely on administrators' estimates for your projected sample size, good luck! I did so in two experimental studies evaluating practice effectiveness. In one, it took me three years to attain a sample size of 39 clients, despite administrator and practitioner assurances that I would have more than 100 in the first year. In the other, I was assured of getting approximately 25–50 clients per year, but due to various unanticipated agency problems only 3 clients had completed the study after 18 months!

Projections may be off because administrators don't anticipate a slackening in new referrals, or forget that many of the referrals they project for your study need to be assigned elsewhere, such as to students in field placements in their agency. They may underestimate attrition problems, such as when clients in a residential treatment program run away before the study is completed, or must be transferred to less restrictive or more restrictive settings due to their good or bad behavior. Sometimes things happen that nobody can anticipate—such as changes in state policies, which require clients to be discharged before they have completed enough sessions of the treatment you are evaluating.

I could go on and on. The myriad pitfalls that I have encountered—and that many of the doctoral students whose dissertations I have supervised have also encountered—have led me to emphasize in my research courses the fact that the hardest part of research is not designing a methodologically rigorous study. Instead, the hardest part is finding a setting in which it will be feasible to carry out such a study, and then—in carrying it out—to avoid real-world practice pitfalls like the ones I have mentioned.

Often, these pitfalls are understandable given the many burdens that confront agencies. We researchers should be sensitive to these burdens, and recognize that things sometimes go awry despite the best intentions and best efforts of agency administrators and practitioners, who must grapple with other important priorities.

How can educators in the human service professions better prepare future researchers for these real-world difficulties? Some doctoral programs require a research practicum as part of such preparation. Doctoral dissertations may help, too. But these steps are not enough. Moreover, students should learn about these difficulties *before* they begin a research practicum or a doctoral dissertation. Although some research texts discuss these issues, more is needed. That's where this book comes in.

This volume fills a gap by focusing exclusively on valuable, real-world illustrations of efforts to implement the gamut of research methods, and by providing invaluable authors' commentaries about their experiences in grappling with a range of challenges: topic selection, problem formulation, measurement, sampling, research design (both quantitative and qualitative), IRBs and ethics, getting funded, problems in data collection, missing data and data analysis, and negotiating with agencies. In addition, the authors discuss the strengths and weaknesses of their own research in ways that illustrate the general strengths and weaknesses of the various research methods. Particularly valuable are the authors' discussions of how the realities of agency settings can pose unanticipated obstacles to the best-laid research plans, and how the authors had to modify their plans and negotiate with research settings when encountering these obstacles.

This book contains chapters written by some of the most highly respected researchers in the human services professions. Reading about the real-world challenges these authors faced throughout the research process provides a perspective that cannot be found elsewhere. The reader will learn many things from this book; especially useful will be learning to anticipate and grapple with these real-world challenges. But it is even more valuable that students and inexperienced researchers who read this book will be comforted, and their enthusiasm about research will be sustained, when they realize that even the best researchers in their profession (and in related professions) encountered difficulties with the real-world challenges that they, too, will inescapably encounter in their own emerging research careers.

Allen Rubin, Ph.D.
Bert Kruger Smith Centennial Professor in Social Work
School of Social Work
University of Texas at Austin

Contributors

Leslie B. Alexander received her M.S.S. and Ph.D. from the Graduate School of Social Work and Social Research at Bryn Mawr College, where she is Professor on the Lelia Woodruff Stokes Fund for Faculty Support and has chaired the College's IRB for a number of years. She is also an Adjunct Professor of Social Work in Psychiatry at the School of Medicine, University of Pennsylvania. Her current research interests include the examination of interpersonal processes in community-based services for the severely mentally ill, and the ethical dilemmas that lay research personnel face in carrying out research tasks in their own communities with vulnerable, often highly stigmatized research participants.

Hoyt Alverson, Ph.D., Professor of Anthropology, Dartmouth College, has conducted and written widely on anthropological research carried out in southern Africa. He is the author of two books, *Mind in the Heart of Darkness* (1978) and *Semantics and Experience* (1994); the former won both the Herskovits Prize of the African Studies Association and First Prize in the University of Chicago Folklore Competition. His most recent research and writing have focused on mental health and employment services for Euro-American, African American, and Hispanic/Latino American populations of the northeastern United States.

Marianne Alverson is Research Ethnographer, New Hampshire–Dartmouth Psychiatric Research Center. She is the author of *Under African Sun* (1987). She is also the author of several articles in professional journals reporting on her ethnographic field studies in New Hampshire on mental health services and on coping with, and recovery from, dual disorders (severe mental illness and addiction to drugs or alcohol). She has consulted regularly with many investigators working through the New Hampshire–Dartmouth Psychiatric Research Center on several aspects of ethnographic research methods employed in a community-based, longitudinal study of severe mental illness.

Jim Baumohl holds a doctorate in social welfare from the University of California, Berkeley, and is Professor and Director of the Doctoral Program at the Graduate School of Social Work and Social Research at Bryn Mawr College. Over the last 30 years he has written about homelessness, the history of alcohol and drug treatment, alcohol and drug control policy, and welfare policy. He is an editor of *Contemporary Drug Problems,* an interdisciplinary and international quarterly. He is currently interested in genial dissipation.

John Brekke, Ph.D., the Frances G. Larson Professor of Social Work Research in the School of Social Work at the University of Southern California, studies psychosocial aspects of schizophrenia. His current research focuses on three related areas: (1) the integration of psychobiological factors into psychosocial rehabilitation for individuals with schizophrenia; (2) the dissemination of evidence-based psychosocial practice for schizophrenia into community-based rehabilitation settings; and (3) the conceptualization and measurement of outcomes in schizophrenia.

Claudia J. Coulton, Ph.D., is the Lillian F. Harris Professor of Urban Social Research in the Mandel School of Applied Social Sciences, Case Western Reserve University, Cleveland. She is Co-Director of the Center on Urban Poverty and Social Change, which she founded in 1988 to conduct applied research, evaluation, and policy analysis related to urban poverty and community building. Dr. Coulton is the author of numerous journal articles, book chapters, and research reports on urban neighborhoods and families, and social welfare policy.

Diane DePanfilis, Ph.D., M.S.W., is Associate Professor and Assistant Dean for Research in the University of Maryland School of Social Work. She teaches research courses in the master's and doctoral programs, and leads a research team studying the impact of various community and child-welfare related interventions. Dr. DePanfilis is coauthor of *Child Protective Services: A Guide for Workers;* coeditor of the *Handbook for Child Protection Practice;* past President of the American Professional Society on the Abuse of Children (APSAC); and was named as the 2004 Research Lecturer of the Year by the University of Maryland, Baltimore. Dr. DePanfilis is particularly interested in ways to bridge the gap between research and practice.

Jeffrey Draine, Ph.D., is an Associate Professor in the School of Social Work and the Department of Psychiatry at the University of Pennsylvania, where he is affiliated with the Center for Mental Health Policy and Services Research. He is also Co-Director of the Center for Mental Health Services and Criminal Justice Research, based at Rutgers University. His work is focused on individuals with psychiatric disabilities and services for them, specifically in the intersection of the mental health and legal systems.

Robert E. Drake, M.D., Ph.D., is the Andrew Thomson Professor of Psychiatry and Community and Family Medicine at Dartmouth Medical School, and the Director of the New Hampshire–Dartmouth Psychiatric Research Center. He has been at Dartmouth for 20 years, and has spent much of that time developing and evaluating innovative community programs for persons with severe mental disorders. He is well known for his work in rehabilitation and health services research.

Barbara J. Friesen, Ph.D., is Professor of Social Work at Portland State University in Portland, Oregon. She serves as the Director of the Ph.D. Program in Social Work and Social Research, and also directs the Research and Training Center on Family Support and Children's Mental Health.

Dr. Friesen studies family and youth perspectives on their needs and their experiences with services, as well as service outcomes. She works to promote family-driven and culturally-responsive services.

Charles Glisson, Ph.D., is University Distinguished Research Professor and Director of the University of Tennessee Children's Mental Health Services Research Center (CMHSRC). He received his doctorate in social work from Washington University, and has directed interdisciplinary NIMH-funded research continuously since founding the CMHSRC 17 years ago. In addition to funding from NIMH, the CMHSRC has received funding from the National Institute of Drug Abuse, Health Resources Services Administration, Child and Maternal Health, Casey Family Program, Silberman Fund, Tennessee Bureau of Tenn Care, and the John D. and Catherine T. MacArthur Foundation. Dr. Glisson's research has focused on the organizational context of children's services, and the effectiveness of mental health, child welfare, and juvenile justice systems.

Daniel Herman, D.S.W., is Assistant Professor of Clinical Epidemiology at the Mailman School of Public Health at Columbia University. He is also a Research Scientist at New York State Psychiatric Institute, where he serves as the Director of Research in the Department of Social Work. Dr. Herman's current focus is on intervention research in the area of homelessness and psychosocial services for adults with severe mental disorders. He believes that researchers should devote more effort to carrying out rigorous evaluations of social work interventions, despite the many difficulties they will encounter.

Leslie Doty Hollingsworth, Ph.D., ACSW, is Associate Professor, University of Michigan School of Social Work. Her research focuses on the adoption and foster care of children in domestic and international contexts. She has published seminal works on identity and adoption. Currently researching parental adherence to child welfare reunification plans, she has recently begun pursuing a developing interest in the intricacies of embryo donation and adoption.

Jill E. Korbin, Ph.D., is currently Associate Dean of the College of Arts and Sciences, Professor of Anthropology, and Co-Director of the Schubert Center for Child Development and Childhood Studies Program at Case Western Reserve University. She received the Margaret Mead Award (1986) from the American Anthropological Association and the Society for Applied Anthropology, a Congressional Science Fellowship (1985–86) from the American Association for the Advancement of Science and the Society for Research in Child Development, and the Wittke Award for Excellence in Undergraduate Teaching (1992) from Case Western Reserve University. Korbin edited the book *Child Abuse and Neglect: Cross-cultural Perspectives* (1981, University of California Press), which was the first volume to examine the relationship of culture and child maltreatment, fatal child abuse, Ohio's Amish population, and the impact of neighborhood factors on child well-being and child maltreatment.

Jean M. Kruzich, Ph.D., is Associate Professor of Social Work at University of Washington in Seattle, and the Chair of the Administration Concentration in the M.S.W. program. Her research foci include identifying the influence of environmental and organizational factors on treatment outcomes, and eliciting consumers' perspectives on their service and treatment experiences.

Jeanne C. Marsh joined the faculty of the University of Chicago School of Social Service Administration in 1978. She now serves as George Herbert Jones Professor. She completed the M.S.W. (1975), Ph.D. (1977, Social Work and Psychology), and a post-doctoral fellowship (1978, in evaluation research, Institute for Social Research)—all at the University of Michigan. Her research focuses on service integration, substance abuse services, and services for women and families. She is currently completing a series of studies examining gender differences in the impact of comprehensive services in substance abuse treatment.

Pamela A. McCaskill is currently a Licensed Psychologist in private practice in the Detroit area, with a specialization in the assessment and treatment of children, adolescents, and families with a variety of presenting problems. Dr. McCaskill received her Ph.D. in Clinical Psychology from Wayne State University in 1997, followed by further training in pediatric psychology during her internship at the University of Florida. She has been active in several community service programs addressing the needs of high-risk adolescents, and has presented on many topics addressing the needs of children, including ADHD, depression, self-esteem, learning disabilities, and parenting the strong-willed child.

Tina Marshall, Ph.D., is a Clinical Research Specialist in the School of Medicine, Department of Psychiatry, University of Maryland, Baltimore. Her research interests include mental health services, particularly services for families of adults with severe mental illness. She's recently learned to drink lots of coffee so that she can keep up with work and her two-year-old daughter.

Mary M. McKay, Ph.D., is a Professor of Psychiatry and Community Medicine at the Mount Sinai School of Medicine, and the Assistant Director of Social Work in Psychiatry at the Mount Sinai Medical Center. Dr. McKay directs a program of federally funded research focused on identifying the mental health and prevention needs of urban youth and their families, and testing community and family-level prevention and service delivery strategies. Dr. McKay has also received two career awards from the National Institute of Mental Health, focused on identifying barriers and facilitators to child mental health service use and testing the impact of collaborative partnerships with parents on overcoming these barriers. Dr. McKay has published extensively and presents nationally and internationally.

Nancy Morrow-Howell, M.S.W., Ph.D., is the Ralph and Muriel Pumphrey Professor of Social Work at the George Warren Brown School of Social Work at Washington University. She teaches gerontology courses and serves as chair of the Ph.D. program. Her interests include community services to the elderly, and productive engagement in later life. Dr. Morrow-Howell is a fellow of the Gerontological Society of America, editor of the Practice Concepts section of *The Gerontologist,* and a national mentor for the Hartford Geriatric Social Work Scholars program.

Cheryl A. Parks, Ph.D., is an Associate Professor of Research at the University of Connecticut School of Social Work, where she teaches research design, substance abuse (theory and intervention), and data analysis. Her research and publications focus primarily on issues related to lesbian identity and alcohol use, lesbian parenting, and gender differences in alcohol use patterns and problems across diverse populations. In 2003, Dr. Parks received a four-year, NIAAA-funded K-award to develop a program of research on the effects of minority sexual identity and culture on alcohol use and alcohol-related problems in women.

Enola K. Proctor, Ph.D., Frank J. Bruno Professor of Social Work Research and Associate Dean for Research at the George Warren Brown School of Social Work at Washington University, directs the Center for Mental Health Services Research at Washington University. Her research interests center on social work practice in health, mental health, and long-term community care, as well as the development of knowledge to guide the delivery and evaluation of clinical social work. She serves as Editor-in-Chief for *Social Work Research.*

Philip A. Rozario, M.S.W., Ph.D., received his doctoral degree from the George Warren Brown School of Social Work and is currently an Assistant Professor at Adelphi University School of Social Work. His gerontological social work research interest includes caregiver well-being, service use of older adults, and productive engagement in later life. He received the 2003–2005 John A. Hartford Geriatric Social Work Faculty Scholars Award for developing his work on meaning construction in the face of chronic illnesses.

Brenda D. Smith is an Assistant Professor in the School of Social Welfare at the University at Albany, State University of New York. She received her Ph.D. in 1999 from the University of Chicago School of Social Service Administration. Her research focuses on service delivery in the child welfare system, organizational influences on practice, and the response of the child welfare system to parental substance use.

Lonnie R. Snowden, Ph.D., is Professor in the School of Social Welfare at the University of California, Berkeley, and Director of the Center for Mental Health Services Research. He also holds faculty appointments in Health Services and Policy Analysis in the U.C. Berkeley School of Public Health and in the Department of Psychology. Professor Snowden has been a mental health services researcher for almost 30 years, focusing on the roles of race, culture, and ethnicity in access to and outcomes of mental health treatment.

Phyllis Solomon, Ph.D., is a Professor in the School of Social Work and Professor of Social Work in Psychiatry at the University of Pennsylvania, where she is affiliated with the Center for Mental Health Policy and Services Research. She has been studying community mental health services for adults with severe mental illness and their families since 1974, when she was deinstitutionalized from a state psychiatric hospital where she conducted research on behavioral interventions for long-term patients. Her research has focused on family interventions, criminal justice and mental illness, consumer-delivered services, and factors related to the receipt of services.

Paul A. Toro, Ph.D., is Associate Professor at Wayne State University in Detroit. He was President of the Society for Community Research and Action (Division 27 of the American Psychological Association) in 2003–04. He and his Research Group on Homelessness and Poverty have conducted a wide range of studies on homelessness over the past two decades, including studies on homeless adults, families, and youth. His studies have compared homeless to matched housed samples, assessed prevalence and public opinion, evaluated interventions, provided careful assessment of mental disorders and substance abuse, tested social psychological theories, collected data across nations, analyzed media and professional coverage, and followed large homeless samples in longitudinal designs. For additional details on his research, see his web site at http://sun.science.wayne.edu/~ptoro/.

Sandra Jo Wilson, Ph.D., is a Research Associate at the Center for Evaluation Research and Methodology at the Vanderbilt Institute for Public Policy Studies. Her research interests are in the areas of meta-analysis, program evaluation, research methodology, and the prevention of antisocial behavior. Her recent research focuses on risk and intervention for juvenile delinquency, the link between antisocial behavior and school failure, and evaluating the impact of programs for the prevention of school violence. In 2003, she won the *Pro Humanitate* Award from the North American Resource Center for Child Welfare for the article reprinted in this volume.

Susan M. Wolfe received her Master of Science degree in Ecological Psychology from Michigan State University, and a Ph.D. in Human Development and Communication Sciences from the University of Texas at Dallas. She is currently a Program Analyst with the United States Department of Health and Human Services, Office of the Inspector General, Office of Evaluation and Inspections, at the Region VI Office in Dallas.

David A. Zanis, Ph.D., is presently an Associate Professor in the School of Social Administration at Temple University, where he teaches social welfare management, research methods, and substance abuse. He has a secondary academic appointment in the Department of Psychiatry, School of Medicine, University of Pennsylvania, where he conducts substance abuse research on several NIDA-funded projects. His interests focus on substance abuse treatment service delivery, batterer's intervention programs, and tobacco.

Allison Zippay, Ph.D., is an Associate Professor in the School of Social Work at Rutgers University. Her research includes work in the areas of poverty, employment policy, and community development. Her qualitative and ethnographic studies encompass poor and low-income groups including displaced workers, teen mothers, and welfare recipients.

Introduction

We owe the idea for the format of this book to the late M. Patrice Golden, whose 1976 volume, *The research experience,* served as an antidote to the typical research textbooks of its day. Just as we have done, her book, now almost 30 years old, provided published research articles that addressed major design approaches, with original commentaries by each of the authors, revealing the "story behind the research." It is one of the few books that students at the Graduate School of Social Work at Bryn Mawr College in the 1970s and '80s remember positively from their social work graduate training. For a research text, that is an accolade worth noting. We kept expecting someone to update the volume, or to produce one that consists of research articles, reflecting the diversity of research activities in which social workers and others in the human services are currently engaged. But nothing of the kind appeared; hence, this volume.

This book recognizes that for most social work and human service students, the research process remains shrouded in mystery and inspires fear and dread. The idea that research can be both fun and useful is not in students' lexicon. Equally surprising to many human service students is that research can have an important relationship to the "real" world of practice. Even for students who majored in the social and behavioral sciences as undergraduates, memories of research methods courses tend to be associated with "something mathematical" or "some type of experiment." This is often even more true for students who are not recent college graduates, of whom there are many in graduate training programs in a range of human service professions. Most students do not associate returning to graduate school with learning more about research, believing that those days are well behind them. They are a captive—but in most cases reluctant—audience.

Most students' notions of what is entailed in the research process come from journal articles that report the results of investigations. Such reports make the entire process of research seem pristine and linear, with no problems or delays. The researcher seems to be omniscient and always in control of every aspect of the research process. It also always appears that the entire operation went smoothly, with no deviations from the original research plan.

This book should also be of interest to those who have recently received advanced degrees in a range of human service professions (including psychology, counseling, nursing, and evaluation), as well as more seasoned researchers, who are trying to implement research outside of university-based settings, with communities and populations that may be less familiar to them.

In this book, the researchers who conducted the reprinted studies tell the other half of the story; what actually happened in the process of conducting the study. Due to space limitations (Primavera & Brodsky, 2004), this portion of a study is usually omitted, or relegated to a paragraph in the journal report of research. But this portion of the story contains precisely the kind of research wisdom and "behind the scenes" activity that students and even experienced research professionals need to learn about. Compromises, delays, and lucky breaks are integral to the research process, and trigger some of the inevitable trade-offs researchers must make in carrying out their research. Some can be anticipated, but others cannot.

Authors' commentaries address many topics: how their research ideas emerged, including the professional and personal experiences that inspired the research; what it took to access their sample; negotiating potential research settings; data collection challenges; cultivating ongoing relationships with research settings; problems with human subjects committees; issues with funding sources; procedures necessary to protect the safety of interviewers and ethnographers; the realities of community research settings that may invalidate seemingly clearly operationalized concepts; and the need for statistical analyses that are responsive to missing data. With these commentaries, students and other readers need not "read between the lines to image the hassles that may have occurred to understand that the research article is a sanitized synopsis of the scientific process, an ex post facto attempt to make more coherent a process that was emergent, uncertain, and messy" (Kirk, 1999, p. xvi). Despite these challenges, research is also fun and rewarding, characteristics that also are not usually described in the typical research article, but are vividly portrayed in the commentaries in this volume.

How did we choose the articles to include? First, we wanted peer-reviewed journal articles. We did not limit the peer-reviewed journals to those most closely identified with social work, because research involving social workers is often not published in journals identified as "social work journals." Second, we wanted the articles to represent the major designs and methods that social workers or other human service researchers routinely employ (such as experimental, and correlational designs and qualitative methods), or designs that are used in the wider research arena and lend themselves well to some social work and human service research problems (such as case control designs and meta-analysis). In addition, we wanted articles that represented primary substantive areas and populations within social work practice and the human services. All of the articles use vulnerable populations, including (among others) the frail elderly, those with mental illness, and displaced workers. In a number of instances, the chosen research study employed a diversity of methods, and could just have easily been located in another of the book's major sections, rather than in the section where it is found.

With three exceptions, at least one member of the research team was a social worker, whether he or she was the lead author of the article or not. This decision reflects the fact that research involving and of use to social workers and other human service professionals is increasingly interdisciplinary. We also limited ourselves to articles published after 1997. (The majority, in fact, were published after 2000.) The articles are not necessarily exemplars of a particular methodological approach or issue, and each article has its particular strengths and weaknesses. Nor are these articles necessarily the favorites of their own authors. However, a testament to the novelty and utility of our vision is the fact that only one of the authors whom we asked to participate turned us down, and that was because of illness. Authors produced their commentaries with amazing speed, responding to our sometimes picayune questions with good humor. Many indicated in emails that the process had actually been fun and enlightening.

It becomes apparent in reading the commentaries that, regardless of the particular design or method that the articles were selected to represent, there are many commonalities in the research process. The types of research conducted by social work and human service researchers require ongoing negotiation with agencies to recruit research participants and to obtain data. This is the case whether one is collecting one's own data (doing primary data collection), contracting with a company or research institute to collect the data, or using agency administrative data.

The researcher also needs to give back to the research setting and to the research participants, either in material goods (such as food or money), or intangible rewards (such as advice and staff training). Researchers are not automatically entitled to data, and need to keep in mind the time, hassle, and potentially negative exposure that agencies may experience when agreeing to participate in research. As others have indicated (see Schilling, Schinke, Kirkham, Meltzer, & Norelius, 1988), researchers should adapt their protocols so that they disturb existing agency routines as little as possible. Researchers also need to understand that while getting the data is of the highest priority to them, it takes a decided back seat to other issues that agencies face—as it should!

The collection of primary data by the researcher offers an opportunity to learn a great deal about the environmental context of the research, and enhances the researcher's ability to interpret his or her data. At the same time, there are distinct trade-offs in terms of the time required for primary data collection. With all research, even including some secondary analysis, investigators should expect that data collection will take about three times as long as anticipated.

Although the ethics of research as presented in most texts focuses on protecting research participants, issues around the safety of the data collectors are rarely addressed, despite the reality that much community-based human service research takes place in settings that may be unwelcoming and even hostile to outsiders. Many of the commentaries discuss these concerns, and the procedures undertaken to ensure the safety of interviewers and ethnographers.

When research is conducted in community-based settings, and data are gathered from and about workers (as well as from and about clients), these agency workers are as much research participants as the clients. Even though workers, in their role as professionals, have an obligation to expand the professional knowledge base, the principle of voluntary participation in research applies to all participants in research. In some research situations, workers may be as vulnerable as clients.

Although authors of the commentaries do not generally depict institutional review boards (IRBs) as ogres, there is no question that the work of IRBs can slow down initial data gathering. In developing research proposals, working with IRBs needs to be included in the overall time frame of study implementation. Further, if more than one setting is involved as a data collection site, more than one IRB may need to approve the research before it can begin. It is not unusual for each IRB to require somewhat different procedures and formats for consent forms, which then need to be reconciled so that ultimately the result is one consent form for any given study. However, occasionally in some multi-site studies, each site may require a slightly different consent form.

Another consistently important point in these commentaries is that the study reported in the selected article was usually a small part of the author's research agenda. Frequently, the study was based on pilot work or on prior research investigations, and was the culmination of years of research work. In other cases, it was the beginning of a process that evolved into future research studies, constituting a career agenda. These continuities suggest that research begets research, and, too frequently, raises far more questions than it answers. But even more important, they reveal that the researchers truly enjoyed doing these research investigations. We hope that their experiences and collective wisdom will inspire future generations of researchers to explore the many uncharted and still-emerging frontiers of research in the human services.

All of the methods addressed in this book are also important to the development of evidence-based practices. Human service experiments, quasi-experiments, and meta-analysis have perhaps the most direct bearing, by providing the most rigorous evidence in support (or nonsupport) of practice interventions. Correlational/observational designs can offer preliminary data about how interventions work in the real world, alerting researchers to factors that they may not have considered but that are necessary for successful implementation of their research. Qualitative and mixed methods offer critical contextual understanding about the environment in which research takes place, including such factors as organizational climate, leadership patterns, and cultural practices. These may affect the research process as well as research outcomes. As Hohmann and Shear (2002) point out, qualitative and mixed methods may allow a researcher to better understand and cope with the "noise" of real life, in planning and implementing research in a range of different community settings. In addition, qualitative and mixed methods can facilitate a more nuanced assessment of the fidelity of the intervention. In other words, was the intervention implemented as designed? Available data can provide an understanding of how services and service interventions are naturally working before or after the implementation of an evidence-based practice.

By presenting commentaries about the process of actually implementing research in tandem with the published articles, we hope to inspire students and other researchers to be more proactive in evaluating research evidence, in terms of its applicability to rapidly emerging debates about the defining parameters of evidence-based practice. Recognizing the strengths and frailties of the research process may promote a healthy skepticism about an easy embrace of the latest listing of evidence-based practices. At the same time, "real world" information and wisdom about actual research processes may promote practitioners' beliefs that they might have something useful to contribute to the evidence-based practice movement.

So, begin reading! We hope that you find the nuanced understandings provided by these authors helpful in thinking through issues related to research development, implementation, and analysis. We also hope that you enjoy reading the commentaries as much as we did. Ultimately, they point out that the research process is an infinitely human process, evoking a range of human emotions, including anger, frustration, and tedium, as well as being one of the greatest sources of professional satisfaction.

REFERENCES

Hohmann, A. A., & Shear, M. K. (2002). Community-based intervention research: Coping with the "noise" of real life in study design. *American Journal of Psychiatry, 159,* 201–207.

Kirk, S. A. (1999). *Social work research methods: Building knowledge for practice.* Washington, DC: NASW Press.

Primavera, J., & Brodsky, A. E. (2004). Introduction to the special issue on the process of community research and action. *American Journal of Community Psychology, 33,* 177–179.

Schilling, R. F., Schinke, S. P., Kirkham, M. A., Meltzer, N. J., & Norelius, K. L. (1988). Social work research in social service agencies: Issues and guidelines. *Journal of Social Service Research, 11,* 75–87.

Human Service Experiments, Quasi-Experiments, and Meta-Analysis

This first section deals with studies that assess the effects of human service programs and clinical service interventions. Experimental designs are absolutely essential to human service research, as they enable researchers to address the primary questions put forth by policy makers and funders: "Are our services effective?" and "For whom are they effective?" The first two articles represent the most rigorous designs, randomized experiments, which achieve the highest level of control among existing research designs. But even in such cases implementation problems can result in a lack of confidence in the conclusions reached about causes and effects. The next three articles demonstrate different procedures that are used in quasi-experimental designs to achieve comparability of comparison groups with experimental groups, and to rule out other alternative explanations for findings. In each of these quasi-experimental studies, the unit of analysis is the individual. However, in order to achieve comparability between experimental and comparison conditions, in two of the studies these groups (experimental and comparison) were derived based on matching (one at the county, and the other at the agency level).

Problems of ensuring fidelity to the model intervention, and possible diffusion of the experimental intervention—as well as ethical issues—are discussed. The commentaries make it clear that implementation is key to ensuring the rigor of the proposed design. In other words, proposing a vigorous design without the ability to implement it as proposed will not achieve the desired study outcomes. Therefore, failure to achieve the intended outcome(s) cannot in that case be attributed to the proposed intervention.

It is also evident that all of these designs can be used to answer questions beyond the outcomes of human service interventions, and may also include process variables such as organizational climate and the experience of human service providers.

The final article in this section addresses methodological issues in meta-analysis, and how the combining of studies may enable the researcher to answer questions that were not specifically posed by the original studies. All three of these approaches—experiments, quasi-experiments, and meta-analysis—are essential to the development and achievement of evidence-based practices.

1

Increasing Access to Child Mental Health Services for Urban Children and Their Caregivers

Mary McKernan McKay, Judith Stoewe,
Kathleen McCadam, and Jude Gonzales

Urban children are at a greater risk of developing psychopathology, yet are less likely to be adequately served by outpatient child mental health services (Griffin, Cicchetti, & Leaf, 1993). There is a growing concern that 50 percent to 75 percent of the children who need such services never have contact with them or drop out prematurely (Kazdin, 1993). Previous research documented the numerous barriers that urban families encounter in attempting to gain access to the child mental health system (Aponte, Zarski, Bixenstene, & Cibik, 1991; Boyd-Franklin, 1993; Flaskerud, 1986; Sue, Fujino, Hu, & Takeuchi, 1991; Wallen, 1992). However, only a few studies have evaluated interventions meant to reduce these barriers and to increase the use of services (Russell, Lang, & Brett, 1987; Shivack & Sullivan, 1991; Szapocznik et al., 1988). This article presents the results of a study that evaluated the combined effects of a telephone intervention and a first-interview engagement intervention, compared to the effect of the telephone intervention alone and of the usual intake procedure, on initial attendance and ongoing retention in services. Implications for future research and recommendations for modifying procedures in urban outpatient child mental health centers are also included.

REVIEW OF THE LITERATURE

The prevalence of mental health difficulties among children has been estimated to range from 17 percent to 26 percent (Brandenburg, Friedman, & Silver, 1987; Tuma, 1989). However, the prevalence of the use of mental health services is substantially lower than the estimated rates of psychiatric disorders (Padgett, Patrick, Bums, Schlesinger, & Cohen, 1993; Regier et al., 1993). Rates of service use are particularly low for children in low-income, urban communities (Griffin et al., 1993). In fact, there is mounting evidence that children with the most serious presenting problems and those whose social situations are the most complex are less likely to be retained beyond the first session and are more likely to discontinue services prematurely (Armstrong, Ishiki, Heiman, Mundt, & Womack, 1984; Bui & Takeuchi, 1992; Cohen & Hesselbart, 1993; Kazdin, 1989, 1993; Miller & Prinz, 1991; Russell et al., 1987; Wahler & Dumas, 1989).

Barriers to the use of mental health services by low-income clients of color have been identified to some extent. Underutilization has been explained by the stigma associated with counseling services, the lack of information regarding available services, inaccessible locations, unresponsive service providers, and the reliance on alternative methods of help (Acosta, 1980; Aponte et al., 1991; Boyd-Franklin, 1993; Flaskerud, 1986; Keefe, Padilla, & Carlos, 1979; Lin, 1983; Muecke, 1983; Sue et al., 1991; Sue & Morishima, 1983; Wallen, 1992).

A growing number of empirical studies have identified differences in the demographic and clinical characteristics of children and families who remain in service and those who drop out (see, for example, Armbruster & Fallon, 1994; Costello, 1993; Kazdin, Mazurick, & Siegel, 1994; Oxford, Boyle, & Szatmari, 1987; Tolan, Ryan, & Jaffe, 1988). However, few studies have focused specifically on interventions that are meant to increase the use of services (Szapocznik et al., 1988). Furthermore, studies that target urban children and families are clearly needed.

There is some evidence that more-focused telephone intake procedures are associated with significant increases in initial attendance rates (Russell et al., 1987; Shivack & Sullivan, 1991). In the most rigorous test of an engagement intervention to date, Szapocznik et al. (1988) successfully engaged adolescent substance abusers and their families through the use of a structural family therapy intervention over the telephone; that is, 57.7 percent of the families in the usual intake condition failed to come to their first clinic appointment, but only 7.1 percent of those in the experimental condition failed to come. There were also indications that the engagement intervention had an impact beyond attendance at intake: 41 percent of the families in the control group, but only 17 percent of those in the experimental group, dropped out of treatment prematurely.

The engagement interventions evaluated in the study reported here are based on a conceptual model for understanding the process of engagement with urban families that was developed from the existing empirical literature. Specifically, the model relies on the recognition of the numerous barriers that interfere with families' involvement with mental health services (McKay, Bennett, Stone, & Gonzales, 1995; Tolan & McKay, 1996). These barriers include within-family impediments (like parental efficacy, low investment in help seeking, and previous negative experiences with mental health services) and external barriers (such as the lack of time and transportation). The primary goal of the study was to evaluate specific engagement interventions that help caregivers invest in seeking help for their children and break down the barriers to the use of services.

METHOD

The impact of a telephone-engagement intervention and a first-interview intervention (combined condition) was examined in relation to three outcome measures: (1) attendance at initial appointments, (2) the average duration of contact with a mental health agency, and (3) the proportion of appointments kept during the study period.

Table 1.1. Demographic Characteristics of the Sample

Characteristic	*n*	%
Age of the child		
1–5 years	7	6
6–9 years	38	35
10–13 years	37	34
Over 14 years	21	19
Missing data	6	6
Gender of the child		
Male	34	31
Female	75	69
Primary caregiver		
Biological mother	68	62
Foster mother	13	13
Grandmother	20	18
Aunt	4	4
Uncle	3	3

Setting and Sample

The study was conducted at an inner-city, child mental health agency. Of the children who were seen at the agency in 1996, 67.3 percent lived with their mothers in single-parent households, and approximately 85 percent of the 450 families who requested services in that year were supported by public assistance. Almost two-thirds of the children seen at the agency are African American, 12 percent are Latino, and the remainder are white.

The 109 caregivers who were involved in the study made consecutive requests for services at the agency. The 109 children who were accepted for services (34 boys and 75 girls) ranged in age from one to over 14 (with a mean age of 10.1 years). Sixty-eight percent of the children lived with their biological mothers in single-parent households and 13 percent resided in foster care (see Table 1.1).

Procedures

For the study, consecutive requests for services at the mental health agency were randomly assigned to one of three conditions: combined engagement intervention (*n* = 35), telephone intervention alone (*n* = 35), and the usual intake procedure (*n* = 39). Random assignment was implemented in two stages. First, adult caregivers requesting services for their children were randomly assigned to speak either to one of the two master's-degree social workers who conducted the telephone-engagement intervention or a third master's-degree social worker, who completed the clinic comparison telephone intake procedure. This assignment was accomplished by evenly dividing the messages from parents for intake appointments among the three social workers.

Following the initial intake telephone call, the families were randomly assigned to therapists for their initial intake appointments and, if appropriate, for ongoing mental health services. At this juncture, a case could be assigned to either one of six master's-level social work trainees who received specific training in engagement skills for first interviews (the second component of the

Table 1.2. Description of Telephone Intervention and Empirical Bases

Target of Intervention	Empirical Basis
1. Clarify the need for mental health care	Lerman & Pottick (1995)
2. Increase the caretaker's investment and efficacy in relation to help seeking	Szapocznik et al. (1988)
3. Identify attitudes about and previous experiences with mental health care	Flaskerud (1986), Muecke (1983), Sue, Fujino, Hu, & Takeuchi (1991), Sue & Morishima (1983), Wallen (1992)
4. Overcome concrete obstacles to access to services	Acosta (1980), Sue & Morishima (1983)

combined engagement condition) or one of 20 other therapists (all of whom were at least master's-level interns who were completing clinical programs in social work, psychology, or psychiatric nursing or fellowship training in child psychiatry) who participated in the clinic comparison condition of the study. All the families were informed about the evaluation component of the study and the specific research focus related to how long children and families remain in services.

Telephone Intervention Alone. This 30-minute intervention was implemented by two master's-level clinicians at the research site. It was meant to help the primary caretakers invest in the help-seeking process by clearly identifying their children's presenting difficulties, framing their actions as having the potential to have an impact on the current situation, and having them take some concrete steps to address the situation even before the initial appointment. In addition, it was meant to explore systematically the barriers to help seeking, in both the family and the environment, such as experiences with previous helpers and issues related to poverty, community violence, and racism. Finally, an active problem-solving approach was used to develop the means to address obstacles to contact with the agency (McKay, McCadam, & Gonzales, 1996). Table 1.2 summarizes the active intervention elements and their empirical bases.

Combined Engagement Intervention. This condition included not only the telephone intervention just described, but also the random assignment of families to therapists who had been specifically trained to focus on the process of engagement in the first interview. The eight-hour engagement training defined the initial interview with a client system as having two primary purposes: to understand why a child and family were seeking mental health services and to engage the child and family in a helping process, if appropriate. Four critical elements of engagement were highlighted in this intervention: (1) the need to clarify the helping process for the client; (2) the importance of establishing a collaborative working relationship with the client; (3) a focus on immediate, practical concerns; and (4) an emphasis on identifying and ameliorating barriers to help seeking (McKay, Nudelman, McCadam, & Gonzales, in press).

Six master's-level social work interns were trained to introduce themselves, the agency's intake process, and possible service options carefully during the first interview. Practice exercises encouraged them to balance the need to obtain intake information with the need to help a child and his or her family "tell their own story" about why they had come to the agency. In this way, a collaborative tone was set from the beginning of the first interview. Furthermore, crisis situations or concrete requests for help in negotiating with other systems, such as a school, were responded to immediately during the first appointment. The training of the interns focused on raising their awareness that many situations necessitate the scheduling of an appointment much sooner than the

Table 1.3. Description of First-Interview Engagement Intervention and Empirical Bases

Target of Intervention	Empirical Basis
1. Clarify the roles of the worker, agency, intake process, and possible service options	Lerman & Pottick (1995), Boyd-Franklin (1993)
2. Set the foundations for a collaborative working relationship	Hatch, Moss, Saran, & Presley-Contrell (1993)
3. Identify concrete, practical concerns that can be immediately addressed	Stanton & Todd (1981)
4. Overcome barriers to ongoing involvement with the agency	Acosta (1980), Sue & Morishima (1983)

following week. Finally, a significant factor in every first interview was the exploration of potential barriers to obtaining ongoing services at the agency, as well as such obstacles as time and transportation. The effect of other types of barriers, particularly previous negative experiences with helping professionals and discouragement by others of seeking professional help, were explored. Differences in the race or ethnicity of the clinician and client were always raised. (See Table 1.3 for a summary of key elements of the first interview intervention and their empirical bases.)

Comparison Telephone Intake Procedures. During the initial telephone call to the agency, a parent or other caregiver speaks with a master's-level social worker. The goal of this conversation, which lasts from 20 to 30 minutes, is to assess the child's need for child mental health services and the fit between the child's needs and the agency's services. The focus of the conversation is on clarifying the presenting problem, identifying relevant referral sources, and obtaining identifying information. The social worker also gives the parent or other caregiver information about the agency's services and, if appropriate, indicates that a therapist will be calling to schedule an intake appointment within the next several days.

Training for Comparison First Interviews. During orientation training at the research site, all the therapists were informed of the diagnostic and demographic information that needed to be obtained during the first meeting with a client. This information included information about presenting problems, family composition and history, social and educational functioning, past psychiatric treatments, and medical problems. The orientation to the first interview emphasized information gathering and diagnostic assessment. The training for the combined engagement protocol also required therapists to gather information. However, it expanded the first meeting's purpose substantially to focus on the process of gathering diagnostic data in a sensitive manner and with a primary focus on helping the client identify obstacles to returning for a second appointment.

Checks for the Integrity of the Intervention. For the telephone engagement intervention, a protocol was developed to address each clinical topic with caregivers systematically. Both master's-level clinicians received training in the implementation of this protocol. Approximately 15 percent of the actual telephone calls were monitored by the first author to ensure the integrity of the intervention. The engagement training for conducting a first interview was also directed by a protocol. Approximately 25 percent of the combined engagement-intervention first interviews were videotaped to ensure the integrity of the treatment. Compliance with the study procedures was found to be high.

Table 1.4. Initial Engagement and Retention Rates for the Three Conditions

	Usual Intake (*N* = 39)		Telephone Alone (*N* = 35)		Combined (*N* = 35)	
	n	%	*n*	%	*n*	%
Families who came at least once	17	44	30	86	31	89
% of sessions attended versus scheduled	101/173	58	151/309	49	241/327	74

Measures. In the study, three outcome measures were of interest. First, the agency's research staff obtained the number of clients who came for their first scheduled intake appointments from the therapists. Next, the number of sessions attended during the 18-week study period was recorded by the agency's computerized tracking system to compute the average number of sessions that each subject attended. Finally, the proportion of appointments scheduled versus the number that were kept was computed using these same data sources.

RESULTS

As was noted earlier, the combined intervention and the telephone-alone conditions were associated with substantial increases in attendance at the initial intake appointments in comparison to the clinic comparison condition (see Table 1.4 for a summary of the results). Although the combined engagement condition evidenced slightly higher initial engagement rates, this difference was not statistically significant. Despite the evidence to suggest that the telephone engagement intervention could increase initial attendance rates, its impact did not extend to the ongoing use of services. On average, families who were assigned to the combined interventions attended 7.3 sessions during the 18-week study period ($F = 6.36$, $p < .05$), whereas those who were seen by comparison therapists averaged 5 and 5.9 sessions (for telephone-alone and the usual intake methods, respectively).

In relation to the proportion of sessions scheduled versus the proportion that were kept during the 18-week study period, families who were assigned to the combined engagement intervention attended 74 percent of the sessions—a 25 percent increase over the families who received the telephone intervention alone and a 16 percent increase over the clinic comparison families.

DISCUSSION

One of the most clinically significant findings of this study was that without more intensive engagement efforts, 56 percent of the cases can be lost between the telephone call to request services and the first intake appointment. This figure is alarming, given that the assessment information gathered during the initial telephone call identified these children as in need of mental health services.

The impact of the telephone engagement intervention was limited to attendance rates at initial intake appointments; it did not extend to ongoing rates of engagement, as other studies have suggested (see, for example, Szapocznik et al., 1988). These findings suggest that the level of the therapists' engagement skills is critical. Therefore, it is not sufficient for therapists to be more responsive to clients during the initial calls to a mental health center; rather, responsiveness and an emphasis on identifying and addressing barriers to the use of services must be continued during face-to-face contact with clients.

The interpretation of the results is limited in several ways. First, the study did not incorporate information from clients about their satisfaction with the agency or the therapists, their motivation to return for future appointments, or the specific barriers that interfered with their use of mental health services. Feedback from the consumers of mental health services is clearly needed to enhance the findings of this study and of the literature on mental health services in general. Feedback from the therapists about the engagement process is also critical if future studies are to specify the complex helping exchanges that occur during early meetings with children and their families. Components of both the telephone intervention and the first interview training were meant to target a range of barriers to help seeking, so more research is clearly required on the types of barriers that are more influential than others in predicting help seeking. Additional refinement and specification of the training are necessary to define more clearly the processes that are more likely to help vulnerable client populations gain access to services.

Another concern regarding the study is the lack of specificity of the clinic comparison therapists' behavior in sessions. Whereas the therapists in the interventions condition were monitored to ensure the integrity of treatment, the therapists in the comparison condition were not. Clearly, a more rigorously designed study is required to replicate the findings of this preliminary evaluation. In future studies, a careful analysis of therapists' behavior in both conditions is needed to gain a better understanding of how such behaviors facilitate or block problem solving in relation to specific barriers to help seeking.

Despite these limitations, there is sufficient evidence to suggest that the provision of intensive engagement training to providers of mental health services and alterations in service delivery systems can influence initial engagement and retention rates. Such adjustments are critical if vulnerable low-income children of color are to receive services. Unless barriers to outpatient mental health services can be addressed, urban children and their families will continue to rely on more costly and restrictive services (Wallen, 1992; Zahner, Pawelkiewicz, DeFrancesco, & Adnopoz, 1992). Furthermore, future studies on the effectiveness of child mental health services will rely on the ability to engage children and their caregivers. Therefore, additional thought and research should focus on developing the means to involve children who need such services the most in such efforts.

REFERENCES

Acosta, F.X. (1980). Self described reasons for premature termination of psychotherapy by Mexican American, black American and Anglo American patients. *Psychological Reports, 47,* 435–443.

Aponte, H.J., Zarski, J., Bixenstene, C., & Cibik, P. (1991). Home/community based services: A two-tier approach. *American Journal of Orthopsychiatry 61,* 577–585.

Armbruster, P., & Fallon, T. (1994). Clinical, socio-demographic, and systems risk factors for attrition in a children's mental health clinic. *American Journal of Orthopsychiatry, 64,* 577–585.

Armstrong, H.E., Ishiki, D., Heiman, J., Mundt, J., & Womack, W. (1984). Service utilization by black and white clientele in an urban community mental health center: Revised assessment of an old problem. *Community Mental Health Journal, 20,* 265–280.

Boyd-Franklin, N. (1993). Black families. In F. Walsh (Ed.), *Normal family process* (pp. 361–376). New York: Guilford Press.

Brandenburg, N.A., Friedman, R.M., & Silver, S.E. (1987). The epidemiology of childhood psychiatric disorders: Prevalence findings from recent studies. *Journal of the American Academy of Child and Adolescent Psychiatry, 29,* 76–83.

Bui, C.T., & Takeuchi, D.T. (1992). Ethnic minority adolescents and the use of community mental health care services. *American Journal of Community Psychology, 20,* 403–417.

Cohen, P., & Hesselbart, C.S. (1993). Demographic factors in the use of children's mental health services. *American Journal of Public Health, 83,* 49–52.

Costello, E.J. (1993). How can epidemiology improve mental health services for children and adolescents? *Journal of the American Academy of Child and Adolescent Psychiatry, 32,* 1106–1114.

Flaskerud, J.H. (1986). The effects of culture-compatible intervention on the utilization of mental health services by minority clients. *Community Mental Health Journal, 22,* 127–140.

Griffin, J.A., Cicchetti, D., & Leaf, P.J. (1993). Characteristics of youths identified from a psychiatric case register as first-time users of services. *Hospital and Community Psychiatry, 44,* 62–65.

Hatch, J., Moss, N., Saran, A., & Presley-Contrell, C. (1993). Community research: Partnership in black communities. *American Journal of Preventive Medicine, 9*(6 Suppl.), 27–31.

Kazdin, A.E. (1989). Hospitalization and antisocial children: Clinical course, follow-up status, and predictors of outcomes. *Advances in Behavior Research and Therapy, 11,* 1–67.

Kazdin, A.E. (1993). Premature termination from treatment among children referred for antisocial behavior. *Journal of Child Psychology & Psychiatry & Allied Disciplines, 31,* 415–425.

Kazdin, A.E., Mazurick, J.L., & Siegel, T.C. (1994). Treatment outcome among children with externalizing disorder who terminate prematurely versus those who complete psychotherapy. *Journal of the American Academy of Child and Adolescent Psychiatry, 33,* 549–557.

Keefe, W.E., Padilla, A.M., & Carlos, M.L. (1979). The Mexican-American extended family as an emotional support system. *Human Organization, 38,* 144–152.

Lerman, P., & Pottick, K.J. (1995). *The parents' perspective.* Switzerland: Harwood Academy.

Lin, T. (1983). Psychiatry and Chinese culture. *Western Journal of Medicine, 139,* 868–874.

McKay, M., Bennett, E., Stone, S., & Gonzales, J. (1995). A comprehensive training model for inner-city social workers. *Arete, 20,* 56–64.

McKay, M., McCadam, K., & Gonzales, J. (1996). Addressing the barriers to mental health services for inner-city children and their caregivers. *Community Mental Health Journal, 32,* 353–361.

McKay, M., Nudelman, R., McCadam, K., & Gonzales, J. (in press). Social work engagement: An approach to involving inner-city children and their families. *Research on Social Work Practice.*

Miller, G.E., & Prinz, R.J. (1991). Enhancement of social learning family intervention for childhood conduct disorder. *Psychological Bulletin, 108,* 291–307.

Muecke, M.A. (1983). In search of healers. *Western Journal of Medicine, 139,* 835–840.

Oxford, D.R., Boyle, M.H., & Szatmari, P. (1987). Ontario Child Health Study: II. Six month prevalence of disorder and rates of service utilization. *Archives of General Psychiatry, 44,* 832–836.

Padgett, D.K., Patrick, C., Bums, B.J., Schlesinger, H.J., & Cohen, J. (1993). The effect of insurance benefit changes on use of child and adolescent outpatient mental health services. *Medical Care, 31,* 96–110.

Regier, D.A., Narrow, W.E., Rae, D.S., Manderscheid, R.W., Locke, B., & Goodwin, F.K. (1993). The de facto U.S. mental and addictive disorders service system: Epidemiologic catchment area prospective one-year prevalence rates of disorders and services. *Archives of General Psychiatry, 50,* 85–94.

Russell, M., Lang, M., & Brett, B. (1987, September). Reducing dropout rates through improved intake procedures. *Social Casework,* 421–425.

Shivack, N., & Sullivan, T. (1991). Use of telephone prompts at an inner-city patient clinic. *Hospital and Community Psychiatry, 40,* 851–853.

Stanton, M.D., & Todd, T.C. (1981). Engaging "resistant" families in treatment. *Family Process, 20,* 161–193.

Sue, S., Fujino, D.C., Hu, L., & Takeuchi, D.T. (1991). Community mental health services for ethnic minority groups: A test of the cultural responsiveness hypothesis. *Journal of Consulting and Clinical Psychology, 59,* 533–540.

Sue, S., & Morishima, J.K. (1983). *The mental health of Asian Americans.* San Francisco: Jossey-Bass.

Szapocznik, J., Perex-Vidal, A., Brickman, A.L., Foote, F.H., Santesban, D., Hervis, O., & Kultines, W.M. (1988). Engaging adolescent drug abusers and their families in treatment: A strategic structural systems approach. *Journal of Consulting and Clinical Psychology, 56,* 552–557.

Tolan, P.H., & McKay, M. (1996). Preventing aggression in urban children: An empirically based family prevention program. *Family Relations: Journal of Applied Family & Child Studies, 45,* 148–155.

Tolan, P.H., Ryan, K., & Jaffe, C. (1988). Adolescents' mental health service use and provider, process and recipient characteristics. *Journal of Clinical Child Psychology, 16,* 317–333.

Tuma, J.M. (1989). Mental health services for children. *American Psychologist, 44,* 188–189.

Wahler, R., & Dumas, J. (1989). Attentional problems in dysfunctional mother–child interactions: An interbehavior model. *Psychological Bulletin, 105,* 116–130.

Wallen, J. (1992). Providing culturally appropriate mental health services for minorities. *Journal of Mental Health Administration, 19,* 288–295.

Zahner, G., Pawelkiewicz, W., DeFrancesco, J.J., & Adnopoz, J. (1992). Children's mental health service needs and utilization patterns in an urban community: An epidemiological assessment. *Journal of the American Academy of Child and Adolescent Psychiatry, 31,* 951–960.

COMMENTARY BY: Mary M. McKay

When I accepted a position in 1995 within a large, midwestern university department of psychiatry as the director of a social work training program, there was growing national evidence that children were not receiving adequate mental health care. The social work training program that I oversaw consisted of a fieldwork unit with multiple MSW field supervisors, as many as 17 master's-level social work interns, and numerous bachelor's-level and predoctoral-level social work trainees. These committed social workers and trainees were charged with the mission of providing mental health services for inner-city youth and their families within a university-based outpatient child mental health clinic. Many also worked as part of numerous community-based youth-focused prevention and intervention projects (see McKay, Bennett, Stone, & Gonzales, 1995, for a description of the child mental health training program, and Tolan & McKay, 1996, for an example of a community-based prevention program). No-show rates for child mental health appointments could sometimes exceed 50 percent within the outpatient clinic, similar to national rates (McKay, McCadam, & Gonzales, 1996). Within the community-based prevention programs, participation rates were substantially higher, at times approaching an 85 percent engagement rate. Thus, this scenario allowed for knowledge about engaging youth and families within the community-based programs to inform the development of innovative strategies to engage "hard to reach" urban youth and their families within the clinic-based services, the focus of the article reprinted here (Tolan & McKay, 1996; McCormick, McKay, Gilling, & Paikoff, 2000).

More specifically, in a large-scale delinquency prevention trial set within urban communities, a conceptual model for understanding barriers to involvement was developed that identified a range of influences at the level of the child, family, community, service delivery system, and provider that could impact a family's decision to participate in a 22-week community-based prevention program (Tolan & McKay, 1996). In response to the identification of multiple barriers believed to interfere with families' participation, a set of systematic engagement interventions was developed to increase rates of involvement. These engagement strategies were developed based upon consultation with prevention workers and parent consumers of the preventive program. This same approach was applied in the child mental health clinic, where a series of meetings was held with both clinic-based mental health providers and parent consumers, to identify barriers to involvement and potential strategies that clinicians could use to enhance engagement, the underpinning of the current article of interest.

As a result of the work completed in the community, the engagement intervention that was developed included a proactive approach, to give youth and their adult caregivers as much

---

Commentary on article: McKay, M. M., Stoewe, J., McCadam, K., & Gonzales, J. (1998). Increasing access to child mental health services for urban children and their caregivers. *Health and Social Work, 23*, 9–15.

information about the community-based program as possible—and to address questions that family members might have, but would consider it impolite to ask (e.g., who is responsible for the program, or why their community was chosen as a site for a preventive intervention) (McKay et al., 1995).

This set of engagement strategies yielded impressive increases in participation rates within the community-based, family-focused prevention programs. For example, prior to the implementation of the engagement intervention described in an article written by Tolan and McKay (1996), of 197 high-risk families identified, 90 (49 percent) completed every session of the program. With the addition of the engagement interventions, 67 percent (year two), 77 percent (year three) and 85 percent (year four) of families completed the prevention program. With these significant results in hand, we began to organize feedback from adults and children seeking mental health care in the clinic-based programs. We held forums in which we sought advice and made adaptations to the engagement strategies deployed in the community-based projects, in order to tailor them to three sets of issues associated with more traditional child mental health service seeking: (1) concerns about mental health care, and stigma associated with mental illness; (2) prior negative experiences of families with mental health care providers specifically, and helpers in general; and (3) perceptions of racism associated with approaching a mental health care institution (McKay et al., 1996; McKay, Nudelman, & McCadam, 1997).

OBSTACLES TO DEPLOYMENT AND TESTING OF INNOVATIVE ENGAGEMENT INTERVENTIONS WITHIN AN OUTPATIENT CHILD MENTAL HEALTH CLINIC: "WE'RE DOING JUST FINE WITHOUT YOU."

One of the most significant obstacles to introducing an innovative practice (and, particularly, a practice-based research project) into a "real world" setting is that procedures and processes are already in place that organize care and can be quite difficult to alter. Further, although *discussions* of evidence-based practice (that is, clinical care strategies that have been previously associated with positive outcomes for youth) were evident in the field, few of these types of child mental health services had moved into real-world clinic settings by the early 1990s (Weisz, Weiss, & Donenberg, 1992).

More specifically related to the article of interest, it was the practice for a highly competent intake worker to speak to each adult caregiver referred for services at the agency research site, and had been so for over a decade. Thus, there was little motivation to alter this entry mechanism, particularly within a busy outpatient program, as the volume of new youth and families referred was, at times, overwhelming. Next, a complex intake system had developed at the site of the research study of interest, which was supported by a strong therapeutic rationale that focused on information gathering and diagnostic assessment, rather than engaging and meeting the immediate, most pressing needs of consumers. In order to begin the study of engagement interventions on the telephone and during the first interview (as described in the article of interest), opportunities to help the agency invest in the project were needed.

Discussions with key agency administrators and providers regarding the literature related to urban youth and family help seeking certainly assisted in setting the stage for the study of interest. However, an important obstacle, confronted from the beginning of the planning related to this study, was the reality that no-shows and missed appointments provided some much-needed downtime for busy providers. In addition, given the limited resources to actually provide care in an inner-city environment, the often-unspoken process driving decisions about entry procedures was related to the need to sort families into those who actually would come to appointments as opposed to those who would experience significant obstacles to involvement. This perspective, both expressed and unstated, was based firmly in the belief that there was little that could be done to address obstacles to care, despite providers' and administrators' firm commitment to be of assistance to youths and their families. Thus, it was only when a set of key opportunities presented themselves—the intake worker going on an extended vacation, and the retirement of a key psychiatrist overseeing the intake process—that this study became possible.

Specifically, as Director of Social Work Training, I offered to oversee the new "engaging" first interview intake process within the outpatient child clinic. In addition, I offered the resources of social work interns to fill in for the full-time intake worker while he was away on vacation. Thus, the research study met very concrete needs of the agency, and relied on a high degree of interest by the social work fieldwork unit, while meeting a significant need within the child mental health services field, to develop and test interventions to overcome obstacles to urban child mental health care.

CHALLENGES RELATED TO REAL-WORLD CLINIC
SAMPLES OF CHILDREN, FAMILIES, AND PROVIDERS

The prevailing conceptual frameworks that have guided innovations within child mental health services over the past two decades have relied heavily upon models that specify treatment conditions for target disorders in clinical populations (Weisz, et al., 1992; Weisz & Hawley, 1998; Weisz, 2000; Weisz, Hawley, Pilkonis, Woody, & Follette, 2000). The range of studies on both the outcomes of treatments, services, and preventive programs has grown exponentially, as witnessed by the volume of reviews, meta-analyses, and reports published in the past six years summarizing the impact of these interventions for children and adolescents (U.S. Public Health Service, 1999; 2000). The model guiding the bulk of these studies (referred to by Weisz as the Medical-Pharmaceutical or "MP" Model) entails a series of controlled laboratory trials, with dissemination, implementation, and deployment occurring at the end of the process.

This model (and the innovative treatments that result) may not be well suited to ultimate use in clinics or community settings because, as Weisz (2000; Weisz, et al., 2000) points out, many of the real-world factors that MP researchers might consider "nuisance variables" and, therefore, rule out or control experimentally, are precisely those variables that need to be understood and addressed if practice innovations are to work well in real clinical practice. These real-world issues (e.g., diverse needs of children, multiple family life stresses that lead to early termination of treatment, limitations in provider skill) may need to be directly addressed within the development and testing of child-focused service innovations if these interventions are to be maximally effective within real-world settings. Within the current study, the wide range of youth served by the clinic, including a diverse age range, different racial and cultural backgrounds of families, and an array of presenting mental health difficulties, could have been considered nuisance variables. Thus, the current study is more in line with calls by Weisz (2000) for the creation of clinic and community intervention development (CID) models that begin with pilot testing within real-world settings, and that attend to "nuisance" characteristics of the service delivery process (e.g., characteristics of clinical populations, preferences of consumers, models that respond to high demand for services and scarcity of service providers in urban communities).

A series of pilot studies preceded the study focused on here (McKay, McCadam, & Gonzales, 1996; McKay, Nudelman, & McCadam, 1997). We were encouraged by the significant positive results that these studies yielded. In addition, the protocol that guided both the telephone engagement intervention and the first interview engagement intervention had been developed so that they could be applied to all youths and their families approaching the agency for service. Rather than being scripted interventions, a series of discussion questions was developed to guide both clinicians and adult caregivers to explore areas that were potentially related to dropping out (see McKay, McCadam, & Gonzales, 1996; McKay, Nudelman, & McCadam, 1997; McKay, Stoewe, McCadam, & Gonzales, 1998 for complete descriptions of the content of the interventions and process of delivery). These questions were designed to explore factors that could interfere with service use, and to identify those resources that could facilitate keeping child mental health appointments.

In addition, training of clinicians conducting the engagement intervention on the telephone with adult caregivers during the first intake call, and social workers conducting first interviews, was meant to develop a set of skills and perspectives believed necessary to enhance initial and ongoing involvement. These skills included: (1) advanced problem-solving techniques to address a range of complex barriers to help seeking (e.g., skills to help the adult caregiver locate solutions to factors that might interfere with help seeking); (2) abilities to encourage families to discuss their fears about mental health care and their prior negative experiences, topics not often discussed but believed to drive decisions regarding premature termination of treatment; and (3) tools used to build collaborative relationships, in order to foster partnerships with both parents and youths to address pressing issues early in the service delivery process (e.g., framing that the parent, youth, and clinician are "all in this together" or are the team that will help build success for the youth). Treatment fidelity was assessed via direct observation by the supervising researcher, and viewing of videotapes of first interview sessions, using coding sheets based upon principles outlined in the intervention protocol. In sum, the protocol, a written guide underpinning both the telephone and first interview engagement intervention, was flexible enough to include a heterogeneous sample of youths and families reflective of real-world clinic populations.

Only providers who voluntarily expressed an interest in being trained and supervised in the two innovative interventions were included in the current study. All others were invited to participate as comparison therapists, with all but one provider refusing to be involved in the study. The voluntary participation of experimental therapists is important in that the engagement methods studied here required a willingness to work with families in highly collaborative ways, and to accept consumers' perceptions as legitimate and worth the time to discuss in a nonjudgmental manner. For example, there is a large literature to support the findings that families of color may hold more negative opinions of mental health providers and diminished hope that services can actually be of help to their children (Boyd-Franklin, 1993). Although voluntary participation was important for the current study, it also creates a potential bias that workers' enthusiasm could contribute to positive findings.

CHALLENGES OF CONDUCTING RESEARCH IN REAL-WORLD SETTINGS: DO RESEARCH METHODS FIT WITHIN CLINICAL CARE SETTINGS?

The current study employed an experimental research design to examine the impact of three distinct study conditions on initial and ongoing involvement in child mental health care: (1) telephone engagement intervention; (2) combined telephone and first interview engagement intervention; and

(3) business as usual. In the case of this study, randomization was possible for a number of reasons that were only partially related to rigorous science or the integrity of the experiment. First, none of the interventions of interest were considered harmful to families. In fact, it was difficult to argue that spending additional time on the telephone or in person with the adult caregiver, addressing barriers to care, could be detrimental to the child mental health care service delivery process. However, since the telephone engagement intervention required additional time spent on the telephone, and the first interview engagement intervention necessitated additional training and supervision, there was little motivation for agency administrators to insist that all families receive such interventions. Thus, acceptance of randomization really was an endorsement of the status quo rather than a clearly felt need to change intake practices for all families seeking care at the agency.

As with any experimental research study, threats to internal validity become critical to understanding outcomes. In this study, a few factors enhanced the rigor of the study, while others weakened the design. For example, since differential attrition was the outcome of interest, this did not pose a threat to interpretation of findings. In addition, since providers supervised by the developer of the engagement interventions were involved in the study (all being social workers or interns within the social work training department), treatment fidelity and monitoring were easier to achieve, given that the researcher was also involved in monitoring experimental interventions and ongoing supervision. However, multiple factors within this research study could not be constrained. For example, inclement weather interfering with family travel to the agency, school holidays, vacations of service providers, and the diversity of skills evidenced by providers in the comparison conditions could not be controlled; however, there is no evidence that these issues significantly influenced results.

The single largest research challenge in planning this study was identifying and tracking the primary dependent variable, involvement in child mental health care. After lengthy discussions, we agreed on three primary outcomes: (1) attendance at the initial intake appointment; (2) the average length of ongoing involvement in care; and (3) the proportion of appointments kept during the study period. First, agency administrators made clear that little staff time could be devoted to support this unfunded study. This meant that any data collected had to be readily available, and its collection could not add any burden to the work lives of inner-city child mental health providers. Thus, the computerized scheduling system supplemented by provider logs was used to track data regarding show rates. We agreed that we would only focus on a behavioral definition of involvement—whether the parent actually brings the child for treatment and how frequently that occurs—because these data were easily retrieved from the agency's centralized scheduling system and could be readily checked for accuracy using provider contact logs.

ETHICAL AND PRACTICE DILEMMAS

Child mental health treatment is primarily a private exchange between child/family and provider. The type of interventions tested in "the study" required provider willingness to make their practice public in two important ways. First, providers were closely supervised, and their interactions on the telephone and during the first interview were topics for both individual and group supervisory conferences. Second, data regarding their results were incorporated into feedback related to how to improve delivery of the engagement intervention, creating the need to reassure providers that outcomes would be examined in relation to the intervention and not seen as a reflection of provider skill.

While not necessarily a challenge when conducting this study, the positive results, along with the two prior trials, built support for the argument that the care of youth referred for mental health could be compromised, and premature dropout was likely, without possibility of exposure to engagement interventions. Therefore, in our next set of studies focused on engagement, we chose not to randomly assign youth and families to experimental and comparison conditions, but rather to expose all participants to the engagement intervention. In essence, it seemed unethical not to provide engagement interventions to all families seeking care for their children.

STRENGTHS AND LIMITATIONS OF THE STUDY

This study involved a relatively small sample of urban adult caregivers and service providers. In addition, it occurred at a single site, with the developer of the interventions actively involved in the research study. Thus, it was not a blind controlled trial. At the time of the writing of the article, these were significant acknowledged limitations of the study. However, since that time these engagement interventions have continued to be refined and tested. For example, in a study of eight child mental health sites implementing these engagement strategies in order to involve urban youths and their families in trauma-specific child mental health services, slightly higher rates of initial and ongoing engagement were achieved across sites without the day-to-day supervision of the developer (see McKay, Hibbert, Hoagwood, Rodriguez, & Murray, 2004, for a more complete description). Thus, studies subsequent to the one discussed here indicate a relatively high degree of generalizability of study findings to other urban child mental health clinics.

RECOMMENDATIONS FOR FUTURE RESEARCH
AND PRACTICE INITIATIVES

It is clear that mechanisms to increase the involvement of urban youth and their families in mental health services are needed. However in order to accomplish this task, community-based agencies and providers might consider the following steps: (1) examine intake procedures and develop interventions to target specific barriers to service use; (2) provide training and supervision to providers, to increase the focus on engagement in first face-to-face meetings with youths and their families; and (3) consider service delivery options with input from consumers regarding innovative services (McKay et al., 2004).

The fact that a substantial portion of youths continue to experience significant mental health issues calls for new models of child mental health services research that address these needs. Enhancing the level of collaboration within research efforts holds promise for addressing these issues. Such efforts bring together university-based researchers who have substantial expertise, knowledge of the literature, and access to resources, with mental health stakeholders and providers who bring strong commitment to the mental health of youth, expertise related to the needs of youths and their families, and an understanding of the practical realities of agency settings and communities.

Although opportunities to collaborate more intensely are available to researchers, these collaborative efforts are not without a specific set of challenges. Collaborative research efforts are labor intensive for both the university-based researcher and the mental health stakeholders.

Furthermore, they require a level of communication and sharing of power that has not necessarily been found in most prior research projects. However, given the imperative to develop new ways to serve our nation's youth, and the fact that innovative child mental health services are likely to fail in community-based settings if they attempt to integrate new services and involve service providers in a noncollaborative manner, such collaborative endeavors are greatly needed (Boyd-Franklin, 1993; Fullilove & Fullilove, 1996).

We know from prior research that the potential effectiveness of child mental health services is limited when those services have been designed and implemented in ways that do not appreciate stressors, particularly those related to poverty and urban community violence exposure, scarce contextual resources (such as after-school or recreational programs for youth), and target groups' core values (such as the importance of extended family and the skills and capabilities of real-world providers) (Boyd-Franklin, 1993). Therefore, the establishment of strong partnerships is critical to ensuring that effective child mental health services are well received within community-based settings, and that innovative programs can be sustained once research funding has ended (Galbraith et al., in press). The engagement interventions discussed here were sustained within the agency long after the study. Ongoing research attention to the impact of collaborative partnerships on child mental health outcomes is clearly needed to further refine the science of collaborative research efforts, and should be considered one of the major agenda items for the field of child mental health services research for at least the next decade.

REFERENCES

Boyd-Franklin, N. (1993). Black families. In F. Walsh (Ed.), *Normal family process* (pp. 361–376). New York: Guilford Press.

Fullilove, M.T. & Fullilove, R.E., III. (1993). Understanding sexual behaviors and drug use among African-Americans: A case study of issues for survey research. In D.G. Ostrow & R.C. Kessler (Eds.), *Methodological issues in AIDS behavioral research* (pp. 117–132). New York: Plenum Press.

Galbraith, J., Stanton, B., Feigelman, S., Ricardo, I., Black, M., & Kalijer, K. (in press). Challenges and rewards of involving community in research: An overview of the "Focus on Kids" HIV-risk reduction program. *Health Education Quarterly*.

McCormick, A., McKay, M., Gilling, G., & Paikoff, R. (2000). Involving families in an urban HIV preventive intervention: How community collaboration addresses barriers to participation, AIDS Education and Prevention, 12, 299–307.

McKay, M., Bennett, E., Stone, S., & Gonzales, J. (1995). A comprehensive training model for inner-city social workers. *Arete, 20,* 56–65.

McKay, M., Hibbert, R., Hoagwood, K., Rodriguez, J., & Murray, L. (2004). Integrating evidence-based engagement interventions into "real world" child mental health settings. *Journal of Brief Treatment and Crisis Intervention, 4,* 177–186.

McKay, M., McCadam, K., & Gonzales, J. (1996). Addressing the barriers to mental health services for inner-city children and their caretakers. *Community Mental Health Journal, 32*(4) 353–361.

McKay, M., Nudelman, R., & McCadam, K. (1997). Involving inner-city families in mental health services: First interview engagement skills. *Research on Social Work Practice, 6,* 462–472.

McKay, M., Stoewe, J., McCadam, K., & Gonzales, J. (1998). Increasing access to child mental health services for urban children and their caregivers. *Health and Social Work, 23,* 9–15.

Tolan, P.H. & McKay, M. (1996). Preventing aggression in urban children: An empirically based family prevention program. *Family Relations: Journal of Applied Family & Child Studies, 45,* 148–155.

U.S. Public Health Service (1999). Mental health: A report of the Surgeon General. Rockville, MD: U.S. Department of Health and Human Services Administration.

U.S. Public Health Service (2000). *Report of the Surgeon General's conference on children's mental health: A national action agenda.* Washington, DC: Department of Health and Human Services.

Weisz, J.R. (2000). Agenda for child and adolescent psychotherapy research: On the need to put science into practice. *Archives of General Psychiatry, 57*(9), 837–838.

Weisz, J.R. & Hawley, K.M. (1998). Finding, evaluating, refining, and applying empirically supported treatments for children and adolescents. *Journal of Clinical Child Psychology, 27*(2), 206–216.

Weisz, J.R., Hawley, K.M., Pilkonis, P.A., Woody, S.R., & Follette, W.C. (2000). Stressing the (other) three Rs in the search for empirically supported treatments: Review procedures, research quality, relevance to practice and the public interest. *Clinical Psychology—Science & Practice, 7*(3), 243–258.

Weisz, J.R., Weiss, B., & Donenberg, G.R. (1992). The lab versus the clinic: Effects of child and adolescent psychotherapy. *American Psychologist, 47*(12), 1578–1585.

2

A Community-Based Trial of Vocational Problem-Solving to Increase Employment Among Methadone Patients

David A. Zanis, Ph.D., Donna Coviello, Ph.D.,
Arthur I. Alterman, Ph.D., and Sharon E. Appling, M.S.W.

INTRODUCTION

Following drug use stabilization, employment has long been considered an important secondary goal for patients enrolled in methadone maintenance treatment programs (MMTPs) (Dole, Nyswander, & Warner, 1968). Several studies have found moderate positive correlations between increased employment, decreased substance use, and positive social functioning (McLellan, Ball, Rosen, & O'Brien, 1981; Siegal et al., 1996; Zanis, McLellan, & Randall, 1994). Overall, employment rates in MMTPs are low and range from 15% to 44% (French, Dennis, McDougal, Karuntzos, & Hubbard, 1992; Hubbard, Rachal, Craddock, & Cavanaugh, 1984; Platt, 1995). Unfortunately, less than 4% of MMTPs provide specific employment services such as counseling job clubs (Etheridge, Craddock, Dunteman, & Hubbard, 1995). Given the low rates of employment, patients' desire for employment services, and the association of employment with improved outcomes, employment interventions appear to be important approaches to explore as potential adjunctive therapies to improve patient functioning.

French et al. (1992) identified programmatic, structural, and client-level factors that contribute to the low rates of employment among clients enrolled in MMTPs. Program factors explain why em-

Source: Zanis, D.A., Coviello, D., Alterman, A.I., Appling, S.E. (2001). A Community-based trial of vocational problem-solving: To increase employment among methadone patients. *Journal of Substance Abuse Treatment, 21,* 19–26. Copyright 2001 Elsevier, Inc. Reprinted with permission.

ployment services are underutilized in MMTPs. Two predominant issues include the lack of available funding to reimburse clinics for providing employment services and the lack of available, standardized, employment interventions to help counselors deliver employment services (Arella, Deren, Randell, & Brewington, 1990; Hall, 1981; Platt & Metzger, 1987). Structural factors include issues such as bias against hiring methadone clients, unavailability of jobs for a particular skill level, and lack of appropriate job-training programs. Patient factors that contribute to low rates of employment include inadequate job skills (e.g., poor reading or mathematics capabilities), competing psychosocial problems (e.g., depression), job-seeking barriers (e.g., transportation), and low motivation to want to obtain employment (Brewington, Arella, Deren, & Randell, 1987; Kidorf, Hollander, King, & Brooner, 1998; Silverman, Chutuape, Bigelow, & Stitzer, 1996; Zanis, Metzger, & McLellan, 1994).

One intent of the present study was to train methadone counselors to deliver a ten-session intervention, Vocational Problem-Solving Skills (VPSS), to unemployed clients (Metzger, Platt, Zanis, & Fureman, 1992). Because the methadone counselor participates as an active and important member in the patient's recovery process, we reasoned that a counselor, if appropriately trained, could be an effective service delivery agent through which unemployed patients could receive individualized vocational counseling services. Thus, a counselor trained in the delivery of vocational services could potentially diminish some structural, programmatic, and client-level barriers associated with unemployment.

To this end, our main hypothesis was to evaluate whether unemployed patients randomized to VPSS counseling would improve their employment functioning compared to patients randomized to a time- and attention-controlled comparison activity.

METHODS

Subjects

A total of 109 patients voluntarily recruited from two MMTPs consented to participate in the randomized controlled clinical trial. To be considered for the project, patients had to meet the following criteria: (1) unemployed or underemployed, defined as working "under the table" less than 10 hours per week; (2) stabilized on methadone and enrolled in the MMTP for a minimum of 3 months; (3) expressed interest and capacity to work at least 20 hours per week; and (4) actively seeking employment as defined by the Bureau of Labor Statistics (BLS, 1994).

Sites

A convenience sample of two community-based methadone programs was selected in an effort to test the intervention in typical community-based settings. Site A had an enrollment of 383 patients, of which 77 (20%) reported current employment. This site employed 10 counselors, of which five voluntarily agreed to participate in the study. All counselors had a minimum of an associate's degree and at least 1 year of experience as a methadone counselor.

Site B enrolled 288 patients, of which 82 (28.5%) were employed. Site B employed nine counselors, of which two had a bachelor's degree and seven had a master's degree. All counselors had at least 1 year of experience as a methadone counselor.

Recruitment and Randomization

Subjects were randomly assigned to receive either 10 individual counseling sessions of VPSS or to a controlled comparison condition consisting of 10 individual sessions of interpersonal problem-solving (IPS). Since the study emphasis was on evaluating the effectiveness of the VPSS condition, the randomization was structured to produce a 3:2 ratio of experimental to control condition. Sixty-two patients were assigned to the VPSS condition and 47 patients were assigned to the IPS condition. Overall, 71 patients were recruited from Site A, with 37 randomized to the VPSS condition and 34 to the IPS condition. A total of 38 patients were recruited from Site B, with 25 randomized to VPSS and 13 to IPS.

Intervention Conditions

All patients, regardless of randomization condition, were required to receive a 30-minute counseling session each week as part of standard treatment services. Each session was designed to focus on generic drug counseling issues (e.g., methadone dose, drug use, attendance in self-help, etc.). This standard counseling session was provided by the same counselor who was trained to deliver the intervention counseling sessions.

Vocational Problem-Solving Skills (VPSS) is a cognitive-based intervention designed to assist chronically unemployed patients transition to work (Metzger et al., 1992). All VPSS sessions were designed to be approximately 30 to 60 minutes in length and delivered within a maximum of a 12-week period. The variation in the length of the sessions and 12-week intervention duration was based on past administrations of the intervention and determined to be a reasonable expectation of service delivery. Both patients and counselors were provided with a manual and workbook, outlining each of the sessions. There are five objectives of the VPSS intervention: (1) help patients understand why they want to work; (2) help patients understand how to overcome current barriers to work; (3) set realistic vocational goals; (4) identify realistic resources to help locate job opportunities; and (5) take appropriate actions to obtain work.

Interpersonal Problem-Solving (IPS) counseling was selected as the comparison condition because it was theoretically similar to the VPSS, was based on a manualized intervention developed by Platt (1980), and provided an opportunity to direct the nature of counseling to focus drug use. The IPS intervention was designed to be delivered in the same frequency and duration of counseling as the subjects in the experimental condition. The goal of IPS counseling was to help patients develop improved problem-solving skills to either reduce drug use or continue abstinence from drug use. The five objectives of the IPS counseling were to: (1) reduce/eliminate illicit drug use or maintain an abstinence plan; (2) understand the utility of social supports in recovery; (3) examine successful and unsuccessful efforts at recovery; (4) formulate realistic recovery plans; and (5) engage in planned activities. Please note: All IPS patients who expressed an interest in receiving employment services were referred to one of two city-based employment programs that offer free employment services.

Counselor Participation

A total of 14 methadone counselors from the two MMTPs were trained to deliver both the VPSS and IPS sessions. Counselor participation was voluntary, and each was compensated by either a US$100 stipend or with free lunches for their participation in the project. All counselors signed a consent form to participate in the study, giving permission for our research team to assess counselor effectiveness.

Counselor Training

Each counselor completed an initial 8-hour training program and received an implementation manual designed to help the counselor deliver the intervention. Prior to implementation of the intervention, all 14 counselors were required to demonstrate an acceptable set of competencies. Counselors were evaluated on a series of hypothetical role-play situations simulated by two independent facilitators.

Upon demonstrated competency of VPSS and IPS skills, counselors were permitted to participate in the study. Additionally, counselors participated in 12 one-hour weekly booster sessions facilitated by the first author as a means to monitor intervention quality and improve service delivery.

Data Collection

A trained independent research assistant assessed patients by interviewing them at baseline, biweekly for 12 weeks, and at 6 months postbaseline. Also, independent urine samples were collected during these assessment periods. The following instruments were administered at baseline and follow-up points of the study.

Addiction Severity Index (ASI). The ASI (McLellan et al., 1980) is a semistructured interview designed to collect historical and recent behavioral information regarding seven areas of functioning: medical, employment, alcohol, drug, legal, family, and psychological. The ASI has demonstrated good validity and reliability in samples of methadone patients (McLellan et al., 1985; Kosten, Rounsaville, & Kleber, 1983). The ASI yields seven composite scores ranging from 0 to 1, with higher scores representative of poorer functioning in the specific domain.

Vocational/Educational Assessment (VEA). The VEA is a 48-item interview created by the authors to measure four domains associated with employment functioning: (1) knowledge of employment resources; (2) attitudes and motivation toward employment; (3) employment barriers; and (4) employment-related behavioral outcomes (income, participation in vocational services, number of job interviews, etc.). This nonstandardized interview was created to measure other possible outcomes associated with employment interventions.

Treatment Services Review (TSR). The TSR, a brief, 5-minute structured interview designed to record the type and frequency of services received during treatment, was administered every 2 weeks for a period of 12 weeks. The TSR has satisfactory validity and reliability within a methadone population and has been used to show relationships between treatment services and patient functioning (McLellan, Arndt, Metzger, Woody, & O'Brien, 1993). The purpose of the TSR was to measure the number of units of service received by the type of service (e.g., employment, drug counseling, etc.).

Chart Review/Employment Verification

Chart reviews were conducted by the project research technician to obtain data on several programmatic variables such as clinic attendance, methadone dose level, attendance, and participation in the intervention conditions. At the 6-month follow-up interview, the research technician verified employment income either through a pay stub or by employer confirmation. Only verifiable employment was included in the analyses. A total of five subjects (5%) reported income that was nonverifiable. None of these persons reported working more than 5 days in the past 30.

RESULTS

Patient Characteristics

Baseline demographics and level of patient functioning were similar between the two intervention conditions except that patients in the VPSS condition (21%) were more likely than control patients (11%) to have a valid driver's license (Table 2.1). Age ranged from 24 to 67, with a mean age of 43.5. The majority of patients were black (61.5%) and most were men (60.5%). Prior to study

Table 2.1. Baseline Demographics

| Background Characteristic | Condition | | Difference |
	Experimental $n = 62$	Control $n = 47$	
Age (mean)	43.5	43.5	
	($SD = 7.8$)	($SD = 4.7$)	
Gender			
Male	61%	60%	
Race			
White	37%	38%	
Black	61%	62%	
Hispanic	2%		
High School Diploma	66%	53%	
Employed (at least 1 day past month)	25%	19%	
Marketable Skill or Trade	66%	66%	
Current Driver's license	26%	11%	$p < 0.05$
Receiving Public Welfare	94%	89%	
Receiving a Pension (VA or SSDI)	15%	19%	
Marital Status			
Married	20%	13%	
Divorced	36%	38%	
Single	34%	43%	
Widowed	10%	6%	
Psychiatric Functioning Previous hospitalization	37%	47%	
Legal History			
Incarcerated > 30 days lifetime	50%	49%	
Currently on probation/parole	10%	9%	
Engaged in illegal activities for profit within the past 30 days	23%	21%	

$N = 109$.

enrollment, mean unemployment was 16 months ($SD = 13$). Over 90% of patients received some form of public welfare (Medicaid, food stamps, cash assistance, etc.). The mean amount of monthly cash assistance (US$285), food stamps (US$150), and work income received (US$153) were not different between conditions.

Pre-enrollment Employment Barriers

The extent of self-identified barriers to obtain work is noted in Table 2.2. Overall, 11% of clients in the control group reported no employment barriers, compared to 5% in the VPSS group. There were no statistical differences between conditions. Importantly, baseline employment functioning was not statistically different as a function of condition (Table 2.3). Patients randomized to the

Table 2.2. Barriers that Contribute to Unemployment by Intervention Condition

| | Condition | | |
| | Experimental | Control | |
Barriers	N = 62	N = 47	Significance
1. No jobs available	52%	57%	ns
2. Drug abuse too severe	47%	36%	ns
3. Poor work history	35%	23%	ns
4. Unwilling to leave public welfare	27%	26%	ns
5. Police record	26%	23%	ns
6. Inadequate education	29%	19%	ns
7. Poor job skills	24%	15%	ns
8. Transportation	23%	21%	ns
9. Poor motivation	21%	21%	ns
10. Unsure how to look for work	19%	17%	ns
11. No current work barriers	5%	11%	ns

Table 2.3. Analysis of Variance of Patient Functioning by Condition and Time

| | Experimental | | | Control | | | |
| | Baseline n = 58 | | 6-Month n = 58 | Baseline | | 6-Month n = 43 | ANCOVA Condition |
ASI Composite Scores	Mean	t-Test	Mean	n = 43 Mean	t-Test	Mean	by Time
Medical	0.17	ns	0.26	0.20	ns	0.22	ns
Alcohol	0.10	*	0.06	0.08	ns	0.05	ns
Drug	0.25	***	0.17	0.22	ns	0.19	ns
Family/Social	0.13	ns	0.17	0.18	ns	0.21	ns
Legal	0.08	ns	0.07	0.09	ns	0.10	ns
Psychiatric	0.29	ns	0.31	0.28	ns	0.31	ns
Employment	0.82	*	0.75	0.86	ns	0.82	ns
Days paid for working	3.70	**	7.60	4.10	ns	5.80	ns
Employment income	US$178	**	US$322	US$125	ns	US$264	ns
Public Assistance	US$292	**	US$249	US$289	ns	US$265	ns
Income from family	US$73	*	US$20	US$79	ns	US$71	ns
Illegal income	US$145	ns	US$56	US$73	ns	US$30	ns
Days of illegal activities	3.20	*	1.00	2.80	ns	2.30	ns

*$p < 0.05$.

**$p < 0.01$.

***$p < 0.001$.

experimental condition worked an average of 3.7 days, had an income of US$178 per month, and had a high ASI employment composite score (0.82). Similarly, patients randomized to the control condition worked an average of 4 days, had a monthly income of US$125, and had an ASI employment composite score of 0.86.

Program Attendance and Services Received

Overall, the mean number of employment sessions received by patients was 5.3 ($SD = 4.2$) in the experimental condition and 0.85 ($SD = 1.9$) in the control condition. Overall, the methadone counselors provided 96% of the employment services, with only 4% of services reported to be received by a referral site. Patients in the control condition received an average of 5.1 IPS counseling sessions. Within the experimental condition, the total number of employment sessions differed significantly by site ($t = 4.7$, df = 56, $p < 0.01$). The mean number of employment sessions in Site B was 8.2 ($SD = 2.8$) compared to Site A's 3.4 ($SD = 3.8$). The primary reasons for not completing the VPSS sessions as identified by patients at the follow-up assessment were continued drug use; psychiatric problems; no longer interested in employment; and the patient became employed. Staff also cited lack of time to provide services, lack of funding to reimburse employment services, and high caseloads as reasons for not delivering services.

Six-Month Findings

Study results are based on the 6-month outcomes of all 101 located patients (93%). Overall, 58/62 (93.5%) VPSS and 43/47 (91.5%) IPS patients completed the assessment. Attrition differences were not detected between groups. At the 6-month follow-up assessment 58.6% (34/58) of the located patients in the experimental condition had been employed one or more days in the past 30 days, whereas only 37.2% (16/43) of the comparison condition had been employed to this extent. For this analysis, employment was defined as working one or more days in the past 30 days. Based on the Yates adjusted chi-square statistic, the employment rate difference between conditions was statistically significant ($\chi^2 = 4.53$, 1 df, $p < 0.05$).

Because employment functioning can be operationalized in several ways, we examined a series of continuous employment measures (net income, number of days paid for working, and the ASI employment composite score) and found no differences in employment functioning between the two intervention groups at the 6-month follow-up point when controlling for baseline differences. These findings are presented in Table 2.3. As can be seen, a series of paired t-tests found that there were several significant within-group differences in the experimental condition from baseline to the 6-month follow-up point, but the differences were not statistically significant across condition and time. Although more patients were employed as a function of condition, neither net income levels nor the mean number of days worked in the past month were statistically significant between conditions when controlling for baseline factors. Also, no other differences in the six areas of change measured by the ASI or other factors associated with obtaining employment (e.g., decrease in illegal income) were detected as a function of intervention condition.

Multinomial Regression Analysis

A series of bivariate analyses were conducted to examine the correlation between potential predictor variables (e.g., intervention condition, gender, race, etc.) and the criterion variable (employed/not employed at least one day in the past 30 days at the 6-month follow-up point). Intercorrelation tables were calculated to identify and then control for possible multicollinearity. Eight variables were then selected that were either demographically important or independently correlated with employment functioning at the 6-month follow-up; these were simultaneously entered into a multinomial regression analysis. The variables included: gender (male vs. female); age (> 40 vs. 40 or less); patient work history (more than 12 vs. 12 or fewer months employed in the past 3 years); patient motivation (continuous); intervention condition (VPSS vs. IPS); ASI medical composite (continuous); transportation barriers (yes or no); and treatment site (Site A vs. Site B).

Because employment functioning can be operationalized in many ways, it was important to examine the factors that predicted different employment patterns. Table 2.4 details the parameters and parameter estimates of a model predicting three types of employment patterns. At the 6-month follow-up point, 53 (54.6%) were considered unemployed (not paid for working in the past 30 days), 19 (19.6%) were termed part-time employees (paid for working between 1 and 14 days), and 25 (25.8%) were considered full-time employees (paid for working 15 or more days in the past 30). The sample size for this analysis was 97; four cases contained missing data at the 6-month follow-up point and were excluded from the analysis. Overall, the model was able to correctly

Table 2.4. Multinominal Regression of Factors that Predict Employment

| | Number of Days Employed | | | |
| | 1 to 14 Days | | 15 to 30 Days | |
	Exp(B)	CI	Exp(B)	CI
Gender				
Male	2.84	0.67–11.99	2.24	0.38–13.23
Female	1.00			
Age				
40 or less	1.00			
> 40	6.79	1.11–41.25*	61.94	3.47–1107.51*
Site				
A	1.00			
B	5.81	1.34–25.12*	14.70	2.46–87.87*
Transportation barrier				
Yes	35.66	4.01–317.31*	26.27	1.85–373.15*
No	1.00			
Length of work history				
>12 months	5.70	1.11–29.28*	34.66	5.09–236.21**
12 months or less	1.00			
Medical ASI score	1.28	0.18–9.28	−0.002	0.00–0.19
Motivation	1.58	1.08–2.33*	2.54	1.55–4.26*
Condition				
Experimental	3.14	0.79–12.48	1.08	0.23–5.24
Control	1.00			

$n = 97$.
*$p < 0.05$.
**$p < 0.01$.

classify 83.7% of cases that did not work; 48% of cases who worked 1 to 14 days; and 73.9% of cases who worked more than 15 days. Five variables (age greater than 40, increased motivation, work history of 12 months or longer, transportation problems, and intervention site) were predictive of both full (15 or more days worked) and part-time (between 1 and 14 days worked) employment patterns. Additionally, lower severity of medical problems predicted full-time employment. Enrollment in the VPSS condition did not predict employment when entered in with the other variables.

DISCUSSION

The 6-month follow-up evaluation found that significantly more VPSS patients obtained employment than patients in the control condition, initially suggesting that VPSS counseling may have increased patient motivation to seek and obtain work. Although a greater percentage of patients who received the VPSS counseling program actually worked, VPSS was not predictive of employment after controlling for other factors.

The finding that other variables (e.g., older persons, those more motivated to work, and those with more extensive work histories) were more likely to be employed has been demonstrated in other studies (Platt, 1995; Zanis, McLellan, & Randell, 1994). Individuals who had reported transportation barriers at baseline were more likely to obtain either full-time or part-time employment. However, at the 6-month follow-up point, these same persons no longer reported transportation as a barrier; thus, the intervention may have contributed to helping patients resolve transportation issues.

Participation at Site B was also associated with increased employment for both intervention conditions. Although the current study was unable to detect a statistically significant difference between intervention conditions within Site B due to the small sample size, we calculated a power analysis to determine that a sample of 130 persons would have been necessary to yield a difference by condition. Importantly, 75% of the clients randomized to VPSS in Site B obtained employment, compared to 62% randomized to IPS counseling resulting in an effect of over 20%. This finding is very encouraging on two counts. First, when compared against a no-treatment intervention, the overall effect could have been somewhat greater, and, secondly, greater observed compliance in the administration of the intervention protocols at Site B was noted during counseling supervision. For example, there was a significant difference in session attendance, with patients from Site B attending an average of 8.2 VPSS sessions compared to 3.4 VPSS sessions among Site A participants. This was concerning, because we had hypothesized that a minimum of eight sessions would serve as an appropriate therapeutic dose of service. Overall, only 40% of the patients assigned to the VPSS condition across both sites completed 8 of the 10 VPSS counseling sessions.

Although participants received more vocational counseling sessions from Site B vs. Site A, subsequent analyses found that the number of sessions did not predict employment. In fact, at Site B those patients who attended fewer VPSS sessions were more likely to be employed at the 6-month follow-up period. One explanation for this finding was that a few VPSS sessions appropriately administered were sufficient to help some patients take action and find employment.

Finally, lower scores on the ASI medical composite score were predictive of full-time employment. This finding has several implications, because many of the patients enrolled in methadone programs have medically related issues that may limit their participation in full-time employment. It remains unknown if these medically related issues are perceived or real barriers toward obtaining employment.

Why Didn't Patients Attend Sessions?

The methadone patients participating in this study reported many barriers to employment, including lack of job skills, lower levels of education, lack of motivation to work, substance abuse, etc. (See Table 2.2.) Interestingly, the most common identified barrier to employment was lack of available jobs. This perceived barrier may have been addressed in the initial counseling sessions, following which patients actively searched for and obtained employment, thus dropping out of sessions. The unemployment rate at the time of the study ranged from 4% to 8% in the immediate five-county area, resulting in the availability of unskilled jobs. Another factor that patients identified as influencing attendance was the duration of sessions (one session each week for a period of 10 weeks). Although the VPSS intervention was designed to help patients develop vocational problem-solving skills, many patients who were interested in securing employment immediately began actively pursuing employment options. To this end, it appears that patients wanted a job, and wanted the counselors to help them find a job, not information on how to problem-solve vocational barriers.

Similarly, although some patients were successful in obtaining work on their own, others required considerable support to obtain and maintain a job. A study by Silverman et al. (1996) suggested that offering methadone patients vouchers to attend vocational sessions could be one avenue by which to reinforce patient participation in vocational training programs. Importantly, incentives may assist in helping patients attend vocational sessions that in turn can help internally motivate patients to take action. Similarly, Kidorf et al. (1998) found that behavioral contingencies can motivate many MM patients to obtain verifiable employment within the community. To this end, it may be that contingency management coupled with skill development training is an issue to further investigate.

It is also important to question the skills, interest, and capacity of methadone counselors to deliver the VPSS intervention. Although counselors demonstrated competency in delivering the intervention and participated in regularly scheduled training sessions, there is little information about the impact of service delivered by the counselor. Because of the large number of counselors in the study it was not possible to statistically test for counselor effectiveness differences, although, based on observation, some counselors were clearly more motivated and effective than others.

Type of Employment

Although there were no differences in employment rates as a function of intervention condition, it was quite surprising that 46% of the participants did obtain employment in the 30 days preceding the 6-month follow-up evaluation. This represents nearly a 100% increase in documented employment from the baseline rate (23% had worked one or more days in the past 30 days). However, the majority (55%) of these new jobs were classified as "under-the-table," but verified, legal jobs. Interestingly, most clients reported that they were not interested in legal, full-time work because of either institutional barriers (e.g., potential loss of Medicaid, inability to obtain methadone) or personal barriers (did not want a regular work schedule, lack of reliable transportation, etc.) that they were not willing to change.

The types of jobs varied but consisted primarily of unskilled ones. Under-the-table jobs consisted mainly of those such as house repair, landscaping, cleaning, and warehouse work. Full-time jobs consisted of grocery store employees, nursing assistants, and custodial and restaurant work. Given some of the personal and systematic barriers faced by these clients (see Table 2.2) and their need to attend a methadone clinic each day, employment in conventional job settings may not be highly desired.

Study Limitations

Several methodological issues should be noted in the interpretation of the study results. First, although each counselor initially demonstrated interest in the project and a minimum set of competencies to deliver the intervention, several of the counselors reported complications in the delivery of the intervention. Issues identified included poor patient attendance of sessions, and inconsistent counselor adherence and compliance to the manuals. Counselors at Site A cited a lack of time to deliver the intervention. Clearly, the lack of adherence measures to monitor counselor delivery of the VPSS and IPS interventions as defined within the manuals may have led to counselor drift in the integrity of the theoretical model. Additionally, while all counselors demonstrated satisfactory competence prior to the start of the study, we were unable to monitor their competency during the delivery of the intervention. Second, the use of the same counselor to deliver both the VPSS and IPS intervention conditions may have resulted in a bias of the services delivered. It is important to note that few control participants reported receiving employment counseling sessions, and both VPSS and IPS patients received equivalent doses of sessions.

Conclusion

Overall, this community-based study found that patients randomly assigned to receive up to 10 VPSS sessions had similar 6-month employment rates compared to patients assigned to a time- and attention-controlled condition. However, almost 50% of the patients had obtained some part-time employment and nearly 25% of these patients were employed on a full-time basis at the 6-month follow-up point, representing a significant increase in the proportion of patients who obtained employment. To this end, we conclude that structured employment interventions may assist unemployed methadone patients in obtaining employment; however, the type of employment services provided must reflect a variety of patient employment needs. Methadone programs should develop opportunities for patients to receive employment counseling services and advocate for employment opportunities within the community.

ACKNOWLEDGMENTS

This project was funded through grants provided by the National Institute on Drug Abuse.

REFERENCES

Arella, L.R., Deren, S., Randell, J., & Brewington, V. (1990). Structural factors that affect provision of vocational/educational services in methadone maintenance treatment programs. *Journal of Applied Rehabilitation Counseling, 21,* 19–26.

Brewington, V., Arella, L., Deren, S., & Randell, J. (1987). Obstacles to the utilization of vocational services: an analysis of the literature. *International Journal of the Addictions, 22,* 1091–1118.

Bureau of Labor Statistics. (1994). *How the government measures employment.* Washington, DC: United States Department of Labor.

Dole, V.P., Nyswander, M.E., & Warner, A. (1968). Successful treatment of 750 criminal addicts. *Journal of the American Medical Association, 206,* 2708–2711.

Etheridge, R.M., Craddock, S.G., Dunteman, G.H., & Hubbard, R.L. (1995). Treatment services in two national studies of community-based drug abuse treatment programs. *Journal of Substance Abuse Treatment, 7,* 9–26.

French, M.T., Dennis, M.L., McDougal, G.L., Karuntzos, G.T., & Hubbard, R.L. (1992). Training and employment programs in methadone treatment: client needs and desires. *Journal of Substance Abuse Treatment, 9,* 293–303.

Hall, S.M., Loeb, P., LeVois, M., & Cooper, J. (1981). Increasing employment in ex-heroin addicts; II. Methadone maintenance sample. *Behavior Therapy, 12,* 453–460.

Hubbard, R.L., Rachal, J.V., Craddock, S.G., & Cavanaugh, E.R. (1984). Treatment outcome prospective study (TOPS): client characteristics and behaviors before, during, and after treatment. In F.M. Tims, & J.P. Ludford (Eds.), *Drug abuse treatment evaluation: strategies, progress, and prospects,* (vol. 51, pp. 42–68) (NIDA research monograph, Rockville, MD).

Kidorf, M., Hollander, J.R., King, V.L., & Brooner, R.K. (1998). Increasing employment of opioid dependent outpatients: an intensive behavioral intervention. *Drug and Alcohol Dependence, 50,* 73–80.

Kosten, T.R., Rounsaville, B.J., & Kleber, H.D. (1983). Concurrent validity of the Addiction Severity Index. *Journal of Nervous and Mental Disorders, 171,* 606–610.

McLellan, A.T., Arndt, I.O., Metzger, D.S., Woody, G.E., & O'Brien, C.P. (1993). The effects of psychosocial services in substance abuse treatment. *Journal of the American Medical Association, 269,* 1953–1959.

McLellan, A.T., Ball, J.C., Rosen, L., & O'Brien, C.P. (1981). Pretreatment source of income and response to Methadone maintenance: a follow-up study. *American Journal of Psychiatry, 138,* 785–789.

McLellan, A.T., Luborsky, L., Cacciola, J., Griffith, J., Evans, F., Barr, H.L., & O'Brien, C.P. (1985). New data from the Addiction Severity Index: reliability and validity in three centers. *Journal of Nervous and Mental Disorders, 173,* 412–422.

McLellan, A.T., Luborsky, L., O'Brien, C.P., & Woody, G.E. (1980). An improved evaluation instrument for substance abuse patients: the Addiction Severity Index. *Journal of Nervous and Mental Disease, 168,* 26–33.

Metzger, D.S., Platt, J.J., Zanis, D., & Fureman, I. (1992). *Vocational problem-solving skills: a structured intervention for unemployed substance abuse treatment clients.* Philadelphia: University of Pennsylvania.

Platt, J.J. (1980). Cognitive interpersonal problem solving skills and the maintenance of treatment success in heroin addicts. *Psychology of Addictive Behaviors, 1,* 5–13.

Platt, J.J. (1995). Vocational rehabilitation of drug abusers. *Psychological Bulletin, 117,* 416–433.

Platt, J.J., & Metzger, D.S. (1987). *Final report, role of work in the rehabilitation of methadone clients.* Rockville, MD: National Institute on Drug Abuse.

Siegal, H.A., Fisher, J.A., Rapp, R.C., Kelleher, C.W., Wagner, J.H., O'Brien, W.F., & Cole, P.A. (1996). Enhancing substance abuse treatment with case management. Its impact on employment. *Journal of Substance Abuse Treatment, 13,* 93–98.

Silverman, K., Chutuape, M.A.D., Bigelow, G.E., & Stitzer, M.L. (1996). Voucher-based reinforcement of attendance by unemployed methadone patients in a job skills training program. *Drug and Alcohol Dependence, 41,* 197–207.

Zanis, D.A., McLellan, A.T., & Randell, M. (1994). Can you trust self-reports of substance users during treatment? *Drug and Alcohol Dependence, 35,* 127–132.

Zanis, D.A., Metzger, D.S., & McLellan, A.T. (1994). Factors associated with employment among methadone patients. *Journal of Substance Abuse Treatment, 11,* 443–447.

COMMENTARY BY: David A. Zanis

GENERAL ISSUES PRIOR TO STUDY IMPLEMENTATION

How and Why We Came to Do the Research

Our research team had investigated the role of employment as a predictor of improved functioning among substance dependent persons enrolled in methadone maintenance treatment programs (MMTP) for many years. Generally, there were three reasons to pursue this issue: (1) Previous studies had found that employment was correlated with improved outcomes; (2) employment could provide individuals with the financial resources, social opportunities, and daily structure to achieve goals; and (3) employment was often identified by clients as a goal.

The published article referenced in this commentary is a result of approximately nine years of work. This includes nearly six years of developmental work and pilot testing, and three years to conduct the study, analyze data, write the article, and submit it for publication. As described in the commentary, the research process involves many twists and turns along the way, always presenting new opportunities and testing slightly different approaches. Not only did our research provide support for our original research question, it also allowed us to formulate many other questions and pursue further inquiry.

In order to fully appreciate the research behind the referenced article, it is critical to have an understanding of the developmental work and pilot testing that was undertaken. Even with good preliminary work, conducting community-based experimental designs presents challenges.

Developmental Work

Developmental work is the process that social scientists go through in formulating research questions and beginning to design research projects. Activities that we conducted included brainstorming ideas with other professional colleagues, discussing with practitioners the clinical utility of the idea, conducting a literature review to understand to what degree others have conducted similar work, and developing partnerships with organizations for possible pilot work.

Initially, we implemented the intervention with one to two persons in various settings (e.g., shelters, drug treatment programs), which resulted in a "draft" intervention manual known as Vocational Problem Solving Skills (VPSS). The VPSS intervention consisted of 10 sessions that were delivered sequentially, and built upon the theoretical framework of Interpersonal Cognitive Problem Solving. The manual was developed for two important reasons. First, it provided clinical

Commentary on article: Zanis, D. A., Coviello, D., Alterman, A. I., & Appling, S. E. (2001). A community-based trial of vocational problem-solving to increase employment among methadone patients. *Journal of Substance Abuse Treatment, 21,* 19–26.

staff with a standard framework to deliver services in a reliable fashion. Second, it provided researchers with a guide by which to evaluate the fidelity of how services were delivered. Thus, the researcher can more effectively control for the content of the services delivered and begin to build a "cause and effect" case for the effectiveness of the intervention.

An additional goal of the developmental work was to produce an intervention that met the requirements of agency standards, governmental requirements, and reimbursement criteria of insurers. Meeting these conditions could lead to a greater likelihood of the intervention being used within community-based methadone programs. Again, various key partners (practitioners, colleagues, etc.) participated in these discussions, to ensure that the materials reflected their views, opinions, and experiences. This consensus-building process is often referred to as content validity development.

Pilot Testing

Following the developmental work, our research team and key partners were satisfied that the manual was ready to be more formally evaluated. Pilot testing is an important and necessary stage of the research process. It allowed our research team to implement and evaluate the entire VPSS intervention for efficacy. About $10,000 in funding for the initial pilot work was secured through a grant for pilot research programs from the University of Pennsylvania. This type of support is often necessary to collect pilot data that can be used for further, more rigorously designed research studies.

Two methadone counselors in a university-affiliated methadone program were trained to deliver the VPSS program with 10 unemployed clients. Clients and counselors were selected based upon convenience for the pilot study. We conducted a process evaluation of the pilot study, which consisted of individual meetings with clients and counselors after each session, geared toward understanding what was learned and obtaining qualitative feedback from both clients and counselors on the sessions. The project director (PD) audiotaped the counseling sessions and was able to rate the sessions for fidelity, content, and process issues, based upon a checklist developed by the investigator and research team. The checklist identified the minimum necessary core components of the VPSS intervention as determined by the consensus team who had reviewed the manual. This pilot project enabled us to monitor the delivery of the manual, obtain participant feedback on the intervention, assess instrumentation, and collect data on the efficacy of the VPSS program. Based on the individual qualitative interviews and client behavioral outcomes (e.g., number of job interviews obtained, hours worked, etc.) it was determined by the counselors, the project staff, and the clients that the VPSS intervention led to improved client vocational outcomes.

Funding

With the preliminary data obtained from the pilot studies, the Principal Investigator (PI) submitted a grant to the National Institute on Drug Abuse (NIDA) to investigate the efficacy of the VPSS to improve employment functioning and reduce drug use. The grant application was an R03 funding mechanism for small grants; the funding amount was approximately $100,000 over a two-year period. Although the application received a good score during the first submission, it was not funded. The comments of the NIDA review committee were addressed and incorporated in a resubmission, and the project scored well enough for funding.

SPECIFIC ISSUES RELATED TO STUDY IMPLEMENTATION

Selection of a Randomized Design

Selection of a randomized design was undertaken because, in theory, it could provide optimal opportunities to measure for cause-and-effect relationships, while ruling out rival hypotheses. Additionally, it would have been less likely for the National Institute on Drug Abuse (NIDA) to fund a less rigorous design. As noted above, we had undertaken extensive pilot work in designing the intervention, and the pilot data suggested that if the VPSS intervention was delivered as designed we could expect to see significant clinical improvement in employment functioning and some improvement related to reduced substance use.

Recruitment

Prior to study implementation, the research team met with staff from both sites and explained the project. We asked staff members to inform their clients about the research study; also, a research assistant gave a letter to each client inviting them to participate in the screening process. Nearly 90 percent of all unemployed clients at both clinics participated in the screening process. Overall recruitment was not a barrier to the implementation of the study for two reasons: (1) The research team and the PI had a strong previous working relationship with the programs, and had developed goodwill with both the agency staff and clients of the programs; and (2) the project itself was conducive to client enrollment because it could result in employment, a desired outcome. Although we had intended to recruit 160 subjects, we were only able to recruit 109 because of a start-up issue at Site B.

Randomization Procedures

We instituted a 3:2 randomization protocol so that more clients could be assigned to the employment intervention condition (VPSS). This unequal randomization protocol allowed us to monitor the delivery of the intervention with more participants. However, on the downside, the lack of an equivalent randomization sequence reduced our capacity to measure differences by intervention condition between sites. Since we experienced significant site differences, the unequal groups within and across conditions limited our statistical power to detect differences within Site A. One limitation of the randomization procedures was not to stratify by condition across sites, which led to unequal distribution of condition within sites.

Site Selection Issues

In our NIDA grant application, we had secured letters of commitment and participation from two methadone maintenance programs located in Philadelphia. We selected two sites because we needed to recruit 160 clients to satisfy our power calculations. Recruitment at each site was conducted over a 12-month period. Initially, the selection and the negotiation of the research sites did not pose a problem. Our team had previously performed research at both sites, and we were familiar with the client population, setting, staff, and administration. Also, we negotiated an informal agreement with each site to provide staff training opportunities, supervision, and research seminars. Moreover, counseling staff viewed the project as an opportunity to develop new skills around employment counseling strategies. The program administrators were enthusiastic because we had developed a system to integrate the VPSS intervention during standard drug counseling sessions—therefore, the treatment programs could receive reimbursement for delivering the service as a counseling session that met most third-party reimbursement criteria.

While the research project was met with equal enthusiasm by the two sites, unexpected issues in the organizational structure changed the dynamics of the study. About one-third of the way through the project, the ownership and management of Site A changed. A new executive director was hired, and there was immediate staff turnover within the program. The research project continued as planned, but the degree of support from the previous administration was no longer available. Because of the change in ownership, staff meetings at Site A were consumed with organizational management issues (e.g., policies, cash-flow issues, inadequate supervision, etc.), and the research project took a secondary role. These dramatic changes in the functioning of the agency affected the counseling staff's enthusiasm. Although only one counselor within the project resigned, the initial "buy in" by the staff had changed from a sense of cooperation to a sense of burden. For example, although it was unrelated to the research project, one counselor filed a grievance with the new management of the clinic for unfair labor practices. Clearly, these issues impacted the counselors' commitment to the research project.

To address the Site A issues, a number of meetings were arranged between the research PI and the new administration. These meetings resulted in a number of promises (e.g., counselor caseloads would not increase, the program would stabilize). When implementation of these promises was delayed significantly, we had invested too much time and resources to withdraw from the site. Furthermore, we did not have enough funding to extend the project and recruit more clients at Site B.

Conversely, Site B was ideal, and the counseling staff and administration participated fully in the study. The staff attended weekly team meetings, completed research project paperwork on time, and provided many insights about how to enhance the quality of the intervention and revise the manual. Within Site B, one counselor had volunteered to serve as the on-site project coordinator. This person took extraordinary interest in the project and was able to address issues on a day-to-day basis. She assisted the research staff in scheduling research appointments, notifying research staff if there were clinic issues, and representing the project during program meetings.

Overall, the issues encountered at Site A presented significant study threats, but our intent was to research the implementation of the intervention in "real world" community-based settings. Needless to say, at the end of the project, we found site differences. In retrospect, we were fortunate that the research study had been implemented at two different clinics. Although the sample size was not sufficient in Site B to yield valid results, it certainly provided reasonable clinical evidence that the intervention was effective. In other words, the effect was achieved, but power was not sufficient to detect the difference due to a small sample size.

Maintaining the Integrity of the Experiment

The PI was responsible for maintaining the study integrity. This was completed by facilitating a weekly research meeting that addressed issues such as recruitment, intervention delivery, follow-up rates, and all aspects of the project. Additionally, the PI was responsible for submitting regular reports to NIDA project officers, and for convening an advisory committee of other researchers to provide project oversight.

Treatment Fidelity and Model Drift

Each participating counselor was required to complete an eight-hour training on the delivery of the intervention. All counselors were given implementation manuals that had step-by-step guidelines on how to deliver the VPSS and IPS sessions. During the training, counselors viewed live demonstrations of how to deliver the intervention and had opportunities to engage in role-play situations. After the training, counselors were asked to read through the manual and practice delivering the sessions in role-plays with other staff. About two weeks later, all counselors were rated by two independent raters on their delivery of the intervention. Each counselor was rated on their capacity to use the common theoretical framework of the VPSS intervention.

Counselors also participated in 12 one-hour ongoing booster sessions that detailed how to deliver each of the 10 counseling sessions. During these sessions, counselors discussed their experiences in the delivery of the interventions. Additionally, each counselor participated in weekly supervision sessions to discuss how to address any difficulties with the delivery of the VPSS or control condition. This activity was valuable at both sites because staff were able to listen to the experiences of their peers. It provided a good perspective on how to deliver the intervention; additionally, it allowed the research staff to listen for issues of intervention drift.

As noted in the article, there were significant site differences in counseling services. There were an average of 8.2 employment sessions at Site B vs. 3.4 sessions at Site A. Staff at Site A attributed the differences in attendance to administrative factors such as staff turnover within the program, increased caseloads, lack of time, and client disinterest. Unfortunately, we were unable to control for the additional burdens that the Site A organization placed on the counseling staff. Because of staff turnover at the agency, the counselors involved in the research were unofficially given additional assignments, which limited their time with clients. At one point during the study, Site A had four vacancies for counseling staff.

From a research perspective, we had procedures in place to collect service delivery data from three different sources: patient self-report, counselor self-report; and counselor documentation on client treatment records. As we collected and compared these data, we began to see differences in the number of counseling sessions provided, type of sessions provided, and length of counseling sessions. For example, when we abstracted data from client records, we found that counselors reported more time spent in counseling sessions, and more sessions provided, when compared against counselor self-reports to our research staff. Similarly, when our research staff interviewed clients, they reported significantly less time participating in counseling sessions, and receiving fewer counseling sessions, than were either reported by their counselor or found in their client records.

We began to investigate these issues immediately to attempt to uncover why there were discrepancies. It seemed that there was considerable variability in how clients and counselors defined the services provided and services received. Every two weeks, we asked clients to report the number of counseling sessions received for various issues (employment, drug use, etc.). Concurrently, we asked counselors to report the same information for services provided. Both counselors and clients were asked to report on the number of sessions, the length of time of the session, and to rate the quality of the session. One main source of variation was that the new Site A administrator developed an internal policy that all counseling sessions were to be recorded in the patient record as 50 minutes in length (the required length of time to receive maximum reimbursement). While these variations in measuring service delivery and monitoring the integrity of the intervention provided for interesting research questions, they did little to help us maintain the integrity of the study. Although we thought we had adequate procedures built into the study design, we were unable to account for some of the unscrupulous behavior of the administration. Clearly a major weakness of study design was our lack of monitoring the counseling sessions through video- or audiotaping. It should be noted that we did not encounter these differences at Site B, and we attribute this to the stability of the program's administration. Counselor and client reports were highly correlated, staff self-reports and client records were almost identical. We were able to maintain high integrity of the study at this site.

Monitoring/Avoiding Remaining Threats to Internal Validity

Despite the use of a randomized design, the following threats to internal validity were present:

- *Compensatory Equalization*—Because counseling staff delivered both the experimental and control conditions, it allowed for the possibility that the counselor might deliver the experimental intervention to the clients in the control group. We tried to account for this threat by having counselors meet in supervision sessions on a weekly basis to discuss how they were delivering both intervention conditions. Importantly, both conditions were manualized and arranged in 10 sequential sessions, and therefore it was somewhat easier to control for drift. Since sessions were not audio- or videotaped, we are uncertain as to what truly happened during the counseling sessions.

- *Demoralization*—When informed about randomization to the IPS condition, several clients in the control condition opted to attend fewer sessions and may not have tried as much to change their behaviors. Initially our client recruitment got off to a slower than expected start. However when the first client in the experimental condition was hired, word filtered throughout the program and we no longer experienced difficulty in recruiting. It also set up a dynamic in that many of the potential participants believed that we would "get them a job." This phrase was commonly used, and some participants would say, "You got Joe a great job, why can't we skip this counseling stuff and just help me get the job." As previously noted, this led to some early attrition from the control condition because participants wanted job referrals, not vocational problem-solving skills.

- *Diffusion*—Because participants in both experimental and control conditions were located in the same methadone program, there was the threat that participants could discuss and share different approaches about how to obtain employment. While we did not observe this behavior, we did notice that once a participant was hired for a job, other persons in the methadone program applied for a position at the same employer.

- *Compensatory Rivalry*—We know of two subjects in the control condition who wanted employment and decided that they really did not need counseling and could just go out and find employment without assistance.

- *Differential Attrition*—We did not see attrition as a threat to the study since we had compensated clients to participate in the follow-up evaluations. Moreover, we had maintained contact with the subjects on a two-week basis to ask about their progress. The project realized high rates of subject completion of the various research assessments. We experienced only a 7 percent attrition rate at the 6-month follow-up point. Of this number, three participants were incarcerated, one had died, and one moved out of the area. Much of this is credited to the good rapport established by the research assistants, and the small compensation ($5.00) paid to subjects for meeting with research staff every two weeks to complete the research assessments.

- *Protocol Deviation*—Because we did not audiotape, videotape, or participate in the actual counseling sessions, the threat of protocol deviation from the manual was present. Our strategies to reduce deviation relied upon the counselors to follow the manual and deliver it as written. Weekly supervision sessions relied upon the counselors to disclose their level of implementation fidelity. Because we believed that a good relationship existed with the counselors, we expected a high level of truthfulness in their reports to us on manual fidelity. When the number of counseling sessions differ between the intervention conditions, a Hawthorne effect could materialize, as participants in one condition receive more attention than the other condition.

Instrumentation

The instruments selected for the study included both standardized assessments commonly used in the field of addiction research (Addiction Severity Index) and a nonstandardized interview designed to measure a variety of employment outcomes. Our early pilot testing allowed us to detect various ways to measure employment. We were interested in capturing as many dimensions of employment as possible, including under-the-table employment and illegal activities. We thought that our internally created instrument was sufficient to reflect the daily employment opportunities for a client population that often consisted of individuals with lower job skills, less education, and greater biopsychosocial risk factors. However, we did experience some challenges in trying to recode responses. For example, one client reported that he worked 3 days per week, but worked 12 hours per day. Another client worked 7 days per week, but only 2 hours per day. These variations in employment patterns can and did create some challenging issues. We decided not to try to recode the number of days worked, since there did not seem to be a standard procedure for this issue. In retrospect, it may have been optimal to determine the overall number of hours worked. This would have allowed us to document a smaller common denominator, enabling us to develop an outcome variable with greater specificity.

Another challenge was validating actual employment in cases where participants reported receiving cash from their jobs. In cases where there was no pay stub to validate employment, the research assistant physically traveled to the workplace to observe that the client was working.

In Table 2.3 of the article, we reported on seven different variables associated with employment and income. Each variable was analyzed both within and across condition in an effort to understand variation. Overall, the consistency of differences found both within and across condition lends credibility to the findings.

Ethical Issues

We did not experience any unusual issues with the IRB, and the project was fully approved by the University's IRB. Additionally, Site B maintained their own IRB and approved the project. Site A did not have an IRB, and the University IRB served as the responsible entity to oversee participant protection. It should be noted that the IRB process took approximately four months to complete; however, we had prepared materials well ahead of time to insure that the materials met the IRB protocols.

One ethical issue that we encountered was how to appropriately address the change in ownership and presenting issues related to Site A. The PI had convened an advisory board of three senior NIDA-funded researchers and the NIDA project officer to discuss opinions on how to proceed. Our main priority was to determine if we should continue with Site A, or stop this portion of the study. Since our objective was to examine the study as part of a community-based trial, we elected to continue with Site A and include Site A in any published reports. It is important to have an advisory board that provides a system of checks and balances on research integrity.

Ethical and Legal Issues Related to Denial of Service

The research project was designed so that no clients would be denied basic services. All clients received standard counseling services and the opportunity to participate in additional counseling sessions. Regardless of condition, clients were referred to local community employment programs to pursue job training or job placement.

Strengths and Limitations of the Study

A clear strength of the study was our ability to collect a high rate of follow-up data. Overall, 93 percent of the study participants completed 6-month post-baseline follow-up interviews. Data on the type of counseling services (e.g., employment, drug use) and number of counseling services provided to participants (as measured by both the participant and the counselor) offered validation that participants in the experimental condition received employment counseling and participants in the control condition did not receive employment counseling. Other strengths included the involvement of counseling staff at Site B, who voluntarily participated in the project and provided feedback about the utility of the intervention within community-based, publicly funded methadone programs. Counselors shared their experiences of implementing the manual-based exercise, which in turn allowed us to modify the manual and include specific field examples.

As previously noted, significant limitations of the study included methodological threats experienced in the project. (These internal validity threats are described above.) The major limitation was the inability to independently monitor the delivery of the intervention (via audiotaping, for example).

Another limitation of the study was low power to independently analyze predictor data within each methadone clinic. The first cut at the data involved simple independent bivariate analyses, which produced significant differences between the experimental and control conditions (see Table 2.3, within-group differences). However, after accounting for baseline differences and performing analyses across conditions, the effects of the intervention were not statistically significant. Additionally the use of regression analyses allowed us to better understand factors that led to employment. This analysis yielded that the variable "site of the intervention" was a significant predictor.

Finally, having to conduct the research within the 2-year limitation of funding was another limitation of the study. In order to satisfy the obligations of our grant, we decided to include two sites. The use of two sites provided a number of methodological challenges because we were unable to have consistency across sites (e.g., counselors had different skills, different incentives, different philosophies within the programs, etc.).

New Hunches

A number of interesting issues emerged during the project, particularly surrounding how clients adapted to employment following hire. One observation led to an additional pilot study that provided case management or "coaching" services to newly hired clients. The case management assisted newly employed clients by describing the culture of work. For example, we found that some clients were unsure how to negotiate time off with their supervisors to address drug abuse issues or medical appointments. In some cases, the clients failed to advocate for their needs because they did not want to divulge their drug use history or treatment enrollment to their supervisor or employer. Unfortunately when this occurred, clients usually made poor judgments by either missing medical appointments or not showing up for work.

MAJOR ADVICE FOR FUTURE RESEARCH IN THE AREA

One of the areas in which we experienced a problem was that about 10 percent of the clients recruited into the study had dropped out within the first two weeks. We implemented an "intent to treat" design in which all recruited participants were included in the final analyses, even if they did not receive a minimal therapeutic dose of control or experimental counseling sessions. It may have been advisable to include only those subjects that had participated in a minimal number of intervention services. It seems that almost all unemployed clients wanted to voluntarily enroll in the project. Possibly an improved format to screen out clients who were not interested in working could be designed. One method that could allow clients who were not interested in work could involve a more rigorous compliance process, in which a minimum of three sessions would have to be attended prior to inclusion in the project. This would then allow a more realistic understanding of the effectiveness of the VPSS program to help clients gain employment.

APPLICATION OF STUDY FINDINGS TO SOCIAL WORK AND HUMAN SERVICE PRACTICE AT BOTH THE MICRO AND MACRO LEVELS

A simple but critical finding of the project was that counseling staff who participated at Site B were able to effectively deliver the intervention, and these services were strongly associated with improved client outcomes. Therefore, at the micro level, counselors were able to implement the manual effectively. At the macro level, as noted in the article, there are major implications regarding the need for continued health insurance for individuals who transition from welfare to the workplace. Few health insurance companies pay for methadone treatment, and of those that do, the reimbursement is not sufficient, in that co-pays are cost-prohibitive for most clients to continue working. Thus, even if clients obtain employment, they need to have health insurance pay for methadone treatment, since it is cost-prohibitive for clients who have low paying jobs.

GENERALIZABILITY OF FINDINGS

The findings presented within the article describe our experience in conducting a research study. The extent to which they are generalizeable to other methadone programs is limited. We set out to create an intervention that could be readily adopted to fit within standard counseling sessions within a methadone treatment setting. If we had considered Sites A and B independently, the experiment would have resulted in a much different understanding of the generalizability of the VPSS program. Based on the reports from clients and counselors, we believe that the VPSS is a reasonably valid counseling approach to help clients obtain employment. The challenge consists in how the intervention is delivered. The integrity of delivery can not be controlled with a manual, but relies upon the supervision, passion, enthusiasm, commitment, capacity, and structure of the organization and staff.

Funding for this project was supported by a grant from the NIDA (R03DA08225).

3

The Impact of Ethnicity on Prospective Functional Outcomes from Community-Based Psychosocial Rehabilitation for Persons with Schizophrenia

Elizabeth S. Phillips, Concepcion Barrio and John S. Brekke

Although there have been only a few studies on ethnicity and psychosocial rehabilitation for individuals with schizophrenia (Baker, Stokes-Thompson, Davis, Gonzo, & Hishinuma, 1999; Jerrell & Wilson, 1997; Telles et al., 1995), cross-ethnic differences have been found in other areas that are notable. For example, two major multinational studies sponsored by the World Health Organization (WHO)—the International Pilot Study of Schizophrenia (IPSS) and the Determinants of Outcome of Severe Mental Disorders (DOSMD)—have revealed that although the incidence of a core schizophrenia syndrome is similar across diverse cultural settings, there are cross-cultural differences in the course and outcome of the illness (Craig, Siegel, Hooper, Lin, & Sartorius, 1997; Sartorius, Jablensky, & Shapiro, 1977). Regardless of the nature of onset and presenting symptoms, there is a marked predominance of favorable outcomes in the centers of developing counties as opposed to the developed nations of Europe and North America. This finding was replicated in a 13-year follow-up of the IPSS cohort (Hopper & Wanderling, 2000). Although the WHO studies have been criticized on the basis of sampling biases and other methodological factors (Cohen, 1988; Lin

This research was supported by National Institute of Mental Health research grant MH43640, and NIMH Independent Scientist Award MH01628, both awarded to the third author.

Phillips, E., Barrio, C., Brekke J.S. (2001). The impact of ethnicity on prospective functional outcomes from community-based psychosocial rehabilitation for persons with schizophrenia. *Journal of Community Psychology, 29,* 657–673. © 2001 John Wiley. This material is used by permission of John Wiley & Sons, Inc.

& Kleinman, 1988), the consensus among many cross-cultural researchers is that collectivistic cultures favor symptom recovery and the restoration of function (Brekke & Barrio, 1997; Hopper & Wanderling, 2000; Karno & Jenkins, 1993; Lin & Kleinman, 1988; Sartorius et al., 1986).

In the United States, cross-ethnic studies on schizophrenia have focused primarily on the expression of symptoms. Fabrega, Mezzich, and Ulrich (1988) examined differences in psychopathology between African Americans and non-minorities and found that the latter were more impaired on items that rated emotional distance and flat affect, as well as on items that rated depressed mood and low self-esteem. Chu, Sallach, Zakeria, and Klein (1985) revealed that African Americans were more likely to exhibit anger, disorientation, asocial behavior, and hallucinations, whereas non-minorities experienced more symptoms of irrelevant speech and delusions.

Tri-ethnic studies comparing non-minorities, Latinos, and African Americans have shown higher levels of paranoia and hysteria for African Americans (Valasquez & Callahan, 1990), and higher somatization for Hispanics (Canino, Rubio-Stipec, Canino, & Escobar, 1992; Escobar, 1987). Recently, Brekke and Barrio (1997) found that non-minorities had a more symptomatic profile than African Americans and Latinos in the United States. They also found support for their hypothesis that ethnic minorities come from a more sociocentric culture, which had a mediating impact on presenting symptoms.

Studies that address the treatment of patients with severe mental disorders have uncovered noteworthy differences as well. For example, it was found that minority patients were more likely to be prescribed higher doses of antipsychotic medications than their non-minority counterparts (Lehman & Steinwachs, 1998). Correspondingly, a study that looked at admission rates to various hospital settings found marked ethnic-related differences (Snowden & Cheung, 1990). In that study, African Americans overutilized hospital services, while those patients of Hispanic origin tended to underutilize services when compared to non-minorities. Snowden and Hu (1997) found that cross-ethnic differences in service utilization among the severely mentally ill were related to variations in how mental health service systems responded to the sociocultural needs of ethnic minority clients.

Related to this, Sue and colleagues found that ethnic minority patients demonstrated a pattern of limited use and premature termination of outpatient services when compared to non-minorities (Sue, 1976, 1977; Sue, McKinney, Allen, & Hall, 1974). The authors called for research and program development to integrate ethnic-sensitive services in an attempt to attract more minorities to community mental health centers (CMHCs). Among their recommendations were to increase minority service providers, develop ethnic-specific services within minority communities, and to develop culturally relevant programming. Ten years after the implementation of most of these suggestions, O'Sullivan, Peterson, Cox, and Kirkeby (1989) replicated Sue and colleagues' studies and found improved follow-up and increased service utilization rates among the ethnic groups studied. Ethnic minorities that had been previously underrepresented in the CMHCs were then represented in proportion to the general population. A recent study (Lau & Zane, 2000) also found that ethnically specific mental health services were more effective than mainstream services for Asian-American clients.

Finally, three studies revealed a relationship between ethnicity and outcomes from psychosocial interventions for individuals with severe and persistent mental illness. A family intervention study by Telles et al. (1995) found no difference when comparing the effectiveness of behavioral family management (BFM) and case management among low-income Latino schizophrenia patients. Contrary to their hypothesis, at one-year follow-up BFM was associated with greater symptomatology. These findings were surprising particularly because aspects of the BFM approach had been culturally modified for the Mexican immigrant sample. These researchers implicate the highly structured program involving communication exercises and directives, which may have been intrusive and stressful. On the other hand, in a study using a single ethnic group Baker et al. (1999) found positive functional outcomes for African Americans participating in an intensive program based on the assertive community treatment model. However, there was no indication how the cultural relevance of the program was determined and how cultural factors were incorporated into the program's design.

In another study, Jerrell and Wilson (1997) collapsed African Americans, Latinos, Asians, and Native Americans into a single ethnic minority group and compared the outcomes from three different community-based treatments for persons diagnosed with dual mental and substance use disorders. In a 6-month intervention, despite ethnic clients having lower psychosocial functioning scores at baseline and receiving less supportive treatment from providers, overall outcomes were equivalent to those of non-minority clients. There was also some evidence for treatment by ethnicity interactions, with the ethnic minority group being more symptomatic in a 12-step intervention, but showing fewer drug and alcohol symptoms in a behavioral skills group.

Altogether, these findings point to the complex role of ethnocultural factors in the treatment of individuals with serious mental illness, and the need for more research in this area (Barrio, 2000). Specifically, since ethnicity has been so rarely investigated in over 20 years of research on community-based rehabilitation services, it is important to investigate ethnic variations in the outcomes from effective intervention models. It will then be possible to determine the need for ethnic-based variations in rehabilitation services for persons with severe mental illness.

The purpose of this study was to examine cross-ethnic variation in prospective functional outcomes from effective community-based psychosocial rehabilitation for persons with schizophrenia. Given the results from previous cross-ethnic studies on other models of community-based care, we proposed that African Americans and Latinos would show poorer functional outcomes over time when compared to non-minorities (Euro-American Caucasians). This hypothesis was also suggested by the lack of an explicit programmatic focus on cultural relevance in the interventions investigated here.

We were concerned about one other confound that was not adequately addressed in previous studies. In making cross-ethnic comparisons, several investigators have argued that a minimally acceptable standard is to use two ethnic minority groups and one non-minority group in a tri-ethnic design (Neff & Hope, 1993; Segall, 1986). This is because the effects of ethnicity and minority status are confounded in cross-ethnic studies in the United States that compare non-minorities to any other one ethnic minority group. With a tri-ethnic design, if differences between ethnic groups persist after the impact of social class is controlled, then the exploration of cultural differences is supported. This study will employ a tri-ethnic strategy with the purpose of examining cross-ethnic variation in prospective functional outcome domains from community-based psychosocial rehabilitation for persons with schizophrenia. Specifically, we hypothesized that ethnicity minority individuals (African American and Latino) would show poorer rehabilitative outcomes over time in the domains of hospitalization, work, social functioning, and independent living when compared to non-minority Caucasians.

METHOD

Design

This study used data from an investigation that was conducted from 1989 to 1994. The parent study employed a quasi-experimental follow-along design of patients admitted consecutively to three community-based intervention programs in Los Angeles (Brekke, Long, Nesbitt, & Sobel, 1997). In a comparison of the three interventions, the two that were high in service intensity were shown to be more effective in improving functional outcomes (Brekke et al., 1997; Brekke, Ansel, Long,

Slade, & Weinstein, 1999). The third intervention was a low-intensity case management program operated by the County Department of Mental Health, which had no particular rehabilitative focus. For the purposes of this study, only data from the two effective psychosocial rehabilitation programs were examined. The programs are described below. Prospective data for this study came from face-to-face interviews done with participants at baseline and then every six months over three years.

A previous tri-ethnic study using the same sample showed that there was no significant association between ethnicity and social class (Brekke & Barrio, 1997); therefore ethnic differences on outcome domains could implicate the role of ethnocultural influences. In this study, the term "non-minority" will refer to Caucasians of European-American origin.

Treatment Programs. Both of the community-based psychosocial rehabilitation sites used in this study have been shown to be effective in improving aspects of functional outcomes (Brekke et al., 1997; Brekke et al., 1999), therefore, they were excellent sites for examining the association of ethnicity with functional rehabilitative change.

Site 1 is a comprehensive rehabilitation program located in urban Los Angeles that provides its members with pre-employment training, job development, and employment with support and follow-up. It offers educational and socialization programs, as well as linkages to other community resources. Based on data presented in Brekke and Test (1992), this site provides an average of 12 hr/month of staff-to-client contact during the first 3 months that members were in the program. This drops to about 5 hr/month by month 12. Twenty-seven percent of the client service contacts were in the vocational area, and 17% focused on independent living skills (Brekke et al., 1997).

Site 2 provides clients with 3 months of intensive training in the areas of socialization and independent living, followed by less intensive ongoing support and rehabilitation. In addition, crisis management services are provided to prevent hospitalizations. This site averaged over 35 hr/month of staff-to-client contact during its 3-month training period, which dropped to about 7 hr/month by month 12. They provided very little vocational training, but 39% of their staff–client contact time involved daily and independent living skills (Brekke & Test, 1992).

Sample

The sample ($n = 98$) was comprised of 25 females and 73 males diagnosed with either schizophrenia or schizoaffective disorder. Forty-two (42%) were non-minority Caucasians, 37 (38%) were African American, and 19 (19%) were Latino. The average age was 33 years ($SD = 7.3$), and the average length of illness was 11.2 years ($SD = 7$). Nearly all of the clients were receiving public assistance and had received treatment in the publicly funded mental health system. There were four study admission criteria: (a) a diagnosis of schizophrenia or schizoaffective disorder; (b) residence in Los Angeles for at least 3 months before study admission; (c) 18–60 years of age; and (d) neither a diagnosis of mental retardation or organic brain syndrome, nor a primary diagnosis of substance dependence. While not a criterion for admission, it was determined in an earlier study that the Latino population was well acculturated (Brekke & Barrio, 1997). Eighty-seven percent were born in the United States and of the 13% born outside the United States, on average 68% of their lives were spent residing in the United States. Additionally, all participants had been exposed to the American public education system.

Sixty-five of the study participants were from site 1 and 33 participants were from site 2. Site 1 had 33 non-minorities (51%), 18 African Americans (28%), and 14 Latinos (21%). Site 2 had 9 non-minorities (27%), 19 African Americans (58%), and 5 Latinos (15%). In the main study analyses, the data from the two sites were pooled. Site effects are addressed in the results.

Diagnostic Procedures. Diagnoses were established through a two-step process. First, admitting clinicians, as part of their intake procedures, diagnosed new members using information from charts and interviews. Following this initial screening, a face-to-face interview was conducted by a licensed, doctorate-level clinician trained in the use of the Schedule for Affective Disorders and Schizophrenia (SADS; Endicott & Spitzer, 1978). The SADS diagnosis was determined through this structured interview as well as a review of clinical records.

Measures

To assess rehabilitative change, two outcome measures were used: the Role Functioning Scale (RFS; Goodman, Sewell, Cooley, & Leavitt, 1993; McPheeters, 1984), and the Strauss and Carpenter Outcome Scale (SCOS; Strauss & Carpenter, 1972). Face-to-face interviews were conducted in English, and administered at baseline and every 6 months over a 3-year period. The primary data gathering instrument was the Community Adjustment Form (Test et al., 1991). Ratings on the RFS and SCOS were derived from the CAF data using procedures outlined in Brekke (1992). Interrater reliability was established during intensive rater training, and during subsequent training assessments throughout the study period (Brekke, 1992; Brekke et al., 1993). The intraclass correlation (ICC) on the work, hospitalization, social functioning, and independent living items ranged from .75 to .98, with an average of .89.

Statistical Analyses

The main analyses for this study were carried out using Hierarchical Linear Modeling (HLM). HLM offers a distinctive perspective to modeling longitudinal data as a response to the developing interest in the application of individual growth models in the social sciences and education (Bryk & Raudenbush, 1987; Francis, Fletcher, Stuebing, Davidson, & Thompson, 1991). It provides a conceptual framework and a set of analytic tools that focus the study of change at the individual client level. This allows for the assessment of both intraindividual and interindividual differences in change. Furthermore, HLM provides a process view of change; that is, a person's score reflects an ongoing process that underlies continuous change in the expression of a variable (e.g., social functioning).

In these analyses, HLM involved a two-stage model of change. At stage 1, each individual's observed score is conceived of as a function of an individual growth trajectory plus random error. This trajectory is determined by the individual's observed scores, which are regressed on time, or a transformation of time. This produces a growth curve. At stage 2 the individual parameters are regressed on a measurable background variable, or covariate (in this study the main covariate was ethnicity), to determine whether there are systematic differences in rate (i.e., slope) or type of change (linear or quadratic) based on the covariate. Final estimates of the growth curve parameters are derived through empirical Bayes estimation, which provides a composite procedure that uses both the information from each participants' data and the information from the covariate in determining final parameter estimates. In other words, each individual's growth curve parameters are estimated with a weighted combination of the level-1 and -2 estimates. This highlights the unique strength of HLM in making individual predictions. For example, if within-subject data is precise, the model heavily weights that information. If between-subject data is strong, that data receives emphasis (Bryk & Raudenbush, 1987). After the individual parameters are estimated, hypothesis testing is used to evaluate the fit of the group linear and quadratic curves in the study sample, as well as the significance of the covariate interaction.

In this study the term "intercept" was used to describe the initial status, or baseline functioning of the groups. The linear slope refers to a straight-line change and can be either positive or negative. The quadratic slope can be also either positive or negative. A positive quadratic slope means that the groups' score dropped from its initial baseline status, then rose again. A negative quadratic slope indicates an initial rise in scores, followed by a decline. Since we tested directional hypotheses, one-tailed tests of statistical significance were applied.

Effect Size. In clinical research, effect size is a useful tool for assessing the practical implications of rejecting the null hypothesis. For this study the product-moment correlations, r (Rosenthal, 1993), were computed for significant HLM findings using the following formula: $r = [t^2/(t^2 + df)]^{1/2}$. The criteria used to assess affect size in clinical research are $r = .10$ is small, $r = .30$ is medium, and $r = .50$ is large.

RESULTS

Status of the Groups at Baseline

Table 3.1 presents baseline data across ethnic groups on the average age at study entry, prognosis, and medication compliance, as well as several clinical and functional variables. The only significant difference was that Latinos and African Americans demonstrated better social functioning at baseline than non-minorities.

Attrition

Two types of attrition were examined: study attrition and treatment attrition. The former concerned participants who dropped out of the study. At 12 and 18 months 88% of the sample was retained. This dropped to 83% at 24 months, 80% at 30 months, and 72% at 36 months. There were no statistically significant differences in dropout rates across the ethnic groups.

Treatment attrition concerned those who exited the rehabilitation programs, but remained in the study protocol. We do not know whether these were planned or unplanned treatment exits.

Table 3.1. Comparison of the Three Ethnic Groups at Baseline

Client Variable (mean and SD)	Caucasian ($n = 42$)	Af-American ($n = 37$)	Latino ($n = 19$)	F, df
Age	32.76 (8.67)	34.49 (8.35)	29.53 (5.33)	$F(2,97) = 2.4$
Prognosis[a]	31.42 (4.57)	32.48 (4.91)	33.68 (2.90)	$F(2,95) = 1.7$
Medication use[b]	157.49 (46.79)	171.53 (27.64)	167.65 (35.27)	$F(2,89) = 1.32$
BPRS[c]	45.45 (15.92)	39.56 (10.48)	44.57 (10.75)	$F(2,95) = 2.1$
Satisfaction with Life[d]	38.53 (14.18)	35.82 (13.85)	44.52 (14.11)	$F(2,90) = 2.2$
Index of Self-Esteem[e]	82.19 (14.72)	83.69 (13.60)	83.34 (15.22)	$F(2,91) = 0.3$
Brief Symptom Inventory[f]	61.37 (35.37)	61.47 (35.97)	75.50 (49.12)	$F(2,89) = 0.9$
Global Assessment Scale	30.86 (9.02)	34.41 (10.29)	35.28 (9.60)	$F(2,95) = 1.4$
RFS Independent Living	2.86 (.84)	3.22 (1.11)	3.21 (.85)	$F(2,95) = 1.68$
RFS Socialization	2.50 (1.73)	3.65 (2.04)	3.53 (1.74)	$F(2,95) = 4.29*$
SCOC Hospitalization	3.33 (1.00)	3.27 (1.07)	3.35 (.61)	$F(2,95) = 0.45$
SCOC Work	0.69 (1.05)	0.84 (1.14)	1.05 (1.08)	$F(2,92) = 0.73$

BPRS = Brief Psychiatric Rating Scale; [a]Measured on the Strauss and Carpenter Prognostic Scale; [b]Number of days on medication in previous 6-month period (Community Adjustment Form; Test et al., 1991); [c]Brief Psychiatric Rating Scale (Overall & Gorham, 1962); [d]Stein and Test (1990); [e]Hudson (1982); [f]Derogatis and Melisaratos (1983).

*$p < .05$.

The exit rate for site 1 was 19% at 6 months, 45% at 12 months, 76% at 18 months, 81% at 24 months, 90% at 30 months, and 91% at 36 months. For site 2 the exit rate was 21% at 6 months, 56% at 12 months, 65% at 18 months, 71% at 24 months, 74% at 30 months, and 79% at 36 months. There were no statistically significant differences in exit rates across the ethnic groups. For the purpose of this study, analyses were done on those participants who stayed in the study protocol, regardless of when they exited treatment. In a previous analysis using this sample plus a usual treatment comparison condition, we found that exiting treatment had a deleterious impact on hospitalization and work outcomes, but not on independent living and social outcomes (Brekke et al., 1997). In this study, due to sample size constraints, we did not separately examine outcomes for those individuals who remained in treatment for the entire 3-year study period.

Functional Outcomes

When examining the functional outcomes, the intercept, linear, and quadratic coefficients were explored for statistical significance. A significant intercept term revealed whether there were differences among the groups at baseline. A significant linear slope illustrated sustained rates of positive or negative change over time in the outcome variables. A significant quadratic slope illustrated a pattern of up-then-down change (negative quadratic) or down-then-up change (positive quadratic). Both linear and quadratic curves (and their combination) were seen as clinically meaningful patterns of change (Brekke et al., 1997; Brekke & Long, 2000). Of major interest was the examination of significant group differences (interaction effects) in the linear and quadratic trajectories with regard to the main covariate, ethnicity. When there were significant effects based on ethnicity, we also analyzed the data using an ethnic minority/non-minority covariate.

Work Outcomes. Figure 3.1 presents the predicted growth curve on the "work" item of the SCOS. There was no ethnicity by intercept interaction, indicating that the groups were equivalent at baseline. The linear term was not significant; but the ethnicity by linear slope interaction was significant, $t(95) = -1.67$, $p < .05$. The quadratic slope was significant, $t(95) = -2.93$, $p < .004$, and the ethnicity by quadratic slope interaction was also significant, $t(95) = 2.47$, $p < .01$. The linear coefficients were .01 for the non-minorities, $-.05$ for the African Americans, and $-.07$ for

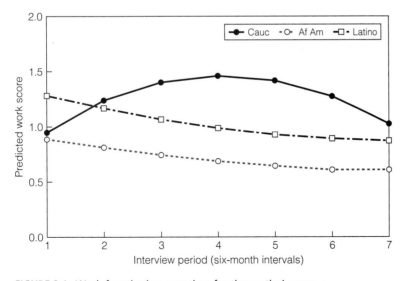

FIGURE 3.1. Work functioning over time for three ethnic groups.

the Latinos. The quadratic coefficients were $-.045$ for non-minorities, .006 for African Americans, and .01 for Latinos. The average effect size for the significant terms was .27. The results indicated that the non-minority group improved over the initial 24 months while in the study, and then they began to decline, but their scores did not drop below their baseline levels. African Americans and Latinos steadily declined from their baseline levels in work functioning over the 36-month study period.

The bi-ethnic (minority/non-minority analyses) revealed the same pattern as the tri-ethnic findings, although the effects were stronger. The groups were equivalent at baseline. The minority status by linear slope interaction was significant at $t(96) = -1.8$, $p < .03$, and the minority status by quadratic slope interaction was significant at $t(96) = -3.01$, $p < .001$. These findings indicated that the work functioning of the non-minority group improved significantly over time whereas the functioning of the ethnic minority group declined over time.

Social Functioning Outcomes. Figure 3.2 presents the predicted growth curves for each group on the social functioning item of the RFS. There was a significant ethnicity by intercept interaction ($t = 2.88$, df, 95, $p < .004$) with Latinos having the highest scores (high scores indicate better functioning), followed by African Americans and then non-minorities. The linear term was significant, $t(95) = 2.57$, $p < .02$, showing that, on the whole, participants improved over time. The ethnicity by linear slope interaction was significant, $t(95) = -1.63$, $p < .05$. The linear coefficients were .16 for non-minorities, .038 for African Americans, and .038 for Latinos, showing that non-minorities improved the most, followed by African Americans and Latinos who had nearly identical change. These findings closely replicated the cross-ethnic findings on work outcomes. The average effect size for the significant terms was .27.

The bi-ethnic analyses revealed the same pattern as the tri-ethnic findings, although the effects of minority status were stronger. The minority group was significantly higher in social functioning than the non-minority group at baseline. The linear term was significant at $t(96) = 2.6$, $p < .01$, and the status by linear slope interaction was significant at $t = -1.9$; $p < .03$, indicating that the non-minority group improved more in social functioning than the minority group.

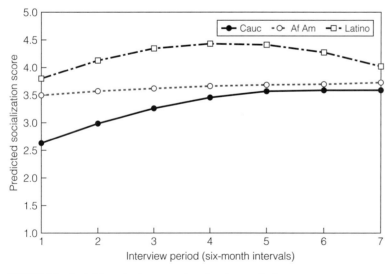

FIGURE 3.2. Social functioning over time for three ethnic groups.

Hospitalization and Independent Living Outcomes. Concerning hospitalization outcomes, there were no differences in any of the initial status, time, or time by ethnicity interactions. Concerning independent living, the ethnic groups were equivalent at baseline. The linear slope was significant, $t(95) = 2.35$, $p < .02$, indicating that the sample improved over time. Neither the quadratic slope nor any of the slope by ethnic group interactions were significant.

Site Effects. Since two program sites were used in this study and the data analysis was done with a sample pooled across sites, we examined the data for site effects. Given that we could not expect sufficient statistical power in each site alone, we looked for any notable divergence in the direction of the findings across sites. Site 1 ($n = 65$) showed more statistically significant findings than site 2 ($n = 33$), but the findings across sites were in similar directions.

Evidence of Gender by Ethnicity Interaction. In an exploratory analysis, Figure 3.3 shows the predicted growth curves for each ethnic group on the "work" item of the SCOC using only males. The results were similar to those shown in Figure 3.1, but they were more pronounced. The quadratic term was significant, $t(72) = -3.156$, $p < .001$, and there was a significant ethnic group by quadratic slope interaction, $t(72) = 2.82$, $p < .003$. The quadratic coefficients were $-.058$ for nonminorities, $.009$ for African Americans, and $.04$ for Latinos. The average effect size for the significant terms was $.33$. When females were examined, no statistical differences were revealed, but the number of female participants was small. There was no evidence for the interactive effects of gender and ethnicity in the areas of socialization, hospitalization, or independent living for the full sample.

To summarize, there were differences found in the domains of work and social functioning in relationship to ethnicity, but not for independent living or hospitalization outcomes. Particularly noteworthy was the pattern from baseline to month 36 for the three groups on the "work" and "social functioning" items. The non-minority group appeared to respond positively to the interventions in both domains, although these improvements began to attenuate after 24 months. Latinos entered into psychosocial rehabilitation with scores either equivalent to, or higher than, the African American and non-minority groups, but they experienced less gain, and in work

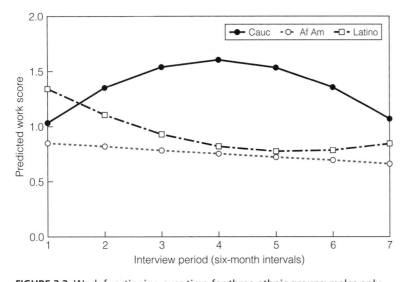

FIGURE 3.3. Work functioning over time for three ethnic groups: males only.

functioning they worsened over time. African Americans showed little change overall. The bi-ethnic findings on social and work functioning were stronger than in the tri-ethnic analyses, and they indicated improvement for the non-minority group, and no change or decline for the ethnic minority group. The cross-ethnic differences in the "work" item were magnified when only male participants were included. In this study, the average effect size was in or near the medium range.

Medication Usage

At each interview period we gathered data on the days that participants were on any psychiatric medication, including anti-psychotic medication, in the previous 180 days. We compared the days on anti-psychotic medication across ethnic groups at each observation period. We found no statistically significant differences across ethnic groups at any time during the study. There were also no cross-ethnic differences in medication dosage at baseline (Brekke & Barrio, 1997). Therefore, the current findings do not appear to be confounded by cross-ethnic differences in medication usage.

DISCUSSION

This study tested the hypothesis that ethnicity minority groups would show poorer outcomes than non-minorities on a number of prospective client outcomes from community-based psychosocial rehabilitation. Using data from programs that had already been shown to result in improved functional outcomes in hospitalization, work, independent living, and social functioning (Brekke et al., 1997; Brekke et al., 1999), this study examined cross-ethnic differences in the rates of change in these domains. The strongest cross-ethnic differences were found in work and social functioning outcomes. In terms of these outcomes, non-minorities experienced considerable gains during the intervention. African Americans showed minimal change, and Latinos appeared to worsen during their participation in the rehabilitation intervention.

These findings have several implications for community-based psychosocial rehabilitation interventions. First, while these interventions were not effective with ethnic minority clients in terms of social and work functioning, there were no differences on independent living and hospitalization outcomes. Therefore, our findings do not show pervasive differential effectiveness across all outcome domains. In fact, on hospitalization, which could be considered to have the most significant cost implications, there were no cross-ethnic differences. However, it is important to highlight the differential effects due to ethnicity on social and work domains because these are two primary functional outcomes targeted by a variety of psychosocial rehabilitation interventions (Mueser, Bond, Drake, & Resnick, 1998; Solomon, 1992).

The finding that both ethnic minority groups did not respond well to the interventions compared to the non-minority group in work and social functioning raises several issues concerning ethnocultural factors and the cultural relevance of treatment programs. Importantly, the use of a tri-ethnic strategy allowed us to determine that ethnic differences were not confounded by minority status. This leads us to consider the dynamics of ethnic culture in explaining the differential effects of the interventions across ethnic groups.

Concerning the cultural relevance of the two treatment programs, while they both had ethnically diverse staff (up to 40% were ethnic minorities), they did not have an explicit focus on race or ethnicity in their service programming. This reflects the field as a whole, since few studies have attended to cultural issues in the treatment of serious psychiatric disorders (Barrio, 2000). Although Community Support Programs (CSPs) have the mandate to be culturally responsive to ethnic minorities (National Institute of Mental Health, 1982; Turner & TenHoor, 1978), the cultural relevance of these programs has not been adequately addressed conceptually or empirically (Barrio, 2000). Moreover, CSP research has not specifically examined differential treatment effects based on ethnicity, and most studies have not provided information about the race/ethnicity of research samples. Although not specific to CSPs, there are a handful of studies that attend to cultural relevance issues in mental health services to ethnic minority groups (Brach & Fraser, 2000; Sue, 1998). These studies reflect an ongoing concern about whether existing programs should be culturally adapted or whether ethnic-specific models of care should be developed to serve ethnic minority populations (Bae & Kung, 2000; Guarnaccia & Parra, 1996; Martinez, 1994; Mays, 1985; Rivera, 1988; Rodriguez, Lessinger, & Guarnaccia, 1992).

In this regard, programs and modalities culturally adapted to identified ethnocultural characteristics and the sociostructural needs of ethnic minorities have demonstrated success in service utilization and outcomes (Lau & Zane, 2000; Lefley & Bestman, 1991; Plummer, 1996; Rivera, 1988; Rodriguez, 1986). These studies suggest that the incorporation of a culturally relevant framework should consider ethnic culture from the perspective of the client-family system, including values, beliefs, and perceptions about health and illness, family practices about caregiving, and the degree of collectivism manifested in interpersonal and prosocial behaviors, while providing individualized psycho-educational services that take into account cultural factors and educational needs (Barrio, 2000). Because the programs in this current study were not culturally adapted and did not involve any specific cultural programming, and given that there were poorer outcomes for the two ethnic minority groups in social and work domains, the implication is that the cross-cultural applicability of these programs could be questioned. As the field in general has paid little attention to cross-cultural issues, this could suggest that researchers, program designers, and clinicians believe that the experience of severe mental illness supersedes any particular cultural or ethnic identification, and that psychosocial interventions need to attend more to the illness than to specific cultural factors. In all, these findings strongly indicate that cultural differences are relevant to psychosocial rehabilitation interventions and that cultural relevance to ethnic minority cultures needs critical attention.

This study also has implications for research in the area of community-based psychosocial intervention. First, literature reviews have found that these interventions show the least consistent outcomes in the areas of social and vocational functioning, while the findings are most consistent with regard to hospitalization and housing outcomes (Mueser et al., 1998; Scott & Dixon, 1995; Solomon, 1992). Our results suggest that social and work functioning are the two areas where differential outcomes due to ethnicity could be the most pronounced. We would therefore recommend that when studies use ethnically diverse samples, they examine their outcomes for cross-ethnic differences. It is also interesting that most literature reviews in this area have not reported the ethnic composition of the samples in the studies they review (Barrio, 2000). Our findings would suggest that this is a problematic practice.

Second, we would encourage program designers and investigators in this area to appraise the cultural orientation from the client's perspective when studying the cross-cultural effects of psychosocial intervention for individuals with severe and persistent mental illness. Information from a careful cultural assessment will help programs identify salient cultural factors, determine the degree of identification with mainstream culture and their ethnic culture, determine client-family practices and cultural preferences, and, on this basis, design or coordinate psychosocial services relevant to the attributes and needs of ethnic minorities being served (Bae & Kung, 2000; Barrio, 2000). Third, as advocated by Betancourt and Lopez (1995), incorporating measures of cultural constructs of interest is essential in the effort to understand the specific cultural mechanisms that are relevant to psychosocial interventions. For example, in the current study a measure of collectivism or sociocentric orientation would have been extremely useful in understanding the cross-ethnic differences.

Although this study did not include measures of cultural constructs, the findings from previous studies using this sample may provide some insight into the differential effects due to ethnicity. Previously, we found that African-American and Latino schizophrenia patients compared to their non-minority counterparts had a more benign symptom profile mediated by higher levels of empathy and social competence (Brekke & Barrio, 1997). These sociocentric cultural mechanisms suggest that a prosocial orientation and a range of interpersonal skills might lead to effective problem-solving behaviors. In terms of the psychosocial interventions used in the current study, we have data to suggest that Latinos who participated in the intervention had significant declines in their scores on sociocentric variables over time (Barrio, in press). It is possible, therefore, that the ideology of the interventions, based on Western behavioral models, that apply values of individualism—independence, self-reliance, competitiveness, autonomous action, and emotional detachment—to persons from collectivistic/sociocentric cultures may not be culturally syntonic. In other words, the interventions could be noxious to participants' sociocentric cultural orientation, and this could explain the poor work and social outcomes from the intervention. Such findings stimulate questions regarding the potential for cultivating sociocentricity and other prosocial cultural qualities that can be incorporated in systems of care. This is a topic for further research, but it is possible that these findings support the claims of Telles et al. (1995) that assertive behavioral interventions are experienced as intrusive and stressful, and could erode the buffering structure provided by more collectivistic cultures.

Given these findings, we would suggest that if the interventions were not supportive of, or even counterposed to, the sociocentric orientation of the ethnic minorities, the impact would be most acutely experienced in social and work domains where the tension between collectivistic and individualistic orientations might be most pronounced. This could explain the differential impact of ethnicity across the four functional outcome domains.

Two other findings from this study deserve comment. In a purely exploratory analysis we found that the differential effect due to ethnicity on work outcomes was most pronounced for male participants, and not present at all for female participants. This suggests that future cross-ethnic study in this area should consider gender as a potentially influential variable. It should also be noted that this is based on a small sample of females. Second, the quadratic trends in the outcome data over time could be related to treatment attrition, in that the rehabilitative changes attenuated once an individual exited the intervention. It is also possible that the nature of rehabilitative change is nonlinear (Brekke et al., 1997).

Before concluding, the following methodological caveats need to be considered. First, the study did not use a random sample of participants from the community; therefore, the study sample cannot be said to represent the population of individuals with schizophrenia. In terms of ethnicity, Latinos were underrepresented and African Americans were overrepresented. Second, the equivalence of the different ethnic groups was established at baseline on numerous variables that have been related to functional outcomes in schizophrenia (Brekke et al., 1997). However, since this was not a randomized design there is always the possibility that the groups were different in ways that could have affected the findings. Third, the Latino sample was small, and while replication is needed on all of these findings, this is particularly true with regard to the Latino sample. Fourth, the ethnic categories used in this study are three broad generalizations and do not account for the inherent heterogeneity within each of the populations. However, each term is useful to refer collectively to a population provided that its diversity is recognized.

Fifth, the two rehabilitation programs were treated as one intervention under the heading of community-based psychosocial rehabilitation. In fact, they were two separate interventions, each with its own strengths and limitations. While this offered statistical power, it also could have obscured specific intervention effects. Sixth, concerning the ethnic differences on social functioning, the significant differences at intercept suggest that the slope findings could be reflective of regression to the mean. Finally, the degree to which these interventions are representative of other community-based psychosocial interventions is unknown.

The findings from this study also suggest several avenues for further research. First, these findings establish the importance of examining ethnicity in interventions involving individuals with schizophrenia. Second, as Betancourt and Lopez (1995) have argued, it is essential that studies on cross-ethnic differences begin to test hypotheses that involve cultural mechanisms to explain cross-ethnic differences. We have suggested several avenues for this research on community-based interventions for individuals diagnosed with schizophrenia. Third, research using larger samples is needed to replicate these results, and replications across program models are essential to establish the generalizability of these findings.

REFERENCES

Bae, S.-W., & Kung, W.M. (2000). Family intervention for Asian Americans with a schizophrenic patient in the family. *American Journal of Orthopsychiatry, 70,* 532–541.

Baker, F.M., Stokes-Thompson, J., Davis, O.A., Gonzo, R., & Hishinuma, E. S. (1999). Two-year outcomes of psychosocial rehabilitation of black patients with chronic mental illness. *Psychiatric Services, 50,* 535–539.

Barrio, C. (2000). The cultural relevance of community support programs. *Psychiatric Services, 51*(7), 879–884.

Barrio, C. (in press). Culture and schizophrenia: A growth curve analysis. *Journal of Nervous and Mental Disease.*

Betancourt, H., & Lopez, S.R. (1993). The study of culture, ethnicity, and race in American psychology. *American Psychologist, 48,* 629–637.

Brach, C., & Fraser, I. (2000). Can cultural competency reduce racial and ethnic health disparities? A review and conceptual model. *Medical Care Research and Review, 57,* 181–217.

Brekke, J. (1992). An examination of the relationships among three outcome scales in schizophrenia. *Journal of Nervous and Mental Disease, 180,* 162–167.

Brekke, J., Levin, S., Wolkon, G., Sobel, G., & Slade, B. (1993). Psychosocial functioning and subjective experience in schizophrenia. *Schizophrenia Bulletin, 19*(3), 599–608.

Brekke, J., & Long, J. (2000). Community-based psychosocial rehabilitation and prospective change in functional, clinical, and subjective experience variables in schizophrenia. *Schizophrenia Bulletin, 26,* 667–680.

Brekke, J., & Test, M.A. (1992). A model for measuring the implementation of community support programs: Results from three sites. *Community Mental Health Journal, 28,* 227–247.

Brekke, J.S., Ansel, M., Long, J., Slade, E., & Weinstein, M. (1999). Intensity and continuity of services and functional outcomes in the rehabilitation of persons with schizophrenia. *Psychiatric Services, 50,* 248–256.

Brekke, J.S., & Barrio, C. (1997). Cross-ethnic symptom differences in schizophrenia: The influence of culture and minority status. *Schizophrenia Bulletin, 23,* 305–316.

Brekke, J.S., Long, J.D., Nesbitt, N., & Sobel, E. (1997). The impact of service characteristics on functional outcomes from community support programs for persons with schizophrenia: A growth curve analysis. *Journal of Consulting and Clinical Psychology, 65,* 464–475.

Bryk, A.S., & Raudenbush, S.W. (1987). Application of hierarchical linear models to assessing change. *Psychological Bulletin, 101,* 147–158.

Canino, I.A., Rubio-Stipec, M., Canino, G., & Escobar, J.I. (1992). Functional somatic symptoms: A cross-ethnic comparison. *American Journal of Orthopsychiatry, 62,* 605–612.

Chu, C., Sallach, H.S., Zakeria, S.A., & Klein, H.E. (1985). Differences in psychopathology between African-American and white schizophrenics. *International Journal of Social Psychiatry, 31,* 252–257.

Cohen, J. (1988). *Statistical power analysis for the behavioral sciences.* Hilldale, NJ: Erlbaum.

Craig, T.J., Siegel, C., Hooper, K., Lin, S., & Sartorius, N. (1997). Outcome in schizophrenia and related disorders compared between developing and developed countries. *British Journal of Psychiatry, 170,* 229–233.

Derogatis, L.R., & Melisaratos, N. (1983). The Brief Symptom Inventory: An introductory report. *Psychological Medicine, 13,* 595–605.

Endicott, J., & Spitzer, R. (1978). A diagnostic interview: The schedule for affective disorders and schizophrenia. *Archives of General Psychiatry, 5,* 837–844.

Escobar, J.I. (1987). Cross-cultural aspects of the somatization trait. *Hospital and Community Psychiatry, 38,* 189–196.

Fabrega, H., Mezzich, J., & Ulrich, R.F. (1988). African-American–White differences in psychopathology in an urban psychiatric population. *Comprehensive Psychiatry, 29,* 285–297.

Francis, D.J., Fletcher, J.M., Stuebing, K.K., Davidson, K.C., & Thompson, N.M. (1991). Analysis of change: Modeling individual growth. *Journal of Consulting and Clinical Psychology, 59,* 27–37.

Goodman, S.H., Sewell, D.R., Cooley, E.L., & Leavitt, N. (1993). Assessing levels of adaptive functioning: The role functioning scale. *Community Mental Health Journal, 29,* 119–131.

Guarnaccia, P., & Parra, P. (1996). Ethnicity, social status, and families' experiences of caring for a mentally ill family member. *Community Mental Health Journal, 32,* 243–260.

Hopper, K., & Wanderling, J. (2000). Revisiting the developed versus the developing country distinction in course and outcome in schizophrenia. *Schizophrenia Bulletin, 26*(4), 835–846.

Hudson, W. (1982). *The clinical measurement package.* Chicago, IL: The Dorsey Press.

Jerrell, J.M., & Wilson, J.L. (1997). Ethnic differences in the treatment of dual mental and substance abuse disorders: A preliminary analysis. *Journal of Substance Abuse Treatment, 14,* 133–140.

Karno, M., & Jenkins, J.H. (1993). Cross-cultural issues in the course and treatment of schizophrenia *Psychiatric Clinics of North America, 16,* 339–350.

Lau, A., & Zane, N. (2000). Examining the effects of ethnic-specific services: An analysis of cost-utilization and treatment outcomes for Asian American clients. *Journal of Community Psychology, 28,* 63–77.

Lefley, H.P., & Bestman, E.W. (1991). Public-academic linkages for culturally sensitive community mental health. *Community Mental Health Journal, 27,* 473–488.

Lehman, A.F., & Steinwachs, D.M. (1998). Patterns of usual care for schizophrenia: Initial results from the schizophrenia patient outcomes research team (PORT) client survey. *Schizophrenia Bulletin, 24,* 11–20.

Lin, K.M., & Kleinman, A.M. (1988). Psychopathology and clinical course of schizophrenia: A cross-cultural perspective. *Schizophrenia Bulletin, 14,* 555–567.

Martinez, C. (1994). Psychiatric treatment of Mexican Americans: A review. In C. Telles & M. Karno (Eds.), *Latino mental health: Current research and policy perspectives* (pp. 227–239). Los Angeles: NIMH.

McPheeters, H.L. (1984). Statewide mental health outcome evaluation: A perspective of two southern states. *Community Mental Health Journal, 20,* 44–55.

Mays, V.M. (1985). The Black American and psychotherapy: The dilemma. *Psychotherapy, 22,* 379–388.

Mueser, K.T., Bond, G.R., Drake, R.E., & Resnick, S.G. (1998). Models of community care for severe mental illness: A review of research on case management. *Schizophrenia Bulletin, 24,* 37–74.

National Institute of Mental Health. (1982). *A network for caring: The Community Support Program of the National Institute of Mental Health* (Publication No. ADM-01-1063). Rockville, MD: Author.

National Institute of Mental Health. (1991). *Caring for people with severe mental disorders: A national plan of research to improve services.* DHHS Publication No. (ADM) 91–1762. Washington, DC: U.S. Government Printing Office.

Neff, J.A., & Hope, S.K. (1993). Race, acculturation, and psychological distress: Fatalism and religiosity as cultural resources. *Journal of Community Psychology, 8,* 3–20.

O'Sullivan, M.J., Peterson, P.D., Cox, G.B., & Kirkeby, J. (1989). Ethnic populations: Community mental health services ten years later. *American Journal of Community Psychology, 17,* 17–30.

Overall, J.E., & Gorham, D.R. (1962). The Brief Psychiatric Rating Scale. *Psychology Report, 10,* 799–812.

Plummer, D.L. (1996). Developing culturally responsive psychosocial rehabilitative programs for African Americans. *Psychiatric Rehabilitation Journal, 19,* 37–43.

Rivera, C. (1988). Culturally sensitive aftercare services for chronically mentally ill Hispanics: The case of the psychoeducational treatment model. *Fordham University Hispanic Research Center Research Bulletin, 11.*

Rodriguez, O. (1986). Overcoming barriers to clinical services among chronically mentally ill Hispanics: Lessons from the evaluation of project COPA. *Fordham University Hispanic Research Center Research Bulletin, 9.*

Rodriguez, O., Lessinger, J., & Guarnaccia, P. (1992). The societal and organizational contexts of culturally sensitive mental health services: Findings from an evaluation of bilingual psychiatric programs. *Journal of Mental Health Administration, 19,* 213–223.

Rosenthal, R. (1993). Cumulating evidence. In G. Keren & C. Lewis (Eds.), *A handbook for data analysis in behavioral sciences: Methodological issues.* Hillsdale, NJ: Lawrence Erlbaum.

Sartorius, N., Jablensky, A., Korten, A., Ernberg, G., Anker, M., Cooper, J.E., & Day, R. (1986). Early manifestations and first contact incidence of schizophrenia in different cultures. *Psychological Medicine, 16,* 909–928.

Sartorius, N., Jablensky, A., & Shapiro, R. (1977). Two-year follow-up of the patients included in the WHO International Pilot Study of Schizophrenia. *Psychological Medicine, 7,* 529–541.

Scott, J.E., & Dixon, B. (1995). Psychological interventions for schizophrenia. *Schizophrenia Bulletin, 4,* 621–660.

Segall, M.H. (1986). Culture and behavior: Psychology in global perspective. *Annual Review of Psychology, 37,* 523–564.

Snowden, L.R., & Cheung, F.K. (1990). Use of mental health services by members of ethnic minority groups. *American Psychologist, 45,* 347–355.

Snowden, L.R., & Hu, T-W. (1997). Ethnic differences in mental health services use among the severely mentally ill. *Journal of Community Psychology, 25,* 235–247.

Solomon, P. (1992). The efficacy of case management services for severely mentally disabled clients. *Community Mental Health Journal, 28,* 163–180.

Stein, L.I., & Test, M.A. (1980). Alternatives to mental hospital treatment: I. Conceptual model treatment program and clinical evaluation. *Archives of General Psychiatry, 37,* 392–397.

Strauss, J.S., & Carpenter, W.T. (1972). The prediction of outcome in schizophrenia: I. Characteristics of outcome. *Archives of General Psychiatry, 27,* 739–746.

Sue, S. (1976). Client's demographic and therapeutic treatment: Differences that make a difference. *Journal of Consulting and Clinical Psychology, 44,* 864.

Sue, S. (1977). Community mental health services to minority groups: Some optimism, some pessimism. *American Psychologist, 2,* 616–624.

Sue, S. (1998). In search of cultural competence in psychotherapy and counseling. *American Psychologist, 53,* 440–448.

Sue, S., McKinney, H., Allen, D., & Hall, J. (1974). Delivery of community mental health services to black and white clients. *Journal of Consulting and Clinical Psychology, 42,* 794–801.

Telles, C., Karno, M., Mintz, J., Paz, G., Arias, M., Tucker, D., & Lopez, S. (1995). Immigrant families coping with schizophrenia: Behavioral family intervention with a low-income Spanish-speaking population. *British Journal of Psychiatry, 167,* 473–479.

Test, M.A., Knoedler, W.H., Allness, D.J., Burke, S.S., Brown, R.L., & Wallisch, L.S. (1991). Long-term community care through an assertive continuous treatment team. In C. Tamminga & S. Schultz (Eds.), *Advances in neuropsychiatry and psychopharmacology: Schizophrenia research* (Vol. I, pp. 239–246). New York: Raven Press.

Turner, J.C., & TenHoor, W.J. (1978). The NIMH Community Support Program: Pilot approach to a needed social reform. *Schizophrenia Bulletin, 4,* 319–349.

Valasquez, R.J., & Callahan, W.J. (1990). MMPIs of Hispanic, Black, & White DSM-III schizophrenics. *Psychological Reports, 66,* 819–822.

WHO. (1979). *Schizophrenia. An international follow-up study.* Chichester: Wiley.

COMMENTARY BY: John S. Brekke

Roll up for the mystery tour.
The magical mystery tour is coming to take you away,
Coming to take you away.

—The Beatles

In more ways than we would like to imagine, a research project in the human services is like a mystery tour. There are plenty of uncharted turns, surprises, consternations, and confusions. But there is also a bit of magic in the inception and sometimes even in the results. This chapter is about the generally unwritten world of social work research, the journey that is well known by researchers but not often revealed in print. It is the magical mystery tour of the lived research project. I will address issues related to the inception, funding, logistics, decisions, hunches, mistakes, good luck, bad luck, and some of the outcomes of this project. I begin by discussing pilot work for this research; then the parent study which generated the data for the accompanying article; followed by the project addressed in the article; and, finally, additional methodological, ethical, and pragmatic issues.

PILOT WORK

By the middle of the 1980s there was optimism that we might be able to successfully treat severely and persistently mentally ill individuals in the community with minimal use of hospitalization, without compromising the quality of life of these vulnerable individuals. With proper treatment we could even significantly enhance their life in the community (see Test, 1984, for a review of the literature at that time). I became engaged in the problem of what these services actually were, what some of the treatment mechanisms might be, and whether there were differential individual responses to these interventions. Before seeking funding for the parent study I did about 18 months of pilot work. We gathered prospective data on about 40 subjects and this gave us important groundwork for the grant in terms of consumer characteristics, recruitment, attrition, performance of the measures, interviewer training, and, most importantly, building collaborative relationships with the agency sites and the County Department of Mental Health. This pilot work was a well-developed dress rehearsal that yielded some publications as well. This kind of foundation is *essential* for most full-scale NIMH proposals and, increasingly, for large private funders. These pilot data and observations were critical to developing the design and hypotheses of the study.

Commentary on article: Phillips, E., Barrio, C., Brekke, J. S. (2001). The impact of ethnicity on prospective functional outcomes from community-based psychosocial rehabilitation for persons with schizophrenia. *Journal of Community Psychology, 29,* 657–673.

I spent a tremendous amount of time at the community service sites that were to become recruitment sites for this study. When gathering data at service sites in the community, there is no way to overestimate the importance of the relationships you build with all levels of staff, from the frontline to the CEO.

PARENT STUDY

The specific questions addressed by the parent study were the following:

1. Considering diagnosis, psychiatric history, premorbid adjustment, overall functioning, and phase of illness, what client variables predict admission and compliance (non-dropout) in different models of community care?

2. Considering time in institutions, symptomatology, work, social, and community functioning, what are the comparative client outcomes from the three models of care over a three-year period?

3. What is the longitudinal character of treatment implementation in the three models of community care? Specifically, (a) considering the types, amounts, and location of daily treatment contact with clients, and the character of the milieu, what are the differences and similarities among the models of care? (b) How do the models of care compare along the dimensions of comprehensiveness, continuity, demand, and the longitudinal nature of care?

4. What are the relationships among client characteristics, the character of treatment implementation, and client outcomes over a three-year period?

The basic features of the parent study design were as follows: 170 subjects diagnosed with schizophrenia or schizoaffective disorder were followed for three years in three models of community-based care that differed as to their rehabilitative focus and their model of service delivery. Two of the programs were model community support programs, reported on in the accompanying article. Data from respondents in the case management/board and care program were not included. The design was quasi-experimental in that there was no attempt to interfere with normal clinical selection procedures, as the naturally occurring services were what we wanted to study. The case management/board and care program was the comparison (usual care) group in the original study. Subjects were selected on a consecutive admission basis. Outcome data came from face-to-face subject interviews conducted every six months over the three-year study period. Subjects were maintained in the study whether they dropped out of treatment or not; therefore we had two kinds of attrition to consider: study attrition and treatment attrition. For example, by the end of the three-year study we maintained roughly 75 percent of the sample in the study, although the majority of the subjects had discontinued the original treatment by that time. Data from an automated information system (AIS) maintained by the Department of Mental Health were used to capture subject history in the public mental health system, as well as to track certain client outcomes during the study period. Daily treatment implementation and global service delivery data were gathered from program staff, client self-report, and AIS sources.

Did we actually complete the parent study design and pursue the questions we set out to address? Yes, but sometimes we did more than proposed, and at other times less.

Concerns and Tradeoffs in the Parent Study Design

Dual Diagnosis in the Sample. One of the strengths of this design was that we would gather data on three existing models of care in the community using a naturalistic design. This would yield us generalizability. However, the comorbid presence of schizophrenia and a substance use disorder diluted the diagnostic purity of the sample, but increased its generalizability. We knew it would increase our recruitment rate but weaken our study retention. We were also unsure about whether the treatment models were adequately designed to handle this dually diagnosed subgroup successfully, and this could dilute the treatment effects that we were interested in. In the end, we decided to exclude individuals who had a diagnosable substance dependence disorder (alcohol or drugs) in the past six months. (They could have a lifetime positive diagnosis). This was ascertained from a pre-enrollment screening, and confirmed by our diagnostic interview after study admission. We relinquished some generalizability for within-group purity, in the interest of capturing treatment effects, and to increase study retention. On a broader note, dual diagnosis can be a confound in a variety of intervention studies that use adolescent and adult samples, whatever their diagnoses, and is important to assess as study inclusion and exclusion criteria are developed.

Service Data. Gathering accurate data on the services delivered was essential for several reasons. One premise of this design was that we had three distinct models of community-based care. They were: (1) a single-site psychosocial rehabilitation clubhouse model with strong focus on work and independent living, (2) a single-site residential lodge model with a preeminent focus on daily living skills and residential placement, and (3) a low-intensity case management model based on an enriched board and care living environment (see Brekke & Test, 1992 and Brekke et al., 1997, for specific program descriptions; and Stroul, 1989, for general model descriptions). Clearly, we needed service data to assess whether the sites continued to offer the same general character of services throughout the study period.

We also intended to describe and analyze the characteristics of the services from each of the three models of care. We had an instrument, the Daily Contact Log (Brekke & Wolkon, 1988; Brekke & Test, 1992) that we had used in pilot work. It required staff to gather daily data on their service delivery to each subject in our study. In addition to the agency staff time, this required an immense amount of research staff time to train the agency staff, and to maintain the integrity of the data gathering over three years. This is a story in itself, but the design problem was that only the two single-site programs could be counted on to gather the DCL data. We would have to rely on County data to monitor the service delivery with the case management sample, as it would be logistically impossible to track each case manager who had contact with clients in case management. The problem was that we were using different data systems to describe the three models of care. One solution was to describe the two single-site models that were the most intensive and most complexly designed using the DCL, and then to describe the case management model using data elements from the County. Another solution would be to have two intensive- program model descriptions using the DCL, and then use the County data to describe the three models on simpler data elements. All three of the program models were County-funded and they used the same reporting data system. We ended up using both solutions at different times.

PROJECT STUDY—ETHNIC VARIATIONS
IN FUNCTIONAL OUTCOMES

We were very interested in the ethnic heterogeneity in the sample in the parent study because of its relationship to generalizability, to subgroup treatment effects, and to possible differences in the characteristics of treatment based on ethnicity. However, the only way we had to guarantee even a remotely adequate sample size for each of three major ethnic groups (Latino, African American and Euro-American) was to purposively over- or undersample the groups, or to just recruit a larger sample than we had planned for until we got the ethnic group numbers we wanted. The issue of what constitutes an "adequate" sample size is a complicated and sometimes technical statistical issue. We were hoping for at least 20 in each group. We also wanted three ethnic groups (one non-minority and two minority) in order to reduce the confound of ethnicity with minority/majority status in the design. We decided against purposive sampling based on ethnicity because we did not want to disrupt the naturalistic design with its focus on generalizability. So, we made budget calculations, and decided to increase the total study sample size so that we would get at least 20–25 Latinos in the sample. This worked, but it stretched our staff and budget quite a bit, and at one point we were not sure we could do it.

The analysis reported in the accompanying article would not have happened except for the interest and effort of two of my former doctoral students who are first authors of this paper. About three-fourths of the way through the study I was doing pilot work for the next phase of my research program, which involved blending psychobiological variables into the study of rehabilitation service outcomes in the community, and this laid the foundation for two future studies (Brekke, Raine, & Thomson, 1995; Brekke et al., 1997; Brekke, Kohrt, & Green, 2001). So, I had laid out my trajectory, and it did not include ethnicity. These doctoral students had other plans. I told them that we had done our best to capture ethnic variation in the sample, but that I did not have the time to venture into the whole area, and I wasn't going on the adventure unless there was someone who would take responsibility for scouring the cross-ethnic and cross-cultural literature in mental health services. The students agreed to lead the way, and I would provide guidance, data, and resources. I also had confidence in these students because we had already published together (Brekke & Barrio, 1997; Brekke & Slade, 1998), and by the time of this project one of them was already in an academic position.

As we began, I told them that there were some data to explore before we could move on. First, if we were going to explore treatment outcome variation, there had to be sufficient change over time in the targeted outcomes for us to explore. Based on previous analyses (Brekke et al., 1997; Brekke et al., 1999), I knew that there was notable treatment change in the two treatment models where we had anticipated change, and that those were the two sites we should include in our analyses. Unfortunately, this meant eliminating subjects, and this would influence the sample size of Latinos. Second, it was important that there be equivalence of the ethnic groups at baseline on our demographic and outcome variables. Without adequate equivalence we would have to do covariance modeling and this could be confounding to our interpretation of the influence of ethnicity on functional outcomes. These preliminary analyses were done on a wide range of variables, and it was decided that we could proceed for three reasons. First, while we had a somewhat marginal sample of Latinos, we could analyze the data using three ethnic groups and then replicate that using the minority/non-minority strata. Second, we discovered that we had equivalence across the three ethnic groups on a wide range of demographic, clinical, and functional variables at baseline. Third, we planned to use hierarchical linear modeling (HLM) (Bryk & Raudenbush, 1992) to analyze the data. HLM can be used to model individual change trajectories over time and to examine if variables like ethnicity have an impact on the magnitude and direction of individual change. It handles missing data very well, and it performs better with more data points. It fit our data and design very well. So, we went forward with testing our cross-ethnic hypotheses. The findings are reported in the accompanying article.

Negotiating Research Sites; Funding and Ethical Issues; Issues Related to Quasi-Experimental Design; Unanticipated Problems and Lucky Breaks

Negotiating the participation of the research sites is a major and fundamental task. In human services research it is essential and critical to success. I always wanted to have my agency contact facilitated by someone I knew the agency would trust. These initial background contacts took time to develop, and they are predicated on involvement in the service community. There is also luck involved. For example, one CEO received his master's degree from the same institution from which I received my Ph.D.

Once in the agency, I have found it very important to start with the highest personnel levels. Without a top-down buy-in, there is little hope of getting the organizational support that will be needed. But once the top is in, it is critical to get the other relevant organizational staff levels to buy in. Spending time with the line staff who will participate in and facilitate the study is critical. My staff and I have become cathartic agents, confidants, problem solvers, advocates, and part of the cleanup crew when necessary.

It is also very important that the staff understands the nature of the project, its importance to the field, how the agency can benefit, as well as the nature of their involvement and the time needed for the collaboration. This all takes time. In this study we needed collaboration and assistance with screening, recruitment, sample follow-along, and some data gathering from the staff. Top management agreed to change the job descriptions of the line staff to include the treatment implementation data gathering we needed. Given all of this commitment from the staff at all levels, I readily agreed to present to the Board of Directors of the agencies when requested, attended agency parties, presented ongoing results to the staff, joined strategic planning committees at the agencies, and spent time comforting staff when they seemed in crisis. My entire staff was trained to do what it took to maintain our relationships. This "schmoozing" time was in the job descriptions of my staff, and their ability to maintain these social aspects of the research was a hiring requirement for me. My project manager was a fine blues harmonica player and he played at agency parties.

There were, however, two things that we would not do in our collaborations with the agency staff. First, while we could publish and present papers together, we had to maintain scientific control of the data and its interpretation. This issue was negotiated before the study began, and then reiterated at later points when relevant. Second, we could not get involved in advocating for staff in their intra-organizational dynamics. This would be perilous; but we did help to problem-solve and support them in some of these struggles. These interpersonal aspects of the research were essential and time consuming, and integral to the success of the study.

We also had several lucky breaks. One was that the study groups across models of care were statistically comparable on nearly all of our outcome and background variables. Our pilot work had suggested that this was possible, but one never knows. Second, the three ethnic groups in the study were comparable across a wide range of critical study variables. These two things made the present project on cross-ethnic treatment responsiveness possible.

Another lucky break was that three of my doctoral students took a course on advanced longitudinal data analysis. They came back from the first class saying that I had sent them to a class that they could not possibly understand. I encouraged them to return, they passed the course, and we built collaborations that resulted in us being able to apply to our data the most sophisticated data analysis technique that was available at that time, hierarchical linear modeling. The introduction to HLM was serendipity at its best, and these cross-departmental collaborations have continued to be mutually reinforcing for years.

Funding Issues. Part of the story of this research includes the vagaries in the race for funding. At the time that financial support was first sought for the parent study (1988), there was a funding mechanism at the National Institutes of Mental Health called a FIRST Award (now defunct as a mechanism), for first time investigators at NIMH. I was able to develop a convincing budget, based on estimates from the pilot work. The parent study was submitted as a FIRST Award to

NIMH. In the first review the study was disapproved, which meant that it didn't make it into the top 50 percent of proposals reviewed. However, the reviewer comments were very positive and very specific. After considering a change of careers (delivering natural gas in northern Minnesota, to be exact), I resubmitted the proposal. The second review resulted in a deferral, which meant that they liked it but I had four weeks to answer several very specific (additional) questions about the proposal. I was told that a funding decision would be based on my written response to the questions that came to me from the scientific review committee. My 15-page response must have sufficed, as I was funded, nearly 14 months after the first submission, and 32 months after pilot data collection began. Published findings from the parent study first appeared more than eight years after we began the early pilot work. There are obvious lessons here.

Ethical Issues. Since we were not manipulating the nature of the treatment delivered or withholding treatment, we did not run into some of the notable ethical problems in human services intervention research. However, we did run into three consternating and potentially damaging problems. First, after I had hired and trained my staff, all study recruitment was held up by the Human Subjects Committee at the Department of Mental Health. The issue was that we wanted to get existing data from them on the services received by our sample during the study, and they believed this violated the subjects' privacy. I suggested that I would get permission from the subjects during consenting, but this did not suffice. After three weeks of negotiation they approved a very unsatisfactory solution. We could get data on all subjects admitted during the study period at the participating agencies, but it could not include client identifiers. I agreed since there was no other option. Luckily, by the end of the study these requirements had changed and we were able to get the data we wanted. But, when the study began, I did not know exactly how we would recover from this situation.

A second situation occurred when the study was being reviewed by a Human Subjects Committee. This study required approval from multiple Institutional Review Boards (IRBs) for human subjects. This is an increasing fact of research life, and multiple reviews are common with research done in the community. Sometimes the various IRBs don't agree on what is acceptable ethical conduct; federal regulations are interpreted differently by different IRBs; and different IRBs may require different levels of review for the study. This study had already been approved by one IRB and was now before another. There was a consumer representative who felt strongly that we should not be able to do the study. This individual's position was quite adamant, but not well supported. After the meeting the Chairperson must have worked something out, because we were quickly approved, but I had no idea how this was done.

Finally, about one year into the study, one of the human subjects committees that had ethical purview over the study decided that no consumers on conservatorships (i.e., public guardianships) could be recruited or maintained in the study. We had no idea how this would impact the study until we discovered that very few of our subjects were conserved. It was a tense few days while we got these data.

Issues Relevant to Quasi-Experiments

Group Comparability. Our study did not involve random assignment of consumers to treatment conditions, nor did it ensure through strata sampling or block randomization that ethnic minorities would be represented equally across treatment groups. This meant that any effectiveness analyses we did were subject to the confound of a selection bias across treatments. We survived this flaw through the grant review process because our aims and hypotheses were focused well beyond treatment effectiveness, and we had ample pilot data for the review committee to believe that we could handle selection bias issues using statistical modeling. Nonetheless, when we did cross-treatment analyses this issue was prominent. If we had too much group nonequivalence this study could have deteriorated into three case studies. We handled this based on solid pilot work that indicated that the three models of treatment had largely equivalent groups. We also had some good luck. As it turned out, there were few statistically significant differences in the subject characteristics across the three models of care. Even more fortunate for us, the ethnic groups were distributed quite evenly across the models of care and there were few significant differences on any of our target variables such as prognosis, symptoms, or functional outcome, across the three ethnic groups.

Selection of Outcome Measures. I was fortunate to have done my Ph.D. work with an outstanding team at the University of Wisconsin–Madison led by Dr. Mary Ann Test. They had been doing research on treatment for schizophrenia in the community for many years. They had developed a battery of life history and psychosocial functioning assessments that I was able to use and build on (Stein and Test, 1980; Test et al. 1991). As we were designing this protocol, it was suggested to me by the Madison team to make certain changes in the protocol such as adding rating items, which I did. I also knew that we would need a particularly convincing set of analyses to establish the equivalence of the study groups, so we added data elements that would provide a good prognostic assessment and more detailed diagnostic data. We ended up with a demanding protocol, but it allowed us to expand the range of questions we could address, and also to build confidence in the data when it came to publishing the results. We also developed a very strong interviewer training protocol in the administration of the measures (Brekke, Levin, Wolkon, Sobel, & Slade, 1993).

Service Delivery Issues. Treatment fidelity concerns the degree to which the treatment is being delivered as it is intended. In this study, we wanted to describe the character of services (Brekke & Test, 1992), and to include service characteristics in our analyses (Brekke et al, 1997; Brekke et al, 1999). Pilot data had suggested that we could count on certain between-model variations on critical service delivery characteristics. There was little awareness of these issues at that time (Brekke, 1988), so our research focus on these issues was timely and it was one of the reasons we were funded.

As the study progressed, we also used the service data in feedback sessions to the agency staff. Given that we could present the data using many units of observation (such as the client, the staff member, or an agency subunit), the data were very interesting to the staff. They could assess the adequacy of their treatment implementation and assess whether they were doing what they thought they were doing. Of course, I was contributing to possible changes in the phenomena I was observing by doing these feedback sessions—but the gain would be in the direction of more treatment fidelity (better adherence to the design of the treatment), so it would certainly not harm the consumers, and we were monitoring the character of the interventions so we would capture the changes if they occurred.

External Validity. External validity was a premium in this design. We used a naturalistic recruitment design in the real world of clinical practice, investigating treatment processes as they happened. These two facets of the design, capturing the clinical population as it existed at the sites (given our admission criteria), and measuring the character of treatment implementation over time, both raised high interest in the project. It allowed us to tout this as a study of usual care in the community, but our pilot data on the consumers and the character of the treatments allowed us to develop hypotheses that were interesting to the field, and that involved variables that many people had interest in, but that had rarely been studied.

New Hunches.   One of the great benefits of being an investigator on the ground level of a study is that you can take advantage of hunches or guesses about potentially important phenomena that you might otherwise miss. The first instance included some conversations we had with consumers during the interviewer training and preparation period for the study. It became clear to us that we needed to capture some subjective aspects of the consumer's lives, such as self-esteem and satisfaction with life. These constructs were not on the radar screen for the field or the funding agency at that time. We quickly included two measures to the study protocol and they have turned out to be very important for understanding treatment outcomes, and for building models of psychosocial outcomes in schizophrenia (Brekke et al., 1993; Bradshaw & Brekke 1999; Brekke & Long, 2000). In some ways we were in the vanguard of this issue.

A second ground-level variable concerned the intrapsychic deficits that represent a general disengagement from the flow of life that can be seen among some individuals with schizophrenia. During the preparation stages of the grant I serendipitously found a measure that captured this phenomenon (Henirichs, Hanlon, & Carpenter, 1984). We began working with it in our interviews, and it seemed to capture a variable on which there was wide variation among individuals with schizophrenia. It also seemed like something that could be potentially important to treatment outcomes, so we included it. This measure has yielded some very interesting findings, and continues to capture the imagination of my students (Brekke & Long, 2000).

Both of these constructs contributed significantly to the development of a psychosocial outcome model in schizophrenia that has been well received in the field, and that has guided much of our subsequent work (Brekke & Long, 2000).

A final issue was measuring the client-to-client interactions at the program sites. We did not intend to measure this construct, but once we were at the agencies we saw its importance. I developed and tested a measure of the character of client–client interactions that we quickly included in our protocol (Brekke & Aisley, 1990). It has been used several times in our analyses (e.g., Brekke & Levin, 1993; Bradshaw & Brekke, 1999).

STRENGTHS AND LIMITATIONS OF THE STUDY

The strengths of the study included its external validity related to consumers and sites, the large sample size (for a clinical protocol), the strong measurement protocol, our use of program process measures, the use of seven prospective data points over three years, low study attrition, and the absence of attrition bias in the sample. There were several limitations. The small sample of Latinos was unfortunate. We did not include measures of cultural mechanisms such as acculturation or collectivism. Finally, the absence of random assignment to conditions limited the internal validity of our conclusions about differential treatment effects. If this had solely been a treatment effectiveness study, I would not have submitted it for funding to NIMH. In other words, if our sole purpose had been to compare the relative effectiveness of the three interventions, random assignment would be required. Given that the overall focus was on individual characteristics, treatment characteristics, and outcomes, the study had notable strengths.

CONCLUSION AND ADVICE

There is a good deal of advice contained between the lines of this commentary, advice about pilot work, consumer involvement, following hunches, and staying close to the ground level of the study. I would just add a few more notions. First, even given the many times that this study could have failed and the raw nerves it engendered, we have gone on to complete three other prospective NIMH-funded studies in this area. Persistence, hard work, and luck all play a continuing role. Second, studying ethnicity is sensitive for a variety of reasons. I strongly recommend working with a multiethnic team. This will increase the probability of a grounded approach. Third, it is helpful to ask the hard and embarrassing questions as you proceed. They yield riches. For example, some very important understanding about the role of ethnic differences came from personal discussions among the staff and investigators. Fourth, when studying ethnic and racial differences it is critical to move beyond these categorical descriptors and to try to measure the mechanisms that underlie the cultural and ethnic differences we study (Betancourt & Lopez, 1993). These mechanisms are the explanatory vehicles for improving our understanding of culture and ethnicity, and they can become the focus of understanding and intervention (Barrio, 2000). Fifth, an interdisciplinary team is critical to any complex study in the human services. We in social work bring a lot to the table, but we have to widen the table to include other specialists with different perspectives and talents. Finally, I will end with a piece of advice from a contemporary of the Beatles, and it is general advice that is relevant to a sound and productive research life. It concerns the thorough grounding of any research in the prominent ideas and research of the time, but also in pushing the field ahead of itself:

Feed your head,
Feed your head,
Feed your head.

—The Jefferson Airplane

REFERENCES

Barrio, C. (2000). The cultural relevancy of community support programs. *Psychiatric Services 51*(7):879–84.

Betancourt, H., & Lopez, S.R. (1993). The study of culture, ethnicity, and race in American psychology. *American Psychologist, 48*(6): 629–637.

Bradshaw, W., & Brekke, J. (1999). Subjective experience in schizophrenia: Factors influencing self-esteem, satisfaction with life, and subjective distress. *American Journal of Orthopsychiatry, 69*: 254–260.

Brekke, J. (1988). What do we really know about community support programs: Strategies for better monitoring. *Hospital and Community Psychiatry, 39*(9): 946–953.

Brekke, J., & Aisley, R. (1990). The client interaction scale: A method for assessing community support programs for persons with chronic mental illness. *Evaluation and the Health Professions, 13*(2): 215–226.

Brekke, J., Ansel, M., Long, J., Slade, E., & Weinstein, M. (1999). The intensity and continuity of services and functional outcomes in the rehabilitation of persons with schizophrenia. *Psychiatric Services 50*(2): 248–256.

Brekke, J., & Barrio, C. (1997). Cross-ethnic symptom differences in schizophrenia: The influence of culture and minority status. *Schizophrenia Bulletin 23*(2): 305–316.

Brekke, J., Kohrt, B., & Green, M. (2001). Neuropsychological functioning as a moderator of the relationship between psychosocial functioning and the subjective experience of self and life in schizophrenia. *Schizophrenia Bulletin 27*(4), 697–708.

Brekke, J., Levin, S., Wolkon, G., Sobel, G. & Slade, E. (1993). Psychosocial functioning and subjective experience in schizophrenia. *Schizophrenia Bulletin, 19*(3), 599–608.

Brekke, J., Long, J., Nesbitt, N., & Sobel, E. (1997). The impact of service characteristics on functional outcomes from community support programs for persons with schizophrenia: A growth curve analysis. *Journal of Consulting and Clinical Psychology 65*(3): 464–475.

Brekke, J., & Long, J. (2000). Community-based psychosocial rehabilitation and prospective change in functional, clinical, and subjective experience variables in schizophrenia. *Schizophrenia Bulletin 26*(3): 667–680.

Brekke, J., Raine, A., Ansel, M., Lencz, T., & Bird, L. (1997). Neuropsychological and psychophysiological correlates of psychosocial functioning in schizophrenia. *Schizophrenia Bulletin 23*(1): 19–28.

Brekke, J., Raine, A., & Thomson, C. (1995). Cognitive and psychophysiological correlates of positive, negative and disorganized symptoms in schizophrenia spectrum disorders. *Psychiatry Research, 57*: 241–250.

Brekke, J., & Slade, E. (1998). Schizophrenia: Breakthroughs in clinical research. In J.Williams & K. Ell (Eds). *Advances in Mental Health Research.* Baltimore, MD: NASW Press.

Brekke, J., & Test, M.A. (1992). Measuring the character of community support programs: Model and results from three sites. *Community Mental Health Journal, 28*(3), 227–247.

Brekke, J., & Wolkon, H.G. (1988). Measuring program implementation in community mental health settings. *Evaluation and the Health Professions, 11*(4): 425–440.

Bryk, A.S., & Raudenbush, S.W. (1992). *Hierarchical Linear Models.* Newbury Park, CA: Sage.

Heinrichs, D.W., Hanlon, T.E., & Carpenter, W.T. (1984). The Quality of Life Scale: An instrument for rating the schizophrenia deficit syndrome. *Schizophrenia Bulletin, 10* (3):388–396.

Levin, S., Brekke, J. (1993). Factors related to integrating persons with chronic mental illness into a social milieu. *Community Mental Health Journal, 29,* 25–34.

Stein, L.I., & Test, M.A. (1980). Alternatives to mental hospital treatment: I. Conceptual model treatment program and clinical evaluation. *Archives of General Psychiatry, 37*: 392–397.

Stroul, B. (1989). Community support systems for persons with long-term mental illness: A conceptual framework. *Psychosocial Rehabilitation Journal, 12*: 9–26.

Test, M.A. (1984). Community support programs. In A.S. Bellack (Ed.), *Treatment and care for Schizophrenia.* New York: Grune and Stratton.

Test, M.A., Knoedler, W.H., Allness, D.J., Burke, S.S., Brown, R.L., & Wallisch, L.S. (1991). Long-term community care through an assertive continuous treatment team. In C. Tamminga & S. Schultz (Eds.), *Advances in Neuropsychiatry and Psychopharmacology,* Volume I: Schizophrenia Research. New York: Raven Press.

4

The Effects of Organizational Climate and Interorganizational Coordination on the Quality and Outcomes of Children's Service Systems

Charles Glisson and Anthony Hemmelgarn

INTRODUCTION

Children are entering state custody in increasingly higher numbers. It is estimated that close to one million children are currently in the custody of state agencies (Barth, Courtney, Berrick, & Albert, 1994; Center for the Study of Social Policy, 1990, 1993; National Center on Child Abuse and Neglect, DHHS, 1996). The majority of these children are in custody for reasons of parental abuse or neglect, and most of the other children who are in custody are there for status offenses (such as truancy or running away) or delinquent behavior. In Tennessee, over 50,000 children are referred to juvenile and family courts each year for abuse, neglect, status offenses, or delinquency, and the number of children placed in state custody each year by these courts has increased by 27% in the last four years and doubled in the past decade (Tennessee Commission on Children and Youth, 1997; Tennessee Council of Juvenile and Family Court Judges, 1995).

As a result of the increasing numbers of children in custody, decreasing resources, and doubts about the effectiveness of systems that serve children in custody, many states have experimented

This research was supported by NIMH grants MH46124 and MH53623.

Glisson, C., Hemmelgarn, A. (1998). The effects of organizational climate and interorganizational coordination on the quality and outcomes of children's service systems. *Child Abuse & Neglect, 22,* 401–421. Copyright 1998 with permission from Elsevier.

with organizational strategies for improving children's service systems (Behar, 1985; Rosenblatt & Attkisson, 1992). These strategies have focused on innovative changes in the organizational configurations of service systems that do not increase costs. For example, it has been argued that the multiple problems faced by children referred for custody require improvements in the interorganizational coordination of services among child welfare, juvenile justice, education, and mental health systems (Burns & Friedman, 1990; Dougherty, Saxe, Cross, & Silverman, 1987; Duchnowski & Friedman, 1990). This argument is based on the belief that the relatively low cost of improving services coordination among these systems will ensure that each child receives the most appropriate services, regardless of which system has first contact with the child. It is assumed that more appropriate services will result in better outcomes for the children.

In spite of the range of efforts in many different states to improve services to children entering state custody by changing organizational configurations, there has been relatively little research to document the outcomes of those efforts. Moreover, most of the efforts to improve these service systems have not taken advantage of the information provided in the organizational effectiveness literature in either designing the changes or in assessing their effects. Of the few studies that have been conducted to document the outcomes of efforts to improve services, most have taken program evaluation approaches with no attempt to measure specific organizational characteristics or to identify each characteristic's unique contribution to service outcomes (Hoagwood, 1997). Thus, with few exceptions, the evaluations of successes and failures have been limited to conclusions about the total effect of a collection of undifferentiated program components and contribute little to understanding the specific organizational components or processes that explain those successes and failures. To date, the results of these evaluations have been disappointing, providing little or no evidence that interorganizational services coordination or other innovative organizational configurations significantly improve service outcomes for children.

This study examines an innovative pilot program in Tennessee designed to improve children's services by reconfiguring the interorganizational mechanisms used to coordinate services. The program (labeled AIMS) created new, autonomous, case management teams to coordinate services from multiple systems to children entering state custody in 12 pilot counties in middle and eastern Tennessee. The study assesses the effects of organizational variables on service quality and outcomes in a sample of 32 public children's services offices located in the 12 pilot counties and 12 matched control counties. The children served by these organizations had been placed in state custody by juvenile and family court judges for neglect, abuse, status offenses, or delinquent behavior. Findings from this study question the effectiveness of interorganizational services coordination and related approaches to improving services. More importantly, the study is the first to provide evidence that organizational climate is a major predictor of the quality and outcomes of children's services.

This study also contributes to the more general human service organization literature concerned with the predictors of organizational effectiveness. Although the impact of *intra*organizational and *inter*organizational variables on effectiveness has been the focus of much of the organizational research conducted in the last several decades, these efforts have most frequently included business and industrial organizations rather than human service organizations. Also, the efforts typically concentrate on only one of the two types of variables and rarely examine both intraorganizational and interorganizational characteristics simultaneously. As a result, there has been little effort to integrate both types of constructs within a single model of effectiveness or to compare their relative effects on outcomes. In this study, we develop and test a model of children's service system effectiveness that includes both intraorganizational and interorganizational variables.

Interorganizational Services Coordination

The study was funded as part of an effort by the National Institute of Mental Health (NIMH) to examine the effect of interorganizational services coordination on service system outcomes (National Institute of Mental Health, 1991; Steinwachs et al., 1992). NIMH and other funders such as the Robert Wood Johnson Foundation have supported several large projects designed to assess the extent to which interorganizational services coordination can improve the effectiveness of organizations that serve populations at risk of chronic mental health problems (Frank & Gaynor, 1994; Goldman, Morrissey, & Ridgely, 1994; Morrissey, Calloway, Bartko, Ridgely, Goldman, & Paulson, 1994). The impetus behind these efforts has come from the belief that the individuals and families most at risk require multiple types of services (Provan & Milward, 1995).

Children who are referred for state custody comprise one such group at risk. These children have been served traditionally by different primary service systems (e.g., child welfare, mental health, juvenile justice, health, education) depending on the configuration of service systems in the state and the particular problems for which the children were referred (e.g., abuse, neglect, truancy, running away, substance abuse, antisocial behavior). However, it has become increasingly evident that children referred for different reasons, as well as their families, share common problems and social histories (Glisson, 1996; Klee & Halfon, 1987; Melton & Flood, 1994). For example, it is not uncommon for a child who has run away to also have broken the law, experienced physical abuse, and been diagnosed as suffering from learning problems. This suggests that these children and their families require a variety of services regardless of the presenting problem that resulted in a referral for state custody.

While interorganizational services coordination appears to be a logical and obvious way of addressing the multiple needs of those individuals most at risk, evaluations of services coordination efforts have been unsuccessful in documenting any major benefits (Hoagwood, 1997). Although the poor findings have been frustrating to those interested in developing mechanisms for improving service effectiveness, this lack of success actually supports some prior theoretical work on interorganizational relationships. While the initial theories of interorganizational relationships assumed coordination was always beneficial, especially for human services (Aiken, Dewar, DiTomaso, Hage, & Zeitz, 1975; Hall, Clark, Giordano, Johnson, & Roekel, 1977), these benefits were questioned in subsequent work. Scott (1985) specifically questioned the benefits of coordination for the mental health sector. This skepticism was based on the potentially positive features associated with both loosely-coupled systems and redundancy (Bendor, 1985; Landau, 1969; Weick, 1976). Scott (1985) suggested that an emphasis on coordination ignores the important roles played by the variety, responsiveness, and redundancy that are found in uncoordinated service systems. Bendor (1985), in particular, pointed out the benefits of having several uncoordinated but parallel systems provide services to the same population. His notion was that such parallel systems create a healthy competitiveness and provide backup systems for any systems that fail.

In spite of the conceptual critiques of services coordination and the limited empirical evidence to date supporting the value of coordination, most of the recent literature continues to argue for the benefits of interorganizational services coordination in the human service sector generally and in the mental health service sector in particular (Alter & Hage, 1993; Glisson, 1994; Goldman et al., 1992; Provan & Milward, 1995). In contrast, this study provides support for the work that questions the benefits of services coordination and suggests alternative organizational strategies for improving services to populations at risk of chronic mental health problems.

The Organizational Climate of Children's Service Organizations

The theoretical and research literature concerning the *inter*organizational coordination of services generally ignores the roles of *intra*organizational factors in effective service delivery. This study provides evidence that this is a critical deficit by identifying one group of intraorganizational variables, service provider attitudes, as a significant predictor of the quality and outcomes of children's services.

The impact of employee attitudes on the performance of work organizations has been the focus of extensive research over the last half century (see early reviews in Hellriegel & Slocum, 1974; James & Jones, 1980; Payne & Pugh, 1975; Schneider, 1975). This research suggests that attitudes shared by employees about their work environment (collectively labeled organizational climate) are important determinants of the organization's effectiveness. While most of this research has been conducted in business and industrial organizations, in recent years attention has been given to worker attitudes in other types of organizations, including government agencies and schools (Ostroff & Schmitt, 1993; Soloman, 1986). However, there has been almost no empirical research on the contribution of organizational climate to human service effectiveness, and none that examines the link between climate and the outcomes of human services that focus on improving individual psychosocial functioning. These human services are provided by mental health, child welfare, alcohol and drug recovery, family violence, and other organizations that focus on the psychological and social dimensions of the people they serve.

Recent studies have confirmed the importance of climate for the effectiveness and efficiency of other types of service organizations (Mayer & Schoorman, 1992; Ostroff & Schmitt, 1993). Although these studies have not focused on the types of human service organizations addressed here, the limited results to date indicate that climate plays as important a role in service organizations as in nonservice businesses and industrial organizations. Moreover, it is likely that climate plays a particularly important role in the performance of public children's service organizations. This assumption is based on the nature of the work required by caseworkers who address the problems experienced by children who are served by these organizations.

The nature of this work requires that caseworkers provide services to children and families who are at risk of a variety of physical and psychosocial problems. Because the effectiveness of these services depends heavily on the relationships formed between service providers and the people who receive the services, the attitudes of the service providers play an especially important role in the outcomes of services. Successful outcomes require caseworkers to be responsive to unexpected problems and individualized needs, tenacious in navigating the complex bureaucratic maze of state and federal regulations, and able to form personal relationships that win the trust and confidence of a variety of children and families. Also, caseworkers must perform their jobs in highly stressful situations that can involve, for example, angry family members or seriously emotionally disturbed children. Therefore, the levels of conflict, role clarity, job satisfaction, cooperation, personalization, and other variables that characterize the shared attitudes and climate of their work environments should be powerful determinants of how caseworkers respond to unexpected problems, the tenacity with which difficult problems are solved, and the affective tone of their work-related interactions with children and families.

Similar to the relationships formed between teachers and their students, successful relationships enable caseworkers to identify, understand, and address each child's individual profile of strengths and needs. Caseworkers must form these relationships in the face of very high caseloads, cope with the stressful nature of working solely with children who have been mistreated or who have behavioral problems, and manage to meet these children's needs in spite of the barriers presented by courts, bureaucratic service systems, and extremely limited resources. A principal reason these relationships are critical to outcomes is because for their work to be successful, caseworkers must be viewed by the children and families they serve as both available and responsive (Dozier, Cue, & Barnett, 1994). This requires that caseworkers react in a timely and supportive manner to what these children say and do, and that their interactions with the children and families be characterized by what Wahler (1994) has described as social continuity. That is, the interactions must be predictable, appropriate, and welcomed over an extended period of time to establish a pattern on which the children and families can depend and anticipate. For these reasons, effective casework relationships are more likely to occur in organizations where caseworkers agree on their roles, are satisfied with their jobs, cooperate with each other, and personalize their work.

Because of the importance of worker attitudes to worker-client interactions, it is important that many public human service organizations are characterized by poor worker attitudes independent of salary, type of clients, and the education and experience of individual workers (Glisson & Durick, 1988). In addition, the organizations have high rates of employee turnover and low job satisfaction when compared to other types of organizations (Soloman, 1986). At the same time, there is considerable variance among public human service organizations in turnover, and worker attitudes range from very negative to modestly positive. This variance provides the opportunity for assessing the relationship between organizational climate and children's service outcomes.

The State-Sponsored Services Coordination Pilot Project

The state-sponsored AIMS pilot project examined in this study was designed to improve the outcomes of children's services through the use of interorganizational services coordination teams. The state implemented the pilot project for 3 years in two separate, six-county areas in middle and eastern Tennessee, respectively. The 12 counties included in the pilot areas ranged from the less populated (15,000) to the moderately populated (150,000). The pilot included rural counties in the poor Appalachian region of the state as well as more populated and prosperous counties, but did not include the state's major urban areas. The pilot services coordination teams could authorize services from any state-supported child welfare, juvenile justice, education, mental health, or health service organization, regardless of the state agency that was given physical custody of the child. It was expected that the teams would increase the level of coordination among the various direct service organizations so that an appropriate array of services and residential placements could be provided to children who entered custody. In addition, a state-level council of the commissioners of the relevant service systems (child welfare, juvenile justice, mental health, education, health) was formed to facilitate the coordination of services by the pilot coordination teams.

The services coordination teams were established in the multi-county pilot areas without making any other changes in the existing direct service systems. It was intended that the teams would reduce duplication of effort, facilitate access to services, and establish mechanisms for ensuring that needed services were provided. A primary goal of the pilot project was to improve authorization, accountability and monitoring procedures. It was assumed that these improvements would enhance the quality and outcomes of services provided to the children by ensuring that the multiple needs of each child and family would be met with the most appropriate services and placements.

NIMH funded this study of the state-sponsored pilot project with the objective of assessing the impact of the services coordination effort and of examining the effects of other organizational factors on the quality and outcomes of services (Glisson & James, 1992). The support from NIMH allowed the research team to follow the development and implementation of the pilot project from its beginning to its end at the state, county, and office levels. Over a 3-year period, research team members worked with state administrators, the pilot services coordination teams, the children's services organizations, and the service system network in each of the 24 counties included in the study. Research team members made weekly visits to the pilot teams, gathered data directly from parents, teachers, caseworkers, and other service providers, and conducted organizational surveys of the caseworkers in the 32 children's service offices.

The longitudinal nature of this study and the time spent in the field with coordination teams, parents, teachers, caseworkers, and other service providers enabled the research team to develop a thorough understanding of the service system issues and problems in each area. Not only did this allow individual children to be followed from the time they entered custody, it also ensured that the research team benefitted from anecdotal evidence and qualitative observations. This information was invaluable in developing an understanding of the roles of organizational climate, caseworker attitudes, and caseworker relationships with children that are discussed here.

An important benefit of the time spent in the field with the services coordination teams, case-workers, and other service providers was the opportunity to observe the actual day to day activities of the new pilot teams and the network of organizations that served the children. This enabled the research team to observe the extent to which each service coordination team actually did what it was designed to do. This is an important issue because it was evident from the field observations that the teams did not always achieve the intended level of responsibility and authority in the custodial and service decisions that affected the children. As a result, there was a great deal of variation across the pilot counties in the extent to which service coordination actually changed as a result of the new pilot teams.

This variation was due to a number of factors. First, referrals for state custody increased statewide after the teams were implemented and the teams were understaffed to respond to the numbers of referrals. Second, juvenile and family court judges in each county varied in the amount of discretionary power they were willing to relinquish to the teams and in some cases allowed the teams very limited power. Third, the team members received minimal training in key areas of mental health and child behavior after joining the teams. This is important because most held bachelor's degrees as their highest degree and had very little formal education in mental health or child behavior. Fourth, the staff in some of the organizations that provided the residential place-ments and services believed that there was no reason to comply with the decisions of the new teams. This was due to the abundance of children entering custody, coupled with the limited resi-dential placements and services that were available. Moreover, state contracts with private agencies for services were not affected by their degree of cooperation with the pilot teams and state facili-ties received more referrals than they could adequately serve.

As a result of these reasons and the varying histories of service coordination within each county that predated the pilot project, service coordination in both the pilot and control areas varied from county to county and even from child to child. The research team measured the actual amount of service coordination experienced by each child in the pilot and control areas so that treatment fidelity in each pilot county could be assessed and compared to that in the control counties (Teague, Drake, & Ackerson, 1995). We were thus able to document our observations that the teams increased service coordination in some counties in the pilot areas, but fell short of the original plan to increase it in all pilot counties.

Hypothesized Model

The study tests a model (Figure 4.1) that links county demographics, organizational characteristics, and the quality and outcomes of services (Glisson & James, 1992). The central construct in the

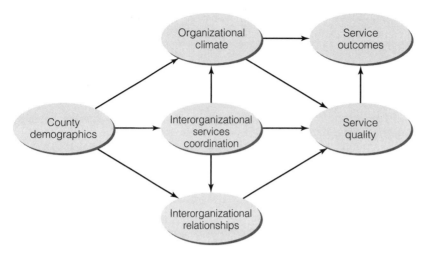

FIGURE 4.1. Hypothesized model.

model is interorganizational services coordination. As explained above, this construct has been the focus of efforts in several states to improve services to children entering state custody. The pilot project was implemented in the study described here for the specific purpose of increasing services coordination. Because services coordination is the manipulated variable in the study, the model depicts services coordination as directly or indirectly affecting all other variables in the model except county demographics. It was hypothesized that increasing services coordination in each pilot county would *directly* affect (1) the climate of the organizations that assumed custody of the children and provided the services that were being coordinated; (2) the quality of the services provided to the children; and (3) the interorganizational relationships among the organizations in the county that assumed custody of children and provided services to them. Two of these constructs, climate and service quality, describe attitudes (climate) and behaviors (service quality) that characterize the caseworkers in the organizations who interact directly with the children. Because the attitudes and behaviors of caseworkers are assumed to be affected by services coordination and are critical elements in the services they provide, these two variables were hypothesized to link services coordination with service outcomes.

The model in Figure 4.1 therefore describes changes in an organizational level variable, services coordination, as affecting service outcomes at the children's level by affecting the attitudes and behaviors of the caseworkers who are responsible for the children. Until now, the mechanisms have not been carefully identified by which organizational level efforts to increase service coordination affect service outcomes. It is explicit in this model that the attitudes and behaviors of those who directly interact with and serve the children must be affected positively if organizational level interventions are to improve service outcomes.

METHODOLOGY

To assess the model shown in Figure 4.1, two additional 6-county control areas (a total of 12 control counties) were selected to match the two pilot areas (a total of 12 pilot counties) county by county on total population, child poverty rates, unemployment, and education levels. Therefore, the study includes a total of 24 counties out of the state's 95 counties. Twelve counties (six pilot counties and six matched control counties) in the sample are located in the middle of the state, and 12 counties (six pilot counties and six matched control counties) are located in the eastern portion. As explained above, the counties selected for the pilot project ranged from the less populated to the moderately populated. Because of the disproportionate amount of resources required to include a major urban area, the 24 sampled counties excluded the four most populated of the state's 95 counties. Although many of the problems associated with children entering custody nationwide are correlated with population density, the highest custody rates, lowest per capita income, and lowest education levels are found in the rural, Appalachian counties represented in the sample. As a result, population size is related to the socioeconomic status of the counties within the sample and the more rural counties have higher rates of poverty and associated problems.

All of the Department of Human Service (DHS) and Department of Youth Development (DYD) offices (32) serving the children in the pilot and control counties were included in the study. At the time of the study, these offices were responsible for the care of over 90% of the children placed in state custody. (Following the study, the children's services offices of DHS and DYD were merged to form the Department of Children's Services.) Whether the children were placed in foster homes, public or private group homes, residential treatment facilities, or large institutions, the children were added to the caseloads of DHS and DYD caseworkers. These caseworkers were the individuals whom government officials and judges held accountable for the well-being of the children. They were responsible for working directly with the children and their families, keeping them informed of custody and service decisions, ensuring the children's well-being, recommending changes in placements and services, and providing information about the children to judges, officials, and other service providers. Moreover, these caseworkers provided the common points of contact among the children and the family members, agencies, service providers, and government officials who were concerned with the children's welfare.

Subjects

Subjects sampled for this study included children entering state custody and the caseworkers in the organizations responsible for their care. The children's parents, surrogate parents, and teachers were also informants in the study. Most of the sampled children in the pilot and control areas were placed in the care of the Department of Human Services (two-thirds) and Department of Youth Development (almost one-third) agencies in their counties of origin. These proportions were equivalent to state-wide statistics for children entering custody during the study period.

A cohort of 600 children was selected from those entering state custody in the 24 counties and followed until state custody was terminated. The 250 children included in this analysis are those children from the initial cohort who remained in custody for at least 1 year. Data were obtained from parents, parent surrogates, and teachers to describe the children's psychosocial functioning when they entered custody and 1 year after entering custody. Data were collected from caseworkers and case files to describe the services the children received during their first 12 months in state custody.

The study depends on outcome measures from those children who remained in custody for at least 1 year because they are the children who are most at risk and who are most likely to be affected by the custody experience. Also, related research has indicated that significant changes in the psychosocial well-being of children who enter custody are difficult to detect in shorter periods of time (Glisson, 1994). Because the capacity to detect change in a child's psychosocial functioning after entering state custody is essential to determining the effects of that experience, observations of the psychosocial well-being of children over a 1 year period provide a critical measure of service outcomes.

In addition to the children, the subjects in the study also included the caseworkers who were responsible for the care of the children. The 32 offices participating in the study varied in size from 10 to 40 employees, with the average being about 15 employees. The smallest included six caseworkers, an office administrator, a supervisor, and secretarial staff, and the largest included 30 caseworkers plus administrative, supervisory, and secretarial staff.

Questionnaires measuring organizational climate and interrelationships among service systems were administered to the caseworkers in the 32 offices that assumed responsibility for the care of the children in the sample. We focused on caseworkers, rather than administrators and secretarial staff, because it is the caseworkers' attitudes and responsiveness to children that are most salient to the casework relationships and service outcomes. Because the climate questionnaires were administered on site in each of the agencies, we were able to obtain a response rate of over 90%. This provided a sample of 260 caseworkers.

Measurement

Service Outcomes. Service outcomes were measured as the improvement in each child's psychosocial functioning during their first year in state custody. This is a particularly useful criterion because it can be applied to a wide variety of children who enter custody for different reasons and with different problem profiles. If services to children who enter state custody are successful, then the psychosocial functioning of a sample of these children should improve, regardless of whether they enter custody for abuse, neglect, status offenses, or delinquency, and regardless of their individual psychological and social histories.

Children manifest problems in psychosocial functioning through externalizing (McMahon, 1994) and internalizing (Ollendeck & King, 1994) behavior. Externalizing behavioral problems are characterized by their disruptive effect and include aggression, rule violation, distractibility, and impulsivity. Internalizing behavioral problems are indicators of a child's personal distress that include anxiety, depression, dependency, and low self-esteem. Externalizing and internalizing behaviors are moderately correlated and are frequently combined to describe a child's overall psychosocial well-being (Achenbach, 1991). Children entering state custody are characterized by high levels of internalizing and externalizing problems regardless of the reason for custody, the particular state agency that assumes responsibility for the child, or the type of residential placement (Glisson, 1996).

Broadband scales from Achenbach's (1991) Child Behavioral Checklist (CBCL) and Teacher Report Form (TRF) provided four of the five indicators used to assess the children's psychosocial functioning. These are the most widely used and extensively validated instruments for measuring children's psychosocial functioning. Broadband scales for measuring both internalizing (e.g., anxious, withdrawn, or inhibited) behavior and externalizing (e.g., aggression, destructive, or antisocial) behavior were included from each of the two instruments. A parent or guardian completed the CBCL and a teacher completed the TRF, providing two measures of both internalizing and externalizing behavior. The raw scale scores for each child were converted to T-scores based on general population norms for age and gender. In addition, the Teacher's Checklist of Children's Peer Relations provided a fifth indicator of psychosocial functioning that describes the child's social skill and social acceptance (Dodge & Somberg, 1987).

All instruments were completed first when the child entered custody and again after the child had been in state custody for 1 year. For the baseline measure taken during the week the child entered custody, a parent or guardian and a teacher used the CBCL and TRF, respectively, to describe the child's behavior prior to custody. One year later, the CBCL was completed by the child's surrogate parent (e.g., foster parent, group home supervisor) and the TRF was completed by the child's teacher to describe the child's behavior after 1 year in custody.

The amount of change in psychosocial functioning was assessed by regressing the 12 month outcome measures on the same measures taken at the time the child entered custody. The residuals from this procedure were then used to indicate changes in the children's functioning over the first year of custody. Negative residuals represent a decrease in psychosocial problem behaviors during the 12 month period and therefore indicate positive service outcomes.

Service Quality. There are very few studies of the quality of children's services (National Research Council, Panel on Research on Child Abuse and Neglect, 1993; Thompson & Wilcox, 1995). However, Behar (1985) describes several characteristics of a high quality service system that is responsive to the needs of multiproblem children. These characteristics include comprehensiveness and continuity.

Comprehensiveness is the extent to which a range of services are provided to a child. A list of 30 different services available to children in state custody in Tennessee was compiled by the research team. A critical responsibility of the caseworker is to ensure that children receive needed services. Comprehensiveness was measured as the number of those services received by each child during his or her first year in custody.

Continuity is the extent to which there are linkages among services received by a child so that the efforts of service providers complement the needs of the child and the efforts of others who are involved in the child's care. A primary task of the child's caseworker is to maintain this continuity through contacts with other service providers. Continuity was measured as the average number of contacts per month that the child's caseworker had with other professionals who provided services to the child.

Additional measures of service quality derive from the alliance that caseworkers form with the children and families they serve. High quality casework services require that the caseworker provides a secure base for the child (and family) by being available and responsive (Dozier, Cue, & Barnett, 1994). *Availability* was measured as the average number of personal contacts (not by telephone or letter) per month that the caseworker had with the child. A second measure of availability was the average number of contacts with the family.

Responsiveness is critical to solving problems that arise with children after they have entered custody. One of the most frequent problems is children being unhappy with or having problems with their residential placements. Although it is not desirable for children to experience multiple residential placements, it is also the case that problems occur within placements that can be resolved only by relocating the child. In previous research, changes in residential placements were associated with a better fit between the child and placement, and interpreted as an indicator of the caseworker's responsiveness to solving problems with placements (Glisson, 1994). Therefore, responsiveness was measured as the changes in residential placements that were made to improve the fit between the residential placement and the child.

Services Coordination. There has been limited organizational research on the interorganizational coordination of services and few acceptable instruments developed to measure the construct (Alter, 1990; Alter & Hage, 1993; Price & Mueller, 1986; Provan & Milward, 1995). The indicators of services coordination used here are based on Mulford and Rogers' (1982) definition of coordination and the elements of service coordination specified by Aiken and colleagues (1975). The coordination of services to children is intended to reduce duplication of effort, facilitate access to information, placements, and services, and establish mechanisms for ensuring accountability. Because children entering custody require a variety of different types of child welfare, mental health, health, and educational services, coordination requires that organizations within a county agree to a common services authorization procedure so that duplicate authorizations are not required for a service or placement to be provided. It also requires that a minimum number of individuals be responsible for ensuring that services are properly delivered. Finally, coordination requires that conflicts of interest be avoided by designating individuals to monitor service delivery other than those who actually provide the services.

The indicators of coordination used in the study are authorization, responsibility, and monitoring. *Authorization* was measured as the number of separate authorizations required for a child to receive services from multiple systems. The fewer required, the greater the coordination. *Responsibility* was measured as the number of individuals responsible for ensuring that needed services were delivered to a child. The lower the number, the greater the coordination. *Monitoring* was measured as the proportion of those monitoring services for each child who also provided service to the child. Because coordination requires a separation of these responsibilities, lower proportions represent greater coordination. Each of the three indicators was reverse scored so that larger numbers indicate increased coordination. The research team collected these data directly from caseworkers at regular intervals for each child in the sample.

Organizational Climate. The Psychological Climate Questionnaire assembled by James and Sells (1981) includes versions of 10 scales used by numerous researchers over the last three decades (Hackman & Oldman, 1975; Porter, Steers, Mowday, & Boulian, 1974; Rizzo, House, & Lirtzman, 1970). Together the scales provide an appraisal of the degree to which employees view their work environment as beneficial versus detrimental to their own well-being and the success of their work (James & James, 1989). Employees' views were assessed with scales measuring fairness, role clarity, role overload, role conflict, cooperation, growth and advancement, job satisfaction, emotional exhaustion, personal accomplishment, and depersonalization. Caseworkers completed these scales anonymously and returned them directly to the research team. Caseworker responses to these scales were aggregated by agency to establish the climate profile of each sampled agency.

Interorganizational Relationships. Seven items were specifically designed for this project to assess the relationships established by each agency with other service organizations (child welfare, juvenile justice, mental health, education, health agencies) that provided services to children in the same county. These items were included within the same questionnaire that measured climate as described above. The seven items included questions about problems in worker cooperation between organizations (*noncooperation*), other organizations attempting to "dump" problem children on the respondent's office (*dumping*), red tape encountered in trying to work with other organizations (*red tape*), placing responsibility on other organizations for problems encountered in their work (*blaming*), unreasonable demands made by other organizations (*unreasonable*), other organizations withholding needed information (*withhold information*), and disputes with other organizations (*disputes*). Responses to each of these items were averaged across workers by agency to describe each agency's interrelationships with the organizations providing services to the children in their care.

County Demographics. Demographic data were available for each county included in the study. Eight demographic variables were chosen: (1) total population of a county; (2) percentage of children living in poverty; (3) percentage of persons 25 years or older who have graduated high school; (4) per capita income; (5) average annual unemployment rate; (6) average annual youth unemployment rate; (7) percentage of children receiving AFDC; and (8) percentage of children suspended from public schools.

RESULTS

Linear structural equation analysis with LISREL VIII was used to examine the hypothesized model shown in Figure 4.1 that describes relationships among multiple latent constructs (Joreskog & Sorbom, 1993). As described above, several manifest or observed indicators are specified as measures for each latent variable. The set of equations that links these manifest indicators to the latent variables is typically referred to as the *measurement model*. A second set of linear equations describes the hypothesized relationships among the latent variables as shown in Figure 4.1. This is referred to as the *structural model*. Together, these two sets of equations provide the basis for a test of the *a priori* hypothesized model against the observed data. Each set of equations was solved separately as described by Anderson and Gerbing (1988), Medsker, Williams, and Holahan (1994), and others. First, the measurement model was assessed to determine if the observed indicators were in fact related to their hypothesized latent constructs. In the second phase, the relationships among the latent variables described in the structural model (shown in Figure 4.1) were tested. Given the distributions of several of the observed variables, estimates for the model were generated by an unweighted least squares (ULS) solution. This solution provides stable estimations without stringent distributional assumptions (Bollen, 1989). Following Browne (1982, 1984), adjustments were made to calculate tests of significance for estimates resulting from the ULS solutions (Bollen, 1989; Joreskog & Sorbom, 1993).

Measurement Model

In the first phase of the analysis, the measurement model was assessed with confirmatory factor analysis. Each indicator was constrained to load on its respective factor (i.e., latent construct) as described in the measurement section above, and all factors were allowed to intercorrelate. Goodness of fit indices were then used to assess model fit.

   Goodness of fit indicators suggested a less than desirable fit in the initial measurement model, $\chi^2(650, N = 250) = 2216.22$, GFI = .84, AGFI = .82, CFI = .82 (see Bentler, 1990; Medsker, Williams, & Holahan, 1994; Mulaik, James, Van Alstine, Bennett, Lind, & Stillwell, 1989). Standardized residuals from this solution provided evidence of specification errors related to the indicators defining service outcomes. To investigate these problems, a separate LISREL analysis was conducted on each construct within our measurement model. Goodness of fit indices confirmed a relatively poor fit for the indicators of service outcome (GFI = .90, AGFI = .71, CFI = .78). This appeared to result from the use of measures from both a parent (or surrogate parent) and a teacher to assess each child's psychosocial functioning, replicating earlier research reporting low correlations between teachers' and parents' behavioral ratings (Achenbach, 1991; Achenbach, McConaughy, & Howell, 1987).

   Based on the above information, a decision was made to retain teacher ratings and omit parental ratings from the outcome measures. Teacher ratings were retained for three reasons. First, previous research has shown that teacher ratings have higher reliability than parent ratings (Achenbach, 1991a; 1991b). Second, three indicators were available from teachers versus only two indicators from parents. Third, children were observed in a similar context by teachers at both the pretest and posttest while this was not true of the parental ratings. The elimination of the parental ratings

Table 4.1. Fit Indices for Measurement Models

Model	Chi-Square	Goodness of Fit (GFI)	Adjusted Goodness of Fit (AGFI)	Comparative Fit Index (CFI)
Six-Variable Model A	χ^2 = 2038.44 with 579 df's	GFI = .85	AGFI = .83	CFI = .83
Five-Variable Model B	χ^2 = 920.59 with 367 df's	GFI = .91	AGFI = .89	CFI = .91

from the indicators of service outcomes substantially improved the fit of the individual construct. With this improvement, all individual constructs had acceptable fit indices (.90 or above). However, as shown in Table 4.1 for Model A, the fit of the overall measurement model remained poor (GFI = .85, AGFI = .83, CFI = .83).

Further examination of the measurement model showed that the two constructs in the model that were measured with a common method (self-report survey) had highly correlated residuals. The self-report survey was administered to caseworkers in each office to measure both organizational climate and interorganizational relationships. One of the two constructs, climate, was measured with several widely-used scales which have been shown in previous research to be linked by a common evaluative factor representing employees' responses to their jobs and organization. The second construct, interorganizational relationships, was measured with seven Likert style items that were created specifically for this project to determine the nature of the working relationships among the agencies that provided services to the children.

Although the residuals of the two constructs were correlated, the measurement model deteriorated further when the indicators from the two constructs were assessed as a single dimension. However, by eliminating interorganizational relationships from the model altogether to create Model B, the overall fit of the measurement model reached an acceptable level (GFI = .91, AGFI = .89, CFI = .91). Both the original six variable measurement model (A) and the reduced five variable measurement model (B) were then used in subsequent analyses of the structural model as described below. The factor loadings for both the original and reduced measurement models are shown in Table 4.2.

The overall fit of the measurement model as well as the fit indices of the individual constructs provide evidence that supports the validity of the measurement model. All relationships between the constructs and their indicators are significant, although as shown in Table 4.2, the individual indicators vary in their loadings. The value of the measurement model is that these loadings specify how each indicator will be weighted in the structural estimation procedures. These weights insure that the relative strengths of the relationships between each construct and its indicators determine the relative contribution of each indicator to the estimation of structural parameters. In the current analysis, *alpha* coefficients were calculated to describe the intercorrelations among the indicators for each construct. They are high for five of the six constructs (between .78 and .89). For service quality, the *alpha* coefficient is .57, reflecting the relative differences among the contributions of the indicators of service quality to the estimation procedures.

Structural Model

As suggested by several researchers (see Anderson & Gerbing, 1988; Medsker, Williams, & Holahan, 1994; Mulaik, James, Van Alstine, Bennett, Lind, & Stilwell, 1989), a two-step approach was taken in which the structural model was evaluated separately from the measurement model. Figure 4.2 shows the estimated parameters of the hypothesized structural model obtained from the six variable measurement model. An important characteristic of this model is the inclusion of both

Table 4.2. Measurement Model Factor Loadings for Manifest Indicators

Variables	Six-Variable Model A	Five-Variable Model B
County Demographics		
Total population	.53	.54
% of children in poverty	−.92	−.91
% of adult H.S. graduates	.80	.79
Per capita income	.75	.75
Unemployment rate	−.85	−.86
Youth unemployment rate	−.74	−.75
% of children AFDC	−.61	−.60
% of school suspensions	.48	.47
Interorganizational Relationships		
Noncooperation	.24	—
Dumping	.66	—
Red tape	.89	—
Blaming	.58	—
Unreasonable demands	.55	—
Withhold information	.53	—
Disputes	.71	—
Service Quality		
Availability (child)	.72	.72
Availability (family)	.67	.67
Continuity	.60	.60
Comprehensiveness	.22	.23
Responsiveness	.16	.15
Services Coordination		
Authorization	.48	.48
Responsibility	.94	.94
Monitoring	.83	.83
Organizational Climate		
Fairness	.64	.73
Role clarity	.45	.34
Role overload	−.62	−.74
Role conflict	−.89	−.88
Cooperation	.45	.45
Growth and advancement	.52	.65
Job satisfaction	.87	.89
Emotional exhaustion	−.84	−.91
Personal accomplishment	.63	.49
Depersonalization	−.84	−.72
Service Outcomes		
Internalizing problems (teacher rating)	.70	.68
Externalizing problems (teacher rating)	.85	.87
Peer relations problems (teacher rating)	.78	.77

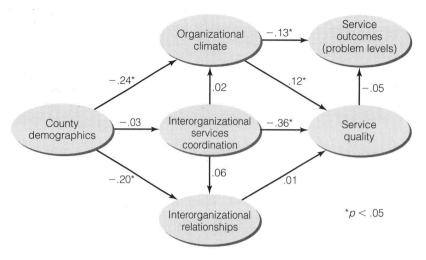

FIGURE 4.2. Parameter estimates for hypothesized six-variable Model A.

organizational and individual level constructs. The statistical rationale for relating organizational or situational characteristics to individual level constructs has been well established for some time (James, Demaree, & Hater, 1980). In fact, it is the effects of the organizational characteristics on the individual child's service quality and outcome that are of particular interest.

In addition to relating organizational and individual variables, the model also estimates relationships among the organizational level variables. These relationships were included in the model to provide estimates of the total effects (both direct and indirect effects) of each organizational level variable on the individual level variables of service quality and service outcomes. The estimates of these effects are assumed to be reliable, but the significance tests of the parameters that describe the relationships that link the organizational characteristics to each other have inflated Type I error rates. This inflated Type I error rate applies to two parameters in the six variable model, the effects of county demographics on organizational climate and on interorganizational relationships. In the five variable model it applies only to one estimate, the relationship between demographics and climate. The Type I errors are not inflated for the significance tests of the parameters describing relationships between the organizational characteristics and the quality and outcomes of services.

As shown in Figure 4.2, several of the parameters describing the effect of the organization on service quality and outcomes are statistically significant. These are the effect of service coordination on service quality, and the effects of organizational climate on both service quality and service outcomes. As shown in Table 4.3, in spite of these significant parameters, the fit indices for the

Table 4.3. Fit Indices for Structural Models

Model	Chi-Square	Goodness of Fit (GFI)	Adjusted Goodness of Fit (AGFI)	Comparative Fit Index (CFI)
Six-Variable Model A	$\chi^2 = 2851.73$ with 584 df's	GFI = .79	AGFI = .76	CFI = .74
Five-Variable Model B	$\chi^2 = 945.79$ with 370 df's	GFI = .91	AGFI = .89	CFI = .91

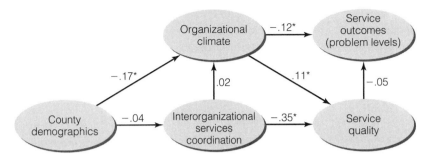

FIGURE 4.3. Parameter estimates for trimmed five-variable Model B.

six-variable structural model (A) are limited by the poor fit of the six variable measurement model (GFI = .79, AGFI = .76, CFI = .74). In contrast, the five variable structural model (B) shown in Figure 4.3 with interorganizational relationships omitted, has stronger fit indices (GFI = .91, AGFI = .89, CFI = .91). An added benefit of Model B is that only one path has an inflated Type I error rate and all other paths in the model remain essentially unchanged.

To summarize the LISREL analysis, the measurement and structural models were improved by eliminating parental ratings as indicators of service outcomes and by removing interorganizational relationships as a latent variable. While the size of the parameters describing the hypothesized paths in the five variable structural model (B) are modest, most are statistically significant. Although the Type I error rate for the significance test of one parameter, the effect of county demographics on climate is inflated, none of the parameters or fit indices are inflated from common method error variance, a frequent criticism of LISREL analyses that report high fit indices and significant paths. Of particular importance are the relative roles played by one *inter*organizational variable in the model, service coordination, and the *intra*organizational variable, climate. Although service coordination has the largest effect on service quality, increased service coordination is related to reduced service quality, quality has no effect on service outcomes, and positive organizational climates are associated with both higher service quality and better service outcomes.

DISCUSSION

This study's most important finding is that improvements in psychosocial functioning are significantly greater for children served by offices with more positive climates. The relationship found between organizational climate and the outcomes of children's services is particularly significant because the measures of these two constructs relied on independent methods. Organizational climate was measured with self-report scales administered to caseworkers in each office, while changes in psychosocial functioning were measured by independent descriptions of children's behaviors provided by their teachers. Therefore, the common method error variance that plagues much of the research using structural modeling and related techniques does not account for any portion of the covariance between the two constructs.

The success that caseworkers have in improving children's psychosocial functioning depends heavily on their consideration of each child's unique needs, the caseworkers' responses to unexpected problems, and their tenacity in navigating bureaucratic and judicial hurdles to achieve the best placement and the most needed services for each child. This requires nonroutinized and individualized casework, personal relationships between the caseworker and child, and a results rather than process oriented approach (Glisson, 1992). These findings suggest that agencies with higher levels of job satisfaction, fairness, role clarity, cooperation, and personalization, and lower levels of role overload, conflict, and emotional exhaustion are more likely to support caseworkers' efforts to accomplish these objectives. In short, positive climates reflect work environments that complement and encourage the type of service provider activities that lead to success.

A second important finding is that improved service quality does not translate into significantly more positive outcomes. This suggests that caseworkers can meet service quality objectives without contributing to improvements in the psychosocial well-being of the children who are served. Although perplexing, a close examination of this finding explains why the process-related requirements for quality service are not necessarily related to outcome criteria. As shown in recent examples from government agencies, process-oriented job requirements are not sufficient for desired service outcomes (Osborne & Gaebler, 1992). This occurs because process-oriented approaches emphasize preprogrammed activities that limit employee discretion and responsiveness to unexpected problems and opportunities. In comparison, results-oriented approaches focus employee attention on the desired outcomes and require employee flexibility and discretion in the development of individualized approaches to reaching those outcomes.

At the same time, most researchers would agree that high quality children's service systems are characterized by the process-oriented indicators used here (i.e., availability, responsiveness, comprehensiveness, and continuity). But consensus about the desirability of these service system characteristics must be distinguished from the conclusion that related process-oriented activities can ensure positive service results. That is to say that these characteristics of quality service are not sufficient for positive service outcomes. This is because effective children's services require nonroutinized, individualized, service decisions that are tailored to each child (Glisson, 1992, 1996). Therefore, decisions that are in the best interests of a particular child may not fit predetermined criteria for service system quality.

The research team identified examples of casework activities in the field that demonstrated how service quality can be unrelated to service outcomes for an individual child. These examples included caseworkers sacrificing service comprehensiveness to ensure that a specific child received maximum use of a single service that was especially important for that child. They also included caseworkers electing to contact only one previous service provider (thus violating the continuity criterion) so that more effort could be placed on gathering information from and working with the specific provider who the caseworker believed was most important to the well-being of a particular child. And many caseworkers recognized that whether a specific child would benefit from being moved to a new residential placement after encountering difficulties in an initial placement (as required by the responsiveness criterion) depended entirely on the characteristics of the child and on the characteristics of the available placements. These workers understood that removing a child from a residential placement in which a child has experienced problems does not in and of itself ensure that the child will experience fewer problems in the next placement. These examples from our field observations show that specific process-oriented service requirements that are in the best interest of one child may not be in the best interest of another. Therefore, process-oriented criteria that define service system quality may not in fact maximize service outcomes for a specific child, depending on the unique circumstances of the case. So although these criteria describe desirable characteristics of service systems generally, they characterize processes that are unrelated to the individualized casework activities that are necessary for positive outcomes.

Although service quality and outcomes are not related in this sample, a very important third finding is that organizational climate was found to positively affect both. Not only were children who were served by agencies with more positive climates more likely to experience improved psychosocial functioning, they also received more comprehensive services, there was more continuity in the services they received, and their caseworkers were more responsive and available. So although the process-oriented service quality variables did not directly affect the results-oriented outcome variables for reasons discussed above, organizational climate had a positive effect on *both* process *and* results. And as in the relationship with outcomes, the measures of climate and service quality ensure that common method error variance does not explain the observed relationship between the two constructs. The positive relationships between climate and both service quality and service outcomes highlight the very important role played by organizational climate in the job performance of caseworkers who engage in highly stressful and demanding job tasks.

A fourth important finding is that although both intra- (climate) and inter- (services coordination) organizational characteristics affect service quality, increased service coordination *decreases* quality. Given the meager results to date of efforts nationwide to improve children's services through interorganizational services coordination and other innovative service configurations, it is significant that services coordination was associated with decreased service quality. Although this finding supports the work of Scott (1985), Bendor (1985), and others who describe the detrimental effects of coordination, and possibly explains numerous failed attempts to improve services with increased coordination, it contradicts several writers who continue to argue for its benefits. Alter and Hage (1993), Provan and Milward (1995), and others have begun more recently to examine the meaning of coordination in relation to multiple interorganizational phenomena, but to date there is little empirical evidence to document these phenomena or to support the value of coordination to service system effectiveness.

These data and our experience in the field suggest that increases in service coordination deflected caseworkers' behaviors from those activities associated with the quality criteria for the children in their caseloads. In areas where coordination increased, caseworkers relinquished responsibility across the board for those activities, based on the incorrect but expedient assumption that they would be assumed by the service coordination teams. In other words, the more pronounced and visible the role of a services coordination team in a given area, the less responsibility caseworkers in the area assumed for the activities associated with the indicators of service quality, regardless of the individual needs of specific children. This did not result in caseworkers in those areas electing to forego quality related processes for only some children, which would have created a null relationship between coordination and quality similar to that described between quality and outcomes. Rather, they were deemphasized for all children in their caseloads, creating a significant negative relationship.

The objective of services coordination is to eliminate parallel, redundant, competing service systems by centralizing service decisions. This centralization ironically can diffuse rather than focus responsibility for casework activities. This happens when those who work directly with a child have less discretion to make key service decisions for the child. By transferring key decisions to those who do not work directly with a child, personal responsibility for the child is reduced for those who do. The important point is that this reduction in personal responsibility is not complemented by a comparable assumption of responsibility by service coordinating teams. Much in the way that the decisions of centralized, managed care gatekeepers frustrate the efforts of health care providers who work directly with patients, services coordination teams that do not work directly with a child are not compelled to assume the same degree of responsibility for the well-being of a child as those who establish a personal relationship with the child. While this may be effective in controlling services and costs as intended in managed care, it cannot be expected to improve service quality or outcomes.

Another salient finding from the study concerns the indicators of service outcomes. Teachers' descriptions of children's psychosocial functioning were found to be better indicators of outcomes than were parents' (or guardians') descriptions. This is consistent with earlier findings about the use of parents and teachers to assess children in custody (Glisson, 1994, 1996). Also, while both teachers and parents have been found to provide valid observations about children's behavior, Achenbach (1991a; 1991b) has reported higher reliability estimates for teachers. It is possible that parents minimize or maximize their accounts of their children's problems, depending on a number of issues related to the circumstances of a case and the unique relationships that exist between the parents and children. For example, parental responses in the current sample could have been influenced by whether a child was entering custody for abuse or neglect (one-third of the sample) where a parent could be implicated, for status offenses (one-third of the sample), or for delinquent behavior (one-third of the sample) where a parent could be the petitioner or could support the petition for state custody.

The finding concerning teachers' assessments is significant because the psychosocial well-being of the children is the most important service outcome that can be assessed for children who are placed in state custody. Aside from the physical safety of the child, family, or community, improvements in the children's psychosocial functioning are minimal goals regardless of the reason for custody or the characteristics of the child. Placing a child in custody addresses the physical safety issue. But if a child's psychosocial functioning does not improve or deteriorates after entering custody, there is no justification other than physical safety for having placed the child in custody. And following the 1976 Wyatt versus Stickney "right to treatment" decision, a dozen federal court decisions have maintained that individuals held in the custody of state human service systems must receive services that are designed to improve their psychosocial functioning.

In summary, findings presented here suggest that service effectiveness is related more to organizational climate, the service provider attitudes that characterize a given service system, than to service system configurations. Although a variety of individual, environmental, and organizational characteristics affect service provider attitudes, almost no research has focused on how such attitudes can be improved in children's service systems. While extensive research on improving climate has been conducted in business and industrial organizations, the successful techniques have not been transported into public agencies that serve children (Mayer & Schoorman, 1992; Ostroff & Schmitt, 1993). There are also unexplored questions about the roles played by related variables such as organizational culture (employee norms and values), which have been found to affect climate in other types of organizations (O'Reilly, Chatman, & Caldwell, 1991; Sheridan, 1992).

Several methodological issues emerge from these findings. First, subsequent research on children's service organizations would benefit from using techniques developed with other types of organizations to experimentally manipulate climate. Not only would this control additional threats to internal validity, it is likely to increase effect sizes. Second, generalization of the current findings beyond the sampled counties requires replication in both urban and rural areas. A final caveat concerns the accuracy of case files that provided data for some of the indicators. Although research assistants worked directly with caseworkers in the field to obtain and verify information from case files, missing and inaccurate data are possible sources of error that could have decreased the effect sizes.

The significant link found between climate and outcomes is important because previous attempts to identify the predictors of children's service system performance have met with very little success. The results of this study provide evidence that these attempts could have failed because they focused on service system configurations rather than on the dimensions of the service system represented by organizational climate and related service provider attitudes. Because many employees of public children's service systems experience high levels of stress, low job satisfaction, high conflict, depersonalization, and burnout, the findings suggest that future research should focus on these types of problems rather than on service configurations as the cause of poor service outcomes.

REFERENCES

Achenbach, T. M. (1991). *Integrative guide for the 1991 CBCL/4-18, YSR, and TRF profiles.* Burlington, VT: University of Vermont Department of Psychiatry.

Achenbach, T. M. (1991a). *Manual for the child behavior checklist/4-18 and 1991 profile.* Burlington, VT: University of Vermont Department of Psychiatry.

Achenbach, T. M. (1991b). *Manual for the teacher's report form and 1991 profile.* Burlington, VT: University of Vermont Department of Psychiatry.

Achenbach, T. M., McConaughy, S. H., & Howell, C. T. (1987). Child/adolescent behavior and emotional problems: Implications of cross-informant correlations for situational specificity. *Psychological Bulletin, 101,* 213–232.

Aiken, A., Dewar, R., DiTomaso, N., Hage, J., & Zeitz, G. (1975). *Coordinating human services.* San Francisco, CA: Jossey-Bass, Inc., Publishers.

Alter, C. (1990). An exploratory study of conflict and coordination in interorganizational service delivery systems. *Academy of Management Journal, 33,* 478–502.

Alter, C., & Hage, J. (1993). *Organizations working together.* Newbury Park, CA: Sage.

Anderson, J. C., & Gerbing, D. W. (1988). Structural equation modeling in practice: A review and recommended two-step approach. *Psychological Bulletin, 103,* 411–423.

Barth, R. P., Courtney, M., Berrick, J. D., & Albert, V. (1994). *From child abuse to permanency planning.* New York: Aldine de Gruyter.

Behar, L. (1985). Changing patterns of state responsibility: A case study of North Carolina. *Journal of Clinical Child Psychology, 14,* 188–195.

Bendor, J. B. (1985). *Parallel systems: Redundancy in government.* Berkeley, CA: University of California Press.

Bentler, P. M. (1990). Comparative fit indexes in structural models. *Psychological Bulletin, 107,* 238–246.

Bollen, K. A. (1989). *Structural equations with latent variables.* New York: Wiley.

Browne, M. W. (1982). Covariance structures. In D. W. Hawkins (Ed.), *Topics in multivariate analysis* (pp. 72–141). Cambridge, MA: Cambridge University Press.

Browne, M. W. (1984). Asymptotic distribution free methods in analysis of covariance structures. *British*

Journal of Mathematical and Statistical Psychology, 37, 62–83.

Burns, B. J., & Friedman, R. M. (1990). Examining the research base for child mental health services and policy. *The Journal of Mental Health Administration, 17,* 87–98.

Center for the Study of Social Policy (1990). *The crisis in foster care: Directions for the 1990s.* Washington, DC: Center for the Study of Social Policy.

Center for the Study of Social Policy (1993). *Kids count data book.* Washington, DC: Center for the Study of Social Policy.

Dodge, K. A., & Somberg, D. (1987). Hostile attributional biases among aggressive boys are exacerbated under conditions of threat to the self. *Child Development, 58,* 213–224.

Dougherty, D. M., Saxe, L. M., Cross, T., & Silverman, N. (1987). *Children's mental health: Problems and services.* Durham, NC: Duke University Press.

Dozier, M., Cue, K. L., & Barnett, L. (1994). Clinicians as caregivers: Role of attachment organization in treatment. *Journal of Consulting and Clinical Psychology, 62,* 793–800.

Duchnowski, A. J., & Friedman, R. M. (1990). Children's mental health: Challenges for the nineties. *The Journal of Mental Health Administration, 17,* 3–12.

Frank, R. G., & Gaynor, M. (1994). Fiscal decentralization of public mental health care and the Robert Wood Johnson Foundation Program on Chronic Mental Illness. *The Milbank Quarterly, 72,* 81–104.

Glisson, C. (1992). Technology and structure in human service organizations. In Hasenfeld (Ed.), *Human services as complex organizations* (pp. 184–202). Beverly Hills, CA: Sage.

Glisson, C. (1994). The effect of services coordination teams on outcomes for children in state custody. *Administration in Social Work, 18,* 1–23.

Glisson, C. (1996). Judicial and service decisions for children entering state custody: The limited role of mental health. *Social Service Review, 70,* 257–281.

Glisson, C., & Durick, M. (1988). Predictors of job satisfaction and organizational commitment in human services organizations. *Administrative Science Quarterly, 33.*

Glisson, C., & James, L. (1992). The interorganizational coordination of services to children in state custody. *Administration in Social Work, 16,* 65–80.

Goldman, H., Morrissey, J., Ridgely, S., Frank, R., Newman, S., & Kennedy, C. (1992). Lessons from the program on chronic mental illness. *Health Affairs, 11,* 51–68.

Goldman, H., Morrissey, J., & Ridgely, S. (1994). Evaluating the Robert Wood Johnson Foundation program on chronic mental illness. *Milbank Quarterly, 72,* 37–48.

Hackman, J., & Oldham, R. (1975). Development of the job diagnostic survey. *Journal of Applied Psychology, 60,* 159–170.

Hall, R., Clark, J., Giordano, P., Johnson, P., & Roekel, M. (1977). Patterns of interorganizational relationships. *Administrative Science Quarterly, 22,* 457–474.

Hellriegel, D., & Slocum, J., Jr. (1974). Organizational climate: Measures, research, and contingencies. *Academy of Management Journal, 17,* 255–280.

Hoagwood, K. (1997). Interpreting nullity: The Fort Bragg experiment—a comparative success or failure? *American Psychologist, 52,* 546–550.

James, L. A., Demaree, R. G., & Hater, J. J. (1980). A statistical rationale for relating situation variables and individual differences. *Organizational Behavior and Human Performance, 25,* 354–364.

James, L. A., & James, L. R. (1989). Integrating work environment perceptions: Explorations into the measurement of meaning. *Journal of Applied Psychology, 74,* 739–751.

James, L. R., & Jones, A. P. (1980). Perceived job characteristics and job satisfaction: An examination of reciprocal causation. *Personnel Psychology, 33,* 97–135.

James, L. R., & Sells, S. B. (1981). Psychological climate: Theoretical perspectives and empirical research. In D. Magnusson (Ed.), *Toward a psychology of situations: An interactional perspective* (pp. 275–295). Hillsdale, NJ: Erlbaum.

Joreskog, K. G., & Sorbom, D. (1993). *LISREL 8 user's reference guide.* Chicago, IL: Scientific Software International, Inc.

Klee, L., & Halfon, N. (1987). Mental health care for foster children in California. *Child Abuse & Neglect, 11,* 63–74.

Landau, M. (1969). Redundancy, rationality, and the problem of duplication and overlap. *Public Administration Review, 29,* 346–358.

Mayer, R. C., & Schoorman, F. D. (1992). Predicting participation and production outcomes through a two-dimensional model of organizational commitment. *Academy of Management Journal, 35,* 671–684.

McMahon, R. J. (1994). Diagnosis, assessment, and treatment of externalizing problems in children: The role of longitudinal data. *Journal of Consulting and Clinical Psychology, 62,* 901–917.

Medsker, G. J., Williams, L. J., & Holahan, P. J. (1994). A review of current practices for evaluating causal models in organizational behavior and human resources management research. *Journal of Management, 20,* 439–464.

Melton, G. B., & Flood, M. F. (1994). Research policy and child maltreatment: Developing the scientific foundation for effective protection of children. *Child Abuse & Neglect, 18,* 1–28.

Morrissey, J. P., Calloway, M., Bartko, W. T., Ridgely, M. S., Goldman, H. H., & Paulson, R. I. (1994). Fiscal decentralization of public mental health care and the Robert Wood Johnson Foundation Program on Chronic Mental Illness. *The Milbank Quarterly, 72,* 49–80.

Mulaik, S. A., James, L. R., Van Alstine, J., Bennett, N., Lind, S., & Stilwell, C. D. (1989). Evaluation of goodness-of-fit indices for structural equation models. *Psychological Bulletin, 105,* 430–435.

Mulford, C., & Rogers, D. (1982). Definitions and models. In D. Rogers & D. Whetten (Eds.), *Interorganizational coordination: Theory, research, and implementation* (pp. 9–31). Ames, IA: Iowa State University Press.

National Center on Child Abuse and Neglect, DHHS (1996). *Child maltreatment 1994: Reports from the states.* Washington, DC: US Government Printing Office.

National Institute of Mental Health (1991). *Caring for people with severe mental disorders: A national plan of research to improve services.* Washington, DC: DHHS (Pub. No. ADM 91–1762).

National Research Council, Panel on Research on Child Abuse and Neglect (1993). *Understanding child abuse and neglect.* Washington, DC: National Academy Press.

Ollendeck, T. H., & King, N. J. (1994). Diagnosis, assessment, and treatment of internalizing problems in children: The role of longitudinal data. *Journal of Consulting and Clinical Psychology, 62,* 918–927.

O'Reilly, C. A., Chatman, J., & Caldwell, D. (1991). People and organizational culture: A profile comparison approach to assessing person-organization fit. *Academy of Management Journal, 34,* 487–516.

Osborne & Gaebler (1992). *Reinventing government.* Reading, MA: Addison-Wesley.

Ostroff, C., & Schmitt, N. (1993). Configurations of organizational effectiveness and efficiency. *Academy of Management Journal, 36,* 1345–1361.

Payne, R., & Pugh, D. (1975). Organization structure and organization climate. In M. D. Dunnette (Ed.), *Handbook of industrial-organizational psychology* (pp. 1125–1174). Chicago, IL: Rand McNally.

Porter, L., Steers, R., Mowday, R., & Boulian, P. (1974). Organizational commitment, job satisfaction, and turnover among psychiatric technicians. *Journal of Applied Psychology, 59,* 603–609.

Price, J. L., & Mueller, C. W. (1986). *Handbook of organizational measurement.* Marshfield, MA: Pitman Publishing, Inc.

Provan, K., & Milward, H. (1995). A preliminary theory of interorganizational network effectiveness: A comparative study of four community mental health systems. *Administrative Science Quarterly, 40,* 1–33.

Rizzo, J., House, R., & Lirtzman, S. (1970). Role conflict and ambiguity in complex organizations. *Administrative Science Quarterly, 15,* 150–163.

Rosenblatt, A., & Attkisson, C. C. (1992). Integrating systems of care in California for youth with severe emotional disturbance. *Journal of Child and Family Studies, 1,* 93–113.

Schneider, B. (1975). Organizational climates: An essay. *Personnel Psychology, Inc., 28,* 447–479.

Scott, W. R. (1985). Systems within systems. *American Behavioral Scientist, 28,* 601–618.

Sheridan, J. E. (1992). Organization culture and employee retention. *Academy of Management Journal, 35,* 1036–1056.

Soloman, E. E. (1986). Private and public sector managers: An empirical investigation of job characteristics and organizational climate. *Journal of Applied Psychology, 71,* 247–259.

Steinwachs, D., Cummum, H., Dorwart, R., Flynn, L., Frank, R., Friedman, M., Herz, M., Mulvey, E., Snowden, L., Test, M., Tremaine, L., & Windle, C. (1992). Service systems research. *Schizophrenia Bulletin, 18,* 627–668.

Teague, G. B., Drake, R. E., & Ackerson, T. H. (1995). Evaluating use of continuous treatment teams for persons with mental illness and substance abuse. *Psychiatric Services, 46,* 689–695.

Tennessee Commission on Children and Youth (1997). *Tennessee kids count: The state of the child in Tennessee, 1996.* Nashville, TN: Tennessee Commission on Children and Youth.

Tennessee Council of Juvenile and Family Court Judges (1995). *1993 and 1994 Tennessee annual juvenile court statistical reports.* Nashville, TN: Tennessee Council of Juvenile and Family Court Judges.

Thompson, R. A., & Wilcox, B. L. (1995). Child maltreatment research: Federal support and policy issues. *American Psychologist, 9,* 789–793.

Wahler, R. G. (1994). Child conduct problems: Disorders in conduct or social continuity? *Journal of Child and Family Studies, 3,* 143–156.

Weick, K. (1976). Educational organizations as loosely coupled systems. *Administrative Science Quarterly, 21,* 1–19.

COMMENTARY BY: Charles Glisson

STUDYING THE ORGANIZATIONAL CONTEXT
OF SOCIAL SERVICES

The Research Problem

The research problem reflects an interest in the organizational context of human service systems that began with my first direct practice experiences over three decades ago. As a newly graduated MSW, I worked first in a large mental health institution and then in a small, community-based, substance abuse treatment program. My direct practice experiences in the two organizations were very different, but in both I encountered organizational characteristics that were counterproductive to successful practice. Rather than supporting service providers' efforts, each organization created barriers to service that decreased service provider effectiveness. For example, the formal divisions of labor in the large mental health institution specified that social workers could provide services to the families of residents but could not provide treatment to the individual residents. This created awkward and inefficient lines of communication where issues discussed with a resident's family could not be shared directly with the resident, but instead were communicated indirectly through a psychologist. In the community substance abuse treatment program, the administration demanded that the same series of treatment protocols be used with each client. The agency would not allow deviations for clients who might benefit from a different combination of treatments or consider the development of new protocols that offered alternative treatments. Although neither organization measured client outcomes and neither wanted to collect data to assess how well they were meeting treatment goals, the two organizations were similar in that both maintained that their services were effective.

Those first practice experiences stimulated a personal interest that continues today in understanding how organizations affect the quality and outcomes of the services they provide. That interest became the focus of my subsequent doctoral training, in which I was introduced to organizational theory from sociology, industrial organizational psychology, and management. This was important because very little organizational theory was included in the mainstream social work literature at the time. Although a sizeable social administration literature existed, it focused largely on administrative practice and not on organizational theory and research. In addition, the social administration literature was separated from the direct practice literature to such an extent that very little connection was made in either literature between administrative practices and direct practice outcomes.

Commentary on article: Glisson, C., Hemmelgarn, A. (1998). The effects of organizational climate and interorganizational coordination on the quality and outcomes of children's service systems. *Child Abuse & Neglect, 22,* 401–421.

In my doctoral training, I was disappointed to find that with few exceptions, the organizational theory and research literature focused almost exclusively on business and industrial organizations. But at the same time, I was excited to discover that studies of business and industrial organizations were examining relationships between organizational characteristics, worker performance, and organizational effectiveness. Although worker performance and organizational effectiveness in most of the studies were unrelated to social work practice, it was exciting to see findings that paralleled my own practice experiences. That is, there was evidence from those studies that organizational procedures, divisions of labor, and decision-making affected the work performance of employees in the *technological core* of the organization (where the product or service was produced or provided). Moreover, the studies suggested that organizational characteristics determined the success of the core technology. In short, organizational characteristics were linked to effectiveness. At that point, I focused my research on understanding the association between organizational characteristics and effectiveness in human service systems.

Beginning with my dissertation, my work was guided by the thesis that the effectiveness of equally trained and equally skilled clinicians varies as a function of the organizations in which they provide services. My objective has been to describe these relationships with the goal of understanding how to design and develop service organizations that maximize the effectiveness of the service providers who work within them.

Methodological and Substantive Developments in the Research

Most organizational studies use correlational approaches. They use either cross-sectional or panel designs to describe organizational characteristics and the relationships between those characteristics and other variables (such as worker performance or organizational effectiveness). The reasons for these correlational designs are twofold. First, it is difficult to find administrators who will allow their organizations to be randomly assigned to experimental conditions or to allow changes to be made by external researchers in the way their organizations function. Second, even quasi-experimental studies of organizational-level interventions are large, complex and expensive. They require multiple organizational sites and both human and financial resources to intervene in those sites. For these reasons, my initial studies were correlational. Later, I was able to obtain the resources required to conduct more complex studies, such as the study included in this text (Glisson & Hemmelgarn, 1998). Over the years, I moved from correlational designs to quasi-experimental designs (represented by the study discussed here) and then to implementing true experimental designs. Currently, I am in the fifth year of implementing a large, true experimental design involving multiple organizational sites, and in the first year of implementing another five-year, true experimental design that also includes multiple sites, both of which are funded by the National Institute of Mental Health.[1]

The study addressed here reflected substantive as well as methodological developments in my research. Methodologically, the quasi-experimental design used in the study was implemented after I had conducted a number of less-expensive cross-sectional and panel studies. Substantively, the study represented a broader focus. I moved from focusing on the impact of the structural characteristics of organizations (e.g., divisions of labor, participation in decision making, hierarchy of authority) to include a focus on organizational climate as the key to understanding the effect of the work environment on service effectiveness. An important difference between the two constructs is that *structure* represents formal patterns of roles and interactions among employees within

---

[1] NIMH R01-MH56563 and R01-66905

a work environment that are prescribed by the organization, and *climate* represents the employees' perceptions of the psychological impact (e.g., emotional exhaustion, depersonalization) of their work environment on them personally. Climate therefore was an important mediating variable that linked organizational characteristics to worker performance.

Almost no organizational research with any type of organization combines interorganizational and intraorganizational constructs in the research questions and design of the same study. The study discussed here was the first to do so with organizations providing child welfare and juvenile justice services. At the time the study was conducted, there was (and continues to be) a general interest among both researchers and service providers in the coordination of services to children and families across multiple service systems. This interest is based on the belief that many of the children and families most at risk require services from more than one service sector and that the services would be more effective if the various systems coordinated their efforts. Although a rational and plausible idea, several organizational scholars argued that coordination has little value for improving services and, indeed, subsequent studies failed to show that coordination improved human service outcomes. Although the empirical evidence to date suggests that outcomes are not improved by services coordination, coordination continues to be emphasized on the basis of its logical appeal and the impression of many practitioners in the field that better coordination should improve outcomes. The study discussed here was one of several efforts to test the effects of interorganizational services coordination. The hypothesized structural model (*Model A* in the article) in my NIMH research proposal specified that interorganizational services coordination would improve organizational climate, service quality, and interorganizational relationships. Further, the model specified that this would result in better service outcomes for the children.

The model originally hypothesized in the NIMH research proposal (*Model A*) was tested exactly as specified in the proposal. And the design and the research questions remained unchanged from those originally proposed. But the results of the study did not support all aspects of the original hypothesized model. As explained above, we expected that services coordination would positively affect climate, service quality, and interorganizational relationships. Instead, coordination was found to have no effect on climate and interorganizational relationships, and to have a negative effect on service quality. While the potential value of coordination for improving services was challenged by these findings, the hypothesized link between organizational climate and both service quality and outcomes was supported. As is frequently the case in research, one door was opened while another was closed, and we turned our interest to understanding more about the role of organizational climate in service quality and outcomes. Following the study, my interest in climate developed further to include organizational culture, and my recent studies have linked structure, culture, and climate in a model of organizational context that explains the attitudes and behaviors of service providers as a function of organizational structure, culture, and climate (Glisson, 2002; Glisson & James, 2002).

Concerns and Compromises in the Design and Conduct of the Study

Although the study was carried out as originally designed in the proposal, there were a number of compromises in the design of the study that were made before the research proposal was written and submitted to NIMH. The compromises reflected the realities of what the state children's service system would agree to do in implementing the pilot study. A constraint in the conduct of most services research funded by NIMH is that funding is available for studying the services but not for providing the services. That is, if an NIMH principal investigator wants to study any type of services, it is usually the case that the services that are the focus of the study cannot be funded by the NIMH research grant. Only the costs of the research activities can be included in most NIH research funding mechanisms. In the study reviewed here, I relied on the state to fund the cost of the pilot coordination teams and on existing funding streams for the services that were coordinated by those teams.

This background is important to understanding why I was unsuccessful in convincing the state to randomly assign regions to the intervention (i.e., pilot coordination teams) and control conditions. Rather than randomly assigning the regions to experimental and control conditions, the state simply picked the regions that they wanted to receive the intervention and the control regions were then selected to match the experimental regions on a number of demographical characteristics.

Counties selected for the control group were those closest to the experimental counties in population size, child poverty rates, unemployment, and education levels. The matching process was systematic in part, but judgment was also involved. Experimental counties were located within each of two of the state's three regions (over 30 counties per region). Counties within these two regions were rank ordered by population. Then similarly ranked counties were identified that were close to experimental counties on the final three criteria, all of which were highly correlated. That is, counties with higher child poverty rates also had higher unemployment and lower education levels. Perhaps most importantly for obtaining funding, we included the demographic characteristics of the selected experimental and control counties in the proposal to show the similarities between the two groups of counties.

We were fortunate that the state wanted to study the effects of the coordination teams, funded the costs of the pilot coordination effort, and allowed us to study the effort. But the trade-off for the research effort was that the state selected the regions in which the coordination teams were to be tested and we were unable to randomly assign the regions to treatment conditions. However, we were able to use matched counties in the control condition, and the NIMH internal review group that evaluated the proposal agreed that the benefits of the study outweighed the deficits created by using matching rather than random assignment.

Funding Sources and Limitations

The study was funded with an R01 research grant from NIMH. The National Institutes of Health (NIH) R01 funding mechanism supports large studies and provides the principal investigator with the maximum authority and flexibility to implement complex research. I was fortunate to receive funding on my first submission (a rare event for R01 proposals), so no revisions were required in my original design and the study was funded as it was proposed initially. It is important to emphasize that this type of large-scale services research is expensive, even when the costs do not include the cost of services. The expense results from conducting and coordinating research activities over a large geographical area, the number of research personnel required to identify subjects and collect data in the field, the length of time required to implement the intervention and follow subjects over time, and the interdisciplinary team of senior researchers that is required to conduct a high-quality study. As a result, large research grants from the National Institutes of Health and other funding agencies are essential to conducting services research of this type.

In addition to providing funds for the research, grants provide autonomy to the research team by separating research funding from the service systems that are being studied. Other avenues for funding research, such as contracts with state or federal agencies for evaluating programs or conducting needs assessments, rarely allow the autonomy or level of funding required for investigators to develop and implement independent programs of research. For example, contracts with state agencies are plagued frequently by political pressure to produce certain findings, inadequate funding to support the most valid and appropriate procedures, and a lack of separation between service providers and researchers that is damaging to independent inquiry.

At the same time, many problems are also encountered with implementing independent research grants. The cooperation of service providers and public officials is necessary and that cooperation can evaporate for any number of reasons. In my own experience over a number of years of funded studies, class action lawsuits that are filed against the service systems, changes in key service system personnel, the election of a new state administration, and administrators becoming concerned about losing control of their employees or service system have disrupted research plans. In the study discussed here, once the state determined how and where the pilot coordination project would be implemented, state officials remained committed to the project and we were able to maintain the required support and collaboration among service providers.

Human Subjects and Ethical Issues

National Institutes of Health study groups and university institutional review boards (IRBs) carefully scrutinize research that includes children. Even in studies that do not randomly assign children to new treatment interventions, there are concerns about coercion, confidentiality, and unanticipated consequences that could result from participation in a study. Although much of my research focuses on system-level variables and interventions, my outcome measures focus on individuals who receive services, and the nature of those services can change as a result of the service system interventions. As a result, the protection of human subjects requires that children and families in these studies be able to provide informed consent to participate, and that any risks be clearly spelled out in the informed consent process. It is common for IRBs to raise concerns about the protection of human subjects, or require procedures that principal investigators believe are unwarranted. In the present case, for example, the university IRB initially wanted letters from each school in each county in each region to approve the research before we implemented the study. This would have included hundreds of schools, most of which would not have had a student in the study once it was implemented. Since we were unable to know in advance which schools the children in the study would be attending, the IRB agreed to approve the study based on receiving approval from the school boards in each county.

During the three decades that I have conducted university-based research, the scrutiny of protocols for the protection of human subjects has increased dramatically. Today, universities and funding agencies are much more vigilant than in the past in requiring that subjects be fully informed about risks, that the risks be reasonable and minimized, that subject confidentiality be fully protected, and that no coercion be used in recruiting subjects. Although review groups at funding agencies and universities can be overly cautious, the increased scrutiny of review groups has resulted in greater attention being given to the protection of human subjects.

Although research with child welfare, juvenile justice, and children's mental health systems can place children at risk, and protections against those risks must be in place, it is also the case that failing to conduct research on systems that serve children also places children at risk. Because of the large gap between what is known about effective services and what is actually practiced in the field, many children referred to child welfare, juvenile justice, and mental health systems receive ineffective services. In addition to children receiving ineffective services, there is evidence that some children actually experience detrimental outcomes as a result of services provided by these systems. That is, there are children who fail to benefit from services and there are children who are worse off from having received inappropriate services. Research has been instrumental in identify-ing these service system deficits, and not conducting research on these service systems would ensure that the service system deficits would remain unknown and uncorrected. Thus, the lack of research can place children at risk.

New Research Directions and Hypotheses Arising from the Study

Several new research directions and hypotheses arose from the findings of this study. Two new studies were designed and implemented as a direct result of the findings; both were five-year studies funded by NIMH R01 grants. The first of the new studies is in its final year, and the second of the new studies is in its first year. The new studies evolved from our finding that organizational climate predicted service outcomes for children, and that organizational climate was tied to the socioeconomic conditions of the county. These findings increased our interest in understanding more about these links, and about how positive work environments could be developed in children's service systems.

There are extensive organizational and community development literatures that describe strategies for improving organizational work environments and developing community support for efforts to introduce innovative programs. However, most of this organizational and community development literature focuses on hard technology, business, and agriculture. We believed that many of these development strategies could be adapted for application in children's service systems. To address these issues, we adapted organizational and community development strategies that had been designed for business and government organizations in a way that was appropriate for children's service systems. We then piloted the new intervention, labeled ARC (for availability, responsiveness, and continuity), for one year in a public children's service system (details of ARC are provided in Glisson, 2002).

On the basis of the pilot data and findings from a number of our related organizational studies, we designed an NIMH proposal to test the effectiveness of the new ARC intervention's impact on the work environments of child welfare and juvenile justice case management teams using a true experimental design. Findings indicated that teams in both urban and rural locations that received the ARC intervention had significantly less role conflict and role overload. Most importantly, all teams receiving the ARC intervention had 41 percent less turnover in case managers than control teams. Significant interactions between location and the intervention indicated that teams working in rural locations experienced even greater benefits from the intervention than urban teams. This was important because the original study found that the teams located in the poorest, most rural counties had the most negative climates. So, the findings from this first follow-up study indicated that organizational development and community development techniques could be used successfully to improve work environments and service quality in public children's service systems. Moreover, the findings suggested that the techniques could be especially effective in impoverished, rural areas.

The second follow-up study was designed on the basis of the findings from the original study and from the first follow-up study. For the second follow-up study, which is currently in year two of five years, we are using a true experimental design to test interventions that are expected to improve services for children referred to juvenile courts in rural Appalachia. These rural counties are the poorest in the state and have the highest rates of referrals to juvenile courts and state custody. Each of the two interventions, one at the micro level and one at the macro level, composes a separate factor in a fully crossed research design that allows the main and interaction effects of the two factors to be assessed.

At the micro level, children and families referred to juvenile courts are randomly assigned within each of eight counties to receive usual services or an evidence-based practice (Multisystemic

Therapy—MST) believed to be effective for reducing delinquent behavior (Henggeler et al, 1998). MST is a home-based intervention that requires therapists to be available on a 24/7 basis, but it had not been systematically tested in remote rural areas. At the macro level, the eight counties are randomly assigned to receive either the ARC intervention or the control condition. In those counties that receive the ARC intervention, a Ph.D. industrial-organizational psychologist is using ARC developmental strategies to support the counties' efforts to reduce delinquency. The ARC specialist works with service providers, courts, schools, and key community opinion leaders to share data and information about barriers to service, and to facilitate efforts of service providers to address the needs of delinquent youth and their families. We expect the best outcomes to occur among children who receive MST in those counties that participate in the ARC intervention.

Strengths and Limitations of the Study

The primary strength of the original study discussed here was its attempt to link both intraorganizational and interorganizational characteristics to service quality and outcomes. By including both types of variables, it became the first study to establish an empirical relationship between organizational climate and service outcomes in child welfare and juvenile justice systems. At the same time, the study added to the growing body of research that failed to confirm the value of interorganizational coordination for service outcomes.

Associated strengths of the study included design and measurement features that contributed to the validity of the conclusions that were drawn about the effects of organizational climate on service outcomes. First, standardized measurement tools and strategies for assessing organizational climate were adapted from the organizational research literature for use in children's service systems. By building on several decades of research on organizational climate in business and industrial organizations, we used established methods of assessing organizational climate. These methods relied on measures that were recognized indicators of organizational climate and depended on a consensus of responses from line workers to describe their work environments. Second, we assessed service outcomes with teacher evaluations of children's functioning. By using different respondents to evaluate climate, service quality, and service outcomes (as opposed to having case managers evaluate both their work environments and service outcomes, for example), the threat of common method error variance was removed from the analysis. That is, studies that depend on the same respondent to measure both independent and dependent variables create the potential for single-source bias that can inflate observed effect sizes through highly correlated error terms. In this study, independent evaluations of organizational climate, service quality, and service outcomes removed this threat.

Another strength of the study was the prospective, repeated assessments of children's functioning that were conducted directly by the research team. By identifying subjects when they were referred for services and following those subjects in real time, we were able to assess the children's functioning at the time they were referred and again after one year. This allowed differences at follow-up to be assessed after controlling for baseline differences using covariate procedures. Many studies of service outcomes use retrospective strategies to assess changes in children's functioning that depend on child welfare or juvenile justice records (which are notoriously unreliable), or on respondents' memories (which can be just as unreliable). By using a prospective design that assessed children's functioning repeatedly in real time, we eliminated these sources of unreliability and increased the validity of our assessments of children's functioning.

Limitations of the study include threats to internal validity and to external validity caused by the lack of random assignment and random selection, respectively. Threats to internal validity are generated by the fact that organizational climate was not manipulated as a part of the design. Contrary to our expectation, the interorganizational coordination program had no impact on climate, and the observed relationship between organizational climate and service outcomes was correlational. That is, we found that offices varied in organizational climate and that children served by offices with more positive climates received higher quality services and enjoyed better outcomes than children served by offices with more negative climates. But because children were not randomly assigned to offices with different organizational climates, we could not conclude that organizational climate *caused* the observed differences in children's outcomes. Almost all studies of organizational climate are correlational and almost no studies in the organizational literature manipulate climate, so there is a need for studies that either randomly assign subjects to different organizational climates or test interventions that are designed to create differences in organizational climate and then assess the impact of those differences.

Another limitation was created by threats to external validity resulting from the use of study sites in 24 counties of one state. Findings cannot be generalized beyond the one state or even beyond the selected regions. As mentioned earlier, rather than being randomly selected, the experimental regions were selected purposively by the state and the control regions were selected to match the experimental regions. It is rare for studies of organizations to incorporate randomly selected sites from a large population of organizations. The difficulty in obtaining the cooperation of a large number of organizations, as well as the logistics and expense of doing the research, results in most organizational research using narrow samples of convenience. As a result, organizational researchers have relied on study replication to generalize findings. However, large-scale nationwide studies of randomly selected children's service organizations are needed to describe the distribution of organizational characteristics such as climate, and to link those organizational variables to a variety of service system characteristics. I am currently participating in an effort being funded by the John T. and Catherine D. MacArthur Foundation to do just that. The study will describe the distribution of organizational climate and culture in a representative, nationwide sample of 200 children's mental health service organizations, and assess the relationships between those variables and other service system characteristics. This study is a companion study to another effort that is examining the role of organizational factors and other variables in the implementation of evidence-based practices among mental health providers who serve children. The objective of these two studies is to gain a better understanding of how to improve children's mental health services by the effective dissemination of evidence-based practices in community mental health organizations.

Advice for Future Research in the Area

Future research on the organizational context of services would benefit from addressing the limitations in internal and external validity described in the previous section. But there are additional issues that face services researchers and practice researchers interested in organizational context and the roles that organizations play in service outcomes and practice effectiveness. This interest has been fueled by the documented gap between science and practice, which suggests that the most effective practices are not being used by the organizations that provide services in the community. A variety of services researchers have begun to incorporate organizational variables in their efforts to study service system effectiveness. And those studying clinical or practice effectiveness are beginning to examine the effects of organizational context on the selection of treatment strategies, treatment fidelity, the therapeutic relationship, and other variables believed to be important to treatment outcomes.

Efforts to incorporate organizational context in both services and practice research would be aided by the use of established research methods from the organizational research literature. Without the knowledge and use of established organizational research methods, there is a danger that services and clinical researchers will encounter barriers or commit errors in their efforts that could otherwise be avoided with the use of established organizational research protocols. "Reinventing the wheel" is an occupational hazard among social and behavioral science researchers when scholars broaden their efforts into new areas of inquiry without benefit of the knowledge gained by other researchers who have studied those areas previously. Common errors in the study of organizational context include a lack of specificity in defining organizational constructs, altering standardized organizational scales, creating scales post hoc by combining items that capitalize on sample-specific covariance structures, not attempting to confirm a priori factor structures, using composition models incorrectly, failing to assess within-organizational agreement in responses, and the use of inappropriate analytic techniques to link group- and individual-level variables (Glisson & James, 2002).

Future research would also benefit from including both organizational culture and organizational climate in the same study. Although the study discussed here focused on the links between organizational climate and service outcomes, there is evidence that organizational culture is as important to organizational success as climate. Both constructs have been studied for decades, but most studies have focused on either culture or climate rather than including both in the same study. Currently, there is confusion about the similarities and differences between the two constructs, which could be addressed by including both constructs in the same studies (Glisson & James, 2002). In addition, most of the research on culture and climate has been conducted in business and industrial organizations, and there is still much to learn about the role each construct plays in the types of organizations that provide social services and other human services.

Future research should move beyond documenting links between organizational context and service outcomes to testing strategies for improving organizational contexts. There are large organizational and community development literatures that address methods for improving organizational context and promoting the introduction of innovative programs in communities, but very little of this work has been in human service organizations. For example, in the two current NIMH funded studies mentioned earlier, we are testing organizational and community development strategies for improving child welfare and juvenile justice teams[2] and the effectiveness of children's mental health services.[3]

Application of Study Findings to Practice

The most important applications of the study's findings are that service systems should focus on creating positive organizational climates to improve service effectiveness. The organizational development literatures describe macro-level interventions that have been successful in improving the organizational climates of business and industrial organizations. Many of these strategies have promise for use in social service organizations, and we have adapted several of these strategies to form our ARC organizational and community development intervention for use in children's service systems. Preliminary data from one of our current studies indicates that our ARC intervention model improves organizational climate and decreases turnover in child welfare and juvenile justice case management teams.

---

[2] R01-MH56563
[3] R01-MH066905

This paper was prepared with the support of NIMH R01-MH56563 and R01-MH R01-MH66905.

REFERENCES

Glisson, C. (2002). The organizational context of children's mental health services. *Clinical Child and Family Psychology Review, 5*(4), 233–253.

Glisson, C., & Hemmelgarn, A. (1998). The effects of organizational climate and interorganizational coordination on the quality and outcomes of children's service systems. *Child Abuse & Neglect 22*(5), 401–421.

Glisson, C., & James, L. R. (2002). The cross-level effects of culture and climate in human service teams. *Journal of Organizational Behavior, 23,* 767–794.

Henggeler, S. W., Schoenwald, S. K., Borduin, C. M., Rowland, M. D., & Cunningham, P. B. (1998). *Multisystemic treatment of antisocial behavior in children and adolescents.* New York: Guilford Press.

5

Confidentiality Intervention: Effects on Provider-Consumer- Family Collaboration

Tina Marshall and Phyllis Solomon

Confidentiality policies were developed to protect people with mental illness from stigma and discrimination that occurs when information about diagnosis and treatment ends up in the wrong hands (U.S. Department of Health and Human Services, 1999). Unfortunately, there are still incidences in which the stigma of mental illness has resulted in denied employment, insurance, education, and other opportunities. For this reason, it is thought that people with mental illnesses will not seek treatment or open up in a trusting manner unless they are assured that what they disclose in the course of the treatment process will be kept confidential. Accordingly, the National Association of Social Workers (NASW) code of ethics emphasizes protecting and safeguarding information obtained during the course of professional service. Although state laws differ regarding the types of information that may be disclosed without client consent (Petrila, 2000), the NASW code of ethics instructs social workers to receive client consent before fulfilling any request for the release of confidential information (Kagle, 2002; NASW, 1999). Social workers are also instructed to "disclose the least amount of confidential information necessary to achieve the desired purpose" (NASW, 1999, p. 10).

Although the importance of confidentiality policies is clear, the implementation of these policies often impedes communication between providers, consumers, and families (Bogart & Solomon, 1999; Lefley, 2000; Marshall & Solomon, 2000). This lack of communication is frequently justified on the presumption that the hardship resulting from mental illness leaves individuals with little or no family contact. However, research indicates that 75% of persons with

Authors' Note: Research for this article was supported by Grant No. 1-R03-MH-61031-01A1 from the National Institute of Mental Health.

schizophrenia have some ongoing contact with family members (Lehman & Steinwachs, 1998). Even consumers who are more severely ill or older tend to have some degree of family contact (Beeler, Rosenthal, & Cohler, 1999). Estimates of the number of adults with mental illness that live with their families vary between 50% and 84% (Beeler et al., 1999; Goldman, 1982; Guarnaccia, 1998; Lefley, 1996; National Institute of Mental Health, 1991).

Furthermore, families, who are often an integral part of consumers' support networks, may well be the first to recognize symptoms of relapse of their relatives (Herz, 1985). Yet, without ongoing contact with mental health providers, families may observe warning signs but have no way to share this information with providers who may intercede to prevent a crisis (Leazenby, 1997). Families have reported feeling frustrated, powerless, dissatisfied, and unconnected with the treatment process. Without information regarding diagnosis, etiology, treatment, and prognosis of their relatives' illness, family members are unable to support treatment goals and promote the recovery process of their relatives (Marsh & Johnson, 1997; Solomon, Draine, Mannion, & Meisel, 1998). For these reasons, best practice guidelines recommend involving families in the treatment of persons with mental illness (American Psychiatric Association, 1997; Dixon et al., 2001; Frances, Docherty, & Kahn, 1996). However, the implementation of confidentiality policies is hindering family involvement and communication with providers and thereby preventing their relatives from receiving support and treatment when they need it the most (Backlar, 1996; Biegel, Song, & Milligan, 1995; DiRienzo-Callahan, 1998; Furlong & Leggatt, 1996; Krauss, 1992; Lefley, 1996; Marsh, 1995; Petrila & Sadoff, 1992; Ryan, 1996; Zipple, Langle, Tyrell, Spaniol, & Fisher, 1997).

Although the code of ethics recommends that social workers discuss confidentiality with clients and other interested parties, research indicates that mental health providers rarely ask clients for their written consent to release information to family members (Marshall & Solomon, 2000, 2003). Furthermore, providers' interpretation and implementation of confidentiality policies vary tremendously. Providers differ in the types of information they believe are confidential, whether verbal agreement or written consent is necessary, and with respect to who is responsible for initiating the consent process (Marshall & Solomon, 2003).

This article reports on findings of a study that examined the effectiveness of an intervention designed to clarify confidentiality policies for the release of information to families. The development of the intervention has been described by the authors in detail in a previous publication (Bogart & Solomon, 1999). The purpose of the intervention was to alleviate inconsistencies in the implementation of confidentiality policies by providing clear and uniform procedures for releasing information to families. The intervention consists of the following three components: a form specifically designed for releasing information to families, two-page policy guidelines, and a 2-hour provider training.

Release Form

Consistent with the NASW code of ethics, the intervention instructs providers to obtain written consent before releasing any confidential information to family members. However, in trying to obtain written consent, providers often discover that only general release forms are available and that these forms are not appropriate for the release of information to families. The model intervention includes a form specifically designed for releasing information to families and/or significant others. The form is included in a previous publication by Solomon, Marshall, Mannion, and Farmer (2002) and may also be received by contacting the primary author. As compared with general release forms, the specific release form has three unique components.

First, general release forms, designed for interagency use, are typically restricted to 30-, 60-, or 90-day time limits or the one-time release of information. The model intervention release form included a 6-month time limit to fulfill statutory requirements of time limits while ensuring that continuity was not disrupted by short time frames that demand frequent updating typically found on general release forms. Second, clients were given the choice to select the types of information they wished to release. Often, general release forms offer a blanket release of information or include categories of information that do not meet the information needs of family members. Providers, consumers, and families from the study site reviewed the 10 categories of information provided on the release form (such as diagnosis, medications and their side-effects, and progress and obstacles to progress) for their appropriateness. Third, the form specified that information would be released verbally rather than requiring formal written correspondence. Verbal release of information was intended to protect clients from printed information accidentally ending up in the wrong hands.

Requiring client consent offers a conservative interpretation of confidentiality statutes. Therefore, the intervention may be adopted in any state and still meet the requirements within the state statutes. The adoption of the specific release form also gives providers the necessary tools to incorporate the procedures in their routine practice.

Procedures

Preliminary research assessing how confidentiality is discussed with persons suffering from mental illness indicated that it is often unclear whether the responsibility for initiating the consent process lies with the provider, consumer, or family member (Marshall & Solomon, 2000). The intervention addresses this issue by instructing providers to routinely initiate a discussion with clients regarding the agency's confidentiality policy. Providers were asked to convey the purpose of confidentiality, exceptions existing under the law, and the agency's procedures for releasing confidential information. Providers were then requested to introduce the release form previously described and to ask clients if they had someone supportive to them to whom they would like to have information about their treatment released. If a client was too ill to make the decision, providers were requested to raise the issue at another time when the client's illness was not exacerbated. Once a client signed a release form, providers were instructed to send a letter to the designated family member to notify them that the form was on file.

Provider Training

All clinical staff members in the intervention agency's participating programs were encouraged to participate in a 2-hour training. Guidelines explaining the procedures and copies of the release form were distributed during the training. Providers unable to attend the training received the materials from their agency supervisor. Trainers reviewed the importance of confidentiality, clarified the types of information that are confidential and that require client consent to be released, presented the procedures for releasing information, and offered case examples to assist providers in addressing implementation issues.

Although it was expected that most clients would sign the form, providers were also encouraged to provide general information to families for whom authorization was not designated. Providers were also informed that client consent was not needed to receive information from family members and were provided with examples of how to keep channels of communication with families open while maintaining their clients' confidentiality. For this reason, the intervention was expected to increase collaboration whether or not clients elected to sign a release form.

METHOD

Site Selection and Comparability

Two agencies offering comparable services were identified by the County Office of Mental Health. Directors from the two agencies were interviewed, and the agencies were determined to be comparable with regard to organizational factors such as reimbursement rates, established policies, provider training for working with families, number of staff members, number of clients served, and client demographics (see Table 5.1). Once the two agencies were found to be comparable, one agency was assigned at random as an intervention agency and the other as the comparison site.

Provider Sample

The provider sample included clinical staff members from the outpatient, partial hospitalization, and case management programs in the participating agencies. At baseline, 59 providers completed a self-administered questionnaire. Of the 11 (90.9%) providers who refused to participate, 10 worked as contract employees in the outpatient program. The response rate for the postquestionnaire was 88.1% (52 providers). The attrition rate was similar to the estimated rate of turnover within the agencies.

Table 5.1. Comparability of the Intervention and Comparison Agencies

	Intervention Agency	Comparison Agency
Geographic location	Suburban	Suburban
Reimbursement rates	Some reimbursement from county for ICM	Some reimbursement from county for ICM
	No reimbursement for outpatient and PH staff	No reimbursement for outpatient and PH staff
Established policies for working with families	No written policy	No written policy
Number of staff members	41	29
Provider training for working with families	No training provided	No training provided
Population by service area	179,176	131,721
Number of clients served	1,135	1,055
Local population of minorities	8%	7%
Percentage of minority clients served	11%	13%
Local population by age group (adults)	63%	64%
Clients served by age group (adults)	84%	84%
Clients served by income (less than $10,000)	86%	81%

NOTE: ICM = intensive case management; PH = partial hospitalization.

Family Sample

Eligible family participants had a relative 18 years or older with a *DSM-IV* (*Diagnostic and Statistical Manual of Mental Disorders,* 4th edition; Am. Psychiatric Assoc., 1994) diagnosis of schizophrenia spectrum or major mood disorders and who was receiving services in the programs participating in the study. Family participants were also required to have in-person or phone contact with their consumer relative at least once a week.

Access to eligible family members was obtained using the following procedures. Providers randomly selected a client file, determined whether the client's family met the study eligibility criteria, and introduced to these clients a research authorization form that permitted the principal investigator to contact them. Each provider was asked to repeat the random selection procedures until they obtained authorization forms from three clients from their caseload.

Permission to contact eligible family participants was obtained from 102 of 174 clients (59%). Common reasons for refusal were that clients were uncomfortable with their family members being contacted or did not want to disturb their family members. In addition, 8 of the 102 families that were contacted (7.8%) did not meet the eligibility criteria and 26 (25.5%) refused to participate. Reasons for family refusal were that "they didn't want to fill out any more surveys," the survey was "too personal," or that they had no contact with providers. Families who had no contact with providers were still encouraged to complete the survey by skipping sections that did not apply. However, some families did not feel that they were providing enough information to be helpful. At baseline, 68 families completed a self-administered questionnaire. The response rate for the postquestionnaire was 85.3% (58 families).

Provider Measures

The following four aspects of collaboration were measured: contact, frequency of contact, array of information shared, and strength of the collaborative relationship. The contact measure captured whether providers had any contact with family members of their clients during the past 6 months. Frequency of contact measured how often the contact occurred. Both items were adapted from Grusky's (1986) family involvement survey. Array of information shared and strength of the collaborative relationship were measured using subscales adapted from Bernheim and Switalski's (1988) staff questionnaire. Examples of items under the array of information shared included providing information to families such as their relative's diagnosis, medications, prognosis, and so forth. The strength of the collaborative relationship measure asked providers to strongly agree, agree, disagree, or strongly disagree with 7 statements such as "Most staff in my agency do not work with families because they do not have the time." The Array of Information Shared subscale exhibited sufficient internal consistency (Cronbach's alpha = .91). However, this was not the case for the Strength of the Collaborative subscale; therefore, each of these items was included into the analysis separately.

Size of provider caseload, provider shift, provider attitudes, and fidelity of the intervention have been identified as factors that may affect collaboration (Hatfield, 1990; Lefley, 1994; Tessler, Gamache, & Fisher, 1991; Wright, 1997) and therefore were included as control variables. Because research indicates that providers who believe that families cause mental illness are less likely to collaborate (Hatfield, 1990; Lefley, 1994; Tessler et al., 1991), provider attitudes were measured by assessing beliefs regarding the causes of mental illness. Rubin's scale (Rubin, Cardenas, Warren, & Pike, 1998) was adapted and eight items were summed to create a Provider Attitude scale (Cronbach's alpha = .73).

Seven items were included to measure fidelity of the intervention. Providers in the intervention agency were asked whether they attended the intervention training (yes = 1, no = 0), whether they read the study guidelines (yes = 1, no = 0), whether they routinely ask clients if they would like to release information to a family member (yes = 1, no = 0), the number of clients on their caseload they asked to sign a release form, whether they reintroduced the form to clients who did not initially sign the form (yes = 1, no = 0), the number of designated family members to whom they sent a letter, and the number of family members designated on release forms whom they contacted (these numbers were divided by the size of their caseloads, and responses were coded into the following categories: 0 = 0%, 1 = 1% to 25%, 2 = 26% to 50%, 3 = 51% to 75%, 4 = 76% to 100%). The seven fidelity questions were summed with scores ranging from 0 (*no fidelity*) to 16 (*high fidelity*). Providers in the comparison agency were not asked these questions and therefore were given a score of 0.

Family Measures

Parallel to the provider measures, the four aspects of collaboration were assessed in the family sample. Contact and frequency of contact were measured using two items adapted from Grusky's (1986) family involvement survey. Array of information shared was measured using two subscales developed by Biegel et al. (1995). For example, the first subscale asked families if they had received information from their relatives' providers such as their relatives' diagnoses, medications, prognoses, and so forth. The second subscale asked families how much information they received (none, very little, some, or a lot). The Cronbach's alphas for the subscales were .89 and .91, respectively. Strength of the collaborative relationship was measured by a single item capturing families' satisfaction with the amount of contact they had with their consumer relatives' providers.

Race/ethnicity, length of time since onset of illness, length of time of relatives' involvement in the agency, support group involvement, family attitudes toward collaboration, and fidelity of the intervention were employed as control variables. Family attitudes toward collaboration was measured using Biegel et al.'s (1995) 10-item subscale (Cronbach's alpha = .80).

Fidelity of the intervention was assessed from the perspective of families with relatives receiving services from the intervention agency. These families were asked whether their relatives were asked for their verbal permission to release information to them (yes = 1, no or unsure = 0), whether their consumer relatives were asked to sign a form permitting providers to release information to them (yes = 1, no or unsure = 0), and if their relatives signed a form, whether they were notified by their relatives' providers of the types of information that may be released to them (yes = 1, no = 0). Responses to the three fidelity questions were summed and scores ranged from 0 (*no fidelity*) to 3 (*high fidelity*). Families connected with the comparison agency were not asked these questions and were given a score of 0.

Analysis

For both families and providers, four sets of multiple regression models were used to assess differences in dependent variable posttest measures (contact, frequency of contact, array of information shared, and strength of the collaborative relationship) between agencies. The models included pretest measures of the dependent variables, a dummy variable for the agency samples, and the control variables previously noted. Descriptive statistics were used to assess the variability for the control variables. Control variables with more than 90% of responses in one category, such as provider shift and family race/ethnicity, were not included in the regression analyses. Variables that were significantly different between agencies, such as the number of years providers worked in mental health and the number of years providers worked in the agency, were included as covariates in the regression analyses. Bonferroni corrections were made for analyses of provider responses to items capturing the strength of the collaborative relationship because separate regression models were used to test this concept.

Whereas power analysis calculations were based on two-sample t tests, the following analyses used multiple regression with a coded dummy variable for the two agency samples (1 = intervention, 0 = comparison agency). As shown by Fleiss (1986), because the independent variable reduces the variability, the sample size required for the regression is smaller; therefore, the sample size of 58 was adequate.

RESULTS

Provider Characteristics

Provider participants included 32 providers from the intervention agency (54%) and 27 providers from the comparison agency (46%). Most providers were employed in the partial hospitalization or the case management programs and were salaried employees. The majority of provider participants were female and White and had graduated from college or graduate school (see Table 5.2).

Family Characteristics

Family participants included 35 families of consumers receiving services in the intervention agency (51.5%) and 33 families of consumers receiving services in the comparison agency (48.5%). Most family respondents were female and White and had at least some college or post-high school education. The majority of the family sample had male relatives, averaging 40 years of age and receiving services in the partial hospitalization program. Most families indicated that they wanted some or a lot of contact with their relatives' providers. However, few families belonged to any groups or organizations that provide support for or advocate on behalf of persons with mental illness and their families (see Table 5.3).

Fidelity of the Intervention

Most providers from the intervention agency reported that they attended the study intervention training ($n = 18$, 69.2%) and read the two-page study intervention guidelines ($n = 23$, 88.5%). There was a significant change from pre- to postintervention (chi-square = 5.243, $df = 1$, $p = .026$) in providers' understanding about their ability to receive information from families without client consent. There was also a significant increase from pre- to postintervention (chi-square = 5.105, $df = 1$, $p = .032$) in the number of providers who reported routinely asking their clients whether they would like to release information to family members or significant others. However, when asked for the number of clients to whom they introduced the study release form, more than half of the providers indicated that they introduced the study release form to fewer than 50% of their caseloads ($n = 14$, 53.8%). More than half of the providers indicated that they did not follow the instruction of the intervention to reintroduce the study release form at a later time to clients who were unable to give consent ($n = 14$, 53.8%). Half of the providers indicated that they had not sent a letter to designated family members to notify them that a release form had been signed ($n = 13$, 50%). More than half of the providers indicated that they contacted fewer than 25% of the family members designated on the release forms ($n = 18$, 69.2%).

Table 5.2. Sociodemographic Characteristics (Provider Sample)

Characteristic	N	Percentage	Characteristic	N	Percentage
Gender			Caseload size		
Male	9	15	75 or more	3	5.1
Female	50	85	50 to 74	4	6.8
Race			25 to 49	8	13.6
Caucasian	52	88	2 to 24	41	69.5
Asian	2	3.4	Missing	3	5.1
African American	2	3.4	Job title		
Hispanic	1	1.7	Therapist	32	54.2
Missing	2	3.4	Director or supervisor	6	10.2
Age (mean = 37.0)			Nurse	3	5.1
Older than 56	7	11.9	Intake worker	2	3.4
46 to 55	7	11.9	Case manager	15	25.5
36 to 45	7	11.9	Intern	1	1.7
24 to 35	34	57.6	Years in mental health (mean = 5.87)		
Missing	4	6.8	11 or more	5	8.5
Education			6 to 10	8	13.6
Some college	2	3.4	2 to 5	29	49.2
College degree	24	40.7	1 or less	10	16.9
Some graduate	13	22	Missing	7	11.9
Graduate degree	20	33.9	Years in agency (mean = 3.95)		
Discipline			11 or more	3	5.1
Psychology	25	42.4	6 to 10	4	6.8
Social work	9	15.3	2 to 5	33	55.9
Nursing	3	5.1	1 or less	12	20.3
Counseling	8	13.6	Missing	7	11.9
None	12	20.3	Caseload: Subjective measure		
Missing	2	3.4	Heavy	17	28.8
Shift			Moderate	25	42.4
Day	53	89.8	Moderate to light	7	11.9
Evening	1	1.7	Light	9	15.3
Both	5	8.5	Missing	1	1.7
Job status			N = 59		
Full-time	45	76.3			
Part-time	14	23.7			

Effects on Collaboration

The results of the regression models presented in Tables 5.4 through 5.7 indicated that families with relatives receiving treatment from the intervention agency were significantly more likely to have had contact with providers during the course of the study than were families from the comparison agency. Although the other regression models indicated that no significant differences were found between the intervention and comparison agencies, families associated with providers who had higher fidelity to the intervention were more likely to report more frequent contact with

Table 5.3. Sociodemographic Characteristics (Family Sample)

Characteristic	N	Percentage	Characteristic	N	Percentage
Gender			Relationship to relative		
Male	16	23.5	Parent	43	63.2
Female	52	76.5	Sibling	14	20.6
Race			Child	2	2.9
Caucasian	63	92.6	Spouse or partner	5	7.4
African American	3	4.4	Other relative	2	2.9
Hispanic	1	1.5	Friend	2	2.9
Missing	1	1.5	Relative's age (mean = 40.39)		
Age (mean = 56.99)			56 or older	6	8.9
Older than 66	22	32.4	46 to 55	11	16.2
56 to 65	17	25.0	36 to 45	31	45.6
46 to 55	15	22.1	24 to 35	15	22.1
36 to 45	8	11.8	Less than 24	4	5.9
24 to 35	4	5.9	Missing	1	1.5
23 and under	2	2.9	Age illness noticed (mean = 20.4)		
Education			46 or older	1	1.5
Less than high school	4	5.9	36 to 45	2	2.9
High school diploma	27	39.7	26 to 35	10	14.7
Some college	19	27.9	20 to 25	16	23.5
College	5	7.4	19 or younger	36	52.9
Some graduate	4	5.9	Missing	3	4.4
Graduate	9	13.2	Age diagnosed (mean = 22.16)		
Income			46 or older	1	1.5
70,000 or more	7	10.3	36 to 45	4	5.9
60 to 69,000	5	7.4	26 to 35	12	17.6
50 to 59,000	4	5.9	20 to 25	17	25.0
40 to 49,000	3	4.4	19 or less	29	42.6
30 to 39,000	7	10.3	Missing	5	7.4
20 to 29,000	12	17.6	Diagnosis		
10 to 19,000	6	8.8	Schizophrenia	32	47.1
Less than 10,000	8	11.8	Bipolar	13	19.1
Missing	16	23.5	Depression	4	5.9
Relative's gender			Other	4	5.9
Male	41	60.3	Missing	15	22.0
Female	27	39.7	N = 68		

providers, receipt of more information from providers, and more satisfaction with the amount of contact they had with providers. All regression models controlled for the length of time since the onset of the relatives' illness, the length of time the relatives have been involved in the agency, the families' involvement in support groups, families' attitudes toward collaboration, and families' pretest response to the variable, which are factors that have been identified as affecting collaboration. None of the regression models for the provider sample were significant.

Table 5.4. Logistic Regression Model: Factors Explaining Family Contact with Providers (Family Sample)

Variable	B	Wald	df	p
Program (outpatient)	−13.06	0.01	2	NS
Program (case management)	−4.24	3.56	1	.04
Support	−0.87	0.41	1	NS
Length of time since onset of illness	−0.08	2.49	1	NS
Relative's involvement with agency	−12.56	0.07	1	NS
Attitudes toward collaboration	−0.00	3.89	1	NS
Fidelity to the intervention	9.35	0.07	1	NS
Relative's support for family involvement	1.09	2.37	1	NS
Pretest response to dependent variable	−0.38	0.14	1	NS
Intervention or comparison agency	−3.75	4.63	1	.03
$N = 58$				
$R^2 = .456$				

NOTE: NS = not significant.

Table 5.5. Linear Regression Model: Factors Explaining the Frequency of Contact with Providers (Family Sample)

Variable	B	t	p
Program	−0.62	−1.23	NS
Support	0.16	0.27	NS
Length of time since onset of illness	0.00	2.26	.03
Relative's involvement with agency	−0.80	−1.16	NS
Attitudes toward collaboration	0.00	1.75	NS
Fidelity to the intervention	−0.21	−0.73	.04
Relative's support for family involvement	0.36	2.23	NS
Pretest response to dependent variable	−0.67	−2.14	.03
Intervention or comparison agency	−0.31	−0.65	NS
$N = 58$			
$R^2 = .579$			

NOTE: NS = not significant.

DISCUSSION AND APPLICATIONS
TO SOCIAL WORK PRACTICE

The intervention evaluated in this study was fairly straightforward. It trained providers regarding the types of information that are confidential and require client consent. It provided uniform procedures for obtaining client consent, including clarifying that consent must be obtained in writing and specifying that it is providers' responsibility to initiate the consent process. The intervention also informed providers that general information may be shared with families without client

Table 5.6. Linear Regression Model: Factors Explaining the Array of Information Shared by Providers (Family Sample)

Variable	B	t	p
Program	2.78	1.79	NS
Support	1.51	0.84	NS
Length of time since onset of illness	0.01	−0.98	NS
Relative's involvement with agency	4.02	1.85	NS
Attitudes toward collaboration	−0.00	−1.16	NS
Fidelity to the intervention	3.69	2.72	.01
Relative's support for family involvement	0.37	0.48	NS
Pretest response to dependent variable	0.44	3.89	.00
Intervention or comparison agency	1.18	0.90	NS
$N = 58$			
$R^2 = .456$			

NOTE: NS = not significant.

Table 5.7. Linear Regression Model: Factors Explaining the Strength of the Collaborative Relationship (Family Sample)

Variable	B	t	p
Program	0.00	0.13	NS
Support	0.00	0.10	NS
Length of time since onset of illness	−0.00	−1.92	NS
Relative's involvement with agency	0.28	0.65	NS
Attitudes toward collaboration	−0.00	−1.18	NS
Fidelity to the intervention	0.41	2.46	.02
Relative's support for family involvement	0.13	0.96	NS
Pretest response to dependent variable	0.60	6.70	.00
Intervention or comparison agency	−0.14	−0.58	NS
$N = 58$			
$R^2 = .727$			

NOTE: NS = not significant.

consent and that information may be received from families without consent and without violating client confidentiality.

The information was offered to participating providers in two different formats: in the form of training and as easy-to-read guidelines. Furthermore, several mechanisms were used to encourage providers to participate in the intervention, such as letters from county mental health authorities specifying the importance of the project, reminders and encouragement by administrators and supervisors, and incentive payments (contract employees received $10 to attend the training).

Despite the simplicity of the intervention, the support, and the incentives, providers did not implement all aspects of the intervention. Although attending the training and reading the guidelines did increase the number of providers who routinely asked their clients whether they would like to release information to families and significantly more providers understood that they could receive information from families without consent, providers did not routinely introduce the release form to clients.

Although we are unable to determine the effectiveness of using the specific release form on provider-consumer-family collaboration due to the lack of full implementation, the training and guidelines, as seen through the family sample, had an effect on provider-consumer-family collaboration. Families in the intervention agency were significantly more likely to have contact with providers during the course of the study than were families in the comparison agency. Although for some families, contact with providers may have included only receiving nonconfidential information or sharing information with providers on a single occasion, the significant increase in families' contact with providers in the intervention agency following the introduction of the intervention indicates that the intervention may serve as a first step toward collaboration. By sharing this nonconfidential information, the providers may learn that the families are trying to be supportive and learn about their relatives' illness. The families may learn that the providers are not trying to shut them out or blame them for their relatives' symptoms. Moreover, if both the providers and the families are clear that the clients' willingness to sign a consent form is standing in the way of further collaboration between all three parties, they may be more likely to raise the option of signing a consent form with clients periodically until clients feel more comfortable with the idea of signing the form and allowing further collaboration to take place. In short, the increase in the number of families having contact with providers in the intervention agency suggests that the intervention may help open the channels of communication between providers, consumers, and families, thereby facilitating further collaboration in the future.

Furthermore, the fidelity variable, a specific measure of the degree to which each provider followed the intervention, was significantly associated with improvements in all aspects of collaboration (frequency of contact, array of information shared, and strength of the collaborative relationship as measured by family satisfaction with the amount of provider contact). These findings suggest that if a greater number of providers in the intervention agency had implemented the model fully, significant improvements in all aspects of collaboration may have been found.

Achieving Full Implementation

Using a Centralized Intake Process   Several factors may have influenced providers' decision to selectively introduce the specific consent form to clients. First, administrative, procedural, and structural modifications recently instituted due to the introduction of managed care may have led to the perception that additional paperwork was unduly burdensome. Therefore, instructing all providers to introduce the specific consent form to every client in their caseloads may have been an unreasonable request.

One step that may be taken to increase the use of the specific consent form without imposing an undue burden on individual providers would be to integrate the form into a centralized intake process. In this case, the intake workers would be responsible for routinely introducing the form to clients. If clients sign the form, it would be the responsibility of intake workers to send the notification letter to the designated family members. Although the intake workers would assist with the administrative burden, it would still be the responsibility of the treating therapists to collaborate with the consumers and families in releasing information.

The partial hospitalization programs in the intervention agency began operating a centralized intake process shortly before the study began to alleviate the burden that the paperwork was imposing on staff members. These programs simply included the specific consent form along with the other forms routinely completed on a mandatory basis. Consequently, within the partial hospitalization programs, one provider was responsible for ensuring that all family consent forms were completed. This procedural change may explain why significant findings were detected only within the family sample. The increases in contact, frequency of contact, array of information shared, and satisfaction with providers reported by families may be attributed to only a few providers adhering to the intervention through the centralized process. This interpretation is further supported by the study finding that indicated families were more likely to have contact with providers from the partial hospitalization program than from the case management program, which did not integrate the study form into a centralized process.

The integration of the specific consent form into a centralized intake process may allow this part of the intervention to be fully implemented so that its effectiveness may be evaluated. However, additional research is needed.

Engaging Contract Employees Another factor that influenced providers' implementation of the intervention was providers' status as contract employees. The original provider inclusion criteria only included providers from the outpatient and partial hospitalization programs. Due to low participation of outpatient providers, the inclusion criteria were expanded to include providers from the case management program. Administrators in both agencies attributed the low participation of outpatient providers to their status as contract employees. Administrators explained that because the employees were paid solely to provide services to clients, the time taken to participate in research, attend training, or attend any other meetings was not reimbursable. Outpatient providers were offered lunch and $10 compensation for attending the introductory session to learn about this research. Those working at that time did attend. However, because these employees worked in several locations, only a few employees worked in the participating agencies at any one time. A total of five offices were shared by approximately 30 employees. Contract employees tended to have irregular schedules, and meetings with clients were scheduled for the entire time they were in the agency, which made scheduling other meetings and trainings close to impossible.

The increasing number of contract employees in managed care mental health systems is likely to have a significant impact on intervention research and the implementation of model interventions. Many contract employees never meet many of their coworkers and have little chance to develop relationships with their supervisors and administrators. Under these circumstances, it is difficult not only to introduce intervention models but also to address implementation issues that arise for providers in their daily practice.

Research indicates that training may lead to effective change when combined with adjusting administrative procedures, providing ongoing supervision and feedback, and modifying financial incentives or penalties (Torrey et al., 2001). Each of these components may be particularly important for engaging contract employees. Special efforts may be needed to compensate for the lack of staff cohesion, the irregular schedules, and the financial disincentives. Furthermore, given the environmental disincentives to implementing new innovations, providers may need to be convinced of the benefits of the intervention for their daily practice. Research has shown that providers are more likely to adopt a new practice if they are convinced that it is worth learning (Torrey et al., 2001).

Next Steps

Further evaluation of the intervention should include the following steps to increase providers' fidelity to the model:

1. introducing the specific consent form as a part of a centralized intake process;

2. offering financial reimbursement to contract employees to offset the expense of attending training and collaborating with families; and

3. offering ongoing consultation over a 2-year period.

Although it is important to increase the number of providers who implement interventions as they were intended, fidelity by all providers in all situations may be an unrealistic goal. If the concept of fidelity is viewed as asymptotic by nature, it makes sense to measure fidelity as a continuous variable rather than as a discrete variable. Furthermore, examining the components of a model and their effect on collaboration may be more informative in understanding methods for improving client outcomes than is simply evaluating the effectiveness of the model as a whole. Future research should include a consumer sample and additional mechanisms, such as reviewing client records, to capture whether the principle components of the intervention have been implemented.

In addition, the eligibility criteria for family participation may be reconsidered for further evaluations. By including in the eligibility criteria that families must have at least weekly contact with their ill relatives, this study targeted families who were potentially supportive prior to the intervention. Additionally, high consumer refusal rates, which were attributed to consumers' discomfort with their families being contacted or not wanting to disturb their family members, indicate that the results of this study may be more reflective of consumers who have close relationships with their families. Future research may choose to broaden the family sample to include families who have been estranged from their relatives and provide additional incentives for participation in the research to reduce high refusal rates. Broadening the family sample would allow for further examination of whether the intervention may serve as an outreach tool for engaging estranged families.

CONCLUSIONS

Although it is commonly noted that unclear confidentiality policies pose a barrier to provider-consumer-family collaboration, this is the first study evaluating the effectiveness of an intervention to clarify confidentiality policies for the release of information to families. Although the intervention was implemented only in part, the results indicated that families with relatives receiving treatment in the intervention agency were significantly more likely to have had contact with providers during the course of the study than were families from the comparison agency. Furthermore, fidelity of the intervention by providers was significantly associated with all aspects of improved collaboration. These preliminary findings suggest that the model intervention, if faithfully implemented, may well enhance collaboration between providers, consumers, and families.

REFERENCES

American Psychiatric Association. (1997). Practice guidelines for the treatment of patients with schizophrenia. *American Journal of Psychiatry, 154* (Suppl.), 1–63.

Backlar, P. (1996). Ethics in community mental health care: Confidentiality and common sense. *Community Mental Health Journal, 32,* 513–518.

Beeler, J., Rosenthal, A., & Cohler, B. (1999). Patterns of family caregiving and support provided to older psychiatric patients in long-term care. *Psychiatric Services, 50,* 1222–1224.

Bernheim, K., & Switalski, T. (1988). Mental health staff and patient's relatives: How they view each other. *Hospital and Community Psychiatry, 39,* 63–68.

Biegel, D., Song, L., & Milligan, S. E. (1995). A comparative analysis of family caregivers' perceived relationships with mental health professionals. *Psychiatric Services, 46,* 477–482.

Bogart, T., & Solomon, P. (1999). Collaborative procedures to share treatment information among mental health care providers, consumers, and families. *Psychiatric Services, 50,* 1321–1325.

DiRienzo-Callahan, C. (1998). Family caregivers and confidentiality. *Psychiatric Services, 49,* 244–245.

Dixon, L., McFarlane, W., Lefley, H., Lucksted, A., Cohen, M., & Falloon, I., et al. (2001). Evidence-based practices for services to families of people with psychiatric disabilities. *Psychiatric Services, 52,* 903–910.

Fleiss, J. (1986). *The design and analysis of clinical experiments.* New York: John Wiley.

Frances, A., Docherty, J., & Kahn, D. (1996). The expert consensus guidelines series: Treatment of schizophrenia. *Journal of Clinical Psychiatry, 57* (Suppl. 12B), 18, 20, 21.

Furlong, M., & Leggatt, M. (1996). Reconciling the patient's right to confidentiality and the family's need to know. *Australian and New Zealand Journal of Psychiatry, 30,* 614–622.

Goldman, H. (1982). Mental illness and family burden: A public health perspective. *Hospital and Community Psychiatry, 33,* 557–559.

Grusky, O. (1986). *Mental health services project interview guide 2: Case manager.* Los Angeles: University of California, Los Angeles, Department of Sociology.

Guarnaccia, P. (1998). Multicultural experiences in family caregiving: A study of African American, European American and Hispanic American families. *New Directions for Mental Health Services, 77,* 45–61.

Hatfield, A. (1990). *Family education in mental illness.* New York: Guilford.

Herz, M. (1985). Prodromal symptoms and prevention of relapse in schizophrenia. *Journal of Clinical Psychiatry, 46,* 22–25.

Kagle, J. (2002). Record-keeping. In A. Roberts & G. Greene (Eds.), *Social workers' desk reference* (pp. 910–911). New York: Oxford University Press.

Krauss, J. (1992). Sorry, that's confidential. *Archives of Psychiatric Nursing, 6,* 255–256.

Leazenby, L. (1997). Confidentiality as a barrier to treatment. *Psychiatric Services, 48,* 1467–1468.

Lefley, H. (1994). An overview of family-professional relationships. In D. Marsh (Ed.), *New directions in the psychological treatment of serious mental illness* (pp. 166–185). Westport, CT: Praeger.

Lefley, H. (1996). *Family caregiving in mental illness.* Thousand Oaks, CA: Sage.

Lefley, H. (2000). Families' perspectives on confidentiality. In J. Gates & B. Arons (Eds.), *Privacy and confidentiality in mental health care* (p. 242). Baltimore, MD: Brooks.

Lehman, A., & Steinwachs, D. (1998). Patterns of usual care for schizophrenia: Initial results from the schizophrenia patient outcomes research team (PORT) client survey. *Schizophrenia Bulletin, 24,* 11–32.

Marsh, D. (1995, January). Confidentiality and the rights of families: Resolving potential conflicts. *Pennsylvania Psychologist,* pp. 1–3.

Marsh, D., & Johnson, D. (1997). The family experience with mental illness: Implications for intervention. *Professional Psychology: Research and Practice, 28,* 229–237.

Marshall, T., & Solomon, P. (2000). Releasing information to families of persons with severe mental illness: A survey of NAMI members. *Psychiatric Services, 51,* 1006–1011.

Marshall, T., & Solomon, P. (2003). Releasing information to families of adults with mental illness: Revisiting professionals' duty. Manuscript submitted for publication.

National Association of Social Workers. (1999). *Code of ethics.* Washington, DC: Author.

National Institute of Mental Health. (1991). *Caring for people with severe mental disorders: A national plan of research to improve services.* Washington, DC: Author.

Petrila, J. (2000). State mental health confidentiality law provisions. In J. Gates & B. Arons (Eds.), *Privacy and confidentiality in mental health care* (p. 242). Baltimore, MD: Brooks.

Petrila, J., & Sadoff, R. (1992). Confidentiality and the family as caregiver. *Hospital and Community Psychiatry, 43,* 136–139.

Rubin, A., Cardenas, J., Warren, K., & Pike, C. (1998). Outdated practitioner views about family culpability and severe mental disorders. *Social Work, 43,* 413–422.

Ryan, C. (1996). Comment on reconciling the patient's right to confidentiality and the family's need to know. *Australian and New Zealand Journal of Psychiatry, 30,* 429–431.

Solomon, P., Draine, J., Mannion, E., & Meisel, M. (1998). Increased contact with community mental health resources as a potential benefit of family education. *Psychiatric Services, 49,* 333–339.

Solomon, P., Marshall, T., Mannion, E., & Farmer, J. (2002). Social workers as consumer and family consultants. In K. Bentley (Ed.), *Social work practice in mental health* (pp. 230–253). Pacific Grove, CA: Brooks/Cole.

Tessler, R., Gamache, G., & Fisher, G. (1991). Patterns of contact of patients' families with mental health professionals and attitudes toward professionals. *Hospital and Community Psychiatry, 42,* 929–935.

Torrey, W., Drake, R., Dixon, L., Burns, B., Flynn, L., & Rush, A., et al. (2001). Implementing evidence-based practices for persons with severe mental illness. *Psychiatric Services, 52,* 45–49.

U.S. Department of Health and Human Services. (1999). *Mental health: A report of the Surgeon General.* Rockville, MD: U.S. Department of Health and Human Services, Substance Abuse and Mental Health Services Administration, Center for Mental Health Services, National Institutes of Mental Health, National Institute of Mental Health.

Wright, E. (1997). The impact of organizational factors on mental health professionals' involvement with families. *Psychiatric Services, 48,* 921–927.

Zipple, A., Langle, S., Tyrell, W., Spaniol, L., & Fisher, H. (1997). Client confidentiality and the family's need to know. In D. Marsh & R. Magee (Eds.), *Ethical and legal issues in professional practice with families* (pp. 238–253). New York: John Wiley.

Commentary by: Tina Marshall

Most people agree that choosing a dissertation topic is one of the hardest things to do. No matter how focused you feel that you are before the exercise takes place, you inevitably learn that your thoughts are leading in several different directions. My professional experience was leading me in the direction of examining services for adults with mental illness. My personal experience and interest drew me toward the family literature. I knew first-hand what it is like to live with someone with severe mental illness. The problem was not *finding* a dissertation topic, it was *choosing* one.

In hindsight, I realize that my dissertation topic chose me. It literally came across my desk at the research center where I was working. I was asked to review and summarize all aspects of confidentiality for the state of Delaware. No small task. In the process of writing the mammoth report, I learned that some state statutes define procedures for releasing information to families, whereas others do not. As I started to dig further into the literature, I found little to no research on the topic. Instead, everywhere I looked I read one-sentence acknowledgments that confidentiality may pose a barrier for communication between families and their ill relative's mental health providers.

As my intrigue in the topic increased, my natural instinct was to try to conduct a personal test of the scope of the problem. I started at home. I asked my mother if she had trouble receiving information from mental health providers when my father was ill. She confirmed that she was told that the information was confidential and that we were virtually shut out of the treatment process. My confidence grew. I was beginning to feel that I may have uncovered a real problem; a problem that had not been examined, and one in great need of attention.

I started speaking to my friends at the National Alliance for the Mentally Ill, a family-consumer advocacy organization for severe mental illness. Over and over I heard stories of family members being told that confidentiality was the reason that they could not receive information about their relative's condition and treatment. I learned that this topic had been on the NAMI policy agenda since the inception of the organization 25 years ago.

The topic had captured me. I raised the issue with everyone I met. In particular, I began to seek out the provider perspective. A colleague allowed me to sit in on a continuing education session that she was conducting with intensive case managers. At one point in the session the group began discussing their contact with the family members of their clients, and I casually asked, "Do you need to get a release signed before speaking with family members or what kind of procedures do you use?" The room erupted into multiple parallel conversations. Some providers asserted that their clients were required to sign a release. Others indicated that release forms weren't necessary since families were a part of the treatment team. Most providers looked confused and admitted that they weren't sure.

Commentary on article: Marshall, T., Solomon, P. (2004). Confidentiality intervention: Effects on provider-consumer-family collaboration. *Research on Social Work Practice, 14,* 3–13.

During this time, I was also conducting fieldwork for another project in which I was in contact with different mental health stakeholders. We were assessing the needs of family members of adults with severe mental illness in a small rural community in Pennsylvania, using surveys, key informant interviews, and focus groups. We integrated questions to assess whether confidentiality might be posing a barrier to provider-family communication. This is when we learned of a tragic event that occurred in the community just a couple of years before.

A young man who had been recently diagnosed with schizophrenia became unresponsive to his medication. His family saw the warning signs that he was decompensating and reached out for help. They called his mental health provider and received no return call. They kept calling and leaving messages, with no response. They called 27 times in the three days before their son became violent against two members of their family. The family members sustained permanent injuries and were unable to maintain their home. The son now lives in a board-and-care home and the parents in a nursing facility. The family later learned that their calls were not returned due to the agency's confidentiality policy.

The tragedy received much publicity in this small community. As a result, when this topic was raised as a part of our project, the mental health authority was eager to address it. We formed a committee with community and hospital mental health providers, families, consumers, and representatives from the county mental health authority to develop procedures for the release of information to families of adults with severe mental illness. I facilitated the committee. We reviewed our state statutes and the statutes of other states that included language regarding the release of information to family members of adults with severe mental illness. I brought in materials collected from other mental health systems that had developed procedures for releasing information to families. It was through this committee that the confidentiality intervention implemented in this study was developed and pilot-tested.

PULLING IT ALL TOGETHER

Up until this point, my work in this area had progressed quite naturally. I was simply interested in the topic and pursued it through any means and opportunity that arose. Serendipitously, two activities propelled the conceptualization of this research study forward and facilitated the development of this topic into a dissertation research study. The first was the development of a journal article, and the second was the submission of a dissertation grant to the National Institute of Mental Health (NIMH). I was encouraged and guided through both activities by the support of my mentor and dissertation chair. Writing these two pieces began my hands-on learning experience with the numerous decisions that are made when formulating a research study.

FORMALIZING THE INTERVENTION

I love to write, so I was quite excited to try to capture what I had learned to date about the inconsistencies in confidentiality statutes. When I began writing the journal article (Bogart & Solomon, 1999)—my very first—I truly didn't know how it would develop. I wrote a few sections and brought them to my dissertation chair, whose comments forced my thoughts into the formal research structure. After passing the article to my mentor numerous times for her comments, I remember feeling so pleased that this problem that had captivated me was so clearly and logically laid out. I thought my article was done. I can clearly remember the cold shock that I felt when my mentor said, "The problem statement looks great. Now what do you recommend that people do about it?" "Recommend?" I thought, "I don't have the experience to recommend." Ironically, it was exactly the experience that I was gaining quite naturally and unexpectedly. With the help of my mentor, I started writing about what we had learned from pilot-testing procedures in the community and through the various conversations I had had over the past months.

In hindsight, it almost seems that this study designed itself, since by this point it was clear that we had to examine the effectiveness of the steps we were recommending. I began writing a dissertation grant to obtain funding from NIMH to support the research.

RIGOR VERSUS FEASIBILITY

As research textbooks suggest, we began with the most rigorous research design and asked ourselves if it was feasible to conduct the study in this manner. Originally, I proposed to survey providers, consumers, and families. My mentor laughed. She pointed out that this was a dissertation study and not my life's work. The most rigorous research design is worthless if it cannot be feasibly conducted. While I would have loved to have included multiple sites in a randomized experiment and to have gathered input from multiple stakeholders, I had to face that this simply wasn't feasible for a dissertation study. So I reined in my thoughts and proposed a pre-post design with a comparison group.

A colleague kindly agreed to conduct the training in the intervention agency, regardless of whether I received the NIMH support to pay her. This was particularly helpful since I did not want the site to associate me with endorsing the intervention. Additionally, the flexibility allowed me to start the study before I received the grant support.

SITE SELECTION

I was quite lucky to be connected to a research center that had strong relationships with the surrounding county mental health authorities. The Director of the center made a call on my behalf and introduced me to the county's Deputy Administrator who helped select two community mental health agencies that were likely to be comparable. She provided a good deal of background information to help me to understand the client population served by these agencies and how representative these clients were of the county in which they lived. We selected two agencies that were 25 miles apart to reduce the likelihood of contamination that could have occurred if staff lived in the same area and talked, by chance, about the research study.

Before my first contact with the agencies, the Deputy Administrator had spoken with the administrators at the two agencies, shared her support for the research study, and encouraged the agencies to participate. When I contacted the agency administrators, my focus was in assessing their interest to participate and gathering information to determine the comparability of the agencies. Both of these objectives were met during the initial interviews. The agency administrators provided demographic characteristics of their staff and turnover rates. They suggested that the study could be conducted with clinical staff from the outpatient and partial hospitalization programs, and introduced me to the program directors.

There were two ways in which the agencies participating in this study differed from the agencies that piloted the confidentiality intervention. The first was that clinicians from outpatient programs were contracted as opposed to being salaried agency staff. Second, the county mental health system that piloted the confidentiality intervention used a centralized intake process for all new clients. In contrast, the primary clinicians completed the intake paperwork with each of their clients in the agencies participating in this study. At the time that the study was designed, I didn't realize the impact that these structural differences would have on providers' participation in the study and fidelity to the intervention.

MAKING CHANGES ON THE FLY

Two months into the recruitment of providers the problems with accessing outpatient clinicians clearly emerged. While case managers and partial hospitalization staff were salaried employees, all outpatient clinicians were hired as contract employees. Consequently, the administrator admitted that he hardly knew most of the clinicians in the outpatient program. Many clinicians worked part-time, coming into the agency only for their scheduled client appointments. In fact, spending additional time in the agency was discouraged due to cramped office quarters. Often four or more clinicians shared a single office, so a clinician would be asked to vacate an office space at the end of a therapy session to make room for another.

Moreover, since outpatient clinicians did not attend staff meetings or in-service seminars it was extremely hard to inform them about the research study. It was even harder to schedule a training session (for the intervention agency). Clinicians were not accustomed to receiving training from their employers. While the agencies required clinicians to be licensed and to maintain their licenses, they attended continuing education sessions on their own and at their own expense.

The primary problem with accessing outpatient clinicians, however, was that clinicians were paid on a fee-for-service basis. Outpatient clinicians were only paid for the time that they spent in therapy sessions with clients. For this reason, the time that they would take to participate in the research study—completing the survey, helping to identify family members to participate, participating in in-depth interviews (*for some*), participating in the training, and potentially changing the way that they practice (*for those in the intervention agency*)—was personal, unpaid time.

Luckily, the agency administrator from the intervention agency recognized this problem and agreed to offer lunch and $10 to any outpatient clinician who would come to an informational session about the research study. Similar informational meetings were set up in the control agency. Flyers and follow-up calls were made to encourage clinicians to participate. Since outpatient clinicians worked irregular schedules, the meetings were also set up at different times of the day and on different days of the week to encourage participation.

Despite the extra activities and incentives, outpatient clinician participation was much lower than expected. Consequently, agency administrators agreed to open the study to staff in the case management program. Three months into the study recruitment, contact was initiated with the directors of the case management programs and I began engaging case managers in the study. Similarly to the other two programs, all clinical staff in the case management programs were eligible to participate in the study. However, even with the addition of the third program the sample size obtained was smaller than expected.

In hindsight, the major lesson learned from this process was the importance of collecting as much information as possible about the participating programs, including their structures and culture, from the onset. The focus of my initial interviews with the agency administrators was to ensure that the agencies were comparable. Fortunately, the trouble that I experienced with outpatient clinicians was similar in both agencies. However, the structure of the outpatient program resulted in difficulties recruiting staff to participate in the research and to faithfully implement the intervention.

Furthermore, a number of unique factors, which could not be fully explored due to the size of the study, were introduced with the inclusion of the outpatient program. For example, outpatient clinicians seemed to operate from a different treatment orientation than case managers or partial hospitalization staff. Unlike the other program staff, clinicians from the outpatient program did not work from a treatment team approach—they had little contact with providers from other programs. The orientation and treatment philosophy of the outpatient providers was to work in isolation with the clients. It is likely that providers with this orientation may have been less willing to implement the intervention, which was expected to promote collaboration between providers, consumers, and families.

Additionally, outpatient clinicians customarily worked with clients on issues of adjustment, personal growth, and development. Therefore, individuals who were "too ill" to engage in this type of work were sent to other programs. For this reason, the caseloads of outpatient clinicians were much more diverse than those of staff from the other two programs. Many clinicians worked with children as well as adults, and had only a few persons with severe mental illness on their caseloads. Even if the outpatient clinicians had been salaried as opposed to contract employees, and their program had been structured similarly to the case management and outpatient programs, it is possible that participation and fidelity to the model may have been low due to differences in treatment philosophy and caseload mix. Uncovering these differences between the programs up front may have led us to choose a different program to participate in the study.

CONDUCTING RESEARCH IN
A NONSTATIC ENVIRONMENT

Unlike the structural program differences, we understood from the beginning that the participating programs were not using a centralized intake process similar to the one in place in piloting agencies. The intervention guidelines were revised accordingly to instruct *all providers* to raise the topic of confidentiality and releasing information to families with each of their clients. While I recognized that this was a change, I didn't realize what a major adjustment to the model that this would be.

Integrating the intervention into a centralized intake process was primarily a systems change, and secondarily a change in provider practice. However, the adjustment to the intervention model called for a change primarily in the way that providers practiced. I learned that while it is hard to facilitate a systems change, facilitating a change in provider practice is even harder. Certainly, the idea that providers would attend a mere two-hour training, leave, and then modify their practice was not realistic. For that reason, it is quite possible that I would have found no results at all if it weren't for an unanticipated modification that occurred during the course of the study.

A few months after the study began, the partial hospitalization program in the intervention agency hired an intake coordinator. This staff person was solely responsible for completing intake paperwork with all new clients. She also completed the forms necessary for clients' annual review. Consequently, the director of the partial hospitalization program instructed the intake coordinator to introduce the intervention's release of information form as a part of her work with all clients. While integrating this task into her daily duties was logical, it was also a substantial modification for the implementation of the intervention.

Luckily, the sample size was big enough to detect some differences between the three programs: outpatient, case management, and partial hospitalization. The study results indicated that families with relatives receiving services from the partial hospitalization program were more likely to have contact with providers. It is likely that this result was due to the change in the way that the partial hospitalization program implemented the intervention. Ironically, if I had learned ahead of time of the director's plan to change the way the intervention was implemented, I would have requested that this change not be made, and fidelity to the intervention may have been so low that positive outcomes may not have been detected.

ACCESSING FAMILY PARTICIPANTS

Paradoxically, one of the trickiest aspects of conducting research with families of adults with mental illness is accessing family participants through mental health agencies. Since so few mental health providers have any contact with families of their adult clients, providers can't simply pull together a list from which we can randomly select families to contact. Instead we asked staff from each agency to review the record of every third client on their caseload. If that client had a diagnosis of schizophrenia spectrum or major mood disorder, they were instructed to ask the client whether they had weekly contact with a family member. If so, the client was asked to sign a written research authorization form so I could contact them about the study. I then contacted these clients by phone, explained the study, and asked for their permission to contact their family member. This sampling strategy had two purposes: first, to obtain a representative sample of families of adults with severe mental illness receiving services at the participating agencies, and second, to keep the burden of identifying eligible families for staff as low as possible.

While the procedures that we put into place were believed to be the most rigorous possible considering the environmental constraints, there were several limitations. Although staff agreed to follow the prescribed recruitment procedures, there was no way to verify that the procedures were rigorously followed. Staff may have approached clients using their own discretion, instead of the random sampling procedure as instructed. (However, when asked if the recruitment procedures were followed, staff indicated that they were.) Furthermore, while staff from the partial hospitalization and case management programs completed three research authorization forms with clients as requested, many outpatient clinicians did not comply with the request. For this reason, we cannot guarantee that the family sample was representative of adult clients with severe mental illness receiving outpatient services. However, since many adult clients with severe mental illness receive an array of services including case management, outpatient, and partial hospitalization, it is likely that clients asked to sign research authorization forms by partial hospitalization and case management staff also received outpatient services.

Naturally, while these procedures kept the burden low for staff, it was extremely time-intensive for me. Follow-up calls were made to staff to remind them to complete the research authorization forms with their clients. Though calls to clients and families allowed me to verify that families were eligible to participate, many clients and families were called a half-dozen times before they could be reached by phone directly. Considering that both the client and family had to agree by phone before the family could even receive a self-administered survey in the mail, it was crucial to have a large pool of eligible clients.

A few months into the study, it became clear that I was not receiving enough research authorization forms from providers to obtain the sample size that I needed for my analysis. The agency administrators suggested that I approach clients in the partial hospitalization program directly by attending the weekly client community meeting. Instead of relying on providers to complete research authorization forms with clients, I took over the recruitment process by explaining the study to clients during the community meetings and asking clients who may have eligible family members to speak with me individually. Clients who volunteered to speak with me were asked for their permission to contact a family member. This effectively changed my sampling strategy from a random sample to a snowball sample; a much weaker sampling procedure. Additionally, I was unable to collect information about clients who refused to allow me to contact their family since I was not approaching clients systematically or in a manner to ensure unduplicated counts. Using the two-prong sampling approach allowed me to collect a larger sample, but at the expense of losing valuable information.

ENHANCING THE RESPONSE RATE

Once we obtained our family sample, the trick was to maintain it. Two mechanisms helped us lower the initial refusal rate and achieve the 85 percent response rate for the self-administered post-survey. First, every family participant received an automatic follow-up reminder card in the mail a week before the survey deadline. Family members who did not respond by the deadline received a follow-up phone call letting them know that the deadline was postponed by one more week if they were still interested in participating. The intense follow-up allowed us to address such problems as surveys getting lost in the mail or on people's dining room tables. Upon follow-up, 13 families asked for the survey to be resent once, and three families asked for the survey to be resent twice. Second, we paid family participants $5 to complete the first survey and $15 to complete the second. All of these activities (contacting participants prior to mailing surveys, two follow-ups, and offering incentive payments) were used because they have been found to increase response rates (Berry & Kanouse, 1987; James & Bolstein, 1990; Monette, Sullivan, & DeJong, 1994).

The most effective strategy to ensure that providers completed the self-administered surveys was one suggested by the program directors in the partial hospitalization and case management programs. The program directors set aside time during their morning staff meeting for staff to complete the pre- and post-self-administered surveys. I facilitated the process by bringing donuts and coffee. I stayed on-site at the agency to answer any questions, and collected the surveys to ensure that staff responses remained confidential. Two follow-up phone calls were also made to providers who were unable to attend meetings. Since provider participation (for partial hospitalization and case management staff) took place during work hours, and as salaried employees they were paid for this time, no extra financial incentives were offered. Only one staff member from the partial hospitalization program (none from the case management program) refused to participate, and the attrition rate was similar to the estimated rate of turnover within the agencies (12 percent).

SELECTING MEASURES: THE ULTIMATE CONSTRAINT

Among the most frustrating aspects of research are the trade-offs faced in selecting outcome measures. There seems to be an inherent contradiction in the goals of research. On the one hand, we are asked to see an issue/problem with new eyes and reconceptualize the way it could be examined. On the other hand, we are then asked to use old "standardized" measures to examine it. Needless to say, for areas in which little research has been done (such as this study), the standardized measures are hard to find.

For this study, we searched for and studied all measures that we could find. In the end, we adapted items from instruments that seemed to fit the best. Though pilot-testing the questionnaires did help to identify some weaknesses, one aspect of my dependent variable was pitifully weak due to measurement problems.

I also learned the importance for future research of including a fidelity measure for this type of study. For many years, researchers did not consider operationalizing the components of intervention models that they were examining. Not only did this make it more difficult to replicate effective interventions, but it was difficult to determine whether an intervention was found to be ineffective simply because it was not implemented as it was designed.

As we developed the intervention model, I operationalized the components and included questions assessing these elements in the questionnaires. I learned, however, that fidelity shouldn't be measured with just a few questions. There is actually a body of literature (McGrew, Bond, Dietzen, & Salyers, 1994; Rapp, 1999; Bond, Evans, Salyers, Williams, & Kim, 2000) that supports the idea that fidelity is better assessed through diverse means (record review, interviews, surveys, etc.) to capture a variety of perspectives from different stakeholders. Though the fidelity measures included in the study are better than no measure at all, there is room for great improvement.

IMPLICATIONS FOR SOCIAL WORK

In conducting research studies, it often feels as if we're *taking* (knowledge and experience) *from* participants. There is a big lapse in time before something is *given back*. Research that examines the effectiveness of an intervention feels natural to me as a social worker. Mental health and social service agencies work hard to help people improve their quality of life. Offering agencies an intervention, especially where the anecdotal information suggests that it may be effective, allows us to partner with our direct service colleagues in finding solutions that work. For this reason, intervention research is particularly rewarding.

Most people come to the field of social work hoping to facilitate change in some aspect of our society. Social workers may shy away from research, thinking that the process is too slow or in-depth to respond to the social issues we face. Not many social problems, however, may be quickly resolved. This study examined an issue that the mental health community has been struggling with for decades. The findings of this small study suggest that the intervention may be effective and is worth pursuing.

I'm currently in the process of writing a grant proposal to continue work in this area. Many of the limitations of this study were due to resource constraints. Further funding would allow me to conduct a full-scale study including consumer, family, and provider samples. The grant support would allow me to revise the intervention model, based on what has been learned in this study. In particular, I would like to examine the effectiveness of implementing the intervention model in a centralized intake system.

Other potential revisions include expanding the training component of the intervention to incorporate skills training for providers in working with families of adults with severe mental illness. Instead of offering the training at one point in time, training and consultation would be offered in three or more short segments over a period of time. The fidelity assessment would be expanded to include interviews with staff, consumers, and families, and reviewing of charts. Hopefully, more work in this area will reveal effective solutions that can easily be implemented within diverse mental health systems.

REFERENCES

Berry, S., & Kanouse, D. (1987). Physician response to a mailed survey: an experiment in timing of payment. *Public Opinion Quarterly, 51,* 102–114.

Bogart, T. & Solomon, P. (1999). Collaborative procedures to share treatment information among mental health care providers, consumers, and families. *Psychiatric Services, 50*(10), 1321–1325.

Bond, G., Evans, L., Salyers, M., Williams, J., & Kim, H. (2000). Measurement of fidelity in psychiatric rehabilitation. *Mental Health Services Research, 2*(2), 75–87.

James, J., & Bolstein, R. (1990). The effect of monetary incentives and follow-up mailings on the response rate and response quality in mail surveys. *Public Opinion Quarterly, 54,* 346–361.

McGrew, J., Bond, G., Dietzen, L., & Salyers, M. (1994). Measuring the fidelity of implementation of a mental health program model. *Journal of Consulting and Clinical Psychology, 62,* 670–678.

Monette, D., Sullivan, T., & DeJong, C. (1994). *Applied social research: tools for human services.* Philadelphia: Harcourt Brace College Publishers.

Rapp, C. (1999). *Best practice fidelity tools.* Lawrence, KS: University of Kansas School of Social Welfare.

6

Are Mainstream Programs for Juvenile Delinquency Less Effective With Minority Youth Than Majority Youth? A Meta-Analysis of Outcomes Research

Sandra Jo Wilson, Mark W. Lipsey, and Haluk Soydan

The mission of the social work profession includes work with marginalized, needy, and economically disadvantaged groups and individuals in society. This often entails services for immigrant and ethnically diverse populations. In the early decades of its development in the United States, the social work profession was called upon to assist newly arrived immigrants, especially in urban and densely populated areas (Addams, 1895; Soydan, 1999). Generations later, the clientele for social work continues to be characterized by ethnic diversity, as well as a multiplicity of languages, religions, and value systems. In other parts of the world, particularly in Europe, social work faces similar circumstances as migration has made populations more diverse (Williams, Soydan, & Johnson, 1998).

Ethnic diversity, in particular, has presented major challenges to social work practice. When people of different ethnic groups are assumed to have different needs or to respond differently to

Authors' Note: The research reported in this article was supported in part by grants from the Centre for Evaluation of Social Services of the National Board of Health and Welfare, Stockholm, Sweden, the National Institute of Mental Health (MH42694 and MH39958), and the Russell Sage Foundation.

services, the methods for serving those groups become a matter of debate. At issue is whether clients of ethnic minority groups should be treated with the same methods, interventions, and programs as the majority population of a particular country. Especially in the United States, the necessity of tailoring social work practice to meet the special needs of ethnically diverse populations has been much discussed (Soydan, Jergeby, Olsson, & Harms-Ringdal, 1999). Such concerns have resulted in various social work practice models for serving ethnic populations, for example, Cultural Awareness (Green, 1995), the Process Stage Approach in Minority Treatment (Lum, 1996), and Ethnic-Sensitive Social Work Practice (Devore & Schlesinger, 1996). These approaches are usually presented as generic models for ethnic minorities that are appropriate to different types of social work services such as family counseling, group counseling, behavior contracting, interpersonal skills training, drug treatment programs, and the like.

However, the need for, and effectiveness of, ethnically tailored social work approaches have been vigorously debated in social work research and practice (Soydan et al., 1999; de Anda, 1997). The nature of the controversy is illustrated by the papers in the volume, *Controversial Issues in Multiculturalism*, edited by de Anda (1997). The questions raised there include: whether the emphasis on multicultural practice has resulted in more effective and appropriate services for ethnic minority clients; whether programs and service delivery systems should be culture-specific in their design; whether the therapeutic process is more effective if the client and the helping professional are of the same ethnic/cultural group; and whether ethnic agencies can more effectively serve ethnic communities than mainstream agencies. Debating whether the emphasis on multicultural practice has resulted in more effective and appropriate services for ethnic minority clients, for instance, John Longres wrote,

> Dr. Brown argues that multicultural practice has brought about more effective and appropriate services. I argue that it has not. . . . In the first place, Dr. Brown is largely talking about appropriateness, not effectiveness. She offers anecdotal evidence to demonstrate that her students, her colleagues, and apparently their clients seem to be satisfied with the counseling they are receiving. This anecdotal evidence hardly stands up to rigorous evaluation and so has to be taken for what it is, the opinion of an educator. Even if her evidence were more rigorously represented, Dr. Brown supplies no evidence of effectiveness: the clients and their helping professionals may feel good, but do the clients behave differently, and have their lives been changed for the better? The evidence suggests that as a collective, people of color are treading water; their lives have not been improved by the growth of a new multicultural sensitivity, however more appropriate it may appear to be. (de Anda, 1997, pp. 18–19).

As this comment indicates, arguments about this issue are seldom based on well-founded empirical knowledge. When relevant evidence is consulted, the results are often surprising. For example, empirical research related to one specific social work intervention, foster care for children who are maltreated or whose parents are unable to care for them, demonstrates that differences between ethnic groups in the outcome of mainstream programs, if they occur at all, do not necessarily favor majority groups. Using data on death rates, Barth and Blackwell (1998) showed that White and Hispanic children in foster care have higher rates of death than their counterparts in the general population, but the death rates for African American foster children are no worse than those for the African American children in the general population. On the other hand, Jonson-Reid and Barth (2000) found that the risk of incarceration following foster care was greater for African American youth than for Hispanic or White youth, even when gender, age at first placement, and characteristics of placement history were controlled.

Although the effectiveness of services in producing positive outcomes for the specific problems to which they are addressed is not the only important consideration in social work practice, it is certainly a critical one. Where such outcomes are concerned, the question of whether culturally tailored or mainstream social work practice is more effective for minority youth is an empirical one. Unfortunately, at present we lack a solid body of research on this issue and where we do have some empirical findings, as in the foster care example above, the results do not always point in the same direction.

The present study was undertaken to assemble otherwise scattered research results about the effectiveness of service programs for minority juvenile delinquents relative to White majority delinquents. It uses the techniques of meta-analysis to address the question of whether mainstream interventions that are not culturally tailored for minority youth have positive outcomes on subsequent antisocial behavior. In addition, those outcomes are compared with the intervention effects for White majority samples to find out if there are any differences in the responsiveness of minority and majority youth to mainstream juvenile delinquency services.

META-ANALYSIS

Meta-analysis is a technique for recording and analyzing the statistical results of a collection of empirical research studies. Central to meta-analysis is the effect size statistic, which represents the quantitative findings of each study in a standardized way that permits comparison across studies. For the intervention studies of interest here, the effect size statistic (ES) is the standardized mean difference (Cohen, 1988; Lipsey & Wilson, 2001), defined as the difference between the treatment and control group means on an outcome variable divided by their pooled standard deviation. This effect size statistic indexes the outcomes for the treatment group relative to the control group in standard deviation units. Thus, ES = .50 indicates that the outcome for the treatment group was more favorable than that for the control group by an amount equivalent to half a standard deviation on the respective outcome measure. For binary outcomes (e.g., arrested/not arrested), the mean difference effect size was derived using Cohen's arcsine transformation for proportion values (Lipsey & Wilson, 2001). If a study assesses the effects of an intervention on more than one outcome, say reoffending and social adjustment, that study would generate two effect sizes, one for each outcome.

The effect size is not the only piece of information recorded about each study that contributes to a meta-analysis. Studies of juvenile delinquency programs involve youth from a variety of different age groups, ethnicities, risk levels, and so forth and use different procedures and methods to evaluate program effectiveness. Of course, the interventions themselves also differ across studies. Thus, in addition to the effect sizes, a meta-analytic database includes detailed information about each study's methods, participants, treatments, and other such descriptive characteristics that may be relevant for understanding the results. Analysis of the coded information from a collection of studies can then investigate relationships between various characteristics of the studies and the effect sizes those studies produce. In addition, statistical techniques can be used to control for many of the sources of error and natural differences between studies so that better estimates of the effects of intervention can be derived (Cooper & Hedges, 1994; Hedges & Olkin, 1985).

The studies included in the meta-analysis presented here are drawn from a database of nearly 500 studies on the effects of intervention with juvenile delinquents (Lipsey, 1992, 1995; Lipsey & Wilson, 1998). This larger synthesis of research results has shown that intervention for juvenile offenders is generally effective at reducing recidivism (Lipsey, 1995), even among serious, violent, or chronic juvenile offenders (Lipsey & Wilson, 1998). However, the results of these analyses have also shown that there is considerable variability in effectiveness across different research studies and that this variability is related to the research methods used, participant characteristics, and format and nature of the treatment. The analysis reported below uses this extensive database to address the relative effects of service programs for minority versus majority juvenile offenders.

METHOD

The database from which the studies for this meta-analysis are drawn includes empirical research on the effects of juvenile delinquency programs conducted between 1950 and 1996, both published and unpublished (Lipsey, 1992; Lipsey & Wilson, 1998). Trained personnel coded over 150 items for each study that describe the methods and procedures, participant samples, treatment and program characteristics, effect sizes, and other important information. Interrater reliability for the coding of effect sizes was .93 and interrater agreement was generally above 80% for items describing study characteristics. For the present analysis, the studies that allowed comparison of the effectiveness of delinquency programs for minority versus majority youth were selected from this database. Specifically, the 141 studies with participant samples comprised at least 60% minority youth, and the 164 studies with at least 60% White participants were selected. The mean percentage of minority youth in the studies selected to represent intervention with ethnic minorities was 82% and the mean percentage of White youth in the comparison studies was about 80%. Among the minority samples, most were predominately African American but Hispanic youth and, in much smaller numbers, other minority youth were also represented (see Table 6.1).

As with all studies in the full database, the selected studies met the following criteria:

- The youth in the study sample were identified as delinquent or displaying antisocial behavior; or, if the youth were not explicitly described as delinquent or antisocial, the study included delinquency or antisocial behavior among its primary outcome variables.

- The youth in treatment were between the ages of 12 and 21 and resided in the United States, Canada, Great Britain, New Zealand, or Australia.

- The research design was an experimental or quasi-experimental comparison of at least one treatment and one control/comparison group.

The selected studies reported intervention effects on a variety of outcome variables. The primary outcome of interest was subsequent delinquent behavior, most commonly measured by police contacts or arrests. Many studies also assessed other outcome variables that we have grouped into broad conceptual domains. Each of these domains covers a variety of specific individual variables, thus results presented for effects in these domains should be interpreted only as broad summaries. The domains we identified include the following outcome constructs. The number of studies contributing outcomes in each category is shown in parentheses.

- Academic achievement: grades and other measures of achievement in various academic subjects ($n = 34$)

- Attitude change: attitudes about delinquency or toward school, work, or community ($n = 57$)

- Behavior problems: nonaggressive behavior problems such as acting out, disruptiveness, and hyperactivity ($n = 23$)

- Employment status: getting or keeping a job, number of jobs held, and the like ($n = 28$)

Table 6.1. Characteristics of the 305 Studies Used in the Meta-Analysis

Variable	N	%[a]	Variable	N	%
General study characteristics			Percentage of sample with prior offenses		
Publication year			None	7	2
1950–1969	43	14	Some (< 50%)	56	19
1970–1979	119	39	Most (≥ 50%)	43	14
1980–1989	116	38	All	143	47
1990–1996	21	7	Some, cannot estimate %	38	12
Missing	6	2	Missing	18	6
Type of publication			Heterogeneity of treatment sample		
Technical report	156	51	Low	107	35
Journal article, chapter	93	31	Moderate	132	43
Dissertation	30	10	High	66	22
Book	24	8	Source of participants for treatment		
Conference paper	2	< 1	Volunteers	18	6
Country in which study was conducted			Referred by parents/friends	1	< 1
United States	280	92	Referred by non–juvenile		
United Kingdom	14	5	justice (JJ) agency	19	6
Canada	9	3	JJ referral (voluntary)	91	30
Other English-speaking country	2	< 1	JJ referral (mandatory)	142	47
Characteristics of juveniles in treatment			Multiple sources	12	4
Gender mix			Solicited by researcher	18	6
No males	9	3	Missing	4	1
Some males (< 50%)	16	5	Treatment characteristics		
Mostly males (≥ 50%)	144	47	Program age		
All males	136	45	Relatively new	187	61
Mean age at time of treatment			Established (2+ years)	113	37
<12.9	14	5	Defunct	1	< 1
13.0–13.9	27	9	Missing	4	1
14.0–14.9	54	18	Program sponsorship		
15.0–15.9	56	18	Research project	85	28
16.0–16.9	67	22	Private agency	29	10
17.0–17.9	38	12	Public agency, non-JJ	54	18
18.0–18.9	11	4	Public agency, JJ	132	43
19.0	27	9	Missing	5	2
Missing	11	4	Duration of treatment (weeks)		
Predominant ethnicity (>60%)			1–10	48	16
African American	80	26	11–20	81	26
Hispanic	19	6	21–30	47	15
Other (Asian, American Indian)	8	3	31–40	66	22
Mixed (minority > 60%)	34	11	41–50	13	4
White	164	54	51 and up	50	17
Delinquency level			Frequency of treatment event		
Predelinquent	89	29	Continuous	57	19
Delinquent	137	45	Daily	55	18
Institutionalized	79	26	2–4 times/week	31	10

Table 6.1. (*Continued*)

Variable	N	%[a]	Variable	N	%
1–2 times/week	90	30	Casework, service brokerage	31	10
Less than weekly	24	8	Counseling, noninstitutional	41	13
Missing	48	16	Counseling, institutional	42	14
Implementation problems			Behavioral, cognitive-behavioral	14	5
Yes	124	41	Employment related	26	9
Possible	67	22	Wilderness/challenge	9	3
No	114	38	Academic services	25	8
Rated amount of meaningful contact			Interpersonal skills	6	2
1 (Trivial)	4	1	Vocational	9	3
2	41	13	Probation and variations	21	7
3	40	13	Other	43	14
4 (Moderate)	67	22	Method characteristics		
5	69	23	What control group receives		
6	61	20	Receives nothing	51	17
7 (Substantial)	23	8	Minimal contact	19	6
Who delivers treatment?			School, treatment as usual	18	6
JJ personnel	91	30	Usual probation services	72	24
School personnel	14	5	Usual institutional treatment	84	28
Public mental health personnel	20	7	Other treatment as usual	49	16
Private mental health personnel	44	14	Placebo	12	4
Non–mental health counselors	66	22	Role of evaluator		
Laypersons	47	15	Delivered treatment	13	4
Researcher	6	2	Planned or supervised treatment	88	29
Other	6	2	Influential, no direct role	52	17
Missing	11	4	Independent of treatment	137	45
Primary treatment format			Missing	15	5
Juvenile alone	8	3	Method of group assignment		
Juvenile and provider	81	27	Random	141	46
Juvenile group	147	48	Matching	80	26
Juvenile and family	19	6	Other nonrandom	84	28
Mixed	41	13	Blinding in data collection		
Other	9	3	No	233	76
Treatment site			Yes	72	24
Public, JJ	98	32	Sample size		
Public, non-JJ site	64	21	Up to 49	57	19
Private	80	26	50–99	65	21
Mixed	43	14	100–199	84	28
Other	20	7	200–299	34	11
Treatment type			300–399	16	5
Multimodal programs			400 and up	49	16
Institutional	16	5			
Noninstitutional	22	7			

[a]Percentages may not add up to 100 because of rounding.

- Family functioning: measures of family relations, parental discipline, family stress, and the like ($n = 15$)

- Internalizing problems: withdrawal, shyness, anxiety, and other similar problems ($n = 23$)

- Peer relations: relations with peers, interpersonal skills, and social adjustment ($n = 31$)

- Psychological adjustment: locus of control, personality adjustment, and the like ($n = 36$)

- School participation: tardiness, truancy, and dropping out ($n = 56$)

- Self-esteem: measures of self-esteem or self-concept ($n = 27$)

CHARACTERISTICS OF THE DELINQUENCY TREATMENT STUDIES

Table 6.1 presents a summary of the 305 studies that comprise the database for this meta-analysis. The characteristics of these studies were generally similar to those for the entire database from which they were drawn. In addition, the characteristics of the studies with minority samples were not appreciably different from those with predominantly White samples. Some of the general features of the studies are as follows:

- The majority of studies were conducted in the United States. Most studies were published subsequent to 1970 with the most common form of publication being technical reports.

- The juvenile samples were largely male with most of the youth age 15 or older. The predominant ethnic classification among minority samples was African American with smaller proportions of mixed and predominantly Hispanic samples.

- Most of the studies involved youth who were delinquent or institutionalized and, for most of the samples, all or the majority of the juveniles had prior offense histories.

- In nearly half of the studies, the treatment was delivered to a group of juveniles (rather than individually) and about one third of the programs were delivered by juvenile justice personnel.

- The most frequent intervention strategies were institutional and noninstitutional counseling and casework or service brokerage-type services, although many other types of service programs were represented.

Nearly half of the studies used random assignment to place youth in treatment or comparison groups. In most of the studies, the youth in the comparison groups received usual or customary services, typically probation or institutionalization.

In addition to the descriptive information already coded on the selected studies, the original reports for those studies using minority samples were examined for statements relating to cultural tailoring of the interventions. We found one report indicating such tailoring (Wooldredge, Hartman, Latessa, & Holmes, 1994) and excluded it from our analyses. Thirteen of the 141 studies with minority youth mentioned using minority service providers with minority delinquents, but the services provided in these cases were not specifically culturally tailored. By all available indications, therefore, the interventions provided to the minority youth, like those provided to the White youth in the comparison studies, were predominantly mainstream services without any special tailoring to the ethnic or cultural characteristics of the juveniles receiving those services.

EFFECTIVENESS OF JUVENILE DELINQUENCY SERVICES

Figure 6.1 reports the mean effect size with its 95% confidence interval for each of the major intervention outcome constructs for minority and White samples. Hedges's (1981) small sample correction was applied to each effect size and all computations with effect sizes were weighted by the inverse sampling variance to reflect the greater stability of estimates based on larger samples (Hedges & Olkin, 1985; Lipsey & Wilson, 2001; Shadish & Haddock, 1994).

For minority youth, the weighted mean effect size for delinquency outcomes across all treatment modalities was .11; for majority youth, the corresponding effect size value was .17. Both these values were statistically significant, as evidenced by confidence intervals that do not include zero. Though the mean effect size for White youth was somewhat larger than that for minority youth, this difference was not statistically significant (as shown by the overlapping confidence intervals for Whites and minorities). To illustrate in more intuitive form what these effect size values mean, Cohen's (1988) arcsine transformation was used to convert them to percentage differences in recidivism rates. If the approximate rate of recidivism for delinquents in control groups is set at 50% (which is very close to the actual rate in the database), the mean effect size of .11 for minority youth is then equivalent to about a 5 percentage point differential, that is, a 45% reoffense rate for treated juveniles compared to 50% for those in the control groups. The mean effect size of .17 for majority youth translates into a 42% reoffense rate for treated juveniles, that is, an 8 percentage point decrease from that for untreated juveniles.

For the other outcome constructs, mean effect sizes for both minority and White juveniles were greater than zero for all outcome categories except family functioning, although not all were statistically significant (confidence intervals for self-esteem and employment status overlapped zero for both groups, and those for internalizing problems and school participation overlapped for the minority samples). Thus, the mainstream interventions represented in these studies, on average,

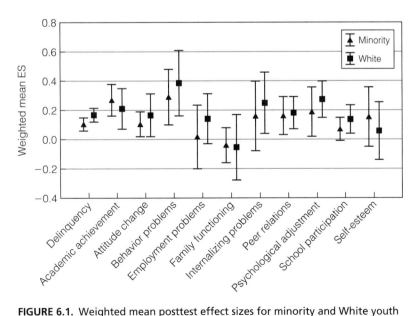

FIGURE 6.1. Weighted mean posttest effect sizes for minority and White youth for each outcome construct.

NOTE: ES = effect size.

had positive effects on both subsequent delinquency and a number of other important outcomes. Of greatest relevance for present purposes, however, were the differences between the minority and White samples on the various outcome constructs. Although the mean effect sizes for White samples were greater than those for minority samples on 7 of the 10 nondelinquency outcome categories, none of the differences in either direction was statistically significant, as evidenced by the highly overlapping confidence intervals. Thus, without exception, across all the outcome domains represented in these intervention studies, there were no significant differences between the overall effects of mainstream intervention services on predominantly minority treatment groups and those on predominantly White treatment groups.

A CLOSER LOOK AT DIFFERENTIAL EFFECTS
ON DELINQUENCY OUTCOMES

The overall mean effect size values in Figure 6.1 give a general affirmative answer to the question of whether mainstream delinquency interventions without special tailoring are as effective for ethnic minority youth as for White youth. However, there is great variability around the mean effects shown there. For the central delinquency outcomes, there was about three times as much effect size variability across studies as would be expected if all the interventions produced the same effect with associated sampling error (the Q-statistic testing effect size heterogeneity was $Q_{305} = 991.5, p < .01$). Differences in delinquency outcomes observed across studies could be due to any of a number of factors, including between-study differences in method and procedure, participant characteristics, amount of treatment, and, of course, type of treatment. Indeed, the results of any one study are jointly determined by the nature of the treatments and participants in the study and the methods used to study them. It is, therefore, informative to investigate the study characteristics associated with larger or smaller effect sizes and, if necessary, to statistically control their influence on the comparison of intervention effects for minority and majority youth. The resulting comparison helps ensure that any difference, or lack of difference, found between the delinquency effect sizes for minority and majority youth represents comparable intervention circumstances and is not simply the result of a different mix of treatments, methods, and the like being used with the different ethnic groups.

The first possible source of effect size variability we examined for delinquency outcomes was differences across studies in methods and procedures. If two researchers use different methods to conduct their studies, and those differences influence the findings, it is difficult to tell whether those findings reflect the effectiveness of the interventions or the influence of the methods used to study them. Thus, methodological differences across studies are nuisance variables that could influence the observed outcomes of intervention differently for minority and majority youth. We therefore sought to identify the methodological characteristics that were related to the observed effect sizes in the studies and statistically control them. We also included several more general nuisance variables in this analysis; for instance, type of publication, which is associated with effect size because of the greater tendency for large effects to be formally published (Dickersin, 1997). For the purposes of this analysis, the studies using minority and majority samples were combined. Once influential between-study differences in method were identified and controlled, intervention effects for minority and majority samples were again compared to determine if any difference appeared.

To investigate the relationship between the methodological characteristics of the studies and the delinquency outcomes observed in those studies, we performed an inverse-variance weighted random effects multiple regression analysis using the delinquency effect sizes for all 305 studies as the dependent variable (Hedges & Olkin, 1985). Next, the regression model was used to predict the overall mean effect size for each study with the method-related independent variables held constant (i.e., assigned the mean value for all studies). This predicted value was added to the residual for each effect size to generate a set of adjusted effect sizes that estimate the effects we would expect if all studies used similar methods.

This regression analysis showed that the delinquency effect sizes were significantly related to certain aspects of the study methods used. The model was significant ($Q_5 = 36.53$, $p < .01$) and about 10% of the variability in delinquency effect sizes was accounted for by the study methods used. The following method-related variables demonstrated the largest relationships with effect size in this analysis.

Pretreatment equivalence of experimental and control groups. Studies in which treatment and control groups were similar prior to treatment (indicated by random assignment to conditions, no pretest statistical differences between groups, and coder ratings of high similarity between treatment and control groups) produced smaller effect sizes than those in which treatment and control groups were not similar.

Type of publication. Unpublished technical reports tended to produce smaller effect sizes than published journal articles, books, and dissertations.

Role of evaluator. Studies in which the evaluator assumed only a research role tended to produce smaller effect sizes. That is, evaluators who were not involved in the design, planning, or delivery of treatment tended to be associated with smaller treatment effects.

Type of treatment received by control participants. Studies in which control participants received more services as part of "treatment as usual" control groups (e.g., institutionalization vs. no treatment or probation) resulted in smaller effect sizes.

Blinding in data collection. Studies in which those collecting outcome data were blind to the group status of participants produced larger effect sizes than those in which data collectors were not blind.

With the effect sizes adjusted for differences between studies on the variables identified as influential in this multiple regression analysis, we then sought to identify the treatment and participant characteristics most strongly related to observed effect sizes. This was accomplished with a second weighted random effects multiple regression analysis that used the method-adjusted effect sizes generated by the procedure described above as the dependent variable. The independent variables for this analysis were organized into four clusters of study characteristics that were entered into the regression hierarchically. The first cluster included such participant characteristics as age, gender, heterogeneity of the sample, delinquency level, and proportion with prior offenses. Note that ethnicity was not included in this analysis because we did not want to control it statistically but, rather, examine it directly at a later stage.

The remaining three clusters involved treatment characteristics. One cluster included general treatment characteristics, including the age of the program, source of participants, and program sponsorship. Another encompassed treatment dose, including implementation quality, treatment duration, treatment frequency per week, total hours of contact, and coder ratings of the intensity and meaningfulness of treatment. The final cluster represented treatment delivery personnel, format of treatment sessions, and treatment site.

The overall model was statistically significant, indicating that the array of study predictors in the model accounted for a significant proportion of the variance between effect sizes ($Q_{21} = 41.20$, $p < .01$). Nearly 15% of the variance among effect sizes was related to the clusters of study characteristics in the model. Of the four clusters of predictor variables, the participant cluster was the largest factor in the model, indicating that the treatment effects varied according to the

Table 6.2. Weighted Mixed Effects Multiple Regression: Reduced Model

Variable	ß	B	p
Participant characteristics			
Delinquents (vs. institutionalized and noninstitutionalized)	.1434	.0946	.012
Prior offenses	.1262	.0807	.035
Treatment characteristics			
Implementation quality	.1604	.0578	.004
Amount of meaningful contact	.1330	.0273	.018
Treatment delivered by juvenile justice personnel	−.1321	−.0918	.025
Regression constant		−.1322	
Overall model	$Q(5) = 31.01, p < .01$		
Residual	$Q(299) = 289.58, ns$		
$R^2 = .10$			
$N = 305$			

characteristics of the juveniles in treatment. The individual variables in this cluster that were most influential are discussed below. The cluster relating to treatment dose was the next most important in the model, with more treatment and fewer implementation problems associated with larger effect sizes. The cluster including the variables describing treatment format and the one involving general program characteristics did not make statistically significant contributions to the overall model.

The next step was to identify the individual participant and treatment variables from the influential clusters that had the strongest relationships to effect size. This was done by dropping in a stepwise fashion the variables that made the smallest contributions to the overall model. The final reduced regression model included five variables (Table 6.2). As the results in Table 6.2 show, two variables relating to the characteristics of the juveniles in the study samples had strong, independent relationships with treatment effect: the participants' delinquency level and the proportion of the juvenile sample with prior delinquent offenses. Participant samples in which all of the juveniles had prior offense records tended to produce larger effect sizes than studies in which fewer participants (or none) had priors. In addition, samples with youth identified as delinquent but not institutionalized tended to show larger effects than those in which the youth were predelinquent (minor offenses but not adjudicated) or already institutionalized. This pattern is not surprising given that predelinquent samples have little delinquent involvement to begin with and thus less room to reduce their involvement as a result of effective treatment. Institutionalized youth, on the other hand, are the most serious offenders and may have problems that are less amenable to the effects of treatment.

Two variables related to treatment dose also showed strong, independent relationships with effect size. Treatments rated by coders as more meaningful in terms of their likelihood of engaging the juvenile were associated with larger effect sizes than those rated as less meaningful. Also, when difficulties in treatment implementation were reported (e.g., not all juveniles received treatment, or treatment delivery was not complete), smaller treatment effects were found, as would be expected. The final variable in the reduced model indicated that interventions delivered by juvenile justice personnel were not as effective as those delivered by mental health personnel and non–mental health counselors.

As in the previous regression analysis with methodological variables, the reduced model representing the key participant and treatment-related variables was used to statistically control for differences between studies on those variables. This was done by using the regression equation to "predict" the effect size value expected when the respective participant and treatment variables were given values equal to their means across all studies. This predicted value was then added to the residual for each effect size to create new effect size values that estimated the effect sizes that would result if all studies were equivalent on the independent variables represented in the regression model.

Minority-Majority Differences with Influential Study Characteristics Controlled

With the most influential study characteristics identified, the relative effects of intervention for minority versus majority samples could be examined while controlling for any differences associated with those study characteristics. The first regression analysis described above produced a set of *method-adjusted* effect sizes for which key methodological differences between studies were held constant. The reduced model from the second regression analysis (Table 6.2) then generated another set of effect sizes from the method-adjusted set for which the influential sample and treatment characteristics were also held constant. This second set of effect sizes, which we will call *equated* effect sizes, statistically controls for all the between-study differences identified by either regression analysis as having a significant relationship to observed effect size values. This level of statistical control permits comparison between studies of minority youth and those of majority youth with increased confidence that any differences in intervention effects, or lack thereof, reflect the role of ethnicity and not other influential study characteristics that happen to be unevenly distributed across the two sets of studies.

Of course, different types of intervention may have different effects, so as a further control, we compared method-adjusted and equated effect sizes separately within each major intervention category. The observed, method-adjusted, and equated effect size means and confidence intervals for minority and majority youth receiving each of the most common types of intervention are shown in Figures 6.2 and 6.3. Figure 6.2 shows counseling-type programs in institutional and

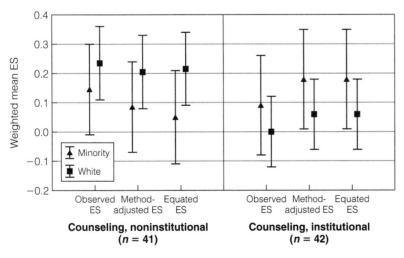

FIGURE 6.2. Mean observed and statistically adjusted effect sizes for minority and White youth for two types of counseling services.
NOTE: ES = effect size.

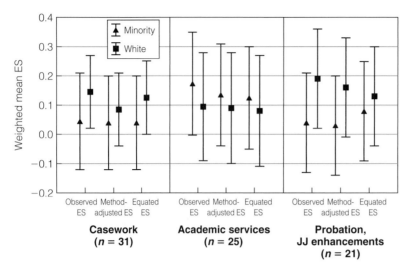

FIGURE 6.3. Mean observed and statistically adjusted effect sizes for minority and White youth for select program types.
NOTE: ES = effect size.

noninstitutional settings. The services in these programs include group and individual counseling, milieu therapy, guided group interaction, family counseling, reality therapy, and the like. Figure 6.3 shows casework and service brokerage-type programs, academic services such as tutoring and special classes, and probation with such juvenile justice enhancements as intensive supervision, restitution, and juvenile justice system education.

There are advantages and disadvantages associated with each of the three forms of effect size means shown in Figures 6.2 and 6.3. The observed means represent the findings of the individual studies as they were originally reported. However, their values are influenced by the various method, participant, and treatment characteristics discussed above, and those characteristics may not be uniform across studies with minority and majority youth. The method-adjusted effect sizes statistically control for between-study differences in method and procedure and thus give the best comparison of the effects actually produced by the treatments that were delivered in the various studies. However, there may be important differences in the participant characteristics (e.g., delinquency level), treatment implementation and amount, personnel, and so forth between the interventions provided to the minority and majority youth in these studies that would yield different effects irrespective of ethnicity. The equated effect sizes simulate a situation in which key methodological, participant, and treatment characteristics are the same for minority and majority youth and thus permit direct comparison. But they represent configurations of method, participant, and treatment characteristics that, to some degree, were not actually provided to the youth in these studies.

With these considerations in mind, it is most appropriate to examine the three types of effect sizes together with attention to any patterns that may illuminate the differences or similarities between delinquency outcomes for minority and majority youth. The most strikingly consistent result in Figures 6.2 and 6.3 is the similarity of the delinquency effects for minority and majority youth across all the treatment types and all forms of the effect size. The overlapping confidence intervals for each pair of means show that the difference between the minority and majority means was not statistically significant for any comparison. Moreover, the pattern of nonsignificant differences does not strongly favor either group. The effect size means for minority youth are somewhat lower than those for majority youth when the interventions are noninstitutional counseling, casework, or enhanced probation services, but they are higher for academic services and counseling in institutional settings.

EFFECTS FOR MINORITY AND MAJORITY YOUTH
RECEIVING THE SAME INTERVENTIONS

The results presented thus far indicate that mainstream treatments without cultural tailoring are as effective for minority youth as they are for majority youth. However, these results are all based on comparisons of different sets of studies, some using samples of minority youth and some using majority youth. Although the use of statistical controls reduces the influence of differences between the sets of studies on characteristics that are irrelevant to the issue of differential effects for minority and majority youth, the possibility remains that other differences that were not controlled still distort the comparisons. The most direct comparison of the effects of delinquency intervention programs for minority versus majority youth comes from studies with both minority and majority participants that report effects separately for each group. Such studies would compare the outcomes for ethnic groups who received the same interventions that were evaluated under the same conditions with the same methods.

Relatively few studies in our database broke out and reported results separately for youth of different ethnicities. Figure 6.4 compares the mean effect sizes for each pair of ethnic groups from those studies that did compare outcomes for those groups. Thus, within each pair of effect size means, the youth in the respective ethnic groups participated side-by-side in the same treatment programs and research studies. Though the numbers are small, the results shown in Figure 6.4 are completely consistent with those from the other analyses reported above. None of the effect size differences between ethnic groups was statistically significant and the nonsignificant trends in those differences were in the direction of larger effects for minority youth than White youth. The limited data that permit direct comparison, therefore, also fail to support the view that the effects of mainstream programs for delinquency favor majority youth and are less effective with minorities.

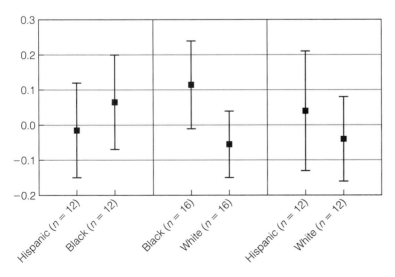

FIGURE 6.4. Differences in mean delinquency effect sizes for minority and majority groups in breakout samples.

DISCUSSION AND APPLICATIONS TO PRACTICE

The analyses reported above provide no evidence that mainstream delinquency intervention programs yield poorer outcomes for minority youth than for White youth despite their general lack of cultural tailoring for minority clientele. A large, representative selection of intervention studies showed no significant differences between minority and White samples in any outcome domain, including effects on delinquency, academic achievement, behavior problems, self-esteem, employment status, peer relations, internalizing problems, attitudes, school participation, family functioning and psychological adjustment. Additional analysis of delinquent reoffending, the major target outcome for these programs, further supported the initial finding of no difference in effects for minority versus White youth. In particular, introducing a range of statistical controls for methodological and substantive differences among the studies into the analysis did not appreciably alter the results. Moreover, direct comparison of outcomes for minority and White youth receiving the same treatments in the same studies using the same methods and measures also showed no differences.

A more interesting, and more definitive, analysis would involve a three-way comparison of the effects of culturally tailored programs for minority youth with the effects of mainstream programs on both minority and White youth. However, too few controlled studies of the outcomes of culturally tailored programs for minorities have been conducted and reported to permit such analysis. The database from which the studies for the meta-analysis presented here were drawn was developed through vigorous search for all qualifying published and unpublished studies conducted between 1950 and 1996, and we believe it provides very good coverage of the extant research for that period. When we examined each of these studies for indications of culturally tailored interventions, however, we found only one (Wooldredge et al., 1994) of the nearly 500 available that clearly involved such tailoring. The effect size for this study was .03, indicating that treatment group youth were not better off than control group youth after participating in culturally tailored treatment. Another 13 reported using minority personnel to provide services to minority youth but gave no indication that the nature of the service itself was otherwise adjusted on the basis of cultural considerations for those youth. The recidivism effect size for the programs with minority service providers was .13. Even if these latter cases are counted as minimal instances of cultural tailoring, there are too few studies to permit an adequate comparison of their outcomes with those of comparable mainstream programs for comparable minority youth. Furthermore, the results of these few studies do not suggest that tailoring by matching the cultural characteristics of juveniles and providers produces better results than mainstream programming. Increased recent interest in culturally sensitive intervention programs may generate enough outcome research to support such comparison in the near future.

It should be noted that the mean effect sizes found for both minority and White youth in this meta-analysis are relatively modest. As Figure 6.1 indicates, there was no outcome domain for which the mean for either group exceeded .40, and most were in the range of .20 and below. The critical delinquency outcomes, in particular, showed a mean effect size of .11 for minority youth and .17 for White youth. By comparison with these values, the mean effect size for over 300 meta-analyses of the outcomes of psychological, educational, and behavioral interventions found by Lipsey and Wilson (1993) was .50.

One possible interpretation of the results presented in this study, therefore, is that the mainstream delinquency intervention programs reviewed are not generally successful in producing positive outcomes. Thus, the lack of any significant differences between the outcomes for minority and White youth demonstrates not that these programs are as equally effective for minorities as Whites despite their lack of cultural tailoring but that they are equally ineffective for both groups of youth. The similarity in the outcomes of mainstream programs for minorities and Whites is only interesting if they have meaningful positive effects on both groups. If the programs do not work, no defensible case could be made for applying them to minority youth no matter how similar the results were to those for White youth.

For several reasons, we do not think the above interpretation of the results is correct. First, numerically small values of the standardized mean difference effect size statistic do not necessarily indicate that the practical significance of the effects is small. The mean effect sizes for the key delinquency reoffense outcomes, for instance, translate into 5–8 percentage point decreases from a 50% recidivism baseline among control groups. This difference, therefore, represents a 10%–16% reduction in the number of juveniles reoffending, which is far from trivial even though one could hope for more.

And, indeed, larger effects on delinquency are represented in the mean effect sizes found. The distributions of effect sizes for minority and White youth summarized by the respective mean values have relatively large variance. That is, the mean values average over a wide range of delinquency effects, some much smaller than the mean but many that are much larger. In other analyses, we have shown that the effects produced by the high-end delinquency interventions are considerable, ranging as high as 40% reductions in recidivism (Lipsey, 1995; Lipsey & Wilson, 1998). One implication of this state of affairs is that the mean effect size is not an especially good summary of the full effect size distribution. Another implication, however, is that the statistically nonsignificant overall difference between the mean for minority youth and that for White youth encompasses the full range of effects, including those of unquestionable practical significance. This can be seen most clearly in Figures 6.2 and 6.3 where the confidence intervals around the mean effect sizes for different types of interventions are very broad, ranging upward to twice or three times the mean value, as well as downward an equivalent amount.

Overall, therefore, we believe the most defensible interpretation of the available research is that mainstream treatments for juvenile delinquents are generally effective and no less effective for ethnic minority youth than White youth. We must emphasize, however, that this does not mean that issues of cultural sensitivity are unimportant to such programs when minority youth are served. It could well be that the effects of programs with cultural tailoring would be larger than those of programs without even though those without do not have differential effects for minority and White youth. The evidence reviewed here only shows that cultural tailoring is not necessary for the programs to have positive outcomes and that the absence of such tailoring does not diminish the effects for minorities relative to Whites. As noted earlier, there are not yet sufficient outcome studies for programs with cultural tailoring to determine if they yield larger effects than comparable programs without such tailoring. In addition, all of the studies included here involved indigenous minority youth, rather than recent immigrants. Thus, our results do not speak to the particular needs of recent immigrant populations or the effectiveness of mainstream intervention for delinquent youth who are newly arrived.

Moreover, even if the major outcomes of mainstream programs for minority youth are comparable to those with White youth, there may be other benefits to culturally sensitive programming. It may well be that the likelihood of participation, the acceptance of the program plan, the ultimate satisfaction with the program experience, and other such factors not commonly measured in outcome studies are less positive for minority youth in mainstream programs than majority youth. This may be especially so for recent immigrant youth. Moreover, if such differences occur, programs especially tailored to specific ethnic groups may well alleviate them. What the evidence reviewed here indicates is only that such tailoring cannot be justified on the grounds that, without it, the programs are ineffective or not as effective as for majority youth. In addition, it is worth noting that in the course of developing culturally sensitive programs, some care must be taken to ensure that such tailoring does not reduce the effectiveness of the mainstream programs that are adapted. Ultimately, we must implement and evaluate a sufficient number and range of culturally tailored programs for delinquent youth to permit a direct assessment of their outcomes and how they compare with those of mainstream programs.

REFERENCES

Addams, J. (1895). *Hull House maps and papers. A presentation of nationalities and wages in a congested district of Chicago, together with comments and essays on problems growing out of the social conditions.* New York: Thomas Y. Crowell.

Barth, R. P., & Blackwell, D. L. (1998). Death rates among California's foster care and former foster care populations. *Children and Youth Services Review, 20,* 577–604.

Cohen, J. (1988). *Statistical power analysis for the behavioral sciences (2nd ed.).* Hillsdale, NJ: Lawrence Erlbaum.

Cooper, H., & Hedges, L. V. (Eds.). (1994). *The handbook of research synthesis.* New York: Russell Sage.

de Anda, D. (Ed.). (1997). *Controversial issues in multiculturalism.* Boston: Allyn and Bacon.

Devore, W., & Schlesinger, E. G. (1996). *Ethnic-sensitive social work practice.* Boston: Allyn and Bacon.

Dickersin, K. (1997). How important is publication bias? A synthesis of available data. *AIDS Education and Prevention, 9,* 15–21.

Green, J. W. (1995). *Cultural awareness in the human services. A multiethnic approach.* Boston: Allyn and Bacon.

Hedges, L. V. (1981). Distribution theory for Glass's estimator of effect size and related estimators. *Journal of Educational Statistics, 6,* 107–128.

Hedges, L. V., & Olkin, I. (1985). *Statistical methods for meta-analysis.* New York: Academic Press.

Jonson-Reid, M., & Barth, R. P. (2000). From placement to prison: The path to adolescent incarceration from child welfare supervised foster or group care. *Children and Youth Services Review, 22,* 493–516.

Lipsey, M. W. (1992). Juvenile delinquency treatment: A meta-analytic inquiry into the variability of effects. In T. D. Cook, H. Cooper, D. S. Cordray, H. Hartmann, L. V. Hedges, R. J. Light, T. A. Louis, & F. Mosteller (Eds.), *Meta-analysis for explanation: A casebook* (pp. 83–127). New York: Russell Sage.

Lipsey, M. W. (1995). What do we learn from 400 research studies on the effectiveness of treatment with juvenile delinquents? In J. McGuire (Ed.), *What works? Reducing reoffending—Guidelines from research and practice* (pp. 63–78). New York: John Wiley.

Lipsey, M. W., & Wilson, D. B. (1993). The efficacy of psychological, educational, and behavioral treatment: Confirmation from meta-analysis. *American Psychologist, 48,* 1181–1209.

Lipsey, M. W., & Wilson, D. B. (1998). Effective intervention for serious juvenile offenders: A synthesis of research. In R. Loeber & D. P. Farrington (Eds.), *Serious and violent juvenile offenders: Risk factors and successful interventions* (pp. 313–345). Thousand Oaks, CA: Sage.

Lipsey, M. W., & Wilson, D. B. (2001). *Practical meta-analysis* (Applied Social Research Methods Series, Vol. 49). Thousand Oaks, CA: Sage.

Lum, D. (1996). *Social work practice and people of color. A process stage approach.* Monterey, CA: Brooks/Cole.

Shadish, W. R., & Haddock, C. K. (1994). Combining estimates of effect size. In H. Cooper & L. V. Hedges (Eds.), *The handbook of research synthesis* (pp. 261–281). New York: Russell Sage.

Soydan, H. (1999). *The history of ideas in social work.* Birmingham, AL: Venture Press.

Soydan, H., Jergeby, U., Olsson, E., & Harms-Ringdal, M. (1999). *Socialt arbete med etniska minoriteter. En litteraturöversikt* [Social work with ethnic minorities. A literature review]. Stockholm: Liber.

Williams, C., Soydan, H., & Johnson, M. R. D. (Eds.). (1998). *Social work and minorities. European perspectives.* London: Routledge.

Wooldredge, J., Hartman, J., Latessa, E., & Holmes, S. (1994). Effectiveness of culturally specific community treatment for African American juvenile felons. *Crime & Delinquency, 40,* 589–598.

COMMENTARY BY: Sandra Jo Wilson

CHOOSING A TOPIC

The meta-analysis on which the article was based was part of a large ongoing project on the effectiveness of interventions for the prevention or treatment of delinquency. Mark Lipsey is the Principal Investigator for the project, and has been collecting evaluation studies of delinquency programs for the meta-analysis since the mid-1980s. Though many chapters and articles other than the one reprinted here have been published over the past decade (e.g., Lipsey, 1992, 1995; Lipsey & D. Wilson, 1998; S. Wilson & Lipsey, 2000), the database is quite large and relatively unexplored. Thus, part of the impetus for the project on minority delinquents was to continue to explore the rich database we have at our disposal. The specific focus of the project on minority youth, however, was suggested by Haluk Soydan of the Center for Evaluation of Social Services in Stockholm, Sweden. Sweden's relatively permissive immigration policy has resulted in a multiethnic population with which Swedish social service agencies are inexperienced. Soydan's question to Mark Lipsey and me was whether the database of delinquency programs might be able to inform his decision making about programming for ethnic minority delinquents in Sweden.

Though Soydan was most interested in the effectiveness of culturally sensitive programming for delinquents, we discovered that delinquency treatment programs were overwhelmingly *not* culturally tailored, at least in the United States. Synthesizing existing research presents a challenge for meta-analysts because we are dependent on the published and unpublished research produced by other researchers. Though we began the project with the intention of investigating the effectiveness of culturally tailored programs, the lack of such studies in the delinquency field resulted in a change of our focus. Because ethnic minority youth seemed to be treated primarily in mainstream programs, we decided that a study of how they fared in the usual services might help answer the question of whether cultural tailoring is necessary for minority delinquents.

Based on the decisions we made at this early stage, we decided to pull out studies from the delinquency treatment database in which the study subjects were ethnic minorities. We performed some interesting analyses and wrote up a short paper for submission to *Research on Social Work Practice*. The focus of that initial draft was only on the minority youth; we described the influence of study methods on the results of research, the differential effectiveness of different types of treatment programs for minorities, and so forth. Several months later, we received three blind reviews from the editor of the journal. He was very positive about the paper and asked us to revise the manuscript based on the reviewers' comments. As we set about that task, a single sentence in one

Commentary on article: Wilson, S. J., Lipsey, M. W., & Soydan H. (2003). Are mainstream programs for juvenile delinquency less effective with minority youth than majority youth? A meta-analysis of outcomes research. *Research on Social Work Practice, 13,* 3–26.

139

reviewer's notes struck us as a good idea. This reviewer said, "perhaps the major emphasis should be on *comparing* the relative outcomes for minority versus majority youths" [my italics]. The tone of the editor's letter suggested that it was not necessary for us to address this particular comment—that the paper would likely be published with only minor editorial changes. But the more we thought about this comment, the more we liked the idea. And though I was tempted at first to take the easy way out and have the paper published as it was, we decided that we needed to undertake a major revision of our analyses with the idea of comparing the effectiveness of programs for minority youth relative to White youth. So, the final paper was born, thanks to an anonymous colleague.

META-ANALYSIS METHODOLOGY

In the following pages, I will discuss some of the methods we used, but focus on the difficulties and questions we encountered during the project. (For anyone wishing to conduct their own meta-analysis, however, Cooper and Hedges (1994) and Lipsey and D. Wilson (2001) are essential texts.)

Criteria for Inclusion and Exclusion

The first step in any meta-analysis involves drawing up a statement of the eligibility criteria for the review. Specifying these criteria requires some careful thought up front but is frequently an iterative process. The volume of research available on juvenile delinquency programs was staggering, and it became necessary to specify some restrictions on the types of studies to be included.

For the juvenile delinquency study as a whole, the eligibility criteria changed over the course of the project. For example, there were many studies of the effectiveness of programs for delinquents that failed to assess the impact of the program on delinquent behavior; these studies focused on psychological adjustment, disruptive classroom behavior, school performance, and other interesting outcomes. Although we were interested in the effects of rehabilitative programs for delinquents in general, we were most interested in whether delinquency programs actually reduce or prevent delinquent behavior. Thus, our criteria changed to specify that candidate studies must have measured delinquent behavior as an outcome. Of course most of the studies in the database measure other outcomes as well.

We also added restrictions on the types of programs we accepted into the study. Pharmaceutical and medical treatments like drug therapy were excluded, partly because some programs were not comparable with the more psychosocial interventions that were the norm in our database. A second reason is what I call the "can of worms" problem. In the end, time and funding requirements dictate how much literature can be included in a synthesis, and meta-analysts must be careful about opening up expensive and time-consuming cans of worms. Keep in mind when excluding studies from a meta-analysis that it must be justifiable under some reasonable standard. We felt that we were justified in excluding pharmaceutical treatments because the community-based practitioners who make up our primary audience would not usually be making a selection between a psychosocial treatment and drug therapy—they would most likely be selecting program options from among a range of psychosocial programs available in their communities. These types of eligibility restrictions kept the sample of potentially eligible studies somewhat circumscribed (although still quite large at 600 studies!) and allowed us to work with a set of delinquency programs that was relatively homogeneous. Thus, a researcher may begin a project with the idea of synthesizing all research on the effectiveness of delinquency programs, but end up with a synthesis of the effects on delinquent behavior of psychosocial interventions.

Although it did not happen in our case, sometimes there is not enough existing research on a topic to permit a meta-analysis. If this happens, it may be necessary to expand the eligibility criteria, so long as the new question to be addressed will be of interest to both the meta-analyst and the intended audience. Of course there are some topics for which meta-analysis is not feasible at all. If the primary research isn't sufficient (even with expanded eligibility criteria), then the meta-analyst should focus his or her energies elsewhere.

Retrieval Bias and the File Drawer Problem

Since the raw material of meta-analysis is the primary research literature, identifying and collecting that literature is a critical part of conducting a review. One of the most widely cited weaknesses of meta-analysis has to do with the comprehensiveness of the literature reviewed (of course this would also be a potential weakness in a traditional narrative review). The reality of academic research is that studies with positive results are more likely to find their way into the published literature, whereas studies with nonsignificant or negative results wind up in the researchers' file drawers (or trash cans). If we had collected only published research, we not only would have reduced our sample of programs by more than half, we might have concluded that juvenile delinquency programs are more effective than they are.

There is another reason to seek out unpublished research when conducting a meta-analysis, which has important practical implications. Unpublished research tends to involve different types of programs, research settings, and methods than the research reported in journal articles. The delinquency programs we found in journal articles were more carefully monitored by researchers and more likely to be done for research purposes. The staffs of these programs were more likely to be affiliated with the research team and to receive more extensive training. The programs in technical reports tended to look more like actual delinquency programs—they were staffed by people who would customarily deliver services to delinquents (e.g., probation officers, social workers) and used training regimens that were fairly typical of community treatment settings. While it is certainly important to know whether a program strategy implemented under ideal conditions is effective (as we might see in a published article), we believe it is equally important (if not more so) to know whether the programs that are typical of real communities are working. If we had not included the unpublished research in our study of delinquency programs, we would not have been able to study these real-world programs and settings.

Coding of Study Characteristics

Once the eligibility criteria are specified and the literature retrieval process is begun, it is time to start coding. The coding process is, I believe, one of the least understood aspects of meta-analysis. There is a huge amount of somewhat tedious work involved in coding, and the task is difficult, time consuming, and expensive. The quality of coding for meta-analysis is a function of both the coding manual and the coders who use it. We do all of our coding directly into a computer database, but a detailed paper coding manual is essential for conducting a good meta-analysis. Mark Lipsey has written an excellent chapter (Lipsey, 1994) that provides some insights on deciding what to code. But how to code it is another question altogether.

The Coding Manual   Table 6.1 from the reprinted article in this chapter shows the large number of different variables we tried to extract from each of the primary articles. Each coding item had to be carefully defined with options for coding the different study characteristics. Although we were familiar with the literature on delinquency programs and used that literature to develop the manual, the response options for different coding items changed once we began coding. For example, the list of treatment delivery personnel (probation officers, police, teachers) grew as different programs used a type of personnel that had not previously been coded.

One of the coding items for the delinquency project involves identifying the method by which subjects were assigned to treatment and comparison groups. Table 6.1 in the reprinted article has three choices for assignment method: random, matching, and other nonrandom. This seems fairly simple on the surface, but the coding manual has an entire page of instructions just for coding this item! Imagine a research study in which the program had only a limited number of slots and more juveniles were referred to the program than could be treated at one time. As a result, the juveniles who were referred after the program had filled up were considered a "waiting list" control group for the research study and were slated to receive the treatment after the data for the study had been collected. This process is thought to approximate random assignment since the youth who were referred later are not expected to be different from those referred earlier. Our coding manual needed to specify that waiting list control groups were proxies for random assignment. Unfortunately, the term "wait list control group" was used in the literature in another way that does not approximate random assignment. Think about a case in which delinquents from one facility in a community are given a program while the youth from a different facility (perhaps in a neighboring town) are scheduled to receive the same program after the delivery personnel have completed the program in the first facility. The waiting list in this case does not approximate random assignment because the youth assigned to the two facilities could be very different from each other. One facility might have more minority youth, youth with more serious offense histories, different staff, and the like. Of course, waiting lists can also be used in true random assignment studies as well. Because of the varying uses of the term "waiting list," the coding manual needed to define and clarify these issues and indicate to the coders how to code the different varieties of waiting list control groups.

Coding the treatment modalities was also surprisingly difficult and changed several times over the course of the project. The first iteration involved a checklist on which the coders indicated the type of treatment. This list grew as new studies with different treatment modalities were added. In addition, most of the programs turned out to have more than one type of treatment, or more than one treatment "ingredient." A second list of supplemental treatments was added to the coding manual to better code the program strategies. Many of the programs had more than two components, however, and the coders found it difficult to identify the most focal treatment ingredient of the many multifaceted programs. To capture the variety of treatment ingredients we uncovered, we developed an even larger list of individual ingredients and coders checked off all the activities present for each program. Unfortunately, this latest scheme was created after the article was published, so we were not able to incorporate the more detailed program coding into our comparisons of White and minority delinquents. But these examples should illustrate how much our coding manual changed over the course of the project.

The Coders   While a small meta-analysis with a limited number of studies or only a few coding items might be done by one person, our meta-analysis project was so large that we needed to hire coders to do most of the coding. Lipsey and I both coded some of the studies in the database, but the majority were coded by graduate students or full-time research assistants. Training and monitoring the coders (even if it is only one person) is critical to achieving high-quality coding. We performed reliability checks on our coders by having two people code a sample of the same studies. We also held weekly coder meetings in which we put forward examples of different coding items and discussed how to code them. Coding is terribly tedious work, yet requires a fairly high level of skill. It takes a very meticulous person to read research articles word-for-word and code the relevant information into a database, yet it is still easy to get bored with the work. It was very difficult to find people with the appropriate skill level who were willing to do such tedious work.

In order to keep our team interested and focused, we used a variety of tactics. First, we encouraged the coders to talk to the project managers and to each other, to ask questions, to offer suggestions, and stay involved in the development of the coding manual. This gave everyone an opportunity to get up from their desks and talk to each other. Since coding is such solitary work, we tried to create opportunities for personal interaction that broke up the day. We also supervised all coding work carefully and kept track of productivity. If one coder was coding fewer studies than the others, we were able to identify the individual and work on ways to increase his or her productivity. Similarly, each study in a meta-analysis is different, and new issues always arise during coding. If a coder stopped asking questions, it usually meant that he or she had glossed over some issue that needed to be addressed. Even the best coders come across situations they haven't seen before, and failure to ask questions is a good clue that a coder is not being mindful. We also tried to alternate coding with other tasks that are less tedious (e.g., conducting telephone interviews for other projects) or reward coders with a "brainless" task (copying, filing, etc.) when they finished a difficult study. In the end, though, keeping the coders on task and working productively involved a balance of inspiration and policing. This managerial and supervisory role was not something my academic training prepared me for—an unfortunate circumstance, given that managing people turns out to be a significant part of large research projects.

Finding Information in Research Studies

Even a well-trained coding team, however, cannot find information to code that isn't there. One of the thorniest problems a meta-analyst faces is that not all eligible studies will provide the details needed for coding. Primary researchers are notorious for leaving key pieces of information out of their publications and technical reports. Some of this, of course, is due to page restrictions in journals, and some is due to the fact that researchers may have a different purpose than providing data for a meta-analyst. Missing information in primary studies can be an indicator of study quality, but not always. Most often, researchers have differing backgrounds and purposes that result in their emphasis on different types of information. Many people are surprised to learn that in 25 percent of the studies we coded for the delinquency meta-analysis, no information was given about the ethnicity of the subjects! Obviously, these had to be excluded from our analysis because we couldn't determine whether the youth were minorities or Whites. In addition, information about the nature of the treatment (a critical part of our coding) was often vague. When missing information causes a study to be excluded from analysis, the results of that analysis may not reflect the true nature of the population of research being evaluated. Unfortunately, the reality is that there is not much a meta-analyst can do to remedy the situation, although there are several techniques available for estimating missing data (Pigott, 1994).

One way to gather further information about a study, however, is to look for other published and unpublished work by the same research team. We found that authors sometimes published the details of their programs, subjects, or implementation quality in different articles than those in which they published the results. Locating these supplemental articles improved our coding of ethnicity, treatment characteristics, implementation quality, and the like. Occasionally, writing or e-mailing an author provided us with more information, but researchers are busy people and responses to our requests were rare, especially if the article was not recent.

Study results are one of the most common types of uncodable or unavailable information. In a meta-analysis, each study contributes an effect size that indexes the results of that study. There are a variety of statistical formulas that allow us to convert the results of statistical tests into effect sizes, but sometimes the data presented in research reports cannot be converted into effect sizes—we may be able to code a positive or negative result overall, but studies without effect sizes are inevitably excluded from most of the interesting analyses. In retrospect, it would have been useful to know how many studies we excluded for uncodable study results. These studies could be compared with those studies that were codable to determine whether the sample of programs in our meta-analysis is representative of delinquency programs in general.

Study Quality

Different meta-analysts advocate different methods for handling the issue of study quality, and researchers seeking to conduct a meta-analysis have several choices. Most meta-analysts believe that the primary studies must exhibit a certain level of methodological rigor to be included in any credible meta-analysis; the debate revolves around the different ideas that researchers have of what "quality" is. One of the most common quality cutoffs (especially with meta-analyses of medical treatments) is randomization. Some meta-analysts exclude any study in which treatment and control subjects are not randomly assigned. We decided, however, that because we were conducting a synthesis of research on social programs, including only randomized studies was unwise. Instead, we required that studies have comparison groups, but subjects did not have to be randomly assigned to them. Since the methods used to conduct a study do influence the results of that study, we believe it is important to include a range of methodologies in a meta-analysis, so that the influence of method on study results can be made explicit. In the minority delinquency meta-analysis, the methods used in the primary studies were associated significantly with the results of those studies. By specifying these influences we were able to understand better how researchers influenced their own results. And, once we made the methods explicit, we were able to control for differences across studies in the quality of their methods. We also found that high-quality randomized studies tended to have different program and treatment characteristics from nonrandomized studies. Since we were interested in how social programs work in actual community settings, we made sure to include the nonrandomized studies in our meta-analysis.

Choice of Statistical Methods

In analyzing the data for the synthesis, we used standard statistical methods for meta-analysis (see Lipsey & Wilson, 2001). This involved examining the distribution of effect sizes to determine whether they were homogenous, or there were differences between the studies that were larger than expected. In our case, we found a considerable amount of heterogeneity among studies; that is, the individual studies produced different outcomes. The goal of any subsequent analysis is to identify study characteristics that account for the heterogeneity. These study characteristics may be features of the method used in the study of the program, attributes of the subjects in the programs, or aspects of the programs themselves. We used a technique analogous to regression analysis to identify the influential study characteristics, though a form of analysis of variance and other techniques may be used. The results of our analyses are presented in the article in a way that makes them appear very straightforward. In reality, there was much behind-the-scenes work that doesn't appear in the research article. This had to do primarily with deciding what variables to analyze, and studying carefully the relationships among those variables. That is, though we wanted to identify the study characteristics (like treatment modality or type of treatment delivery personnel) that produced larger (or smaller) program effects, it turned out that many of our study characteristics were interrelated.

To illustrate this, imagine a situation with two delinquency programs (instead of an entire meta-analytic database). One program is an intensive probation intervention that involves frequent contact between probation officer and juvenile, electronic monitoring, and the like. The community in which this program is housed has a large Hispanic population, thus many of the youth in this program are Hispanic. The second program is a casework-type program in which the youths and their families are assigned to a caseworker who then endeavors to find the services that are most appropriate for each case. This program in this particular community involves mostly White youth. The evaluations of these two programs used different methods. The first program is state-run and was evaluated by a local evaluator who was unable to randomly assign youth to experimental and control groups. As a result, the youth in the experimental intensive probation program tended to have more severe problems than the youth assigned to the control group in that study. The second program also had a local evaluator, but a limited number of caseworkers was available. As a result, not all eligible youth could participate and the youth were randomly assigned to receive either casework or traditional probation. The results of the two evaluations showed that the difference between Program 1 and its control group was much larger than the difference between Program 2 and its control group. Does that mean that intensive probation services are more effective than casework? Or, does it mean that Hispanic youth are more amenable to treatment than White youth? Or, could it be that the methods used to evaluate Program 1 were such that the program looked better than it should have? Disentangling these types of issues is the key to a good meta-analysis. The regression analyses we conducted enabled us to identify the variables most strongly associated with study effects, while controlling for relationships among the variables. Examination of a few individual variables was also necessary, however.

For example, when we found that treatments delivered by juvenile justice personnel tended to be less effective than those delivered by other service personnel, we wanted to make sure that the programs delivered by juvenile justice personnel did not all use the same method or have the same treatment modality. If that had been the case, then we couldn't be sure whether our finding that the personnel influenced study outcomes was truly due to the personnel or due to the method or treatment modality. This required that we carefully examine the relationships among all the study characteristics and check the distributions of the individual variables. We performed various cross-tabulations (of, for example, type of treatment personnel with method of group assignment) to ensure that the influential variables we identified were not completely confounded with each other.

In addition, when we found that minority youth did not seem to fare any worse than majority youth in mainstream programs, it was important to make sure that minority youth were not more likely to receive a certain type of program. Because this was a particularly critical issue, we followed up with the additional analyses that compared the subset of programs in which minority and White youth participated side-by-side in the same programs. This gave us more confidence in our finding that minority youth fared equally well in mainstream programs as their White peers. These kinds of background analyses do not often show up in a published article, but they enable a researcher to be more confident in the results that are presented in the article.

PRACTICALITIES

As meta-analysts, we are lucky that we do not have to negotiate with stakeholders, staff, and subjects. At our university, we are not subject to the Institutional Review Board (IRB) since our research is not considered human subjects research. Different universities and funding agencies, however, have different regulations for meta-analysis. Some universities consider meta-analysis to be human subjects research and require IRB sign-off as exempt research. In any case, it is wise to check the regulations with funders and IRB review committees well in advance of starting a meta-analysis project.

As in all research, obtaining funding is an integral part of any project. We were fortunate in this case that Soydan's Center for the Evaluation of Social Services was interested in funding the project. We had already done the bulk of the work as part of the larger project (which has been funded over the years by the National Institute of Mental Health and the Russell Sage Foundation). However, in all of our development work to obtain funding for this and other projects, we have been faced with similar difficulties. Reviewers for grant proposals are often not familiar with the technical details of conducting meta-analysis and (because no human subjects, stakeholders, and field settings are involved) may assume that meta-analysis is an inexpensive research method. While meta-analysis may be cheaper than conducting a large community-based demonstration project, it often costs more than reviewers expect. Some of our efforts to obtain funding for meta-analysis projects have been criticized by reviewers for being too expensive. As meta-analysis in social science fields becomes more common and the details of the methodology become better known, perhaps funding opportunities will be more commensurate with the actual costs of the research.

STRENGTHS AND LIMITATIONS

The biggest limitation of the article is, I believe, the limited description of the treatment programs. We used very broad treatment categories and there are certainly differences between programs in these categories. A more detailed study of the different program ingredients and the effectiveness of these ingredients would certainly be relevant to social work practice. Of course we couldn't answer all of the interesting questions in a single article, and chose to focus on comparing minority and White delinquents instead. But one of the things I struggle with as a meta-analyst is how to apply the results of my work in the "real world." How can policy makers and practitioners make use of my findings? Does it help them to know that we found mainstream delinquency programs to be equally effective for minority juveniles as for Whites? While I find that the actual process of conducting a meta-analysis is interesting and fun and satisfies my curiosity about various topics, I endeavor to find ways that other people might find our work interesting and useful. I am not sure that the results of our project will stimulate any change in social work practice—and, in fact, I sometimes worry that the results might be used to preserve the status quo. Just because we found that minorities fared equally well in mainstream programs doesn't mean that issues of cultural sensitivity are unimportant or that culturally tailored programs wouldn't be beneficial. But, if mainstream programs work just as well for minorities and different treatment strategies are equally effective, practitioners can perhaps focus more energy on improving the delivery of programs rather than on finding the perfect program.

The biggest strength of the article is also one of the strengths of meta-analysis in general. As evidence-based practice becomes infused into the practice of social work, meta-analysis becomes more applicable and useful to social workers. Evidence-based practice requires that programs and courses of treatment have demonstrable evidence of their effectiveness. A single evaluation study of a program may show that the program is effective, but the program may only be effective in the particular setting in which it was evaluated, or for youth that have similar characteristics to those in the evaluation study. Meta-analysis, however—by dealing with the full range of subjects, treatments, and research circumstances in a body of research—can present a synthesis of empirical findings that has more scope, depth, and generality than any one study can provide.

FINAL WORDS

As a graduate student learning how to do research, I heard my professors say that research always takes longer and is more expensive than expected, and never turns out as planned. But confident graduate students never seem to listen to this advice. Of course my professors were right, but I had to figure that out for myself. Research is hard, and it takes a long time, is expensive, and the project you thought you were going to do is rarely the one you end up doing. Knowing these things doesn't keep us from getting discouraged. Learning how to manage people, maintain flexibility, and stay positive is as important as understanding the technical aspects of research.

REFERENCES

Cooper, H., & Hedges, L. V. (Eds.). (1994). *The handbook of research synthesis*. New York: Russell Sage.

Lipsey, M. W. (1992). Juvenile delinquency treatment: A meta-analytic inquiry into the variability of effects. In T. D. Cook, H. Cooper, D. S. Cordray, H. Hartmann, L. V. Hedges, R. J. Light, T. A. Louis, & F. Mosteller (Eds.), *Meta-analysis for explanation: A casebook* (pp. 83–127). New York: Russell Sage.

Lipsey, M. W. (1994). Identifying potentially interesting variables and analysis opportunities. In H. Cooper & L. V. Hedges (Eds.), *The handbook of research synthesis* (pp. 111–124). New York: Russell Sage.

Lipsey, M. W. (1995). What do we learn from 400 research studies on the effectiveness of treatment with juvenile delinquents? In J. McGuire (Ed.), *What works? Reducing reoffending—Guidelines from research and practice* (pp. 63–78). New York: Wiley.

Lipsey, M. W., & Wilson, D. B. (1998). Effective intervention for serious juvenile offenders: A synthesis of research. In R. Loeber & D. P. Farrington (Eds.), *Serious and violent juvenile offenders: Risk factors and successful interventions* (pp. 313–345). Thousand Oaks, CA: Sage.

Lipsey, M. W., & Wilson, D. B. (2001). *Practical meta-analysis*. Applied Social Research Methods Series, vol. 49. Thousand Oaks, CA: Sage.

Pigott, T. D. (1994). Methods for handling missing data in research synthesis. In H. Cooper & L. V. Hedges (Eds.), *The handbook of research synthesis* (pp. 163–176). New York: Russell Sage.

Wilson, S. J., & Lipsey, M. W. (2000). Wilderness challenge programs for delinquent youth: A meta-analysis of outcome evaluations. *Evaluation and Program Planning, 23,* 1–12.

Correlational/Observational Designs

The research studies in this section exemplify what are commonly referred to as observational studies. In these designs, the researcher does not intervene by manipulating the independent variable(s). As a result, the researcher needs to determine whether there is any naturally occurring relationship between the independent and dependent variables. For this reason, these designs are also frequently referred to as correlational designs. The most common of these are cross-sectional, in that all data for both the independent and dependent variables are collected at the same time. The fact that both independent and dependent variables are obtained at the same time makes determining the directionality of the relationship between them or the temporal ordering of variables problematic. Since the dependent variable is what is being explained or predicted, the researcher must be assured that the independent variable occurred prior to the dependent variable. A phenomenon (a variable) that occurs after cannot explain or predict a phenomenon (a variable) that occurs before. The directionality problem makes it difficult to claim cause-and-effect relationships. One of the commentaries specifically discusses this directionality problem.

Longitudinal designs compensate for this temporal order problem by collecting data over time; this process makes it very clear that the independent variable(s) occurred before the dependent variable. When collecting data over time, the researcher must be able to gather these data from each of the original participants, at each of the data collection points. However, this can be a particular problem when doing primary data collection from participants who may be difficult to locate and/or may refuse to be reinterviewed. Hence, one of the commentaries discusses how the amount of missing data necessitated changing the analysis procedure. This problem can also occur in secondary data analysis, when using agency administrative data.

Case control designs consist of groups constituted on the basis of the presence or absence of a characteristic of interest to the study. One group has the characteristic of interest (cases) and the other group does not have the characteristic of interest (controls). In these designs, the characteristic of interest is the outcome or dependent variable; for example, homeless or not, sexually abused or not, or victim of domestic violence or not. Major concerns with these designs are assuring that the two groups are mutually exclusive, with controls never being cases, and that the two groups come from the same population. If the two groups come from different populations, it is not clear whether the differences are related to the outcome of interest or to the characteristics of the different populations.

Unfortunately, case control designs are not frequently used in human services. They should be used more often—we sometimes find studies in journals that inappropriately talk about risk factors for homelessness or child abuse, for example, when the sample only contains homeless individuals or victims of child abuse. Case control designs can be useful in providing direction for the development of evidence-based practices for at-risk groups. Other observational/correlational designs provide preliminary evidence for potential evidence-based practices.

7

Client-Service Matching in Substance Abuse Treatment for Women with Children

Brenda D. Smith, Ph.D. and Jeanne C. Marsh, Ph.D.

INTRODUCTION

Growing recognition of the large number of problems that co-occur with substance abuse has fostered interest in matching client needs with appropriate services. Many providers, policy makers, and researchers have observed that medical, psychiatric, economic, family, and legal problems contribute to the development of substance abuse problems and can serve as impediments to their reduction. Some argue substance abuse treatment is more effective when health, mental health, parenting, housing, and legal issues are addressed along with substance abuse issues (McLellan & McKay, 1998). Further, some believe *matching* services to clients' diverse medical, psychological, and social needs contributes positively to client retention in treatment, satisfaction, and outcome. However, others suggest the overall effectiveness of substance abuse treatment may be reduced if limited resources are diverted from primary substance abuse treatment activities (Fiorentine, 1998). Some evidence supports both positions.

This study focuses on the relation between the provision of health and social services and specific substance abuse treatment outcomes. It examines service delivery in a large public service system and focuses on a traditionally underserved client population: women with children. Specifically, the study examines the impact of health and social services matched to client-identified needs on the treatment outcomes of substance use and client satisfaction.

Reprinted from Smith, B. D., Marsh, J. C. (2002). Client-service matching in substance abuse treatment for women with children. *Journal of Substance Abuse Treatment, 22,* 161–168. Copyright 2002 with permission from Elsevier.

Background

Health and social services seem to improve substance abuse treatment outcomes, especially, perhaps, when services are tailored to individual client needs (Hser, 1995; Hser, Polinsky, Maglione, & Anglin, 1999; Joe, Simpson, & Hubbard, 1991; Marlatt, 1988). McLellan and colleagues conducted a series of studies showing the majority of treatment clients have a substantial number of addiction-related problems; the severity of these problems is generally a negative predictor of outcome; services directed at these problems can be delivered in treatment settings; and these services can be effective in improving the results of substance abuse treatment (McLellan & McKay, 1998). In a study specifically focused on matching services to service needs, McLellan et al. (1997) randomly assigned men and women to either a standard or matched service condition. Clients in the matched condition were provided with three individual sessions in the areas of employment, family/social relations, or psychiatric health if these were identified needs based on the Addiction Severity Index (ASI). Findings showed matched clients were more likely than standard clients to complete treatment and to show improvement in psychiatric and employment areas. In addition, both groups showed significant reductions in substance use, but matched clients were significantly less likely to be retreated for substance abuse problems during the 6-month follow-up period. This study points to possible advantages of service matching. It also raises several questions to be addressed in studies of service matching: (1) how should treatment providers and researchers identify client problems or service needs?; (2) which service characteristics should be matched?; (3) how will service delivery and service matches be measured?; and (4) how will treatment outcomes be defined and measured?

Identifying Client Problems and Service Needs. Researchers have attempted to relate client characteristics, such as age, race, gender, socioeconomic status, IQ, and marital status, to treatment outcome. In general, this research has shown weak and inconsistent results (Hser, 1995; Marsh & Miller, 1985; McLellan & Alterman, 1991). Research focusing specifically on client problems and needs has provided more promising direction (Joe et al., 1991; McLellan et al., 1997; McLellan & McKay, 1998). In the study described above, McLellan et al. (1997) identified client needs with the ASI, an assessment interview in which clients are asked to report their level of functioning in seven major areas including alcohol and substance abuse. Hser et al. (1999) defined client service needs as explicit client requests for services. Their study emphasizes the importance of client opinions, rather than staff opinions, when assessing service needs. More work is needed to determine the optimum means of assessing client service needs.

Which Service Characteristics Are Matched. Often substance abuse treatment has been conceptualized in terms of setting or modality (i.e., inpatient, outpatient, partial hospitalization, methadone maintenance). In general, studies assessing the effect of matching clients to the most appropriate treatment modality have found no improvement in client outcomes (McLellan & McKay, 1998). McLellan et al. (1997) wrote, "Our initial attempts to 'match' substance abuse patients from an employee assistance program to an optimal setting or program failed. Scientifically, we found no differential predictors of better outcomes by setting or program" (p. 730). McLellan and Alterman (1991) and others point out a variety of services can be provided within any one setting and those services represent the active ingredients of treatment most likely to affect outcome. As a result, in recent studies, treatment has been conceptualized in terms of specific services, such as counseling, health care, child care, and employment services. In some studies, services have been measured in terms of program contact in a particular area (Marsh, D'Aunno, & Smith, 2000). In others, particularly those utilizing the Treatment Services Review (McLellan, Alterman, Cacciola, Metzger, & O'Brien, 1992), services have been measured in terms of contact with a specialist (e.g., doctor, nurse, family therapist, employment specialist) and/or as engagement in discussion sessions (e.g., group or individual counseling about drug problems, family therapy sessions, AA/NA meetings).

Measuring Service Delivery and Service Matches. Service delivery and service-need matches can be measured in several ways including: the overall number of services received, the number of needed or requested services received, and the ratio of matched service needs to the total number of service needs. Studies suggest clients receiving more services have better outcomes (Broome, Simpson, & Joe, 1999; McLellan, Arndt, Metzger, Woody, & O'Brien, 1993; McLellan et al., 1998). A question remains as to whether a higher number of *any* services will have the same positive effects as a similar number of services *matched* to client needs.

Studies of matched services, measured either as a total number or as a ratio, have taken two major directions. First, studies have examined the proportion of client-identified needs that are met in substance abuse programs. Recent research shows in substance abuse services overall, substantial proportions of client needs are not met. For example, Joe et al. (1991) found in a large sample of methadone maintenance clients in 21 clinics in Texas, 46% received the services they felt they needed. Marsh et al. (2000) found among a sample of women clients in Illinois, the percentage of clients receiving services for identified needs ranged from 79% for HIV counseling to 4% for housing assistance. Second, service matching research has examined the capacity for both met and unmet service needs to predict treatment outcomes. In general, there appears to be a relation between met service needs and positive treatment outcomes, but little relation between unmet needs and outcome. At least two studies have focused specifically on the effects of unmet or unresolved needs. Joe et al. (1991) found unmet needs were unrelated to treatment satisfaction or to retention in treatment. And Fiorentine (1998) found unresolved needs, defined as problems identified at treatment entry for which clients continued to desire assistance, were unrelated to treatment engagement or to drug use. However, in a study of 171 clients participating in a community-based drug treatment program, Hser et al. (1999) found clients with higher ratios of met service needs both stayed in treatment longer and showed more improvement in corresponding problem areas than did clients with lower ratios of met service needs.

Defining and Measuring Substance Abuse Treatment Outcomes. Defining and measuring client outcomes constitutes another challenge when assessing the effects of service matching. Although the primary outcome of interest in substance abuse services research has been level of substance use, other outcomes of interest include: (1) retention in services; (2) satisfaction with services; and (3) health and social functioning in areas where services were received, such as employment, housing, or mental health. A first critical question has been whether the provision of health and social services, in addition to substance abuse services, can affect social functioning as well as substance use. Studies by McLellan and colleagues (McLellan et al., 1993; McLellan et al., 1998) have shown substance abuse services alone have positive effects on substance use but very little impact beyond that. However, when substance abuse services are enhanced with health and social services, particularly employment counseling, family therapy, and psychiatric sessions, substance use decreases and social functioning improves. These findings led the authors to conclude "addiction services combined with social services are the 'necessary and sufficient' conditions for truly effective treatment" (McLellan et al., 1993, p. 1498).

A second key question centers on which treatment outcomes are affected by tailored or matched services. Overall, the research to date suggests when clients receive services responding to identified needs, clients tend to stay in services longer (Hser et al., 1999), reduce their substance use (Woody et al., 1984), and improve functioning in areas where they have received targeted services (McLellan et al., 1997; Woody et al., 1984). A primary concern remains whether matched services compromise reductions in substance use typically achieved in substance abuse treatment.

A summary of existing research points to possible enhancement of treatment outcomes when client-identified service needs are matched with services delivered. Yet, this research leaves several questions unanswered. Does the provision of services matched to needs affect outcomes differently than the provision of any health and social services? Will matched service needs improve treatment outcomes when many service needs remain unmet? What types of treatment outcomes are most clearly related to matched services? Do certain types of matched services relate to certain types of treatment outcomes? And, do findings of the possible advantages of service matching in largely white, male, employed samples translate to female, largely African American, and unemployed samples?

It is the purpose of this research to illustrate approaches for addressing some remaining questions related to client-service matching. The research addresses the question of whether treatment outcomes are affected when substance abuse treatment is expanded to address a range of health and social needs. Specifically, the research examines the impact of matching client-identified needs for counseling and ancillary services on the treatment outcomes of substance use and client satisfaction. It assesses whether matched service needs relate to treatment outcomes, independent of the total number of health and social services a client receives. By identifying the relation between specific service types and specific outcomes, the study examines which ingredients of substance abuse treatment relate to which substance abuse outcomes. Finally, this study focuses on a sample that is female, predominantly African American, mostly unemployed, and involved with public services. This multiproblem sample with many service needs reflects the population typically served by public human service systems in the US.

METHODS

Study Design

The study is an analysis of survey data collected for an evaluation of an enhanced substance abuse treatment program for clients of the child welfare system (see Marsh et al., 2000). The evaluation study contained three groups: enhanced treatment, regular treatment, and a control group comprised of child welfare clients identified as substance users who may or may not have attended substance abuse treatment. This study uses data from all evaluation participants who had attended substance abuse treatment in the 24 months prior to being interviewed.

Sample and Procedure

Survey respondents came from a randomly selected sample of women with children who had contact with the Illinois child welfare system. Introductory letters invited respondents to call to set up a private interview, either at their treatment site or at a university office.[1] The study followed procedures to protect human subjects; survey respondents provided written informed consent; and the study was monitored by a university institutional review board. Of the 673 sample members,

---

[1] A $25 incentive was offered to each respondent, and $40 was provided to treatment sites for helping to locate each respondent.

203 were located and 199 completed interviews for a response rate of 30%. Of these, 183 met the criterion for this study of having attended treatment within the past 24 months.

Response Bias Assessment

The low survey response rate heightens concern that survey respondents differ from nonrespondents in ways that could affect the study findings. Administrative data on all sample members enabled us to compare respondents to nonrespondents to assess possible bias in 31 separate variables including demographic characteristics, severity and type of substance use problems, employment status, and income. The two groups did not differ on 25 of the variables examined. Nonetheless, the results of these analyses show that respondents were: (1) more likely to be African American and married; (2) less likely to have health coverage (including Medicaid); (3) more likely to use heroin and methadone treatment; and (4) more likely to have currently open child welfare cases. Whereas these findings suggest certain ways the respondents differ from nonrespondents, and indicate certain ways (e.g., medical coverage, child welfare case, heroin use) respondents may face greater obstacles than nonrespondents, it is difficult to assess all possible effects of response bias on the study findings. In the best case, the study findings could be generalized to urban mothers having some involvement with the child welfare system. However, the low response rate suggests just as with studies using nonprobability sampling techniques, caution should be used in generalizing the findings.

Measures

The survey instrument contained sections on substance use and substance abuse treatment, service need and service receipt, demographic and family characteristics, health and mental health, and experiences in the child welfare system. Respondents were asked about the use of alcohol and six illicit substances including: marijuana, hallucinogens, cocaine, heroin, recreational methadone, and sedatives. Respondents were asked about use of each substance in their lifetime, in the past 24 months, and in the past 30 days. The instrument also contained detailed questions on eight types of substance abuse treatment including: self-help meetings, detoxification, halfway houses, long- and short-term residential care, outpatient and intensive outpatient, and methadone treatment. Respondents were asked about attendance in each treatment type in the past 24 months and past 30 days. Study variables are described in Table 7.1.

Description of Survey Respondents

The respondents in this study share characteristics of poor urban women who are clients of substance abuse treatment facilities and the child welfare system. The respondents range in age from 22 to 49, with a mean age of 33. The vast majority (83%) of the study participants are African American; 11% are white; 2% are Hispanic; and the remainder are other or unidentified. About half have completed high school; just over one-fourth are employed, and a similar percentage have annual incomes over $10,000 per year. Just over half of the respondents were involved with the child welfare system at the time of the interview. A similar portion had children at home, whereas the remainder had all of their children placed in substitute care. Most respondents reported their physical health (93%) and emotional health (88%) to be good; 7% of the respondents reported their physical health to be poor or very poor, and 12% reported their emotional health to be poor or very poor. In other indicators of health and mental health, 26% reported having a chronic illness, and 19% reported a psychiatric hospitalization in the past 6 months. Most respondents (79%) reported smoking regularly during the past year. Cocaine is the illicit substance used by most respondents; 60% reported using cocaine in the 30 days prior to entering treatment.

Table 7.1. Variable Definitions

Variable	Definition
Dependent variables	
Substance use	Respondents were asked whether their current substance use was less than, greater than, or about the same as it was before starting treatment. This is a dichotomous variable indicating whether or not a respondent reported less substance abuse than before starting treatment. Twenty-eight percent of respondents reported that their substance use was the same or greater than before starting treatment; 72% of respondents reported that their substance abuse was less than before starting treatment.
Client satisfaction with treatment (Treatment helped a lot)	In a section of the survey focusing on satisfaction with services, respondents were asked about the extent to which a treatment program had helped them to control substance use. This is a dichotomous variable indicating whether or not a respondent reported that treatment had helped a great deal. Forty percent of respondents reported that treatment had helped somewhat or not at all; 60% of respondents reported that the treatment program had helped a great deal.
Independent variables	
Number of services	A continuous variable indicating the total number of supplementary services a respondent received at her treatment facility.
Number of matched service needs	A continuous variable indicating the number of a respondent's matched service needs. When an expressed service need corresponds to a service received, it is counted as a matched service need.
Matched services ratio	The ratio of matched service needs to reported service needs.
Matched ancillary service needs	A dichotomous variable indicating a matched service of legal help, housing, or job training.
	Thirteen percent of the respondents had an ancillary services match.
Matched counseling service needs	A dichotomous variable indicating a matched service of domestic violence counseling, sexual abuse counseling, or family counseling. Twenty-four percent of the respondents had a counseling service match.
Substance use prior to treatment	A continuous variable indicating the number of days in the 30 days prior to entering treatment that a respondent reported using the 4 substances used most by these respondents: cocaine, heroin, marijuana, and alcohol (5 drinks or more).
Days in treatment	A continuous variable indicating the number of days from the time a respondent entered treatment and either the interview date or the treatment exit date.
Attended treatment in last 30 days	A dichotomous variable indicating whether or not a respondent was attending substance abuse treatment in the 30 days prior to the interview.

Statistical Analysis

We conducted bivariate Chi-Squares and *t*-tests to assess the association between several service use variables and the dependent variables. Multivariate logistic regression models were conducted to assess whether matched services remain associated with the dependent variables after accounting for factors such as the severity of substance use, length of treatment, number of service needs, and total number of services used.

RESULTS

Matched Service Needs

Table 7.2 shows the percentage of study respondents reporting needs for a range of services. Medical care, job training, and housing assistance were the types of services for which the highest portion of respondents reported a need. The table also shows service receipt for all study respondents and for the subset of respondents who had reported a service need. In general, the table reflects a substantial portion of respondents reporting a service need did not receive services corresponding to the need. Unmatched service needs were particularly high for legal help, housing assistance, medical check-ups, and job training.

Association Between Matched Service Needs and Treatment Effects

Table 7.3 shows bivariate relationships between two treatment outcomes and three measures of service use: the total number of services used, the total number of matched service needs, and a matched services ratio. At a bivariate level, all three services variables are positively associated with client satisfaction. The number of services used is associated with reporting less substance use, but neither measure of *matched* service needs is significantly associated with reporting less substance

Table 7.2. Reported Service Needs and Service Receipt

		Percent Reporting Service Receipt	
Service	Percent Reporting Service Need	Of All Respondents	Of Those Reporting a Service Need
Medical care	70%	16%—check up 30%—reproductive	13%—check up 29%—reproductive
Child care	46%	27%	44%
Domestic violence counseling	32%	43%	47%
Family counseling	54%	25%	28%
Job training/counseling	62%	16%	16%
Housing assistance	56%	6%	10%
Legal help	33%	7%	8%
Assistance with public benefits	45%	18%	28%

n = 183.

Table 7.3. *T*-test of Treatment Outcomes by Service Need and Use Indicators

		Number of Services Used				Number of Met Service Needs				Ratio of Met Service Needs to Expressed Service Needs			
		Mean	SD	t	p	Mean	SD	t	p	Mean	SD	t	p
Treatment helped a lot	Yes (*n* = 110)	5.4	3.05	4.29	< .001	1.32	1.56	2.84	.005	.26	.33	3.32	.001
	No (*n* = 73)	3.6	2.45			.77	1.06			.12	.23		
Less substance use	Yes (*n* = 132)	4.9	2.91	1.98	.05	1.18	1.41	1.29	.20	.22	.31	1.37	.17
	No (*n* = 51)	4.0	2.95			.88	1.39			.16	.37		

use. Thus, these relationships suggest matched service needs are related to the perception that treatment is helpful, but not to reports of less substance abuse.

Types of Matched Service Needs

We explored whether the two treatment outcomes were related to types of matched services in Chi-Squares tests of these relationships. Matched counseling services (domestic violence services, family counseling) were associated, albeit weakly, with reports of less substance use ($\chi^2 = 3.756$, $p = .05$); matched ancillary services (housing, job training, legal services) were associated with client satisfaction ($\chi^2 = 6.213$, $p = .01$).

A multivariate test of one of these relationships is shown in Table 7.4. Model 1 indicates when controlling for client and service characteristics, matched ancillary services remain positively associated with client satisfaction. Model 2 addresses the question: Is client satisfaction related to matched services, per se, or is it simply receipt of supplementary services in general that relates to client satisfaction? When the variable for the total number of services used is included in Model 2, the effect of matched ancillary services is not significant. This model suggests while matched ancillary services might be related to client satisfaction, this relationship may be largely accounted for by the receipt of supplementary services in general.

Table 7.4. Logistic Regression of Service Need Matching and Client Satisfaction

| | Treatment Helped a Lot | | | | | |
| | Model 1 | | | Model 2 | | |
Variable	B	SE	Odds Ratio	B	SE	Odds Ratio
Match concrete service needs	1.19†	.64	3.28	.13	.75	1.14
Days in treatment	.0014†	.0008	1.001	.0013	.0008	1.001
Treatment in last 30 days	1.2**	.39	3.32	1.05**	.40	2.86
Substance use prior to treatment	.0004	.014	1.00	−.006	.014	.99
High school education	.71*	.37	2.03	.69†	.38	1.99
Income >$10,000	−.49	.42	.61	−.58	.44	.56
Children at home	.72*	.37	2.06	.82†	.39	2.28
Physical health good	−1.34	.84	.26	−1.22	.89	.29
Emotional health good	1.99**	.76	7.32	2.10**	.77	8.1
Used alcohol prior to treatment	.005	.41	1.005	−.04	.42	.96
Used cocaine prior to treatment	.37	.44	1.44	.46	.45	1.59
Used marijuana prior to treatment	−.23	.50	.79	−.12	.52	.88
Used heroin prior to treatment	−.96†	.52	.38	−.73	.54	.48
Number of needs	−.04	.09	.96	−.02	.10	.98
Number of services used				.23**	.08	1.25
Constant	−2.03	1.09		−3.09	1.22	
	−2 log likelihood 246.159 ($\chi^2 = 48.76$, df 14, $p < .001$)			−2 log likelihood 188.825 ($\chi^2 = 57.33$, df 15, $p < .001$)		

*$p < .05$.

**$p < .01$.

†$p < .10$.

DISCUSSION

Data Limitations

In addition to the low survey response rate and the possible areas of response bias suggested above, several data limitations should be considered when evaluating the study findings. First, the study relies on data collected for another purpose. Consequently, the study design is not ideally suited to address the research questions. In particular, the cross-sectional evaluation survey relies on retrospective reports of substance use, service needs, and service use. Second, many of the measures are limited. The analysis rests on dichotomous measures of ongoing substance use and satisfaction with services. The measures of service use do not reflect treatment quality or intensity. Plus, substance use and service use are measured through self reports only. Despite these important limitations, we believe the study, at minimum, illustrates approaches to addressing some key remaining questions about matching services to service needs.

Discussion of Findings

Albeit tempered by the data limitations discussed above, the following findings are suggested by this study: (1) The substance abuse treatment clients in this study—poor, urban women with children, who had participated in substance abuse treatment program and who had contact with the child welfare system—reported many service needs. Overall, few of these needs were addressed by their substance abuse treatment programs. (2) Clients receiving more health and social services reported better outcomes, both in substance use and in satisfaction with services. (3) When services were matched to needs, matched counseling services were associated with reports of less substance use, and matched ancillary services (legal help, housing, job training) were associated with client satisfaction. (4) When the total number of services a client received was taken into account, the relationships between matched services and treatment outcome lost statistical significance.

A salient, if unsurprising, finding is the substance abuse treatment clients in this study had many service needs and relatively few (between 8% and 44%) were met. Ancillary service needs, such as legal help, housing assistance, and job training were less likely to be matched than counseling service needs. The study also found, for many services, service receipt was unrelated to clients' service needs. Respondents reporting a need for job training, for example, were as likely as respondents overall to receive job training.

This finding is not surprising when considering service provision in large public systems. Within any given treatment program, the most typical practice is to provide a standard protocol of services to each client in the program. This is consistent with the practice of matching clients to setting or modality rather than services, and does not result in meeting a significant number of specific client needs. The practice of conducting a thorough assessment that could permit tailoring or matching services to needs is not standard.

The second finding, that clients who used more services were more likely to report that treatment helped and to report less substance use, is consistent with findings of other studies (Broome et al., 1999; Marsh et al., 2000; McLellan et al., 1993, 1994, 1997, 1998). As with subjects of other studies, for these clients of public service systems, there seems to be a dosage effect operating, such that clients who receive more services have better outcomes.

Third, the study begins to specify which individually tailored services might relate to which treatment outcomes. Although the relationships identified are weak, possibly due to the limited number of matched services, the relationships between counseling services and reporting less substance use, and between ancillary services and client satisfaction merit further study. A post hoc explanation suggests while counseling activities engaged clients in treatment in a way that enabled them to reduce their substance use, the provision of ancillary services enhanced clients' lives more broadly, increasing their satisfaction with the program, or their perception that it was helpful.

Finally, this study examined the relative impact of matched services and total number of services. For this group of women substance abuse clients having many service needs, the total number of health and social services received had a stronger association with treatment outcomes than did services specifically matched to needs. These relationships could be better explored if more service needs were matched. The treatment clients surveyed in this study reported an average of nearly five service needs, but had only one matched service need. Still, this finding raises questions about the efficacy of service matching in a context of many unmet service needs.

Although the data limitations suggest caution in interpretation and generalization, this study contributes to a body of research indicating substance abuse treatment is enhanced when health and social services are provided. The study suggests direction to future studies addressing the value of matching services to client-identified needs. In particular, the study points to the value of future research that will more clearly specify the conditions under which tailored services will improve substance abuse treatment outcomes.

ACKNOWLEDGMENTS

This research was supported by the Illinois Department of Children and Family Services, the Office of Alcohol and Substance Abuse of the Illinois Department of Human Services, and the Children and Family Research Center at the University of Illinois, Urbana-Champaign, IL. Portions of this paper were presented at the Society for Social Work and Research Annual Conference, San Diego, CA, January 18, 2002.

REFERENCES

Broome, K. M., Simpson, D. D., & Joe, G. W. (1999). Patient and program attributes related to treatment process indicators in DATOS. *Drug and Alcohol Dependence, 57,* 127–135.

Fiorentine, R. (1998). Effective drug treatment: testing the distal needs hypothesis. *Journal of Substance Abuse Treatment, 15*(4), 281–289.

Hser, Y. (1995). A referral system that matches drug users to treatment program: existing research and relevant issues. *Journal of Drug Issues, 25,* 153–168.

Hser, Y., Polinsky, M. L., Maglione, M., & Anglin, M. D. (1999). Matching clients' needs with drug treatment services. *Journal of Substance Abuse Treatment, 16*(4), 299–305.

Joe, G. W., Simpson, D. D., & Hubbard, R. L. (1991). Unmet service needs in methadone maintenance. *International Journal of the Addictions, 26,* 1–22.

Marlatt, G. A. (1988). Matching clients to treatment: treatment models and stages of change. In D. M. Donovan & G. A. Marlatt (Eds.), *Assessment of*

addictive behaviors: the Guilford Behavioral Assessment Series (pp. 474–483). New York: Guilford Press.

Marsh, J. C., D'Aunno, T. A., & Smith, B. D. (2000). Increasing access and providing social services to improve drug abuse treatment for women with children. *Addiction, 95*(8), 1237–1247.

Marsh, J. C., & Miller, N. A. (1985). Female clients in substance abuse treatment. *International Journal of the Addictions, 20* (6/7), 995–1019.

McLellan, A. T., & Alterman, A. I. (1991). Patient treatment matching: a conceptual and methodological review with suggestions for future research. In R. W. Pickens, C. G. Leukefeld, & C. R. Schuster (Eds.), *Improving drug abuse treatment.* NIDA Research Monograph 106, Washington, DC: DHHS publication number (ADM) 91–1754.

McLellan, A. T., Alterman, A. I., Cacciola, J., Metzger, D., & O'Brien, C. P. (1992). A new measure of substance abuse treatment: initial studies of the Treatment Services Review. *Journal of Nervous and Mental Disease, 180*(2), 101–110.

McLellan, A. T., Alterman, A. I., Metzger, D. S., Grissom, G. R., Woody, G. E., Luborsky, L., & O'Brien, C. P. (1994). Similarity of outcome predictors across opiate, cocaine, and alcohol treatments: role of treatment services. *Journal of Consulting and Clinical Psychology, 62*(6), 1141–1158.

McLellan, A. T., Arndt, I. O., Metzger, D. S., Woody, G. E., & O'Brien, C. P. (1993). The effects of psychosocial services in substance abuse treatment. *Journal of the American Medical Association, 269*(15), 1953–1959.

McLellan, A. T., Grissom, G. R., Zanis, D., Randall, M., Brill, P., & O'Brien, C. P. (1997). Problem-service matching in addiction treatment: a prospective study in four programs. *Archives of General Psychiatry, 54,* 730–735.

McLellan, T. A., Hagan, T. A., Levine, M., Gould, F., Meyers, K., Bencivengo, M., & Durrell, J. (1998). Supplemental social services improve outcomes in public addiction treatment. *Addiction, 93*(10), 1489–1499.

McLellan, T. A., & McKay, J. R. (1998). The treatment of addiction: what can research offer practice? In S. Lamb, M. R. Greenlick, & D. McCarty (Eds.), *Bridging the gap between practice and research: forging partnerships with community-based drug and alcohol treatment.* Washington, DC: National Academy Press.

Woody, G. E., McLellan, T. A., Luborsky, L., O'Brien, C. P., Blaine, J., Fox, S., Herman, I., & Beck, A. T. (1984). Psychiatric severity as a predictor of benefits from psychotherapy. *American Journal of Psychiatry, 141*(10), 1171–1177.

COMMENTARY BY: Jeanne C. Marsh and Brenda D. Smith

Learning from clients and soliciting their perception of their own service needs is a fundamental social work value and one that provides the organizing framework for our *Journal of Substance Abuse Treatment* article. This article builds on a series of prior studies conducted by the authors in the areas of substance abuse and child welfare services. Before working on this study, one author had completed a series of studies documenting the value of comprehensive services in the provision of substance abuse treatment for women (Marsh, 1982; Marsh & Miller, 1985). The second author had conducted an in-depth survey of mothers involved in the child welfare system who had delivered a substance-exposed infant. The results revealed both the significant service needs of these clients and the failure of the child welfare system to meet these needs (Smith, 2003). Immediately prior to work on the client-service matching paper, we both had collaborated on an evaluation of a program that integrated substance abuse and child welfare services for women involved in the child welfare system (Marsh, D'Aunno, & Smith, 2000).

As social work researchers, we were predisposed to pursue research questions related to clients' perspectives about service effectiveness. Our experience had shown us that we have few well-specified and tested models of service delivery in child welfare or substance abuse. However, we have fewer models to guide the integration of the delivery of substance abuse and child welfare services. Further, we knew from practice that child welfare services may consist primarily of parent training sessions, whereas substance abuse treatment can be limited to individual and/or group counseling sessions. We were concerned about the prevalence of so-called "cookie cutter" services in public social services, in which an assessment of client service needs is lacking and there is no effort to tailor service provision to specific client conditions (see Smith & Donovan, 2003, for a description of service delivery in child welfare settings).

Our predisposition for meeting client-specified needs influenced decision making at every stage of the research process, including (1) specification of the research question, (2) determination of the research design, (3) definition and measurement of the independent and dependent variables, and (4) analysis and interpretation of the data. This predisposition influenced the "true story behind the stylized story" that was ultimately accepted for publication. It is the "true story" that is the focus of this book and this commentary. The commentary is organized according to the research decisions relevant to this cross-sectional study that used data collected for another purpose. Specifically, we examine decisions related to articulating the research question, the research design,

---

Commentary on article: Smith, B. D., Marsh, J. C. (2002). Client-service matching in substance abuse treatment for women with children. *Journal of Substance Abuse Treatment, 22,* 161–168.

measuring independent and dependent variables, and analyzing and interpreting the strengths and limitations of the research.

DECISIONS ABOUT THE RESEARCH QUESTION

The basic question that concerned us in this research was whether treatment outcomes could be affected by the simple practice of asking clients what they need and then providing these services. Meeting client-specified needs is fundamental to good social work, but it has not received significant attention in child welfare or substance abuse. At the time we wrote the article, however, the idea of meeting client-specified needs had received some focus in the substance abuse literature under the rubric of patient-treatment *matching*. The concern at that time was related to matching patient types to setting or program types (rather than problems to services). McLellan and colleagues (1997) wrote that "this idea of 'matching' the right types of patients to the right kinds of programs has been as attractive to clinicians and administrators as it has been elusive to those who have tried to accomplish it" (p. 730). Influenced by this interest in the substance abuse treatment literature, we conceptualized our concern with meeting client-specified needs in terms of client-service matching. We carefully conceptualized the matching construct by drawing distinctions between the (mostly unsuccessful) patient-setting matching efforts in the literature and our interest in client-specified needs-service matching. Ultimately, we defined our research question objective as examining the impact of health and social services matched to client-identified needs on the treatment outcomes of substance use and client satisfaction.

DECISIONS ABOUT THE RESEARCH DESIGN

Some of the challenges we faced when conducting our study on needs-service matching resulted from the fact that we were using data collected for another study. As mentioned, the original study was a program evaluation that focused on the effects of an enhanced services program on substance abuse outcomes for women involved in the child welfare system. The evaluation data included items relevant to our research question; nonetheless, using the evaluation data presented us with some challenging decisions as we proceeded with the new study. The original study was quasi-experimental. This study used data from all evaluation participants who had attended substance abuse treatment. Thus, it used only parts of the data from the original quasi-experimental study, and study subjects were no longer differentiated according to types of treatment.

Ruling Out Alternative Explanations

A primary challenge in cross-sectional studies is that of establishing causal connections between independent and dependent variables. Given the purpose of our research, we were particularly interested in examining whether matched services "caused" changes in outcome variables. We know that causal inferences can be drawn appropriately when: (1) there is appropriate temporal ordering (i.e., when data collection for the independent variable precedes in time data collection for the dependent variable); (2) there is co-variation between independent and dependent variable; and (3) plausible alternative explanations can be eliminated. In some studies, various features of a particular research design contribute to the strength of the causal inference, e.g., by building—in a time lag between the measurement of variables in panel designs or by eliminating explanations related to selection in randomized experimentation. However, in cross-sectional studies that do not use random assignment, researchers must rely on theory and statistical manipulations to strengthen causal connections.

In this study, respondents reported on the services they needed, the services they received, their satisfaction with services and previous and current drug use—all at the same time in the same survey interview. As a result, reports of services needed and used were retrospective. The survey asked respondents about current drug use, and asked them to retrospectively recall aspects of their past drug use, drug treatment experience, service needs, and service receipt. Some of the respondents were currently attending treatment at the time of the interview, so they did not have to remember very far back when asked about "when you started treatment." Some respondents, however, had to remember as far back as two years earlier. It's likely that the quality of these responses varied. This was a tradeoff we needed to make to be able to use data from a one-time cross-sectional study as compared with a longitudinal study. Thus, we posited the temporal ordering of the independent and dependent variables and relied on client recall to empirically establish time-ordering between independent and dependent variables. When we developed the statistical model, we assumed the matched services were received prior to the client's assessment of the outcome variables of satisfaction and drug use. Further, we used statistical measures both to establish covariation and to rule out alternative explanations.

A likely alternative explanation in much social work research relates to selection, that is, the concern that findings are unique to the particular group participating in a study. In this study, subjects came from a probability sample, so that helped to rule out alternative explanations related to sample selection bias, one type of selection problem. We did not rely on service providers, for example, to recommend study subjects. The sample of potential subjects was randomly selected from the state administrative database of women with children who had contact with the Illinois child welfare system. However, even with this probability sample, a low survey response rate (related to the procedures used to recruit participants, described below) raised questions about another type of selection problem: response bias, or the possibility that survey respondents differed from nonrespondents. We were fortunate in this case to have administrative data on all sample members, whether they responded to the survey or not. With these data we were able to compare respondents to nonrespondents in characteristics such as number of children, age, race, and type of maltreatment allegation. Fortunately, we found that the respondents looked very much like the nonrespondents in these comparisons.

Survey Response

Although this study had the advantage of using a probability sample to select clients into the study sample from a population of mothers involved in the public child welfare system in Cook County, Illinois, as discussed above, the methods used to gain participation from sample members resulted in a low response rate. Sample members were contacted by letter to invite them to set up an interview at a treatment facility or university office. In addition, information about substance abuse treatment centers that sample members had attended was available from the database, and these substance abuse treatment centers were recruited to help contact sample members. Still, participating in the study required substantial initiative and follow-through on the part of the respondents. Given our experiences working with the population in the study (very poor women, mostly unemployed, and involved with public services), we should have recommended that the survey research organization we contracted with for data collection use a more proactive approach. We knew that this is a highly mobile population, reducing the chances that sample members would even receive an initial letter. In addition, a portion of the sample did not have telephone access, reducing the chances for phone follow-up. (In fact, contact was never established with 55 percent of the sample.) Many sample members faced transportation challenges, so requiring respondents to come to a treatment facility to complete the survey posed an additional barrier to participation. As mentioned, we had contracted with a survey research organization to oversee data collection. The advantage of this approach was that the survey research professionals could take over this demanding and challenging aspect of the study. The disadvantage was that we were a step removed from the data collection. If we had been more directly involved, perhaps we might have observed the challenges early on and intervened to modify the data collection strategy in ways that could have increased the survey response rate.

Ethics of Informed Consent

Each survey respondent provided informed consent for participation in the study. However, sample members had not given advance consent for the two state agencies to release contact information to the evaluation team. Nevertheless, the survey research organization we contracted with for data collection had access to contact information for all sample members. At the time, such access was considered justified because the evaluation study was considered an internal study of the Illinois Departments of Children and Family Services and Alcohol and Substance Abuse. State agency staff were involved in the early phases of the study; we were conducting the evaluation study at their request. Since the time when the evaluation data were collected, some state agencies have modified their practices regarding release of client contact information. It is possible that if the evaluation study were conducted today, all sample members would have had to sign a release explicitly providing access to their contact information. Under these procedures, it is possible some portion of the sample would disallow access to their information. Such approaches for the release of client contact information highlight a dilemma in the use of administrative data—the protection of client privacy can result in restricted samples when using administrative data.

DECISIONS ABOUT MEASUREMENT

Measuring a Service Match: Different Ways to Measure Have Different Benefits

To address the relationship between matched service needs and substance abuse treatment outcomes, we had several decisions to make. First, as outlined in our article, we considered various ways to operationalize a needs-service match. Measuring service use and service matches is one of the more challenging aspects of research in this area. No single measure grasps the full complexity of needs-service matching. We initially measured service use in three ways: as a ratio of met service needs to expressed service needs, as the total number of met service needs, and as the total number of services used (regardless of match to expressed need). Each of the alternative measures has advantages in different contexts. A ratio of met needs to expressed needs provides a relative measure of met needs, but two persons with the same ratio of met needs could have very different numbers of met and unmet needs. For example, a respondent with 1 service match for 2 needs (a ratio of .5) has 1 met need and only 1 unmet need, whereas another respondent with 3 service matches for 6 needs (also a ratio of .5) has 3 met needs and 3 unmet needs. Needs-services matches can also be operationalized as the total number of met needs. This measure can address comprehensiveness of service provision, but it fails to account for differences in the magnitude of unmet needs. A respondent with 3 matched services for 6 needs (a total of 3 matched needs) is likely to differ from a respondent with 3 matched services for 3 needs (also a total of 3 matched needs). Finally, the total number of services received, regardless of match, addresses the phenomenon we encountered in which clients sometimes received services even though they expressed no need for the service. A client might receive 3 services matched to needs and another 2 services addressing unexpressed needs. (Interestingly, we found that at the bivariate level all three measures of service receipt were associated with client satisfaction, but only the total number of services received was associated with a reduced likelihood of substance use.)

Another aspect of service matching involves the type of service matches. We decided to create separate variables for two types of service matches: concrete (or ancillary) services, and counseling services. The decision to make this distinction grew from our observation that the likelihood of service matches varied according to service type. Whereas service matches were low generally, they were particularly low for concrete services such as housing, public assistance, and legal assistance. Because the likelihood of service matches differed for the two types of services, we wondered if outcomes associated with matches of the two types of service might vary as well.

Having decided to address the two types of matches, we then had to decide how to specifically operationalize them. We might have created relatively complex variables such as a ratio of concrete services received to expressed concrete needs, but our limited sample size and the distribution of such ratio variables (primarily the fact that so many respondents had either no matched services or only one of any type), led us to decide to create dichotomous variables indicating any concrete services match versus no concrete services match, and any counseling services match versus no counseling services match. Hence, our choices in how to operationalize the match types were largely affected by practical considerations, such as the distribution of our data and limitations associated with the sample size. Without such limitations, we might have been able to operationalize the match type variables in ways that more closely reflected the conceptual complexity of needs-service matches.

Thus, we created variables to reflect the number of different service types respondents received, and whether or not respondents received any services to match their expressed concrete service needs or counseling service needs. In doing so, we understood that such variables indicate only a part of the complexity of service use. These variables, for example, do not reflect the number of sessions received of any given service type. A respondent who received three sessions total of a service, such as counseling, and another respondent who received three sessions per week over a sustained period of time would both be coded as having received one service type. Whether they would be coded as having a counseling services match would depend on whether they indicated counseling as a needed service. If not, even though they received counseling, they would not be coded as having a counseling services match. In addition, the quality of counseling and other types of services is likely to vary, yet our measures do not account for varying quality. Clearly, our study is limited by the fact that measures of service intensity and quality were not included.

The lack of more complex variables on service use was partly a consequence of using data collected for another purpose. If we had designed our survey with this study of service matching in mind, the survey might have contained more questions to elicit details about service receipt. The evaluation study was primarily focused on the overall effects of an enhanced services package, and of the effects of receiving any of some particular service types. It was not primarily concerned with the details of service needs and service matching. Furthermore, the evaluation survey was very long. It included substantial detail on current and past substance use for a long list of different types of substances. It also included a long list of questions about each respondent's children (up to nine children).

Our rationale for using a self-reported measure of substance use had much to do with wanting to simplify the data collection, and partly with our desire to focus the research on the clients' perspectives. The self-reported measure surely is affected by the possibility of social desirability bias. As they all had contact with child protective services, these respondents may have felt pressures to minimize or disguise their substance use. To defend our use of the self-reported measure, we cited research indicating that self-report measures have validity when compared to other measures. Still, we understand that there are some good reasons for suspicion of self reports, especially for these respondents who faced such scrutiny from public services and who had so much at stake. A better test of our research questions about the effects of matched services versus any services on substance use might have used a variety of outcome measures of substance use, including self reports and other tests. Respondent reports of whether their substance use was less than, the same as, or more than before starting treatment might have been compared to other measures, such as hair or urine tests, assessing substance use before treatment and at the time of the survey. Obviously, such tests would have required a more elaborate study design, including more than one time of data collection.

Choosing Dependent Variables That Reflect the Clients' Perspectives

Substance use is an obvious outcome variable to assess for persons in drug treatment, but there are many aspects of substance use and many ways to measure it. We had collected a range of data on current and past substance use. All of the data was self-reported from survey respondents, so any measures involving tests (such as urine screens) or third-party observations were not an option. The evaluation survey had included questions on amount of substance use in the 30 days prior to the interview, the types of substance use in the past 30 days, and how current use level compared to the use level prior to treatment. In the evaluation study, we initially considered some continuous outcome variables that indicated the amount of commonly used illicit substances and alcohol used in the past 30 days, for example. However, these continuous variables had very skewed distributions (68 percent of respondents reported no substance use in the 30 days prior to the interview). Hence, for the evaluation analysis, we decided to create a dichotomous variable distinguishing some use in the 30 days prior to the survey interview from no use in the 30 days before the interview.

In this study, we wanted to avoid using an all-or-nothing, abstinence-focused approach in the conceptualization of substance use. Rather, we wanted to consider a more flexible harm-reduction approach. Consequently, we focused on a survey question in which respondents reported whether their substance use was less, more, or the same since starting treatment. Both because we considered a report of less use to be substantively distinct from a report of the same or more use, and because we preferred a dichotomous outcome variable to a three-category variable for ease of statistical manipulation, we created a dichotomous dependent variable distinguishing respondents who reported less substance use posttreatment from those who reported the same or more substance use.

Unlike the evaluation study, in this matching study, we did not want to focus only on the substance use dependent variable. We wanted a second dependent variable that reflected clients' assessment of the treatment experience, regardless of its effect on posttreatment substance use. The concept we focused on, client satisfaction with treatment, which was indicated by respondent reports that "treatment helped a lot," reflects our view that substance abuse treatment clients might want something other than, or in addition to, reduced substance use from substance abuse treatment. This second dependent variable distinguished clients who reported having been helped "a great deal" (for whatever reason) by substance abuse treatment from those who reported having been helped only "somewhat" or "not at all." With this second dependent variable we were acknowledging that a client might achieve reduced substance abuse from substance abuse treatment, yet not feel helped substantially; or, conversely, a client might feel helped a great deal, even without reduced substance abuse. We thought that such feelings of being helped could be a first step toward later reduced substance abuse, or toward other positive outcomes. As with the other dependent variable, we had both substantive and practical reasons for making this second dependent variable a dichotomous variable. Substantively, we felt that very satisfied clients were distinct from somewhat or unsatisfied clients; practically, the dichotomous variable allowed us to conduct similar types of analysis with the two dependent variables.

In sum, the outcome variables we created and used in our analysis partly reflected decisions based on conceptualization, and partly reflected decisions made for more mundane and practical reasons. For example, we chose a substance use outcome variable that reflected client reports of improvement, rather than their reports of any use versus no use, because we recognized that client perceptions of improvement have substantive and conceptual importance distinct from reports of abstinence. At the same time, however, the variables we created also reflect the distribution of the data (highly skewed distributions led us to dichotomize some variables, for example) and our preference for variables coded in ways that we found easier to use (two categories versus three categories, for example). Finally, our choices were made in the context of having survey data collected for another purpose.

DECISIONS ABOUT INTERPRETATION AND
GENERALIZATION OF FINDINGS

Several significant findings emerged from this research. These findings clearly support the idea that meeting client-identified service needs improves treatment effectiveness. They also show a strong relation between the absolute number of services provided and outcomes, measured in terms of reduced substance use and client satisfaction. But we had to ask ourselves, "How do we interpret these findings? How much confidence can we place in them?"

Our answer to the question of how much confidence we could place in these findings ultimately depended on our assessment of the overall strengths and limitations of the study. The reviewers and editors of the journal to which we submitted the article had to make this same judgment. In order to decide whether or not to publish the article, they had to ask themselves how much confidence they were willing to place in the findings. They had to assess the overall strengths and weaknesses of the study.

As authors, our sense was that the strengths of this study derived from the fact that it was well conceptualized, with high relevance for practice. Basic practice issues related to the value of assessment for tailoring services to client needs, and the relation of tailored services to outcomes, were conceptualized and tested in terms of client-service matching. The conceptualizations and measurement drew heavily on the social work understanding that clients know best what their service needs are. Understanding the impact of client-specified services was a topic of great practice relevance. Happily, the article reviewers and journal editor agreed with us. They liked our conceptualization of client-service matching very much. Because the journal editor was an expert in the area of substance abuse treatment and had written an important article on client-service matching, it was gratifying that he liked our conceptualization. Further, we believed the study's primary limitations derived from the survey data we used, data that had originally been collected for another purpose. Under ideal circumstances, we might have conducted a brand new study using instruments specifically designed to address our questions about needs-service matching. The reviewers and editors agreed with us on this point, too. They asked us to revise the article to emphasize our conceptualization and tone down our focus on the study findings. Particular weaknesses included the survey response rate, the use of cross-sectional data relying on retrospective reports, and limitations to generalizability of findings.

Low Survey Response Rate

The low survey response rate (30 percent) was a particular concern. We were applying a rule of thumb of 75–85 percent for an adequate response rate in services research. Clearly, the response rate of 30 percent in this study was far from the mark. Given the low response rate, a saving grace was that we had administrative data about the entire sample. We could use these data to examine how survey respondents compared to sample members who did not participate. Essentially, we hoped to use these data to determine that respondents did not differ from nonrespondents in ways that could affect study findings. To determine this, we compared respondents to nonrespondents on 31 demographic characteristics. This analysis showed that the two groups did not differ on 25 of 29 variables analyzed.

Using Cross-Sectional Data Involving Retrospective Reports

The cross-sectional design used in the study presented limitations in two ways. First, as previously discussed, cross-sectional designs lack features that support strong causal inferences. In cross-sectional studies the variables presumed to occur at different points in time are measured at the same time. Second, the researcher must rely on respondents' capacity to recall events that occurred in the past as the basis for time ordering among variables. Confidence in the findings is reduced by this reliance on retrospective reports.

Generalizability of the Findings

Finally, under ideal circumstances we would expect that our study findings could be generalized to other populations of poor mothers involved with child protective services who had participated in drug treatment. Two considerations undermined our capacity to generalize to other groups in this study, however. First, even though we determined that the respondent sample was comparable to the overall population from which it was probabilistically drawn, the low response rate left some possibility that it was not representative. Thus, even though we were able to test for obvious response bias in a number of demographic characteristics (as described above), we could not confidently generalize to this study sample frame. Second, even if we felt confident in generalizing to the sample frame used for this study, the study was conducted in a place (Chicago) and at a time (late 1990s) that may have had distinctive characteristics.

Summary and Conclusions

A primary lesson to be learned from the commentary on this study is that the conceptualization of research problems and research questions is very important. As a consequence of strong conceptualization, we were able to make a contribution, despite some substantial problems with the data. That is, given that the problems were clearly described, the conclusions could be placed in the proper perspective. As we noted in our article, our study has flaws, but it sets out a conceptualization and rationale that future researchers can use. We hope that future researchers will use the conceptualization we put forth to address similar research questions with a stronger design and better data.

REFERENCES

Marsh, J. C. (1982). Public issues and private problems: Women and drug use. *Journal of Social Issues, 38*: 153–166.

Marsh, J. C. & Miller, N. A. (1985). Female clients in substance abuse treatment. *The International Journal of the Addictions, 20*(6&7), 995–1019.

Marsh, J. C., D'Aunno, T. A. & Smith, B. A. (2000). Increasing access and providing social services to improve drug abuse treatment for women with children. *Addiction, 95*(8), 1237–1247.

McLellan, A. T., Grissom, G. R., Zanis, D., Randall, M., Brill, P., & O'Brien, C. P. (1997). Problem-service "matching" in addiction treatment. *Archives of General Psychiatry, 54* (August), 730–735.

Smith, B. D. (2003). How parental drug use and drug treatment compliance relate to family reunification. *Child Welfare, 82*(3), 335–365.

Smith, B. D. & Donovan, S. E. F. (2003). Child welfare practice in organizational and institutional context. *Social Service Review* 77(4), 541–563.

8

How Much Is Enough? Perspectives of Care Recipients and Professionals on the Sufficiency of In-Home Care

Nancy Morrow-Howell, Ph.D., Enola Proctor, Ph.D.,
and Philip Rozario, M.S.W.

As the home-care industry has grown, so too have concerns about the quality of in-home care (Applebaum, Mollica, & Tilley, 1997–1998). In response, the health and human service sectors have stepped up efforts to assess and improve quality of care (Applebaum, 1995). Although family and friends provide considerably more care than formal providers (Kosberg & Cairl, 1992; Morrow-Howell, Proctor, Dore, & Kaplan, 1998; Strawbridge & Wallhagen, 1992), relatively little attention has focused on assessing and improving the quality of in-home care provided by the informal sector.

As with the assessment of quality of care in general, research on the quality of home care is challenged by definitional issues (Capitman, Abrahams, & Ritter, 1997). Reflecting the complexity of the concept "quality of care," different criteria are used to define and measure quality (McGlynn, 1997). Accordingly, there is lack of consensus as to what constitutes quality home care. Further challenges surround the issue of who should rate quality. Which home care consumer should be considered in assessing quality (Applebaum et al., 1997–1998), and which stakeholders should rate quality?

This work was funded by the Agency for Health Care Policy and Research Grant R01 HS-6406-01 as well as a Faculty Award from the George Warren Brown School of Social Work, Washington University in St. Louis, Missouri. From Morrow-Howell, N., Proctor, E., Rozario, P. (2001). How much is enough? Perspectives of care recipients and professionals on the sufficiency of In-home care. *The Gerontologist, 41,* 723–732. Copyright 2001 The Gerontological Society of American. Reproduced by permission of the publisher.

This study seeks to increase knowledge about the variance in the assessment of quality of home care related to rater role. There are many roles assumed by people related to the home care industry—care recipient, informal caregiver, professional caregivers, clinical case managers, financial case managers, etc. We seek to understand if people systematically view and thus rate home care quality differently, depending on their role. Specifically, we focus on two raters: care recipients and professionals. Among the many potential domains of quality of care, we focus on one: the sufficiency of the amount of care provided by informal and formal caregivers to meet the dependency needs of frail elders in activities of daily living (ADL).

Related Literature

Conceptions and Indicators of Quality.—Various attributes are used to conceptualize and evaluate the quality of care. With respect to health care in general, Donabedian (1992) identified six attributes of quality: effectiveness, efficiency, cost-effectiveness, acceptability, legitimacy, and equity. The aspect of health care addressed in this study, home care, has been typically evaluated in terms of prevented nursing home placements, costs, and such elder outcomes as functional status and mortality. Attention to more proximal indicators of quality, particularly features of the in-home care per se, is more recent. For example, Ory and Duncker (1992) called for reconceptualizing outcomes to include the adequacy of care. Morrow-Howell, Proctor, and Berg-Weger (1993) addressed the adequacy of informal care for elderly patients discharged home from the hospital, documenting concerns that discharge planners expressed about informal caregivers' abilities to perform the tasks expected of them in posthospital care.

Health care has also been evaluated in terms of the extent to which services meet needs for assistance, an aspect of quality that may be particularly germane to care recipients. McGlynn (1997) noted that patients tend to evaluate care in terms of its responsiveness to their individual needs. Morrow-Howell, Proctor, and Dore (1998) conceptualized adequacy in terms of the extent to which services meet needs for assistance. Consistent with this approach, Skinner, Steinwachs, Handley, and colleagues (1999) postulated that outcomes of care (for persons with severe and persistent mental illness) would be better when services meet needs for assistance. Particularly in postacute care, meeting needs for functional assistance is an important component of quality. Over the past 2 decades there have been trends for patients leaving the hospital after shorter stays at higher levels of dependency and with increased need for care (Coe et al., 1986; Kosekoff et al., 1990). Mamon, Steinwachs, Fahey, and colleagues (1992) found that 97% of patients discharged home after hospitalization had need for care at 2 weeks postdischarge.

Stakeholder Perspectives on Quality.—As McGlynn (1997) has noted, "quality is in the eye of the beholder; that is, expectations and the value associated with different aspects of care are likely to vary among different stakeholders" (p. 9). In assessing the quality of home care, the relevant perspectives include those of the elder-care recipient, any one of a number of family members (some providing care and some not), and the formal care providers (the home care aides themselves, their supervisors, or the care managers; Wagner, 1988). Additionally, funders and regulators are key stakeholders. Each of the various constituencies or stakeholders in the home-care industry has a legitimate and perhaps unique perspective; their motivations, values, and criteria may be truly different (Kaufert, 1983). Each perspective may be differentially important in planning or evaluating programs and services. For example, discrepancy between the need for a service (as assessed by providers) and the demand for that service (as expressed by consumers) is critical in program planning; that is, there is a risk that services will be structured by providers for hypothetical target populations (Wilson & Netting, 1987). Patient perspective, particularly patient satisfaction, has been regarded as an "indispensable" reflection of the quality of care (Donabedian, 1988, p. 1746); and Skinner, Steinwachs, Handley, and colleagues (1999) noted that by "listening to the consumer and designing systems of care that are more responsive to meeting needs defined by the consumer, more effective—and accountable—delivery systems are likely" (p. 117). Yet particularly in gerontology, in which elderly subjects may be too sick or cognitively impaired to participate in interviews, researchers may depend on proxy informants. Thus, differences introduced by rater role may threaten the validity or interpretation of quality of care measurement (Tennstedt, Skinner, Sullivan, & McKinlay, 1992).

Related Work on Rater Perspectives.—Incongruence between professional and lay perspectives of service needs and preferences is well-documented (Avant & Dressel, 1980; Keith, 1975; Riesenfield, Newcomer, Berlant, & Dempsey, 1972; Wilson & Netting, 1987). For example, Wilson and Netting (1987) found that elders identified fewer problems and needs than health professionals did, whereas professionals perceived that the elderly adults had more access to services (transportation, specifically) than did the elderly adults themselves. Epstein, Hall, Tognetti, and colleagues (1989) reported low correlations between patient and proxy ratings of satisfaction with health care. Factors associated with satisfaction with hospital discharge plans are different for patient and family raters (Proctor, Morrow-Howell, Albaz, & Weir, 1992). Patient ratings were associated with involvement in the decision-making process, social support, and physical condition; family ratings were associated with length of hospital stay, discharge planning processes, and discharge destination. Efforts to improve satisfaction ratings may be different depending on which consumer group is being considered.

The study of systematic differences between various raters of health status has a somewhat longer history. Moderate to weak associations have been documented between self-rated health and physician-rated health, with older adults generally rating their health more positively than physicians do (Friedsam & Martin, 1963; Kivinen, Halonen, Eronen, & Nissinen, 1998; Rothman, Hedrick, Bulcroft, Hickam, & Rubenstein, 1991; Streib, Suchman, & Phillips, 1958; Maddox, 1964). Additionally, self-rated health has been found to be a better predictor of future health-related outcomes (Maddox & Douglas, 1973) and health service use (Markides, 1979).

Similarly, systematic differences are observed in various raters' assessments of elders' functional ability (Rubenstein, Schairer, Wieland, & Kane, 1984; Dodge, Janz, & Clark, 1994). As with health status, older adults tend to report higher levels of functioning, with family members reporting the lowest levels, and professionals (nurses) assigning intermediate ratings (Rubenstein et al., 1984). Further, the closer the relationship and the more frequent the contact, the lower the family members' perception of the elder's functional and health status is (Rubenstein et al., 1984; Rothman et al., 1991).

Several researchers have tested explanations for differences between ratings of health and function. Kivinen and colleagues (1998) postulated that it is the differential perception of the effect of age that explains the difference in rating of health status between patients and physicians. After controlling for medical condition, they found that age of the patient did not relate to self-rated health whereas it did relate to assessments by physician, with older patients assessed as being in poorer health. Other researchers have suggested that characteristics of the elders as well as the family proxies affect ratings of the elder's health and functional status (Kiyak, Teri, & Borson, 1994; Magaziner, Simonsick, Kashner, et al., 1988; Rothman, Hedrick, Bulcroft, Hickam, & Rubenstein, 1991; Poulshock & Deimling, 1984; Hooyman, Gonyea, & Montgomery, 1985). Better agreement between patient and family raters has been associated with better mental health and cognitive ability of the patients (Magaziner et al., 1988; Kiyak, Teri, & Borson, 1994). Family proxies experiencing greater burden or psychological distress report greater impairment in health and functional ability of the care recipient. This suggests that family members perceive higher disability to correspond with burden they feel or to justify nursing home placement or formal service use they may feel they need (Rothman et al., 1991). Finally, it has been suggested that the disabled elder may seek to conceal disability so as not to burden caregivers, deny disability as a coping mechanisms, or use a different time frame in the evaluation of their ability (Rubenstein et al., 1984).

Study Focus and Conceptualization

This study addressed the issue of stakeholder perspectives on the quality of in-home supportive care. Quality is conceptualized and measured in terms of the sufficiency of the amount of care received to meet specific functional dependency needs. Who says how much is enough help with activities of daily living—the care recipient, the informal or formal care provider, the professional care manager, or the public payer? In this study, we focused on the care-recipient perspective versus the professional perspective of a nurse researcher. Both formal and informal care are considered when assessing sufficiency of care, which is very important in the context of community care (Capitman et al., 1997).

This study addressed four research questions:

1. Do care recipients and professionals vary in their assessment of physical functioning ability, and if so, what specific functional areas (ADL and instrumental activities of daily living [IADL] areas) contribute to the variation?

2. Do care recipients and professionals vary in their assessment of the sufficiency of care? That is, do care recipients and professionals have different perspectives on whether enough help is provided?

3. What specific functional need areas (ADL and IADL areas) contribute to the variation in raters' assessment of sufficiency of care?

4. What factors are associated with sufficiency of care from these two different perspectives?

Although previous literature consistently demonstrates that older adults rate their functional ability higher than either family members or health care professionals do, we sought to replicate this finding in a sample of chronically ill elders recently discharged home from the hospital. The last three questions have the potential to add new knowledge regarding rater role.

METHODS

Parent Study

The data for this study were derived from a larger, prospective study of postacute care for older adults with chronic heart disease. To accomplish the aims of the parent study, the researchers recruited 253 older adults between June, 1990, and October, 1991, while the participants were hospitalized at a large Midwestern urban teaching hospital. Subjects met the following criteria: they were 65 years of age or older, were diagnosed with congestive heart failure (CHF), were served by a discharge planner, and were discharged to a home setting. CHF is a particularly appropriate diagnosis for studying postacute home care, given its prevalence among elderly persons, high public health costs, and the importance of supportive home care to maintain gains achieved during hospitalization (Bonneux, Baredregt, Meeter, Bonsel, & van der Mass, 1994). Given the aims of the parent study, we selected patients served by discharge planners to ensure a sample with need for home care and one that received a mix of informal and formal services.

Discharge planners identified patients who met study criteria, whom research assistants approached to explain the study; 82% of patients contacted consented to participate. We approached a family member at the instruction of the discharge planner when patients were too ill or cognitively impaired to participate. In 35% of the cases, this family collateral provided consent and completed data collection for purposes of the larger study.

Data Collection

At the time of hospital discharge, a research assistant abstracted the medical records. At 2 weeks post-discharge, a research assistant completed a telephone survey with the study participant or the collateral. Within 48 hours of this telephone interview, a registered nurse (RN) research assistant completed an in-home interview. Both the telephone and in-home interview focused on functional ability and informal and formal assistance received to meet the patient's ADL and IADL needs. We recognize that two data collection methods are used (telephone and in-home interviews) and that this may confound our findings in that differences attributed to rater role may result from differing data collection methods. Yet the advantages of this approach outweigh this risk, as we describe below.

During the telephone interview, the research assistant relied on the study participant's self-report. We viewed the telephone interview as the preferred approach to data collection in self-report data because, compared with an in-person interview, it minimizes cues and the influence of the interviewer. In contrast, we viewed the in-person interview as conducive to obtaining a professional clinical assessment. During the in-home interview, the nurse research assistant had access to a broader range of information she could draw from the study participant, the family members present at the interview, and clinical observations to make a professional assessment of functional ability and sufficiency of care provided. Thus, we obtained concurrent assessment of physical functioning ability and the sufficiency of care through the telephone interview (self-report from the study participant) and the in-home interview (clinical report of nurse research assistant).

Sample Subset

Addressing the research questions posed in this article required that (a) the care recipient be capable of providing self-report and (b) each subject provide both a telephone interview and concurrent in-home interview. Although the requisite sample for these analyses is select and, in our case, small ($n = 85$), such a sample is necessary to answer questions about rater perspectives that are important both substantively and methodologically. Despite limits to statistical power, the subsetted sample provides a scarce opportunity to examine issues in quality of care measurement that are critical in both gerontology and health services research.

Accordingly, we subset the sample from the larger study as follows. Of the 253 eligible patients at the time of discharge, 209 were available to participate in a telephone survey 2 weeks post discharge. In this 2-week period, 39 patients died, were readmitted to the hospital, or entered a nursing home before information could be gathered; this number reflects the unstable condition of CHF and the high readmission and mortality rate associated with this condition (Bonneux et al., 1994). Five patients refused to participate in the 2-week interview. Of the 209 study participants completing the 2-week postdischarge telephone interview, in-home interviews were completed on 149. In-home interviews were not completed for two reasons: (a) the participant lived more than 2 hours from the study site and in-home interviews were not requested because of the excessive travel time and (b) the participant consented to the telephone interview but not to the in-home assessment. Thus, 149 observations had concurrent telephone and in-home interviews at the 2-week postdischarge observation point. Finally, to compare care recipients with professionals, we include only those 85 observations for which the older adult completed the telephone interview rather than a family proxy.

Bivariate analyses were completed to compare the 85 elders in this study sample with the 124 elders who were available for the 2-week follow-up interview but were not included in this particular analysis (as mentioned above, 209 study participants completed the first follow-up interview). There are no gender, race, or socioeconomic status (SES) differences between the two groups; however, the 85 elders in this study were more functional ($t = 9.39$, $p < .01$) and younger ($t = -3.79$, $p < .01$) than elders who did not participate. This difference results from the elimination of study participants whose family proxies provided the information because the elder was not able, most often by virtue of illness or dependency. This sample bias limits generalizability, which is discussed below.

As noted above, achieving a valid subsample to address differences in rater perspective is associated with limits to both analytic power and generalizability. In the functional area-by-area analysis reported below, four cell sizes were too small for valid tests of statistical difference (transfer, toileting, walking, and eating). Thus we eliminated these areas from the comparison of self-report and professional assessment. In regard to generalizability, those care recipients too ill or too cognitively impaired to participate in the telephone interview are different from those who can participate, and indeed the amount of care they receive and their perceptions of the sufficiency of this care could be different. Thus we can generalize only to care recipients who can participate in telephone interviews regarding their conditions and their care arrangements. This generalizability issue would plague any such study no matter how big the sample size because one can never measure and compare self-report perspective from study participants incapable of self-report.

Dependent Variables

The two dependent variables in this study, physical functioning ability and sufficiency of care, were obtained from both the care-recipient and the professional perspectives. For the care-recipient perspective, research assistants (Masters in social work students) conducted telephone interviews with each care recipient, capturing the dependent variables through self-report. To obtain a professional perspective, we trained geriatric nurse practitioners to conduct the in-home assessments using all relevant information available in the interview as well as observation to inform their ratings of functional ability and sufficiency of care. To increase reliability, we used only two nurses for the study. Both nurses had RN degrees and were active and experienced geriatric practitioners.

Physical functioning ability was assessed using the OARS (Older Americans Resources and Services Multidimensional Functional Assesssment Questionnaire) instrument (Duke University Center for Study of Aging and Human Development, 1978), which has seven ADLs (transfer, walking, toileting, bathing, grooming, dressing, and eating), and six IADLs (meal preparation, shopping, money management, travel, housekeeping, and medicine administration). In each area, functional ability is captured with a three-level response: able to perform activity with no help (2), able to perform with some help (1), or completely unable to perform (0). The summative measure ranges from 0 to 26, with higher scores reflecting greater functional ability. Telephone interviews captured the care recipients' self-report of functional ability, whereas the nurses assessed functional ability through clinical interviewing during the in-home interview.

Sufficiency of care reflects the extent to which the informal and formal assistance is seen as enough to meet subjects' ADL and IADL needs. The measurement tool used to capture the sufficiency of care was developed by the authors for studying posthospital care; reliability was established through tests on 20 subjects (Morrow-Howell, Proctor, and Dore, 1998). Test-retest reliability, established on subject telephone self-report on two consecutive days, was .87, using a weighted kappa. Interrater reliability of the instrument across two professionals, who conducted simultaneous in-home assessments, was .81, again using a weighted kappa (Morrow-Howell, Proctor, & Dore, 1998).

Procedures for scoring sufficiency of care were as follows. In areas of the OARS instrument in which function in an ADL or IADL area was rated as independent, we asked no further questions about that specific function. In ADL or IADL areas with any dependency, further information was captured about who provided assistance with the task, how often assistance was received from formal and informal sources, and how sufficient this help was. "Sufficiency of care" was rated, specific to each area of functional need, using a 4-point scale on which 1 = without help at most times; 2 = usually does not have enough help; 3 = usually has enough, but on occasion help is not available when needed; and 4 = always enough help. As with the functional-ability ratings, care-recipient ratings of sufficiency were self-reports obtained during the telephone interviews; professional ratings of sufficiency of care were nurse assessments from the in-home interviews.

To compare care recipient and professional ratings, we calculated two summative scores, averaging the rated sufficiency of care across areas of functional dependence—one score reflecting the care recipient's overall sufficiency of care and one reflecting the professional (nurse) assessment of the overall sufficiency of care. The quantity ratings (1–4) in each area of need were summed and divided by the number of identified dependency areas, producing an average sufficiency rating. These scores were therefore able to control for difference in care-recipient and professional perspective in functional ability, as follows. If a care recipient reported functional dependency in three areas (transportation, meal preparation, and housekeeping, for example), the three sufficiency ratings in each need area were summed and divided by three. If, however, the nurse assessed more areas of dependency (for example, four areas, including transportation, meal preparation, housekeeping, and medicine administration), her score would be an average of four sufficiency ratings. Each summative sufficiency rating—one for care recipient and one for professional—ranged from 1 (never enough help) to 4 (always enough help). Scores were thus comparable across rater, regardless of differences between the raters in assessing the patient's functional ability.

Independent Variables

A variety of independent variables were measured for purposes of exploring their contribution to the dependent variable sufficiency of care from care recipient and professional perspectives. Demographic characteristics were extracted from the medical record and included age in years, gender, and race recorded dichotomously as White and African American. Marital status was recorded as currently married and not currently married. Socioeconomic status was assessed from patient response to questions for the Hollingshead Index of Social Class; this measure uses education and occupation to assign subjects a rating of 11 to 77, with lower numbers representing higher social status (Hollingshead, 1957).

The care recipient's health characteristics were ascertained by the nurse during the in-home assessment. Cognitive ability was assessed using the Short Blessed Mental Status exam, which yields a score of 0 to 28, with higher scores indicating more cognitive impairment (Blessed et al., 1968). The Chronic Conditions Checklist from the OARS instrument (Fillenbaum, 1988) captured the existence of 32 chronic medical conditions, weighted by the extent to which the condition interferes with activity (from 0 [no limitation] to 3 [severe limitation]).

The informal care situation was captured through four variables obtained as part of the in-home interview. The identity of primary caregiver was recorded as spouse, adult child, or other. If other caregivers assisted in any way, a dichotomous variable captured the involvement of secondary caregiver. Co-residence of the caregiver and care recipient was also recorded dichotomously. The study participant provided information about the health of primary caregiver, using a 4-point rating scale of excellent to poor. During the in-home interview, the nurse also queried about the level of formal care. Formal care was measured through the number of hours of in-home care provided by agency staff, volunteers, or any paid helper during the previous month.

Statistical Analysis

The univariate distributions of the independent and dependent variables were examined and descriptive statistics are presented in Table 8.1. The extreme skew on the number of hours of formal assistance per month warranted attention. This variable was log transformed, resulting in a more symmetric distribution, and the logged variable was used in regression analysis. Dependent t tests were used to compare care recipient and professional ratings on functional ability and sufficiency of care. Similarly, we used dependent t tests to compare the functional ability ratings and the sufficiency of care ratings on each ADL and IADL area to determine the sources of variation in the summative scores. Thus, functional ratings as well as sufficiency ratings were compared between care recipients and professionals in bathing, grooming, toileting, and so forth. In cases in which sufficiency ratings were compared within each ADL and IADL area, we compared care recipients to professionals only when both raters assessed a functional dependency in the area and therefore provided a sufficiency of care rating in that area (i.e., sufficiency ratings in the area of

Table 8.1. Description of Sample ($n = 85$)

Items Measured	Percentage	Mean (*SD*)	Range	Skew
Independent Variables				
Age		76.9 years (6.5)	65–94	0.18
Gender	66% female			
Race	61% African American			
Marital status	71% not married			
Socioeconomic status		56.4 (18.0)	11–77	−0.70
Cognitive status		6.8 (5.1)	0–19	0.49
Interference from chronic conditions		9.8 (4.5)	2–27	0.72
Identity of caregiver	Spouse 17%			
	Child 43%			
	Other 40%			
Presence of 2ndary	72% had other helper			
Co-residence	52% co-reside			
Health of caregiver	Poor 6%			
	Fair 26%			
	Good 52%			
	Excellent 16%			
Hours of formal help		48.6 hrs (144)	0–906	4.9
Logged hours of formal help		1.76 (1.0)	0–4.2	0.35
Dependent Variables				
Functioning (care recipient)		19.32 (4.2)	4–25	−0.81
Functioning (professional)		17.51 (4.1)	8–24	−0.21
Sufficiency (care recipient)		3.21 (0.84)	1–4	−0.93
Sufficiency (professional)		2.73 (0.76)	1–4	−0.48

bathing could only be compared if both care recipient and professional reported a dependency in that area and therefore provided a sufficiency of care rating in bathing). Although this strategy results in the loss of sample size within each cell, it enables the comparison of sufficiency ratings that are freed from the rater bias that is known to exist in the assessment of functional ability.

We used analysis of variance techniques through the SAS general linear model procedure to test the relationship of the independent variables to the sufficiency of care measures (Cody & Smith, 1997). Main effect and repeated measure models were both used. We used repeated measures analysis of variance to test the interactions of the independent variables and rater identity on sufficiency of care. Given the number of interactions to be tested, we tested each interaction separately, after controlling for all independent variables and rater role. The caregiver identity variable was dummy coded. Because of the substantial correlation between spousal caregiver and marital status in this sample ($r = .71$) as well as the lack of a statistically significant association with the sufficiency of care ratings, we eliminated caregiver identity from the regressions to reduce the number of independent variables being tested. The only model with a significant interaction term is presented.

RESULTS

Do Care Recipients and Professionals Vary in Their Assessment of Physical Functioning Ability? If So, What Specific Functional Areas Are the Sources of the Variation?

As would be predicted from previous work, the older adults receiving in-home supportive care rated their functional ability higher than nurse researcher assistants did, $t(84) = -5.57$, $p = .0001$. As seen in Table 8.1, care recipients rated their functional status approximately 2 points higher on the 26-point scale of physical functioning (19.32 vs. 17.51). Ratings from each of the ADL and IADL areas are compared in Table 8.2. For each functional area, in which scores range from 0 to 2,

Table 8.2. Physical Functioning Ability: Differences Between Care Recipient and Professional Ratings by Functional Area ($n = 85$)

Functional Area	Significant Difference Between Raters?	Higher Score
Medications	Yes ($p = .00$)	Care recipient
Transfer	Yes ($p = .00$)	Care recipient
Toileting	Yes ($p = .00$)	Care recipient
Walking	Yes ($p = .00$)	Care recipient
Bathing	Yes ($p = .01$)	Nurse
Grooming	Yes ($p = .00$)	Care recipient
Dressing	Yes ($p = .00$)	Care recipient
Eating	Yes ($p = .00$)	Care recipient
Meal preparation	No ($p = .29$)	Not applicable
Shopping	Yes ($p = .00$)	Care recipient
Money management	Yes ($p = .00$)	Care recipient
Transportation	Yes ($p = .01$)	Care recipient
Housekeeping	No ($p = .22$)	Not applicable

the mean care recipient rating was compared with the mean professional rating. As can be seen, care recipients rated their functioning higher in all but three ADL and IADL areas. Nurses rated the older adults as more functional in the activity of bathing than did the care recipients themselves. In two areas—meal preparation and housekeeping—professional and care-recipient ratings of functional ability were not significantly different.

Do Care Recipients and Professionals Vary in Their Assessment of the Sufficiency of Care?

As seen in Table 8.1, professionals tended to rate the amount of care as less sufficient than the care recipients did (2.73 vs. 3.21); ($t(84) = -4.9$, $p = .0001$). On average, the nurses were almost one-half a point lower on the 4-point scale.

What Specific Functional Need Areas Contribute to the Variation in Raters' Assessment of Sufficiency of Care?

Ratings in each of nine ADL and IADL areas are compared in Table 8.3. Four functional areas (transfer, toileting, walking, and eating) were eliminated because the number of pairs of ratings was less than five. For each functional area in which both the care recipient and nurse agreed that there was a dependency, the mean care recipient rating of sufficiency of care was compared with the mean professional rating. As can be seen, the sufficiency ratings did not vary in three functional need areas. However, it should be noted that sample size drops quite low in two of these comparisons, and lack of statistical power could explain the null finding. Care recipients rated the sufficiency of care higher in five need areas (note that the marginally significant difference in medications is included, given a p value of .06 and a small sample size). Nurses rated assistance in the area of transportation as more sufficient than did care recipients.

What Factors Are Associated with Sufficiency of Care from the Two Different Perspectives?

Analysis of variance reveals that three variables have main effects on sufficiency of care: coresidence of care recipient and care receiver, health of caregiver, and rater identity (see Table 8.4).

Table 8.3. Sufficiency of Care: Differences Between Care Recipient and Professional Ratings by Functional Need Area

Functional Need Area	Number of Pairs of Ratings	Significant Difference Between Raters?	Higher Score
Medications	23	Yes ($p = .06$)	Care recipient
Bathing	41	Yes ($p = .00$)	Care recipient
Grooming	11	No ($p = .66$)	Not applicable
Dressing	8	No ($p = .41$)	Not applicable
Meal preparation	24	No ($p = .11$)	Not applicable
Shopping	69	Yes ($p = .00$)	Care recipient
Money management	21	Yes ($p = .00$)	Care recipient
Transportation	56	Yes ($p = .00$)	Nurse
Housekeeping	77	Yes ($p = .01$)	Care recipient

Table 8.4. Factors Associated With Sufficiency of Care (Dependent Variable)

Variable	Estimate	St. Error	Probability
Age	.02	.01	.07
Nonwhite	−.19	.16	.27
Female	.09	.15	.56
SES	.001	.004	.74
Married	.15	.18	.39
Interference from chronic conditions	−.01	.02	.48
Cognitive status	−.02	.02	.33
Coresidence	.36	.17	.04
Presence of secondary caregiver	.18	.16	.24
Caregiver health	.26	.09	.01
Hours of formal services	−.10	.07	.18
Rater identity (care recipient/professional)	.54	.10	.0001
Rater identity × formal services	−.19	.08	.02

Notes: Sample Size = 79; Model F = 3.224, p = .001; Model R^2 = .54. SES = socioeconomic status.

Two of these variables relate to the informal care system. Care was rated as more sufficient when care recipients lived with their caregivers and when caregivers were healthier. As reflected in earlier analyses, identity of the rater is related to sufficiency of care, with professional ratings being lower than care-recipient ratings. When the two informal support variables were tested in interactions with rater identity, the interaction effects were not significant. Thus, these variables are related to the sufficiency ratings, regardless of whether the rater was a care recipient or a professional. Of the 11 interaction terms tested, only 1 interaction was significantly associated with sufficiency of care. We found no main effect for amount of formal services and no relationship between formal services and sufficiency of care from the perspective of care recipients. However, for professionals, higher amounts of formal care were associated with lower sufficiency ratings.

DISCUSSION

We acknowledge both weaknesses and strengths in our conceptualization and measurement of the dependent variable, sufficiency of in-home care. The construct, sufficiency of care to meet elders' functional dependency needs, is but one aspect of the broader construct of quality of care. Our focus on the amount or quantity of care does not capture the important aspect of quality, or how good that care is. Yet quantity seems to be a minimal component of quality; how can care be construed as "quality" when there isn't enough care?

Consistent with a few other examples in the quality of care literature (e.g., Skinner et al., 1999), we chose to measure our dependent variable, sufficiency of care, within specific areas of functional needs, with two important consequences. First, our data can reveal variations in sufficiency of care across the various ADL and IADL areas for which care is needed and provided. Findings thus have the potential to pinpoint specific areas of challenge or difficulty in providing enough care, as well as highlight areas of care for which the care provider and care recipient have different perspectives. Second, the resultant aggregate ratings of sufficiency should be more reliable than global ratings that are not tied to specifics.

This study's findings replicate and build on prior work demonstrating that older adults rate their functional abilities higher than professionals. The study adds new knowledge regarding differences in perspectives by documenting that the assessments of sufficiency of care also vary by rater role. In general, care recipients rate amount of care as more sufficient compared with how professionals rate it. These findings are very consistent with related work that suggests older adults rate their functional ability and health higher than professionals do, as well as identify fewer problems and needs.

These data suggest that variance between nurse ratings and care recipient ratings of physical function derives from both ADL and IADL areas. In 10 out of 13 activities, care recipients rated their functional ability higher than nurses did. The nurses rated functional ability higher in only one area—bathing. Perhaps dependent elders are more conservative about their abilities in the area of bathing out of fear of falling in the bathroom.

When considering the source of variance from ADL and IADL areas in the sufficiency ratings, the pattern is less clear than in functional assessments. Care recipients rate their care as more sufficient in five out of nine need areas, with no statistical difference between the two ratings in three areas. In regard to transportation, nurses assessed the amount of help to be more sufficient. It may be that nurses view the amount of transportation as sufficient if it is enough to get the care recipient to necessary destinations, like medical appointments. The care recipient may view other trips as important as well, such as those for social visits or pleasure outings; the care recipient may assess help as less than enough if these trips are not occurring, whereas the nurse may view these types of trips as more discretionary.

Although this study does contribute to understanding how raters' assessment of care varies, we did not capture information about why ratings are different. It is likely that care recipients are motivated to report sufficient levels of assistance for two reasons. First, as Donabedian noted, "unless special precautions are taken, patients may be reluctant to reveal their opinions for fear of alienating their medical attendants" (1988, p. 1746). Particularly with elderly adults, Woodruff and Applebaum (1996) suggested that consumers' perspectives may be influenced by their strong desire to remain independent and in their current living situations. Care recipients may lower their own standard of acceptability in regard to meal preparation, bathing, housekeeping, and so forth when faced with the reality of their needs and their available resources. Second, care recipients may not be willing to criticize their care providers, especially family members, by assigning low sufficiency ratings. On the other hand, professionals may maintain their standards of acceptable quantity of care across care recipients, with less threat (certainly less personal repercussions) about the consequences of the deficiencies. Additionally, they could be less concerned about judging care providers as deficient in some way. Our findings point to the need for further research on motivations leading to differences in ratings between different stakeholders in home care.

There are some similarities in factors associated with sufficiency ratings between the two perspectives. Two variables are important predictors from both perspectives: coresidence of caregiver and care recipient, and health of the caregiver. These two variables had main effects but no interaction effects in the regression analyses, reflecting the salience of these independent variables for both care recipient and professional. Remarkably, only characteristics of the informal caregiving network were related to the sufficiency of care ratings irrespective of rater. These findings speak to the critical role of informal caregivers in the community long-term care system. The proximity and the health of the primary helper affect the perceived sufficiency of the amount of assistance received. These findings suggest that if we are to increase the quality of in-home supportive care, we should focus on programs and policies that shore up the informal system.

In addition to caregiver proximity and caregiver health, one other independent variable affected professionals' ratings of the sufficiency of care: amount of formal service. (In this sample of chronically ill elders in the post-acute period, there are comparatively high levels of formal service, which was planned as part of the parent study.) Interestingly, nurses rated care as less sufficient in situations with higher levels of formal care. Although counterintuitive, this finding is not infrequent in services research and often indicates limitations in measurement—specifically the inability to adequately capture and control for sickness or need level. That is, sicker or more dependent elders usually receive more formal care, yet despite higher levels of care, their care arrangements remain less adequate because of the high demands of the care situation. In this particular study, we might interpret this association to mean that, in the professional assessment, the addition of formal services does not bring the amount of care up to a sufficient level (or in the few cases in which there are only formal services involved, formal services alone are not enough). These interpretations are consistent with our finding that caregiver proximity is a critical factor; often, formal providers are not as accessible or proximate as informal providers. In short, these findings suggest that a focus on formal care at expense of informal care is not sufficient to improve the quality of in-home supportive care.

Ratings of the sufficiency of care did not vary significantly by elder age, gender, race, or SES, whether from the perspective of care recipient or of the professional. This failure to find disparities in the sufficiency of care for various demographic groups, including those at risk for poorer health outcomes, may be reassuring from a social justice perspective.

Important implications from this study are that raters of sufficiency of in-home supportive care are not interchangeable, and that information source is a critical factor in quality of care studies. Both care recipient and professional ratings are valid because sufficiency perspectives may be based on different standards and different values—but they are not interchangeable. Program evaluators and researchers need to determine which perspective is most appropriate for the situation under study. Professional ratings may be more related to medical outcomes, such as readmission or morbidity, whereas care recipient ratings may be more related to quality of life or satisfaction measures. Program developers and funders also need to pay close attention to the source of information in needs assessments. As Rosow (1964) stated many years ago, problems of old age can be divided into two groups: those that they actually have or think they have and those the professionals think they have. More recently, Lenert, Ziegler, Lee, Sommi, and Mahmoud (2000) pointed out that substituting providers' views for those of patients might lead to overtreatment of patients. In sum, these findings confirm that rater perspective is likely to have consequences for health service planning, delivery, and evaluations, and that various stakeholders define quality differently, which translates into different expectations of the health care system and thus differing evaluations of quality (McGlynn, 1997).

REFERENCES

Applebaum, R. (1995). Quality and quality assurance. In G. Maddox (Ed.), *Encyclopedia of aging* (pp. 786–787). New York: Springer.

Applebaum, R., Mollica, R., & Tilley, J. (1997–1998). Assuring homecare quality: A case study of state strategies. *Generations, Winter,* 57–63.

Avant, W., & Dressel, P. (1980). Perceiving needs by staff and elderly clients: The impact of training and client contact. *The Gerontologist, 20,* 71–77.

Blessed, G., Tomlinson, B., & Roth, M. (1968). The association between quantitative measures of dementia and of senile change in the cerebral grey matter of elderly subjects. *British Journal of Psychiatry, 114,* 797–811.

Bonneux, L., Baredregt, J., Meeter, K., Bonsel, G., & van der Mass, P. (1994). Estimating clinical morbidity due to ischemic heart disease and congestive heart failure. *American Journal of Public Health, 84,* 20–28.

Capitman, J., Abrahams, R., & Ritter, G. (1997). Measuring the adequacy of home care for frail elders. *The Gerontologist, 37,* 303–313.

Cody, R., & Smith, J. K. (1997). Applied Statistics and the SAS Programming Language (4th ed.) [Computer software]. Upper Saddle River, NJ: Prentice Hall.

Coe, M., Wilkenson, A., & Patterson, P. (1986). *Preliminary evidence on the impact of DRG's: Dependency at Discharge* (Final report). Beaverton, OR: Northwest Oregon Health Systems.

Dodge, J., Janz, N., & Clark, N. (1994). Self-management of the health care regimen: A comparison of nurses' and cardiac patients' perceptions. *Patient Education and Counseling, 23,* 73–82.

Donabedian, A. (1988). The quality of care: How can it be assessed? *Journal of the American Medical Association, 260,* 1743–1748.

Donabedian, A. (1992). The role of outcomes in quality assessment and assurance. *Quality Review Bulletin, 18,* 356.

Duke University Center for Study of Aging and Human Development. (1978). *Multi-dimensional functional assessment: The OARS methodology (2nd edition).* Durham, North Carolina: Author.

Epstein, A. M., Hall, J. A., Tognetti, M., Son, L., & Conant, L. (1989). Using proxies to evaluate quality of life. *Medical Care, 27,* S91–S98.

Fillenbaum, G. (1988). *"Multidimensional functional assessment of older adults.* Hillsdale, NJ: Erlbaum.

Friedsam, H. J., & Martin, H. W. (1963). A comparison of self- and physician's health ratings in an older population. *Journal of Health and Social Behavior, 4,* 173–183.

Hollingshead, A. (1957). *A two-factor index of social position.* Unpublished manuscript.

Hooyman, N., Gonyea, J., & Montgomery, R. (1985). The impact of in-home services termination for caregivers. *The Gerontologist, 25,* 141–145.

Kaufert, J. M. (1983). Functional ability indices: Measurement problems in assessing their validity. *Archives of Physical Medicine and Rehabilitation, 64,* 260–267.

Keith, P. (1975). Evaluation of services for the aged by professionals and the elderly. *Social Service Review, 49,* 271–278.

Kivinen, P., Halonen, P., Eronen, M., & Nissinen, A. (1998). Self-rated health, physician-rated health and associated factors among elderly men: The Finnish cohorts of the Seven Countries Study. *Age and Ageing, 27,* 41–47.

Kiyak, H. A., Teri, L., & Borson, S. (1994). Physical and functional health assessment in normal aging and in Alzheimer's disease: Self-reports vs family reports. *The Gerontologist, 34,* 324–330.

Kosberg, J., & Cairl, R. (1992). Burden and competence in caregivers of Alzheimer's disease patients. *Journal of Gerontological Social Work, 18,* 85–97.

Kosekoff, J., Kahn, K. L., Rogers, W. H., Reinisch, E. J., Sherwood, M. J., Rubenstein, L. V., Draper, D., Roth, C. P., Chew, C., & Brook, R. H. (1990). Prospective payment system and impairment at discharge. *Journal of American Medical Association, 265,* 1980–1983.

Lenert, L., Ziegler, J., Lee, T., Sommi, R., & Mahmoud, R. (2000). Differences in health values among patients, families members, and providers for outcomes in schizophrenia. *Medical Care, 38,* 1011–1021.

Maddox, G. L. (1964). Self-assessment of health status: A longitudinal study of selected elderly subjects. *Journal of Chronic Disease, 17,* 449–460.

Maddox, G. L., & Douglas, E. B. (1973). Self-assessment of health: A longitudinal study of elderly subjects. *Journal of Health and Social Behavior, 14,* 87–93.

Magaziner, J., Simonsick, E. M., Kashner, T. M., & Hebel, J. (1988). Patient-proxy response comparability on measure of patient health and functional status. *Journal of Clinical Epidemiology, 41,* 1065–1074.

Mamon, J., Steinwachs, D. M., Fahey, M., Bone, L. R., Oktay, J., & Klein, L. (1992). Impact of hospital discharge planning on meeting patient needs after returning home. *Home Services Research, 27,* 155–175.

Markides, M. (1979). Self-rated health. *Research on Aging, 1,* 98–112.

McGlynn, E. A. (1997). Six challenges in measuring the quality of health care. *Health Affairs, 16,* 7–21.

Morrow-Howell, N., Proctor, E., & Berg-Weger, M. (1993). Adequacy of informal care for elderly patients going home from the hospital: Discharge planner perspectives. *Journal of Applied Gerontology, 12*(2), 188–205.

Morrow-Howell, N., Proctor, E. K., & Dore, P. (1998). Adequacy of care: The concept and its measurement. *Research on Social Work Practice, 8,* 86–102.

Morrow-Howell, N., Proctor, E., Dore, R., & Kaplan, S. (1998). Post-acute services to older patients with heart disease. *Journal of Applied Gerontology, 17,* 150–171.

Ory, M. G., & Duncker, A. P. (1992). *In-home care for older people: Health and supportive services.* Newbury Park, CA: Sage.

Poulshock, S. W., & Deimling, G. T. (1984). Families caring for elders in residence: Issues in the measurement of burden. *Journal of Gerontology, 39,* 230–239.

Proctor, E., Morrow-Howell, N., Albaz, R., & Weir, C. (1992). Patient and family satisfaction with discharge plans. *Medical Care, 30,* 262–275.

Riesenfield, M., Newcomer, R., Berlant, P., & Dempsey, W. (1972). Perceptions of public service needs: The urban elderly and the public agency. *The Gerontologist, 12,* 185–190.

Rosow, I. (1964). *Housing and social integration of the aged.* Cleveland, OH: Case Western Reserve University.

Rothman, M. L., Hedrick, S. C., Bulcroft, K. A., Hickam, D. H., & Rubenstein, L. Z. (1991). The validity of proxy-generated scores in measures of patient health status. *Medical Care, 29,* 115–124.

Rubenstein, L., Schairer, C., Wieland, D., & Kane, R. (1984). Systematic biases in functional status assessments of elderly adults: Effects of different data sources. *Journal of Gerontology, 39,* 686–691.

Skinner, E., Steinwachs, D., Handley, K., Lehman, A., Fahey, M., & Lyles, C. (1999). Met and unmet needs for assistance and quality of life for people with severe and persistent mental disorders. *Mental Health Services Research, 1,* 109–118.

Strawbridge, W., & Wallhagen, M. (1992). Is all in the family always best? *Journal of Aging Studies, 6,* 81–92.

Streib, G. F., Suchman, E. A., & Phillips, B. S. (1958). An analysis of the validity of health questionnaires. *Social Forces, 36,* 223–232.

Tennstedt, S. L., Skinner, K. M., Sullivan, L. M., & McKinlay, J. B. (1992). Response comparability of family and staff proxies for nursing home residents. *American Journal of Public Health, 82,* 747–749.

Wagner, D. (1988). Who defines quality: Consumers or professionals? *Caring, 7,* 26–28.

Wilson, C. C., & Netting, F. E. (1987). Comparison of self- and health professionals' ratings of the health of community-based elderly. *International Journal of Aging and Human Development, 25,* 11–25.

Woodruff, L., & Applebaum, R. (1996). Assuring the quality of in-home supportive services. *Journal of Aging Studies, 10,* 157–169.

COMMENTARY BY: Nancy L. Morrow-Howell, Enola K. Proctor, and Philip A. Rozario

OVERVIEW OF STUDY QUESTIONS AND METHODS

The article in this volume derived from a larger study, of which we first give an overview. In 1990, we were awarded a three-year grant by the Agency for Health Care Policy and Research (now called Agency for Healthcare Research and Quality). Our study, entitled Adequacy of Home Care for Chronically Ill Elderly (RO1 HS 6406-01, Proctor and Morrow-Howell), focused on post-acute care for Medicare patients with congestive heart failure. The study aimed to assess the adequacy of care following hospital discharge, to identify factors associated with adequacy of care, and to isolate the impact of care plan adequacy on six-month health and functioning outcomes. The study was relevant, given the "quicker and sicker" phenomenon in acute care; that is, Medicare-covered patients were being discharged after shorter hospital stays, in less-recovered states, and were more reliant on informal and formal in-home care. We argued that the expensive inpatient care could be undermined by inadequate care in the weeks following discharge, and that policy makers and health services administrators would benefit from increased understanding of postacute care.

The study was a prospective longitudinal study. We recruited 253 patients over the age of 65 who had congestive heart failure, were hospitalized for heart or heart-related issues, were served by a discharge planner, and were discharged to a community rather than institutional setting. We gained consent for participation while the person was in the hospital, and we interviewed the participants at hospital discharge, 2, 6, 10, and 14 weeks postdischarge, with both telephone and in-person interviews. We also gathered information from the social workers doing the discharge planning as well as from medical records.

We collected information that captured patient characteristics (demographic, social support, health, mental health, functional ability), family characteristics (living arrangements, caregiver identity, caregiver health), and characteristics of the informal and formal services received (what types of services and how much). We developed a measure of care plan adequacy that captured the extent to which needs for assistance were met. First, we assessed the study participant's functional ability in 14 activities of daily living (walking, toileting, bathing, traveling, shopping, meal preparation, medicine administration, etc.). If the person reported that she needed help in an area, we

Commentary on article: Morrow-Howell, N. L., Proctor, E. K., & Rozario, P. A. (2001). How much is enough? Perspectives of care recipients and professionals on the sufficiency of in-home care. *The Gerontologist, 41,* 723–732.

asked how much help was received. Finally, the respondent rated the sufficiency of the help, from "never enough help" to "always enough help."

We collected data at multiple points in the post-acute period in order to capture patient change and services received. Telephone interviews were completed at 2, 6, 10, and 14 weeks post-discharge. Both telephone and in-home interviews were done at the first and third postdischarge interview. In-home interviews were necessary to complete measures that required clinical judgment or face-to-face communication (like the Mini-Mental State Exam that we used to assess cognitive function). However, we did not eliminate the telephone interviews at these observation points. Instead we retained the telephone interview content throughout all four waves and simply added new content that we obtained through the two in-home interviews. We did this to avoid switching data collection methods on any of the variables. Also, we did not want to rely totally on an in-home interview at any observation point because we knew that we would not be able to accomplish in-home interviews with all participants (due to refusal of an in-home visit or long travel distance to the home). Thus, telephone interviews were used to capture most of the information; and nurse research assistants went into the home on two occasions to augment data with measures that required face-to-face contact. This study design had the advantage of allowing us to pose our research question about rater role, because the concurrent assessment of care plan adequacy was obtained from two sources: telephone self report and face-to-face clinical interview (and the exact procedures for the concurrent assessment are described below).

The following table captures basic elements of our design as described above.

In-hospital data collection	Postdischarge data collection			
• Informed consent • Abstract medical record • Interviews with patients and discharge planners	2 weeks	6 weeks	10 weeks	14 weeks
	Telephone (self report)	Telephone (self report)	Telephone (self report)	Telephone (self report)
	In-home (professional assessment)		In-home (professional assessment)	

FIGURE 8.1. Concurrent assessment

A primary concern was retaining study participants over the 14-week observation period. We assured study recruits that we would schedule interviews at their convenience and pay them $10 for each interview (thus, $20 total when telephone and in-home were conducted). We worked hard to track and retain study participants by mailing birthday and holiday cards and calling several times to remind them of scheduled interviews. Fourteen study participants chose to withdraw from the study, and we eliminated 13 more because of complications that prevented the valid collection of data (for example, in one case, the family collateral lost contact with the patient and could not provide adequate information; in several other cases, we tried multiple times to interview the participants, who never refused but always postponed). Despite our success in retaining study participants, there was a high rate of attrition in this sample, largely due to the unstable condition of the degenerative disease of congestive heart failure. Across the 14-week observation period, we lost subjects to death, nursing home admission, or multiple hospital readmissions during the observation period. Of the 253 study participants who gave consent in the hospital, less than half in the community over the observation period, without any hospital readmissions.

SUBSET OF STUDY FOR THE ARTICLE

Our original study proposal had six major research questions and associated hypotheses. The published article addresses one of the original study questions. In the proposal, we posed the question "How do professionals and patients rate the adequacy of care for chronically ill Medicare beneficiaries discharged home from the hospital?" We hypothesized that adequacy ratings would vary by rater role, with professionals rating the care plans as less adequate than patients. We stated this hypothesis because previous work had established that older adults, family members, and professionals have different perspectives on functional ability as well as needs for assistance.

We had two occasions to compare professional and self report of care plan adequacy; and we chose the 2-week observation period for this analysis because the 10-week observation, where both telephone and in-home interviews also were done, had a smaller sample size due to attrition. Thus, we chose to address the study questions using data collected at hospitalization and at the first telephone and in-home interview postdischarge.

CHALLENGES AND TRADEOFFS
IN STUDY DESIGN AND CONDUCT

Challenge #1: Increasing Control through Study Design

In studying postacute care for chronically ill elderly, we deemed it important to control for some illness factors by focusing on one disease. We picked congestive heart failure (CHF) because it is prevalent and associated with high rates of health care utilization. Thus, knowledge gained would be generalizable to a larger number of Medicare patients than other diagnoses, and interventions to improve outcomes might have more of an impact on health costs. Yet we found it very challenging to achieve the control we desired through this design feature. There is much heterogeneity among CHF patients, in terms of illness severity and services needs. Furthermore, our study participants had a chronic, debilitating disease that, in general, progresses over time; their health status was often unstable over the observation period. Thus, we needed to control illness severity through several measures so that we could have statistical control in addition to design control of illness. Accordingly, we measured illness severity at each wave, using standardized measures of CHF symptoms and health status, and we controlled illness severity by using these measures in our statistical analyses.

We began the study with the protocol to recruit only patients hospitalized for CHF, yet we learned that the admitting diagnosis was often a condition very related to CHF, but not CHF per se. For example, CHF patients are vulnerable to pneumonia, so pneumonia was often the admitting diagnosis when heart failure was a critical part of the diagnostic picture. However, we did not extend our inclusion criteria to *any* admitted patient having CHF because some very irrelevant admitting diagnosis might have been included. For example, we would not want to include a person with CHF admitted for a hip fracture. Thus, we changed our protocol and used the criteria that CHF had to be among the reasons for hospitalization. To ensure this, our study team regularly reviewed the diagnoses of patients referred to the study to determine eligibility.

Challenge #2: Including Cognitively Impaired Study Participants

From previous literature, we knew that as many as 30 percent of CHF patients could be cognitively impaired at the time of hospitalization (either chronically or acutely). A critical decision was whether to include or exclude cognitively impaired patients. Including cognitively impaired patients would increase subject heterogeneity (the sample would include the full range of cognitive function) and be more representative of CHF patients, thereby enhancing generalizability. It would also require flexibility in data collection, in that we would have to interview collateral sources if the patient's cognitive abilities prevented self report. If we eliminated cognitively impaired patients, we would decrease generalizability, in that the sample would be restricted to CHF patients with higher cognitive function. However, we would have more control of the quality of the data collected; that is, we could collect all information from patient self report and not substitute proxy respondents. We chose to develop protocols to include cognitively impaired elders to have maximum generalizability, yet this decision had its challenges.

As part of the referral procedure, we queried hospital staff (mostly social workers but sometimes floor nurses) about the cognitive ability of the patient to provide informed consent and study data. When the person was deemed too cognitively impaired to participate, we asked for their permission to contact a family member to participate on their behalf. We approached that family member for consent and asked them to participate in the interviews. To the extent possible, we included cognitively impaired persons in explaining the study and gaining consent from the family collaterals.

In 35 percent of the cases, the family collaterals (or proxies) served as the information source. There is a small literature reviewing the effects of information source on the validity of information; clearly, some variables were more affected by data source than others. For example, family proxies were probably more accurate about service use or CHF symptoms than about more subjective information regarding perceived social support or extent of depressive symptoms. This issue is particularly relevant, given that our article examined the effect of information source (or rater role) on assessments of the adequacy of care. For this particular research question, we used only observations for which the source of information was the patient (eliminating observations where family proxies were the informants) so that we could cleanly compare patient perspective to nurse professional perspective. But in other analyses, we included information on all subjects, whether patient self report or family proxies, recognizing the possibility of introducing some measurement error but opting for a more representative and larger sample. It is a very interesting research dilemma that there is no way to assess the discrepancy of self report versus professional report when the study participant is cognitively impaired, as the information from cognitively impaired elders may be seriously flawed, if obtainable at all.

Challenge #3: Dealing with Hospital Readmissions

Although we were aware of high rates of readmission of CHF patients (and, indeed, used this to rationalize focusing on this diagnosis for our study of postacute care), we did not fully appreciate the challenge of readmission at the outset of our study. Forty-one percent of the sample subjects were readmitted at least once in our 14-week study period. Twelve percent had two readmissions. Some readmissions occurred very soon after discharge, even before our 2-week interview. Although readmission was an outcome of interest, the sample size for our longitudinal study of care plans and other six-month outcomes was jeopardized. Thus, we made the decision to follow patients through another hospitalization and discharge to the community. At the time of the first readmission, we started the data collection again, redoing the baseline interview during the hospital readmission and restarting the calendar, in terms of the postdischarge interviews. This protocol introduced a repeated measure into the design, but allowed us to follow vulnerable study participants for longer periods of postacute care. If a study participant was readmitted a second time, we classified the observation as "readmitted twice" and "completed the study." In some cases, a study participant was close to the final 14-week postdischarge interview when she was readmitted. Thus, we needed to complete a second round of data collection and follow this person into postacute care again. Accordingly, the study's data collection period ran longer than we planned.

Challenge #4: Dealing with Study Participants' Requests for Help

When our research assistants called or visited study participants in the postacute period, they were often mistaken as service providers. During the consent process and as needed in subsequent contacts, the RAs clarified their positions to study participants and their family members; and we trained the RAs to deal with requests for help. The fact that the RAs were usually social work students heightened their awareness of the difficult situations of some of the study participants. The RAs were instructed to clarify the limits of their research role and to ensure that the study participants had the names and telephone numbers of professionals involved in their care (which we acknowledge is an intervention, though necessary from an ethical standpoint). If the study participant was in an abusive or neglectful situation, we were obligated reporters to the Missouri Department of Health and Senior Services; and RAs were instructed to bring the case to the attention of the principal investigators who would assist in making the hotline call. We have learned through this and other research projects that the assumption of a research role often presents ethical dilemmas for social work students; we take extra care to hire students who are aware of this tension and willing to discuss difficult situations and not intervene prematurely.

Challenge #5: Achieving Concurrent Assessments of Adequacy of Care

Our study design called for the "concurrent" rating of care plan adequacy by study participants and nurse professionals. This protocol, which was critical to answer the research question about rater role, called for the simultaneous assessments of the postacute care arrangements by the professional and the patient. Thus, at the 2-week and 10-week interviews, we arranged for both a telephone interview to get patient self report and an in-home interview to get the professional assessment. Both interviews focused on the informal and formal assistance provided to address functional impairment (all other information gathered in the interviews was different, and study participants did not complain of redundancy). As explained in the article, the telephone interview was conducive to self report by the study participant and the in-home interview was conducive to clinical observation and professional judgment.

The biggest practical challenge was completing the two interviews at the same time or concurrently. We operationalized "concurrent" to mean that the two interviews were conducted within a 48-hour period. The RAs set up the telephone interview at a time agreeable to the study participant, informed the study participant that a nurse interviewer would be calling shortly to schedule the second part of the interview, and got the necessary information to the nurse to schedule the in-home visit. The nurses were trained to call the study participant immediately after receiving notice that the telephone interview had been scheduled. We kept track of the time of the two interviews to monitor our adherence to the "48 hour" protocol. We aimed for an 80 percent success rate and we reviewed these data regularly. We problem-solved as needed to adhere to this protocol, and it took constant vigilance to achieve an adequate level of attainment. It is clear that any concurrent ratings must be within some specified time frame (the operationalization of "concurrent"), under the assumption that the study participants' conditions and service arrangements are constant throughout that period. In this study, we decided that we could not accomplish a smaller time interval between interviews; yet we acknowledge that changes could occur in this two-day period. For example, there could be intervening life events and changes in health and services received between the two interviews, but scheduling the interviews closer together was not often possible.

RESEARCH SITE

Our topic of postacute care for Medicare patients was compelling to funders because of the "quicker and sicker" phenomenon; at the same time, social workers were under pressure in this environment to arrange discharges more quickly and deal with patients who were more medically unstable. The hospital administration and social workers thus appreciated the importance of the study but were not eager to take on any new demands. Our protocol called for the social workers to identify patients that met study criteria and fill out referral forms. We also conducted a 15–30 minute interview with the social worker around the time of the patient's discharge. To increase the study's appeal to the social workers, we had budgeted money to pay the social workers $5 for each interview, and we tried to schedule interviews over the lunch break. We also supplied treats (donuts, Halloween candy, etc.) for all the hospital staff involved in our project, and posted signs expressing our gratitude for their participation. The research assistant who was responsible for following up with referrals and interviewing the social workers was very skilled and likable, and the protocols worked well. However, it was not fail-proof, and all eligible study participants were not referred to the study. Because it was very hard to obtain records to indicate which patients were eligible but not referred, we could only estimate this with the help of administrative staff responsible for hospital records.

We were fortunate that in this time of rapid hospital change, administration and staff remained constant enough for us to collect the data as planned. Very often this is not the case in agency-based research. Also, our study was facilitated by our ability to pay the social workers as study participants when they completed an interview. In other public agencies, we have not been able to use such financial incentives for staff participation.

ETHICAL ISSUES

We discussed earlier the issue of including cognitively impaired patients in our sample, and the protocol to solicit participation of a family proxy. But, as indicated above, we relied on the social workers and nurses to determine patients' ability to give informed consent and provide study information. In order to ease the burden of the referral process, we did not ask them to use a standardized instrument or more formal clinical or legal protocols. Thus, social workers may have excluded some patients who had the capacity to participate and included some who did not really understand the research project and their involvement. Yet participation was voluntary, in that study participants could refuse any phone contact, and the response to our telephone calls was almost always very positive. The information collected was about needs and services and was not of a sensitive nature. Thus, we assessed the risk of participation as minimal.

Social workers were also viewed as research subjects, given that they participated in an interview. Thus, they provided informed consent and could not be coerced to participate, despite encouragement from department administrators. One social worker did refuse to participate in referral or interview activities.

As mentioned previously, our research assistants encountered situations where study participants were clearly in need of assistance or counseling. In cases of abuse and neglect, we were mandated reporters and placed hotline calls to state officials. We reported on three or four such situations throughout the data collection period. However, there were other serious situations, short of abuse or neglect, that we thought merited intervention. Thus, we designed appropriate protocols in conjunction with social work administrators. In extreme cases and *only with the agreement* of the study participant, the project directors called the hospital discharge planners and gave them the pertinent information about the patient's situation. (If the study participant refused the help, we did not intervene in any way.) We did this only rarely, knowing that we were introducing an intervention in a longitudinal study of the service system as it was naturally occurring. Also, it was inappropriate to extend the social worker's involvement with the client beyond the standard practice associated with the hospital position.

On a few occasions, family members of study participants called our study offices, usually to learn more about the study. We comfortably shared information about study objectives and general methodology, but we did not share any information about the study participant. When family members called to request services, we clarified that we were researchers and encouraged them to contact the professionals involved in the care of their family member. On a few occasions, a family member would call and try to learn specific information about their family member's condition or care arrangements, and we would explain research protocols and the confidentiality of the data we collected. These conversations were challenging on only a few occasions, and in these cases, the RA would refer the caller to the PIs.

STATISTICAL ANALYSES

In the published article, we give detailed explanation of the final sample size in the rater-role analysis, and this accounting required comprehensive records during the data collection process. Our final sample is small ($n = 85$), which is the major tradeoff for attaining a measurement of one phenomenon from two different raters within 48 hours of each other. We argue that the requisite sample for this analysis is select; "despite limits to statistical power, the subsetted sample provides a scarce opportunity to examine issues in quality of care measurement that are critical in both gerontology and health services research" (page 175). Of course, power depends on the specific analysis, and for dependent *t*-tests to compare overall adequacy scores, we had adequate power. Also, we used a repeated measures approach in multiple regression, given that each study participant provided two observations—one with the professional rating of adequacy and one with the self-reported adequacy. This approach increased our power. Yet we did a functional area-by-area analysis (for example, comparing adequacy ratings in each area of functional need, such as shopping, meal preparation, etc.). In this series of dependent *t*-tests, four cell sizes were too small for valid tests of statistical difference (transfer, toileting, walking, and eating). Thus we eliminated these areas from the comparison of self report and professional assessment. Also, we mention in the article that the lack of statistical power cannot be ruled out as an explanation for null findings.

As in the case of any study design short of an experiment, there are limits to conclusions about causality. However, the nature of the variables in this study allowed causal conclusions. We can claim that rater role caused the differences in ratings, since rater role is immutable. That is, because rater role and the rating of the adequacy of care are correlated, we can conclude the rater role affects the ratings because the ratings cannot affect the rater role.

STRENGTHS AND LIMITATIONS OF THE STUDY

We enumerate several strengths and limitations of the study in our published paper. As is often the case, our strengths and limitations are not independent. For example, it is a strength to control variance in discharge planning procedures and postacute service options by focusing on a specific geographic area. This also allowed us to conduct in-home interviews with most of the study sample because travel distance was reasonable. However, generalizability was limited accordingly. (In every peer review process for the manuscripts resulting from the parent project, we needed to defend having only one study site and to describe the extent to which the findings were generalizable.) Also, it is a strength that we were able to conduct concurrent assessments of care plans from self report and professional assessment, but we were limited in our ability to achieve a large enough sample for a wider range of analyses.

APPLICATION OF FINDINGS

We believe that the major finding of this study reinforces a very important idea for researchers, practitioners, and evaluators: the perspectives about adequacy of care (and indeed more widely, the quality of care) differ across various stakeholder groups. Thus, researchers cannot rely on varying sources of information without introducing error, practitioners need to communicate specifically with all involved stakeholders and not make assumptions about agreement, and program evaluators have different outcomes assessments to consider. We conclude that stakeholder perspectives can be both valid and different; and substitutability of information source is not always appropriate in quality-of-care research.

We believe that documenting discrepancy in perspective by each specific area of need (housekeeping, meal preparation, etc.) is very useful for targeting improvements in the service system. For example, we document a discrepant view of the sufficiency of transportation assistance. Nurses were more likely than older adults to view the amount of transportation assistance as sufficient. We propose that this discrepancy stems from different priorities for travel—for example, getting to medical appointments versus getting to social outings or religious services. This discrepancy in perspective clearly warrants further investigation as we develop transportation services for our aging society.

Finally, we think that this study demonstrates the importance of null findings. We fail to document differences in sufficiency of care by elder age, gender, race, or SES. The most vulnerable elderly are not less likely to rate the assistance they receive as less sufficient and professionals are not observing a difference. We argue that this is good news from a health disparities perspective.

9

Predicting Incarceration of Clients of a Psychiatric Probation and Parole Service

Phyllis Solomon, Ph.D., Jeffrey Draine, Ph.D., and Steven C. Marcus, Ph.D.

According to the criminalization hypothesis, more restrictive involuntary hospitalization criteria have increased the use of criminal arrest as a management strategy for persons who have severe mental illness (1–3). Although longitudinal data to test this assumption are lacking (2, 4), a large number of individuals with severe mental illness are involved with the criminal justice system (5–11). It was recently estimated that 16 percent of jail inmates and 16 percent of persons on probation have a mental illness (5). These statistics raise the question of whether jails are being used as an alternative to treatment for persons who have severe mental illness.

We studied one aspect of this hypothesis—the decision to incarcerate persons who are in violation of stipulations of probation or parole. For those who are mentally ill, probation or parole stipulations frequently include compliance with prescribed psychiatric medication and specific housing arrangements. Noncompliance with these treatment stipulations may result in incarceration. Recent research on involvement in mental health treatment among probationers and parolees with psychiatric disorders has shown that more intensive treatment monitoring seems to result in a greater chance of incarceration for these clients.

This finding could be attributed to greater surveillance and awareness of violations of conditions of probation or parole by case managers and other mental health care providers. Through this process, mental health providers augment the monitoring function of probation and parole officers (12). Intensive supervision of probation or parole has been associated with a higher rate of incarceration as a result of more frequent observation and a greater scope of surveillance (13–15).

Solomon and Draine (11) found that case managers used reincarceration as a mechanism for obtaining needed treatment for psychiatric probationers and parolees who were perceived to be decompensating, were unwilling to sign a voluntary admission for hospitalization, and were unable to be committed on an involuntary order because of restrictive admission criteria. It was easier for the case managers to reincarcerate these clients on a technical violation than to hospitalize them. Given that the jail system under study had a well-developed mental health treatment program, the case managers could be reasonably assured that the clients would receive psychiatric treatment.

Investigators who have examined factors that explain reincarceration of mentally ill offenders have concluded that these explanatory factors are the same as for non–mentally ill offenders—that is, sociodemographic characteristics and criminal history (16–18). Even in a study of a group of offenders with severe psychiatric illness, Feder (19) found that psychiatric treatment variables did not explain rearrest. However, she did find that although mentally ill offenders were less likely to be reincarcerated, they were more likely to have committed a technical violation. Other researchers have found that rates of technical violations were related to the interaction of the offenders' degree of psychopathology and their diagnosis (20).

These findings suggest that among mentally ill offenders, characteristics of the psychiatric illness and treatment variables both may explain reincarceration for a technical violation. If jails are used as treatment facilities for mentally ill offenders, it is likely that characteristics of the psychiatric illness and patterns of mental health service use will explain reincarceration for technical violations of probationers and parolees and not explain reincarceration for a new offense.

This study assessed whether the incarcerations that took place during a 15-month study period in a population of persons with mental illness who were on probation or parole occurred more for reasons of noncompliance with stipulated psychiatric treatment than for new criminal activities. Specifically, the investigators hypothesized that among psychiatric clients who were on probation or parole, clinical characteristics, psychiatric status, and use of mental health services would be associated with incarceration for a technical violation and not for a new offense when sociodemographic characteristics and criminal history were controlled for.

METHODS

Setting

The setting for the study was the probation and parole system of a large city on the East Coast of the United States. This county probation and parole system supervises individuals who are sentenced to probation or who are paroled from sentences of less than two years. Under this system, the distinction between community supervision for probation and parole is minimal. Both probation and parole are supervised by the same officers using the same procedures.

At the time of the study, two specialized probation units were assigned psychiatric cases. Because these units did not provide clinical services, the "psychiatric" designation was an administrative one rather than a clinical one. Clients were assigned to the psychiatric units for a variety of reasons, including at the discretion of sentencing judges. Many clients were assigned to psychiatric probation or parole because they had a history of mental health treatment.

Recruitment of Study Participants

Because of the heterogeneity of the population on psychiatric probation or parole, potential study participants were screened with a standardized diagnostic tool to determine their history of serious mental illness. The researchers attempted to screen and interview each new client assigned to psychiatric probation or parole. New clients were defined as those who were newly sentenced to probation; newly paroled clients; current clients receiving a new, additional probation sentence; or continuing clients returning to community supervision after a stay in jail.

The researchers were present at the psychiatric probation and parole offices from January 1995 to July 1997 to monitor intakes. The four investigators over the course of the study were the second author, two doctoral students in social welfare who had professional experience in the criminal justice system, and a full-time study coordinator with Ph.D.-level training in ethnographic research methods. An attempt was made to contact each new client until a sample of 250 was obtained. New clients were approached in the office or were referred to the researchers by probation and parole officers.

The researchers kept a running list of new referrals to the psychiatric probation and parole units. New referrals over the recruitment period totaled 1,006. The study participants had to be actively supervised by officers to be eligible for the study. Thus the researchers concentrated their recruitment efforts on clients who were reporting to psychiatric probation and parole offices. They monitored the sign-in logs for names of clients from the new referral list and approached clients in the waiting area or asked officers to refer clients for the study. A total of 440 clients were asked to consent to participate in the screening interview. Of these, 327 (74 percent) consented to be screened for the study.

The only data collected for clients who refused to participate in the study were observer estimates of age, sex, and ethnicity. There were no differences in these characteristics between participants and those who refused to participate. Clients who provided voluntary informed consent were briefly interviewed and then screened for lifetime diagnoses of depression, mania, and schizophrenia with the Quick Diagnostic Interview Schedule (QDIS) (21–23), which is an abridged computerized version of the Diagnostic Interview Schedule. The interviewer read QDIS items to the study participants and entered their responses directly into the computerized program on a notebook computer. Individuals who screened positive for lifetime occurrences of major depression, mania, or schizophrenia were asked to consent to participate in the study.

Follow-Up Data Collection

The sample of 250 was monitored with use of a protocol that included interviews with the client and with probation and parole officers about each client every three months for one year or until the client was incarcerated, whichever came first. The client interview assessed quality of life, service use, motivation to cooperate with criminal justice stipulations and mental health treatment, substance use, and mental health status.

Informed consent procedures that had been approved by the institutional review board were used for both the screening phase and the follow-up phase of the study. At each subsequent interview point, clients were reminded of their right to refuse to continue to participate in the study without affecting their legal or treatment status. The clients' incarceration data were tracked for 15 months— three months beyond the one-year interview. Data were obtained for all clients from at least one time point; one or more expected waves of data were missing for 98 clients (39 percent).

Symptoms were assessed with the Brief Psychiatric Rating Scale (BPRS) (24,25). Interviewers were trained to agreement with one another on the use of the BPRS. The entire interview period was used for rating observations. The interviewer probed for objective symptom reports at the end of the interview. Subscales were constructed for anxiety and depression, thought disturbance, and hostility (26).

The sections on the severity of drug and alcohol use from the Addiction Severity Index (ASI) (27,28) were used to assess addiction. Client responses were anchored by using the calendar follow-back method to improve the validity of reports of substance use (29). Cutoff scores for drug and alcohol problems were estimated with the use of patterns of responses to the ASI items that would indicate a clinically significant problem with drug or alcohol use for individuals with severe mental illness.

A measure of attitudes toward psychiatric medication was also used (30). This measure was a modification of a self-report scale of medication compliance developed by Hogan and colleagues (31). Clients were also asked about their participation in psychiatric treatment and compliance with probation or parole supervision.

Interviews with officers included assessments of the severity of substance use developed for clinicians' use (32) and assessments of dangerousness to self or others, grave disability, and lack of impulse control (33, 34). These latter assessments were included because they indicate criteria for involuntary hospitalization, which may be an alternative to incarceration. The officers were also asked questions that paralleled the questions asked of clients about the clients' motivation to participate in treatment, to comply with the terms of probation or parole, or to take psychiatric medications.

A list of 24 strategies an officer might use in working with a client who has a mental health problem was included. The officers were asked whether they had used each strategy in the previous three months. These items covered strategies that focused on monitoring, access to treatment, and coercion.

Criminal justice system databases were checked regularly for incarcerations. Several sources of information were used to determine whether incarcerations were for new charges or for technical violations. They included reports filed by officers as well as open-ended interviews conducted with both clients and officers about each incarceration. Information from these sources was analyzed to allow each incarceration to be classified as being primarily for a new charge or for a technical violation.

ANALYSIS

For the purposes of analysis, variables were conceptualized in terms of eight conceptual blocks: sociodemographic characteristics, clinical characteristics, criminal history, service use during the follow-up period, motivation to comply with treatment and probation or parole, symptoms, officers' reports, and officers' strategies. The sociodemographic variables were age, male sex, education, African-American ethnicity—a majority of the sample—and never married. The clinical variables were diagnosis of schizophrenia, diagnosis of depression, diagnosis of mania, self-reported psychiatric treatment before first life-time arrest, self-reported previous psychiatric hospitalization, and self-reported alcohol or drug problem.

The criminal history variables were three or more self-reported previous lifetime arrests and self-reported arrest as a juvenile. Variables related to service use during the follow-up period were any reported use of inpatient hospitalization, emergency services, medical care, therapy, vocational services, substance abuse treatment, or intensive case management. Variables related to motivation to comply with treatment and probation were self-reported lack of compliance with probation or medication, self-reported low motivation for compliance with medication, mental health treatment or probation, and a low rating by the client of the helpfulness of psychiatric medication.

Symptom variables were significant severity ratings for alcohol and drug addiction on the ASI and significant ratings for anxiety and depression, thought disturbance, and hostility on the BPRS. Characteristics of officers' reports were lack of compliance with medications or the stipulations of probation or parole or observed low motivation for compliance with medication, mental health treatment, or probation or parole and officer assessments of client's danger to self, danger to others, grave disability, or lack of impulse control. Finally, the characteristics of officers' strategies were any officer report of routine supervision strategies, collaboration with mental health professionals to supervise the mutual client, a threat to incarcerate the client, and an attempt to hospitalize the client involuntarily.

The first analysis was designed to determine the factors associated with incarceration for new criminal behavior. The purpose of the second analysis was to identify factors associated with technical violations of probation. Both analyses used the group that had no arrests for comparison. Bivariate associations were assessed with chi square analyses (35).

Multivariate prediction models were fitted with use of proportional hazards regression. This longitudinal analysis accounted for time and censored for clients who were not incarcerated over the follow-up period (36). Variables were dichotomized at clinically significant cutoff points for ease of interpretation of resulting risk ratios. Stepwise models were constructed by using variables from the conceptual blocks as potential factors.

The first proportional hazards model predicted any incarceration for a new charge compared with no incarceration, excluding clients who were incarcerated for technical violations. The second model predicted any incarceration for a technical violation, excluding those who were incarcerated for a new charge. Logistic regression was used to directly compare clients incarcerated on a new charge with those incarcerated on a technical violation. To prevent cases from being excluded from the multivariate analyses, means replacement (by arrest group) was used to account for item nonresponse (37). Effect size was assessed by risk ratios (proportional hazards) and odds ratios (logistic). Statistical significance of the effect was assessed with the Wald chi square statistic (38). The statistical package SAS (SAS Institute, Cary, NC) was used for the statistical analyses.

RESULTS

Of the 327 clients screened for lifetime occurrences of major depression, mania, or schizophrenia, 254 (78 percent) screened positive for one or more of these illnesses and thus were eligible for the study. Four eligible clients refused to give consent. Sociodemographic and other characteristics of the sample are summarized in Table 9.1. The results of the QDIS are summarized in Table 9.2.

Probation officers provided detailed case information for 197 clients. Among the 180 for whom complete data from officers were provided, 159 (88 percent) were on probation and 40 (22 percent) were on parole. Nine (5 percent) were on both probation and parole. In 78 of the 191 cases for which data were available (41 percent), this was the client's first experience with either probation or parole; of these, 76 were on probation and two were on parole.

Of the 250 clients in our sample, 85 (34 percent) were incarcerated within 15 months of the baseline interview, which is consistent with rearrest rates of 24 to 56 percent found among individuals with mental illness (39). Of these incarcerations, 41 (16 percent of the sample) were for technical reasons and 44 (18 percent) were for new criminal charges.

Clients reported using a substantial mix of psychiatric services when they were living in the community. Of the 250 clients, 100 (40 percent) were hospitalized during the follow-up period, and 77 (31 percent) reported receiving psychiatric crisis services. A total of 169 (68 percent) reported receiving any individual, family, or group therapy at some point. Ninety-seven (39 percent) reported receiving substance abuse treatment, and 78 (31 percent) reported receiving intensive case management.

Table 9.1. Characteristics of a Sample of Clients of a Psychiatric Probation and Parole Service

Characteristic	*N* or Mean ± SD	%
Male sex (*N* = 250)	183	73
Ethnicity (*N* = 249)		
African-American	161	65
White	57	23
Hispanic	20	8
Mixed or other	11	5
Currently using psychiatric medication (*N* = 247)	139	56
Homeless at time of interview (*N* = 249)	27	11
Drug or alcohol use at the time of arrest (*N* = 248)		
Alcohol	50	20
Drugs	33	13
Both drugs and alcohol	39	16
Ever arrested as a juvenile (*N* = 249)	94	38
Age in years (*N* = 247)	34.6 ± 9.1	
Number of years of education (*N* = 249)	11.1 ± 2.4	
Number of arrests during lifetime (*N* = 246)	7 ± 9.9	

Table 9.2. Psychiatric Diagnoses of 250 Clients of a Psychiatric Probation and Parole Service, as Determined by the Quick Diagnostic Interview Schedule

Diagnosis	*N*	%
Schizophrenia only	37	15
Mania only	10	4
Depression only	65	26
Both schizophrenia and mania	4	2
Both schizophrenia and depression	46	18
Both mania and depression	34	14
Schizophrenia, mania, and depression	54	22

As indicated in Table 9.3, three variables were predictive of both incarceration on a new charge and arrest for a technical violation in the multivariate models. Participants who doubted the helpfulness of psychiatric medications were almost five times as likely to be incarcerated for a new charge than not incarcerated at all and three times as likely to be incarcerated on a technical violation than not incarcerated.

Clients for whom officers reported low treatment motivation were nearly eight times as likely to be incarcerated on a technical violation than not to be incarcerated and almost three times as likely to be incarcerated for a new charge than not incarcerated. In both categories, officers' assessment of dangerousness to others was a significant risk factor for incarceration.

Four variables were associated with incarceration for a new charge but not with incarceration for a technical violation. Middle to older age (age 36 to 50 years), higher educational attainment,

Table 9.3. Odds Ratios of Incarceration for a New Charge versus No Incarceration and Incarceration for a Technical Violation versus No Incarceration in a Sample of Mental Health Clients on Probation or Parole, as Determined by a Proportional Hazards Model

Variable	New Charge Versus No Incarceration Over 15 Months ($N = 209$)		Technical Violation Versus No Incarceration Over 15 Months ($N = 206$)	
	Odds Ratio	95% CI	Odds Ratio	95% CI
Age of 36 to 50 years	.36*	.18–.74		
Never married			3.18**	1.39–7.26
Education at high school level or above	.42**	.22–.08		
More than three arrests during lifetime			4.03***	1.87–8.71
Arrested before age 20 years			.38**	.19–.80
Any client report of noncompliance with psychiatric care			.13***	.05–.39
Any psychiatric hospitalization during follow-up period			3.84**	1.58–9.33
Any group or individual therapy during follow-up period			.16***	.05–.49
Client's belief that psychiatric medications are not helpful	4.89**	1.76–13.63	3.10*	1.04–9.28
Client is taking psychiatric medication			9.46***	2.61–34.33
Any officer report of low treatment motivation	2.72**	1.35–5.49	7.78***	3.28–18.46
Any officer assessment of danger to self			.20***	.09–.48
Any officer assessment of danger to others	2.68**	1.32–5.40	3.79***	1.71–8.39
Any officer assessment of disability	.36**	.18–.70		
Routine pattern of supervision by officers	.24***	.12–.47		

*$p < .05$

**$p < .01$

***$p < .001$

officers' assessment of disability, and a routine pattern of client supervision by officers were all associated with a lower risk of incarceration for a new charge.

Eight variables were associated with incarceration on a technical violation but were not associated with incarceration for a new charge. Four of these variables were associated with a greater risk of incarceration for a technical violation. Individuals who had never been married, who had been incarcerated more than three times during their lifetime, or who had any psychiatric hospitalization during the follow-up period were three to four times as likely to be incarcerated for technical reasons than not to be incarcerated.

Participants who had been prescribed psychiatric medication were more than nine times as likely to be incarcerated on a technical violation than not incarcerated at all. A first arrest before the age of 20 years; any client report of noncompliance; receipt of any individual, family, or group therapy; and officers' assessment of danger to self were associated with a lower risk of incarceration on a technical violation.

In the logistic regression analysis that directly compared clients who were incarcerated for new charges with those who were incarcerated for a technical violation of probation, two variables showed significant differences. Clients who were incarcerated on a technical violation were six times as likely to have received any intensive case management services (odds ratio = 6.09, 95% CI = 1.7 to 21.7; $\chi^2 = 8.34$, $df = 1$, $p < .01$) and more likely to have had high scores on the hostility subscale of the BPRS (odds ratio = 3.0, 95% CI = 1.1 to 7.9; χ^2 = 4.86, df = 1, p < .05) than those who were incarcerated for a new charge.

DISCUSSION AND CONCLUSIONS

The results of this study support the hypothesis that among clients of a psychiatric probation and parole service the use of mental health services would explain incarceration for technical violations. Services seem to have an inconsistent effect on incarceration for technical violations. Engagement in any form of therapy and client-reported noncompliance with mental health treatment appeared to protect against incarceration for a technical violation, whereas taking a prescribed medication, being hospitalized during the follow-up period, and receiving intensive case management services were associated with a higher likelihood of incarceration for a technical violation. These apparent inconsistencies can be reconciled in the context of the functions of probation and parole.

A primary function of probation and parole officers is monitoring stipulations of probation and parole, which include compliance with psychiatric treatment. Mental health providers, particularly case managers, can enhance the monitoring of persons who are on probation. Medication prescription protocols require clients to make visits to mental health services for medication checks. Similarly, the nature of intensive case management services means observing clients' appointment-keeping behavior as well as their engagement in behaviors that could lead to new criminal charges. Recent release from a psychiatric hospital probably triggers greater monitoring of clients' behavior by mental health care providers. Thus failure to keep appointments and engagement in activities that may lead to criminal behavior may result in mental health care providers' contacting probation and parole officers about noncompliance.

In some cases, providers cooperate with officers to leverage compliance under threat of incarceration. Previous research has shown that officers who interact with mental health care providers are more likely to use threats of incarceration with their clients (40). Such threats may escalate to the point that the officer initiates incarceration.

The result for reports of noncompliance initially appears counterintuitive. It is easier to understand this result in terms of reduced monitoring opportunity than in terms of noncompliance. Noncompliance means that clients were at least participating in mental health services, but not at the expected level. Consequently there is less opportunity for mental health providers to observe activities that violate the client's probation or parole stipulations.

Marginal engagement in mental health services may also reduce the incentive for officers to monitor these clients as closely, and hence they may leave the monitoring to the mental health system. Officers may be comfortable knowing that they can document at least some level of participation in mental health services, which may explain the lack of routine supervision by the officers, in turn explaining incarceration on technical violations. This approach may have implications for mandated services more generally. Although the mandate may provide incentives for clients to be nominally involved in treatment, it cannot explain the quality or the depth of the treatment.

Probation and parole officers help their clients avoid criminal behavior. Incarceration for a technical violation may be used as a preventive measure to keep clients from engaging in criminal behavior that could result in an incarceration for a new charge. Officers who view mental health treatment for these clients as a means of reducing criminal behavior may resort to incarceration as a strategy for treatment and greater subsequent compliance with treatment after release from jail.

Consistent with this reasoning is the finding that clients with low motivation and more negative attitudes about mental health treatment had a greater likelihood of being incarcerated for a technical violation. These negative attitudes were also associated with incarceration for a new charge. This finding seems to indicate that a lack of engagement with mental health services is associated with continued criminal behavior.

As in previous research, clinical characteristics did not play a role in either type of incarceration, but psychiatric status, specifically dangerousness to others, was related to both incarceration for a technical violation and incarceration for a new criminal charge, and dangerousness to self was protective against a technical violation.

The association between dangerousness to others and incarceration for a technical violation can readily be understood in terms of yet another function of officers—protecting public safety. Given that the jail in this study had a comprehensive mental health treatment system, including inpatient psychiatric beds, it is likely that clients who were dangerous to others would have received treatment if they had been sent to the jail. This mental health system has strict commitment criteria. Consequently case managers may find it easier to obtain hospitalization for their clients in the jail (41).

Consistent with previous research on reincarceration, criminal history was related to incarceration for a technical violation but did not predict incarceration for a new charge. A client's criminal history probably influences officers' decisions about technical violations. Officers thus may use incarceration for a technical violation as a strategy to prevent criminal behavior that will ultimately result in a new criminal charge.

Also paralleling the results of previous research, sociodemographic characteristics helped explain both types of incarceration, but these characteristics differed for each type. Clients who went to jail for a technical violation were less likely to have ever been married. Persons on probation who have fulfilled fewer social expectations may not have the attendant social networks to support treatment or compliance with conditions of probation or parole. Thus officers may need to resort to other strategies to encourage compliance with treatment.

On the basis of these findings it appears that incarceration for a technical violation is not being used pervasively for treatment purposes, although it does occur. This type of incarceration is used more to control the client and as a strategy for encouraging clients to comply with treatment when they are living in the community under court stipulations. In some cases mental health providers and probation and parole officers work together toward clinical goals for the client. These alliances between the mental health system and the criminal justice system are not formally structured but occur on an ad hoc basis. If formalized arrangements between the mental health and criminal justice systems are pursued, policy planners will need to carefully weigh the benefits of service coordination against the clients' increased risk of incarceration.

Criminal justice systems vary in the extent to which they have specialized probation and parole units. Future research could examine the interaction between mental health services and probation and parole agencies in several service contexts. As we gain a better understanding of this interactive process, interventions or service models may be developed. Such approaches could provide an opportunity for studies of these service innovations. The implications of this and related research would tap into the current interest in outpatient commitment and mental health courts.

ACKNOWLEDGMENTS

This research was funded by grant R01-MH-54445 from the National Institute of Mental Health. The authors acknowledge the contributions of Jonathan David, Ph.D., in coordinating data collection and Kim Nieves, M.S.W., in data collection and management. The authors thank Tony Sasselli, Fran Ronkowski, and Jim Rubolina.

REFERENCES

1. Abramson M: The criminalization of mentally disordered behavior. *Hospital and Community Psychiatry* 23:101–105, 1972

2. Teplin L: The criminalization of the mentally ill: speculation in search of data. *Psychological Bulletin* 94:54–67, 1983

3. Teplin L: The criminalization hypothesis: myth, misnomer, or management strategy? In *Law and mental health: Major developments and research needs.* Edited by Shah SA, Sales BD. Washington, DC: National Institute of Mental Health, 1991

4. Hiday VA: Civil commitment and arrests: an investigation of the criminalization thesis. *Journal of Nervous and Mental Disease* 180:184–191, 1992

5. Ditton PM: Mental health and treatment of inmates and probationers. Washington, DC: Bureau of Justice Statistics, 1999

6. Teplin LA: The prevalence of severe mental disorder among urban jail detainees: comparison with the Epidemiologic Catchment Area program. *American Journal of Public Health* 80:663–669, 1990

7. Teplin LA, Abram KM, McClelland GM: Mentally disordered women in jail: who receives services? *American Journal of Public Health* 87:604–609, 1997

8. Guy E, Platt JJ, Zwerling I, et al: Mental health status of prisoners in an urban jail. *Criminal Justice and Behavior* 12:29–53, 1985

9. Lamb HR, Grant RW: The mentally ill in an urban county jail. *Archives of General Psychiatry* 39:17–22, 1982

10. Lamb HR, Grant RW: Mentally ill women in a county jail. *Archives of General Psychiatry* 40:363–368, 1983

11. Solomon P, Draine J: Issues in serving the forensic client. *Social Work* 40:25–33, 1995

12. Solomon P, Draine J: One year outcomes of a randomized trial of case management with seriously mentally ill clients leaving jail. *Evaluation Review* 19:256–273, 1995

13. Gottfredson MR, Mitchell-Herzfeld SD, Flanagan TJ: Another look at the effectiveness of parole supervision. *Journal of Research in Crime and Delinquency* 19:277–298, 1982

14. Martin SS, Scarpitti RF: An intensive case management approach for paroled IV drug users. *Journal of Drug Issues* 23:43–59, 1993

15. Tonry M: Stated and latent functions of ISP. *Crime and Delinquency* 36:174–191, 1990

16. Bonta J, Law M, Hanson K: The prediction of criminal and violent recidivism among mentally disordered offenders: a meta-analysis. *Psychological Bulletin* 123:123–142, 1998

17. Feder L: A profile of mentally ill offenders and their adjustment in the community. *Journal of Psychiatry and the Law* 19:79–98, 1991

18. Schellenberg EG, Wasylenski D, Webster D: A review of arrests among psychiatric patients. *International Journal of Law and Psychiatry* 15:251–264, 1992

19. Feder L: A profile of mentally ill offenders and their adjustment in the community. *Journal of Psychiatry and the Law* 19:79–98, 1991

20. Toch H, Adams K: Pathology and disruptiveness among prison inmates. *Journal of Research in Crime and Delinquency* 23:7–21, 1986

21. Bucholz KK, Marion SL, Shayka JJ, et al: A short computer interview for obtaining psychiatric diagnoses. *Psychiatric Services* 47:293–297, 1996

22. Bovings L, Helzer J, Croughan J, et al: National Institute of Mental Health Diagnostic Interview Schedule. *Archives of General Psychiatry* 38:381–389, 1981

23. Spengler P, Wittchen HU: Procedural validity of standardized symptom questions of psychotic symptoms: a comparison of the DIS with two clinical methods. *Comprehensive Psychiatry* 29:309–322, 1988

24. Overall J, Gorham D: The Brief Psychiatric Rating Scale. *Psychological Reports* 10:799–812

25. Lukoff D, Liberman RP, Nuechterlein K: Symptom monitoring in the rehabilitation of schizophrenic patients. *Schizophrenia Bulletin* 12:578–602, 1986

26. Guy W: ECDEU *Assessment Manual for Psychopharmacology,* revised ed. Rockville, Md, National Institute of Mental Health, 1976

27. Zanis DA, McLellan AT, Corse S: Is the Addiction Severity Index a reliable and valid instrument among clients with severe and persistent mental illness and substance use disorders? *Community Mental Health Journal* 33:213–227, 1997

28. McLellan AT, Luborsky L, Cacciola J, et al: New data from the Addiction Severity Index: reliability and validity in three centers. *Journal of Nervous and Mental Disease* 173:412–422, 1985

29. Fals-Stewart W, O'Farrell TJ, Freitas TT, et al: The timeline follow-back reports of psychoactive substance use by drug-abusing patients:

psychometric properties. *Journal of Consulting and Clinical Psychology* 68:134–144, 2000

30. Sullivan G: *Rehospitalization of the seriously mentally ill in Mississippi: Conceptual models, study design, and implementation.* Santa Barbara, CA: Rand, 1989

31. Hogan TP, Awad AG, Eastwood R: A self-report scale predictive of drug compliance in schizophrenia. *Psychological Medicine* 13:177–183, 1983

32. Drake R, Osher F, Wallach M: Alcohol use and abuse in schizophrenia: a prospective community study. *Journal of Nervous and Mental Disease* 177:408–414, 1989

33. Segal S, Watson M, Goldfinger S, et al: Civil commitment in the psychiatric emergency room: I. The assessment of dangerousness by emergency room clinicians. *Archives of General Psychiatry* 45:748–752, 1988

34. Segal S, Watson M, Goldfinger S, et al: Civil commitment in the psychiatric emergency room: III. Disposition as a function of mental disorder and dangerousness indicators. *Archives of General Psychiatry* 45:759–763, 1988

35. Rosner B: *Fundamentals of biostatistics,* 4th ed. Belmont, MA: Duxbury, 1995

36. Allison PD: *Survival analysis using the SAS system: a practical guide.* Cary, NC: SAS Institute, 1995

37. Hosmer DW, Lemeshow S: *Applied logistic regression.* New York: Wiley, 1989

38. Taylor MA, Amir N: The problem of missing clinical data for research in psychopathology: some solution guidelines. *Journal of Nervous and Mental Disease* 182:222–229, 1994

39. Hiday VA: Mental illness and the criminal justice system. In *A handbook for the study of mental health.* Edited by Horwitz A, Scheid T. Cambridge, England: Cambridge University Press, 1999

40. Draine J, Solomon P: Threats of incarceration in a psychiatric probation and parole service. *American Journal of Orthopsychiatry* 71:262–267, 2001

41. Solomon P, Rogers R, Draine J, et al: Interaction of the criminal justice system and psychiatric professionals in which civil commitment standards are prohibitive. *Bulletin of the American Academy of Psychiatry and the Law* 23:117–128, 1995

COMMENTARY BY: Phyllis Solomon and Jeffrey Draine

THE EMERGENCE OF THE RESEARCH STUDY

The story behind this study begins with an earlier investigation of a randomized design of adults with severe mental illness leaving jail who were also homeless, funded by the National Institute of Mental Health (NIMH) (Solomon & Draine, 1995a). We collaborated closely with the mental health service in the jail system, a very extensive mental health service that included inpatient and ambulatory services in the jail that were created to respond to court decrees. With the assistance of mental health workers, doing initial screenings for homelessness and severe mental illness, 200 of their clients who consented to the study were randomized to one of three conditions upon release from jail:

- An Assertive Community Treatment (ACT) Team, which included four case managers, a supervising psychiatrist, a resident fellow in forensic psychiatry, and a housing specialist. Sixty clients were assigned to this experimental condition.

- Forensic Intensive Case Managers, who were individual case managers who specialized in working with adults with severe mental illness involved in the criminal justice system. This was a program already in operation at the time of the study. Sixty clients were assigned to this control condition.

- Usual system of care, which was referral to community mental health agencies. Eighty were assigned to this control condition. In order to maintain statistical power, more were assigned to this condition in anticipation of greater attrition.

Being grounded in the values and expectations of mental health professionals, it was assumed that ACT, an intensive and comprehensive mental health service, would likely lead to greater benefits for homeless individuals with mental illness leaving jail. These benefits would include more stable housing, reduced symptoms, fewer functional deficits, more paid employment, more friends, more social activities, fewer hospitalizations, less time in jail, and fewer arrests. However, contrary to the proposed hypothesis, there were no differences between the conditions with regard to functional, behavioral, psychosocial, and criminal justice outcomes. Although there was not a statistically significant difference, there was a clear tendency for those in the experimental ACT condition to have the highest percentage of rearrest, 60 percent, while intensive forensic case management

Commentary on article: Solomon, P., Draine, J., Marcus, S. (2002). Predicting incarceration of clients of a psychiatric probation and parole service. *Psychiatric Services, 53*, 50–56.

had 40 percent, and usual care, 36 percent (Solomon & Draine, 1995a). This was a quite puzzling outcome that needed to be explained.

To make sense of this, we went to two sources, the case managers, and the research literature in criminal justice. From the ACT case managers, we found that they were collaborating very closely with probation and parole officers, working as a team with them to supervise clients' compliance with their stipulations of probation and parole. In addition, the case managers learned to ask judges for stipulations on their clients' probation and parole, which included the requirement that clients report to case managers and take their psychiatric medication as a condition of serving time in the community. Therefore, if the clients did not comply with the psychiatrists' orders, they were at risk of technical violations. The team case managers had concluded that when clients did not comply with medication orders, the availability of the extensive and accessible mental health service in the jail often made a trip to jail for a probation violation an easier means to access emergency psychiatric treatment than dealing with the city's mental health system's more restrictive criteria for civil commitment. This collusion with the criminal justice system certainly explained some of the difference in incarceration by the three conditions. The further explanation came from the criminology literature. We followed a lead to read the work by Michael Tonry on Intensive Supervision and Parole (ISP). We found his 1990 paper on the stated and latent functions of ISP, which explained how increased supervision of high risk probationers and parolees also resulted in higher incarceration rates because of the increased likelihood that they would be observed in actions that violated their probation and parole (Tonry, 1990). This increased surveillance resulting in increased incarceration was the dynamic we were observing in our study. Thus, the mental health blinders were off, and we began to see these interactions as true intersystem interactions requiring an understanding of criminal justice, as well as mental health professional work.

From these study findings emerged our interest in examining whether jail was used as an alternative facility for mental health treatment when individuals with severe mental illness did not use or could not get into psychiatric treatment. We also found that some individuals who entered our study were not released from jail in time to enter the study community treatment conditions, as they would go from the jail to the state psychiatric hospital and back to jail. The study was only funded for three years, which was common practice for a research demonstration grant that funded the service. The study generated a number of ideas about the use of coercion and surveillance with this population (Draine & Solomon, 1994; Draine, Solomon, & Meyerson, 1994; Solomon, Draine, & Meyerson, 1994; Solomon & Draine, 1995b&c; Solomon, Rogers, Draine, & Meyerson, 1995). As was discussed in the article, the most important idea was one that we have since found in another study: If mental health providers merely monitor clients with regard to adherence to prescribed treatment, without providing rehabilitation services, incarceration is more likely to occur than in conditions with less monitoring.

TRADE OFFS IN DESIGN

Our first thought was to address the issue of jail as an alternative to treatment by following up individuals with severe mental illness for whom involuntary commitment petitions were filed in the city mental health system. The commitment process in Philadelphia is more adversarial than in most jurisdictions within Pennsylvania. Community mental health workers in Philadelphia often chafe under a perceived higher burden of demonstrating sufficient cause for a commitment for a client when they are convinced it is warranted. Workers tell many anecdotal stories of what happens to people who are denied these commitments. The working hypothesis was that those who were denied involuntary psychiatric hospitalization were more likely to go to jail in the follow-up period than those who were hospitalized.

This seemed like a great approach to studying the issue, but then the reality of feasibility hit. Although there seem to be a high number of persons with severe mental illness in jail, arrest and incarceration are low base rate phenomena. Consequently, it would require an enormous sample size to follow in order to have a high enough rate of incarceration to explain this dependent variable. Without doing this, there would not be enough variance. For example, if only 3% were incarcerated in a year, 97% were not incarcerated. It would take years to accrue such a large sample and then follow them for an additional year to allow for possible incarceration. This would just not be feasible. This approach was therefore abandoned. We needed an alternative setting where the sample would have a higher base rate of incarceration. We needed to look to those already involved in the criminal justice system where there is a high likelihood of continued criminal involvement. Probation and parole appeared to be a good option as the rates of incarceration among this already criminally involved population are relatively high.

NEGOTIATING THE SETTING

From the earlier study, we knew the supervisor in the psychiatric probation and parole unit of the city. However, for political reasons, he was no longer in the court system. But luckily we were introduced to Kay Harris, a social worker, then chair of the Criminal Justice department at Temple University, who had a long research career examining the workings of the criminal justice system. Since we were crossing from the familiar mental health services domain into the criminal justice system, we needed a guide. We met with Kay, who expressed interest in our questions and in helping us work our way through the court system to seek their cooperation. Professor Harris took us to meet the Executive Director of the court system, Dr. Geoff Gallas.

Another lucky break was that Dr. Gallas had been a researcher in a previous life and, after listening to our study idea and receiving Professor Harris's imprimatur for our research, he sent us with Professor Harris through the bureaucracy he directed. Although we knew pretty much that we needed to be in the psychiatric probation unit, we had to work our way through Philadelphia's byzantine City Hall. Each door was opened either by familiarity with Professor Harris, assurance of Dr. Gallas's approval, or a combination of these factors. We finally arrived at the specialized probation and parole offices, where, among other specialized units (Hispanic Offenders, Developmentally Disabled Offenders, and Sex Offenders), there were two psychiatric units. With the endorsement of the court administrator, the supervisor and his staff met with us to explain the unit procedures, policies, forms, and available data in order to design the grant proposal, so that the research could be feasibly conducted. We were then able to write the grant application as well as draft a very specific letter of support that clearly indicated exactly what the court would do to ensure our access to the sample and data that were required for the study. Dr. Gallas then had this text word-processed on the court administrator's stationery, with his signature. A very specific letter is required for grant submission to the National Institutes of Health (NIH) institutes (which include NIMH) so the committee that reviews the study for scientific merit is convinced of the feasibility of the proposed study. Feasibility of studies is an extremely important criterion in assessing proposals for possible funding. The committee members need to know that the executive within the proposed setting understands and agrees to cooperate with the study, so reviewers are assured that the researchers can obtain the necessary sample size and data.

HUMAN SUBJECTS ISSUES

At the time that we designed the study we did not feel that we needed a Certificate of Confidentiality (these certificates guarantee confidentiality of identifying information of research subjects, and are intended to protect privacy from a diversity of legal actions), as the information we were seeking from the subjects was the same that probation/parole officers had access to as well. For example, we were going to ask about drug use, but the officers have the option of requesting drug screens. We would not be asking about engagement in any criminal activities other than what is in the public record or information to which the officers have access. However, the NIMH review committee disagreed with our position. The reviewers' position, as stated in the summary sheets (the reviewers' critiques of the research proposal, addressing conceptualization, significance, methodology, human subjects, budget, and inclusion of minorities, women, and children), was that "information that is not revealed to the probation/parole officer is very likely to emerge during the course of the study. Furthermore, the applicant states that subjects will be told that information obtained will not be shared with their probation or parole officers. It is unclear whether the investigators are obligated to tell subjects that certain reporting requirements exist. It is also unclear what action will be taken if client interviews reveal behavior that might be seen as potentially dangerous or criminal."

Given these review comments, we agreed to apply for and did receive a Certificate of Confidentiality. The NIMH was barred from funding the grant until we responded to human subjects concerns to the satisfaction of the NIMH program officer assigned to the application. At the time (1994), Certificates of Confidentiality had been used for some time at the National Institute of Drug Abuse, but were not as commonly used at NIMH. The Certificate assured subjects that their identity, and thus any data from their interviews, would not be revealed to anyone outside the research study team. In other words, the information on any specific individual could not be subpoenaed. The only exception to revealing personal information was in cases where there was imminent danger to self or others. Certificates of Confidentiality were created so that individuals asked to volunteer for research were more likely to be truthful in interviews regarding topics that might include incriminating information about themselves. To this end, the simple description of the certificate language in the consent form highlighted the fact that research staff would not be forced to identify any participant in the research, and thus could not release any data that may be incriminating, in court or other legal proceedings. Currently, Certificates of Confidentiality are quite widely used in research that investigates issues that may prompt legal actions. These certificates are relatively easy to obtain from NIMH, regardless of funding source or even for unfunded research related to the study of mental health issues.

It is also important to note that since the subjects in this research were involved in the criminal justice system, the university's Institutional Review Board was required by federal regulations to have someone who works in the criminal justice system on the review panel at the time this grant application was reviewed. This meant that a criminal justice staff person needed to be identified and then be willing to participate in this review process.

The NIMH review committee was concerned about what we would do if we became aware of dangerous or criminal behavior. We set out a procedure for handling such situations. The following describes implementation of this procedure. In about two cases, the research assistant did encounter clients who were acutely ill to the extent that he was concerned for their safety. In these situations, he discussed them with us and we set out a plan of action. In one case, it included encouraging the client to seek treatment. When he didn't, we told him that we planned to call the crisis service. He then proceeded to call the psychiatric emergency crisis service himself.

Safety of the interviewer was another concern. This was less of a concern about the clients than about the environments in which the clients lived, since many interviews were conducted in the clients' homes. The neighborhoods where the clients lived were some of the most dangerous in the city, where people would stand waving bags of drugs to attract cars to pull over. The research assistant had conducted the initial interviews with the subjects in the probation and parole offices, so he knew the clients. If interviews could be conducted in the offices or other agreed-upon locations, that was preferable, but not always feasible. Often clients would not show up for interviews. Most of our interviews were conducted by the research assistant or the research coordinator (the second author). These interviewers were both older and extremely savvy about handling themselves in these communities. We were extremely cautious about who we hired for this research assistant position. We did not hire some younger eager individuals, because we were not convinced that they could handle themselves in these environments. Today, the use of cell phones helps mitigate concerns about interviewer safety, but at the time of this study's data collection, they were not very prevalent.

IDENTIFYING AND OPERATIONALIZING THE SAMPLE

Because we wanted to test the criminalization hypothesis, this research investigation required a sample of individuals with severe mental illness. This hypothesis assumes that mentally ill individuals enter the criminal justice system due to a lack of access to mental health treatment. The criminalization hypothesis emerged in response to deinstitutionalization and its attendant restrictive psychiatric hospital admission policies, and to observations of what was thought to be large numbers of individuals with mental illness in the criminal justice system. Consequently, we needed to be able to obtain a sample of individuals who were diagnosed with a severe psychiatric disorder. These psychiatric probation/parole units, the setting for obtaining our sample, were not clinical programs—they are termed psychiatric only because of their focus on supervising people who were perceived to have mental health problems. In most cases, having a psychiatric problem was determined by the past service history of the parolee or probationer. However, individuals could be sent to these units by judges and court administrators for reasons no more clinically sophisticated than the person was acting "weird" or "out of it," or occasionally because the probationer/parolee was thought to be particularly vulnerable with respect to harming self or others or being preyed on by others. These units were thought to be a good resource for supervising such individuals.

Because these units did not diagnose or treat these individuals, they did not have records with detailed and reliable clinical information, including psychiatric diagnoses, that we were accustomed to in clinical mental health facilities. We had thought that possibly the mental health evaluation unit at the court would be able to assist, as they would probably have evaluated these individuals and made a diagnosis. However, it turned out that there was no systematic procedure guiding who was evaluated in this unit. Again, psychiatric evaluations were based on a referral by a judge, an attorney, or other court personnel, but there would be many potential subjects for our study who would likely not have been evaluated. Consequently, we realized that we would have to conduct our own diagnostic assessment. As described in the article, our screening used an instrument that can be administered by trained non–mental health professionals and had been used in community epidemiological studies, the Q-DIS.

Another decision we made in the design of the study was that we wanted subjects to be new intakes, within a month or two of entering these psychiatric probation/parole units. This way we would not have clients in the study who were at different points in the probation and parole process. This passed the review procedure at NIMH with no criticisms. However, problems were encountered soon after we began recruiting and enrolling subjects into the study. The research assistant who was recruiting came back one day and presented us with the problem of how we operationally defined "new intakes" for purposes of our study, since he was unable to determine study eligibility for some individuals. For example, what we found was that, after having been in jail, clients could return to these units to complete their community service from a prior sentence. The question was whether this individual was a "new intake" for purposes of our study. The entire team discussed the different possibilities and decided which clients would be and would not be eligible for the study. This resulted in the specific operationalization of a new case as delineated in the article. This points out how important it is to operationally define a study's eligibility criteria. Otherwise, a research assistant is unable to make the determination about a subject's study eligibility on the spur of the moment in the field.

SAMPLE RECRUITMENT AND DATA COLLECTION PROCEDURES

The original application had probation and parole officers calling the research office when eligible subjects showed up for appointments with officers. However, we quickly realized that this was not going to happen. We needed to have a research assistant in the office an extensive amount of time to monitor new intakes. The research assistant assumed responsibility for reviewing the intake log of clients signing in for appointments, and learned how to recognize new cases. When cases were ambiguous, the coordinator would get more detail from the probation/parole officers, and the officers would help the assistant to understand the circumstances of a case. But the research assistant had to take the initiative to do this, as probation/parole officers were more concerned with other things than our study.

This process of the assistant spending time in these offices also contributed to our understanding of the procedures followed by probation and parole officers. We found, for instance, that officers were empowered to send a client to jail for a brief period of time, less than a week in many cases, before having to inform the judges. Officers could then visit their clients in jail to reiterate the conditions of probation and parole, and their expectations for the clients. Some referred to this as a "shock incarceration" that demonstrated to clients that the officer was serious about their complying with their stipulations. These types of observations were essential to our understanding of the study's dependent variable, which will be discussed later.

Such observations are among the substantial benefits of primary data collection, and part of what makes primary data collection worth the cost. There is essentially an element of participant observation in every primary data collection. While those who rely on administrative data may benefit from larger sample sizes for analysis and perhaps samples that are more representative of larger populations, those collecting primary data are intimately connected with the context of data collection. We were particularly lucky to have a research assistant who had a Ph.D. in Folklore, with training in ethnography. He reveled in keeping an informal eye on how the units operated. We greatly benefited from this research assistant's trained observation and reflection about office functioning. It helped us understand how decisions were made. This taught us the need to formalize the use of qualitative methods within a quantitative study in future research studies. This mixed epistemology is exceedingly important for understanding the context of research studies and, often, the operationalization of important study concepts as well.

OPERATIONALIZATION OF THE DEPENDENT VARIABLE

A problem similar to operationalizing "new intakes" arose in differentiating "new" from "technical" charges. In designing the study it seemed that it would be no problem to distinguish between probationers/parolees who would be incarcerated for new crimes versus technical violations. However, of the 85 individuals reincarcerated, many had a mix of new charges and technical violations. Individuals arrested for a new charge, for instance, may also be considered for a technical violation, because they were on probation or parole at the time, and criminal activity is a violation of their stipulations for completing their sentence in the community. Conversely, the pursuit of some technical violations could result in new charges. For example, if it was found that the reason a person was repeatedly going to the Jersey Shore (a technical violation of the stipulation to stay in the jurisdiction of their probation/parole) was to buy drugs, then a new charge could be added to the technical violation. Probation and parole officers have a great deal of discretion as to whether to charge an offender with a technical violation, new charge, or both. Testing our hypothesis required that we categorize these incarcerations as resulting primarily from technical violations or new charges. The idea of categorizing reincarceration into these two components came from the first author's earlier work in conceptualizing readmission to psychiatric hospitals, where it was apparent that although rehospitalization appeared to have a clear empirical referent, it has numerous conceptual meanings (Solomon & Doll, 1979). There are various pathway factors (leading to hospital admission) and gateway factors (decisions to admit to the hospital) that explain rehospitalization, resulting in differing factors explaining these various concepts of hospitalization. For example, an individual can be rehospitalized because of an exacerbation of the illness, or because a family member needs respite, or because there are not appropriate community mental health alternatives. How one conceptually delineates complex constructs can result in very different findings.

To code these reincarcerations into one of these two categories required an in-depth examination of each reincarceration. One source of data was the post-incarceration interviews we conducted with both clients and their officers, which elicited each individual's version of the event. We also acquired the violation report that each officer sent to the sentencing judge outlining the event. With these various data, and informed by our understanding of how these units operated, we examined each case. Most cases were clear as to whether the incarceration was primarily motivated by a new charge or a technical violation. About a dozen cases, though, required in-depth discussion by the whole research team after each member of the team read the data to make a final decision on the coding.

LONGITUDINAL ASPECT

The design of the study required interviews to be conducted with both the clients and the officers every three months. It took great persistence to keep finding the clients every three months. Although these clients were obligated to report to the probation and parole offices on a regular basis, if they did not show up for their scheduled appointments, the officers were required to make contact with the client. If the officer was unable to contact the client by phone, he/she was to go into the community to find the client. Very often the officers did not make the effort to locate the client. Thus, it became apparent that we could not always count on officers knowing where to locate our subjects. In a number of cases, our research assistant was better able to find clients than some of the officers. It also helped that the same research assistant followed them over the course of the study, so the clients knew him. We paid subjects an incentive payment, which helped.

However, in some cases these individuals did not want to be found, which made it extremely difficult. Some officers were far more difficult to obtain data from than clients—officers who did not want to be bothered with the study, and from whom it was very difficult to obtain completed data forms every three months on their clients who were in our study. This may have produced some bias, in that data from certain officers tended to be consistently missing. But we could not force officers to participate in the study. Officers did sign consents for interviews that we conducted with them about their philosophy of probation and parole, but not for providing information about their clients. Participating in the study was not a requirement of their job and was purely voluntary. We had to rely on the officers' goodwill.

The proposed statistical procedure, event history analysis, allowed us to have some loss of quarters without losing all data on that client. However, because of difficulties in collecting all the data of interest from both probationers/parolees and their officers, we had a significant amount of missing data. If we ran the analysis as proposed, based on data from all waves of data collection, the cases available for analysis would have been substantially reduced. Our response was to maximize the potential of the multiple data waves while keeping a longitudinal data analysis. To do this, we operationalized many of the variables over the whole course of the follow-up period, instead of by wave of data collection. For example, instead of a variable operationalized as "received outpatient therapy in the last three-month period," we would use a variable operationalized as "ever received outpatient therapy." In this way, we could use the data from a case that had only two waves of data collection, which would have normally been deleted from an event history analysis, using time-sensitive variables by wave. Event history analysis requires enough data points (usually at least three) to impute the missing data points. If missing data points cannot be imputed from the existing data, the case is eliminated from the analysis. The trade-off was to include all cases and maximize available data for power in analysis, even though this meant less than optimal operationalization of variables in a time-sensitive manner.

SUMMARY AND CONCLUSIONS

This study points to the importance of truly understanding the setting and context in which research takes place. Primary data collection provides an opportunity to use naturalistic observation in the data collection settings. Such observation could be more systematically included in the design and conceptualization of proposed studies. This design-integrated way of mixing methodologies provides a richness and depth to the data for use in explaining one's findings, as well as the ability to operationalize variables and establish inclusion and exclusion sample criteria. Too often, researchers do not realize that in addition to operationalizing their concepts, they also have to operationalize their sample criteria. Over the years of doing mental health services research, it has become clear that one learns about the policies and operations of service systems from implementing research studies.

REFERENCES

Draine, J., & Solomon, P. (1994). Jail recidivism and the intensity of case management services among homeless persons with mental illness leaving jail. *The Journal of Psychiatry and Law 22*, 245–261.

Draine, J., Solomon, P., & Meyerson, A. (1994). Predictors of reincarceration among patients who received psychiatric services in jail. *Hospital and Community Psychiatry 45*, 163–167.

Solomon, P., & Doll, W. (1979). The varieties of readmission: The case against the use of recidivism rates as a measure of program effectiveness. *American Journal of Orthopsychiatry 49,* 230–239.

Solomon, P., & Draine, J. (1995a). One-year outcomes of a randomized trial of case management with seriously mentally ill clients leaving jail. *Evaluation Review 19,* 256–273.

Solomon, P., & Draine, J. (1995b). Issues in serving the forensic client. *Social Work 40,* 25–33.

Solomon, P., & Draine, J. (1995c). Jail recidivism in a forensic case management program. *Health and Social Work 20,* 167–173.

Solomon, P., Draine, J. & Meyerson, A. (1994). Jail recidivism and receipt of community mental health services. *Hospital and Community Psychiatry 45,* 793–797.

Solomon, P, Rogers, R., Draine, J., & Meyerson, A. (1995). Interaction of the criminal justice system and psychiatric professionals in which civil commitment standards are prohibitive. *Bulletin of the American Academy of Psychiatry and the Law 23,* 117–128.

Tonry, M. (1990). Stated and latent functions of ISP. *Crime and Delinquency 36,* 174–191.

10

Adverse Childhood Experiences: Are They Risk Factors for Adult Homelessness?

Daniel B. Herman, D.S.W., Ezra S. Susser, M.D., Dr.P.H., Elmer L. Struening, Ph.D., and Bruce L. Link, Ph.D.

INTRODUCTION

Recent research indicates that 5 to 15 million Americans have experienced an episode of homelessness during their lifetimes.[1,2] Structural factors such as labor market changes, an inadequate supply of low-cost housing, and cuts in income assistance programs have created the social conditions in which homelessness has grown during the past 15 years.[3,4] Individual-level risk factors—those personal characteristics and circumstances that make certain persons more vulnerable to becoming homeless under these conditions—have also been identified. These include poverty, gender (more males than females are homeless), ethnicity (homelessness affects more African Americans than members of other groups), age group (most homeless persons are between 30 and 39 years old), and psychiatric and substance abuse disorders.[5]

The purpose of this study was to determine whether adverse childhood experiences are risk factors for adult homelessness. A substantial body of epidemiological research provides strong evidence that such experiences, especially physical or sexual abuse and inadequate parental care, are risk factors for negative psychiatric outcomes in adulthood.[6-13] Meanwhile, studies of homeless persons have found remarkably high prevalences of adverse experiences during childhood, primarily histories of out-of-home care (foster, group, or institutional care) and running away from home.[14-20] The high prevalence of childhood adversity in samples of homeless people, taken together with the epidemiological literature that links such adverse experiences to adult psychiatric

From Herman, D. B., Susser, E. S., Struening, E. L., & Link, B. L. (1997). Adverse childhood experiences: Are they risk factors for adult homelessness? *American Journal of Public Health, 87,* 249–255. Reprinted with permission.

status, have led some researchers to speculate that early experiences may also be risk factors for adult homelessness.[5, 21]

Nonetheless, the research to date, while suggestive, has been unable to clearly demonstrate a causal association between adverse childhood experiences and adult homelessness. First, with some notable exceptions,[21, 22] data on the prevalence of such experiences in a suitable nonhomeless comparison group have generally not been available. In addition, measures of adverse childhood experiences have generally been restricted to foster care and running away,[5] variables which, at best, are limited proxy measures of childhood adversity. Finally, most studies to date have employed sampling methods that overrepresent persons who use shelters and whose homelessness is particularly long term.

The present study was designed to build on prior research by examining the connection between childhood adversity and adult homelessness with more definitive methods. It employed a national probability sample of formerly homeless persons and a comparison group of never-homeless persons. In addition, the study used measures of early adversity that more directly assessed a conceptually meaningful set of childhood risks, namely physical and sexual abuse and inadequate parental care.

METHODS

Sample

The data are from the follow-up phase of the Comprehensive Nationwide Study of Knowledge, Attitudes and Beliefs about Homelessness. The first phase of this study, the methods and results of which are described in detail elsewhere,[1] was a nationwide random-digit-dial telephone survey of 1507 adult residents of US households conducted between August and November of 1990. Although the primary purpose of this study was to describe public attitudes toward homelessness and homeless persons, the survey also found that a surprisingly large proportion of respondents reported that they themselves had been homeless at some time in their lives. The study estimated the lifetime prevalence of literal homelessness at over 7%, considerably higher than had been suggested by previous studies of currently homeless samples.

To confirm this unexpected finding and to further document the nature of the homeless experiences that were reported in the initial survey, a follow-up telephone study was conducted in 1994. As described elsewhere,[23] in the follow-up study efforts were made to reinterview all 169 respondents from the initial sample who reported having been homeless at some time in their adult lives, as well as a sample of never-homeless control subjects. The control subjects we sought to reinterview were purposely selected to overrepresent those considered to be at especially high risk for homelessness on the basis of risk profiles developed with data from the initial survey. To accomplish this goal, we used logistic regression to identify the following predictors of adult homelessness: homelessness as a child; renting as opposed to owning one's living quarters; family income below $20,000; having friends or family who were poor; having been on public assistance; and hospitalization for mental illness. On the basis of the logistic regression results, we determined each respondent's predicted probability of homelessness. We then sampled as control subjects all respondents with a predicted probability greater than .20, 85% of those with a probability between .10 and .20, and 37% of those with a probability of less than .10.

Although the aims of the initial study of attitudes toward homeless people did not involve recontacting respondents, 58% of the sampled respondents who were still living were relocated and reinterviewed. Of the ever-homeless respondents, 92 (54%) were successfully reinterviewed, and

395 (57%) of the never-homeless control subjects were successfully reinterviewed, yielding a total of 487 respondents for the follow-up phase of the study. The similar follow-up rates for the homeless and nonhomeless groups is reassuring with regard to possible selection bias. A bias of large magnitude would depend on different follow-up rates in the homeless and nonhomeless groups and, in addition, on some interaction between these follow-up rates and the risk factors. Therefore, the strong relationships we report below are highly unlikely to be accounted for by selection bias.

As described fully in a previous paper,[23] results were weighted to ensure that certain types of people were not over- or underrepresented in our analyses. Thus, we took into account not only the sampling scheme of the original random-digit-dial survey but also the scheme employed in the follow-up interview phase. In this way, we preserved the representativeness of the original sample, which was designed to reflect all households with telephones in the United States. Table 10.1 shows the demographic characteristics of the sample after appropriate weights were applied. We somewhat overrepresented those with more than a high school education, women, people aged 25 through 54 years, and married people in comparison with 1990 census data (not shown). Because we conducted our interview in English, our sample underrepresented Hispanics.

Table 10.1. Demographic Characteristics of Respondents (Weighted Percentages[a]): 1994 Follow-Up to the Comprehensive Nationwide Study of Knowledge, Attitudes and Beliefs about Homelessness (_n_ = 487)

Characteristic	%
Sex	
Female	56.8
Male	43.2
Race/ethnicity	
White	85.4
African American	8.5
Hispanic	3.3
Other	2.8
Age, y	
18–24	4.3
25–54	67.6
55–64	11.6
65+	16.5
Marital status	
Married	64.6
Not married	35.4
Education	
< high school graduate	13.5
High school graduate	32.7
Some college or more	53.8
Adult homelessness	
Ever	4.3
Never	95.7

[a]Weighted as described in text to reflect all households with telephones in the United States in 1994.

We classified subjects as positive for lifetime adult homelessness if they met our definition of adult homelessness in the follow-up phase of the study, since more in-depth information about homelessness was elicited during the follow-up. We defined homelessness as having had to sleep overnight in a shelter, an abandoned building, a vehicle, or out in the open because the respondent did not have a place to live (see our previously published report[23] for a complete description of our criteria).

Measures

Drawing on previous epidemiological work on childhood adversities and their association with subsequent adult social and psychiatric problems, we focused on childhood physical and sexual abuse and inadequate parental care as primary risk factors. To assess the quality of parental care during childhood, we employed a scale adapted from the Childhood Experience of Care and Abuse Interview developed by Bifulco and colleagues. This measure, which focuses on perceptions of parental antipathy and indifference toward the child, has been used successfully in several published studies of the relationship between childhood adversity and adult psychopathology,[8, 24–27] and evidence establishing its validity and reliability has been reported elsewhere.[28] In collaboration with the original measure's authors, we developed a seven-item condensed version of the measure suitable for use in a telephone survey. In our version, subjects were asked to respond ("always," "usually," "sometimes," or "never") to the following questions in relation to their mother or their primary female caretaker during most of their childhood: Was she concerned about your worries? Was she very hard to please? Was she interested in how you did at school? Did she make you feel unwanted? Was she interested in who your friends were? Was she very critical of you? Was she there if you needed her? The subjects were then asked the same questions in relation to their father or their primary male caretaker during most of their childhood. Following Bifulco and colleagues, we refer to this scale as measuring the overall construct of "lack of care" in childhood.

A total score for each parent or parent figure was computed by summing the responses to each item (always = 3, usually = 2, sometimes = 1, never = 0), using reverse scoring for positively worded questions. This procedure yielded scores for lack of care from each parent ranging from 0 to 21, with higher scores indicating higher levels of lack of care. The mean score for lack of care from mother was 3.8 (SD = 3.9; α = .82) and the mean for lack of care from father was 5.4 (SD = 4.9; alpha = .86). In the analyses that follow, we define subjects as having experienced lack of care if they scored in the highest 10th percentile of the distributions of lack of care scores for *either* parent (corresponding to a score of greater than 10 for mother's lack of care or greater than 12 for father's lack of care). Analyses (not reported here) using different cutpoints (15th, 20th, and 25th percentiles) and continuous-scale scores yielded similar results. Analyses using lack of care from mother only and lack of care from father only also produced comparable results.

Childhood physical abuse was rated as present if the respondent answered yes to the following single question: Before you were 18, were you ever severely beaten by an adult and badly bruised or injured? Childhood sexual abuse was deemed present if the subject answered yes to the question, Have you ever been sexually molested, abused, or raped? *and* the respondent reported that she or he was under age 18 when the abuse first occurred.

Data Analysis

We compared the risk of adult homelessness among persons reporting adverse childhood experiences with the risk among those without such experiences. In univariate analyses, we computed odds ratios with 95% confidence intervals by standard methods.[29] We used odds ratios to maintain consistency between univariate and multivariate analyses. Readers can, in addition, easily compute relative risks from the data provided in the tables. We also compared the risk of homelessness associated with various combinations of adverse childhood experiences with the risk among a group of subjects with no reported childhood adversities.

In logistic regression analyses, we then examined the association between adverse childhood experiences and homelessness, adjusting for the following potential confounding variables: sex; age (in years); ethnicity (African American vs other); urban vs rural current residence; socioeconomic status of family of origin (father's Nam-Powers-Terrie Occupational Status Score,[30] a continuous score between 0 and 100; if no father was present, mother's occupational prestige was substituted); receipt of welfare during childhood (whether, before the subject was 17, the family ever received welfare or public assistance); and current depressive symptoms (a continuous score between 0 and 24 on an eight-item scale using items from the Center for Epidemiologic Studies Depression scale[31] [$\alpha = .84$]). We included current depressive symptoms as a covariate to control for the possible effect of depressed current mood on recall of childhood experiences.[32]

Standard statistical packages (SPSS, SAS), which assume simple random sampling, produce incorrect standard errors for a complex survey design such as ours. Therefore, the software program SUDAAN,[33] which provides accurate estimates of standard errors for complex survey designs, was used to calculate all confidence intervals and significance tests.

RESULTS

Four percent of the weighted sample reported at least one episode of adult lifetime homelessness (Table 10.1). Sixteen percent of the weighted sample met our criteria for having experienced lack of care from a parent or parental figure during childhood (Table 10.2). Lack of care was significantly more common among women than among men (19% vs 11%, $P < .05$). Twenty-four percent of the weighted sample (29% of women and 17% of men, $P < .005$) were classified as having experienced either lack of care or abuse (Table 10.2). These figures compare well with data reported in the British studies from which our measure was derived; Bifulco and colleagues found that roughly 20% of a representative sample of working-class London mothers experienced lack of care and slightly under one third experienced lack of care or abuse in childhood[28] (the authors have yet to report such data on men).

Physical abuse during childhood was reported by 7% of the weighted sample and childhood sexual abuse was reported by just under 10%, with sexual abuse significantly more common among

Table 10.2. Prevalence of Adverse Childhood Experiences (Weighted Percentages[a]) by Adult Homelessness: 1994 Follow-Up to the Comprehensive Nationwide Study of Knowledge, Attitudes and Beliefs about Homelessness ($n = 487$)

Type of Adversity	Ever Homeless, %	Never Homeless, %	Total Sample, %
Lack of care	66.0	13.3	15.6
Physical abuse	47.8	5.5	7.3
Sexual abuse	14.7	9.3	9.6
Lack of care plus either type of abuse	53.9	4.8	6.9
Any childhood adversity	68.5	21.9	24.0

[a]Weighted as described in text to reflect all households with telephones in the United States in 1994.

women (14% in women vs 4% in men, $p < .005$). Although the accuracy of national prevalence data on child abuse is disputed, these estimates are similar to much published data in this area.[13, 34] For instance, the estimated prevalence of retrospectively reported childhood sexual abuse (through age 15 only) found in the Los Angeles Epidemiologic Catchment Area study was 5.3% overall, with women significantly more likely to have been abused.[35] The most comprehensive recent study of physical violence toward children in the United States estimated the annual incidence rate of "abusive violence" (using a somewhat broader definition than our own) to be 110 per 1000 children.[36]

These risk factors tended to overlap. The odds of having been physically abused were 16 times greater among those who experienced lack of care than among those who did not experience lack of care, while the odds of having been sexually abused were 3 times greater among those with lack of care than among those without. Similarly the odds of sexual abuse were 3 times greater among those who were physically abused than among those who were not physically abused.

Table 10.3 presents the results of analyses that assess the degree to which lack of care and abuse increase individuals' risk of lifetime homelessness. The unadjusted odds ratio (OR) for lack of care was 12.7 (95% confidence interval [CI] = 5.0, 31.9) and the unadjusted odds ratio for physical abuse was 15.8 (95% CI = 5.9, 42.1). There was a nonsignificant trend in the expected direction for sexual abuse (unadjusted OR = 1.7, 95% CI = 0.6, 4.6). The pattern of results remained when we assessed the strength of the association between each childhood risk factor and lifetime homelessness while adjusting for the other respective childhood risk factors. The risk of homelessness

Table 10.3. Relationship between Adverse Childhood Experiences and Adult Homelessness (Weighted Percentages[a]): 1994 Follow-Up to the Comprehensive Nationwide Study of Knowledge, Attitudes and Beliefs about Homelessness ($n = 487$)

Type of Adversity	% Who Have Been Homeless[a]	Unadjusted OR (95% CI)	Adjusted OR[b] (95% CI)
Lack of care			
Yes	18.4	12.7 (5.0, 31.9)	6.6 (2.5, 17.6)
No	1.7		
Physical abuse			
Yes	27.8	15.8 (5.9, 42.1)	6.0 (2.1, 17.4)
No	2.4		
Sexual abuse			
Yes	6.4	1.7 (0.6, 4.6)	0.8 (0.7, 7.4)
No	4.1		
Lack of care plus either type of abuse[c]			
Yes	33.3	26.0 (9.2, 73.6)	...
No	1.9		
Any childhood adversity			
Yes	12.5	7.8 (3.0, 19.9)	...
No	1.8		

Note. CI = confidence interval; OR = odds ratio.

[a]Weighted as described in text to reflect all households with telephones in the United States in 1994.

[b]Adjusted for the effect of each risk factor.

[c]Persons with both factors (Yes) are compared with persons with neither factor (No). Persons with one factor present ($n = 83$) are excluded.

associated with lack of care from *both* mother and father (unadjusted OR = 16.7) was not appreciably higher than the risk conferred by lack of care from mother alone (unadjusted OR = 16).

The combination of lack of care and either type of abuse increased subjects' risk of homelessness by a factor of 26 (unadjusted OR = 26.0, 95% CI = 9.2, 73.6) compared with the risk among subjects with no reported childhood adversity (no lack of care, physical abuse, or sexual abuse). The experience of any childhood adversity increased subjects' risk of homelessness by a factor of 8 (unadjusted OR = 7.8; 95% CI = 3.0, 19.9).

We performed logistic regression analyses to control for the possibility of confounding by respondent's sex, age, ethnicity, urban vs rural current residence, parental socioeconomic status, receipt of welfare during childhood, and current depressive symptoms. In these analyses, lack of care (adjusted OR = 13.1, 95% CI = 4.7, 36.2) and physical abuse (adjusted OR = 18.0, 95% CI = 5.4, 59.5) continued to be strongly associated with homelessness, while sexual abuse again showed a nonsignificant trend in the expected direction (adjusted OR = 1.6, 95% CI = 0.5, 5.2). The combination of lack of care and either type of abuse was associated with an adjusted odds ratio of 38.9 (95% CI = 11.3, 133.6), while the adjusted odds ratio for any childhood adversity was 7.4 (95% CI = 2.6, 20.1). We also tested for interactions between each risk factor and the potential confounders, but found none to be significant.

We investigated the possibility of gender differences in two ways. First, odds ratios indicating the strength of association between respective risk factors and the outcome were computed separately for men and women. For lack of care (men = 15.7, women = 15.1), sexual abuse (men = 1.8, women = 2.1), and the combined variable indicating any childhood risk (men = 10.5, women = 8.1), the odds ratios were very similar. For physical abuse, the odds ratio was greater for women than for men (25.2 vs 10.7). Using separate logistic regression models, we then tested for the presence of significant interactions between sex and each separate risk factor, as well as between sex and the combined risk factor. No significant interaction was found. Since no conclusive pattern of differences by sex was apparent, we reported the findings unstratified by sex.

DISCUSSION

We found the combination of lack of care and either physical or sexual abuse during childhood to be associated with a dramatically elevated risk of adult homelessness (unadjusted OR = 26.0). In addition, both lack of care and physical abuse, when considered alone, were associated with highly significant increases in the risk of homelessness in both univariate and multivariate tests. Sexual abuse showed a nonsignificant trend in the expected direction in both univariate and multivariate analyses.

Although our findings are consistent with previous studies that found other indicators of childhood adversity (i.e., out-of-home care and running away from home) to be prevalent in homeless samples, we believe this to be the first epidemiologic study to firmly establish that specific adverse childhood experiences are indeed risk factors for adult homelessness. In addition to using an appropriate comparison group, our study employed measures of childhood adversity that were drawn from a highly regarded previous body of work that links such childhood experiences with elevated risk for psychiatric disorder. We have extended this research by demonstrating that adverse childhood experiences are also risk factors for an important social outcome.

We emphasize that these adversities "cause" homelessness only within a broad social context that allows for the existence of widespread homelessness.[37] Absent these structural conditions (e.g., the inadequate supply of affordable housing), it is unlikely that childhood adversity would frequently lead to adult homelessness.

Causal Pathways

There are likely to be multiple causal pathways through which these risks might operate. In earlier work, Susser[15] emphasized the possibility that childhood adversity may predispose individuals to homelessness because effective kin support is presumably less often present in families in which such adversity occurs. Since the family of origin is seen as an important potential source of assistance to individuals in trouble, it follows that if this resource is less available, the risk of homelessness would be increased.[38] Furthermore, the work of Brown and colleagues suggests that other sources of social support during adulthood may also be strongly compromised, albeit less directly, by adverse childhood experiences. In Brown and Moran's research on working-class women, childhood adversity has been found to predict a range of subsequent interpersonal problems including social isolation or development of relationships with people who are undependable support figures.[26] Consistent with these findings, evidence for the role of social isolation as a mediating factor in the link between abuse during childhood and adult homelessness among Vietnam-era war veterans has been reported by Rosenheck and Fontana.[22]

In the present study, measures of social support were restricted to current indicators only, limiting our ability to formally test the role of social support as a mediating variable. Nonetheless, the associations we observed between childhood adversity and several measures of current social support were consistent with this hypothesized causal pathway. For instance, being currently divorced or separated from a spouse was significantly associated with lack of care (OR = 4.8, 95% CI = 2.5, 9.4) and physical abuse (OR = 4.6, 95% CI = 2.0, 10.4) and associated at the trend level with sexual abuse (OR = 2.1, 95% CI = 0.8, 5.8). Speaking to relatives less often than once a month was also significantly associated with lack of care (OR = 2.9, 95% CI = 1.1, 8.2) and physical abuse (OR = 5.2, 95% CI = 1.7, 15.4), as was having two or fewer close friends living nearby (OR = 3.1, 95% CI = 1.8, 5.40 for lack of care; OR = 4.6, 95% CI = 2.2, 9.7 for physical abuse). Neither of these variables was significantly associated with sexual abuse.

Another potential causal pathway linking childhood adversity to adult homelessness involves the likelihood that such adversity elevates individuals' risk for psychiatric disorders such as depression and substance abuse, both of which appear to be likely risk factors for homelessness.[5] In this model, the development of one or more such disorder would follow childhood adversity and subsequently cause adult homelessness, perhaps by reducing individuals' ability to earn adequate income and thus to maintain stable housing. To explore this possibility in our data, we assessed whether the strength of the association between the childhood risk factors and homelessness would be significantly reduced by adding as covariates into the logistic models described above self-reported indicators of serious mental disorder (lifetime history of psychiatric hospitalization) and substance abuse problems (lifetime history of treatment in a drug or alcohol detoxification program). Although the results did not support the hypothesized relationship, our cross-sectional method does not permit us to definitively rule out the possibility that mental disorder may indeed mediate the relationship between childhood risk factors and adult homelessness.

Limitations

Recall bias is a potential threat to the validity of our findings, since the measures of risk factors and homelessness were collected retrospectively. Specifically, if respondents who reported that they had been homeless were more likely to recall adverse childhood experiences (or conversely, if those reporting adverse childhood experiences were more likely to recall having been homeless), the odds ratios we observed would have been artificially inflated. While this is possible, we find it improbable that such bias could account for differences in risk as strong as the ones we observed.

Furthermore, our findings are consistent with those of other studies that did not rely on subjective ratings of childhood experience or self-reported measures of homelessness.[14, 16–18, 21] Finally, the fact that we controlled for current depressive symptoms in our multivariate analyses also served to protect against the potential effects of current mood on recall of childhood experiences.

Although we employed reliable, multiple-item measures of childhood lack of care, our measures of abuse were more limited. As noted previously, the difficulties inherent in assessing abuse histories are well documented[39, 40] and may in part account for the inconclusive results we obtained regarding sexual abuse.

A strength of our sampling method—interviewing currently housed individuals about prior lifetime homelessness—is also a potential weakness in that the sample may underrepresent persons with particularly long homeless experiences who do not reacquire stable housing. Since we sampled households only (and not shelters and other locations where long-term homeless persons may reside), such persons would not have had the opportunity to be selected into our sample. Thus, the risk factors we studied may increase the risk of entry into homelessness only among those persons whose ultimate duration of homelessness is less likely to be chronic. However, other studies with the opposite sampling bias (i.e., overrepresenting persons with long-term homelessness) have generated results consistent with those reported here.[14, 17–20] Furthermore, since our sample was a nationally representative probability sample of all US households with telephones, the potential sampling bias is probably smaller than that in research relying on convenience samples of limited shelter or street locations.

Definitive claims about cause are difficult to make in observational studies. Even so, we believe that our design is a strong one. We have limited ourselves to examining risks that occurred during childhood and an outcome that occurred during adulthood. The temporal order between risk and outcome is clear, and we have statistically controlled for potential confounders. In the case of childhood-related risk for adult homelessness, we would also argue that prospective strategies would be very costly and, given the high rate of attrition likely to occur in a sample containing subjects at elevated risk for homelessness, would not necessarily provide a more solid basis for causal inference.

Our data are difficult to compare with those from previous studies that focused on the role of out-of-home care as a risk factor for homelessness.[14, 15, 17–20] We did investigate out-of-home care in our sample and found it to be roughly twice as prevalent among the homeless as among the nonhomeless (4.8% vs 2.6%). The 4.8% prevalence rate among the homeless group is substantially lower than has typically been reported in studies of currently homeless populations. A plausible explanation consistent with this discrepancy is that out-of-home care may be more strongly associated with duration of homelessness than with its initial onset. Our data do not permit us to directly assess this hypothesis.

As a final caveat, we emphasize that by focusing on childhood risk factors, we are not attempting to explain all cases of homelessness. Despite the strong relationship we found between adverse childhood experiences and homelessness, roughly one third of the persons in our sample who became homeless as adults reported no lack of care, while roughly one half of those who became homeless reported no childhood physical abuse.

CONCLUSIONS

Our results lend strong support to the hypothesized link between adverse childhood experiences and adult homelessness, confirming what a number of previous studies have suggested. These results are consistent with a rapidly growing body of research indicating that abuse and neglect during childhood are also potent risk factors for a number of psychiatric disorders, including depression, anxiety, and substance abuse.[9, 12, 41–43] A definitive understanding of the mechanisms through which these risk factors operate awaits future research that is explicitly designed to test hypotheses about such mechanisms. Nonetheless, these findings suggest that interventions that can effectively reduce the incidence of child abuse and neglect may ultimately yield a large dividend by preventing critical social problems including homelessness and the enormous social costs that these problems engender.

ACKNOWLEDGMENTS

This study was supported in part by National Institute of Mental Health (NIMH) grant MH46101 (Bruce Link, principal investigator) and by an NIMH Scientist Development Award (K20 MH01204) to Dr. Herman.

REFERENCES

1. Link B, Susser E, Stueve A, Phelan J, Moore R, Struening E. Lifetime and five-year prevalence of homelessness in the United States. *Am J Public Health.* 1994;84:1907–1912.

2. Jahiel R. The size of the homeless population. In: Jahiel R, ed. *Homelessness: A Prevention-Oriented Approach.* Baltimore, MD: Johns Hopkins University Press; 1992.

3. Burt M, Cohen B. *America's Homeless: Numbers, Characteristics, and Programs That Serve Them.* Washington, DC: Urban Institute Press; 1989.

4. Rossi P. *Down and Out in America: The Origins of Homelessness.* Chicago, IL: University of Chicago Press; 1989.

5. Susser E, Moore R, Link B. Risk factors for homelessness. *Am J Epidemiol.* 1993;15:546–556.

6. Brown G, Harris T. *The Social Origins of Depression: A Study of Psychiatric Disorder in Women.* London, England: Tavistock Publications; 1978.

7. Harris T, Brown G, Bifulco A. Loss of parent in childhood and adult psychiatric disorder: a tentative overall model. *Dev Psychopathol.* 1990;2:311–328.

8. Bifulco A, Brown G, Adler Z. Early sexual abuse and clinical depression in adult life. *Br J Psychiatry.* 1991;159:115–122.

9. Bryer J, Nelson B, Miller J, Krol P. Childhood sexual and physical abuse as factors in adult psychiatric illness. *Am J Psychiatry.* 1987;144:1426–1430.

10. McLeod J. Childhood parental loss and adult depression. *J Health Soc Behav.* 1991;32:205–220.

11. Rutter M. *Maternal Deprivation Reassessed.* Harmondsworth, England: Penguin; 1981.

12. Straus M, Kantor G. Corporal punishment of adolescents by parents: a risk factor in the epidemiology of depression, suicide, alcohol abuse, child abuse, and wife beating. *Adolescence.* 1994;29:543–561.

13. Finkelhor D, Araji S, Baron L, Browne A, Peters S, Wyatt G. *A Sourcebook on Child Sexual Abuse.* Beverly Hills, CA: Sage Publications; 1986.

14. Susser E, Struening E, Conover S. Childhood experiences of homeless men. *Am J Psychiatry.* 1987;144:1599–1601.

15. Susser E, Lin S, Conover S, Struening E. Childhood antecedents of homelessness in psychiatric patients. *Am J Psychiatry.* 1991;148:1026–1030.

16. Herman D, Susser E, Struening E. Childhood out-of-home care and current depressive symptoms among homeless adults. *Am J Public Health.* 1994;84:1849–1851.

17. Piliavin I, Sosin M, Westerfelt A, Matsueda R. The duration of homeless careers: an exploratory study. *Soc Serv Rev.* 1993;67:576–598.

18. Sosin M, Colson P, Grossman S. *Homelessness in Chicago: Poverty, Pathology, Social Institutions and Social Change.* Chicago, IL: Chicago Community Trust; 1988.

19. Sosin M, Piliavin I, Westerfelt H. Toward a longitudinal analysis of homelessness. *J Soc Issues.* 1990;46:157–174.

20. Winkleby M, Rockhill B, Jatulis D, Fortmann S. The medical origins of homelessness. *Am J Public Health.* 1992;82:1394–1398.

21. Koegel P, Melamid E, Burnam M A. Childhood risk factors for homelessness among homeless adults. *Am J Public Health.* 1995;85:1642–1649.

22. Rosenheck R, Fontana A. A model of homelessness among male veterans of the Vietnam War generation. *Am J. Psychiatry.* 1994;151:421–427.

23. Link B, Phelan J, Bresnahan M, Stueve A, Moore R, Susser E. Lifetime and five-year prevalence of homelessness in the United States: new evidence on an old debate. *Am J Orthopsychiatry.* 1995;65:347–354.

24. Bifulco A, Brown G, Harris T. Childhood loss of parent, lack of adequate parental care and adult depression: a replication. *J Affect Disord.* 1987;12:115–128.

25. Bifulco A, Harris T, Brown G. Mourning or early inadequate care? Reexamining the relationship of maternal loss in childhood with adult depression and anxiety. *Dev Psychopathol.* 1992;4:433–449.

26. Brown G, Moran P. Clinical and psychosocial origins of chronic depressive episodes, I: a community survey. *Br J Psychiatry.* 1994; 165:447–456.

27. Harris T, Brown G, Bifulco A. Loss of parent in childhood and adult psychiatric disorder: the role of lack of adequate parental care. *Psychol Med.* 1986;16:641–659.

28. Bifulco A, Brown G, Harris T. Childhood experience of care and abuse (CECA): a retrospective interview measure. *J Child Psychol Psychiatry.* 1994;35:1419–1435.

29. Fleiss J. *Statistical Methods for Rates and Proportions.* New York, NY:John Wiley & Sons Inc; 1981.

30. Terrie W E, Nam C B. *1990 and 1980 Nam-Powers-Terrie Occupational Status Scores.* Tallahassee, Fla: Florida State University, Center for the Study of Population; 1994. Working Paper Series 94–118.

31. Radloff L. The CES-D scale: a self-report depression scale for research in the general population. *Appl Psychol Meas.* 1977;1:385–401.

32. Brewin C, Andrews B, Gotlib I. Psychopathology and early experience: a reappraisal of retrospective reports. *Psychol Bull.* 1993;113:82–98.

33. Shah B, Barnwell B, Hunt P, LaVange L. *SUDAAN User's Manual: Professional Software for Survey Data Analysis for Multi-Stage Sample Designs, Release 6.0.* Research Triangle Park, NC: Research Triangle Institute; 1992.

34. Wauchope B, Straus M. Physical punishment and physical abuse of American children: incidence rates by age, gender, and occupational class. In: Straus M, Gelles R, eds. *Physical Violence in American Families: Risk Factors and Adaptations to Violence in 8415 Families.* New Brunswick, NJ: Transaction Publishers; 1990.

35. Siegel J M, Sorenson S B, Golding J M, Burnam M A, Stein J A. The prevalence of childhood sexual assault. *Am J Epidemiol.* 1987;126:1141–1153.

36. Wolfner G D, Gelles R J. A profile of violence toward children: a national study. *Child Abuse Negl.* 1993;17:197–212.

37. Koegel P, Burnam M A. Getting nowhere: homeless people, aimless policy. In: Steinberg J, Lyon D, Vaiana M, eds. *Urban America—Policy Choices for Los Angeles and the Nation.* Santa Monica, Calif: RAND Corp; 1992.

38. Snow D A, Anderson L. *Down on Their Luck: A Study of Homeless Street People.* Berkeley, CA: University of California Press; 1993.

39. Zuravin S J. Research definitions of child physical abuse and neglect: current problems. In: Starr R H Jr, Wolfe D A, eds. *The Effects of Child Abuse and Neglect: Issues and Research.* New York: Guilford Press; 1991.

40. Salter AC. Epidemiology of child sexual abuse. In: O'Donahue W, Geer J H, eds. *The Sexual Abuse of Children: Theory and Research.* Hillsdale, NJ: Lawerence Erlbaum Associates; 1992.

41. Burnam M, Stein J, Golding J, et al. Sexual assault and mental disorders in a community population. *J Consult Clin Psychol.* 1988;56:843–850.

42. Kessler R, Magee W. Childhood adversities and adult depression: basic patterns of association in a US national survey. *Psychol Med.* 1993;23: 673–690.

43. Kendler K, Kessler R, Neale M, Heath A, Eaves L. The prediction of major depression in women: toward an integrated etiologic model. *Am J Psychiatry.* 1993;150:1139–1148.

COMMENTARY BY: Dan Herman

BACKGROUND

My interest in the area of homelessness dates back to my first job as a professional social worker in New York City during the early 1980s. At that time, the problem of widespread urban homelessness was just emerging as a major issue demanding attention from both the political sector and public health and social service agencies in the city. I was working then as a program planner for the local mental health authority, which was becoming increasingly involved with this problem because the link between homelessness and mental health issues and service needs was quickly coming to the fore. One of the early steps undertaken by the agency was the implementation of a survey of housing and service needs of homeless shelter residents. To design and carry out the study, we turned to a group of academic researchers affiliated with Columbia University and New York State Psychiatric Institute (NYSPI). My role was to serve as liaison between the city agency and the research team, primarily to help specify the questions that the city wanted answered and to help the researchers negotiate access to the shelter system.

Several years after the completion of the study, which (I'm proud to report) did ultimately contribute to the development of enhanced housing and services for homeless mentally ill shelter residents, I returned to school to pursue a doctorate in social work at Columbia. One of my mentors, Professor David Fanshel, was a well-known researcher in the area of child welfare and foster care who had recently published an influential book entitled *Foster Children in Life Course Perspectives,* employing multivariate statistical methods to examine continuities and discontinuities over the life course of children in out-of-home care. Both the substance and the methodology of this work had a significant influence on my choice of dissertation topic. I was then fortunate enough to gain access to the data collected in the city's needs assessment study, allowing me to complete a dissertation investigating continuities over the life course of homeless men (Herman, 1991).

One of the questions that interested me was the relationship between out-of-home care during childhood and subsequent homelessness. This evolved from the observation by shelter staff and others working with homeless adults that out-of-home care was frequently reported by their clients. I examined, as part of the dissertation, the prevalence of such experiences in this sample and explored the relationship between out-of-home care and a number of outcomes including psychiatric hospitalization, criminal behavior, and psychiatric symptoms. Unfortunately, the data set I had did not permit me to investigate one of my key questions—Does out-of-home care (or other adverse childhood experience) "cause" homelessness?—because I had no suitable comparison group of nonhomeless persons.

Commentary on article: Herman, D. B., Susser, E. S., Struening, E. L., & Link, B. L. (1997). Adverse Childhood experiences: Are they risk factors for adult homelessness? *American Journal of Public Health, 87,* 249–255.

After receiving my doctorate in 1991, I became a full-time member of the staff of NYSPI, where I joined a research team carrying out a follow-up study of the shelter cohort studied in the needs assessment survey described above. While in this position, I was encouraged to apply for a National Institute of Mental Health (NIMH) career development grant (a so-called "K award") to obtain support for additional training in research methods. Building on my dissertation research, I successfully applied for a grant entitled "Childhood Experiences and Adult Alcohol, Drug and Mental Health Outcomes." This five-year award supported my further training in services research and epidemiologic methods through coursework and mentored research. One of my mentors on this grant was Bruce Link, a well-known sociologist and epidemiologist at Columbia who, for many years, had been studying stigma, particularly as it pertained to disadvantaged groups including persons with mental illness (Link, Struening, Rahav, Phelan, & Nuttbrock, 1997). Dr. Link and his colleagues had just been funded to carry out a follow-up study of a major national survey on attitudes toward homelessness and homeless persons.

Although Dr. Link's original research question focused on public attitudes toward homelessness, he also sought to estimate the lifetime prevalence of homelessness in the study population (and, by extrapolation, in the housed U.S. population in general). He and other homelessness researchers saw this as an important question for several reasons. For one, it would provide important information about the scope of the homelessness problem. Specifically, lifetime prevalence data could be used to complement existing estimates of the number of persons in shelters or on the streets at any one point in time, to give researchers and policymakers a more accurate estimate of the overall scale of the phenomenon. Furthermore, researchers including Dr. Link convincingly argued that information about the characteristics and service needs of persons who are homeless had been seriously biased by reliance on data obtained from currently homeless samples that tend to overrepresent persons whose homelessness is long-term while underrepresenting those with shorter homeless episodes. Dr. Link contended that this problem contributed to an overestimate of the presence of particular characteristics, including mental disorders and substance abuse problems, in the homeless population.

In their original study, a random-digit-dial telephone survey of a representative sample of U.S. households, Dr. Link's team found a surprisingly high prevalence—over 7 percent—of lifetime homelessness. To confirm this finding and to gather more detail on the nature of the homeless experiences reported by respondents, he received funding from NIMH to carry out a second telephone survey. In this study, those who had reported episodes of homelessness in the original survey would be reinterviewed, along with a comparison group of subjects who had not been homeless. I realized that Dr. Link's study provided a serendipitous opportunity to investigate the question that had interested me for some time—does the experience of adversity in childhood increase the risk of subsequent homelessness in adulthood? Assuming that the study could reliably distinguish between persons who had been homeless at some point in their lives, and that we could employ reasonably valid retrospective measures of childhood adversity, a relatively simple case-control design would be appropriate for the question at hand.

This "case-control" design is commonly used in epidemiology to assess the relationship between one or more "exposures" and an outcome of interest (typically a disease). The design involves comparing how frequently or how much of the exposure is present among persons with the disease (cases) relative to an appropriate comparison group of persons without the disease (controls). This method stands in contrast to so-called "cohort" studies in which persons who have experienced a particular "exposure" and persons without such exposure are followed over time, the proportion of each group that develops the outcome of interest is measured, and the rates in the two groups are then compared. A key advantage of case-control studies is that they can be completed much more quickly and inexpensively than cohort studies since they do not involve lengthy follow-up. They can also be used when the outcome of interest is relatively rare, since the researcher essentially starts with a group that has already experienced the outcome. The internal validity of case-control studies can easily be derailed, however, by measurement and sampling problems. Especially critical is that cases and controls must be drawn from the same "source population" so that they are truly comparable. The current study would meet this criterion since both cases (persons in the sample with homelessness histories) and controls (persons without such histories) would come from the same overall sample. Interested readers should see Rothman, 2002, or another introductory epidemiology text for a discussion of basic design issues in case-control studies.

MEASURING ADVERSITY

As I've noted, my original research question focused on whether or not there is a causal association between out-of-home care during childhood (i.e., foster care, group homes, or other institutions) and adult homelessness. This question grew out of data from numerous descriptive studies, as well as clinicians' reports, suggesting that these experiences were common in samples of homeless persons (for example, see Koegel, Melamid, & Burnam, 1995). These data were often used to support the contention that significant numbers of young adults were becoming homeless as they "aged out" of out-of-home care and were left without adequate follow-up services when they reached adulthood. Critics questioned this conclusion on two major grounds. First, they correctly pointed out that, in the absence of nonhomeless comparison groups, it was unjustified to conclude that the rates of out-of-home care reported in these studies demonstrated that such experiences were causally related to homelessness. Furthermore, critics noted that, even with valid comparison groups, the presence of out-of-home care could be viewed as a marker of other characteristics and adverse childhood experiences that might predispose persons to become homeless as adults. Thus, since out-of-home care frequently follows abuse or neglect during childhood, it could be that abuse and neglect (and/or other factors associated with these experiences) are the true risk factors for adult homelessness.

Since the Link study would furnish an analogous "never-homeless" group that could be compared with persons who had been homeless, I was confident that the first of these methodological weaknesses would clearly be addressed in the new study. To confront the second problem, I realized that it would be essential to employ a broader construct than out-of-home care as the major independent variable; it would also be important to capture data on physical and sexual abuse and the broad domain of "emotional neglect." In the course of my postdoctoral training I had been introduced to the work of George Brown and Tiril Harris, who had done groundbreaking research on the impact of social factors in the genesis of depression among working class women in London (Brown & Harris, 1978). In revisiting their newer publications, I learned about ongoing efforts focusing on the particular role of childhood adversity as a risk factor. As part of this effort, a member of Brown's team, psychologist Antonia Bifulco, had developed an interview measure called the Childhood Experience of Care and Abuse (CECA), intended to retrospectively measure a broad range of "neglectful and abusive experiences of parents and others in the child's environment" (Bifulco, Brown, & Harris, 1994). This measure seemed that it might be appropriate to our needs, since it would permit us to capture a relatively wide view of childhood adversity.

Overcoming a bit of personal trepidation—Why, I wondered, would a world-renowned figure like George Brown be willing to extend his team's resources to a fledgling social work researcher in New York?—I contacted the London group and explained the study we were planning, requesting their help and permission to use the CECA. They were very responsive to my request but I was disappointed to learn that the CECA, at least in its original form, was clearly not suitable for the task at hand. This was because it is a lengthy measure in which the subject is encouraged to describe, in a detailed narrative form, the "story" of his or her childhood to a highly trained interviewer who then uses a complex coding scheme to generate ratings of childhood adversity. Such a method, typical of the mixed-method approach to measurement employed by Brown's group, was clearly infeasible in our traditional telephone survey design. To my surprise, however, Professor Brown offered to train me on the CECA, and to collaborate with our team in developing a brief version of the measure that would be appropriate for our research design. I jumped at the opportunity and later that year traveled to London, where I participated in a weeklong training seminar and developed a close working relationship with Dr. Bifulco and other key members of the research team.

Over the next several months, we worked on creating and pilot-testing a brief scale measuring "lack of care" (LOC) and abuse that, while compatible with the original measure, would be appropriate for our survey. This was a challenging task, given the length and complexity of the original measure and the obvious limitations imposed by our methodology. Furthermore, since my research questions were a relatively minor "add-on" to the purposes of the planned study, I knew that time constraints in the interview would limit us to a small number of questions. To simplify our task (and to preserve space for the measure of LOC), we decided to identify brief single-item measures of the sexual and physical abuse domains, since this method had been used in earlier telephone surveys of nationally representative samples, also permitting us to validate our estimates against previously collected data. We therefore selected two items (one for each type of abuse) that closely approximated the questions that had been used in these earlier epidemiologic studies. For LOC, we set about drafting and piloting a set of Likert-scale questions designed to tap parental antipathy and indifference, the two major dimensions of the LOC construct. We received invaluable assistance in this task from Dr. Bifulco, who helped us to develop a set of items that we felt would closely approximate the same construct studied by the British group.

ANALYTIC ISSUES

I have skipped discussion of what is the most important and typically the most difficult phase in implementing an empirical study—collection of the data. This is because the data collection process (as well as coding, cleaning, and data entry) for this study was carried out by a private contractor under the supervision of Dr. Link. After receiving the data from the contractor, other members of the research team performed further reliability checks and developed a weighting scheme so that the analytic data set would accurately reflect the U.S. household population. Once these steps were completed, I was in the enviable position of receiving from Dr. Link a weighted, clean data file that I was then able to import into SPSS for analysis. Making use of contractors to collect data is common, especially in telephone surveys, and may have significant logistical and cost advantages; however, the research team must still maintain primary responsibility for human subjects protection issues as well as remaining ultimately accountable for questions of sampling and data quality.

In my preliminary analyses, it soon became obvious that lack of care and physical abuse were very strongly associated with both lifetime and recent homelessness in these data. I distinctly recall showing these early data runs to my mentor, Dr. Ezra Susser, who excitedly responded,

"Congratulations! These are once-in-a-lifetime findings!" Being a new (and naïve) researcher, I had no idea at the time how unusually strong these associations were. In the years since, over the course of numerous studies, never again have I seen such clear-cut and strong results in any studies that I've been involved in—and, if Dr. Susser proves correct, I probably never will.

After assuring myself, via multiple checks, that I had made no obvious errors in the bivariate analyses, I set out to consider the possible effects of confounding and bias. Uncontrolled confounding is a common threat to internal validity in nonexperimental studies, including case-control designs. In this research, we were especially concerned that the observed association between childhood adversity and adult homelessness could have been confounded by a range of variables, including characteristics of the subject's family background and current status measures. With respect to family background, for instance, we were aware that both adult homelessness and adverse childhood experiences could be associated with lower socioeconomic status of the family of origin. If this were true, the association we observed between childhood adversity and adult homelessness could be spurious (that is, accounted for by their both being associated with socio-economic status). In fact, when my hypothesis was first put forward in our group, several members of the team rather strongly suspected that this would prove to be the case. This is why we ran a multivariate logistic regression analysis in which we examined the relationship between the childhood adversities of interest and adult homelessness, while adjusting for a set of potential confounders including measures of socioeconomic status in the family of origin. As reported in the results section of the paper, the results of this analysis were essentially identical to the unadjusted analysis, leading us to conclude that confounding by these variables was unlikely to account for the observed associations.

A related area of concern that we attempted to address in the multivariate analysis was the possibility that recall of childhood experiences could be biased by respondents' current psychological state, something that had been suggested by a review of the literature on the validity of retrospective recall of childhood events (Brewin, Andrews, & Gotlib, 1993). This potential problem existed because our case-control design relied on retrospective reporting by respondents of their childhood experiences. If, as some evidence suggested, current depressed mood increased the likelihood that respondents would report more negative ratings of their childhood experiences (and current depressed mood was associated with previous homelessness), it would be important to attempt to control for this potential bias. We did this by including a measure of current depressive symptoms in the multivariate analysis described above.

This step, while probably useful, clearly did not entirely remove the potential validity threat associated with biased recall of childhood adversity. As noted in the published article, the potential problems associated with our reliance on retrospective recall of adverse childhood experiences were a significant concern. Specifically, if subjects who had experienced homelessness as adults were more likely to recall childhood adversity (or conversely, if never-homeless subjects were less likely to recall such adversity), the associations we observed between childhood adversity and adult homelessness would have been biased upward. Since the study was completed, further research on the validity of retrospective recall of childhood adversity has been published, including a recent comprehensive review of research in this area (Hardt & Rutter, 2004). This review provides reassurance as well as reason for concern. After considering the available body of research that examined the degree of concordance between contemporaneous and retrospective reports of childhood adversity, the authors conclude that "when abuse or neglect is retrospectively reported to have taken place, these positive reports are likely to be correct" (p. 270); however, such reports are seen as typically providing an underestimate of the incidence of such events. Somewhat more worrisome, however, is their second major conclusion: persons who are more "well-functioning" in adulthood may be less likely to report (due to forgetting or other factors) adversities that occurred in early life when compared with people who are "suffering social impairment," and that such misreporting does not seem to stem from current mood state. If this bias occurred in our study, there is the real possibility that it could have artificially inflated the odds ratios we observed. Reassuringly, the magnitude of this bias in the studies reviewed was rather small, causing me to remain confident that the very strong effects we reported are unlikely to be entirely accounted for by such bias.

WHAT ABOUT OUT-OF-HOME CARE?

As noted above, the original impetus for this study was previous data suggesting that foster care and other out-of-home care were extremely common among samples of homeless persons. In our study, although such experiences were roughly twice as common in the ever-homeless group compared with the never-homeless group, the prevalence of out-of-home care among the homeless group (4.8%) was dramatically lower than had been reported in earlier studies. The explanation we offered is that out-of-home care may be more strongly associated with long-term rather than episodic homelessness; therefore, previous studies that tended to oversample chronically homeless populations would naturally have observed higher rates of such care. Furthermore, most of the earlier research sampled exclusively shelter residents who are likely to have significantly different characteristics and homeless histories than our subjects who reported lifetime homelessness. In fact, in our study, the most common places respondents reporting lifetime literal homelessness stayed in were vehicles and makeshift housing rather than shelters (Link, Phelan, Bresnahan, Stueve, Moore, & Susser, 1995).

TYPE III ERROR? A THOUGHT-PROVOKING CRITIQUE

Looking back, I remain reasonably confident that this is a strong study overall. To my knowledge, there have been no published studies whose results contradict our findings and we have heard no major methodological criticisms. However, two colleagues, Sharon Schwartz and Kenneth Carpenter, published a valuable and thought-provoking article that challenged the way in which we framed the research question and the broad interpretation of our findings (Schwartz & Carpenter, 1999). Their article focuses on problems associated with research that "provides the right answer for the wrong question"—a phenomenon they call "Type III" error.

Schwartz and Carpenter first distinguish studies that seek to assess the causes of variation in risk for a particular outcome *between individuals* within a given population from studies that aim to determine the causes of differences *between populations* or time periods. In the field of drug abuse, for instance, an example of the former would be a study examining whether school failure increases the risk of cocaine dependency, while an example of the latter would be research seeking to explain why the statewide rate of cocaine use differs between California and Wyoming. Both of these questions are potentially important and may have very different answers. Furthermore, factors identified as increasing risk for cocaine use at the individual level may not hold constant in different populations or at different points in time. The authors argue that researchers interested in reducing the overall incidence of a condition in a population frequently err by studying interindividual differences that, while they may contribute to increased risk for developing that condition, are irrelevant to determining the overall rate of the condition in the population. This, according to Schwartz and Carpenter, is an example of Type III error that is common in public health research (and also clearly applies to social work).

The authors offer our study to exemplify how Type III is manifest in research on homelessness. They correctly note that the overall rate of homelessness in the U.S. increased dramatically after the 1980s, stimulating a great deal of research on the causes of this problem. Much of this research, including our study, focused on the characteristics (individual-level risk factors) differentiating homeless from domiciled persons. Arguing that the overall rate of homelessness is largely determined by structural factors such as the supply of affordable housing, the authors contend that differences between persons who are and are not undomiciled at a given point in time may be relevant to the question of who becomes homeless but not to why the amount of homelessness has risen over time. This has been referred to by others as the "musical chairs" phenomenon, in which the number of affordable housing slots is fixed and those who become homeless are the persons least able to compete due to individual factors such as mental illness, substance abuse, childhood adversity, etc. Citing our study (and several others), Schwartz and Carpenter continue that "even researchers who recognize that these are distinct issues with distinct causes often conclude that both types of studies are important for reducing the rate of homelessness," while in fact "homelessness represents a situation in which information about interindividual differences (i.e., individual-level risk factors) is not necessary for reducing the rate of homelessness because the causes of the current amount of homelessness and the causes of interindividual differences in homelessness are distinct" (pp. 1177–1178).

How well-deserved is this critique? Clearly, Schwartz and Carpenter make an important (and essentially irrefutable) case regarding the need to carefully distinguish between questions and methods pertaining to the causes of the incidence or prevalence of a condition in a population and those relating to the distribution of that condition within a population. Furthermore, the area of homelessness serves as an excellent example of a social problem around which such confusion can easily occur. Looking back at our paper, however, I believe that we were rather careful to emphasize that we viewed structural factors, specifically "labor market changes, an inadequate supply of housing, and cuts in income assistance programs" as the primary causes of the recent growth in homelessness, while referring to individual-level risk factors as "those personal characteristics and circumstances that make certain persons more vulnerable to becoming homeless under these conditions" (see Introduction). Discussing our findings, we emphasized that "these [childhood] adversities 'cause' homelessness only within a broad social context that allows for the existence of widespread homelessness" (see Discussion).

I suspect, then, that Schwartz and Carpenter took us to task primarily on the basis of our concluding sentence which addressed the policy implications of our results:

> ...these findings suggest that interventions that can effectively reduce the incidence of child abuse and neglect may ultimately yield a large dividend by preventing critical social problems including homelessness and the enormous social costs that these problems engender.

In retrospect, I can see how this statement, although obviously well-intentioned (and perhaps relevant to the prevention of other conditions such as mental disorders and other health conditions), does not logically flow from our conceptualization of the research problem or our findings, if one assumes that the overall rate of homelessness is entirely unrelated to the distribution of individual-level risk factors (as do Schwartz and Carpenter). Today, I find myself agreeing more than disagreeing with the fundamental criticism offered by these authors, at least as it applies to this concluding statement. However, I do believe that it's debatable since, in my view, the "musical chairs" metaphor tends to oversimplify the broad processes that generate homelessness.

I would argue that while the rate of homelessness is indeed, to a great extent, determined by the number of "chairs" (i.e., the number of units of affordable housing), there are clearly other factors that influence the prevalence of homelessness in a particular population or geographical area. This can be demonstrated by a simple thought experiment. Assume that you are a middle-class professional adult, with no serious psychiatric or medical problems, living in your own home in a small city. Living in other homes nearby are your parents, and several siblings. It is difficult to imagine any circumstances that would lead to your becoming literally homeless, since, even assuming total loss of income, it is likely that you would be able to receive support (either money or a place to stay) from your extended family or other members of your network. This is relatively insensitive to whether the supply of low-cost housing in the community is small or great. Now imagine that you are the same person but you have recently become psychotic due to the onset of bipolar disorder, leading you to behave in a self-destructive and unpredictable manner. This causes you to lose your job, your savings, and your possessions. You also grow suspicious of your family members and friends who want nothing to do with you because of your untreated mental illness and drinking problems. There is an excellent chance that you could end up sleeping on the street or in a local shelter. Again, this is relatively independent of whether the supply of low-cost housing is small or great.

POSTSCRIPT: FUTURE RESEARCH DIRECTIONS

No research of which I am aware has challenged the general proposition that childhood adversity is an individual-level risk factor for adult homelessness. Nonetheless, an outstanding question that is especially important from a prevention perspective concerns the mechanism(s) through which childhood adversity increases risk for adult homelessness—something that we speculated on but were unable to convincingly address given our design limitations. Clearly, then, research is needed that focuses in more depth on particular causal pathways between childhood adversity and adult homelessness. Such research, rather than simply examining risk factors and outcomes, would need to adopt a true life-course perspective. This perspective assumes that changes and events over the subsequent life history of affected persons moderate the impact of adverse childhood experiences. Typically requiring longitudinal approaches, this program of research would be designed to investigate the complex sequences and mechanisms through which early adversities lead to later experiences and conditions (including both social, familial, and environmental influences as well as internal psychological resources) that in turn increase or reduce the risk of later outcomes.

At the broader level, this study can be seen as part of an ever-growing research literature that links adverse childhood experiences to a remarkably wide number of disparate adult outcomes in the areas of health, mental health, and social functioning. Although we did not publish these results, we found in our own data that LOC and abuse were significantly and positively associated with marital divorce or separation, victimization, having been in jail or prison, unemployment, and poverty. In these domains as well, it would seem that the key questions at this point concern the causal pathways through which childhood adversity leads to negative health and psychosocial outcomes.

REFERENCES

Bifulco, A., Brown, G., & Harris, T. (1994). Childhood experience of care and abuse (CECA): A retrospective interview measure. *Journal of Child Psychiatry and Psychology and Allied Disciplines, 35*(8), 1419–1435.

Brewin, C., Andrews, B., & Gotlib, I. (1993). Psychopathology and early experience: A reappraisal of retrospective reports. *Psychological Bulletin, 113*(1), 82–98.

Brown, G., & Harris, T. (1978). *The social origins of depression: A study of psychiatric disorder in women.* London: Tavistock Publications.

Hardt, J., & Rutter, M. (2004). Validity of adult retrospective reports of adverse childhood experiences: Review of the evidence. *Journal of Child Psychology & Psychiatry, 45*(2), 260–273.

Herman, D. (1991). *Homeless men in New York City's public shelters: A life course perspective.* Unpublished dissertation, Columbia University.

Koegel, P., Melamid, E., & Burnam, M. A. (1995). Childhood risk factors for homelessness among homeless adults. *American Journal of Public Health, 85*(12), 1642–1649.

Link, B., Phelan, J., Bresnahan, M., Stueve, A., Moore, R. E., & Susser, E. (1995). Lifetime and five-year prevalence of homelessness in the United States: New evidence on an old debate. *American Journal of Orthopsychiatry, 65*(3), 347–354.

Link, B. G., Struening, E. L., Rahav, M., Phelan, J. C., & Nuttbrock, L. (1997). On stigma and its consequences: Evidence from a longitudinal study of men with dual diagnoses of mental illness and substance abuse. *Journal of Health & Social Behavior, 38*(2), 177–190.

Rothman, K. J. (2002). *Epidemiology: An introduction.* New York: Oxford University Press.

Schwartz, S., & Carpenter, K. (1999). The right answer for the wrong question: Consequences of type III error for public health research. *American Journal of Public Health, 89*(8), 1175–1180.

A Comparison of Homeless
and Matched Housed Adolescents
on Family Environment Variables

Susan M. Wolfe, Paul A. Toro, and Pamela A. McCaskill

Each year many adolescents run away or are "thrown away" from their homes. Estimates for homelessness among adolescents range from 575,000 (Finkelhor, Hotaling, & Sedlak, 1990) to more than 1 million (U.S. General Accounting Office, 1989). Early research in this area focused on the psychological deviance of runaways, and these youth were classified as juvenile delinquents (Robertson, 1992). In the 1970s, the literature began to focus on the multiple causes for runaway behavior, including family problems. At the same time, it became clear that not all adolescents in shelters and on the streets had run away from home but that many had been pushed or thrown out by their parents.[1]

Adolescent homelessness is a serious problem for several reasons. Adolescents generally lack the skills and education necessary to obtain jobs that pay well enough to support themselves. Many homeless adolescents turn to crimes like prostitution and drug dealing in order to survive. Such youth living on the streets are in danger of becoming victims of crime and suffering significant health problems. Shelters and other services are necessary to prevent them from remaining on the streets. Although shelters often provide family counseling and other valuable services as well as a place to sleep, they require substantial resources to operate. The necessity of interventions to prevent adolescents from becoming homeless in the first place seems to be indicated; however, research has not identified the most effective intervention points for this population.

---

[1]In this article, we generally use the term *homeless* to describe the full range of adolescents homeless without their parents, including the runaways, throwaways, street youth, and other groups described in the existing literature.

From Wolfe, S., Toro, P., McCaskill, P. (1999) A comparison of homelessness and matched housed adolescents on family environment variables. *Journal of Research on Adolescence, 9,* 53–66. Copyright 1999 Blackwell Publishing. Reprinted with permission.

Many studies have focused on the family problems of homeless youth. Family problems studied have included maltreatment, conflict, and parental drug and alcohol abuse (e.g., Gutierres & Reich, 1981; Powers, Jaklitsch, & Eckenrode, 1989; Roberts, 1981, 1982; Stiffman, 1989; Zide & Cherry, 1992). Studies have consistently found high rates of physical, sexual, and emotional abuse among homeless adolescents. In a study on status offenders, sexual abuse was seven times higher among the runaways as compared to other members of the group (Famularo, Kinscherff, Fenton, & Bolduc, 1990). Findings of other studies have found that as many as 78% of homeless adolescents self-reported significant physical violence perpetrated by their parents during the year prior to the runaway episode (Farber, Kinast, McCoard, & Falkner, 1984). Homeless adolescents as a group report experiencing low levels of care and acceptance (Dadds, Braddock, Cuers, Elliott, & Kelly, 1993). Neglect has been reported by as many as 43% of homeless adolescents (Boesky, Toro, & Wright, 1995; Powers, Eckenrode, & Jaklitsch, 1990), and the act of throwing an underage adolescent out of the home could itself be viewed as a form of abuse or neglect.

Families of homeless adolescents are often highly conflictual (Feitel, Margetson, Chamas, & Lipman, 1992; Loeb, Burke, & Boglarsky, 1986; Spillane-Grieco, 1984). Conflict was long considered to be a normal part of parent–adolescent relations; however, more recent work has found that excessive conflict in family relations during adolescence is indicative of problems (Bandura, 1964; Hall, 1987; Rutter, Graham, Chadwick, & Yule, 1976). It becomes especially problematic when the conflict results in the adolescent running away or being thrown out of the home.

Studies on homeless youth have several methodological limitations (Robertson, 1992). Most studies use small samples of participants, and the homeless youth are often recruited from a single, nonrepresentative shelter or street site. Control or comparison groups are seldom included, and data on the reliability and validity of instruments frequently are not provided.

The goals of this study were: (a) to compare family environments of homeless adolescents residing in shelters to a matched comparison group; (b) to develop a methodology that would include a large and representative sample of homeless adolescents, a comparison group, and measures that are standardized with demonstrated reliability and validity; and (c) to identify factors relevant for future study to facilitate our understanding of the contributions of family factors to the problems of homeless youths. Based upon our review of the literature, we expected that greater levels of maltreatment and parental treatment of mental illness and substance abuse would be found among homeless as compared to housed youth. We also expected that homeless youth would perceive less support from family members than housed youth and would experience higher rates of verbal and physical aggression from parents. Finally, we expected that the families of homeless youth would be characterized as less cohesive, allowing for less expression, and less supportive of independence.

METHOD

Participants

Homeless Youth. A total of 118 homeless adolescents were recruited over a 14-month period (February 1993–April 1994) from six different shelters from throughout a large midwestern metropolitan area (1990 population over 4 million). Homeless youth were defined as adolescents (ages 12–17) who had spent the previous night at a youth shelter. The original design included adolescents residing on the streets; however, service providers reported that youth under the age of 18 tend to stay off the streets in the city studied (as in most other midwestern cities) because it is too dangerous and cold. They either go to formal shelters or stay with friends or family members.

Although it would have been preferable to include those who were staying with friends or family members, efforts indicated they were not easily accessible.

Data were obtained from each of the shelters to determine how many adolescents utilized their services annually. The sample was selected in proportion to the number of youth served by each shelter during a 1-year period. Service utilization data indicated that very few of the homeless youth used multiple shelters in the area. Four of the shelters included were suburban, and the other two were located in urban areas. Three shelters served both men and women, two served women only, and one served men only. Annual caseloads of adolescents (under age 18) served by each shelter ranged from 20 to 317. Most of the sample were homeless for the first time (66.9%), and most had been homeless for only a short period (life-time homelessness was 1 month or less for 74.6%). Analysis of reasons for leaving home indicated that 56 (47.5%) of the homeless youth were runaways, 30 (25.4%) were throwaways, and 32 (27.1%) were service seekers. Service seekers were those adolescents whose parents brought them to the shelter to obtain counseling and other services and to have some time to cool off following a period of intense conflict. Both the adolescent and the parents expected them to return home after a brief period at the shelter.

Housed Comparison Group. The comparison group consisted of 118 housed youths who were matched on age (within 1 year), gender, and neighborhood socioeconomic status. Homeless adolescents were asked to nominate 5 to 10 same-sex friends who lived in the neighborhood in which they last resided with their parent(s) or guardian(s). Letters explaining the study were sent to the parents of these youth. These letters were followed by phone calls to obtain verbal permission and schedule an interview if both the adolescents and their parents agreed to participation. The final sample consisted of two types of matches. The first kind (58 matched pairs) included housed teens who were matched to the homeless teen who nominated them. The housed teens in these matched pairs generally came from the same or a nearby neighborhood (based on zip code boundaries). Largely because of incomplete information provided on addresses and phone numbers (and to a lesser extent because some homeless adolescents refused to provide peer nominations), many of the homeless teens could not be precisely matched to the youth they nominated. The housed adolescents in the remaining 60 pairs were chosen from the list of another homeless adolescent who came from a similar neighborhood, as defined by the median family income of the zip code area. Across both types of matches, most housed–homeless pairs ($n = 104$) were matched on median neighborhood family income plus or minus $15,000 (the remainder were matched plus or minus $25,000). All pairs were matched on age (within 1 year) and gender. Background characteristics of both groups are provided in Table 11.1. There were no significant differences ($p > .10$) between the two groups on the three matching criteria or on any of the other characteristics in the table.

Measures

Background Characteristics. Demographic and other background information collected included gender, race, age, time homeless, reason for homelessness, parental educational and occupational status, and median family income of the adolescent's neighborhood (based on zip code boundaries). Reason for homelessness was used to code adolescents into three categories: runaway (had voluntarily left home, $N = 56$); throwaway (forced to leave home by parents, $N = 29$); or service seeker (parents sent to shelter for cooling off period with understanding they would return home, $N = 33$). These variables were later used for within-group analyses of the homeless population to determine whether there were significant differences between the different types of homeless adolescents.

Table 11.1. Background Characteristics of the Homeless and Housed Samples

	Homeless		Housed	
	N	Percentage	*N*	Percentage
Race				
White	53	44.9	63	53.4
Nonwhite[a]	65	55.1	55	46.6
Gender				
Male	35	29.7	35	29.7
Female	83	70.3	83	70.3
	M	*SD*	*M*	*SD*
Age	14.68	1.32	14.81	1.41
Parental education[b]	12.77	1.95	12.66	1.57
Parental occupation[c]	39.30	20.13	39.02	17.01
Neighborhood income[d]	28,605	13,353	29,825	12,010

Note: The homeless and housed groups did not differ significantly on any of the six characteristics in this table ($p > .10$, based on analyses of variance and chi-square tests). $N = 118$.

[a]Most in this group were African American (103 of total 120). [b]Highest number of years completed by mother or father. [c]Highest occupational status achieved by mother or father, based on a 100-point scale (Stevens & Featherman, 1981). A mean score of 39 falls within the range of blue-collar positions. [d]Neighborhood median family income (in dollars) is based on the zip code in which the adolescent most recently lived.

Diagnostic Interview Schedule for Children (DISC). The DISC (Version 2.3) is a structured instrument that obtains self-reported data from children and adolescents and produces diagnoses based on *Diagnostic and Statistical Manual of Mental Disorders* (3rd ed., revised; *DSM–III–R;* American Psychiatric Association, 1987) criteria. It was originally developed for the National Institute of Mental Health's Epidemiological Catchment Area program to determine the prevalence of mental disorders and related service needs for children in the United States. It allows lay interviewers to obtain data that can be scored to arrive at an accurate and reliable diagnosis of child and adolescent psychiatric disorders (Shaffer et al., 1993). The questions are in a standard order such that the exact wording of all probes is specified. No interpretation by the interviewer is required, and there is no need for extensive clinical training.

The DISC has demonstrated excellent interrater reliability. In initial field studies, interrater reliability was 97% (36 of 37 clinicians and lay interviewers had perfect agreement). Clinicians and lay interviewers have been found not to differ from one another when using the DISC to make diagnoses (Shaffer et al., 1993). Numerous revisions leading to Version 2.3 have improved the psychometric qualities of the measure to the point that it is considered the best available structured research interview yielding *DSM–III–R* (1987) diagnoses for adolescents (Piacentini et al., 1993; Schwab-Stone et al., 1993; Weinstein, 1988, 1990).

A previous study comparing these two groups for prevalence of mental disorders determined that the two groups differed significantly only for behavioral disorders (a combination of attention deficit hyperactivity disorder, oppositional defiant disorder, and conduct disorder), and alcohol abuse or dependency (reference omitted at this time for blind review). Variables were dummy coded 0 for no diagnosis and 1 for a positive diagnosis of a behavioral disorder and alcohol abuse or dependency.

Inventory of Childhood Events (ICE). The ICE measures perceived childhood experiences and family history by having the respondent rate frequencies of parenting behaviors on a 5-point scale. It was developed for use with marginal populations (Passero, Zax, & Zozus, 1991;

Zozus & Zax, 1991) and adapted for adolescents in this study. Subscales used included a maltreatment index (8 items, α = .74), violence observed between parents (3 items, α = .76), perceived love from parents (10 items, α = .82), and scolding behaviors of parents (6 items, α = .85). When this measure was used in a study of homeless adults (mostly ages 18–35), 1- to 2-week test–retest reliabilities for subscales similar to those used here ranged from .62 to .83 (Wolfe & Toro, 1992).

Family Environment Scale (FES). The FES was used to assess the social climate of the family (Moos & Moos, 1994). The Cohesion, Expressiveness, Conflict, and Independence scales were included in this interview protocol. This was a 36-item, true/false, questionnaire that assessed the self-reported social environment characteristics of the adolescents' families. Some strengths of this measure are that it is theoretically based, standardized, and normed, and the items are easily understood by respondents (Grotevant & Carlson, 1989, p. 314). Although its lack of adequate testing with lower socioeconomic groups limits the certainty with which we can make conclusions about the results, the research team decided to use this measure because of the exploratory nature of this study. There is evidence of sufficient reliability (internal consistency alphas of .61 to .78 and test–retest reliability estimates of .68 to .87), and considerable validity data now also exists (Moos & Moos, 1994). One- to 2-week test–retest reliability coefficients for the FES scales used here, as obtained in a study of homeless young adults, ranged from .71 to .83 (Wolfe & Toro, 1992). KR20 coefficients were computed for the four scales, and results indicated that only the cohesiveness and conflict scales were sufficiently reliable to retain for analyses (KR20 coefficients = .7936 and .7177, respectively).

Social Network Interview (SNI). The SNI is an adaptation of the Network Interview (Rappaport et al., 1985) and was used to assess family structure and support. It requires participants to list those persons in their social network whom they consider important and with whom they have had contact in the past 6 months. For each network member nominated, several questions are asked, including their relationship to the participant, frequency of contact, provision of help, and how well they get along. A number of studies have documented the accuracy of such self-reported network data through corroboration by others (Hammer, 1984). This study used four indexes reflecting the size and level of contact with family members, the extent to which the youth feels he or she gets along with family members, and the proportion of family members listed in the network that provide support. One- to 2-week test–retest reliability coefficients for these four SNI indexes, based on a study of homeless young adults, ranged from .71 to .95 (Wolfe & Toro, 1992).

Conflict Tactics Scales (CTS). The extent of violence perpetrated by the parent toward the child and by the child toward the parent was assessed by the CTS (Straus, 1979, 1990). Six subscales were used: Parent to child reasoning, verbal aggression, physical aggression, and child to parent reasoning, verbal aggression, and physical aggression. Across several studies, internal consistency alphas have ranged from .50 to .88 for these scales. Validity data indicate that the CTS scales correlate with several risk factors for family violence (e.g., unemployment and heavy drinking; Straus, 1990). The CTS is the most widely used measure of domestic violence and has been used to assess differences across cultures and socioeconomic groups. It has also been used in recent studies of homeless families and single adults (e.g., Goodman, 1991; Toro et al., 1995).

Results of reliability analyses for this sample of adolescents indicated that both of the reasoning scales (child to parent and parent to child) did not have sufficient reliability (.57 and .59), so they were not included in the analyses. The remaining scales, the child to parent verbal aggression (α = .77) and physical aggression (α = .80) and the parent to child verbal aggression (α = .79) and physical aggression (α = .88) demonstrated good internal consistency.

Interviews were conducted by full-time staff interviewers and graduate and advanced under-graduate students in psychology. Interviewers were trained in establishing rapport, practical and safety issues, and the administration of each measure. For homeless youth, the interviewer would visit the shelter and randomly select a youth from a list of current residents. To allow youth to be candid, interviews were generally conducted in a private room at the shelter. Interviews with housed youth were conducted in a private place at their homes. Because some youth were illiterate, all measures were administered verbally to youth in both groups by the interviewer, who recorded responses on standardized answer sheets. Both homeless and housed participants were paid $5 after completing the interview.

RESULTS

Homeless versus Housed Adolescents

Four multivariate analyses of covariance (MANCOVA) tests were used to analyze the differences between homeless and housed adolescents on the various scales. Because both alcohol abuse or dependence and conduct disorder were found to be more prevalent among the homeless group, they were entered as covariates to partial out their possible effects on the outcomes. Results are presented in Table 11.2.

Table 11.2. MANCOVA Results for Family Variables

Variable	Homeless		Housed			
	M^a	SD	M	SD	F	η^2
Childhood events[b]					3.10*	.053
Maltreatment index	1.03	.70	.69	.64	9.52**	.041
Mother–Father violence	1.32	1.18	1.02	1.00	1.37	.006
Parental love	1.97	.80	2.19	.87	1.95	.008
Parental scolding	1.79	1.05	1.45	1.05	3.30	.015
Family climate[c]					12.41**	.097
Conflict	5.19	2.04	4.41	1.82	13.65**	.056
Cohesiveness	4.30	2.81	6.25	2.18	24.46**	.096
Social network interview[d]					2.41*	.041
Family network size	7.08	3.78	6.41	3.00	1.80	.008
Family contact	3.17	.67	3.37	.55	4.22**	.018
Gets along with family	2.89	.77	3.12	.66	2.71	.012
Family support network	3.66	3.02	3.72	2.14	3.40*	.015
Conflict tactics[e]					7.08**	.111
Child verbal aggression	2.88	1.54	1.98	1.41	10.03**	.042
Child physical aggression	1.56	1.43	.78	.90	0.95	.004
Parent verbal aggression	3.33	1.44	2.48	1.34	12.95**	.053
Parent physical aggression	.66	.81	.44	.63	19.81**	.079

Note: MANCOVA = multivariate analysis of covariance. $N = 118$.

[a]Means reported are the observed means. [b]For all F tests involving these variables from the Inventory of Childhood Events, $df = 1, 223$. [c]For all F tests involving these variables from the Family Environment Scales, $df = 1, 231$. [d]For all F tests involving these variables from the Social Network Interview, $df = 1, 231$. [e]For all F tests involving these variables from the Conflict Tactics Scales, $df = 1, 230$.

*$p < .05$, **$p < .01$.

Results of the first MANCOVA indicated there was a significant multivariate effect of group (housed vs. homeless) for the ICE variables, $F(4, 220) = 2.82$, $p < .05$. Although the results were significant, the effect size ($\eta^2 = .049$) was small. Univariate F tests indicated that there was a significant group difference for parental maltreatment. Homeless adolescents reported significantly more parental maltreatment.

Results of the second MANCOVA indicated there was a significant multivariate group effect of group for the family social climate, as assessed by the FES, $F(2, 230) = 12.41$, $p < .01$ (a medium effect size, $\eta^2 = .097$). Univariate comparisons indicated that there was significantly more conflict and less cohesion in the families of the homeless adolescents compared to the housed adolescents.

Results of the third MANCOVA indicated that there was a significant multivariate effect of group for the social network variables, $F(4, 228) = 2.41$, $p = .05$ (a small effect size, $\eta^2 = .041$). Univariate comparisons indicated that only the frequency of contact with family was significant.

Results of the fourth MANCOVA indicated that there was a significant multivariate group effect for the conflict tactics variables, $F(4, 227) = 7.08$, $p < .01$ (a medium effect size, $\eta^2 = .111$). Univariate comparisons indicated that there were significant group differences for the amount of child to parent verbal aggression and parent to child verbal and physical aggression. Only child to parent physical aggression was not significant.

DISCUSSION

The results supported our predictions that homeless adolescents would show a wide range of problems on family environment variables. The study expands on the research literature on homeless adolescents by finding that these problems are not only extensive but differentiate the homeless from similar housed adolescents who do not leave home. In fact, despite being carefully matched on a variety of background characteristics and controlling for the possible effects of behavioral disorders and alcohol use, the homeless differed from the housed group on virtually every family variable measured, with small to moderate effects of housing status. In addition to its use of careful matching procedures, this study improved upon previous studies in several other ways. The use of probability sampling methods and the inclusion of the full range of shelters serving both urban and suburban areas provided a more representative sample of homeless adolescents. The interview included instruments with demonstrated reliability and validity and the relatively large sample size enhanced statistical power.

Findings of this study have implications for further research. A number of studies (e.g., Shields, Cicchetti, & Ryan, 1994) have found that maltreated children have problems in regulating their behaviors and tend to be aggressive, disruptive, and noncompliant. Findings of previous analyses indicating that the homeless youth demonstrate a significantly higher rate of behavioral disorders are consistent with these findings. Results of this study indicate that maltreatment appears to be associated with adolescents leaving home; however, it is not clear that the maltreatment is the cause of their running. It is possible that their running is simply an extension of their unregulated behaviors that possibly elicit the maltreatment. Because these data were self-reported by the adolescents, it is also possible that they exaggerated their responses to justify leaving home or because they were angry with the parents who asked them to leave.

The possibility that adolescent problem behavior may account for increased parental aggression, decreased cohesion, and increased conflict among the homeless adolescent group should not be ruled out completely, despite our having controlled for them in the analyses. It is possible that the parents are reacting to the adolescents' problem behaviors by becoming more aggressive and argumentative. Results of this study indicated that these homeless adolescents are more verbally aggressive toward their parents, in addition to the higher rates of problem behaviors and alcohol use. It is highly possible that as parents' and adolescents' negative interactions increase, someone reaches his or her limit, and the adolescent either leaves or is asked to leave, or both agree upon a cooling off period to de-escalate the conflict.

Despite the methodological improvements made in this study, there were some limitations. First, the study was cross-sectional. Family environments and parent and adolescent behaviors develop over a long period of time, and this study measured some of these behaviors at a time when the family system was most likely at its highest level of disequilibrium. Longitudinal studies would be useful for determining whether the homeless episode was merely the climax of a specific struggle within the family or whether it is a harbinger of more negative things to come. On one hand, it is possible that the homeless episode was the culmination of a series of problem behaviors and conflicts. With the passage of time and through the shelter interventions provided, the negative family interaction cycle may be turned around. It is equally likely that this homeless episode is just one further step in a progression toward familial disaffiliation by the adolescent.

A second limitation is the reliance upon a single source for data. The information regarding parenting practices and behaviors that was collected for this study is based upon the perceptions of the adolescents and may be distorted by their subjective realities. However, in their research on perceptions of parent–adolescent interactions by family members and outsiders, Noller and Callan (1988) found that adolescent ratings more closely approximated those of outsiders than did those of parents. Future research could still benefit from including adolescent perceptions, perceptions of other family members, as well as ratings by outsiders to gain a more comprehensive view of family interaction patterns.

A third limitation was that the study included only those youths who were residing in shelters. Although it was determined that there was no significant population of street youth in this particular locality, conversations with service providers confirmed that there were runaway and throwaway adolescents residing with older friends or families of friends. Methodologies need to be developed to locate and include this group in future studies.

A final limitation was that this study, like most others, was atheoretical. Studies grounded in a theoretical perspective would be helpful in determining the mechanisms underlying the family and adolescent problems. These results point to several theoretical perspectives that may be useful in designing future studies. Reports of less perceived maternal love indicate that studies grounded in attachment theory may be useful to explain some of the relational dynamics. Research grounded in aggression theories may be useful for explaining the high rates of verbal and physical aggression perpetrated by parents and adolescents. The parenting styles literature developed by Baumrind (1968, 1978, 1991a) may have utility for examining the differences in family environment, particularly the independence and expressiveness dimensions. The vast literature on the development of autonomy and parenting may also be a good foundation for studying the overall interactions in the context of the adolescent developmental processes.

The results of this study demonstrate that comparative studies of this type are not only feasible but may be useful for identifying factors that are uniquely associated with adolescent homelessness. The study's results also point to the need to improve upon methodologies, measurement, and theoretical grounding of future studies of homeless adolescents.

ACKNOWLEDGMENTS

This research was supported by funds provided to Paul A. Toro by Wayne State University. We thank Lisa Boesky, Nyama Reed, Jerry Rogers, Steven Schoeberlein, Virginia Szymanski, and others associated with our Research Group on Homelessness and Poverty for their help with participant recruitment, data collection, and data analysis. Thanks to the two anonymous reviewers who provided constructive feedback for revisions to this article. Also, we thank the youth shelters and homeless and other youth who participated in this research.

REFERENCES

American Psychiatric Association. (1987). *Diagnostic and statistical manual of mental disorders* (3rd ed., rev.). Washington, DC: Author.

Bandura, A. (1964). The stormy decade: Fact or fiction. *Psychology in the Schools, 1,* 224–231.

Baumrind, D. (1968). Authoritarian vs. authoritative control. *Adolescence, 3,* 255–272.

Baumrind, D. (1978). Parental disciplinary pattern and social competence in children. *Youth and Society, 9,* 239–276.

Baumrind, D. (1991a). Parenting styles and adolescent development. In R. M. Lerner, A. C. Petersen, & J. Brooks-Gunn (Eds.), *Encyclopedia of adolescence* (Vol. 2, pp. 746–758). New York: Garland.

Boesky, L. M., Toro, P. A., & Wright, K. (October, 1995). *Maltreatment in a probability sample of homeless adolescents: A subgroup comparison.* Paper presented at the Annual Meeting of the American Public Health Association, San Diego, CA.

Dadds, M. R., Braddock, D., Cuers, S., Elliott, A., & Kelly, A. (1993). Personal and family distress in homeless adolescents. *Community Mental Health Journal, 29,* 413–422.

Famularo, R., Kinscherff, R., Fenton, T., & Bolduc, S. M. (1990). Child maltreatment histories among runaway and delinquent children. *Clinical Pediatrics, 29,* 713–718.

Farber, E. D., Kinast, C., McCoard, W. D., & Falkner, D. (1984). Violence in families of adolescent runaways. *Child Abuse & Neglect, 8,* 295–299.

Feitel, B., Margetson, N., Chamas, J., & Lipman, C. (1992). Psychosocial background and behavioral and emotional disorders of homeless and runaway youth. *Hospital and Community Psychiatry, 43,* 155–159.

Finkelhor, D., Hotaling, G., & Sedlak, A. (1990). *Missing, abducted, runaway, and throwaway children in America, first report: Numbers and characteristics from national incidence studies.* Washington, DC: Office of Justice Programs, Office of Juvenile Justice and Delinquency Prevention.

Goodman, L. A. (1991). The prevalence of abuse in the lives of homeless and housed poor mothers: A comparison study. *American Journal of Orthopsychiatry, 61,* 489–500.

Grotevant, H. D., & Carlson, C. I. (1989). *Family assessment: A guide to methods and measures.* New York: Guilford.

Gutierres, S. E., & Reich, J. W. (1981). A developmental perspective on runaway behavior: Its relationship to child abuse. *Child Welfare, 60,* 89–94.

Hall, J. A. (1987). Parent–adolescent conflict: An empirical review. *Adolescence, 22,* 767–789.

Hammer, M. (1984). Explorations into the meaning of social network interview data. *Social Networks, 6,* 341–371.

Loeb, R. C., Burke, T. A., & Boglarsky, C. A. (1986). A large-scale comparison of perspectives on parenting between teenage runaways and nonrunaways. *Adolescence, 21,* 921–930.

Moos, R. H., & Moos, B. S. (1994). *Family Environment Scale manual* (3rd. ed.). Palo Alto, CA: Consulting Psychologists Press.

Noller, P., & Callan, V. J. (1988). Understanding parent–adolescent interactions: Perceptions of family members and outsiders. *Developmental Psychology, 24,* 707–714.

Passero, J. M., Zax, M., & Zozus, R. T., Jr. (1991). Social network utilization as related to family history among the homeless. *Journal of Community Psychology, 19,* 70–78.

Piacentini, J., Shaffer, D., Fisher, P., Schwab-Stone, M., Davies, M., & Gioia, P. (1993). The Diagnostic Interview Schedule for Children—Revised Version: III. Concurrent validity. *Journal of the American Academy of Child and Adolescent Psychiatry, 32,* 658–665.

Powers, J. L., Eckenrode, J., & Jaklitsch, B. (1990). Maltreatment among runaway and homeless youth. *Child Abuse & Neglect, 14,* 87–98.

Powers, J. L., Jaklitsch, B., & Eckenrode, J. (1989). Behavioral characteristics of maltreatment among runaway and homeless youth. *Early Child Development and Care, 42,* 127–139.

Rappaport, J., Seidman, E., Toro, P. A., McFadden, L. S., Reischl, T. M., Roberts, L. J., Salem, D. A., Stein, C. H., & Zimmerman, M. A. (1985). Finishing the unfinished business: Collaborative research with a mutual help organization. *Social Policy, 15,* 12–24.

Roberts, A. R. (1981). *Runaways and non-runaways in an American suburb: An exploratory study of adolescent and parental coping.* (Criminal Justice Center Monograph No. 13). New York: John Jay Press.

Roberts, A. R. (1982). Stress and coping patterns among adolescent runaways. *Journal of Social Service Research, 5,* 15–27.

Robertson, J. M. (1992). Homeless and runaway youths: A review of the literature. In M. J. Robertson and M. Greenblatt (Eds.), *Homelessness: A national perspective* (pp. 287–298). New York: Plenum.

Rutter, M., Graham, P., Chadwick, O., & Yule, W. (1976). Adolescent turmoil: Fact or fiction? *Journal of Child Psychology and Psychiatry, 17,* 35–36.

Schwab-Stone, M., Fisher, P., Piacentini, J., Shaffer, D., Davies, M., & Briggs, M. (1993). The Diagnostic Interview Schedule for Children—Revised Version: II. Test–retest reliability. *Journal of the American Academy of Child and Adolescent Psychiatry, 32,* 652–657.

Shaffer, D., Schwab-Stone, M., Fisher, P. C., Piacentini, J., Davies, M., Conners, C. K., & Regier, D. (1993). The Diagnostic Interview Schedule for Children—Revised Version. Preparation, field testing, interrater reliability and acceptability. *Journal of the American Academy of Child and Adolescent Psychiatry, 32,* 643–650.

Shields, A. M., Cicchetti, D., & Ryan, R. M. (1994). The development of emotional and behavioral self-regulation and social competence among maltreated school-age children. *Development and Psychopathology, 6,* 57–75.

Spillane-Grieco, E. (1984). Characteristics of a helpful relationship: A study of empathic understanding and positive regard between runaways and their parents. *Adolescence, 19,* 63–75.

Stevens, G., & Featherman, D. (1981). A revised socioeconomic index of occupational status. *Social Science Research, 10,* 364–395.

Stiffman, A. R. (1989). Physical and sexual abuse in runaway youths. *Child Abuse & Neglect, 13,* 417–426.

Straus, M. A. (1979). Measuring intrafamily conflict and violence: The Conflict Tactics (CT) Scales. *Journal of Marriage and the Family, 41,* 75–88.

Straus, M. A. (1990). The Conflict Tactics Scales and its critics: An evaluation and new data on validity and reliability. In M. A. Straus, & R. J. Gelles (Eds.), *Physical violence in American families: Risk factors and adaptations to violence in 8145 families* (pp. 49–73). New Brunswick, NJ: Transaction Publisher.

Toro, P. A., Bellavia, C., Daeschler, C., Owens, B., Wall, D. D., Passero, J. M., & Thomas, D. M. (1995). Distinguishing homelessness from poverty: A comparative study. *Journal of Consulting and Clinical Psychology, 63,* 280–289.

U.S. General Accounting Office. (1989). *Homelessness: Homeless and runaway youth receiving services at federally funded shelters.* Washington, DC: Government Printing Office.

Weinstein, S. (1988). Comparison of the DISC with clinicians' *DSM–III* diagnosis in psychiatric inpatients. *Journal of the American Academy of Child and Adolescent Psychiatry, 28,* 53–60.

Weinstein, S. (1990). Convergence of *DSM–III* diagnosis and self-reported symptoms in child and adolescent psychiatry. *Journal of the American Academy of Child and Adolescent Psychiatry, 30,* 627–635.

Wolfe, S. M., & Toro, P. A. (1992). *Pilot/reliability study: People and transitions in housing (PATH) project.* Unpublished manuscript, Wayne State University, Detroit, MI.

Zide, M. R., & Cherry, A. L. (1992). A typology of runaway youths: An empirically based definition. *Child and Adolescent Social Work Journal, 9,* 155–168.

Zozus, R. T., & Zax, M. (1991). Perceptions of childhood: Exploring possible etiological factors in homelessness. *Hospital and Community Psychiatry, 42,* 535–537.

COMMENTARY BY: Paul A. Toro, Susan Wolfe, and Pamela McCaskill

In 1992, when we were designing our Homeless Adolescent Comparison (HAC) study (McCaskill, Toro, & Wolfe, 1998; Wolfe, Toro, & McCaskill, 1999), we were aware of no existing study that compared homeless adolescents to an appropriate comparison group of housed adolescents matched on demographic and geographic variables. There were a number of completed studies that compared homeless to general adolescent samples (e.g., Windle, 1989; Yates, MacKenzie, Pennbridge, & Cohen, 1988) and there were a few case control studies that compared homeless and matched housed adults (e.g., Shinn, Knickman, & Weitzman, 1991). Having just completed data collection on our own case control study involving homeless adults (Toro et al., 1995), we were eager to apply this methodology to homeless adolescents.

THE RESEARCH AND POLITICAL CONTEXT FOR OUR RESEARCH

The many needs of homeless adolescents have been well documented in our own HAC study papers (cited above), a few of our more recent papers reporting on a larger case control study involving homeless adolescents (e.g., Heinze, Toro, & Urberg, 2004), as well as various review papers produced by our Research Group on Homelessness and Poverty and others (e.g., Haber & Toro, 2004; Robertson, 1991; Robertson & Toro, 1999; Toro, Lombardo, & Yapchai, 2003). These reports suggest high rates of substance abuse, mental disorders and psychological distress, learning disabilities, delinquency, risky sexual behaviors, family violence, and other negative experiences and characteristics among homeless youth samples. Despite our awareness of these problems, there was very little research on homeless youth available back in 1992, certainly in relation to the larger literature on homeless adults (Robertson, 1991; Toro, 1998).

Despite the vacuum of good studies at the time, there was great interest in homelessness developing among the media, politicians, and social scientists (Buck & Toro, 2004), and large amounts of federal grant monies were rapidly becoming available. Many policymakers seemed to view homelessness as a national crisis in need of immediate assistance, including sound research to identify why this problem appeared to be growing at such an alarming pace. As young community psychologists with a genuine personal concern about marginalized people in our society, the availability of grant funds made it more tempting for us to consider this line of ostensibly risky research.

Commentary on article: Wolfe, S., Toro, P., McCaskill, P. (1999). A comparison of homeless and matched housed adolescents on family environment variables. *Journal of Research on Adolescence, 9*, 53–66.

The HAC study became a significant preliminary study (funded with "seed money" from Wayne State University), which we effectively used to help us obtain federal funds to conduct a much larger study with a similar case control design (see citations on previous page).

THE VALUE OF THE CASE CONTROL DESIGN
FOR UNDERSTANDING HOMELESSNESS

Whether one is interested in homeless adolescents, homeless adults, or homeless families (the three main subgroups of the homeless; see Toro, 1998), it is difficult to develop a firm research understanding of the causes of homelessness. As psychologists, we were very interested in developing such an understanding. However, it was clear to us that the experimental design could not be used for this purpose. The likely causes of homelessness are complex social phenomena to which it is practically and ethically impossible to randomly assign people. Thus we cannot assign persons to being chronic substance abusers versus not, or to severe poverty versus not, and then observe whether one group is more likely to become homeless over time. One good way to shed some light on the possible causes of homelessness is to conduct careful case control studies.

Commonly used by epidemiologists, the case control design takes one group of interest (e.g., persons with AIDS) and compares this group with another group that is similar on a number of obvious dimensions (e.g., age, race, gender, socioeconomic status) so as to understand what might be "causing" the groups to differ (e.g., being homosexual, injecting illicit drugs). Various advantages and disadvantages of the case control design will be discussed in a later section.

Sampling Issues: Homeless Youth

At the time when we were designing our HAC study in 1992, there were a few different choices for sampling homeless youth. One approach surveyed large groups of teens in the general population and identified youth from this pool who have a history of homelessness (e.g., Windle, 1989). This approach underrepresents youth who have longer histories of homelessness or institutional histories. A second approach drew from service settings such as medical clinics (e.g., Yates et al., 1988). Such studies describe youth seeking services, who may be very different from those who do not seek help. A third approach sampled from street locations where homeless youth were known to congregate (e.g., Robertson, Koegel, & Ferguson, 1989). This street-sampling method, especially if it includes youth who are 18 or older, generally yields a much more deviant profile of homeless youth. Furthermore, it was becoming clear to us that street youth represent a small portion of the broader homeless adolescent sample and in many, if not most, cities in America (including Detroit), such youth, at least ones under age 18, were very difficult to find. We opted for a fourth sampling strategy in our HAC study: collecting a probability sample of homeless youth (aged 12–17) from a wide range of shelters targeted to homeless youth (which, in Detroit, as in most other cities, were all quite separate from the larger number of shelters for homeless adults and families). In 1992, we were quite impressed with a few existing studies of homeless adults that had also used such probability sampling methods, including one study of our own that we had recently started (Koegel, Burnam, & Farr, 1988; Toro et al., 1999). In the HAC case, we sampled from six shelters based on the size of each one's annual caseload.

We felt it important to focus on youth under age 18 because society treats "youth" who are 18 or older much differently than those who are legally minors. Minors cannot easily obtain their own independent housing, and in most states, including Michigan, minors away from home without the permission of their guardian are considered to be "breaking the law." Furthermore, based on our review of the existing research literature on homeless youth, as well as our own and others' studies on homeless adults (including many "young adults" aged 18–25), we suspected that the needs and characteristics of homeless adolescent minors might be very different from those of "young adults" who are homeless.

Sampling Issues: Housed Comparison Youth

The approach to sampling an appropriate comparison group of nonhomeless persons used in our first case control study involving homeless adults (Toro et al., 1995) was to obtain very poor housed adults from soup kitchens and other food programs. This approach, unfortunately, would not work for obtaining homeless or poor housed adolescent minors. Although many homeless and poor adults (mainly men) and some homeless and poor families (generally young women with young children) can be found at such sites, few minors "on their own" can be found at food programs in Detroit, as in most other U.S. cities. We considered going door-to-door in poor neighborhoods (perhaps the same ones from which our homeless adolescents originally came), but soon realized that such time-consuming work would tax our modest resources. After discussing our hopes for a matched housed sample with some local advocates for homeless youth, we settled on a much more efficient strategy to obtain a matched housed group: we asked the homeless youth in our study to nominate same-age youth in their neighborhoods of origin. We encouraged the nomination of "acquaintances" rather than "close friends" for a number of reasons. In particular, if we got too many of the nominations who were close friends, we were worried that many of the nominations would have prior experiences with homelessness themselves, thus weakening the comparison we set out to make in the case control design (i.e., comparing homeless to similar housed youth).

Even with the focus on getting "acquaintances," we still ended up with some housed youth ($n = 21$, 17% of the total 118) who had been homeless sometime in the past. This problem of "contamination," not mentioned by Wolfe et al. (1999), is common in case control designs: one must take steps to assure that none of the "controls" are, in fact, "cases." In our study, we carefully assessed both the housed and the homeless to obtain their lifetime history of homelessness. Because the 17 percent rate of prior homelessness in the housed sample was at least somewhat higher than would be expected in normative samples of adolescents (rates have ranged from 9–15 percent; see Ringwalt, Greene, & Iachan, 1994; Windle, 1989), we also conducted a separate set of analyses excluding these previously homeless youth in the housed sample. Luckily, the findings from this set of analyses (comparing the homeless to the never-homeless housed) were very similar to what we found when comparing the total housed and homeless samples (see McCaskill et al., 1998). Thus, the inclusion of the "previously homeless" among the larger housed sample did not "wash out" or otherwise alter the housed–homeless differences we were expecting. So, in the Wolfe et al. (1999) paper, we decided to retain the small number of "previously homeless" in the housed sample.

Measurement Issues

Aside from some of our own early studies and a few other exceptions (e.g., Koegel et al., 1988; Morse, Calsyn, Allen, Tempelhoff, & Smith, 1992), it appeared to us that few studies on homeless people paid adequate attention to the psychometric properties of the measures used. Many existing studies at the time appeared to have been hastily put together, using a simple set of questions, then obtained a sample at one particular site in one particular part of a particular city, and then proceeded to draw conclusions about the problems and needs of homeless people on this basis. For example, among homeless adults, very high rates of mental disorders were often reported when, upon closer scrutiny, it was apparent that unreliable assessment tools had been used, that substance abuse had been lumped in with other types of mental illness, and/or that samples were not representative (Toro, 1998). In our HAC study, we attempted to identify measures with sound reliability and validity data. We also added measures that had yet to be used by most other researchers investigating homelessness (e.g., ones assessing social support/networks and family background), and made sure that all measures took into account the context of the lives of the homeless youth.

Ethical Issues

Interviewer Safety. We have always had to attend closely to the safety of our interviewers in all our research on the homeless. Safety was particularly worrisome in our early studies, in which we sampled homeless people on the streets, in parks, bus stations, and other public places—we even attempted some interviews in abandoned buildings (Toro et al., 1999). Safety has been less of a concern in our research on homeless adolescents, because few are found on the streets, and the shelters where we do most of the sampling are relatively safe environments (though the neighborhoods around them can sometimes be less than fully safe). However, in our longitudinal research (including our current study following homeless and matched housed adolescents), we have encountered some worrisome situations. Since most initially homeless people (especially adolescents) become housed over time, our longitudinal studies usually place interviewers in private homes. We have observed drug dealing, verbal abuse, drunkenness, "shady characters," and other troubling circumstances in such home visits. To protect the safety of our interviewers, we typically send them to homes in pairs, with cell phones to be used in case of emergency. We also train the interviewers carefully, so that they develop their "street smarts" and learn to avoid or leave potentially dangerous situations (even if this means that we are unable to collect important follow-up data). Although we have developed some written guidelines and other materials to assist in such interviewer training, we have found that the best training takes place "in the field," and by "sharing" among interviewers that takes place informally as well as in regular interviewer meetings.

Giving Money to Homeless People. It is quite clear that the homeless, including the HAC youth, have high rates of substance abuse. Many argue that researchers should not pay homeless people to encourage their participation in research because they might use the money to buy drugs or alcohol, or use the money in other irresponsible ways. Our stance on this issue is that we have no right to judge what participants do with their money. We simply have a working relationship in which we pay them for their time (similar to an employer–employee relationship). While giving participants food vouchers or some other form of compensation might seem desirable, it may also be seen by some potential participants as paternalistic, and might decrease participation in the research. Furthermore, vouchers can also be exchanged for money, producing the same sort of problem they were designed to avoid.

Dilemmas in Maintaining Confidentiality. While conducting interviews, sometimes in very public places, we have to attend to making sure that others do not overhear us. In our HAC study, we had to try to identify an interview spot out of earshot of shelter staff (for homeless youth) and parents and other family members (for housed youth). We occasionally were privy to criminal activity, and interviewed participants who were high on drugs or alcohol. Our stance is that we must maintain confidentiality at all times, unless the person is at imminent risk of harming self or others. Thus, we will not report criminal acts, unless someone is being or is likely to be physically harmed by them. The most frequent situation in which we have had to break confidentiality concerns child abuse. Over the course of interviewing thousands of homeless people over the past 20 years, including the homeless adolescents in the HAC study, there have been several occasions where we have reported suspected ongoing abuse against minors. These minors have sometimes been our research participants (e.g., HAC adolescents) and sometimes others in the home (e.g., young children or infants). There have also been a few occasions in which adults or adolescents have been actively suicidal and we have sought professional intervention. Typically, in cases of both child abuse and suicide risk, we attempt to discuss our intention to break confidentiality with the participant before doing so. We have yet to encounter a serious risk of imminent homicide or serious bodily harm, but this is another situation that could prompt us to break confidentiality.

SOME PRACTICAL ISSUES

Involving Students in Applied Community Research

Our HAC study, like most of our other research, involved various graduate and undergraduate students, as well as postdoctoral and other staff, in major roles. We believe that the best way to learn about such research is by doing it, rather than simply reading about it in books or hearing about it in courses. There are a number of advantages, and a few disadvantages, of involving students and other trainees in such research. Probably the greatest advantage is that a constant flow of "new blood" leads us to consider new types of research and new ways of interpreting the research we have already done. Another advantage of having students is the energy they bring to the research. There have been a number of periods over the past 20 years when our team had little or no funds to conduct research. We have often (especially in the earlier studies) had to rely on "volunteer" student assistants—with their energy, plus the added incentives of needing to do theses and/or gaining research experience—to get the research done. This was the case in the HAC study. The main disadvantage of relying on volunteer students is that the research often takes longer to complete than when grant funds can pay full-time staff to do the work. Both graduate and undergraduate students have many different demands on their time, and sometimes do not follow through to complete projects.

Getting Ahead in Academia versus Helping the Community

In pursuit of success in an academic setting, we have sometimes felt caught between our community-oriented values and the need to get ahead in a university environment. In part because developing close community contacts is essential for the type of research we do, and also because we enjoy interacting with "real" people in the community, we spend a fair amount of time with people outside the university. This takes us away from writing papers and grant proposals—the activities that are most likely to lead to rewards in academia.

Grants

Obtaining grant funds, especially large ones from federal sources, has become increasingly important at universities in recent years. Because there remain few (if any) sources of research funding specifically targeted to homelessness, some researchers who studied homelessness in the 1980s and 1990s have begun to study other topics that currently have better funding potential (e.g., HIV/AIDS, violence). It is disheartening to see the "faddish" nature of grant funding. It makes it difficult to pursue one program of research over many years. In order to obtain funding for the large expansion of the HAC study we are now engaged in, we had to target the research to substance abuse (since funding is coming from the National Institute of Alcohol Abuse and Alcoholism).

Helping Service Providers versus Homeless People

In the HAC study and in many of our other research projects, our community connections tend to be with agencies that provide services to the homeless, or policy makers who oversee and/or fund such services. Although we believe these to be productive involvements for both the community leaders and ourselves, a nagging concern remains that our efforts may be having little impact on truly reducing the prevalence of homelessness. Establishing strong services does not necessarily translate into a better life for the homeless people whom we ultimately aim to help. Furthermore, helping agencies to garner more resources to assist those who are already homeless does nothing to prevent the flow of people into homelessness in the future (see our discussion below on preventive interventions).

The Importance of Personal Relationships

In conducting the HAC study and our various other research projects, it has been critical that we cultivate personal relationships in the community. In order to actually do this, the researchers must have some real assistance to offer the leaders with whom they interact. We have found that offering to provide data to improve grant proposals, locating student volunteers, or providing staff training have been highly valued by the agencies with which we interact. Community–researcher relationships need to be a "two-way street" in which both parties benefit from the exchange. Decision makers will not often approach you or listen seriously to you if they don't have a trusting relationship at the outset. Many community leaders have experienced being "burned" by researchers who promised a great deal but delivered little. Once the data are collected, researchers often lose motivation to maintain community ties. It is important to be "persistent and stable." For instance, in Detroit, people come back to our team again and again because they know we are here for the long term and can be helpful to them, as we have been in the past. Such leaders get repeatedly rewarded for contacting us, and refer colleagues to us. In doing research that has real policy relevance, community researchers must recognize that some time will have to be spent in nurturing such community relationships. This is not just a "chore" that makes the research possible, but can be enjoyable and stimulating.

Designing Interventions for Homeless Youth

The knowledge we have gained from the HAC study and our subsequent research on homeless youth has led us to consider the design of effective interventions—to assist youth who have been homeless, as well as to prevent youth from becoming homeless in the first place.

Comprehensive and Family-Focused Treatment Programs

Robertson and Toro (1999) have advocated for a comprehensive array of services tailored to the specific needs of homeless adolescents. The need to tailor services follows from the heterogeneity of needs seen among homeless youth (and their families), as documented by our HAC studies and many others. Given that homelessness among adolescents nearly always occurs in a family context, we would also argue that interventions be provided in such a context. One general category of comprehensive interventions involves intensive case management. These interventions work closely with homeless clients, attempting to meet both their long- and short-term needs, including permanent housing, education, job training and placement, and linkages to services in mental health, substance abuse, and health care. Interventions that can provide only one or two narrow services (e.g., mental health, substance abuse, housing, or education) may have limited effectiveness with the multiproblem cases that tend to be common among homeless adolescents. In one such intensive intervention for street youth in Seattle, Cauce et al. (1994) found that, relative to youth in a regular case management program, youth assigned to the intensive case management program showed reduced externalizing behaviors and improved quality of life ratings over an initial three months.

Preventing Homelessness

Discussions of how to prevent homelessness are relatively new in the research literature (e.g., Lindblom, 1996; Shinn & Baumohl, 1999; Toro et al., 2003). Our HAC study and others suggest that one approach that might have potential for accomplishing prevention is to identify groups known to be "at risk" for later homelessness. Such groups would include children and youth with histories of residential instability, foster care, and other out-of-home placements (all experiences that were common in our HAC homeless sample). Adolescents who are "aging out" of the foster-care system appear to be particularly vulnerable to homelessness (Courtney, Piliavin, Grogan-Taylor, & Nesmith, 2001). Teenage mothers with children are another at-risk group (Greene & Ringwalt, 1998; we have also included teenage mothers in our studies on homeless youth). These mothers tend to drop out of school, thus increasing their chance of becoming unemployed and dependent on social welfare services for economic survival. Case control designs could be useful here; for example, using a similar approach to that used in the HAC study, teen mothers could be matched with similar teens who have not given birth. Both groups could be compared and even tracked over time to identify the risks associated with being a teen mother. Experimental designs could also be useful; for example, youth "aging out" of foster care could be randomly assigned to receiving an intensive program designed to prevent their homelessness (and perhaps other poor outcomes) or to a control group. If after being followed over time, the program does, indeed, prevent homelessness, then we have documented a "probable cause" of homelessness in this group (i.e., being left to "fend for themselves" without the supports the program offers).

ADVANTAGES AND DISADVANTAGES
OF THE CASE CONTROL DESIGN

One advantage of the case control design is that it tends to enhance external validity by typically studying "real people" in the "real world" (as opposed to the "sterile" laboratory). Because of its real-world focus, the case control design can also help uncover relationships between variables of interest that we might not have thought of in advance. For example, in our HAC study, we expected that parent violence against the homeless adolescents would be common; we did not necessarily expect that the levels of violence seen in the homeless adolescents against their parents would be high as well. These findings suggested that a "process" of negative parent–adolescent interaction might exist, and that family-oriented (rather than individual) interventions might be warranted. Another advantage of the case control design is its efficiency. Experiments, at least those in applied contexts, can be much more costly to implement.

Though the case control design can help us "rule out" some factors that might be potential "causes" of homelessness, it is still, in the end, a correlational design that does not allow firm causal inferences. In the case of the HAC study, we can conclude that the differences observed between the homeless and housed youth on various family environment variables are not due to gender, race, age, or obvious socioeconomic factors (see Wolfe et al., 1999; pp. 56–57). However, many other factors might operate to "confound" the relationship seen between housing status and family environment, and we do not know for sure whether the poor family environments produced the homelessness, or vice versa. Longitudinal studies, such as the one now being done in follow-up to the HAC study, could help untangle the temporal ordering of effects.

A related disadvantage of the case control design is that it sometimes only "hints" at the true "cause" one is seeking. In the case of AIDS, for example, identifying that a very high percentage of those with AIDS are homosexual men does not tell us exactly *why* these men are at risk. However, once epidemiologists identify that homosexuals are at risk, they can then "hone in" on one of the causes (in this case, the HIV virus that is transmitted by the exchange of various bodily fluids, such as occurs in anal sex that is common among homosexual men).

Although not a limitation of the case control design per se, our HAC study, as noted by Wolfe et al. (1999), also suffered from the total reliance on one source of information (i.e., the youth themselves). Other sources that could supplement youth self-report are parent report, record data (e.g., from school or the juvenile justice system), and direct behavioral observation (e.g., of parent–youth interactions). Recent findings from the large expansion of the HAC study have found reasonable agreement between different data sources on even quite sensitive topics (e.g., correlations between youth and parent reports on substance use/abuse ranged from .47 to .51).

CONCLUSION

Despite its limitations, the case control design, as applied in the HAC study, has both scientific and practical implications. It helps highlight some factors that are closely associated with youth homelessness and may be causes of it. It calls attention to the serious needs of this group and can give service providers ideas about how best to assist homeless youth.

REFERENCES

Buck, P. O., & Toro, P. A. (2004). Images of homelessness in the media. In S. Barrow et al. (Eds.), *Encyclopedia of homelessness* (pp. 301–308). Great Barrington, MA: Berkshire Publishing/Sage.

Cauce, A. M., Morgan, C. J., Wagner, V., Moore, E., Sy, J., Wurzbacher, K., Weeden, K., Tomlin, S., & Blanchard, T. (1994). Effectiveness of intensive case management for homeless adolescents: Results of a 3-month follow-up. *Journal of Emotional and Behavioral Disorders, 2,* 219–227.

Courtney, M. E., Piliavin, I., Grogan-Kaylor, A., & Nesmith, A. (2001). Foster youth transitions to adulthood: A longitudinal view of youth leaving care. *Child Welfare, 80,* 685–717.

Greene, J. M., & Ringwalt, C. L. (1998). Pregnancy among three national samples of runaway and homeless youth. *Journal of Adolescent Health, 23,* 370–377.

Haber, M., & Toro, P. A. (2004). Homelessness among families, children and adolescents: An ecological–developmental perspective. *Child and Family Psychology Review, 7,* 123–164.

Heinze, H., Toro, P. A., & Urberg, K. A. (2004). Delinquent behaviors and affiliation with male and female peers. *Journal of Clinical Child and Adolescent Psychology, 33,* 336–346.

Koegel, P., Burnam, A., & Farr, R. K. (1988). The prevalence of specific psychiatric disorders among homeless individuals in the inner city of Los Angeles. *Archives of General Psychiatry, 45,* 1085–1092.

Lindbloom, E. N. (2003). Preventing homelessness. In J. Baumohl (Ed.), *Homelessness in America* (pp. 187–200). Phoenix: Oryx Press.

McCaskill, P. A., Toro, P. A., & Wolfe, S. M. (1998). Homeless and matched housed adolescents: A comparative study of psychopathology. *Journal of Clinical Child Psychology, 27,* 306–319.

Morse, G., Calsyn, R. J., Allen, G., Tempelhoff, B., & Smith, R. (1992). Experimental comparison of the effects of three treatment programs for homeless mentally ill people. *Hospital and Community Psychiatry, 43,* 1005–1010.

Ringwalt, C. L., Greene, J. M., & Iachan, R. (1994, November). Prevalence and characteristics of youth in households with runaway and homeless experience. Presentation at the Annual Meeting of the American Public Health Association, Washington, DC.

Robertson, M. J. (1991). Homeless youth: An overview of recent literature. In J. H. Kryder-Coe, L. M. Salamon, & J. M. Molnar (Eds.), *Homeless children and youth: A new American dilemma* (pp. 33–68). London: Transaction Publishers.

Robertson, M. J., Koegel, P., & Ferguson, L. (1989). Alcohol use and abuse among homeless adolescents in Hollywood. *Contemporary Drug Problems,* Fall, 415–452.

Robertson, M. J., & Toro, P. A. (1999). Homeless youth: Research, intervention, and policy. In L. Fosburg, & D. Dennis (Eds.), *Practical lessons: The 1998 National Symposium on Homelessness Research.* Washington, DC: U.S. Department of Housing and Urban Development.

Shinn, M., & Baumohl, J. (1999). Rethinking the prevention of homelessness. In L. Fosburg, & D. Dennis (Eds.), *Practical lessons: The 1998 National Symposium on Homelessness Research.* Washington, DC: U.S. Department of Housing and Urban Development.

Shinn, M., Knickman, J., & Weitzman, B. C. (1991). Social relationships and vulnerability to becoming homeless among poor families. *American Psychologist, 46,* 1180–1187.

Toro, P. A. (1998). Homelessness. In A. Bellack, & M. Hersen (Eds.), *Comprehensive clinical psychology,* Ch. 8, in Vol. 9, Applications in diverse populations, pp. 119–135, New York: Pergamon.

Toro, P. A., Bellavia, C., Daeschler, C., Owens, B., Wall, D. D., Passero, J. M., & Thomas, D. M. (1995). Distinguishing homelessness from poverty: A comparative study. *Journal of Consulting and Clinical Psychology, 63,* 280–289.

Toro, P. A., Lombardo, S., & Yapchai, C. J. (2003). Homelessness, childhood. In T. P. Gullotta, & M. Bloom (Eds.), *Encyclopedia of primary prevention and health promotion,* (pp. 561–570). New York: Kluwer.

Toro, P. A., Rabideau, J. M. P., Bellavia, C. W., Daeschler, C. V., Wall, D. D., Thomas, D. M., & Smith, S. J. (1997). Evaluating an intervention for homeless persons: Results of a field experiment. *Journal of Consulting and Clinical Psychology, 65,* 476–484.

Toro, P. A., Wolfe, S. M., Bellavia, C. W., Thomas, D. M., Rowland, L. L., Daeschler, C. V., & McCaskill, P. A. (1999). Obtaining representative samples of homeless persons: A two-city study. *Journal of Community Psychology, 27,* 157–178.

Windle, M. (1989). Substance use and abuse among adolescent runaways: A four-year follow-up study. *Journal of Youth and Adolescence, 18,* 331–344.

Wolfe, S. M., Toro, P. A., & McCaskill, P. A. (1999). A comparison of homeless and matched housed adolescents on family environment variables. *Journal of Research on Adolescence, 9,* 53–66.

Yates, G. L., MacKenzie, R., Pennbridge, J., & Cohen, E. (1988). A risk profile comparison of runaway and non-runaway youth. *American Journal of Public Health, 78,* 820–821.

SECTION III

Qualitative Methods

Within the last decade or so, the standard armamentarium of research methods, essential for researchers in the human services, has expanded to include qualitative data gathering and analysis. Although none of these methods are new, their necessity and legitimacy in human services research has increased. Some of the authors in this section reported having difficulty getting funding for their research through traditional funding sources; some noted difficulty in publishing their results. There are increasingly more refereed journals that both welcome and encourage qualitative submissions. Some of these journals are specifically devoted to qualitative methods; others accept research that includes both quantitative and qualitative approaches.

We include three different qualitative approaches in this section—intensive interviews, focus groups, and ethnography. For all, the importance of "giving voice" to respondents, using their own words to describe and interpret their social worlds and experiences, is key. The methods also lend themselves to research participants whose social worlds are less known to most researchers, including the dually diagnosed, lesbians, and displaced workers. These are all populations who benefit from social work and human service interventions.

All of the selections indicate that qualitative approaches are every bit as systematic as quantitative approaches, with careful articulation of all decision points reached, including any changes in focus during the course of data collection, and the rationales for such decisions. These accounts in the write-up of study findings are essential to communicate clearly the systematic process involved in qualitative research studies, and to assure that the important decisions made during data collection and analysis are transparent.

Some of the commentaries discuss the use of audio taping and verbatim transcriptions of the tapes as the major source of raw data for the analysis. Although one usually thinks of sampling in qualitative approaches as nonrandom, without the use of explicit sampling frames, probability sampling is sometimes used within a primarily qualitative interview study format. Although software programs for qualitative data analysis have been available for some time, authors of research studies in this section either did not use them, or stopped using them early in the analysis process. The hard work of organizing the often massive amount of text, and conceptualizing themes, remains the job of the investigator. How useful the available qualitative software programs may be in the effort to organize, manipulate, and link themes is a personal choice.

Some institutional review boards (IRBs) are still unaccustomed to reviewing qualitative studies, and have difficulty understanding these approaches—particularly ethnography. IRBs are accustomed to the tradition of written informed consent. However, there are ways to document informed consent that are equally ethical (i.e., having participants verbally acknowledge agreement on audio recordings).

Qualitative approaches contribute to evidence-based practices by providing more nuanced understanding of the lives of individuals who may be hidden from public view. These approaches can offer a window into both the facilitating and impeding environmental factors that form the critical context in which human service interventions are located. These approaches can also offer understanding about why established evidence-based practices may not work in a given environment.

12

Lesbian Identity Development: An Examination of Differences across Generations*

Cheryl A. Parks, Ph.D.

A s is the case with any identity formation, that of lesbians is a developmental process (Garnets & Kimmel, 1993). Early theoretical models described a linear and orderly progression from feelings of marginality to acceptance of identity (Cass, 1979, 1984; Troiden, 1989), while more recent theories suggest a wide variability in the timing, sequence, and outcome of developmental events (Kahn, 1991; Radonsky & Borders, 1995; Rust, 1993). Individual lesbians report a range of family, social, and historical circumstances that affect the timing and character of their coming-out experience.[†] Understanding and appreciation of that experience requires an awareness of the social and historical context in which it occurs.

This paper presents selected findings of a qualitative, life-history interview study of 31 Caucasian, nonurban, self-identified lesbian social drinkers, conducted between September 1995 and October 1996. The study examined both sexual identity development and alcohol use over the life course (Parks, in press). The focus here are those findings related to the identity development processes described by the three generations of lesbians represented (45 and over, 30–44, and under 30 years old).

*Based on a poster session presented at the 1998 Annual Meeting of the American Orthopsychiatric Association, Arlington, VA, while the author was on faculty at Florida State University School of Social Work, Tallahassee.

[†]"Coming out" refers to the notion that lesbians and gay men self-identify as homosexual, and subsequently disclose to others their sexual preference. Although some have defined it as an event associated with one's first same-sex encounter (Vance & Green, 1984) or as one or more episodes of social disclosure (Franke & Leary, 1991), the present study, in keeping with the bulk of the literature (Gonsiorek & Rudolph, 1991), defines coming out as the overall developmental process of coming to terms with one's homosexuality, extending from first awareness to identity acceptance.

From Parks, C. (1999) Lesbian Identity development: An examination of differences across generations. *American Journal of Orthopsychiatry, 69*, 347–361. Reprinted with permission.

METHODOLOGY

This study employed a modification of the in-depth, phenomenologically based interview process outlined by Seidman (1991). Following a semistructured interview format focused on life history, current experience, and present understanding, the context, details, and meanings of respondents' coming-out and alcohol-use experiences were explored. This approach encouraged examination of the social, historical, and cultural contexts surrounding the lived experience of study participants. Respondents were able to convey their own understandings of the meanings and significance they have assigned to the events and circumstances of their lives.

Setting and Sample

Through a combination of convenience and snowball sampling (Biernacki & Waldorf, 1981), 31 self-identified lesbians living in rural and small urban areas of southeastern Pennsylvania were recruited to participate in intensive, life-history interviews. To identify an initial pool of potential participants, the researcher distributed questionnaires to all females in attendance at an annual picnic sponsored by a local homophile organization. Eleven respondents met all criteria for selection. These participants and personal contacts of the researcher referred subsequent volunteers. The researcher was not acquainted with any of the study participants.

Participants were required to be self-identified lesbians, age 21 and older, who were moderate to heavy users of alcohol. These criteria reflected the study's focus on alcohol use and identity development (additional details regarding alcohol and drug use selection criteria are available elsewhere [Parks, in press]). The study further limited participants to non-Hispanic Caucasians who had no visible stigmatizing conditions (e.g., physical disability), since race and disability may exert independent and confounding effects on both alcohol use and lesbian identification. Adequate representation and examination of these effects were not possible within the present study design.

All respondents lived a significant distance from the nearest large urban center. Many identified that urban area as a potential resource for social and recreational activities, though most ventured only occasionally into "the City," which contained a large network of gay/lesbian-identified bars, businesses, and other resources. The areas in which respondents lived provided only a limited number of gay-identified resources.

The 31 study participants ranged in age from 23 to 79 years. Most had been born or lived the majority of their childhood and adult years in the study locale. A majority held college ($N = 10$) and graduate ($N = 7$) degrees, and only two had not completed high school. All but five were employed full-time in fields ranging from manufacturing and industry to social services and medicine. Incomes ranged from a low of $9,000 to a high of $85,000 annually, with the greatest variability being among those older than 45. A majority ($N = 18$) owned their own homes, many ($N = 14$) lived alone, and a majority ($N = 17$) defined their present relationship status by some level of exclusive involvement with another woman. Six had been previously married, five had had children, and four were living with their own or their partners' child(ren).

Data Collection and Analysis

A 2½–3-hour semistructured interview was conducted with each respondent, usually in the respondent's home. Prior to the interview, the researcher reviewed the purpose of the study and provided each respondent with an informed-consent agreement for signature. All interviews were audio-taped and the researcher recorded, in writing, responses to face-sheet questions administered at the beginning of each session. Examples of interview questions included: "Take me back to when you first thought you might be lesbian. What was going on in your life at the time? What happened?" and "What is it like for you today as a lesbian?" Additional probes were used to elicit details and clarify the chronology of events described. The researcher took minimal notes during the interview; impressions and observations were recorded after each session.

Each interview produced five separate sources of data: the questionnaire; the interview face sheet; the interview tapes; a typed verbatim transcript of each interview; and the researcher's notes recorded after each session. In addition, following transcription, the researcher produced a two-page biographical sketch of each respondent and a time-line denoting ages when individual respondents first engaged in specific forms of dating and sexual behavior. Finally, data obtained from the questionnaires, face sheets, and researcher's notes were coded into three data matrices to provide a visual summary of descriptive characteristics representing the entire respondent group. Each data source was coded for identification. Codes and signed consent forms were maintained in separate locations, and names were edited out of transcripts to protect the confidentiality of respondents. Each woman was assigned a pseudonym for reference.

Tape transcription and analysis of verbatim transcripts began in October 1995. Analysis continued throughout and following the data-gathering process. This integration of data collection and analysis provided an opportunity to identify emergent categories within completed interviews and to explore these categories with future respondents.

Using a generalized, issue-focused analysis (Weiss, 1994), the researcher read each transcript individually and coded excerpts according to the concept or category addressed. Similarly coded passages were sorted into excerpt files, then coded into more narrow topic areas. This process of coding and sorting allowed identification of emergent categories for further analysis. Patterns and connections among excerpts within categories began to define major trends, and their variants, that linked the experiences of individual participants. This local integration preceded and continued throughout inclusive integration, the final process by which themes and connections among categories were derived. The analysis concluded with the production of a conceptual model describing the correspondence between lesbian identity development and alcohol use. The present paper discusses only the identity development component of that model.

FINDINGS

Respondents were born between 1917 and 1972; they reached the age of 18 between 1935 and 1990. Over this span of 55 years, huge changes occurred in public awareness and popular attitudes about homosexuality (Miller, 1995; Spencer, 1995). Analysis revealed similarities within and differences between respondents' life stories that reflected these historical changes. These similarities and differences identified respondents within one of three distinct generations or eras in gay and lesbian history: those 45 and older (the pre-Stonewall era); those 30–44 (the gay liberation era); and those under age 30 (the gay rights era).

Across generations, respondents described thoughts, feelings, and actions that defined, for them, a recognition and acceptance of lesbian identity. An internal progression from self-awareness to self-definition was inextricably linked to each individual's social awareness of, and access to, other lesbians and lesbian-defined events. Phases in the identity development process, as revealed in respondents' life stories, reflected this interaction. Respondents reported a general progression from awareness (internal recognition of feelings), through exploration (beginning and undefined sexual and social contact) and immersion (high exposure and involvement in lesbian-defined events, limited selectivity), into synthesis (defined identity and more selectivity in contact with

Table 12.1. Mean Ages of Lesbian Identity Developmental Events by Group

Event	Pre-Stonewall (ages 45–79, N = 11)		Liberation (ages 33–42, N = 12)		Gay Rights (ages 23–29, N = 8)		Total (ages 23–79, N = 31)	
	Age	(Range)	Age	(Range)	Age	(Range)	Age	(Range)
Self-awareness	18.8	(9–37)	17.0	(12–24)	14.6	(10–18)	17.0	(9–37)
First social contact	23.9	(18–38)	21.7	(15–33)	19.3	(12–24)	21.9	(12–38)
First sexual involvement	22.8	(18–43)	21.1	(15–33)	20.5	(18–26)	21.5	(15–43)
First disclosure	24.9	(17–41)	22.6	(15–33)	21.0	(18–23)	23.0	(15–41)
First self-labeling	31.9	(20–50)	25.5	(16–33)	20.3	(12–27)	26.4	(12–50)

lesbian groups and activities). Examination of the timing and sequence of events associated with each phase revealed several differences across generations (see Table 12.1).

Pre-Stonewall Era

Eleven women, ages 45–79 at the time of this study, reached adulthood (age 18) before the Stonewall Riots of 1969.[*] This was an era characterized by historians as oppressive and punitive for homosexuals (Miller, 1995; Spencer, 1995). Small gay and lesbian enclaves had begun to emerge (Faderman, 1991), and public debate about the morality and threat of homosexuality reached unprecedented heights. It was a time marked by suspicion of female same-sex friendships, by psychiatric labeling of lesbians as "sick," and by political wrangling over their fitness for military service.

The events and themes characterizing this era were most prominent in coastal, urban, and political centers of the United States. Study respondents grew up in small towns and rural locales far removed from these "big city" concerns. Their geography served as a sort of shelter, a "closet" that muffled the noise of public consternation as effectively as it muted information. As a result, most of these women experienced this era not as overtly oppressive and punitive, but as silent. It was a time of "not knowing" and of being "closeted" from opportunities or options to find out.

Self-Awareness and Early Life Experiences. Respondents described their early childhood and adolescent experiences as they first became aware of feelings of same-sex attraction. The two oldest respondents talked about that awareness, which occurred for them in the 1930s, as an experience marked by the pervasive silence of the era:

> SKI (79): At 14, I decided I would never get married. I decided that being a housewife, getting married, you know, looking after a man, taking care of him, no this was not for me. I just…no…I mean what I liked to look at were the young women walking down the street. [Interviewer: Did you know that at 14?] Yes, oh yes, I knew that but I had never heard of anything like this so I didn't know what it was. It just…it's kind of weird when you think about it in today's world where everything…well, at the age of almost 12 I didn't realize my mother was pregnant until very shortly before she had the baby. That's how closed everything was in that era.

[*]On June 17, 1969, patrons of the Stonewall Inn, a gay bar in Greenwich Village, resisted arrest and battled with police for three nights, marking the start of the gay liberation movement (Spencer, 1995).

The younger members of this cohort, those in their mid-forties to early sixties, spent all or part of their adolescence or early adulthood in the tumultuous climate of the 1960s. They, too, encountered silence, but a silence sometimes breached by the cautionary admonishments from different adults in their lives. Many of these women denied any realization of same-sex feelings during adolescence, while others recalled feeling "different" even earlier:

MEL (61): Although there were people that I was attached to...I didn't interpret that in any way at all. I mean it wasn't part of our world to talk about lesbianism or even homosexuality. It wasn't recognized as something you decided that I knew about.

MAY (49): I just felt that...I feel different, you know. I mean, I certainly didn't talk about those things at nine or ten but it was going on in my head. I just knew I had feelings.

Within this group, fewer than half of the women recognized or acknowledged a same-sex attraction or feeling of being different before the age of 18. Those who did experienced both guilt and a sometimes painful sense of aloneness. The majority first identified these feelings between the ages of 19 and 21 (1963–1971). For them, awareness arrived simultaneously with either a first contact with another lesbian or with the initiation of same-sex sexual involvement. These contacts, made during college or through work, helped a few to clarify earlier feelings and experiences; for others, they were a new, provocative, and not altogether welcome stimulus:

RAY (49): I was working with a female, a friend of mine. A guy that worked with us evidently thought that I...and she was going through a rough time and she was straight and...well, I was straight too, as far as I knew, and he got us together and we started running around....I knew then...that's why probably when I dated in high school there was never any real feelings. [Like] the minute that happened, I knew. Then I tried to kid myself afterwards cuz it wasn't the norm.

SIS (45): I think I was just not ready to call it anything and to really sit myself down and decide. It's like, well, put it off and you won't have to worry about it.

Family and peers also played a role as these women embarked on their individual journeys of sexual discovery. Members of their families were as unaware or reluctant to speak of homosexuality as were the women themselves. Few heard any references, from family members, to the possibility of same-sex attractions throughout adolescence and early adulthood. Silence about homosexuality was also pervasive among peers and at school. Most within this group heard nothing; those who did recalled jesting remarks or vague rumors that carried a generally negative tone. A few recalled that certain colors, worn on certain days, identified a person as "queer." It was a designation that had little meaning in their lives at the time:

SIS: I guess that it was not the normal thing. That...what I went through...there was a woman, a teacher in high school that...that people made mention of that and that was weird. It was kinda that thing, like I think that person is...not bad but...but different and that wasn't a good different kind of thing.

MAY: Then it was like...queer cuz Thursday was queer day, you know. I think [it] was universal with all schools but I didn't even really know what that meant.

Dating boys is a common experience for teenage girls, and this was true for a majority of these women as well. While most dated boys in high school and college, only three became sexually involved with a male partner before having sexual contact with a woman. None identified heterosexual dating as an overt attempt to deny or conceal feelings of same-sex attraction; they did so to fit in, to meet perceived expectations of others, or because it was possible:

> DEE (79): The only reason I went out with him was because my two best girl friends were having dates all the time. I...think I did it more because it was the thing to do and because the opportunity presented itself.

Exploration: Making Contact and Early Sexual Involvement. Self-awareness did not predict the age or circumstances in which these women first made contact or became involved with others like themselves. Only one made a deliberate effort, upon graduation from high school, to find other women with whom she could share her romantic and sexual interest. For the others, contact was initiated either by someone else expressing interest or as an evolution within an existing same-sex friendship:

> MEL: During the first year that she worked there she made a pass at me and, uh, I had no idea that she was thinking on these lines but, um, I responded and we started seeing a lot of each other after work and within several months she moved in with me in my apartment.

> RO (50): Then I worked at [a factory] and I met this girl and we just hit it off. We got along good and...you know, I mean, we just started...seeing each other and things, you know, led on. And that's how I got into it.

Only four women had any social contact with other lesbians before they became intimately involved with another woman. These social groups provided a medium through which they were able to meet and develop a friendship before engaging with their first same-sex partner. Of the remainder, most experienced their first romantic or sexual involvement in isolation from and prior to any social contact with others. Six women saw this first sexual involvement as an isolated event, one that provided no conclusive definition of their sexual preference:

> MEL: We had this very close relationship, we had this relationship and, uh, it lasted for almost two years, I think, and...although I was involved with her, I didn't know at this point that, that I really couldn't choose how my life was going to be.

The majority of these 11 women experienced a first sexual involvement with another woman by the age of 22; only three delayed that experience until their mid-twenties or later. Most also became socially involved with lesbians other than a partner by the age of 25. For a few, social involvement preceded sexual contact; for others, it occurred within a few weeks. For most, this first sexual experience preceded social involvement by two to ten years.

Immersion into Synthesis: Identity Acceptance and Disclosure. These women had few known resources through which to make contact with other lesbians. Within their small communities, there were no bars or other locales in which to meet; they relied on happenstance or trips to "the City" to find one another. Thus, four of them did not move through an immersion phase, as earlier defined, in their acceptance of lesbian identity. They progressed from exploration into synthesis following a more introspective, oft-times lonely, path.

Three pathways* to identity acceptance and disclosure were apparent in the coming-out stories of this group of 11 women. The first, followed in its entirety only by Ski, reflects the lesbian

---

*This term was selected to suggest the life journey depicted, retrospectively, in the accounts provided by respondents. It is not meant to imply that they held a vision of their destinations as they began to respond to the awareness of their same-sex attractions. Rather, all had made a variety of choices and decisions at different points and, in looking back, they and the researcher were able to trace the "pathway" their lives had followed.

version of every (heterosexual) girl's romantic dream: girl meets girl, they fall in love, pursue careers, and live together happily ever after:

Ski met her first and only partner at age 16. The two women identified and acknowledged their attraction to one another a year later. Following college, they established a household, pursued careers, and remained together until her partner's death 52 years later (in 1986). Throughout this period, Ski struggled with her sexual identity only twice—at age 19, due to religious conflicts and awareness of the risks attached to public exposure, and again at 50, due to the religious question. Neither she nor her partner ever disclosed their relationship to anyone and it was never challenged. As a couple, they became involved in a small network of other female couples with whom they routinely socialized. Nobody in this network spoke of lesbians or homosexuality. Ski identified herself as lesbian at age 50, became involved in a network of younger lesbian friends at 69 (after her partner's death), and publicly disclosed her identity for the first time at the age of 77.

A second path, characterized as "try (and retreat), try (and retreat), try again," represented a more isolated and lonely experience. Followed by just three respondents, that route included a relatively brief (up to 2–3 years) first involvement, a retreat of a year or more into hetero- or asexuality, a second relationship "try," another retreat, and try again. The first retreat served to define the meaning and "fit" of the first same-sex involvement; it ended with a recognition, and at least beginning acceptance, of a preference for the company of women. It was a retreat characterized by a high degree of introspection, silence about identity concerns, and isolation from other similarly inclined individuals. The second involvement was again brief and usually unfulfilling, though it served two purposes: clarification of remaining questions about lesbian identity, and development of a social connection with at least one other lesbian. These women, like Ski, did not immerse themselves in lesbian-defined networks and activities; they often were unaware that any even existed. Rather, they progressed almost seamlessly from an exploration of their attraction into quiet acknowledgment and acceptance of that preference.

The transition was not so smooth for the remainder of this cohort. "Live fast, play hard, and think about tomorrow later" characterized the mood, attitude, and behavior of the seven respondents on this third pathway. It was identified by the presence of a large, female friendship group that gave primacy to social and recreational pursuits. Initially, most members did not define themselves as lesbian, though sexual involvement between and among members was presumed. Members might have dated or engaged in very brief sexual encounters with men as well. Romantic and sexual liaisons occurred frequently, for brief periods, and in rapid succession. Priority was given to action, having fun, and finding pleasure; the nature and meaning of all this activity was not discussed, and seldom even considered.

This was a pathway that "caught" respondents; as they became entangled in the action and the relationships, a silence enfolded them. They did not talk within the group, and outside of it they could not. With age, they began to slow down, to consider what they were doing and what they had done. Most surfaced from this immersion recognizing that they had "become lesbian," and that it was an identity they could accept. Most have now entered into longer-term relationships and participate, with their partners, in a more selective network of lesbian friends.

Self-identification and disclosure of a lesbian identity are two developmental events often associated with "healthy" self-acceptance (Levine, 1997; Radonsky & Borders, 1995). Nearly all in this cohort had disclosed feelings of attraction or "being different" prior to acknowledging a self-identification as lesbian. On average, they did not label themselves as gay or lesbian until they were in their thirties (range: 20–50). Prior to that, and usually within 2–10 years of awareness, they talked about these feelings and their meaning with a close female friend or partner. All identified these early disclosures as necessary precursors to lesbian identification. Though all eventually disclosed to other gay and lesbian individuals, few revealed themselves to straight friends, at work, to family members, or to clergy. All remained quiet with health care providers, employers, and neighbors. In sum, most maintained the silence with which they were so familiar from their youth. All defined this silence as a reflection of the times; only one also regarded her silence as indicative of her struggle with self-acceptance.

Silence surrounds the lives of these women. They grew up in an era when sexuality was not discussed; there were no cues, models, or information about what feeling "different" might mean. Respondents had to find their own ways to explore and to name the unfamiliar feelings and impulses they experienced. They did so in isolation, either alone or with groups of others who were as silent and naïve as they were. All spoke, in their interviews, about the hardships imposed by this silence and isolation. All expressed an acute awareness that that legacy remains alive and present in their lives today:

> DEE: I have never been ashamed of the fact that I'm a lesbian. I don't go, and I would never go out and broadcast it or flaunt it because I'm from the era when you didn't do that. I had to hide it for so long, for so many years when I worked, that now it's second nature.

Liberation Era

Arriving on the American scene in 1969, gay liberation was a relative latecomer to that period of the '60s usually associated with black civil rights, women's liberation, and anti-War protests, as well as with hippies, drugs, and free love. Gay liberation did not gain the visibility and public recognition garnered by these earlier movements and '60s phenomena. It did, however, benefit from the experience and momentum of activists involved on these other fronts (Adam, 1987) as well as from the relaxation of attitudes (particularly sexual) that these earlier movements generated. From 1969 until the mid to late 1970s, gays and lesbians became more visible as they began to speak up; in some quarters, they began to be heard, and they now envisioned a new freedom—freedom to be gay without fear, to feel proud, to no longer have to hide.

It was a short-lived dream. A strong conservatism swept the country in the late '70s and early '80s. Homosexuality rocketed to the top of the Moral Majority hit list. The gay liberation movement had splintered and was unable to marshal the unity needed to fight this onslaught. Gays and lesbians across the country found themselves once again looking for cover (Miller, 1995).

Twelve of the present study respondents were children and teenagers (ages 7–15) in the year this era began; by its end in the early 1980s, all had become adults. Like their older counterparts, most grew up in the small towns and suburbs where they live today. In this era, geographic location provided a less fortified shelter than it had for the older respondents. Media coverage of "liberation" events penetrated the lives and consciousness of residents in even the smallest of America's towns and suburbs. Information (most of it negative) was now accessible; resources for contact and support were not, except to those in large urban centers. The small town "shelter" continued to serve as a closet, but it now had a glass door; options remained limited even as a "look outside" became possible. Just as insiders could see out, others were able to look inside. Consequently, the women of this era experienced a new freedom that was accompanied by a frightening sense of vulnerability.

Self-Awareness and Early Life Experiences. Awareness came early for respondents of this era, almost two years earlier, on average, than it had for their older counterparts (see Table 12.1).

Seven experienced either feelings of being different or a same-sex attraction before the age of 18; five of them defined these feelings as "homosexual":

> SIA (41): When I first had inklings that I was gay, I guess I was about 13 or 14 but...and then the first woman...or girl that I ever was with...we just like kissed and stuff like that. I was like 15.

Five women described themselves as naïve, "clueless," or unaffected as adolescents because they did not associate what they had heard about homosexuality with their own experience. They became aware of same-sex sexual feelings during college or shortly thereafter. In every instance, it was the personal disclosure of a friend that prompted self-awareness:

> SNO (38): Yeah, I was real naïve...very naïve. I mean I went through a couple years of college and hung around everybody. Everybody thought I was gay and I didn't even probably know what the word meant. And...so it wasn't really until I got involved and experienced it that I really thought about it.

> KIP (36): I think because she was drunk and apparently she had been attracted to me, which I didn't even pick up on, but then she just sort of blurted that out. "What would you say if I told you I was gay?" And, initially, I was angry because I thought we were closer than that.

As a group, these women were exposed to more, and earlier, information and discussion about gay and lesbian issues than their predecessors. They were also more mobile, traveling with sports teams, working summers in distant locales, attending colleges farther from home. These conditions may provide a partial explanation for their earlier self-awareness, but, as the quotes above suggest, they did not guarantee it.

Experiences with family, peers, and school reveal other notable differences between this and the older group that may have influenced awareness or denial. Most of these women's families displayed a reluctance to talk about sexuality during the respondents' adolescence and young adulthood. However, the respondents believed that silence reflected discomfort and avoidance, not lack of awareness. Several heard overt comments about homosexuality, invariably negative, from parents or other family members. In most cases, it was the family learning about an extended family member "suspected" of being gay that prompted such comments:

> ACE (33): My mother told me it wasn't normal. Everybody in my family told me it wasn't normal.

Heightened public awareness of homosexuality in this era was most evident in respondents' descriptions of the remarks they heard from peers, some as early as grade school. "Queer" days and vague rumors virtually disappeared as the majority of these women recalled overtly hostile and derogatory remarks made about "those kind of people." Whether they knew what they were saying or not, other kids made it clear that homosexuality was not acceptable. Respondents sometimes joined in this chorus, either because they did not yet see themselves as "one of them" or because they did:

> CAT (33): I remember hearing things but a lot of it was derogatory...you know, queers and fags....When I was in second grade some kid called me a faggot and I remember I cried. I had no idea what it meant, I just knew it wasn't, like, a nice name.

> CAS (36): My friends and I always made fun of gay people growing up. I mean that was just, you know...kids.

SIA (on having kissed a girl others identified as gay): Well I totally, like, denied that...I was mean...I just pretended that I didn't have any part in it at all. And I started, you know, bad-mouthing her along with my friend...denying...absolutely denying it...trying to push all the blame on her, you know.

A majority of these respondents followed convention and began to date boys while in high school, doing so at about the same age as those in the older group. Whether due to lack of interest or an early awareness of a preference for girls, four did not date boys at all. Of the eight who were heterosexually involved, dating progressed into a sexual relationship for all but two. Most became involved with boys in order to fit in; only one did so in an effort to deny her same-sex feelings:

KIP: It was pretty empty, it was pretty meaningless, it was...very unemotional, very detached. I just sort of did that 'cause I thought that's what we were supposed to do. Uh, they were there, you know [laugh].

Generally, heterosexual involvement again preceded self-awareness of a same-sex interest, but this time only by a year. Early awareness did not predict or preclude that involvement. The women in this group displayed a slightly higher rate of heterosexual involvement than their predecessors, a change likely reflecting the larger cultural climate of sexual freedom and exploration.

Exploration: Making Contact and Early Sexual Involvement. Early self-awareness had a much stronger bearing on the timing and circumstances of respondents' first same-sex sexual relationship. Four who experienced early self-awareness initiated that involvement while still in high school. Attributing their actions to abusive home situations and a rejection of same-sex feelings, three others delayed involvement until their late twenties and thirties.

Four of the five remaining respondents found that self-awareness coincided with social contact and sexual involvement. Each discovered an interest in women through friendships formed in college and at work. It was the identity disclosure and initiative of others in these settings that prompted their self-exploration. The final member of this group did not think of herself as potentially lesbian throughout high school or college. Yet, at 19:

CAT: The thought occurred to me that I would like to sleep with a woman but I didn't know quite how to go about that, you know, how to say "excuse me [laugh] I want to try this, would you like to volunteer?" So I made the decision that if it found me, I would decide what to do about it then.

It "found her" at the age of 22. A friend initiated their relationship with a disclosure of identity and interest.

Most of these women knew about homosexuality, or gays and lesbians, prior to self-awareness and sexual contact with another woman. As a group, they became socially and sexually involved approximately two years earlier than the pre-Stonewall respondents, though they displayed more individual variability in the timing of that contact. Four became sexually involved 3–6 years prior to any social contact with other lesbians; three delayed a year or more between social contact and sexual involvement. The other five became socially and sexually involved almost simultaneously.

Immersion into Synthesis: Identity Acceptance and Disclosure. There was, in the 1970s and early '80s, an atmosphere of sexual freedom that invited experimentation on the part of many young adults throughout the U.S. Information about gays and lesbians, and some limited resources by which to make contact, also became available to the women of this cohort. This convergence of freedom and information allowed these respondents a high degree of fluidity in their sexual exploration. Their first same-sex experiences were viewed as temporary and nondefining by most of them; half also pursued additional sexual contacts with men. After these initial experiences, all were involved within various (lesbian) social groups and subsequently pursued both long- and short-term relationships with other women. Thus, for this cohort, immersion involved both a high level of social contact with other lesbians and sexual activity within both lesbian and heterosexual domains.

No discernible pathways, and few patterns, to self-labeling and identity acceptance revealed themselves in the coming-out stories of these 12 women. On average, they assumed the label just after the age of 25, over six years earlier than those of the pre-Stonewall era. Two accepted the identity while still in high school, and four did so between the ages of 20 and 23. The remaining six self-labeled after the age of 27, though three of these continue, on some level, to struggle with self-acceptance.

There are two striking features in the stories of these women: their level of heterosexual involvement following a lesbian experience and the sexual confusion reported about many of their partners. Six reported sexual encounters with men after their first lesbian involvement. Two who engaged in one-night stands with men did so while under the influence of alcohol or drugs; the others were involved more extensively and defined it as an exploration of the heterosexual option or as a deliberate test of their sexuality.

A number of these women ended their first (and subsequent) relationships because of a partner's identity struggle and return to heterosexuality. This occurred only once among the older respondents, suggesting that it may have been a phenomenon of this later era. It reflects, perhaps, a convergence of the "free love" of the '60s and the gay liberation of the '70s:

> CAS (describing how she saw it in 1979): At least [they] were giving it a shot for a short time. People bounced around a lot in those days.

Her phrase provides a fitting image of the unpredictability of the life experiences of these 12 women. They did, indeed, bounce around a lot. Each pursued a unique and unpatterned series of lesbian involvements ranging from long- and short-term commitments, to dating without commitment, to promiscuity. A majority had been "in love" at least once; most had suffered the disillusionment of that love being lost. A few "cheated," others had been "cheated on," and some reported both. Only two expressed confidence in the potential longevity of their present relationship; the others, whether "single" or "involved," harbored an uncertainty about the future that is both a reflection of past experiences and a more global perception of the "lesbian life-style" today:

> SIA: I think that it would be nice to be in . . . to be in a . . . as far as being a lesbian, it would be nice if there could be more permanence, if people did stick together more, work things out more.

Amidst all the choices, information, and relationship activity available to these respondents, all confronted decisions about when and to whom they would disclose their sexual identity. All disclosed, on average, two years earlier than their older counterparts, and they did so more quickly after first self-awareness. More disclosed earlier to a wider range of individuals and groups, including parents and siblings. Confrontations by parents and friends also provoked more of these disclosures. Despite this generally higher level of openness (and confrontation), half of these women remained "closeted" to more than half of the groups and individuals discussed, and no respondent was "out" to them all.

Overall, the women of this era confronted a much wider array of opportunities and challenges than the pre-Stonewall women. They had access to far more information and people to help make sense of their feelings and experiences. They and their partners had greater freedom and more options. They were also more exposed: to each other; to the negative images of "their kind" portrayed by the media; and to the risks of being found out, or sanctioned, by others because of that exposure. This tension between freedom and exposure permeated their coming-out stories. Some contrasted that tension with the silence and isolation experienced by older lesbians and recognized the change as progress. Others viewed it as evidence that not enough progress had been made. Most remained hopeful, but not optimistic, that further change might be possible:

> PJ (33): I mean these movements, if they keep getting stronger and stronger I think we're going to see a lot more changes for us, thank God. They're not moving as rapidly as I think they should be.

Gay Rights Era

Eight respondents, ages 23–29, achieved adulthood between 1985 and 1991. They had grown up during the liberation era and, as adolescents, experienced the groundswell of anti-gay rhetoric provoked by the advent of AIDS. As they entered adulthood, they witnessed the rising tide of gay rights activism and the public "outing" of celebrities. They heard about the AIDS quilt, gay-bashing, and the lesbian baby boom. Of all respondents to this study, they alone grew up with early and frequent exposure to gays and lesbians as a visible and defined group. As adults, they have learned to define that group, and themselves, as a minority.

However, these women also grew up within small towns and suburbs, removed from urban centers of gay activism and lesbian-identified activities and services. Access to others like themselves was limited by their "closeted" environs; the media served as the primary (and, in this era, more open) "door" to information. A part of the media reflected a more neutral, less flamboyant, and sometimes even positive image of gay life (Fejes & Petrich, 1993). Under the onslaught of AIDS, media also promoted a "normalized" message advocating sexual responsibility and caution. Still, other sources continued to incite and reflect the persistent negativity and condemnation characteristic of earlier times.

Self-Awareness and Early Life Experiences.   Prior to adolescence, all of the women of this era had had at least a vague and distant awareness of the existence of gays and lesbians. By the time they were 18, all had confronted personal sensations and experiences that brought these images closer to home—half of them by age 14, the others 1–4 years later. None described feelings of "being different" or "not normal"; rather, all recognized a real, and sometimes troubling, attraction to female friends:

> LEA (24): In my head I wanted to be a family, I wanted to be a mother and have a husband and have a child. And that's what I always wanted in my head. And then, when I started feeling feelings for women, I was…it was really hard, cuz I didn't…I knew in my head what I wanted and I didn't want that to be it. And so I just kinda, I just kept pushing it away.

Though they recognized the connection between image and sensation, most did not define their feelings, or themselves, as lesbian while still in high school. The majority either paid little attention to the whole matter or actively attempted to "push it away." Only one both recognized the connection and labeled her feelings as lesbian before 18:

> GIL (29): I remember being at dances, um, in middle school and maybe if you become physical with a woman, um, like even if you're just kidding around, you're hugging or whatever, I remember that I liked that and I remember being like, "Wow! This is nice, I don't want this

to stop," or, "I wonder if I could do this again, if she'd get upset." So...I really realized that I knew that I was gay, like, seventh or eighth grade.

ALI (23): I was attracted to my best friend, which I hadn't really paid much attention to, I just kinda blew that off.

As adolescents and in high school, respondents had a tacit understanding that these feelings were not to be spoken. Whether a topic to be ignored or one with which to struggle, homosexuality was an issue about which they would remain silent for a few more years. Their families joined them in that silence. None of these women heard any mention of homosexuality, either positive or negative, from family members throughout childhood and adolescence. Most families did not actively prohibit such discussion; rather, respondents either perceived the silence as normal or used it as a means to protect their family members from additional burdens:

LEA: There was always something going on in my family so I didn't want to go, I didn't want to add to any problems or anything.

RED (26): I never got the impression...it wasn't no one wanted to talk about it or anything like that. It was just...was not something that was in daily conversation, you know, or even came up. I couldn't remember it ever coming up, negative or positive.

A tacit agreement to remain silent also existed between most of these women and their peers. In contrast to the overt hostility experienced by so many of their liberation-era predecessors, only two of these women found their school-age peers to be negative or hostile to gay and lesbian issues. Others could not recall hearing the topic mentioned except as an occasional, offhand remark. Their peers were not unaware of homosexuality; it was simply a topic that failed to command their attention.

Amidst the noise of increased media information and the silence of families and friends, these women confronted or ignored their feelings of attraction to other women as they dated (7 of the 8), became sexually involved with boys (4), were engaged to be married (3), and went on to marry and have children (2). Only one of these respondents described her heterosexual involvement as an overt attempt to deny her attraction to women. The others dated or became sexually involved as a rebellious gesture, because boys were available, or because their interest in girls was not yet strong enough to pursue:

LEA: I don't know why, I just didn't want any....I guess because the more I was feeling it, I...I don't know if I thought it was going to show or what, but I just didn't want anybody...it was...it was weird because it was OK for people to say I was a pig or a sleaze or anything. That was OK with me. I just didn't want anybody to think I was gay.

JAZ (25): I did date men, yes. Yes. And there wasn't really ever a thought of dating women or...I mean, it was just sorta in this fantasy world. And I don't think I've ever...I was ever...attracted enough to women to ever do something.

As a group, these eight women reported no overt pressure or perceived expectations that they would become involved heterosexually. Yet, they dated earlier, did so more frequently, and engaged in more sexual activity than the women of the two older cohorts. They were also the first group in which the average age of same-sex awareness preceded that of heterosexual involvement. This seeming contradiction becomes understandable in light of the contradictions of the era. Majority cultural norms were supportive of early heterosexual dating. Information about homosexuality was widely available yet not openly discussed. This was not the pervasive silence of the pre-Stonewall era; it was a close silence among family and friends, one even more potent in its contrast to the media noise. In that silence, these women "heard" about expected and tolerated forms of sexual behavior. Though they reported no consciousness of these expectations, they followed them.

Exploration and Immersion into Synthesis. This group progressed from early awareness to identity acceptance and disclosure within a more compressed time frame than the other respondents in this study. In addition to experiencing all "identity events" at an earlier average age than their predecessors, they did so over a shorter span of years (see Table 12.1). They also, on average, reversed two patterns followed by earlier generations. Within this group, social contact with other lesbians preceded sexual involvement, and self-identification as lesbian preceded first disclosure of same-sex interest to others. Within these more general trends, they also displayed a wide variability in their individual pathways.

All of these women experienced either a first social contact with other lesbians or sexual involvement with another woman by the age of 21. The most common route to finding like-minded others was college, where four of these eight respondents met and became involved with their first partners. The other four found lesbians with whom to socialize through work and recreational domains, which ultimately led them to their first lesbian relationships.

For most of these women, self-identification as lesbian occurred within the context of these social groups and prior to a same-sex sexual involvement. They were the first group to experience immersion as primarily a social, rather than sexual, phase in the coming-out process. Two of them, however, were not socially connected with other lesbians when they initiated their first same-sex sexual relationship; they also experienced a lengthy delay (2 years) between sexual involvement and self-identification. Neither had attended to her sexual feelings in high school and each believed this first contact was to be a singular event in her life:

JAZ: We were really closeted even within ourselves. So much so that I don't think either one of us understood or faced it. We never really talked about the lesb...being lesbian. We were just in love with each other and it was hidden from everybody and it wasn't until we were breaking up that I personally started to look at myself and realized that I was gay.

Following that first involvement, both retreated from dating to clarify the meaning of that experience. Through contact and discussion with straight and lesbian friends, they began to define themselves as lesbian. By the time of this study, both were again dating and enjoying regular social contact within a large network of lesbian friends.

Three women described their coming out as a natural progression from first awareness to identity acceptance. They found acceptance to be a relatively easy and unremarkable achievement:

GIL: So if that's...a coming-out story, that's about it. It just was, just a general progression, there was no major, like, "Whoa!" or anything that I remember being specifically emotional, I guess, about it.

Others defined the process as more of an internal and very personal struggle. They found themselves wanting to resist their own discovery that lesbian relationships were more satisfying than heterosexuality. Consequently, these five women described a conscious, sometimes painful, and frequently lonely self-examination. Most attributed that struggle more to fear about the reactions of others than to any discomfort of their own:

JAZ: I just keep remembering myself in this room. And just kinda thinking about...you know...I remember thinking about negative consequences...of it, you know. Cuz I wasn't out to anybody. So I'd go through the whole family thing, friends thing, work thing. And I sort of . . . but I'd weigh it against how comfortable it made me feel . . . to be gay.

The coming-out stories of these young women contain a more deliberate and contemplative character than those of their predecessors. They did not have the closet of silence and isolation into which the pre-Stonewall women were able to retreat, nor did they have the (liberation-era) predictability that unequivocal condemnation can provide. Rather, these women faced the visibility, ambiguity, and contradictions that the combination of information, social acceptance, and intolerance confers. Some progressed quickly, going from one relationship to the next and from awareness into self-acceptance. Others moved more slowly, retreating between relationships, engaging socially with other lesbians, and struggling with that self-definition. Regardless of the pace, all maintained a strong consciousness of the meanings and consequences that their actions might impart. This deliberate and contemplative approach was well suited to balancing the competing and contradictory forces pervading the era.

That approach is evident, as well, in the decisions to disclose made by these women. As a group, they disclosed at an earlier age and to more people than the prior generations. Two of them did so in response to parental confrontations, before they had themselves accepted a lesbian identity. Others, though they were also confronted, did not disclose until they were confident of the identity themselves. (At the time of this study, just one respondent had not disclosed to her parents—out of fear that they would challenge custody of her children.) With disclosure, the women found a new, supportive, and more open relationship with their families than they had previously enjoyed. Although respondents in the other two groups had also considered the costs and benefits of disclosure, they did not report the same degree of conscious deliberation, the same careful weighing of risks against freedoms, that characterized the decisions of these eight women.

Overall, these women of the gay-rights era inherited both opportunities and challenges carried forward from the days of liberation. They were exposed for a greater portion of their lives to more (and more conflicting) information than their predecessors. To some small extent, "being gay" had been "normalized" within certain segments of the straight world, while it continued to provoke fear, outrage, and violence within others. The women of this era encountered the "noise" of this conflict, the "close silence" of family and peers, and the limited options afforded by their small towns and communities. Faced with these contradictions and the competing demands provoked by heightened public awareness, they found few clear boundaries within which to operate. They had to define their own boundaries, consciously considering their options and weighing the risks, or opportunities, those options might afford. They are confronting that task, most quite successfully, as they live with "being out" today.

CONCLUSIONS

Within limits imposed by the qualitative methodology employed, the present findings have several implications for practice with lesbian clients. Different generations devise coping strategies for survival resonant with the obstacles and conflicts perceived and encountered. As social change occurs, individuals may or may not make adaptations in these strategies. Changes in public visibility and tolerance of lesbianism are simultaneously perceived as a protection and a threat within different age groups. Visibility has not translated into a consistent availability of resources nor willingness on the part of older lesbians to access resources that are available. Clinicians need to be cognizant of the history and diversity contained within the lesbian population if they are to respond effectively to the unique experiences and needs of each generation.

As suggested by the stories of these 31 women, coming out is not a linear and orderly sequence of events culminating in a predictable outcome. Summary data reveal a progression—from self-awareness in adolescence, to self-labeling and identity acceptance in early adulthood (see Table 12.1) —comparable to that found in previous research (Garnets & Kimmel, 1993). Lost within these summaries, however, is the wide variability in the sequence, timing, and outcome of developmental events described by the individuals in this study. Within and across age groups, respondents reported a variety of historical, social, family, and individual circumstances affecting their coming-out experience.

The historical periods in which respondents came of age contribute to understanding some of their differences, both developmentally and currently. The women of the pre-Stonewall era confronted a pervasive silence about (homo)sexuality, and an isolation from all things lesbian, as they struggled to define the meaning of their experiences. In subsequent eras, they carried this legacy of silence even as they felt its protective cloak begin to slip away. Their encounters with liberation and gay rights, while enlightening and exciting for some, provoked new anxieties and a troubling sense of vulnerability among many. They live carefully today, wary and sometimes fearful of all the openness, yet empowered by the "gay right-ness" of the identity they now claim.

The younger women, who grew up in succeeding eras, encountered neither the limits nor the protections that silence affords. They discovered more quickly the meanings and risks attached to their feelings and their behavior. Those who came out during the liberation era suffered the tensions and disillusionments of that transitional epoch. They are more cautious and protective now. Though most accept who they are, they do not have the same sense of normalcy expressed by those just a decade younger. These "young ones," more open and deliberate in their actions, are also encouraged, rather than dismayed, by the history of their predecessors. In it, and in their own histories, they have found contentment with their lives today and a sense of optimism about the future.

Geography provides another dimension for understanding the coming-out process of these women. Though resources and information have become more available in urban areas, lesbians living in small towns and rural areas remain more confined in their options. Because they are less anonymous, nonurban women, especially those over age 45, may be more cautious about identifying and using the resources that are available.

Researchers and clinicians alike often assume that a lesbian's disclosure decisions reflect the degree to which she is comfortable and accepting of her sexual identity. Thus, the decision to "pass" tends to be regarded as evidence of identity conflict. That assumption is not supported by the findings of this study. The decisions of respondents had more to do with issues of perceived safety and tolerance—for themselves and others—than any other consideration. Withholding of disclosure from family members, and sometimes from coworkers or friends, is often motivated by concern about the comfort and sensitivities of these other people. The women in this study regard themselves as "normal," despite their awareness that others do not share that view.

Clinicians need to respect and trust the disclosure decisions their lesbian clients have determined to be most suitable to their individual circumstances. "Pathologizing" these decisions displays a serious breach of respect for the individual dignity and self-determination of the client. Insistence upon disclosure that precedes or runs counter to a lesbian client's readiness may prove extremely harmful to the client, to the person in whom she has now confided, and, ultimately, to the therapeutic process. If, on the other hand, a woman has either disclosed prematurely or wishes to take that action after some years of "passing," clinicians are well positioned to help address the psychosocial implications of these choices.

These generational, geographic, and individual variations in coming out highlight the importance to clinicians of understanding both the history and the diversity of this population. Lesbian history is a relatively new and not well documented field of study. The significance of changed (and changing) public attitudes and policies regarding homosexuality is not well understood by human service practitioners or their lesbian clients. Though homosexuality is more visible, and perceived by many to be better tolerated than even a decade ago, one cannot assume that all lesbians find this to be a welcome development. Individuals, whether "established" lesbians or those just coming out, will likely meet this new openness with reactions and strategies carved out of their personal past. What may be perceived by some as a new opportunity, will strike others as a threatening vulnerability. As clinicians, we are challenged to understand, and must be prepared to respect, that diversity of response.

REFERENCES

Adam, B. D. (1987). *The rise of a gay and lesbian movement.* Boston: Twayne.

Biernacki, P., & Waldorf, D. (1981). Snowball sampling: Problems and techniques of chain referral sampling. *Sociological Methods and Research, 10*(2), 141–163.

Cass, V. (1979). Homosexual identity formation: A theoretical model. *Journal of Homosexuality, 4*(3), 219–235.

Cass, V. (1984). Homosexual identity formation: Testing a theoretical model. *Journal of Sex Research, 20*(2), 143–167.

Faderman, L. (1991). *Odd girls and twilight lovers: A history of lesbian life in twentieth-century America.* New York: Columbia University Press.

Fejes, F., &. Petrich, K. (1993). Invisibility, homophobia and heterosexism: Lesbians, gays, and the media. *Critical Studies in Mass Communication, 10,* 396–422.

Franke, R., &. Leary, M. R. (1991). Disclosure of sexual orientation by lesbians and gay men: A comparison of private and public processes. *Journal of Social and Clinical Psychology, 10*(3), 262–269.

Garnets, L. D., &. Kimmel, D. C. (1993). Introduction: Lesbian and gay male dimensions in the psychological study of human diversity. In L. D. Garnets, & D. C. Kimmel (Eds.), *Psychological perspectives on lesbian and gay male experiences* (pp. 1–51). New York: Columbia University Press.

Gonsiorek, J. C., &. Rudolph, J. R. (1991). Homosexual identity: Coming out and other developmental events. In J. C. Gonsiorek, &. J. D. Weinrich (Eds.), *Homosexuality: Research implications for public policy* (pp. 161–176). Newbury Park, CA: Sage Publications.

Kahn, M. J. (1991). Factors affecting the coming out process for lesbians. *Journal of Homosexuality, 21*(3), 47–70.

Levine, H. (1997). A further exploration of the lesbian identity development process and its measurement. *Journal of Homosexuality, 34*(2), 67–78.

Miller, N. (1995). *Out of the past: Gay and lesbian history from 1869 to the present.* New York: Vintage Books.

Parks, C. A. (in press). Lesbian social drinking: The role of alcohol in growing up and living as lesbian. *Contemporary Drug Problems.*

Radonsky, V. E., &. Borders, L. D. (1995). Factors influencing lesbians' direct disclosure of their sexual orientation. *Journal of Gay and Lesbian Psychotherapy, 2*(3), 17–37.

Rust, P. C. (1993). "Coming out" in the age of social constructionism: Sexual identity formation among lesbian and bisexual women. *Gender and Society, 7*(1), 50–77.

Seidman, I. E. (1991). *Interviewing as qualitative research: A guide for researchers in education and the social sciences.* New York: Teachers College Press.

Spencer, C. (1995). *Homosexuality in history.* New York: Harcourt Brace & Company.

Troiden, R. R. (1989). The formation of homosexual identities. *Journal of Homosexuality, 17*(1/2), 43–73.

Vance, B. K., & Green, V. (1984). Lesbian identities: An examination of sexual behavior and sex role attribution as related to age of initial same-sex sexual encounter. *Psychology of Women Quarterly, 8*(3), 293–307.

Weiss, R. S. (1994). *Learning from strangers: The art and method of qualitative interview studies.* New York: Free Press.

COMMENTARY BY: Cheryl A. Parks

The thought that I might conduct a qualitative study as my dissertation was not even on the radar screen when I first began my doctoral work. I was a confirmed "quantoid"—I liked statistics, relished in being identified as a positivist and, quite honestly, had very little knowledge or understanding of the nature or value of qualitative approaches. I wanted to do something meaningful, something "scientific," something (bottom line) that I could finish and hopefully, some day, turn into a publication or two. Quantitative research, statistics, something with lots of numbers to crunch—that was real research, that's what I understood was publishable, and that was what I intended to do!

With that as my starting point, I have to say there are definite benefits to the two-year (or longer) process of course work, intensive study and dialogue, writing, and further study that precedes the work of conducting and writing a dissertation. In addition to the expected immersion into new content areas and approaches to research, there is the opportunity to clarify interests, determine a research focus, and hone the analytic skills necessary to complete that first major independent research project. For me, the process included acquiring an understanding and appreciation for qualitative research methods. But that's getting ahead of this story. As I often heard then, and now frequently restate, the research problem must guide selection of the method (Gambrill, 1995), not the other way around, and that is, in fact, how this story started.

CHOOSING A TOPIC

Like many of my colleagues at the time, and like many students I have met since, my interests in beginning the doctoral program at Bryn Mawr College were fairly broad (read: unfocused) and offered innumerable (read: overwhelming) possibilities for research. Yet, two topics of both personal and professional interest—lesbian identity and alcohol use—were persistent in capturing my attention. In addition to 16 years of clinical experience working with individuals and families affected by alcoholism, I had also witnessed the sometimes debilitating effects and changing patterns of alcohol use and abuse, with and without treatment, in the lives of family and friends. As a private practitioner in a small urban community, I had also gained a reputation as a "gay-friendly" therapist although I was not yet "out" as a gay woman in many domains of my life. The juxtaposition of this personal and professional "history," and the seeming inconsistencies between what I knew (professionally and academically) and what I had experienced vis-à-vis alcoholism and recovery and gay identity, acted as a sort of honing device to focus my research

Commentary on article: Parks, C. (1999) Lesbian identity development: An examination of differences across generations. *American Journal of Orthopsychiatry, 69,* 347–361.

interests. Yet, by virtue of the very personal character of these two topics (for me), I also questioned their legitimacy as areas for objective research inquiry. This was another reason (I thought at the time) to pursue a positivist—by definition, more objective—quantitative approach in my dissertation.

Delving into the alcoholism literature (I opted at first to avoid lesbian identity as it felt too risky), it became quickly apparent that most alcohol research focused on men, and that there was a gap in research focused on women's experiences. That allowed me to make my first topic decision—I would focus on women's drinking. In pursuing that body of literature, I repeatedly "ran into" statements identifying lesbians as a special population group, and one that appeared to experience higher levels of drinking and more alcohol-related problems than heterosexual women (Hughes & Wilsnack, 1994). My avoidance wasn't working! So, I read what I could find of a very limited literature on lesbians' alcohol use, discovering far more questions than answers. By then I was hooked. I wanted to know how lesbians' and heterosexual women's drinking differed, but more importantly, I wanted to understand why.

These two overly broad and quite vague questions, while interesting to me, offered little direction as to how to proceed. Holding onto my quantoid roots, I entertained the idea of conducting a survey to compare patterns of use and problems experienced by heterosexual versus lesbian respondents. Aside from the obvious difficulties of trying to randomly sample a largely hidden population, or the equally problematic issues surrounding use of convenience samples, this approach would limit me to addressing only the first of my two questions. Yet, it was really the second question—Why?—I was most interested in pursuing. Fast-forward to my final semester, with two courses on qualitative methods and clinical research (plus further immersion in the literature on lesbian identity and alcohol use) now completed, and my resistance to using a qualitative approach had waned considerably. By then my focus had also changed. I was much more interested in within-group comparisons (lesbians who did and did not report heavy drinking), than in between-group (lesbian versus heterosexual) differences. Much of the literature then available attributed heavy drinking among lesbians to the stress of lesbian identity and to the centrality of the gay bar to socialization (Hughes & Wilsnack, 1994; McKirnan & Peterson, 1989). I wanted to examine different assumptions underlying that conclusion (e.g., the nature of identity stress, the role of the bar as a constant) and to explore what other motivating and constraining forces might contribute to lesbians' heavy drinking.

SELECTING A DESIGN

My newfound respect for qualitative research notwithstanding, I had a difficult time fully surrendering the use of any type of quantitative approach to my research question. Initially, I proposed a mixed-method approach of conducting a convenience sample survey (to measure the extent of heavy drinking) and follow-up interviews with a randomly selected subsample of survey respondents (to explore stressors, bar attendance, other factors). Knowing that as a doctoral student I needed the consensus and approval of my faculty committee in order to proceed, I initially discussed this strategy informally with a few faculty members. Somewhat to my surprise, and contrary to what I've since learned is a more common experience, it was the survey rather than the qualitative portion of my proposal that received the most challenge. Based on informal feedback I received, I reframed the survey as a recruitment and screening tool only (severely cutting back on the number and type of questions asked and on the number of surveys to be distributed) and expanded the focus of the interview to include discussion of identity development as well. At this point, I had moved completely, although not entirely voluntarily, into the qualitative camp—or so I thought.

The process of obtaining approval by my dissertation committee both revealed my continued positivist leanings and also presented an additional challenge to getting started. Although I can no longer remember the details, my first formal proposal was rejected at least in part because I had included several within-group comparisons (based on age and levels of alcohol use) that were unsupportable within my qualitative design. Even my resubmitted, approved proposal prompted the admonishment to "take off your starchy positivist suit and put on your clinical smoking jacket" from Dr. Jim Baumohl, my dissertation chair (advice to which I would repeatedly return throughout the dissertation process). To their credit (and my gratitude), although the members of my committee had not encouraged a qualitative dissertation, once that was identified as the necessary approach to address the questions I was asking, they continuously held me to the requirements of that methodology. But in doing so, they also created some ripples in what appears in the published literature as (and what I had imagined would be) the smooth unfolding of the research process.

Timing is everything! In the first round with my committee (late May), a few elements of my proposed research were tentatively approved. I would focus on lesbians' alcohol use by recruiting and conducting intensive interviews with a convenience/snowball sample of approximately 25 to 30 adult, self-identified lesbians who were heavy drinkers. A proposed recruitment plan and procedures outlined for obtaining informed consent and maintaining confidentiality of respondent information were also given the okay. The committee would reconvene in late September to consider final approval of suggested revisions to the proposal. (This May–September hiatus is, I think, a ripple unique to dissertation research). However, a significant step in my recruitment plan required me to attend an annual local picnic attended by a large number of lesbians in the area—in early September. Missing this event would severely impair my proposed recruitment strategy and create another delay in starting the study. I decided to move forward and, with the permission of the picnic sponsors, distributed copies of my recruitment survey to women at the picnic.

That decision "worked." Of 70 surveys distributed, 57 were returned and 30 (of which 6 met the original selection criteria) indicated the respondents' willingness to participate in an interview. I had about a fifth of my proposed sample! Although I could not actually begin interviewing until I received final committee approval, I had found a group of women willing to talk to me! When I received approval three weeks later (without changes in the sampling strategy), I was ready to begin.

CONDUCTING THE STUDY AND PRELIMINARY ANALYSIS

Three weeks is not an overly long delay between first contact (the survey) and follow-up (a telephone call), but it was enough that potential respondents required reminders about the survey completed and a renewed request for their participation. It was also enough of a delay that contact information, particularly availability, had changed for some (telephone numbers, best times to call, and interview availability were requested in the recruitment survey). Ultimately, the six qualified volunteers were contacted and scheduled, but it took six weeks to get this small number of interviews completed. By then it was Thanksgiving, and none of the original six had been able to offer the name of another woman who might be interested in participating. I had hit a wall!

A "silver lining" of qualitative research is that data analysis proceeds simultaneously with data collection, and several tasks, including transcription of interview tapes, can be completed on a scheduled or impromptu basis during lulls in the active data collection process. So, although I had not planned it that way, I had adequate time between September and January to interview, transcribe, and begin the analytic process with these six respondents. (In retrospect, I would now recommend to anyone doing qualitative research to plan this "slow" pace of interviewing to allow time for immersion with the data, early on and throughout the study.)

There were several benefits to this simultaneous, and early, analytic process, but two stand out in relation to their impact on sampling. The first (I'll talk about the second later) was the early recognition that one of my original selection criteria—current heavy drinkers—was too narrow, both conceptually and in terms of obtaining a reasonable sample. These first six women reported marked variability in their levels of alcohol use over time, and it was just a matter of timing that my recruitment survey identified them as current (past 30 days) heavy drinkers. A reasonable assumption was that women identified as moderate or light drinkers in my recruitment survey might at one time also have been heavy drinkers. My committee was persuaded by this analysis and argument and allowed me to "open up" my sample selection criteria to include moderate drinkers as well. Suddenly another 10 respondents to surveys distributed at the picnic "qualified" for inclusion! Four months, though, is a long time to wait for follow-up. By that January, one of the 10 was no longer interested and I was unable to find four others. Five were still interested and agreed to participate; so, several hours of phone calls and numerous rescheduled appointments later, a total of 11 completed interviews were obtained from that first recruitment event.

Though the expanded selection criteria allowed the pace of my interviewing to pick up speed, I was having little luck with the "snowball" part of my sampling strategy. Only two of the original 11 respondents identified one other potential participant, and neither of them offered additional referrals. Six months into the study, I was well short of the number of participants I had originally proposed, and it was beginning to seem that achieving saturation in my data (Seidman, 1991; Weiss, 1994) would be an unattainable goal. But discouragement is not defeat, and the notorious obsession doctoral students have with their research resulted, for me, in a couple of lucky breaks. Friends (tired of my incessant worrying), and research students (by this time I was also teaching and—surprise!—I just happened to mention my research from time to time) who were interested in my study, offered to recruit their friends and acquaintances as participants. One of those contacts generated a "snowball" of eight interviews, three others resulted in snowballs of five, three, and two interviews each, and most were with women from areas beyond my original locale.

Four new referral networks proved to be both a blessing and a curse. The blessing was that I suddenly had a wealth of referrals and more potential respondents than I could possibly need. The curse was that, with new referrals coming in from so many different sources, contact information was not always accurate or complete and several whose names I was given either did not meet the selection criteria or had a misunderstanding of what the study would entail. As a result, I spent considerable time on the phone, attempting contacts, describing the study, and conducting screening interviews, only to find that several potential interviewees were unavailable, unqualified, or had reconsidered their willingness to participate. This is not a complaint, nor meant to sound ungrateful—I might still be doing this study rather than writing about it if not for these referrals—but it is meant to convey some of the disappointments, frustrations, and blind alleys that are hidden within that simple published statement that "a convenience/snowball sample was used." Anticipating that these ripples in the research process are bound to occur might help to better (i.e., less anxiously) take them in stride.

Actually conducting the interviews presented still other challenges, opportunities, and concerns to be addressed. Agreeing to be interviewed is not a small contribution made by research respondents; in my case, they were giving me not only two–three hours of their time (on average), but also an opportunity to learn about some very personal, and often sensitive, areas of their lives. The communities and networks from which respondents were recruited were relatively small and close-knit, so many respondents knew others who had been interviewed or knew of me (the researcher) as a clinician in the area. Providing assurances of confidentiality, obtaining informed consent, and scheduling interviews in private locations at their convenience were all givens in the planning and conduct of the study, and were in place to address some of these issues. However, as the interviewing progressed, other unanticipated concerns also arose. Some respondents seemed inattentive to and unconcerned about informed consent (causing some ethical concern that the consent obtained was truly informed); a few were mildly to overtly suspect of my "agenda" (questioning whether I might diagnose them as having an alcohol problem) or of the possibility of breaches in confidentiality (requiring repeated assurances throughout the interview, and reminders that they could withdraw at any time; also, some respondents would casually ask about or refer to interviews conducted with friends, seemingly "testing" my resolve to maintain the confidentiality of all participants). Finally, my "closeness" to the research topics, and the effect that it would have on my ability to maintain objectivity and distance and not impose my own biases into the interviews, provoked additional concern and attention throughout the interviewing. This was sometimes exacerbated by how much I truly liked and enjoyed a particular respondent or interview, by respondents raising topics that were particularly interesting but tangential to the topic at hand (e.g., lesbian parenting), or by respondents' offers of food, drink, and future social contact made during and after the interview process (all such offers, except the occasional acceptance of a soda while interviewing, were refused). Actively attending to these issues, through self-reflection and consultation with peers and advisors, was a necessary and ongoing component of the interviewing and analysis processes.

Earlier I alluded to a second benefit that arose out of simultaneously engaging in data collection and analysis within qualitative research. I will turn to that discussion now because it, in conjunction with the reflexivity just mentioned, had a bearing both on my sampling strategy and on my ability to recognize when I had interviewed enough respondents. Somewhere around interview number 13 or 14, two things began to happen. First, there was the surge in potential respondent referrals described earlier. Then, based on preliminary analysis of earlier interviews, I began to recognize that the "coming-out" stories of respondents who were in their twenties were sounding very different from those of women who were just 10–15 years older. Before starting the research, I had anticipated differences between those in their late forties or older and women who were younger (due to social changes affecting openness about and visibility of homosexuality since Stonewall and other events of the late 1960s and early '70s; see Miller, 1995, for more on lesbian and gay history in the U.S.), but this distinction within that younger group came as something of a surprise. My original (admittedly unquestioned and wrongheaded) assumptions had been that "coming out" was basically a linear process (as described in the literature), and that it had changed very little in the two decades during which I had taken that journey. To really hear the stories of these younger, twenty-something women (a task made easier, I think, by my clinical background, if not by my personal history), I had to actively challenge both of those assumptions and, particularly during the final analysis, better attend to the historical, social, and cultural events described by respondents as backdrops to their "coming-out" process. In the end, this added an unexpected, richer, and much-needed dimension to my overall analysis.

A more immediate effect of this recognition of age differences, however, was that I began to impose an age criterion on my sampling. Rather than continuing to interview any woman over the age of 21 who met my identity and alcohol-use criteria, I began to specifically seek out women within the three age cohorts that seemed to be emerging from the preliminary analysis—those under 30, 30–44, and 45 and older. While this added another constraint to finding eligible participants, it also allowed me to be more focused in my sampling/recruitment, and to recognize more readily when I had reached saturation with each age group. Saturation occurred fairly quickly with the youngest respondents—after just six interviews, I was hearing very little that was new or different—so I concluded with this cohort after eight interviews. With the older and oldest groups, reflecting a broader range of ages and thus experiences, I reached this point of saturation after 12 and 11 interviews, respectively. Finally, after 13 months, contact with 102 potential respondents, and 31 taped interviews, I was done—all that was left to do was the final analysis and then writing it up. A piece of cake!

FINAL ANALYSIS

The thing that stands out most for me as I recall this phase of my research is the paper—piles and piles of original transcripts (over 1200 pages, typed, single-spaced) intermixed with other piles of "excerpt files" and still others of process notes, reference materials, and sundry other items that I was convinced would be absolutely critical to completing this analysis. At the time, I had had very limited exposure to computer-based qualitative analysis programs, and what little I knew convinced me to do my analysis the old fashioned way—with scissors, tape, and cardboard boxes. It probably was not the most efficient approach—and I hate to think about the number of trees ultimately lost to the process—but, feeling the pressure to get the dissertation done, I didn't want to divert energy into learning a new computer program as well. Looking back, that was neither a good nor a bad decision, based on the quality of the technology available at the time. Today, that technology is much improved, and I would recommend taking the time to learn one computer program well before undertaking a qualitative interview study. If nothing else, it will save some trees and help to reduce some of the feelings of chaos that all that paper can instill.

Just as there was overlap in the interviewing and preliminary analysis phases of this research, there was considerable overlap as well in the final analysis and writing phases. Confronting all of that raw data, I needed to find some way of organizing and making sense of it. First, I reread and resorted everything, adding items to many initial excerpt files, discarding others, and creating new files as new ideas began to surface. Having noted the differences in cohorts previously described, I returned to the literature on lesbian history to learn more about the different sociocultural contexts affecting different generations. The temporal "life history" character of my interviews and the "historical record" of cultural change led naturally to a developmental focus in my analysis, and suggested a beginning outline of chapters for the dissertation. Beginning to write about that history, my research methodology, and the women as they lived today (Chapters 1–3) provided some sense of coherence and of moving forward in the analytic process. In moving back and forth—from reading the literature, to writing, to reading and coding transcripts—new perspectives and ways of thinking about "the data" began to emerge. All that paper and all those cardboard boxes gradually began to take on some semblance of order.

It was during this immersion in analysis and writing that my original concerns about the science (i.e., objectivity, reliability, credibility, generalizability) of qualitative analysis resurfaced. Having already confronted one bias while conducting the interviews, I was even more concerned that others were still out there, hidden, lurking and ready to disqualify any interpretations or conclusions that I might presume to make. To counter this concern (and the equally powerful fear that any such biases revealed would also disqualify me from completing the Ph.D!), I actively sought feedback and tested my interpretations with others. One advantage of dissertation research is having a committee of faculty available for such consultation, and my committee was particularly good at helping me to uncover untested assumptions. While "going native" is a risk of qualitative, particularly ethnographic, research, "being native" provided me the benefit of access to friends and acquaintances (none of whom I had interviewed) who could recognize (or refute) my interpretations as credible and reflective of their own experiences (Sandelowski, 1986). At the same time, being a "native," a therapist, and a part of one of the communities from which several respondents were recruited might have facilitated trust and rapport with some respondents while limiting the responses of others, both of these reactions affecting the reliability of the data collected (Miles & Huberman, 1994). Again, by checking my interpretations with other members of the community, and by taking advantage of an opportunity to present preliminary findings at a professional conference of practitioners, I was able to receive additional feedback and gain confidence in the validity, reliability, and transferability of my findings. Receiving a pass on the dissertation and defense was a final confirmation that my study had indeed met the standards of scientific inquiry!

AFTERWORD

It has been almost 7 years since I completed the 18-month process of data collection, analysis, and writing described in these pages. Revisiting that experience by writing this commentary has been nostalgic, a little bit painful, and a stimulating reminder of the questions that initiated my research career. Relating that experience to where I am today offers one perspective on the relative strengths and limitations of the research described, and on any advice for future research that I might offer; relating my findings to social work and human service practice is another. Because it is a more limited discussion, I will start with the latter.

In preparing to write this commentary, I reread the proposal submitted to my committee in 1995. I was startled to see how superficially I had addressed the potential application of this research to social work practice, particularly given that I was a social worker in practice at the time it was written! That self-conscious admission aside, and recognizing the limits to generalizability of an $N = 31$ qualitative study, I believe there are areas in which this study's findings can be applied to practice. Two, discussed in the accompanying article (Parks, 1999b), are introduced as cautions to clinicians—to carefully consider the meanings and risks associated with changes in public visibility, and with identity disclosure, for the individuals seeking their assistance. The differences in meanings and risks reported, by cohort, among these 31 women suggest the possibility of even greater variability among women not represented in this study—particularly lesbians of color and lesbians who would not volunteer as participants in a study requiring such disclosure. I have suggested similar applications, related to findings on alcohol use and the correspondence between identity development and drinking, elsewhere (Parks, 1999a, 1999c).

In contrast to the minimal attention I gave to practice, my discussion within the proposal of future research applications was far more extensive. Remembering my quantoid roots, I saw my dissertation as the first phase in an ongoing research agenda. I proposed that the dissertation would result in a beginning conceptualization of a model for understanding lesbians' alcohol use. That would be followed by further qualitative study and an elaboration of the model with other groups of lesbians. Finally, I intended to conduct a population-based test of the model using quantitative research methods. Such was the imagination of an ambitious but naively optimistic and novice researcher! Yet, due to some lucky breaks, fortuitous insights, and great support, the first of these goals was, I believe, achieved.

As the first phase in an ongoing research agenda, this study has both strengths and limitations. Its primary strength, in my view, lies in its resonance with the lived experience of the many women who have heard or seen its findings through presentations and in print. The proposed model, which describes a correspondence between lesbian identity development and alcohol use that also accounts for differences across cohorts, makes sense to women of vastly different sociohistorical backgrounds. Placement of that model within a framework of bicultural competence also serves to depathologize lesbians' alcohol use, and suggests a competency-based model for interventions when that use becomes problematic (Parks, 1999a). Finally, in proposing a conceptual model, this research provides fertile ground for the future generation of research hypotheses and testing using quantitative procedures. At the same time, the study and the proposed model are limited by the size and composition of the sample on which they are based. Generalizability is constrained by the selection criteria imposed and the sampling method used. Selection criteria specifically excluded women of color and women who were either light drinkers or in recovery; the required self-identification as lesbian and use of convenience/snowball sampling effectively excluded women who were not publicly "out" or who were socially isolated. A second phase of qualitative research is now needed to include the voices of these and other women who have been overlooked or excluded from this and other studies focused on lesbians' experiences.

In requesting these commentaries, the editors suggested that we include any major advice for future research in this area. I have three points I would like to add to those I have already made. As I started on this study, I was cautioned about two things—that my topic was too narrow, and that a qualitative dissertation would limit both my publication and future employment prospects. Because they resonated with my own concerns, these cautions nearly succeeded in steering me away from the choice I had made. But—and this speaks to the first piece of advice—I had fallen in love with the topic, it was personal, it was meaningful and important to me, and my questions demanded a qualitative approach. Yet with all of that, I still became discouraged, suffered through boredom, and questioned the value and sanity of what I was doing at different points in the process. So, before choosing a qualitative dissertation, be sure of your commitment to your topic and be prepared to defend that choice, repeatedly, to others as well as to yourself. If that research is on a topic with which you have a personal connection, be sure you have plenty of advisors with whom you can periodically check for assumptions and biases—but, also, from whom you will receive encouragement and support to forge ahead.

Second, lesbians' alcohol use *is* narrow, and it seemed a particularly risky and circumscribed choice in the mid-1990s. But, again, timing is important. I was fortunate in pursuing this topic just as it also was beginning to receive attention from the Gay and Lesbian Medical Association (Dean, et al., 2000) and designation by the National Institutes of Health as a research priority. The topic remains understudied and riddled with methodological limitations. Interested researchers would be well advised to examine existing critiques of previous studies, as well as suggested techniques by which to address limitations, before embarking on new research with this population.

Finally, with three dissertation-based publications and having recently been awarded tenure, I now consider the warnings about limited publication and employment opportunities to be unfounded. In recent years, there has been a virtual explosion of new journals addressing gay and lesbian populations, as well as a modest increase in venues for publication of qualitative studies. Although challenges to qualitative publication endure, new venues and a growing literature on qualitative research (Padgett, 2004) suggest that this tide may be turning as well.

REFERENCES

Dean, L., Meyer, I., Robinson, K., Sell, R. L., Sember, R., Silenzio, V., Bowen, D. J., Bradford, J., Rothblum, E., Scout, M., White, J., Dunn, P., Lawrence, A., Wolfe, D., & Xavier, J. (2000). Lesbian, gay, bisexual, and transgender health: Findings and concerns. *Journal of the Gay and Lesbian Medical Association, 4*(3), 101–151.

Gambrill, E. (1995). Less marketing and more scholarship. *Social Work Research, 19*(1), 38–47.

Hughes, T. L., & Wilsnack, S. C. (1994). Research on lesbians and alcohol: Gaps and implications. Special Focus: Women and Alcohol. *Alcohol Health and Research World, 18*(4), 202–205.

McKirnan, D. J., & Peterson, P. L. (1989). Psychosocial and cultural factors in alcohol and drug abuse: An analysis of a homosexual community. *Addictive Behaviors, 14*, 555–563.

Miles, M. B., & Huberman, A. M. (1994). *Qualitative data analysis: An expanded sourcebook*. Thousand Oaks, CA: Sage Publications.

Miller, N. (1995). *Out of the past: Gay and lesbian history from 1869 to the present*. NY: Vintage.

Padgett, D. K. (2004). *The qualitative research experience*. Ontario, Canada: Wadsworth.

Parks, C. A. (1999a). Bicultural competence: A mediating factor affecting alcohol use practices and problems among lesbian social drinkers. *Journal of Drug Issues, 29*(1), 135–154.

Parks, C. A. (1999b). Lesbian identity development: An examination of differences across generations. *American Journal of Orthopsychiatry, 69*(3), 347–361.

Parks, C. A. (1999c). Lesbian social drinking: The role of alcohol in growing up and living as lesbian. *Contemporary Drug Problems, 26*(1), 75–129.

Sandelowski, M. (1986). The problem of rigor in qualitative research. *Advances in Nursing Science, 8*(3), 27–37.

Seidman, I. E. (1991*). Interviewing as qualitative research: A guide for researchers in education and the social sciences*. New York: Teachers College Press.

Weiss, R. S. (1994). *Learning from strangers: The art and method of qualitative interview studies*. New York: The Free Press.

13

Dynamics of Income Packaging: A 10-Year Longitudinal Study

Allison Zippay

As welfare recipients have increased their participation in the labor force under the implementation of the Personal Responsibility and Work Opportunity Reconciliation Act of 1996 (P.L.104-193), heightened attention has been given to the practice of "income packaging," by which individuals variously combine paid employment, unreported odd jobs, social services, and other income sources to make ends meet (Edin & Lein, 1997; Zucchino, 1998). Going beyond welfare recipients, the practice has long been routine across many groups of working poor and low-income individuals and is assumed to affect decisions regarding both employment and social services utilization (Gilboy, 1938; Pfeffer, 1997; Rank, 1994). However, few empirical in-depth studies have examined the long-term dynamics and effects of such resource pooling, including its use as a means to supplement low wages.

This article examines the dynamics of income packaging among displaced steelworkers, who experienced extensive downward mobility after losing jobs because of plant closures in the 1980s. Using a longitudinal research design to collect both qualitative and quantitative data, I interviewed a sample of 102 randomly selected displaced workers from a community in western Pennsylvania in 1987, a time when a majority were unemployed or underemployed and heavily dependent on social services. In 1997 I interviewed some of the respondents again to examine changes in their income and employment over 10 years, the dynamics of their use of social services, their pooling of multiple income sources to make ends meet, and their use of social assistance as a supplement to low-wage work. Although the results of the study are not generalizable, they offer information to guide further research and can enhance an understanding of some of the interactive effects of social services use and work behavior.

BACKGROUND

Income Packaging

Several qualitative studies have collected information on the ways in which low-income individuals use resources from multiple sources as a strategy of economic support. Edin and Lein (1997) conducted in-person interviews with 379 welfare- and wage-reliant single mothers and found that all but one of the welfare-reliant respondents were receiving income from other sources, including relatives, friends, boyfriends, churches, social agencies, paid employment, or unreported side jobs, and that many of the wage-reliant mothers were drawing on similar sources to supplement earned income. Interviewing inner-city residents of Philadelphia who worked as day-haul farm workers, Pfeffer (1997) found that two-thirds lived in households that received public assistance and that they typically drew on resources from family, friends, social agencies, and unreported side work such as doing household repairs, refurbishing scavenged furniture, or providing homemaker services to elderly neighbors. Other qualitative studies also found that poor and low-income households typically draw on a variety of economic sources, including odd jobs, scavenging, bartering, and cash and in-kind assistance from relatives and friends (Edin, 1991; Perrucci, Perrucci, Targ, & Targ, 1988; Rank, 1994; Stack, 1974; Zucchino, 1998).

Research also suggests that the practice of income packaging is the historical norm. A review of the administrative records of a representative sample of 2,180 Massachusetts residents who received federal work relief in 1936 found that 45 percent supplemented their relief benefits with additional jobs and money from boarders or renters and that the majority also received food, clothing, and other assistance from social agencies (Gilboy, 1938, 1940). Almost identical results were found in a national survey of relief recipients (Works Progress Administration, 1937). Although the role and value of an income versus a services approach to assistance has long been a focus of debate in the social welfare system (Gilbert & Specht, 1986; Leiby, 1978; Levitan, 1998), much of the empirical research suggests that a key feature of income packaging among many poor and low-income groups has been the ways in which its resources are strategically combined.

Work Effects

Income packaging typically includes the use of social services programs as well as reported or unreported work, and a large body of literature has examined the work disincentive and incentive effects of various forms of cash assistance and social program regulations (Garfinkel, 1971; Greenberg, 1970; Moffitt, 1992; Pechman & Timpane, 1975; Portney & Danziger, 1988; Wise, 1985). Studies of the employment effects of cash assistance programs, including unemployment insurance, disability insurance, and Aid to Families with Dependent Children, have found small to moderate aggregate reductions in average hours worked, with the size of the effect varying according to variables such as gender, labor market conditions, benefit reduction rates, and the size and duration of the income guarantee (Betson, Greenberg, & Kasten, 1980; Danziger, Haveman, & Plotnick, 1981; Hamermesh, 1977; Tella, 1971; Watts & Rees, 1975). Economists have demonstrated that benefits from unemployment insurance and various disability programs typically produce a "reservation wage" effect in which individuals with a time-specified guaranteed income prolong their unemployment by choosing not to work at a job below a certain wage, and some have noted the positive effects of using insurance guarantees to prolong job searches to secure the most appropriate employment (Ehrenberg & Oaxaca, 1976; McCue & Reed, 1996; Sahib, 1996; Welch, 1977; Zagonari, 1995).

Such labor effects often are analyzed in terms of the income and substitution effects proposed by standard consumer theory (Devine & Kiefer, 1991; Helfgott, 1980). The income effect predicts that if nonwage income rises (from a lottery win or a social services program, for example), holding wages steady, hours of work will go down. The substitution effect predicts that if nonwage income remains constant and the wage rate increases, the demand for leisure decreases (increasing work incentives because of the opportunity for leisure). Because these effects seldom occur in isolation and because other factors also affect work and leisure decisions, labor supply behavior is difficult to predict.

Despite the difficulties of predicting labor participation, strong income effects have long been assumed by many social critics to play a predominant role in the behavior of many social program participants (Banfield, 1970; Gilder, 1982; Murray, 1984). Income and reservation wage effects are clearly present for some individuals in certain circumstances. However, it also could be argued that social program participation in the form of income or in-kind assistance allows some people to accept and keep a low-wage job that otherwise would not provide adequate economic support. This assumption is implicit in programs such as the earned income tax credit and the extended Medicaid coverage sometimes available to those exiting welfare (Ellwood, 1988; Ozawa, 1995; Seipel, 2000).

Studies of how low-income individuals package social services, work, and assistance from family and friends can begin to explore in more detail the methods and rationales for resource pooling and the effect such packaging has on individual decisions regarding job search, employment, and retention of low-wage jobs. Such studies also can examine how packaging such diverse sources can help people with economic and occupational transitions as they seek job or status upgrades.

Setting

The setting for the study was the Shenango Valley in western Pennsylvania. Made up of several small towns with a combined population of about 60,000, the Shenango Valley is 90 miles north of Pittsburgh. For more than a century, manufacturing dominated the local economy and employed the majority of the workforce. Between 1980 and 1984 seven local steel fabrication and production plants closed, displacing approximately 6,500 workers. The closures led to additional closures and workforce reductions among some local supplier industries, and unemployment levels rose to 24 percent in 1983.

During the 1980s, job growth in the valley was slow and primarily in the low-wage services sector. But by the early 1990s a more diverse expansion was underway. A new highway opened to connect the area more directly to Pittsburgh, making commuting to the metropolitan region for work viable. An aging population brought increased demand for workers in the health services. Several manufacturing mini-mills opened operations in the valley, and two long-established local pipe mills experienced a rising demand for their products and expanded their labor force. These developments prompted some increases in the total number of manufacturing jobs, although services positions continued to dominate the economy. By 1997 the unemployment rate in the area had dropped to 5.3 percent, and the local poverty rate had fallen from 18 percent in 1983 to 12 percent (Penn Northwest Development Corp., 1997).

METHOD

First Wave of Interviews: 1987

In 1987 I conducted in-person in-depth interviews with 102 randomly selected displaced steel-workers who resided in the Shenango Valley and had been employed as hourly blue-collar laborers at two steel fabrication plants that closed in 1983 and 1984. The sampling frame was a list compiled by the United Steelworkers of America of all hourly manufacturing workers at the plants. The interviews were conducted in the respondents' homes or in a community center, and the response rate was 86 percent.

It is estimated that approximately 10 percent of the local steelworkers who were displaced in the 1980s relocated beyond a 60-mile radius of the valley to obtain employment, and another 20 percent traveled that distance to look for work but decided not to relocate (primarily because they could not find stable or high-paying employment). The 1987 study included interviews with 10 respondents who had relocated from the area (Zippay, 1991b). Those results are not reported in this article because the longitudinal study was focused on workers who had remained in the valley.

The study used a mixed-methods approach (Tashakkori & Teddlie, 1998) in which a structured questionnaire was used to collect both quantitative and qualitative data. Information was gathered on income and employment status, social and emotional reactions to the plant closings, social services utilization, job search and job training efforts, and social network characteristics. Structured in-person interviews also were conducted with 22 social services directors and community leaders to gather information on caseload changes that social services experienced in the wake of the plant closings (Zippay, 1991a).

Second Wave of Interviews: 1997

In 1997 I conducted telephone interviews with 87 respondents who had been interviewed in 1987. I used a mixed-methods approach in which a structured questionnaire was used to gather primarily qualitative data, as well as some quantitative information (Patton, 1990; Tashakkori & Teddlie, 1998). Information was collected on the respondents' current employment status, social services utilization, income sources, work history, and job-training efforts. The qualitative data were analyzed using cross-case analysis in which responses for each question were grouped and coded according to patterns and themes (Patton). To verify themes, data were triangulated through in-person interviews with six directors of social services, employment, and community agencies. Data on local employment levels and social services use were gathered from county and state documents.

I made attempts to contact all of the original 102 respondents. Five were deceased, two refused an interview, and eight could not be located through listings in the phone directory or post office. The response rate was 90 percent. Of those who could not be located, four were over age 65 and the others were middle age. The absence of forwarding addresses may have been because of local or more distant relocation resulting from retirement, employment, or other reasons.

Respondent Characteristics

The 87 respondents interviewed in 1997 ranged in age from 42 to 79 years, with a mean age of 54. All were men except one, 90 percent were white, and 10 percent were African American. Before the plant closings in the early 1980s, most had worked solely in manufacturing, and their seniority at the plants had averaged 16 years. In 1983 their average hourly wage while working at the plants was $12, and their average annual income was $25,000. Seventy-three percent of their fathers had been manufacturing workers, and almost all of the respondents were lifetime residents of the valley. Eighty-five percent had at least a high school diploma, and 15 percent had less than a high school education.

FINDINGS

Income and Employment Status: 1987

At the time of the first interview in 1987, four years after the plant closings, income and employment rates among the displaced workers had plummeted. Of the 102 respondents, 35 were not working—14 were unemployed and actively seeking work, 11 were discouraged by job search failures and had withdrawn from the labor force, eight had retired, and two were disabled. A high 27 percent of respondents reported household incomes below the federal poverty line, and median household incomes were $14,500 (compared with a national median of $30,853). Of the 65 respondents who were working, 60 percent were employed in low-wage services sector jobs, with the most common being janitor, security guard, and delivery truck driver. Average hourly wages were $6.50 and one-half of the jobs carried no health benefits.

Income Sources and Job Search: 1987

During the first interview in 1987, the respondents were asked to list their sources of income and to describe their job search processes. In the first year after their job losses, all of the respondents collected unemployment insurance, which was available to them for 52 weeks (because of high local and national unemployment), and most families supplemented their unemployment insurance by drawing on savings. As they began to seek employment, their job searches followed a similar pattern: Most respondents filed dozens of in-person applications for nonfactory blue-collar positions or for mill work at any plants still operating within a 60-mile radius of the valley. However, only two of the job seekers obtained manufacturing positions in the first year, and only 15 were working in manufacturing by 1987. Because low-wage services sector jobs were viewed by many as more acceptable for secondary earners, female spouses were often the first members of the family to take jobs at fast-food restaurants or at retail stores. In 1987, 70 percent ($n = 58$) of female spouses were working, and 90 percent were employed in services jobs. Of these, half had gone to work after the plant closings to help support the family, and 29 spouses assumed the role of primary earner.

As their unemployment insurance expired, many of the respondents began, with resignation, to take low-wage services jobs, and in 1987, 60 percent of the 65 respondents who were employed were working in this sector, with a modal wage of $3.35 (the minimum wage at that time). A majority also reported that they picked up odd jobs whenever they could get them, with the most common being roofing, house painting, and yard work. These jobs were frequently described as a needed supplement to minimum wage work:

> I was packin' ice cream at the Brookfield Dairy for $3.35 an hour and installed carpet on the side.

★   ★   ★

> I mowed lawns for bowlin' money.

★   ★   ★

> I did any kind of odd job I could find—mostly roofing and carpentry—while I was washin' dishes at Tully's [restaurant] for $3.35. I could never have made it on just the Tully's money.

With the local surfeit of unemployed and underemployed people, the availability of such odd jobs was limited, and the former blue-collar workers described a variety of means they used to pick up a little extra income. One respondent sold firewood that he cut from his yard. Another hung a sign offering to hand-wash cars for $1 a vehicle. One attended flea markets to sell wood and crafts that he made. Several respondents sold cars or boats or other possessions or had yard sales. About 8 percent of the respondents described bartering as a way to get goods or services—they exchanged a roofing job for some carpentry work or did a plumbing job in return for an auto repair.

> We were about to give up a campsite we had, but the camp director let us run camp activities in exchange for the site.

Most respondents, however, said they did such services for each other as a norm of their friendship, without a formal expectation of return.

Many respondents also drew on family members for assistance. Older children were sometimes encouraged to take paper routes, baby-sit, or do odd jobs. When able, some adult parents helped respondents with mortgages, buying groceries, baby-sitting, or small purchases, and several respondents moved in with their parents.

> My wife's father helps us out—if not I'd a been on food stamps or welfare. He brings over a bag of groceries or sometimes he gives me $35 for [snow] shoveling his driveway.

★   ★   ★

> We had bought a house but couldn't keep up with the payments. So we rented the house and moved in with my parents.

It is important to note, however, that many of the parents of the respondents were not economically well-off and were limited in the assistance they could offer. Most had been blue-collar workers, many were retired and living on fixed incomes, and others were unemployed or underemployed.

The availability of family members as suppliers of assistance represented a network resource—a social contact who could potentially provide material or services support (Granovetter, 1995; Lin, 1999). It was clear from the respondents' open-ended comments that network members were often key participants in their economic survival strategies of bartering, loans, and other forms of assistance. In 1987 data were collected on the size and composition of the respondents' social networks, with the finding that most networks were dominated by kin, and that the networks of the respondents who were poor and those who were not working were significantly smaller (Zippay, 1990). Respondents from households with incomes below the federal poverty line had a mean network size of 22.5 compared with 42.8 among people who were not poor ($t = 3.77$, $df = 94.82$, $p < .000$). Excluding work colleagues from the count, people who were employed had a mean network size of 40.4, compared with 25 for those who were not working ($t = 2.20$, $df = 96$, $p < .03$). Although data were not collected on the precise levels or types of support provided by network contacts, the findings indicate that the people who were poor and unemployed had fewer and less diverse network contacts on whom to draw for income and support.

All 102 respondents reported that a primary means by which they made ends meet after the plant closings was to cut back on expenses. Most said that they got rid of "all the extras" and described cost-cutting activities that included eating hot dogs instead of steak, shopping at discount stores, curtailing social activities, and reducing the insurance on their cars.

> We cut back on everything—car insurance, cable TV, everything. We used our savings, sold a motorcycle, and bought generic groceries.

★   ★   ★

We don't buy nothin' we don't need. Don't go out—even quit goin' to McDonalds.

During the first three years after their job losses, as people's savings dwindled and unemployment or underemployment continued, increasing numbers of respondents turned to various social services for assistance. All of the respondents used at least one social program, and many used several: 64 percent had used food pantries or government food distribution programs, 35 percent had received food stamps, and 36 percent had used a utility bill assistance program sponsored by the local Salvation Army. In 1987, four years after the plant closings, 69 percent of the respondents were still using one or more social programs, including food stamps, Aid to Families with Dependent Children, general assistance, food pantries and food banks, Supplemental Security Income, unemployment insurance (among those that had lost another job), counseling services, and WIC, the supplemental nutrition program for women, infants, and children. Thirty-four respondents were receiving a partial pension from the mill (available to those age 40 or older with at least 20 years of service), and 10 were drawing social security. Eight respondents were participating in job training funded by the federal Job Training Partnership Act of 1982 (P.L. 97-300).

These patterns of social services use were corroborated by data from local social services agencies. For example, government surplus food distributed through the local emergency management office increased from 4,000 families in 1981 to 12,000 in 1983 and dropped to 8,000 in 1986. Public welfare cases at the Mercer County Assistance Office rose from 7,200 in 1981 to 13,000 in 1983 and fell slightly to 12,000 in 1986 (Zippay, 1991b).

A majority ($n = 17$) of the 22 social services directors who were interviewed for the study commented that it was typically a female spouse who made the first phone call for information, often noting that her husband was too embarrassed or depressed to seek aid. Formerly middle income and steadily employed, most of the respondents' families had not recently used social services and were hesitant to apply. As two of the respondents described:

I feel it is a last resort. You feel too proud to take it.

★   ★   ★

I waited till we were rock bottom before we took food stamps even though I knew we had qualified for a long time.

Thus, all of the 102 respondents who were interviewed in 1987 drew on multiple sources of income in the first four years after the plant closings, with the most common being social insurance and social services programs, regular employment, side jobs, and assistance from family members. Ninety-six of the 102 respondents simultaneously used social programs and reported or unreported work for some period in the four years after their job loss. Despite drawing on multiple sources, however, each source typically added only incremental amounts to the families' lower-income budgets. As two respondents noted:

You scrimp and save and set your sights lower. You do a roofing job, get some help from your folks, or sell some possessions. But it is never enough and you always worry.

★   ★   ★

I told my son—you and I are like chickens scratching in the backyard. We aren't rich, we aren't poor. A chicken scratches from sunrise to sunset. We do the same—you scratch, scratch, scratch to get enough to get by.

Table 13.1. Status Changes among Respondents: 1987–1997

Status	1987 (*N* = 102) (%)	1997 (*N* = 87) (%)
Unemployed	14	.01
Poverty	27	7
Use of social services	69	9
Employed in low-wage services sector	60	15
Average hourly wage	$6.50	$12.14

Employment and Income Status: 1997

Some of the changes that respondents experienced from 1987 to 1997 are listed in Table 13.1. Ten years after their first interview, the economic and employment status of a majority of the respondents had improved. Of the 87 respondents, 62 (71 percent) were employed, 17 (19 percent) were retired, four were disabled, and one was unemployed and actively seeking work. Two respondents were temporarily laid off, and one was discouraged and had withdrawn from the labor force. Of the 62 that were working, only nine (15 percent) were working in low-wage services sector jobs. Twenty-nine (47 percent) were employed in manufacturing, 10 (16 percent) were in nonfactory blue-collar positions, and nine (15 percent) held professional, supervisory, or technical jobs. Their average hourly wage had risen to $12.14, and median household income was $32,500. Over the course of 10 years, 40 percent of the respondents had participated in some form of job training or education, ranging from a bachelor's degree in education to a six-month course in engine repair. Comparing the average hourly wages of the nonretired respondents who had participated in training with those who had not, higher earnings were associated with advanced training, including college-level study or training in a technical trade ($13.80 versus $10.97; [$t = 2.13$, $df = 39.44$, $p < .039$]). Entry-level training of one year or less (such as six months of computer programming) did not result in higher wages, and not one of the respondents who had participated in entry-level training had a job related to that training in 1997.

Although most of the respondents had made income gains since 1987, a majority had earnings that were lower in value than their earnings as steelworkers in 1983. In constant dollars, the average wage of $12.14 an hour represented a loss of 48 percent from the $12 mean they were earning in 1983. Those employed in low-wage services sector positions averaged $6.42 an hour compared with $13.35 for manufacturing jobs and $15.93 for other blue-collar positions (such as carpenter or electrician). Half of the low-wage services jobs were part-time, and three-fourths carried no health insurance benefits.

Other Income Sources: 1997

By 1997, as their income and employment status rose, the respondents who were most actively engaged in packaging income from multiple sources to make ends meet included those in the low-wage services sector, retirees, those who were disabled, and others not in the labor force.

All of the nine respondents who were employed in low-wage services sector jobs had at least one additional income source, and most had three or more: Five were collecting a partial pension from their former mill jobs; three were working odd jobs, including raising honey bees, refurbishing old cars, and hauling trash; and six had working spouses. Of the 17 retirees, all were drawing on both social security and mill pensions, four had part-time jobs, three had working spouses, and one was using a social services program (a local food bank).

By 1997 only eight of the 87 respondents were using one or more social programs (excluding the retirement benefits of social security and pensions). Among those who used social services, seven were not working because of physical disabilities or unemployment, and the programs they used included food stamps, food pantries, general assistance, WIC, and Medicaid. Four had spouses who were employed, and those who were disabled collected social security disability insurance or worker's compensation.

When the low-income respondents were asked how they made ends meet in 1997, two themes emerged—"belt-tightening," and using resources from multiple sources. As in 1987, those who were in low-income categories talked about "pinching pennies" and cutting out the extras. Because this situation had extended for more than 10 years, many of them have also talked about a change in expectations:

> I used to have a JCPenny's taste. Now I'm satisfied with Wal-Mart. I've lowered my standards and expectations and am very careful with my finances. You learn to appreciate what you have.

★ ★ ★

> You set your standards lower. Material goods aren't everything. If you have big expectations, you are in trouble.

Among these respondents, packaging resources from multiple sources was described as a routine matter of common sense and economic survival, and typically involved juggling a patchwork of regular and odd jobs, scouting alternative resources, drawing on support from family and friends, and conserving spending.

> I work nights part-time as a security guard and part-time as a custodian. My wife works days and I watch the kids till she comes home. We get a little help from the in-laws and we watch every penny we spend.

★ ★ ★

> People make a go of it however they can. Two jobs, wives work, kids have paper routes. It's a survival thing.

Although fewer respondents were combining income sources to make ends meet, many of the respondents who had higher incomes also drew on multiple sources as a routine means for increasing their incomes and resources. These multiple sources included spousal earnings, second jobs, unreported side jobs, gifts from family members, interest from investments, savings, retirement and social insurance programs, financial aid for children attending college, and others.

Temporary Assistance and Wage Supplements

Over the course of 10 years, the proportion of respondents using social services dropped from 69 percent to 9 percent. Although their use of social services typically extended for four to seven years after their initial job losses, it had no negative effect on employment and earnings in 1997. Among nonretirees, use of social services in 1987 was not associated in 1997 with higher levels of unemployment or part-time employment, or lower hourly wages. The respondents interviewed in 1997 were asked to describe the role of social services in their lives during the past 10 years. The common theme in their responses was "temporary" assistance: Social insurance and social services programs had helped get them through tough times when money was scarce and helped them make ends meet when they were unemployed or working in low-wage jobs.

The importance of supplements to low-wage work was also emphasized by the 17 nonretired respondents who were collecting partial pensions from the mill. In open-ended questions the majority said that the guaranteed income provided by the pensions made it easier for them to accept available minimum wage jobs rather than hold out for higher-paying blue-collar or manufacturing jobs. As one respondent who was working as a security guard noted, "My job pays low, but my pension makes up for the lower wages."

The special role of income supports also was emphasized by the 40 percent of respondents who had participated in some form of job training or education during the preceding 10 years. Cognizant of the changing postindustrial economy, the majority of the respondents under age 55 had expressed in 1987 a desire to obtain additional training or skills. Because the underfunded local Job Training Partnership Act program could not accommodate its thousands of applicants, the majority of those who desired training had to finance it themselves. Among the respondents who had not participated in training or education, the most common reason was that they could not afford it—they could not support their family while they took the time for education. Conversely, among those who did participate, one of the most common reasons was that they had a means of financing the training and supporting their family: financial aid, savings, or the earnings of a spouse. This was particularly true for those participating in more advanced training (and who subsequently received the greatest financial gains from that education). As described by a respondent in 1987 who went to law school:

> After the mill closed I was working at [a local plant] and got injured on the job. I was laid up and collecting worker's comp and restless and started to study for the LSAT [law school entrance exam]. I had a college degree and had always wanted to go to law school—I applied and got in. My wife was working as a nurse—that paid the bills while I was in school. I couldn't have done it otherwise.

DISCUSSION

In the first years following their initial job losses, income packaging was a universal economic strategy among these respondents, with 100 percent drawing on income and assistance from multiple sources, including regular employment, odd jobs, social insurance, social services, spousal earnings, friends and relatives, and bartering. Ninety-six percent drew simultaneously on income from work (reported or unreported) and social programs at some point during this period. The respondents' use of social services and income packaging over 10 years had various effects on employment. As reported by the respondents in 1987, most used their guaranteed income from unemployment insurance to prolong their search for jobs at a self-set reservation wage. Few attained it, however, and most waited to accept low-wage services positions until their unemployment insurance expired and it was clear that they had no other employment options.

In the following years, social services and guaranteed incomes, including partial pensions from former mill jobs, were most often used as a supplement to low-paying jobs. In what could be called a "supplemental" wage effect, many respondents commented that other forms of assistance enabled them to take and keep low-wage jobs because their earnings were supported by other sources. Some respondents used multiple sources to support their pursuit of advanced job training, which later resulted in higher wages and a reduction in needed supports. Because these sources often simultaneously included reported and unreported wage and nonwage income, income and substitution effects were intertwined and not isolated and neatly predictable. Although most respondents used social services and remained in a low-income category for several years after the plant closings, their use of social services did not have any long-term negative effects on levels of employment or earnings. The small percentage of respondents who had a more sustained use of social services did so primarily because of long-term physical disability.

Although the results of this study are not generalizable, the findings can inform further research in this area. The income packaging practiced by these respondents is not exclusive to poor and low-income individuals, but the sources, levels, and purposes are different from those of other groups and classes. Middle- and upper-income families often package dual incomes, interest from investments, gifts from family members, inheritances, or corporate bonuses or perks to maintain or extend certain standards of living. Among poor and low-income households, those sources are more likely to include social welfare programs and a variety of odd jobs and to maintain more minimal standards.

In the past, many critiques of the social welfare system have been framed with the assumption that individuals either work or depend on social services. Increasingly, empirical research is illustrating how rare such a dichotomy is and how complex, dynamic, and diverse are the sources of income and assistance that enable people to make ends meet. A better understanding of income packaging can help policymakers attend to the ways in which various social programs and income sources serve in combination to sustain or build families and how the availability of various resources affects decisions regarding job searches, retention of low-wage employment, and occupational transitions. This is particularly important in the wake of the Personal Responsibility and Work Opportunity Reconciliation Act as many social welfare professionals have increased their involvement in employment issues.

The challenge for policymakers and planners is multifaceted: to understand how people pool resources and with what effects, to assess which individuals have fewer resources on which to draw, to understand how resource packaging can further economic mobility and social stability, and to design ways to support the positive aspects of packaging. In social work practice, case managers can frame and approach income packaging as normative, assist individuals with the development of strategies for packaging, and facilitate consumers' connections to resources that promote both social and economic growth. Research on income packaging also reinforces the importance for the profession of a continued examination of the substantive and temporal role of social programs as wage supplements and their effects on both individual and structural labor market activity.

REFERENCES

Banfield, E. (1970). *The unheavenly city*. Boston: Little, Brown.

Betson, D., Greenberg, D., & Kasten, R. (1980). A micro-simulation model for analyzing alternative welfare reform proposals: An application to the program for better jobs and income. In R. Haveman, & K. Hollenbeck (Eds.), *Microeconomic simulation models for public policy analysis*. New York: Academic Press.

Danziger, S., Haveman, R., & Plotnick, R. (1981). How income transfer programs affect work, savings, and income distribution: A critical view. *Journal of Economic Literature, 19,* 975–1028.

Devine, T., & Kiefer, N. (1991). *Empirical labor economics: The search approach*. New York: Oxford University Press.

Edin, K. (1991). Surviving the welfare system: How AFDC recipients make ends meet in Chicago. *Social Problems, 38,* 462–474.

Edin, K., & Lein, I. (1997). *Making ends meet: How single mothers survive welfare and low-wage work*. New York: Russell Sage Foundation.

Ehrenberg, R. G., & Oaxaca, R. (1976). Unemployment insurance, duration of unemployment, and subsequent wage gain. *American Economic Review, 66,* 754–766.

Ellwood, D. (1988). *Poor support: Poverty in the American family*. New York: Basic Books.

Garfinkel, I. (1971). *The work and human investment incentives of negative income tax and wage-subsidy programs*. Discussion paper, Institute for Research on Poverty, University of Wisconsin, Madison.

Gilbert, N., & Specht, H. (1986). *Dimensions of social welfare policy*. Baltimore: Johns Hopkins University Press.

Gilboy, E. W. (1938). The expenditures of the unemployed. *American Sociological Review, 3,* 801–814.

Gilboy, E. W. (1940). *Applicants for work relief: A study of Massachusetts families under the FERA and WPA.* Cambridge, MA: Harvard University Press.

Gilder, G. (1982). *Wealth and poverty.* New York: Bantam Books.

Granovetter, M. (1995). *Getting a job* (2nd ed.). Chicago: University of Chicago Press.

Greenberg, D. (1970). *Income guarantees and the working poor. The effect of income maintenance programs on the hours of work of male family heads.* Santa Monica, CA: Rand.

Hamermesh, D. S. (1977). *Jobless pay and the economy.* Baltimore: Johns Hopkins University Press.

Helfgott, R. B. (1980). *Labor economics* (2nd ed.). New York: Random House.

Job Training and Partnership Act of 1982, P.L. 97–300, 96 Stat. 1322.

Leiby, J. (1978). *A history of social welfare and social work in the United States.* New York: Columbia University Press.

Levitan, S. (1998). *Programs in aid of the poor.* Baltimore: Johns Hopkins University Press.

Lin, N. (1999). Social networks and status attainment. *Annual Review of Sociology 25,* 467–487.

McCue, K., & Reed, W. R. (1996). New evidence on workers' willingness to pay for job attributes. *Southern Economic Journal, 62,* 627–652.

Moffitt, R. (1992). Incentive effects of the U.S. welfare system: A review. *Journal of Economic Literature, 24,* 1–61.

Murray, C. (1984). *Losing ground: American social policy, 1950–1980.* New York: Basic Books.

Ozawa, M. (1995, December). The earned income tax credit: Its effects and its significance. *Social Service Review, 69,* 563–582.

Patton, M. Q. (1990). *Qualitative evaluation and research methods.* Newbury Park, CA: Sage Publications.

Pechman, J. A., & Timpane, P. M. (Eds.). (1975). *Work incentives and income guarantees.* Washington, DC: Brookings Institution.

Penn Northwest Development Corp. (1997). *Mercer County industrial guide.* Mercer, PA: Author.

Perrucci, C. C., Perrucci, R., Targ, D. B., & Targ, H. R. (1988). *Plant closings.* New York: Aldine de Gruyter.

Personal Responsibility and Work Opportunity Reconciliation Act of 1996, P.L. 104-193, 110 Stat. 2105.

Pfeffer, M. J. (1997). Work versus welfare in the ethnic transformation of a Philadelphia labor market. *Social Science Quarterly, 78,* 452–471.

Portney, K., & Danziger, S. (Eds.). (1988). *The distributional impacts of public policies.* New York: St. Martin's Press.

Rank, M. R. (1994). *Living on the edge: The realities of welfare in America.* New York: Columbia University Press.

Sahib, P. R. (1996, April). Investigating the effect of the optimality constraint on parameter estimates in a job search model. *Canadian Journal of Economics, 29*(Part I), S62–S64.

Seipel, M. M. O. (2000). Tax reform for low-wage workers. *Social Work, 45,* 65–72.

Stack, C. (1974). *All our kin: Strategies for survival in a black community.* New York: Harper & Row.

Tashakkori, A., & Teddlie, C. (1998). *Mixed methodology.* Thousand Oaks, CA: Sage Publications.

Tella, A. (1971). *The hours of work and family income response to negative income tax plans.* Kalamazoo, MI: W. E. Upjohn Institute for Employment Research.

Watts, H. W., & Rees, A. (Eds.). (1975). *Final report of the New Jersey graduated work incentive experiment* (Vols. 1, 2, 3). Madison, WI: Institute for Research on Poverty.

Welch, F. (1977). What have we learned from empirical studies of Unemployment Insurance? *Industrial and Labor Relations Review, 30,* 451–461.

Wise, J. (Ed.). (1985). *Social experimentation.* Chicago: University of Chicago Press.

Works Progress Administration, Division of Social Research. (1937). *Survey of cases certified for works program employment in 13 cities* (Series IV, No. 2). Washington, DC: Author.

Zagonari, F. (1995, November). Decision-making processes under uncertainty: An econometric analysis. *Economic Journal, 105,* 1403–1414.

Zippay, A. (1990). The limits of intimates: Social networks and economic status. *Journal of Applied Social Sciences, 15,* 75–95.

Zippay, A. (1991a). *From middle income to poor: Downward mobility among displaced steelworkers.* New York: Praeger.

Zippay, A. (1991b). Job training and relocation experiences among displaced industrial workers. *Evaluation Review, 15,* 555–569.

Zucchino, D. (1998). *Myth of the welfare queen.* New York: Scribner.

COMMENTARY BY: Allison Zippay

INTRODUCTION

In-depth interviewing has been described as finding out what is "*in and on* someone else's mind" (Patton, 1990, p. 278). It is the job of the interviewer to engage respondents in a guided conversation that delves into an experience or phenomenon that we typically know little about. The quality of data obtained is determined in part by the skills of the interviewer: the ability to establish rapport, elicit rich stories and detail, probe for clarification, and facilitate a substantive exchange (Patton, 2002; Seidman, 1998). It is a sizable challenge. And it is best fueled by curiosity about the topic being explored and a fascination with the people and conversations that reveal the nature of that phenomenon.

BACKGROUND

My curiosity with the stories of displaced steelworkers had its origins in my upbringing in the geographic area in which this study took place. It was fueled by an interest in labor history and the stories of grandparents, uncles, and acquaintances about what appeared to be a mysterious and fearsome work environment: a world of enormous physical plants, flying sparks and molten steel, and intense noise and heat. Some of the respondents interviewed for this study described it vividly:

> You would walk into the foundry from upstairs...and into a dungeon. Then you'd be hit with the noise and the dirt. The plant was so old the windows were stained brown; a brown light would filter in. You could hear the noise from the street, the banging on steel.
>
> The first day I came to work I walked down the steps into the foundry. There was steam and smoke belching. Like hell itself. I said, "Oh God, what have I done?"

When the factories in this mill-dominated region began to close in the 1980s, I was struck by the multifaceted expressions of loss. Despite the difficult work environment, former steelworkers appeared to be mourning not only the passing of a steady employer and a good paying job, but also the lapse of an attachment to a culture that included pride in their trade and strong bonds with a tight-knit community of fellow steelworkers. With few other blue-collar jobs available locally, there were rumors of former mill workers making ends meet by flipping hamburgers at fast-food restaurants for minimum wage, picking up odd jobs, and drawing on a patchwork of social and community services. Nationwide, there were stories of former manufacturing workers from

---

Commentary on article: Zippay, A. (2001). Dynamics of income packaging: A 10-year longitudinal study. *Social Work, 47,* 291–300.

rustbelt towns across the country making up a new class of working poor. How were these formerly well-paid workers managing these economic transitions?

I decided to gather empirical evidence that tracked shifts in income and employment by talking directly to former steelworkers in one community. In-depth interviews were used to obtain the stories behind the numbers on displacement and income loss, and to hear their accounts of mill work, job loss and job search, and making ends meet. The study was longitudinal, with data collected in two phases. A first set of in-person, in-depth interviews was conducted in 1987, about 4 years after the first plant closings. Follow-up interviews were administered 10 years later with the same respondents (Zippay, 1991a, 1991b, 2001). The methods described below begin with a recounting of the initial phase of this longitudinal study.

METHODS: PHASE 1

Planning

All research studies begin with a planning and learning phase, and it typically starts with an immersion in the research literature on the topic to understand what is and is not known about the subject. In a qualitative design that uses in-depth interviews, that learning phase also involves some level of immersion in the community of the respondents. Respondents' comments are reflective of their particular context and experiences. To be able to probe and make sense of these responses, researchers need to gain knowledge and insight into the language, culture, experiences, and perspectives of the interviewees (Denzin & Lincoln, 1994; Rubin & Rubin, 1995). Getting to know the community and its members can also facilitate access to information and respondents, because it is often difficult for a stranger or someone outside of the community to gain trust and confidences without a community contact or "known sponsor" (Patton, 2002).

Immersion for this study took several forms as I spent several months at the study site observing and gathering information. I arranged to tour one of the mills still operating in the area to get a visual and tactile sense of work in that environment. Interviews were scheduled with key community leaders including the mayor, planning officials, clergy, and local union representatives to gather their views regarding the impact of the closings. Information was collected from employment and welfare offices, realtors, local newspapers, and community development officials regarding changes in unemployment rates, welfare use, housing prices, and economic development efforts. I spent time at community events and social gatherings talking to current and former steelworkers and local residents about millwork, unemployment, making ends meet, and community. I wrote field notes and drafted a set of research questions. Next I had to locate a sample of respondents.

Sampling

The mills had closed four years prior to the start of the study. Where were these former employees? I started with the contacts I had already made at the local union office, and obtained a list from the United Steelworkers of America of all of the hourly manufacturing employees who had worked at the mills at the time of the shutdowns.

The sampling methods used to recruit respondents for in-depth interviews are the same as those that can be employed in any other quantitative or qualitative research design including random, purposeful, and snowball sampling (Berg, 2003; Patton, 2002). I was looking for a sample that would be similar in composition to the population of manufacturing workers at the plants, large enough to be credible and provide theme saturation, and feasible to interview in the time I had available for field work (Patton, 2002). Using the list provided by the United Steelworkers as a sampling frame, a systematic random sampling method was employed to select every *n*th name of the lists, with a target of 100 interviews.

The local telephone directory and post office forwarding were used to track down current addresses and phone numbers. I kept a list of names for which I had no current addresses, and would ask my community contacts if they knew any of them and how they could be reached. All but a few were found. This location effort was eased by the relatively small size of the community, the fact that most people were still living at their previous address, and that only about 10 percent of the sample had relocated out of town.

Recruitment

Why would respondents agree to give up an hour or more of their time to talk about personal issues with a stranger? Sometimes they don't. And sometimes incentives are used: money, a gift or voucher, food, or an interviewer with whom they are acquainted. But often participation is generated by the respondent's desire to have a voice; to tell their story and perhaps have some input or effect on public discourse (Padgett, 1998; Weiss, 1994). Other factors also help, including a reputable, prestigious, or known institutional sponsor for the research, a convenient interview time and location, and a well-written, persuasive invitation to participate (including a description of the study, the value of the respondent's input, a guarantee of confidentiality or anonymity, and the potential impact of the research) (Berg, 2003; Patton, 2002).

For this study no monetary or material incentives were available. The recruitment letter described the purposes and university sponsor of the study, and offered a chance for them to share their stories about millwork, plant closings, job search, and employment with a researcher who had a local connection. At that time many of the respondents were still unemployed or employed part-time and taking an hour or two for an extended interview was not an expressed concern. Many were angry about their job and income losses and eager to relay their experiences for a study that might contribute to public and policy debates on the topic. I followed the recruitment letter with a phone call to answer questions and schedule a time for the interview. The response rate was 84 percent.

The Interview Process

Most of the interviews with the former steelworkers were conducted at kitchen tables in their homes. As part of my planning for the study I had laid out a timeline for these interviews based on the number of respondents and the number of weeks I had available to spend in the field. But—as many qualitative researchers quickly learn—that schedule had to be continually revised and extended. The time it took to connect with respondents to schedule their interviews was often longer than anticipated. And once scheduled, some forgot their appointments, got cold feet, or had unexpected obligations that resulted in additional time spent reconnecting and rescheduling.

But once they commenced, those interviews were a joy to conduct! Many new qualitative researchers worry about the reception they will get from respondents, and are uneasy about being perceived as intruding into the personal space and time of the interviewee. It has been my experience that, once the interview gets underway, most respondents relish the opportunity to tell their story. Most people like to talk about themselves and are encouraged by the attentiveness and curiosity of an interviewer. The telling of a narrative is also often spurred when respondents feel that their situation has been misjudged or ignored, and many are motivated by the opportunity to have input into a public debate as results are distributed to a wider audience. That was certainly the case in this study. Many of the displaced steelworkers felt that they were misunderstood and were "out of sight and out of mind" of policy makers (Palmer & Sawhill, 1984; Zippay, 1991b). Their frustration helped to spur participation.

The Questionnaire

The purpose of an open-ended question in a qualitative interview is to get the respondent to talk. It is a directed conversation that aims to elicit rich detail and elaboration (Seidman, 1998; Weiss, 1994). That is the *opposite* of a closed-ended quantitative item, which requires that an answer be precise and categorical. There are several survey methods that qualitative interviewers use to draw out these rich and vivid responses. The interviews may be informal, guided conversations in which no questionnaire is used; they may employ a "topic guide" in which the interviewer covers a series of subjects, with the questions and their sequence guided by the course of conversation; or they may use a set of structured open-ended questions (or a combination or closed- and open-ended items) (Patton, 2002; Wengraf, 2001).

A structured questionnaire was used for both phases of this study, because I wanted to obtain some quantitative as well as qualitative information from a set of closed- and open-ended questions. *Probes* were used with the open-ended questions to follow up the respondents' comments, to gather details, and to explore unanticipated issues or themes.

Qualitative structured questionnaires are composed with the same deliberation as those used in quantitative research. Generating rich, detailed responses is facilitated by the phrasing and sequencing of a question, as well as the interviewer's skills of engagement. Questions that require nonthreatening, descriptive responses are good icebreakers and allow time for rapport to develop. Items dealing with the most sensitive issues are often placed in the middle of the interview, as the respondents have warmed to a topic and have begun to tell their story. The interviews typically wind down with less delicate qualitative questions and with demographic items (Berg, 2004; Patton, 2002).

A similar strategy was applied in both phases of this study. The interviews began with a few straightforward, closed-ended questions: How long were you employed at the mill? What was your job title? Next came a series of items that began with description and moved to opinion: Describe for me the job that you did at the mill. What did you like about working in the mill? What did you dislike? Having recounted their work life as it had been, the questions then moved into its loss: the circumstances surrounding the plant shutdowns, their reactions, unemployment, job search, and making ends meet. The most sensitive questions, including those dealing with emotional problems and sustained income loss, were placed in the middle of the interview. Demographics and a question regarding their vision of their future closed the interview. I carried cards that listed a phone number for a local community service hotline to distribute to respondents who had indicated that they were interested in further information or assistance with mental health or other service issues.

As noted, most of the men and women relished talking about their work in the mill, and their depictions were often vivid and detailed. But not everyone was talkative or eloquent. A few were morose, some were timid, and others simply quiet. Sometimes rapport developed over the course of the interview (through engagement techniques including initial informal conversation, nonverbal cues that showed attention and interest, and persistent probing), and their answers became more detailed as the conversation progressed. But those strategies did not work with everyone, and there were a few whose responses were mostly cursory throughout. On the other extreme were respondents whose gab knew few bounds and for whom the conversation was in frequent need of redirection. The literature on qualitative research methods provides many tips on techniques to employ to either encourage or limit detailed responses from interviewees (Berg, 2003; Morgan, 1988; Rubin & Rubin, 1995).

After each interview, I headed to a coffee shop, library, or office to write up field observations and clarify and complete the notes I had written on the questionnaire so that they were coherent and legible. Even those vivid interviews that seem initially to be seared into memory can quickly fade or become blurred as time passes and the numbers of interviews mount. Observations were edited and recorded as soon as possible after completing the interview, to facilitate accurate recollections. From notes taken during the interview, I wrote an ethnographic sketch that included descriptions of the respondent's demeanor, dwelling, and neighborhood. These observations provided one more element of "thick description" (Geertz, 1973) in furthering an understanding of the meaning and context of the respondents' experiences.

Data Analysis

The long, rich, and detailed stories that are so welcome during the course of an in-depth interview can subsequently draw sighs as they add volume to the hundreds of pages of transcripts that must then be analyzed. The analysis of the information collected via in-depth interviews is a labor-intensive and time-consuming process, and simultaneously painstaking and enthralling. Data can be *managed* with the assistance of computer software programs, but the actual analysis must originate from the researcher. The rewards include "eureka" moments, which occur as themes emerge and ideas coalesce from hundreds of comments and pieces of text, and the analytic puzzle begins to take shape.

Because I had collected some quantitative as well as qualitative data, the analysis was begun by entering the quantitative data into an SPSS file and running frequencies that provided a demographic profile of the respondents. The qualitative data were entered into a word processing program (the original study was conducted prior to the advent of user-friendly qualitative software). The answers to each open-ended question were entered into separate files and coded with a number for each respondent. For example, the 102 answers to the question "What did you like about your job at the mill?" were typed in succession and numbered from 1 to 102. That format provided the transcripts for a cross-case analysis.

The analysis of the qualitative data began with a *case* analysis using the survey instrument. Each interview (or case) was read from start to finish to review the chronology of each respondent's experience with job loss, job search, employment, social service use, and income packaging. Initial notes on patterns and themes were recorded, and some preliminary categorical coding was done on the demographics of age and employment status.

Next a cross-case analysis was conducted. All of the answers for each open-ended question were read, and initial themes and patterns were noted. Quotes that were rich in detail or captured the essence of a particular theme were highlighted and noted for possible use in the reporting of results. Substantive content is not always neatly contained within a particular answer (comments regarding depression, for example, might surface throughout the interview), and these scattered references were located and regrouped for coding and analysis. Sometimes certain items or themes were counted and that information was made numeric and entered into the SPSS file.

Axial, or categorical, coding (Berg, 2003) on the cross-case analysis followed. The data were sorted and reanalyzed according to demographic variables such as age, employment status, and education, and initial codes including job search process, use of social services, and social network composition. Sometimes the text was cut and pasted via word processing to cluster and sort the responses according to age, employment status, etc. Other times a color-coded highlighter was used to manually mark passages associated with a particular demographic or theme. Selective coding followed as this process of sorting and reanalyzing occurred over and over as new themes or associations arose, and variables were combined and reexamined (Boyatzis, 1998; Newman, 2004).

Analyzing qualitative data is time consuming because of the volume of text involved, the repeated readings necessary for multilayered coding, and the contemplation required to make sense of it all. For this study, some patterns and themes were evident immediately, whereas others emerged over time as successive layers of analysis revealed nuance, meaning, or possible explanations for behaviors or situations. Sometimes themes were conspicuous through the repetition of words or phrases across many respondents ("I've been depressed . . ."). Other times a theme was embedded in an oblique phrase or metaphor ("I feel like a piece of paper that someone crumpled up and threw into the wastebasket"), and meaning was gleaned from multiple clues and the context of the interview as a whole. Spending concentrated blocks of time with the text and becoming immersed in the data help to focus and facilitate the process.

Data from the other sources used in this study (interviews with human services executives, documents, socioeconomic indices) were analyzed separately. They were then incorporated into the overall analysis to facilitate an understanding of the context of emerging themes, provide ideas for selective coding, offer confirmatory evidence, or expose inconsistencies that required examination. This source triangulation provided multiple perspectives and pieces of evidence with which to assemble a more holistic understanding, and to strengthen the validity and credibility of the study (Tashakkori & Teddlie, 1998).

LONGITUDINAL STUDY: PHASE 2

I had tentative plans from the outset of the study to reinterview the respondents after 10 years, with one of the purposes of the research being to track long-term shifts in employment and income. Prior to the second phase of the study, I checked local telephone directories and updated the addresses of the respondents. This process was eased once again by the high numbers of respondents whose addresses and telephone numbers had remained the same. Letters of request for a second interview were sent to all of the Phase 1 respondents, and 87 of the original 102 were located and interviewed for Phase 2. Because of resource limitations, the second round of interviews was conducted by telephone. Conducting in-depth interviews via telephone can be tricky, because it is usually more difficult to develop rapport minus in-person exchanges, and answers may be less rich and descriptive (as people are less likely to expound on the phone). These particular telephone interviews were aided by the fact that it was a second survey; rapport had been previously established, the respondents were familiar with the interviewer and the format, and they were invested in the process of having their story told. The interview format was the same as in Phase 1, with both closed- and open-ended items, but there were fewer questions, and fewer that sought long descriptive answers. Without a face-to-face contact, the techniques used to encourage conversation and description had to rely on voice inflection, tone, and verbal exchange. These included speaking with a warm tone and a "smile in the voice," careful listening, and well-placed probes.

Although the information obtained from the telephone interviews was detailed and rich enough to inform the research questions, it was thinner overall than that collected face-to-face.

Several factors affected those responses. During the first interview the conversations of many respondents were fueled by anger at the recent plant closings, but ten years later many were resigned and more subdued in their responses. Recognizing that people are less likely to give lengthy answers on the phone, the questions were purposefully structured to generate more concise responses. And there is no question that elaboration was contained by the absence of the opportunities present in face-to-face engagement, including the ability to respond to nonverbal cues and to imbue the exchange with a visual attentiveness and enthusiasm.

The methods used to analyze the data were the same as those described for Phase 1, with the addition of a comparative analysis across Phases 1 and 2. The respondents' questionnaires for Phases 1 and 2 were paired, and read for themes based on chronology across the decade. The cross-case analysis was likewise compared across the time periods.

Respondent Feedback

Sharing the results of an in-depth study with respondents can be part of a trust-building interchange as both parties give and receive information. It is also a way for researchers to validate their interpretations by obtaining respondents' feedback on these constructions. In keeping with the conceptual framework of qualitative methods, the process can maintain the centrality of the "voice" of study participants (Denzin & Lincoln, 1994; Patton, 2002). Many of the respondents in this study were eager to hear how others who had lost their mill jobs were faring. I had stated in the first introductory letter that they would receive a copy of the results, and many asked about it during the interview. I had mailed a summary of the initial quantitative and qualitative findings—minus any names or identifiers—to all of the respondents following the completion of Phase 1. I did a limited "member checking" to verify these interpretations and findings with study participants (Lincoln & Guba, 1985; Padgett, 1998) by phoning five of the respondents to get their feedback on that summary. I had also provided all respondents with a phone number and address in the letter that accompanied the summary, and encouraged them to reply to me with questions or comments. Other qualitative studies have used member-checking techniques that provide a greater quantity of *ongoing* feedback. These include bringing individuals from the sample population into focus groups to allow input into questionnaire development, and collecting focus group feedback from respondents at various stages of the coding and analysis process (Patton, 2002).

Ethics

The rights and privacy of the respondents were protected in several ways, with the protocols for both phases of the study approved by a university institutional review board (IRB). Letters of introduction and consent were sent to the respondents prior to each phase of the study delineating the sponsors and purpose of the research, and respondents' rights including voluntary participation, the option to terminate the interview at any time, and a guarantee of confidentiality. Plans for a 10-year longitudinal study were tentative at the outset of the study, and the request for a second interview was initiated in a letter and consent form sent to the respondents prior to the second phase. Anticipating that the sensitive topics of some survey questions might elicit emotional discomfort or requests for further information, a phone number for a community service hotline was distributed at the end of the Phase 1 interview, and was provided over the telephone at the end of the Phase 2 survey. To protect privacy and confidentiality, no names or identifiers were used in any of the write-ups of the results.

CREDIBILITY

The methods and parameters of this longitudinal study were determined by the research purpose, the research questions, and available resources. Each phase of the study was funded by a small grant that covered administrative costs, data entry, and my time in the field. I chose to be the sole interviewer on the project, because I wanted the consistency that was inherent in that role, and because I had funded time to do the interviews. I also enjoy the work and, as an observer and ethnographer, wanted a high level of immersion in the field. Qualitative interviewers have been described as an "extension of the instrument," and having one interviewer limits the variability in qualitative survey administration that can come with interviewers who have different styles, abilities, and training (Patton, 2002). As the only questioner, I was consistent in my techniques of building rapport, covering all of the survey items and topics, using inflection and tone, and developing probes and follow-up questions. That approach also had its weaknesses. While I focused on maintaining a neutral affect throughout, my perspectives, bias, and skill deficits invariably influenced the data obtained (Charmaz & Mitchell, 1997). I also acted as the primary analyst on the project, with interrater reliability used for some of the coding. The same strengths and limitations applied: the consistency of the process and a high level of familiarity with the data were intended to enhance its credibility and facilitate a multilayered analysis, but my particular lens or perspective circumscribed the process. Consequently, a number of other sources and methods were applied to supplement that evidence and its review.

In both phases of this study, the data collection techniques and the multimethod design were employed as a check on consistency, confirmability, and credibility (terms often used in qualitative research in place of "validity" and "reliability," to more accurately convey the standards sought in exploratory research with nonrandom samples) (LeCompte & Goetz, 1982; Patton, 2002; Tashakkori & Teddlie, 1998). These design and analysis components included the structured questionnaire (in which the questions asked of respondents were consistent), comparing quantitative to qualitative responses, member checking, making some qualitative data numeric to confirm emerging patterns, using verbatim words of the respondents to illustrate and authenticate themes, and triangulating evidence from multiple sources (including interviews with community services executives, and secondary data such as poverty rates and public assistance caseloads).

RELEVANCE

One of the themes that emerged during the first round of interviews for this study was the fact that many of the steelworkers felt that they participated in a work environment that was quite apart from that of many other Americans: an almost surreal surrounding that was noisy, hot, dirty, and physically challenging, and with a strong sense of camaraderie and shared experience among coworkers. As one respondent noted:

> Working in a mill is kind of like another world. Unless you were born and raised in a steel town and accepted that life—I don't think people would work there.

In-depth interviewing is a method of gaining insight into social worlds and phenomena about which we may have little knowledge or experience. Within social welfare, the lives and experiences of our consumers are often remote from those of most policy and decision makers. There are no welfare recipients or homeless or displaced steelworkers in the House or Senate. Distilling the themes that emerge from qualitative in–depth interviews is one way that we can begin to recognize and convey the situations of distressed groups to a wider audience. This longitudinal study of displaced steelworkers examined the ways in which able-bodied individuals with strong past ties to the labor market packaged income from a variety of sources (including social services) to weather economic transitions. It underscores how different are the contexts and situations of the low-income groups with which we work, and how critical it is to understand those differences in formulating effective program and policy responses. That is the hallmark and contribution of methods of in-depth interviews to studies in social welfare: gaining insight into experiences and phenomena about which little is known, to develop future research questions and empirically based problem-solving techniques.

REFERENCES

Berg, B. L. (2003). *Qualitative research methods for the social sciences* (5th ed.). Boston: Pearson Education.

Boyatzis, R. (1998). *Transforming qualitative information: Thematic analysis and code development.* Thousand Oaks, CA: Sage.

Charmaz, K., & Mitchell, R. G., Jr. (1977). The myth of silent authorship. In R. Hertz (Ed.), *Reflexivity and voice.* Thousand Oaks, CA: Sage.

Denzin, N. K., & Lincoln, Y. S. (Eds.). (1994). *Handbook of qualitative research.* Thousand Oaks, CA: Sage.

Geertz, C. (1973). *The interpretation of cultures: Selected essays.* New York: Basic Books.

LeCompte, M. D., & Goetz, J. D. (1982). Problems of reliability and validity in ethnographic research. *Review of Educational Research, 52*(1), 31–60.

Lincoln, Y. S., & Guba, E. G. (1985). *Naturalistic inquiry.* Beverly Hills, CA: Sage.

Morgan, D. L. (1988). *Focus groups as qualitative research.* Newbury Park, CA: Sage.

Neuman, W. L. (2004). *Basics of social research: Qualitative and quantitative approaches.* Boston: Pearson Education.

Padgett, D. (1998). *Qualitative research methods in social work research.* Thousand Oaks, CA: Sage.

Palmer, J. L., & Sawhill, I. V. (Eds.). (1984). *The Reagan record.* Cambridge, MA: Ballinger Publishing Company.

Patton, M. Q. (1990). *Qualitative evaluation and research methods* (2nd ed.). Newbury Park, CA: Sage.

Patton, M. Q. (2002). *Qualitative research and evaluation methods* (3rd ed.). Thousand Oaks, CA: Sage.

Rubin, H. J., & Rubin, I. S. (1995). *Qualitative interviewing: The art of hearing data.* Thousand Oaks, CA: Sage.

Seidman, I. (1998). *Interviewing as qualitative research: A guide for researchers in education and the social sciences.* New York: Columbia University Teachers College Press.

Tashakkori, A., & Teddlie, C. (1998). *Mixed methodology: Combining qualitative and quantitative approaches.* Thousand Oaks, CA: Sage.

Weiss, R. S. (1996). *Learning from strangers: The art and method of qualitative interview studies.* New York: Free Press.

Wengraf, T. (2001). *Qualitative research interviewing: Semi-structured, biographical, and narrative methods.* Thousand Oaks, CA: Sage.

Zippay, A. (1991a). Job training and relocation experiences among displaced industrial workers. *Evaluation Review, 15*(5), 555–570.

Zippay, A. (1991b). *From middle income to poor: Downward mobility among displaced steelworkers.* New York: Praeger Publishers.

Zippay, A. (December 2001). The role of social capital in reclaiming human capital. *Journal of Sociology and Social Welfare, 28*(4), 99–120.

14

Voices of African American Families: Perspectives on Residential Treatment

Jean M. Kruzich, Barbara J. Friesen, Tracy Williams-Murphy, and M. J. Longley

The relationships among institutions, professionals, and families are changing as the multiple benefits of the importance of involving families in services for their children are recognized. Koroloff, Friesen, Reilly, and Rinkin (1996) summarized the change:

> In less than two decades, the participation of parents and other family members who care for children with serious emotional disorders has expanded from limited "patient" or "client" roles to a wide range of planning, decision making and evaluation roles (p. 409).

These changing relationships, which parallel those in other child disability fields, are prompted by research linking family participation to positive outcomes for children (Burks, 1995; Carlo, 1993; Carlo & Shennum, 1989; Curry, 1991), by legal mandates (Koroloff et al., 1996), and by the development of a strong family movement in children's mental health (Bryant-Comstock, Huff, & VanDenBerg, 1996).

In addition, there is a small but growing body of research on relationships between families and residential treatment programs (Baker, Heller, Blacher, & Pfeiffer, 1995; Johnson, 1999; Laufer, 1990; Shennum & Carlo, 1995). Although there are a number of studies about the participation of families of color in special education (Bennett, 1988; Harry, 1992; Harry, Allen, & McLaughlin, 1995), to our knowledge there are no studies that report the perspectives of families of color about their involvement in residential programs. This is despite the fact that children of color are frequently overrepresented in residential treatment programs (Coker, Menz,

Johnson, & McAlees, 1996). African Americans make up approximately 12 percent of the total population, yet they are about 25 percent to 30 percent of the children in community-based programs (Singh, 1996) and 26 percent of the juveniles (from 10 to 19 years of age) in residential facilities (Hoberman, 1992).

This article reports on a series of focus groups with caregivers whose children were in residential treatment settings. We describe the common experiences of all family members and then highlight the unique themes reflected in the comments of African American family members.

METHOD

Because little research existed, we designed an exploratory study to identify issues of central concern to families whose children were in residential treatment. The use of qualitative research methodology was selected to gather rich descriptive data directly from family members whose children were or had been in residential care for treatment for emotional disorders.

Respondents

Four focus groups were held at two annual national meetings of the Federation of Families for Children's Mental Health, a national family support and advocacy organization. Some focus group participants were contacted through coordinators of statewide family advocacy organizations and were provided with information prior to the conference; others were recruited during the conference.

The first three focus groups met at the annual meeting in 1996 and included 18 family members. Fourteen of the participants were mothers; four were fathers. All but two of the participants were non–African American caregivers. Although participants shared common experiences and concerns, the two African American family members in the initial focus groups identified a number of unique concerns not voiced by other group members. To further explore these concerns, a fourth focus group comprised of nine African American family members from around the country was conducted the following year at the federation's annual meeting, using the same recruitment strategies used the previous year. Participants in the fourth focus group included four mothers, two fathers, one grandmother, one foster mother, and one aunt. The children's ages ranged from five to 18 years.

Data Collection and Procedure

We used a semistructured interview guide to facilitate discussion; it included five questions: (1) What kind of contact did you have with your child when s/he entered residential treatment, especially in the first six weeks? (2) How were you involved in your child's education and treatment while s/he was in residential treatment? (3) What were some things that supported your involvement in residential treatment? (4) What were barriers or things that got in the way of your being involved? Were there things that made it difficult for you to be as involved as you wanted to be? (5) What are your recommendations for change?

All four focus groups were held in meeting rooms at the conference hotels. Each focus group met for approximately one and one-half hours. A moderator facilitated discussion and an observer took notes and taped the session with an audiocassette recorder. The moderator for each focus group reflected the predominant ethnic makeup of the group. Participants signed consent forms at the time of the meeting and received a stipend for their participation.

Data Analysis

Focus group sessions were audiotaped, transcribed verbatim, and read into a computer program, the Ethnograph (Seidel, Friese, & Leonard, 1995), producing a numbered transcript to assist in coding and sorting the narrative data. Data were analyzed using the constant comparative approach whereby comments are coded and codes are compared with each other to derive a set of themes that classify the data (Strauss & Corbin, 1990). Three research team members reviewed the content of the files and developed initial categories and preliminary coding. One member of the research team coded the transcripts, and a second member coded a 20 percent sample to check interrater reliability. The results were compared, the third member of the research team arbitrated differences, and the transcripts were recoded to eliminate discrepancies. Later, to provide an additional validity check on emerging themes, a fourth person independently identified themes from the verbatim transcript without the Ethnograph coding. Interrater reliability attained through this process was greater than 95 percent.

FINDINGS

The first section of the findings addresses common perspectives of African American and non–African American family members regarding their experiences with residential treatment. The remainder of the findings focuses exclusively on the unique concerns of African American participants.

Commonalities across All Focus Groups

Concerns or perspectives shared by African American and non–African American family members were related to initial and ongoing contact with their children, the importance of being involved in their children's education and treatment planning, and recommendations for change.

Initial Family Member–Child Contact

Family members across all groups shared positive and negative experiences about their initial contact with the residential treatment program. The discussions involved the decision to place their child in residential treatment, the child's entry into the program, and the level and type of contact allowed.

Programs varied widely in the degree to which they encouraged or discouraged family involvement during the initial weeks or months of treatment. In some cases family members were told in advance that during an "adjustment period" there could be no contact with their children. Family members' experiences reflected varying degrees of flexibility around this policy. One mother noted that although program staff initially requested no contact, they responded to her plea:

> Because he was five they requested that we give him two weeks before contact, but because of his age, I requested that I contact him sooner. We did contact by phone for the first two weeks before I visited.

Another family caretaker had a very different experience. She reported that the day after she hospitalized her child for evaluation, she was told that he had been moved to a residential program. The residential program staff said: "You cannot talk to your child for 90 days because he is our child."

Ongoing Contact while in Placement

One of the most important issues that surfaced for all family members was maintaining contact with their children in the form of in-person visits and telephone calls. Many family members expressed concerns about visiting, especially the inflexibility of rules and policies. Several commented on the lack of communication between the facility and the home, particularly in notifying family members when privileges had been diminished or suspended. African American and other family members alike cited instances where visits were canceled as a consequence of a child's misbehavior:

> The punishment was like taking time away from the family. I drove two hours to see him and find out that he did something wrong about an hour or so before I got there. They would cut out two hours off his visit time.

Some family members had access to their child through daily calls; the expense of long distance rates and the ability of the child to take or initiate a call limited other families. Some family members also reported that their phone contact was dependent on their child's behavior and were concerned that "they use that as a punishment...not being allowed to speak to me when he was being punished. That is very unfair." Many family members raised the financial expense of maintaining contact with their children who were in residential treatment. Regarding off-campus visits, one family member commented: "You take them out for dinner, you try to spend some time doing whatever. It's expensive."

Involvement in Education and Treatment Planning

Although all family members emphasized the importance of being involved in treatment decisions, their experiences varied widely. One family member remarked: "I was very involved right from the beginning...I have been involved in everything...I'm thought of as staff, that's how often I am there." Another family member's experience was similar, but she contrasted her own participation with that of others: "When my daughter was in residential, there was very little involvement with the families. My case was an exception, not the rule. I was the first parent ever to attend a treatment team for their child."

Recommendations for Change

Families were asked to make recommendations for change that would support and encourage family involvement. Common themes among all family members were the need to be respected, valued, and more involved in making decisions about their children's treatment. They felt that residential facilities should be more flexible with scheduling visiting and more sensitive to individual family situations. They asked for meetings with other family members, additional information about the program, financial support for visiting and phone calls, and an increase in interagency collaboration during treatment and through transition.

Unique Concerns of African American Family Members

African American family members discussed at length a number of unique issues not raised by non–African American family members. These included separation of child from family and community, use of medication, cultural and racial dissimilarity, staff stereotyping, communal responsibility, and need for advocacy for other African American children in the facility.

Separation of Child from Family and Community. African American family members expressed intense apprehension around the initial decision to place their children in residential treatment. One family member expressed concern that staff would interpret the child's placement as relinquishing the child: "You have to let staff know that under no circumstances I'm giving this child to you—he still belongs to me. This is something of mine that I am allowing you to help me with." Others spoke of their fears that separation from family and community and limitations placed on family–child contact would be experienced by their children as abandonment: "She was the only African American child there. Then she was cut off from everything that she knew.... I was concerned about her feeling that this was a final separation, that she had been discarded because of her behavior. It was very crucial that she knew that I was there." Another family member stated the difficulty in more stark terms: "It is terrifying. It is not scary, it is terrifying to be the only one, miles and miles away from home, and all you can do is go along with everything they say."

A major difference between African American and non–African American family members was the frequent doubt expressed by African American family members about whether their children could possibly be well-served in any residential treatment setting. Rather than recommending changes in residential treatment policies and programs, the vast majority of African American family members' comments focused on redirecting resources so that community support would be sufficient to keep their children out of residential treatment.

A number of family members recommended more services in the community "to try and help a lot of the kids so they do not have to go." Another person suggested a change in allocation of funding: "Take some of the monies that we are paying these residential facilities and make it so that we have psychologists or therapists, all those things, and special ed teachers so they can function from their home." Over and over again family members spoke of the need for supports so that their children would not need to be sent away. The strongest statement came from a family member who saw residential treatment as warehousing children:

> I think that we need to look at other avenues as far as treating these children. We talk about being human and we talk about other countries and talk about what is taking place all over the world, but I see us doing an injustice to children in this country.

Use of Medication. African American family members' grave concerns about the use of medication with their children included possible differential effects of psychotropic medications based on biological factors, questions about overmedication, use of drug therapy as the only treatment intervention, and fears about possible racist experimentation. One family member commented on research that he felt indicated that medication "doesn't always work the same for the African American as it does for the white male or female." Another family member stated: "I don't think there is enough research that has been done on the effects of medication on blacks in general, and especially the black male." A third family member questioned residential treatment staffs' decisions to prescribe medications "because they play funny things with our kids sometimes, like with medication."

Participants also expressed concerns about overreliance on medication:

> They were leaning more toward medication. I thought there would be behavior management or more teaching stress management, or conflict resolution.... It seemed like when he first got there all they wanted to do was medicate.

Another family member, in a thinly veiled reference to the Tuskegee experiments (Gamble, 1993), suggested that the decision to use medication may not be guided by a desire to help: "If there is any type of medication, you are being injected almost like you are a test case, almost like there is just a lot of research done."

Cultural and Racial Dissimilarity. Even when residential treatment programs' espoused philosophy and policies address the importance of cultural competence, actual practice will be determined by the behavior of staff as they interact with children and their families. Racial and cultural dissimilarities between staff and children were a major concern for African American parents for a variety of reasons. As one mother stated: "The people who work in the program are not African Americans or Latinos. It is very demeaning when people speak about your family life, where you live, like it is some foreign country." Another participant's remarks underscore the value that he placed on a cultural match between his child and counselor and his repeated, futile attempts to obtain it:

> I didn't mind skin; we look at them as an individual. But in our time with our son and the times he has been in residential, he has always had a white social worker or clinician, and we have always tried to stress to get a black clinician or Hispanic because basically we share the same culture. But we could never get that.

Another participant listed a host of universities in the area and expressed her frustration and puzzlement with the lack of ethnic diversity among residential treatment providers: "I know they graduate people from those neighborhoods of color. How can you have no one?"

The cultural incongruity between African American children and staff was seen as hampering effective intervention with their children. A mother remarked that a staff person thinking s/he fixed her child by teaching him how to cry highlights the staff's lack of shared experience: "When we all know you don't do much crying in the housing projects because people will whip your butt."

Stereotyping by Staff. Many African American family members described how staff members' negative stereotypes potentially affected the assessment, diagnosis, and staff understanding of the culture of their child and family. They identified instances where stereotypes appeared to lead to differential treatment of their children, and actions they took to counteract these problems. One mother said that because her child was African American, "they said his problems were social. I said: 'No, it is not because of his environment, his neighborhood, or his color. It is because he has an emotional and mental problem.'" Another mother believed that because her child was African American he was misdiagnosed with a more severe diagnosis: "My son had Tourette's, but he was misdiagnosed at six as being schizophrenic." The perception of staff stereotyping leading to inaccurate diagnoses was mentioned by another family member who worked in a state mental health division: "I have found often times that one doctor will diagnose all the children the same, just because they are black."

In addition to concerns about the accuracy of the clinical assessment and diagnosis of their children, African American family members worried about how staff prejudice negatively affected their care. As one family member remarked: "If all staff are white and the only experience they have with African American kids is just the experience of them in the hospital setting, you are going to bring your prejudices right into the workplace." Speaking of her son's therapist, another family member said "he had such ideas, from too much TV. He obviously had preconceived ideas; he really opened up and told me some of his stereotypes. I went, 'That is utterly ridiculous.' But he had them and that is the way they deal with our children." A family member, recalling African

Americans' historical persecution, remarked that some staff "are sons and daughters of Ku Klux Klansmen." Another family member spoke of staff labeling her son and other African American children as potentially dangerous, which led to discriminatory treatment:

> They didn't want him to wear an Afro; they didn't want him to have his hair in braids. They had a disagreement with him hanging around with other black kids. The social worker told me that the other kids [the white kids] said they looked like a gang when they walked together, and they were afraid. So they separated him from the other [black] kids.

Family members also experienced staff stereotyping in relation to themselves. One mother remarked: "They make assumptions, they don't ask. . . . She's black, and she's single, so she must be dumb. Never mind that I can talk about Goethe and I can do calculus and geometry."

One of the ways family members attempted to promote good quality of care for their children was through monitoring case records and paperwork. One father thought his son had been unfairly labeled as dangerous. He said that "the most important thing I gained is documentation. . . . The only record you have is what is in the record, what is written. If the papers don't read right, you can lose it all." Another family member said:

> There has to be some kind of monitoring of paperwork and write-up of these kids. . . . The next person that deals with him . . . they look for what has already been written. . . . That's how they deal with them. That vicious cycle has to be broken.

A parent, who acknowledged difficulties with residential staff, took a tape recorder to a meeting in an attempt to have a record: "I was not allowed to use it. Because when I had my tape recorder there, they refused to talk." Although both African American and non–African American family members talked about the importance of being involved in their children's treatment, African American family members were unique in their focus on involvement and documentation as a way to protect their children.

Communal Responsibility and Advocacy. African American families expressed feelings of responsibility not only for their own children but also for other children and their families. One parent expressed this sense of communal responsibility for all African American children:

> When you are a vocal parent in these settings . . . these other kids tend to tag onto you, your voices, in their treatment. . . . You are sharing your visit not only with your child but with someone else's child. . . . It is really sad.

Family members often viewed themselves as spokespersons for other families and as advocates for other children. They expressed concern about the well-being of children whose family members were not involved. One family member remarked: "Just imagine when the parents don't come and get involved and don't see what is going on." Although recognizing different levels of family participation, they remained nonjudgmental about the absences:

> It is not a matter of not caring and not everybody has a strong voice, which is why there always has to be people like us at the table who speak out not only for our children but for other families who are not as educated or as informed. That is why we have to do this and not in turn stereotype and say: "Well, nobody has been here, so nobody cares." Maybe nobody has been because they weren't allowed to come, they weren't made to feel welcome, because it was just one more beat down so that they give up, frustrated. We shouldn't forget that.

DISCUSSION

Reviewing the themes family members identified in light of African Americans' historical experience and research studies provides a fuller context for the issues that surfaced in the focus groups. In this discussion we concentrate on resources available for practitioners and administrators striving to increase the degree to which culturally competent services for African American families and youths are provided.

Separation of Child from Family and Community

Historically African Americans have done everything possible to help ensure that members stayed in the community. Martin and Martin (1995) in their analysis of the black experience and social work noted: "Few problems in black history and black life have created greater fear, anxiety and dread in black people than the problem of loss and separation" (p. 139). Keeping African Americans within the community and away from white-controlled institutions was a way to help ensure safety. African Americans are more likely than other groups to fear mental health treatment and hospitalization (Lawson, 1996; Sussman, Robins, & Earls, 1987). These concerns may affect practitioners as well. A recent study of 141 African American social work practitioners found that they were more likely to recommend mental health services for troubled Caucasian youth than for African Americans (Fletcher, 1997). The study's author suggested that the difference might be the result of concerns about how African American adolescents would fare in the mental health system.

Residential treatment represents an extreme case of family–child separation, often involving long distances and limited contact. This concern of African American parents about the welfare of their children when they are away from the family, however, is not limited to situations involving out-of-home placement. For example, Smith (1989) discussed the conflict that middle-class African American parents face in relation to the school system, the societal institution that is most involved with their children's lives. Parents have seen authority and power used as a tool of discrimination, but their children need to be in school, so they must "turn a child over to people who appear to be representing that structure of power and authority" (Smith, p. 131).

Kalyanpur and Rao (1991) suggested using techniques that increase the ability of African American families to gain a sense of mastery and control. These may include general strategies such as involving families in treatment planning and decision making as well as specific responses to the conditions associated with out-of-home placement.

Concerns about Medication

Concerns about the safety of African American children focused on the effects, dosages, and appropriate use of medication. African American family members' beliefs that medications have a differential effect related to race are supported in recent psychopharmacological literature (U.S. Department of Health and Human Services, 2001). Findings reveal greater problems for African Americans than white people in metabolizing antianxiety and depression medications (Strickland, Stein, Lin, Risby, & Fong, 1997). A number of studies have found that African Americans may experience more negative side effects from tricyclic antidepressants and lithium (Lawson, 1996; Meyers, 1993). In addition, concerns have recently been raised about the overreliance on stimulant medication for children labeled as hyperactive (Tyson, 2000).

Family concerns about differential treatment in the use and dosage of medications for African Americans also have empirical support. In a recent study of four hospital emergency rooms, African

American adults were more likely to receive psychiatric medications, more doses, and more injections of antipsychotic medications than were Caucasian patients. However, when clinicians made efforts to engage African American patients in the evaluation and treatment process, there was a decrease in the amount of antipsychotic medication prescribed (Segal, Bola, & Watson, 1996).

Information about possible differential effects of medication by racial or ethnic group and clinicians' racial bias should be incorporated into professional training. The Surgeon General's report, *Mental Health: Culture, Race and Ethnicity,* notes the importance of clinicians' becoming sensitized to the possibility of a significant proportion of ethnic minority patients responding to lower-than-usual doses (U.S. Department of Health and Human Services, 2001). In addition, practitioners should carefully communicate with family members about the purpose, action, and potential side effects of any medication.

Cultural Dissimilarity and Staff Stereotyping

Most African American families in this study raised concerns that racism and lack of culturally competent staff would lead to differential and suboptimal treatment for their children. Proctor and Davis (1994) identified the most widespread concern of ethnic minority clients working with majority workers as the fear that the majority workers harbor ill will to members of the clients' race. If that concern is removed or not an issue for the client, a second concern—"Does the practitioner have sufficient knowledge of my world to be of real assistance to me?"—may be a more difficult issue to address. The level of segregation in employment, housing, and education in the United States means "many white practitioners have virtually no meaningful contact with minorities before seeing them as clients" (Proctor & Davis, p. 318). For example, O'Donnell (1999) found that workers had little understanding of why African American fathers might avoid contact with the child welfare system and recommended training as a way to promote effective outreach.

The influence of stereotyping is apparent in the assessment of African Americans receiving mental health and educational services. A disproportionate number of African American adults are diagnosed with more severe diagnoses such as schizophrenia as opposed to an anxiety or mood disorder (Baker & Bell, 2000; Neighbors, 1997; Snowden & Cheung, 1990; U.S. Department of Health and Human Services, 2001). Segal et al. (1996) found that clinicians in emergency rooms spent significantly less time assessing African American patients than other patients. African American children, particularly males, are six times more likely to be diagnosed with schizophrenia (Milazzo-Sayre, Benson, Rosenstein, & Manderscheid, 1986). African American children have consistently been overrepresented in special education programs over the past 20 years (Patton, 1998). Although African Americans are 16 percent of the nation's school population, they represent 35 percent of the special education population (Harry & Anderson, 1994). African American males are also overrepresented in the receipt of corporal punishment—at close to four times the rate that would be expected—and receive almost three times the rate of suspension that would be expected based on their proportion in the school population (Harry & Anderson).

African Americans also have differential access to services. In comparison to white people, African American adolescents have been less likely to receive mental health services, more likely to be placed in the juvenile justice system, and more likely to be in out-of-home care than to be served in their own homes (McCabe et al., 1999; Stehno, 1982).

Every effort should be made to recruit, train, and support a diverse staff reflective of the population served. Many of the African American families in this study expressed the desire for cultural similarity of worker and child. The importance of "cultural match" for positive client outcomes is an area of increasing study and debate (Snowden, Hu, & Jerrell, 1995). Even if cultural congruity were the most desirable, it is unlikely that it will be available in residential treatment and social services settings in the near future (Fong & Gibbs, 1995). This reality heightens the importance of the professional training programs including curricula that address the impact of culture, race, and ethnicity on mental health and mental health services (U.S. Department of Health and Human Services, 2001).

To address this issue, practitioners need both formal training and opportunities to gain experience with the cultural context of African American families. Involving family members in staff training has been found to be a useful strategy for increasing communication and understanding among families and staff (Bailey, Buysse, Smith, & Elam, 1992). Practitioners need the ability to deal with justifiable cultural mistrust and racial anger (Ridley, Chih, & Olivera, 2000). A number of cross-cultural authors noted the responsibility of professionals to make the client sufficiently comfortable so that racial differences can be acknowledged (Green, 1999; Paniagua, 1998) and client concerns about goodwill, understanding, and competence expressed (Proctor & Davis, 1994).

Communal Responsibility and Advocacy

One of the major differences between African American and non–African American family members' perspectives was the collective identity expressed by many African American families. Iglehart and Becerra (1995) linked the development of this collective identity to institutionalized racism:

> In the face of exclusionary and separatist practices, the African American philosophy espoused historically has been one of African Americans helping African Americans. This self-help ethos encouraged African Americans to feel a responsibility for helping those who were less fortunate (p. 162).

The sense of collective identity is a unique strength, as evidenced by the concern that participants expressed for other children in residential treatment. It may also build a sense of family for children in out-of-home placements who may not have ready access to their own families. Institutional changes are needed to collectively support African American children. These may range from concrete resources, such as family resource rooms where groups can meet, to expanded roles for family members on visits, boards, or advisory committees. Meaningful family participation and the allocation of space and resources can reflect a program's commitment to the importance of families in treatment progress and return of children to home and community.

STUDY LIMITATIONS AND FUTURE DIRECTIONS

The major limitation of this study was its sample size. A larger sample size would permit analysis of within-group variation in terms of gender, different ethnicities, age of the children, and level of involvement while the child was in residential care. Although we chose not to seek objective data on socioeconomic status, the African American participants in this study appeared to be relatively affluent and well-educated. The high level of unanimity revealed in their perspectives may reflect the relative homogeneity among focus group participants. Future research efforts would benefit from study samples that include a wider range of social and economic status to better capture the variation that exists. Nevertheless, these findings address a gap in our knowledge of family member perceptions about residential treatment, in particular the unique concerns voiced by a sample of African American family members.

REFERENCES

Bailey, D. B., Jr., Buysse, V., Smith, T., & Elam, J. (1992). The effects and perceptions of family involvement in program decisions about family-centered practices. *Evaluation and Program Planning, 15,* 23–32.

Baker, B. L., Heller, T. L., Blacher, J., & Pfeiffer, S. (1995). Staff attitudes toward family involvement in residential treatment centers for children. *Psychiatric Services, 46,* 60–65.

Baker, F. M., & Bell, C. C. (2000). Issues in the psychiatric treatment of African Americans. *Psychiatric Services, 50,* 360–368.

Bennett, A. T. (1988). Gateways to powerlessness: Incorporating Hispanic deaf children and families into formal schooling. *Disability, Handicap and Society, 3,* 119–151.

Bryant-Comstock, S., Huff, B., & VanDenBerg, J. (1996). The evolution of the family advocacy movement. In B. A. Stroul (Ed.), *Children's mental health: Creating systems of care in a changing society* (pp. 359–374). Baltimore: Paul H. Brookes.

Burks, J. (1995). Edgewood Children's Center outcome study 1991/1992. *Residential Treatment for Children and Youth, 13,* 31–40.

Carlo, P. (1993). Parent education vs. parent involvement: Which type of efforts work best to reunify families? *Journal of Social Service Research, 17,* 135–150.

Carlo, P., & Shennum, W. (1989). Family reunification efforts that work: A three-year follow-up study of children in residential treatment. *Child and Adolescent Social Work, 6,* 211–216.

Coker, C. C., Menz, F. E., Johnson, L. A., & McAlees, D. C. (1996). *Improving school outcomes and community benefits for minority youth with serious emotional disturbances: A synthesis of the research literature.* Menomonie: University of Wisconsin-Stout, School of Education and Human Services, Rehabilitation Research and Training Center.

Curry, J. F. (1991). Outcome research on residential treatment: Implications and suggested directions. *American Journal of Orthopsychiatry, 61,* 348–357.

Fletcher, B. F. (1997). Same-race practice: Do we expect too much or too little? *Child Welfare, 76*(1), 213–237.

Fong, L., & Gibbs, J. (1995). Facilitating services to multicultural communities in a dominant culture setting: An organizational perspective. *Administration in Social Work, 19,* 1–24.

Gamble, V. N. (1993). A legacy of distrust: African Americans and medical research. *American Journal of Preventative Medicine, 9,* 35–38.

Green, J. W. (1999). *Cultural awareness in the human services* (3rd ed.). Needham Heights, MA: Allyn & Bacon.

Harry, B. (1992). *Culturally diverse families and the special education system: Communication and empowerment.* New York: Teacher's College Press.

Harry, B., Allen, N., & McLaughlin, M. (1995). Communication versus compliance: African-American parents' involvement in special education. *Exceptional Children, 61,* 364–377.

Harry, B., & Anderson, M. G. (1994). The disproportionate placement of African American males in special education programs: A critique of the process. *Journal of Negro Education, 63,* 602–619.

Hoberman, H. M. (1992). Ethnic minority status and adolescent mental health services utilization. *Journal of Mental Health Administration, 19,* 246–267.

Iglehart, A., & Becerra, R. (1995). *Social services and the ethnic community.* Boston: Allyn & Bacon.

Johnson, M. M. (1999). Multiple dimensions of family-centered practice in residential group care: Implications regarding the role of stakeholders. *Child & Youth Care Forum, 28,* 123–141.

Kalyanpur, M., & Rao, S. S. (1991). Empowering low-income black families of handicapped children. *American Journal of Orthopsychiatry, 61,* 523–532.

Koroloff, N. M., Friesen, B. J., Reilly, L., & Rinkin, J. (1996). The role of family members in systems of care. In B. A. Stroul (Ed.), *Children's mental health: Creating systems of care in a changing society* (pp. 409–426). Baltimore, MD: Paul H. Brookes.

Laufer, Z. (1990). Family ties as viewed by child care and treatment personnel in residential settings for children aged 6–14. *Child & Youth Care Quarterly, 19,* 49–57.

Lawson, W. B. (1996). The art and science of the psychopharmacology of African Americans. *Mount Sinai Journal of Medicine, 63,* 301–305.

Martin, E. P., & Martin, J. M. (1995). *Social work and the black experience.* Washington, DC: NASW Press.

McCabe, K., Yeh, M., Hough, R. L., Landsverk, J., Hurlbut, M. S., Culver, S. W., & Reynolds, B. (1999). Racial/ethnic representation across five public sectors of care for youth. *Journal of Emotional and Behavioral Disorders, 7,* 72–82.

Meyers, H. F. (1993). Biopsychosocial perspective on depression in African Americans. In K. M. Lin, R. F. Poland, & G. Nakasaki (Eds.), *Psychopharmacology and psychobiology of ethnicity* (pp. 201–222). Washington, DC: American Psychiatric Press.

Milazzo-Sayre, L. J., Benson, P. R., Rosenstein, M. J., & Manderscheid, R. W. (1986). Use of inpatient psychiatric services by children and youth under age 18, United States, 1980. *Mental Health Statistical Note, 17*(175), 1–39.

Neighbors, H. W. (1997). The (mis)diagnosis of mental disorder in African Americans. *African American research perspectives* [Online]. Available: www.isr.umich.edu/regd/prba/win97/misdiagnosis.html.

O'Donnell, J. M. (1999). Involvement of African American fathers in kinship foster care services. *Social Work, 44*, 428–421.

Paniagua, F. A. (1998). *Assessing and treating culturally diverse clients: A practical guide* (2nd ed.). Thousand Oaks, CA: Sage Publications.

Patton, J. M. (1998). The disproportionate representation of African American males in special education: Looking behind the curtain for understanding and solutions. *Journal of Special Education, 32*, 25–31.

Proctor, E. K., & Davis, L. E. (1994). The challenge of racial difference: Skills for clinical practice. *Social Work, 39*, 314–323.

Ridley, C. R., Chih, D., & Olivera, R. J. (2000). Training in cultural schemas: An antidote to unintentional racism in clinical practice. *American Journal of Orthopsychiatry, 70*, 65–72.

Segal, S. P., Bola, J. R., & Watson, M. A. (1996). Race, quality of care, and antipsychotic prescribing practices in psychiatric emergency services. *Psychiatric Services, 47*, 282–286.

Seidel, J., Friese, S., & Leonard, D. (1995). *The Ethnograph v 4.0: A user's guide.* Amherst, MA: Qualis Research Associates.

Shennum, W. A., & Carlo, P. (1995). A look at residential treatment from the child's point of view. *Residential Treatment for Children & Youth, 12*, 31–45.

Singh, N. (1996). Cultural diversity in the 21st century: Beyond E. pluribus unum. *Journal of Child and Family Studies, 5*, 121–136.

Smith, J. W. (1989). Black middle class education in the 1980s. In A. F. Coner-Edwards, & J. S. Spurlock (Eds.), *Black families in crisis: The middle class* (pp. 129–139). New York: Brunner/Mazel.

Snowden, L. R., & Cheung, F. K. (1990). Use of inpatient mental health services by members of ethnic minority groups. *American Psychologist, 45*, 347–355.

Snowden, L. R., Hu, T., & Jerrell, J. (1995). Emergency care avoidance: Ethnic matching, and participation in minority-serving programs. *Community Mental Health Journal, 31*, 463–473.

Stehno, S. M. (1982). Differential treatment of minority children in service systems. *Social Work, 27*, 39–45.

Strauss, A., & Corbin, J. (1990). *Basics of qualitative research.* Newbury Park, CA: Sage Publications.

Strickland, T., Stein, R., Lin, K., Risby, E., & Fong, R. (1997). The pharmacologic treatment of anxiety and depression in African Americans. *Archives of Family Medicine, 6*, 371–375.

Sussman, L. N., Robins, L. N., & Earls, F. (1987). Treatment seeking for depression by black and white Americans. *Social Science Medicine, 24*, 187–196.

Tyson, K. (2000). Using the teacher–student relationship to help children diagnosed as hyperactive: An application of intrapsychic humanism. *Children & Youth Care Forum, 29*, 265–289.

U.S. Department of Health and Human Services. (2001). *Mental health: Culture, race and ethnicity— A supplement to mental health: A report of the Surgeon General.* Rockville, MD: Substance Abuse and Mental Health Services Administration, Center for Mental Health Services.

COMMENTARY BY: Jean M. Kruzich and Barbara J. Friesen

RESEARCH CONTEXT

The focus groups addressed in this article were undertaken in the first phase of a five-year project designed to study the participation of parents and other caregivers of children with mental health problems in the children's treatment and other aspects of service. The focus was on children and youth who were placed out of the home for the purpose of mental health treatment. The entire project included exploratory research designed to map the conceptual territory related to family participation in out-of-home treatment settings, followed by a quantitative survey of family members whose children were in out-of-home care. Our overriding goal was to change residential treatment policies to be more responsive to families. We saw how research based on family members' perspectives had been important in helping mental health practice and policy move away from parent blaming (Rapp, Kisthardt, Gowdy, & Hanson, 1994), and we were hopeful that our study would support more family-friendly policies in out-of-home care.

In the exploratory phase, we wanted to learn about the relevant dimensions and processes of participation, and to identify policies and practices that encouraged and supported participation, along with barriers that prevented families from participating as fully as they wanted to. For this first phase, to learn about the experiences of families whose children have been placed in out-of-home care, focus groups were particularly suited to our research purpose. Focus groups have the benefit of being efficient, eliciting extensive information from a number of people in a relatively short period of time. Another strength is that individuals are likely to feel less vulnerable in a group than in a one-to-one interview, and feel a greater degree of control, relative to individual interviewees, over how much they feel under pressure to contribute to the discussion (Farquhar, 1999). In addition, the group interaction often produces ideas and insights that may not occur when conducting an individual interview (Krueger & Casey, 2000). For these reasons, focus groups were chosen as an effective way to identify appropriate questions and response alternatives for the survey instrument we planned to develop.

Initially there was no plan to examine differences between African American and non–African American caregivers. However, the first three focus groups included two African American parents who identified a number of issues that appeared to be substantially different from those raised by the non–African American members of the groups. Both our interest in further exploration

Commentary on article: Kruzich, J., Friesen, B., Williams-Murphy, T., & Longley, M. (2002). Voices of African American families: Perspectives on residential treatment. *Social Work, 47,* 461–470.

and our resources to accomplish it were bolstered by the composition of our research team, which included an African American woman and an Alaskan Native woman, both of whom brought an intense interest and considerable expertise in the area of diversity and children's mental health.

IMPLEMENTATION OF RESEARCH DESIGN

Identifying and Recruiting Participants

We wanted to meet with family members who had a child who was currently or had been in out-of-home treatment for mental health problems. There is no easily accessible sampling frame for this population. Although we could have approached a number of local residential treatment centers to get in touch with parents who would be interested in talking with us, such an approach would necessarily reflect the experiences of parents from only a few programs, and we were interested in obtaining the broadest possible range of experiences and responses. In addition we also believed that parents would be more forthcoming about their experience if they did not need to identify where their child was in care. It also freed us, the researchers, from being identified with residential treatment providers, and thus secured a more independent status vis-à-vis the respondents. We expected that this would enhance a sense of trust and willingness to share their experiences with us.

We decided that the annual conference of the Federation of Families for Children's Mental Health provided an excellent opportunity to reach families from a broad geographic area. The Federation is a national family support and advocacy organization focusing on children's mental health issues. The Federation's annual conference in Washington, DC, is attended by 800–1000 family members each year, and thus was a setting likely to include a sufficient number of parents with residential treatment experience to participate in our group interviews.

Multiple methods were used to identify and recruit participants. Each year (1994 and 1995) we notified the Federation of Families staff of our desire to conduct focus groups at the annual meeting, and Federation staff helped to make logistical arrangements for the groups. Our research staff sent faxes describing the project to statewide family organizations in every state, asking family organization staff to help identify families who would be attending the Federation of Families' conference, had experience with residential treatment or other out-of-home treatment settings, and might be willing to participate in focus groups at the conference. We provided the times and places of the groups, and, as much as possible, enrolled potential participants in advance of the conference. We also used snowball or network sampling, asking potential participants to contact other families who had a child in residential treatment.

At the conference, notices explaining the focus groups' purpose, times, and locations were posted at the conference registration desk and other visible locations (see Appendix A for Focus Group Fact Sheet). Announcements about the opportunity to participate were also made in a number of the conference sessions. Focus group respondents included family members from 11 different states representing all regions of the United States. Although our interest in soliciting diverse views about families' experiences with their children's out-of-home placements was stimulated by the comments of two African American women in the first round of focus groups, we wanted to more broadly target people of color to learn about their experiences. The participants who came to the fourth focus group meeting, however, were all African American parents and other caregivers, with no other races or ethnicities represented. Since the conference provided a sizeable number of scholarships, attendees represented an economically diverse group. In the African

American focus group, however, all of the family members appeared to be solidly middle or upper middle class. It may be that African American conference participants from lower socioeconomic groups were less likely to participate in our focus group. A focus group member's comment that "there always have to be people like us at the table who speak not only for our children but for other families who are not as educated, not as informed" supports the notion that lower-income African Americans may be less comfortable and willing to participate in research studies.

Constructing the Interview Guide

Prior to organizing the focus groups and collecting the data, we carefully read the literature on family involvement in out-of-home treatment. Based on the literature review and conversations with parents, we constructed a series of questions—the questioning route—to use in the focus groups. The interview guide was semistructured, allowing flexibility in the process of interviewing. Open-ended questions allowed us to elicit participants' subjective experiences, in their own words, of having a child placed in out-of-home care, and to learn what was most important to them. This is especially relevant in giving voice to culturally diverse people and populations at risk, whose voices have not been heard in discourses about social and organizational policies. (See Appendix B for focus group introduction, questions and probes).

While federal regulations classify focus groups as eligible for an expedited review, the Human Subjects Research Review Committee (HSRRC) at Portland State University required a full review because the study was part of a federally funded grant. Portland State's Institutional Review Board approved the research protocol, including consent forms, for this phase of data collection. Interestingly, when the research team prepared the first-person scenarios for the HSRRC submission, we included one hypothetical member who was anxious before the group but was reassured by the structure and atmosphere. In fact, when we conducted the groups, we saw no sign of anxiety or reticence on the part of participants; most seemed eager to share their experiences. At the end of the session, several of them thanked the researchers for conducting this inquiry, noting its importance, and commenting that getting the perspective of family members was a much-needed but rare occurrence.

DATA COLLECTION

When participants arrived at the room where the focus group was to be held, they were greeted by members of the research team and invited to help themselves to food and beverages. Participants were offered another copy of the one-page explanation of the focus group, which included information about a $30 honorarium for participants, and given a consent form to read, sign, and return. They were informed that the honorarium would be distributed at the end of the session. The session began with caregivers responding in writing to questions about demographics, the frequency of their contact with their children, and their assessment of whether the amount of contact they had was sufficient.

The first "public" question asked by the lead facilitator asked for information about their contact with their children who were in out-of-home placement, a question we chose because it was concrete and factual, not of a personal nature, thus relatively nonthreatening, and underscored the commonality among participants. In the first three focus groups, which consisted primarily of non–African American participants, the lead and assistant moderator were white. An assistant moderator participated in each group with responsibilities for monitoring the recording equipment and taking notes throughout the discussion. For the African American focus group, an African

American member of the research team served as the lead facilitator with a white assistant facilitator.

In the first three focus groups, composed primarily of non–African Americans, participants mostly stayed within the structure of the prepared questions and probes, adding details and issues that we had not anticipated. Members of the fourth group, composed solely of African American caregivers, were responsive to the initial questions but also went beyond the constraints and foci of the prepared questions. The focus of the questions was about caregiver participation when children were in out-of-home placement. However, many of the African American caregivers went outside of this boundary, discussing their concerns about the appropriate treatment and safety of their children, and questioning why out-of-home placement was necessary. The facilitators did not try to constrain or control this discussion, as it seemed entirely appropriate, and was stimulated by our questions about caregivers' roles in relation to out-of-home settings. This is consistent with the emergent process typical of qualitative research.

DATA ANALYSIS

Data Reduction and Coding

Analysis of focus group data has two basic parts: one mechanical and another interpretive. Because the four focus groups generated over 120 pages of textual data for analysis, the mechanical part of the analysis was greatly facilitated by the use of computer programs. A word processing program was used to prepare the text for entry into a qualitative analysis software program, the Ethnograph (Seidel, Friese, & Leonard, 1995). The choice of a specific software program is based on the kind of project, database, and analysis being used (Weitzman & Miles, 1995). Since our interest was in description and conceptual ordering, and not theory development, we chose a program particularly suited for detailed, line-by-line multiple code applications that would allow overlap or nest-coded "chunks" (the ranges of text that codes are applied to). Ethnograph offered a more efficient way of coding than a word processing program and had the benefit of providing a visual schema of the nested codes. In retrospect, we felt the minimal amount of time spent learning Ethnograph was well worth the benefits we gained from its use.

A major issue was how to reduce the data to a more manageable form that would allow us to discover themes and relationships in the data. The interpretive part of analysis involves determining the criteria for organizing the textual data into useful segments, and the subsequent search for patterns within these subdivisions to draw meaningful conclusions (Knodel, 1993). Codes are terms related to a verbal episode; most often our episodes were a phrase or several sentences, but some were entire paragraphs. The interview questions provided the basis for the a priori themes or initial categories used in our codebook, and we treated them as tentative and subject to redefinition. Our codes were organized hierarchically, with subthemes collapsed under larger themes.

Coding began with all the research team members reading and independently coding portions of the transcripts. We then met to compare our independent coding and agree on common codes and definitions. Multiple research team members would once again independently read a sample of the transcripts and code it with an updated version of the codebook. This process was continued with further refining until we reached saturation, at which point additional coding was confirming our codebook and all incidents could be readily classified. As we proceeded with the analysis, we identified themes that were not originally incorporated into the interview guide but nevertheless arose, and were subsequently added to the codebook and included in the analysis.

One example from the African American focus group was the concern that parents raised about actual or perceived misuse or overuse of medication with their child. While none of the project staff had read anything in the literature to this effect, a review of the psychopharmacology research literature revealed that indeed there was evidence for differential effects with African Americans. These issues fell outside of our coding scheme, with its focus on parent participation. Since medication concerns did not fit within the classifications used in the initial version of the codebook, an additional category titled "Issues" was added, along with various subcategories of parental concern with the quality of treatment, and was included in the revised codebook. This example illustrates an advantage of qualitative approaches to research: participants' ideas and experiences are allowed to emerge, unconstrained by the specificity of structured questions. A second example from the African American respondents was the concern expressed by a number of family members about their child's safety while in the residential facility. Safety was an important issue to them, but one that did not fit into our coding scheme with its primary focus on barriers and supports to family participation. Once again, another subcategory was added to the codebook.

The researchers performed an analysis very similar to the procedures outlined by Strauss and Corbin (1990). We began the analysis process with a provisional list of codes that were drawn from the interview guide. For example, the first question in the interview guide asked about the kinds of contact participants had while their children were in out-of-home treatment. Our initial codebook included "visiting" as a category with subcategories for setting (facility, home, off-campus), and distinguished between two types of facility visits: controlled, in which agency staff regulates the timing and/or frequency of visiting, and flexible, in which family members have input on the timing and/or frequency of visiting. It was not until we had coded a good deal of the transcripts that other codes emerged as important aspects of visiting. An example of one such property attribute was whether family visits at the treatment facility were integrated into the treatment milieu or occurred only in a designated visiting area isolated from staff and other residents and families.

The next stage in the analysis was making connections between parental experiences and race, with the aim of understanding the unique behaviors, attitudes, and feelings that African American family members had toward their experience of involvement in their child's residential treatment.

EVALUATING QUALITATIVE RESEARCH

The criteria to be used to assess rigor is a hotly contested issue by researchers of varying paradigmatic stances. Positivists and postpositivists posit an external reality that can be observed and described and in which the researcher is a neutral observer who gathers data, whereas constructivists assume that there are multiple social realities and that knowledge is not discovered but created by the observer (Padgett, 1998). While validity, random sampling, reliability, and generalizability are useful strategies to increase rigor in quantitative research, trustworthiness standards have been developed by qualitative researchers to evaluate the validity of qualitative study findings and how they are reported. Threats to credibility and trustworthiness can be grouped under three broad headings: reactivity, researcher bias, and respondent bias (Padgett, 1998). Analytic triangulation, or the use of multiple coders to ensure the categories and themes, was one strategy that we used. An audit trail including descriptions of the iterative processes of data collection, coding, and interpretation provided further safeguards.

The racial diversity of the research team included costs and benefits. The presence of an ethnically diverse research team to develop codes and code the transcripts probably helped to increase the extent to which family members perceptions' were accurately reflected. While helping neutralize potential group identification bias, the team's diversity also increased the amount of time needed to reach agreements and complete the data analysis. Pilot testing the questions with family members, having moderators culturally similar to focus group participants, and situating the groups in a location that was welcoming and comfortable were also important. Our subsequent presentations of focus group findings at the Federation of Families annual conference, which included focus group participants, was a form of member checking that enhanced the trustworthiness of the data analysis; for one of the two presentations, a participant from the African American focus group was a copresenter with members of the research team. However, focus group members did not read the analysis, and we cannot assume that other African American members shared the same perspective on the results as the African American focus group member who was a copresenter.

Reliability

In this study, we were particularly interested in providing exploratory information that could aid in the development and conceptualization of a survey instrument. While duplication of results was not important, it was important that research team members shared the same understanding of codes, and that sufficient detail was provided in the write-up that the research process could be replicated. Intercoder reliability was calculated using this formula: reliability = number of agreements/total number of agreements + disagreements (Miles & Huberman, 1994). Project staff involved in coding included project investigators as well as research associates. The fact that some project staff had family members who had been in out-of-home treatment added a source of expertise that supported all coders' willingness to disagree and not feel pressure to conform.

Sampling

In exploratory studies, the quality of the study is not determined by the size or randomness of the sample, as the research goal is not to generalize but rather to go into depth with a small number of people. Thus, qualitative research seeks to compose a group of people who have something in common, and to include individuals who are "information-rich" (Krueger & Casey, 2000). The addition of a fourth focus group targeted for the purpose of increasing the sample's persons of color is an example of theoretical sampling, in which the characteristics of the sample are determined as the study progresses. Though this study would have benefited from having focus groups comprised of respondents from other ethnic groups, the grant timeline and budget did not allow additional focus groups.

Reflexivity

Analysis and interpretation of qualitative data require the researchers to continually question their interpretations. Within qualitative research, reflexivity, or the ability to examine oneself, is a major way of addressing the impact of social factors that can impinge on a study (Adamson & Donovan, 2002). In this study, it was particularly important to consider through the reflexive process the impact of race. Researchers need to be able to identify their taken-for-granted knowledge, and be open to studying what they are no longer aware of. Having a diverse research staff involved in coding (which included African American, Native American, and white members) was particularly valuable. The fact that the team also included individuals who had experience with a family member receiving out-of-home mental health treatment, and represented varied disciplines (education and social work), were also helpful in considering diverse and alternative explanations.

One example of the reflexive process is related to the research team's discussion of the use of terminology; in one instance, for example, whether to use the word "stereotyping" or "racism" as a subheading. African American family members described incidents in which they perceived that staff treated their children and them negatively because of race. A definition of racism is any attitude, action, institutional structure, or social policy that subordinates persons or groups because of their color. Stereotyping is defined as having inaccurate, preconceived notions that are held about all people who are members of a particular group—for example, racial, religious, or sexual stereotyping (Sue, 2003). All members of the research team ended up agreeing that either term would be an accurate description, and that it was important not to minimize family members' experience. However, our shared goal of creating more family-friendly practices in out-of-home treatment ultimately led to deciding to use the term "stereotyping," because we believed that journal readers would be more open to the study findings.

Another decision around language was how to refer to the race of the study participants. Generally, research studies use "white and black" or "white and nonwhite," with the white sample serving as the norm. Because the major focus of this article was African Americans, we made a conscious decision to refer to other groups as non–African American, and by doing so, not refer to white as the norm.

While the coinvestigators for this study had published in a wide range of venues, neither had experienced the degree of difficulty they faced in getting this manuscript into print. We first sent the manuscript to a well-respected interdisciplinary journal, and received very divergent reviews. One reviewer adamantly stated that there was nothing in the study findings that was not already known; a second reviewer recommended some minor revisions and areas for reorganization. The editor chose to reject the paper. When this manuscript was submitted to a second journal, one reviewer described the analysis as "exceptionally rigorous" and noted that the study "could make an invaluable contribution to improving the quality of care provided to African American families," whereas another reviewer characterized the study as a "very elementary representation of an exploratory qualitative investigation" and was particularly critical of the sample size.

Literature that addresses the lack of research about ethnic minorities suggests that our experience is not unique. Cox (1990), in a survey of management scholars who had written on race or ethnicity, found that researchers from both minority and majority groups had frequently experienced pressure not to do such research, albeit for different reasons. The majority of the survey respondents believed that methodological obstacles, including the need for using qualitative designs and sample-size issues, increased the difficulty of conducting and publishing such research. Cox (1990) suggests that reviewers' unfamiliarity with the relevant research and high levels of personal bias in the review process relate to the lack of consensus on acceptable methods, thus hampering publication on race and ethnic issues in management journals. Sue (1999) posits that the difficulties of doing such research, together with psychology's overemphasis on internal as opposed to external validity, has hindered the development of ethnic minority research.

Generalizability

Our focus groups allowed us to identify important variations in family members' perceptions of their involvement in residential treatment. However, our study design was not intended to identify the distribution of these opinions, issues, and meaning in the target population. A more useful concept would seem to be that of transferability.

Transferability is considered to be the parallel to the positivistic concept of generalizability, except that the reader, not the researcher, decides if the results can be applied to a second situation

(Krueger & Casey, 2000). Thus, we were not conducting a study in order to generalize our findings to the larger population of parents whose children have received mental health services in out-of-home treatment settings. Instead, we were interested in providing "thick description" (sufficiently detailed information about participants' experiences), so that readers can make their own judgments about the relevance or applicability of the findings for their situation.

LESSONS LEARNED

The lessons gained from these focus groups ranged from very practical issues to important conceptual and methodological matters. Beginning with the practical, we learned a great deal about managing the microphones and audio recording when serving food. One obvious lesson is to avoid crunchy food, and ask participants to keep paper shuffling and other noise to a minimum. We used an "omni-mike" that picked up the contributions of participants without the need to raise their voices unnaturally, but it also recorded noises such as crunching of celery and corn chips.

Recruitment

While many qualitative studies using focus groups recruit respondents through impersonal means, we believe that the personalized recruitment strategy was crucial to having a sufficient number of focus group members. Over half of the focus group members had personally met or heard one of the study's principal investigators speak. In addition, the Federation chapter staff who were contacted by project staff and asked to invite prospective group members were known to each of the group members. We do not believe the focus group research (particularly the African American focus group) could have been done without those family members having a relationship with the Federation chapter staff, a conclusion shared by other researchers who have conducted focus groups with marginalized populations (Jarrett, 1993). Such an approach to recruitment does raise questions of selection bias, and of how focus group participants may vary from other parents experiencing the same situation.

Sampling

Our experience with this study led to a heightened appreciation of the importance of maintaining a flexible approach to the sampling frame, allowing the characteristics of the sample to be determined as the study progresses. Retrospectively, it is apparent to us that the fourth focus group was more fruitful and focused because it was composed of family members who shared a common background and culture. A key assumption of the focus group literature is that individuals with common concerns and experiences will be more willing to share viewpoints and disclose personal information (Jarrett, 1993). It is difficult to imagine trying to collect and understand the experiences of a group that was more diverse than the African American focus group. Future studies should include focus groups of parents from a variety of cultural and ethnic backgrounds, as well as participants who represent a broader range of class and income categories.

New Knowledge

In addition to learning a great deal about parents' perceptions, responses, and feelings about their experience with residential treatment, we also gained new knowledge about current practices in out-of-home care settings. From the first three focus groups, the issue of "contingencies"—that is, contact of children and parents being dependent on the behavior of the children, their peers, or their parents—was a concept that we had been aware of, but had not known was so widespread. Another phenomenon that surprised the research team was the apparently still-widespread practice of restricting contact between children and their families when they entered the treatment program "for a period of adjustment," despite the fact that this practice is rooted in outdated theory, and that contemporary practice emphasizes family involvement. The open-ended questions used in the group interviewing allowed the emergence of these findings that were not originally the focus of study.

Our experience in conducting this research underscored the importance of researchers being open not only to the feelings and experiences of participants but also to new information that they may contribute. As Rapp et al. (1994) note, "We must be willing to elevate consumers from the role of client to the roles of teacher and partner in a collective learning enterprise."

REFERENCES

Adamson, J., & Donovan, J. L. (2002). Research in black and white. *Qualitative Health Research, 12,* 816–825.

Cox, T. (1990). Problems with research by organizational scholars on issues of race and ethnicity. *Journal of Applied Behavioral Science, 26,* 5–23.

Farquhar, C. (1999). Are focus groups suitable for "sensitive" topics? In R.S. Barbour, & J. Kitzinger (Eds.), *Developing focus group research: Politics, theory and practice* (pp. 47–63). London: Sage Publications.

Jarrett, R. (1993). Focus group interviewing with low-income minority populations: A research experience. In D. L. Morgan (Ed.), *Successful focus groups: Advancing the state of the art* (pp. 184–201). Newbury Park, CA: Sage Publications.

Knodel, J. (1993). The design and analysis of focus group studies. In D. L. Morgan (Ed.), *Successful focus groups: Advancing the state of the art* (pp. 35–50). Newbury Park, CA: Sage Publications.

Krueger, R. A., & Casey, M. A. (2000). *Focus groups: 3rd Ed. A practical guide for applied research.* Newbury Park, CA: Sage Publications.

Miles, M. B., & Huberman, A. M. (1994). *Qualitative data analysis: An expanded sourcebook.* Thousand Oaks, CA: Sage Publications.

Padgett, D. (1998). *Qualitative methods in social work research: Challenges and rewards.* Thousand Oaks, CA: Sage.

Rapp, C. A., Kisthardt, W., Gowdy, E., & Hanson, J. (1994). Amplifying the consumer voice: Qualitative methods, empowerment, and mental health research. In E. Sherman, & W. J. Reid (Eds.), *Qualitative research in social work* (pp. 381–395). New York: Columbia University Press.

Seidel, J., Friese, S., & Leonard, D. (1995). *The Ethnograph v 4.0: A user's guide.* Amherst, MA: Qualis Research Associates.

Strauss, A., & Corbin, J. (1990). *Basics of qualitative research: Grounded theory procedures and techniques.* Newbury Park, CA: Sage Publications.

Sue, D. W. (2003). *Overcoming our racism: The journey to liberation.* San Francisco: John Wiley and Sons.

Sue, S. (1999). Science, ethnicity and bias: Where have we gone wrong? *American Psychologist, 54,* 1070–1077.

Weitzman, E. A., & Miles, M. B. (1995). *Computer programs for qualitative data analysis.* Thousand Oaks, CA: Sage Publications.

APPENDIX A: FOCUS GROUP FACT SHEET

Focus Groups
Family Participation in Residential Treatment Programs
(Scheduled at the Federation of Families Annual Meeting November 11 & 12, 1994)

WHO IS SPONSORING THESE GROUPS? The groups are sponsored by the Research and Training Center on Family Support and Children's Mental Health at Portland State University, Portland, Oregon. Barbara Friesen and Jean Kruzich are the principal investigators for the research project, and will serve as facilitators for the focus groups.

WHAT IS THE PURPOSE OF THESE GROUPS? The meetings are being held to gather information for a study of parent/family member participation in residential treatment. We want to hear from family members about a variety of issues having to do with their involvement while their children are in residential care. The information will be used to design a questionnaire and interviews to be used in a study of residential programs.

WHO SHOULD PARTICIPATE? Family members whose children are or have been in a residential treatment program to address emotional, behavioral, or mental problems. Each group will consist of 6-8 family members; preferably people who don't know each other and whose children have not been in the same residential programs.

HOW WILL THE GROUPS WORK? The facilitators will give a short introduction, and then ask group members to discuss 4-5 questions, sharing their experiences and ideas. The sessions will be tape-recorded, and then transcribed (typed) so that the facilitators (Barbara and Jean) can carefully review what group members have to say. All information will be reported anonymously. We will want to use members' exact words in our report, but will not identify who said what, nor list who the members of the focus groups were.

WHERE WILL THE GROUPS BE HELD? HOW LONG WILL THEY TAKE? OTHER DETAILS? The focus groups will be held in the conference coordinator's suite (Scott Bryant-Comstock). We'll leave you a message at the conference hotel once we know the room number. We'll also give you a short information sheet to complete and bring to the meeting. Each group will take one and one-half hours. Refreshments will be provided. Each group participant will be paid $30.00 at the end of the focus group session.

HOW CAN I FIND OUT MORE ABOUT HOW THIS INFORMATION IS USED? Group members can ask to be sent a copy of any reports or articles that are produced using the focus group information. In addition, participants who are willing to review and comment on copies of the study questionnaire or interview guide will be invited to do so.

WHAT IF I HAVE OTHER QUESTIONS? Through Thursday afternoon (November 10, 1994) call Barbara Friesen (503) 725-4166 or Katie Schultze (503) 725-4159. From Thursday evening through the rest of the Federation Annual Meeting, call Barbara Friesen at the conference hotel.

APPENDIX B: FOCUS GROUP INTRODUCTION
AND FOCUS GROUP QUESTIONS AND PROBES

FAMILY PARTICIPATION IN RESIDENTIAL TREATMENT
(90 MINUTES)

Introduction. We are Jean Kruzich and Barbara Friesen from the Research and Training Center on Family Support and Children's Mental Health in Portland, Oregon. We're getting ready to do a study about parents' involvement in residential treatment programs for their children. That study will look at current ways that families participate, and identify ways that programs can support family involvement. Your first-hand experience will be of great help to us in figuring out what questions we should be asking, and what we should find out more about.

Meeting together in a group like this allows us to learn a lot because we can get so many ideas at once. We have four main questions that we'd like you to discuss; Jean and I will keep quiet for the most part, except to clarify something. Your ideas may be similar about some issues, and different in other ways, and that's great—we want to hear what all of you have to say. As you know, we're tape-recording the session, and we'll have someone type out the recording so we can read it very carefully. So when you speak, please begin by identifying yourself (e.g., "This is Barbara") for the typist.

As we said, there are four questions to discuss in about an hour (15 minutes each, more or less). Questions? Let's begin by introducing yourselves—give your name, and say how long your child was in residential treatment.

1. **First, we'd like to hear about the contact you had with your child when s/he was in residential treatment.**

   - What kind of contact did you have? (Visits to facility, home visits, letters, phone, etc.)
   - Who decided how much contact you and your child had?
   - Did this change over time?

2. **In what ways were you involved with your child's education and treatment while s/he was in residential treatment?**

   - Planning, implementing, evaluating services
   - Treatment for yourself or family
   - What about decisions about daily issues, e.g., clothing, diet, religious preferences, cultural practices, privileges, chores?
   - What was the most important aspect of your involvement?

3. **What did residential staff/program do to support your involvement?**

4. **Were there things that made it difficult for you to be involved as much as you wanted to be?**

   - Related to your own circumstances (e.g., distance, geography, culture, finances, religion)?
   - Related to residential program (e.g., visiting hours, policy on parent contact/involvement, other)?

5. **In addition to involvement in your child's treatment, did you have involvement/ input in other ways?**

   ■ How? (advisory committee, parent meetings, meetings with administrator)

   ■ How did agency support?

   ■ Barriers? (any special circumstances—e.g., transition into specific neighborhoods, rites of passage, others)

   ■ Were you able to influence the program to reflect your family or community's culture (food, holidays, customs, religion)?

6. **If you could make one change in the way families are involved in residential treatment, what would it be?**

15

Social Patterns of Substance-Use among People with Dual Diagnoses

Hoyt Alverson, Marianne Alverson, and Robert E. Drake

INTRODUCTION

Impairment in social functioning is a central feature of substance-use disorder. Diagnostic criteria specify that use of a substance becomes problematic when normal social activities are altered or reduced (American Psychiatric Association, 1994). For people with severe mental illness, several studies indicate that co-occurring substance disorder is associated with increased family problems and disruption in familial living arrangements (Blankertz & Cnaan, 1994; Dixon, McNary, & Lehman, 1995; Kashner *et al.,* 1991; McHugo, Paskus, & Drake, 1993; Test, Wallish, Allness, & Ripp, 1989; Westermeyer & Walzer, 1975). Loss of familial support may be catastrophic for this population because they often live with marginal social, financial, and other resources. For example, studies suggest that loss of familial support may lead to homelessness or incarceration (Caton *et al.,* 1994; Clark, 1996).

At the same time, substance abuse and dependence often take place in social contexts, with peers facilitating and reinforcing use. For persons with severe mental illness, several studies show that substance-use is social and that patients report socializing as a primary motivator for use (Bergman & Harris, 1985; Dixon, Haas, Weiden, Sweeney, & Frances, 1991; Hekimian & Gershon, 1968; Mueser, Nishith, Tracy, DeGirolamo, & Molinaro, 1995; Test *et al.,* 1989; Warner *et al.,* 1994). For example, Warner *et al.* (1994) found that "activity with friends" was the most commonly reported reason for substance-use among outpatients with severe mental illness.

Clinicians commonly express concern that psychiatric patients are abandoning needed familial supports in favor of antisocial, drug-abusing peer groups that take advantage of these patients because of their disability payments and hasten their slide into homelessness or incarceration. Despite these concerns, there have been few detailed studies of the social networks of individuals with dual

From Alverson, H., Alverson, M., Drake, R. E. (2001). Social patterns of substance-use among people with dual diagnoses. *Mental Health Services Research, 3,* 3–14. Reprinted with permission of the publisher.

diagnosis. Trumbetta, Mueser, Quimby, Bebout, and Teague (1999) examined network data on homeless dually diagnosed patients in Washington, DC, and found that having fewer addicts and more AA/NA members in one's social networks predicted recovery from substance-use disorder.

The purpose of this report is to present ethnographic data supplemented with certain of those obtained in formal surveys and interviews, which reveal important variations in features of study participants' social networks. More specifically, we attempt in this paper to suggest answers to the following questions. What is the social context of these individuals' substance-abusing behaviors? Are there distinctive social patterns of use? How do dually diagnosed individuals relate to peers, families, and mental health clinicians? What are the implications of the findings for clinical services?

ETHNOGRAPHIC METHOD

The etiology, prognosis, and treatment of mental illness have long been known to exhibit economic, social group, as well as (sub-) cultural effects. For this reason ethnographic research among the mentally ill has become an important and well-justified domain of research in the health sciences (Alverson, Alverson, Drake, & Becker, 1998; Alverson, Becker, & Drake, 1995; Estroff, 1981, 1991; Romanucci-Ross, Moerman, & Tancredi, 1997). Much of this work draws inspiration, method, and epistemology from the cross-cultural study of personality, cognition, and psychopathology (Berry, 1992; Cole, 1996; Dasen, 1988; Kleinman, 1980; Verma & Bagley, 1988).

Ethnography has been a favored method of inquiry where little is known of the cultural milieu and social group structure among people being investigated, or where there is a desire to document the ways in which people talk about, and bestow meaning upon, events in their lives. A subject's personal and sociocultural situatedness or perspective is often accessible only by combining direct observation with discourse recorded in specific settings or contexts (Fetterman, 1989; Jorgensen, 1989; Spradley, 1980).

Unfortunately for much research, most people, most of the time behave or act in a state of half-conscious awareness of their behavior. The cognitive and emotive meanings, the reasons for and purposes of behavior, usually "become clear" to any person in retrospect, when one thinks or tells about it. Such retrospective self-narration supplies characteristic "meaning" (reasons, justifications, motives, and goals) that may well have not been (consciously) operative at the time of the action. "Storied experience" (what people come to believe about their behavior as a function of how it is cast in verbal performances or self-reflection) is often at variance with contemporaneous cognizing of actual behavior. And yet, it is often such storied experience that later guides or informs actual subsequent thought or action. For these reasons, participation in, and observation of, ongoing lives and interviewing about past events together provide a potentially rich or "thick description" of one's lived-world and storied self-identity (Geertz, 1973; Kleinman, 1988; McAdams, 1993; Rosenwald & Ochberg, 1992; Sarbin, 1986).

In the study reported here the principal field ethnographer, M. Alverson, established a welcome acceptance not only among study participants but also among numerous others—their families, friends, and associates. These others provided independent and valuable information from many and varied perspectives about study participants, thereby enriching, augmenting, qualifying, or contextualizing participants' own testimony and action. This kind of consensual validation of one's thoughts and actions are not obtainable by survey interviewing of randomly selected individuals from heterogeneous population aggregates. The ethnographer became a regular, intimate, but unobtrusive participant in their day-to-day lives following these clients and others on a regular basis for 2 years. She shared with them activities and experiences at many of their regular haunts engaging in observation, conversation, and informal interviewing in the many real-world contexts and settings in which their lives, including mental illness and substance abuse, are situated and expressed.

The willingness of these clients (and others) to participate in this ethnography, to part with valuable information, and to reveal intimate aspects of their lives, could only occur if two conditions were met: (1) a relationship of trust and mutual confidence between ethnographer and study participants were built, and (2) they came to feel a genuine equity in the valued outcomes exchanged between them and the ethnographer. The ethnographer met these conditions by participating in clients' daily lives primarily on terms and conditions of reciprocity negotiated with or set down by them (Denzin, 1989; Ferrell & Hamm, 1998; Jorgensen, 1989; Judd, Smith, & Kidder, 1991).

THE NEW HAMPSHIRE DUAL DIAGNOSIS STUDY
AND ETHNOGRAPHIC SUBSTUDY

The New Hampshire Dual Diagnosis Study, built upon a statewide treatment system put in place in 1988, was designed to assess, by randomized clinical trial, the clinical and cost effectiveness of two treatment regimes among dually diagnosed clients (Drake *et al.,* 1998). The clinical trial compared patient outcomes from two treatments: (1) integrated and coordinated mental health services delivered by "assertive community treatment" (ACT) and (2) standard case management. A total of 223 such persons (57 women, 166 men) from two cities and five small towns in New Hampshire were assigned randomly to one of the two treatments. The study participants were interviewed and evaluated regularly (every 6 months) by structured interview-questionnaire over the course of the next 3 years. Results of the clinical trial have been previously reported (Clark *et al.,* 1998; Drake *et al.,* 1998). Because of the small number of participants in the ethnographic substudy and because the ethnography was concluded 3 years before completion of the clinical trials, the ethnography did not attempt to evaluate outcome differences.

Data collection in the larger study—in addition to that obtained in the ethnography—consisted of baseline and semiannual follow-up administration of the following formal instruments and schedules (Drake *et al.,* 1998):

a. Structured Clinical Interview for *DSM-III-R* to establish severe mental illness and co-occuring substance-use disorder;

b. Portions of the Uniform Client Data Inventory to obtain basic demographic information;

c. The Time-Line Follow-Back to assess days of alcohol or drug-use or both over the 6 months prior to baseline;

d. Sections of the Addiction Severity Index to assess abuse and dependency;

e. A self-reported chronology of housing history and institutional stays supplemented with official records thereof;

f. The Quality of Life Interview—a "subjective" and "objective" representation of perceived quality of life;

g. The Expanded Brief Psychiatric Rating Scale to assess current symptom expression;

h. Service Utilization Interview to assess utilization of health services.

Follow-up interviews utilized the same instruments except for (b) and sections of other instruments dealing with past life-history information. These instruments were supplemented by case managers' assessments of clients, using the following rating scales: (a) the Alcohol Use Scale, (b) the Drug Use Scale, (c) the Substance Abuse Treatment Scale. Regular testing of urine for substance-use also took place.

Although these instruments elicited a great quantity of information with satisfactory reliability (some of which we report later), they did not reveal in detail or with contextual richness many important aspects of the social context and social functions of substance-use and many other activities of clients' daily lives. By way of brief illustration, one client reported, in response to questions contained in a formal interview, that he had been employed by his brother during a portion of the study period. This response was coded in the database as "kin support" and "gaining employment." Further the client reported not using drugs. The ethnographic study documented clearly that the brother in question was (is) one of the city's known drug dealers, who was employing his SMI-SUD afflicted brother as a mule in the drug operation, and was paying him in part with drugs. The brother did have a lawn care business, which to some extent, was a front for the drug operation. The client stated that he was working for his brother in that business. In this case, as in many others, we see that a simple response to a seemingly straightforward interview question entails a seriously misleading implication or intentional deception about the nature and purpose of this reported "employment."

More generally, the matrix of social relationships and social activities within which substance-use is couched is a complex structure of action. Clients do not typically carry around in their heads detailed or accurate characterizations of this structure as a whole or how its constituents fit together. Similarly, clients' tacit knowledge of the social contexts of their substance-use is not readily accessible to introspection or propositional expression. Moreover, respondents often do not give full or candid answers to questions, even to those few, which they could in principle answer, when asked face-to-face to disclose information that may contain adverse personal or social demands.

Standardized instruments use prompting questions and answer codings that are decontextualized and usually very general. Asking good, probative, nuanced, yet acceptable questions of someone about individual social relationships and activities requires, in addition to good rapport, detailed knowledge of social context and of biography. So, to augment and enrich the intertemporal method of the interviews and administration of formal instruments, an ethnographic study of a small subsample of this study population located in one city was planned and carried out over 2 years, 1990–92. During this time 19 clients of the 223 included in the larger study were selected by means of a combination of "accidental" and "purposive" sampling procedures (Judd, Smith, & Kidder, 1991) to be participants in the ethnographic substudy. During the 2 years one died of substance abuse and three others dropped out. Of 15 client/informants officially still in the study at the end of the 2-year period, eleven are male, four female. Because of the sample size and the nature of the data collected we do not seek to generalize the findings to some larger population. Rather, we present the findings as data, which can validly motivate further study and sensitize clinicians to issues of clients' social world that have so far not come to light in other research.

The ethnography collected considerable data that bear on and reveal important aspects of clients' substance-use, including especially the sites and activities of their social networks in general and the composition and activities of their substance-use networks, in particular. The latter provided opportunities conducive to obtaining information on study participants' proffered motivations for using addictive substances as well as their claimed abilities or inability to control or want to quit their use. The ethnography, in short, examined important *social functions* of substance-use.

SOCIAL PATTERNS OF SUBSTANCE-USE

Among the clients participating in the ethnography and among dozens of others informally observed, the social organization or patterning of an individual's substance-use was found to fall into one (or sometimes two) of four distinct, different, and usually mutually exclusive types. Further, how clients perceived and responded to case managers' entreaties to quit using or to clinical interventions in general were observed to differ with each social pattern of use, mainly because of the varying social resources associated with each pattern, which variably support, constrain, or discourage substance-use.

The discourse presented later is in clients' own words extracted from conversations, some of which were held within, and some outside the settings of substance-use. None of the reported conversation was elicited in structured interviews. The quotes often composed portions or aspects of clients' "life stories," which typically "dribbled" out in informal chats, which took place over many months in many settings. Limitations of space preclude even sketching the larger life-stories from which the quoted material is taken. Likewise the ethnographer's observations of clients' and others' behavior cannot be included in this brief report. All of these together—observation, dialog, life-stories—should and will in later publications be woven into an integrated description of clients' life-worlds. Meanwhile we present the conversational data to indicate from the clients' situation and perspective something about the social patterns of substance-use.

Pattern One

"The Solitary User," comprises those whose addictive substance of choice is alcohol. These are loners who prefer to drink as their budget allows, rarely, if ever, sharing or reciprocating over time with other clients in the mental health center. Among the study participants these are the clients for whom social intercourse in general seems to be daunting or difficult.

> People at the Mental Health Center don't like me 'cause I don't bum anything off them. They're always hitting me up for cigarettes. I try not to, but I give it to them anyway. I try not to bum off them, but they still come bumming to me!

Hoarding resources, these clients are more likely than are other users to refuse formal contact with the mental health center. Repeatedly they claim being misunderstood or not listened to by mental health professionals. They resent case managers who concentrate treatment solely or largely on sobriety because it does not address their "real problems."

> X (the case manager) is happy if I don't drink, then he thinks everything is OK. He's not concerned with the real issue, my depressions. They come whether I drink or not. There's nothing I can do about it. The meds don't help. X makes no attempt to understand me. He doesn't listen to me. He only has one focus.

Avoiding case managers and group therapy, these clients do not deny the need for therapy, frequently wishing they could afford private care.

> I don't like them (case managers) coming around. I don't like going to group. The others always talk. They're smarter than me. I'm a burnout. I'd rather have private therapy.

Although some of these clients may have experimented with drugs, they generally prefer alcohol, fearing the illegality of drug use and contacts with drug users.

There are too many drug users at AA meetings. I think that's a bad trend. There's a big difference between drink and drugs. Drugs are illegal. Drug users are criminals—dangerous. I don't want to be near them.

Typically, if these clients run out of funds for liquor before their next paycheck, they eat at soup kitchens and may in a few cases appeal to certain others (typically not fellow addicts) for extra cash. Without such extra support, however, use is usually heavier at the beginning of the month when they receive SSI/SSDI or other payments. Clients typically endure a dry spell at the end of the month, attending AA meetings, while waiting for the next monthly check. Many clients point to such a dry spell as proof of their ability to control use.

I bought a six pack and two quarts of wine. I'll go to AA when I'm out [of liquor].

If there is regular family support, which includes cash or groceries, the client is more likely to be able to continue drinking throughout the month. With such extra financial resources, these clients confine themselves to their room, discontinue picking up their medication, and switch from beer to hard liquor. Because of their relative social isolation, they admit to putting themselves at greater risk of injury or even dying from intoxication.

If I don't get it (medication), I'm more likely to go on a vodka binge, and vodka is my undoing.

When such an escalation of liquor consumption occurs, these clients are unlikely to contact case managers for help, because they resent or fear sobriety-talk, which in their minds is about issues separate from what causes their binge drinking.

They have a one-track approach: sobriety first. Sobriety is defined as NO drinks. There is no difference between these two or three beers I'm drinking now and vodka. For me there IS a difference. Vodka is my undoing, not these few beers.

The only client to die from substance abuse during the 2-year study had no financial constraints and drank alone. Locking herself up in her room with hard liquor, she refused all contacts with her case manager.

I feel suicidal when I drink. I don't want to be here. Nothing really makes a difference. I feel this way all the time.

Pattern Two

"The Street Corner Clique," comprises those clients who are members of a small substance-use social network (outside the mental health center) based in the neighborhood, bar, or residential setting. This pattern is observed with regular alcohol use and occasionally marijuana. Clients share, in addition to addictive substances, numerous other material items and social transactions with a small group of friends or acquaintances, who may or may not themselves be psychiatric patients. Substance-use is only one among many resources and activities that they enjoy together as a group.

Client: [speaking with ethnographer while sitting with friends in her local bar] *We play cards, tell stories. We take trips, go on picnics with the dues of members. In this club you have "Gemeinschaft" not just "Gesellschaft."* ["Gemeinschaft" means "face-to-face group/community"; "Gesellschaft" means "anonymous social system." Clearly this client is very well educated.]

Ethnographer: *Is this the only place you feel it?*

Client: *Yes. I have no family, and there certainly is none at mental health or the SRO* [abstinence-oriented, mental health housing where she lives]. *And T* [her case manager] *wouldn't come here. He hasn't even seen it, and he doesn't approve.*

Pointing to their small group's limited financial resources as proof, clients in this pattern refer to themselves as "in control." In such a small network, one member's decision to try sobriety reduces the liquor funds for the group as a whole. Members have all had pressures to slow down or stop drinking, so they respect another member's abstinence efforts by not offering drinks, waiting for the urge for sobriety to pass. With the loss of a member, the individuals in a smaller group may feel more vulnerable or insecure in their habit, and may wrestle with questions of sobriety themselves. Those clients, who were observed to move from Pattern Two use to sobriety, easily apply their considerable interpersonal skills from their substance use group to their treatment sobriety groups. The following snippets of conversation take place variously between a client in Pattern One, called here, #1; a client formerly in Pattern Two use, called here #2; and the ethnographer, M. Alverson. Notice client #2's considerable "discourse competence" (interaction management, information management, and subtle referential appositeness of contributions)

#2 [talking in the hallway with ethnographer minutes before treatment sobriety group, client interrupts the conversation to hug and greet group members as they come in.]

#2: [Turning to ethnographer] *Did you see the scratches on her arm?*

Ethnographer: *No.*

#2: *She's not suicidal but she tries to hurt herself. She has lousy self-esteem, like me. I'm trying to get her into CTT.*

Ethnographer: *Why?*

#2: *It's supposed to give more time, and she needs lots of support.*

#1 [Lone drinker after sobriety group session.] *I wanted to tell her that when you black out from drinking it means you drink too much and the more you drink, the more you're going to be in that situation. But I just couldn't speak up. I've always been shy. I was shy in school. I had a terrible stuttering problem when I was growing up, I know, though, I've got to learn to speak up.*

#2 [At the same group, #2 tried to persuade a member to drink less] *I've been able to use the money I used to drink up for things—like a TV.*

#1: *I don't like groups. They don't understand. I don't want to be around people that don't understand.*

#2 [Drawing out #1 in group.] *Remember when we were roommates at the hospital together? I didn't appreciate it then, but I sure do now—how good it was to room with you.*

No response

#2: *You were so nice. We did have good times, didn't we?*

#1: *Yeah, we made cocoa together.*

#2: *And remember when we used to talk about our children together?*

#1: *Yeah, when I held my little Sammy in my bed with me, all the bad feelings went away.*

Pattern Three

"The User Syndicate," comprises substance-users who are members of a large, thriving substance-use social network operating within and around the Mental Health Center itself. From there certain individuals go out occasionally to locate or secure resources (including information) to be shared with members as a whole. Those in this pattern consume alcohol or drugs or both and may also, along with others in the network, abusively use their medications (hoarding, stockpiling, trading, or combining pharmaceuticals with street-drugs or alcohol). All of them—clients of the Mental Health Center—boast of steady, persistent, "controlled" substance-use with minor impairment and only occasional adverse consequences for their mental health. While asserting their "controlled use," they confidently point to "limits"—that unlike some others outside their "syndicate," they would not sell off personal belongings to support their substance-use.

Y drinks all the time—buys a case of beer, keeps half of it in his refrigerator and half of it in the bedroom. He just drinks through it, then buys another case. Y is always drinking. I would never go that far. I'd never sell my stuff. People who have to sell their stuff to use! I'm not like that.

I can stop. I don't use every day. I don't sell off my stuff like some of them do.

Clients in pattern three are circumspect regarding illegal activity, engaging in no more than low-risk crime (such as shoplifting) to support their habits. At or near the Mental Health Center, they daily seek and share with each other news of locations in the city where donations or surplus commodities are being distributed to the homeless. Together they go to line up for handout food or clothing to obtain living essentials without wasting precious cash needed for addictive substances.

Because every client in the group is expected to share cigarettes and trade portions of their monthly check for substance-use, those that generously include cash windfall or gifts, meds, meals, and sex in the barter are particularly highly regarded. Clients coming in new to the Mental Health Center are actively recruited to join. Giving things and other favors away is to store social obligations against possible personal shortfalls ahead. Unilateral social exchange in effect buys one insurance. This includes steady access to drugs and alcohol. Members are prevailed upon to share whatever they can as often as possible.

I get the cocaine, share it with T, then she gives me food.

I barter as much as possible. It's more common now 'cause most people don't have money . . . the more people you know, the better off you are in life.

If you don't have money, like me, you gotta know a lot of people.

These clients view their substance-use as leading a "normal" life.

Beer's what everybody does. Look at the ads in football, it's mainstream America.

I was just going along with my friend. Coke's got nothing to do with my problems. Other people drink, go to cocktail parties and have a good time. The nurse at the hospital uses pot. I know doctors that drink. Dr. X. drinks cocktails. A lot of people enjoy themselves that way. That's what I do with cocaine. I don't see any difference. I could go cold turkey any time.

Although they themselves do not engage in high crimes to support their substance-use, they do buy small, regular amounts from those clients who, acting as couriers, bring in drugs obtained from outside dealers to the Mental Health Center. As long as these client-couriers provide drugs to the group on a regular and discrete basis, the group conceals their identity from inquiring officials and provides a hideout for those escaping the law. If, however, the client-courier escalates personal use to the point that mental illness symptoms and drug-use appear out of control, members of the group will inform on him/her to mental health personnel. This "ratting" has the effect of getting help for an out-of-control member and protecting the group from a crack-down that conspicuous behavior might invite.

Participants in this substance-use pattern have striven for sobriety for short spells. Word of this gets around fast. Because the group has multiple sources of funding, any one member's defection does not affect the group as a whole. Although a member seeking sobriety is not pressured or propositioned to join in substance-use, such a client will often be left to sit alone at a table, cut off from usual reciprocities such as cigarette swaps. In this situation a "shunned" client will spend more time at the sobriety club in the Mental Health Center where "substance abuse" is not a topic and where directed activities provide some diversion. Isolation from the usual, larger group of support and reciprocities, even if one is engaged in treatment, usually insures that such effort at sobriety is short-lived.

By avoiding detection (abetted by staying away from conspicuously illegal behavior), clients in Pattern Three have little experience with long-term periods of sobriety. Substance-use, no more and no less than picking up meds or swapping cigarettes, is how members identify the Mental Health Center. It's the place to hang out to do and get what one wants. Suffering from symptoms or stigma of mental illness, these clients feel an important connection to the Mental Health Center and the reciprocities thriving within it to satisfy their needs for acceptance in an otherwise hostile world.

> People who have mental illness tend to be more friendly. The outside world is cold. . . . You know, it makes you feel good to feel the support among the mental health clients. They show concern for each other. We all know each other. We've all been there before. I'm an alumni going into a neutral territory, a safe zone.

Pattern Four

"Entrepreneurial Substance Providers," includes those clients who take on the role of creating and maintaining the flow of alcohol and drugs for themselves and to the Pattern Three syndicate. They are actively engaged in arranging reciprocities and procuring supplies from outside and delivering alcohol and drugs to other clients. They command considerable social skills and can describe contacts they artfully make outside the Mental Health Center and the circle of those in the "mental health system" in bars, on streets, in jail. They act as liaison between mental health client users and distributors in the city.

> You have to plan it out and have some kind of strategy and that gives you something to do. It's something to keep you from getting bored, and it takes some intelligence.

> You get more friends on the outside because you have to talk to people to find it, to get it. You meet people.

Just like their case managers, these clients believe they are providing a useful service to clients, and upon occasion they boast of such accomplishments to one another and the ethnographer.

> Client [describing reasons for distributing cocaine to fellow clients]: *They oughta make it legal. What we got here is pure, powdery drugs, so it's more potent, and that's why we feel better.*

Ethnographer: *What did your case manager say when you told her you were using and selling cocaine?*

Client: *I don't know. Nothin' much. That's why she wants to see me today, but I don't feel like getting preached at. What does she know? She don't help me find a job or nothin'. There's nothin' for me to do. I got a good mind. I gotta have somethin' to do.*

These clients describe themselves as being on a "roller-coaster" existence. Persistent, escalating use leads to selling off personal belongings.

I got high off cocaine, and I wanted more, so I sold my amplifier, and then I sold my leather jacket. Now all I got left is the radio.

It also leads to multiple criminal activities, to homelessness, and eventually to hospitalization or incarceration. These clients are risk-takers and appear to be "higher functioning." They exhibit fewer side effects from medication. If they survive "hitting bottom" with drug-related violence, hospitalizations, arrests, and other traumatic experiences, they may grow weary of their roller-coaster life and risk continuing the sobriety that was forced upon them in hospital, jail, or on probation, to change their life.

I just don't want to go to prison or to hospital anymore, and the only way that'll happen is if I stop using.

Each time the ethnographer accompanied a client returning "home" from hospital or jail with determination to remain sober and "get a life," the same outcome was observed. The client received little or no support for sobriety and within days returned to the expected procuring of drugs and sharing, increasing use and dependency, until the next institutionalization.

SOCIAL PATTERNS OF USE AND REPORTED "QUALITY OF LIFE"

In Table 15.1, 16 client participants of the ethnographic study are listed along with the sites where their social networks are situated, the social pattern of their substance-use, and the relationship of the client to his/her case manager in the client's expressed opinions. (Client "0" died before the study was completed.)

As the table illustrates, there is—in this small sample anyway—a positive association between social patterning of drug use and the size and variety in the client's social networks generally. Those in Patterns Three and Four tend to belong to larger, functionally and geographically more varied social groupings than do those in substance-use Patterns One or Two. The latter have fewer and smaller social networks generally and are on the whole less gregarious and, in some cases, less socially skilled than those in Patterns Three and Four. On the other hand, the variation in the observed and self-reported quality of clients' relationships to their case managers seems to be unrelated to differences in the social pattern of substance-use. This is not surprising because case managers used the same kinds of interventions and treatments with all study clients, irrespective of their social patterns of substance-use.

The sample size here is too small to establish definitively whether there are important correlations among use networks, social networks, current or past familial ties, and satisfaction with social relationships and activities. There are however some interesting suggestive connections contained in data obtained from administration of the Quality of Life Interview (QOLI) administered as part

Table 15.1. Clients' Social Networks

Client	Site/SN[a]	SUSN[b]	Case Manager[c]
#0	7,4	1	0
#1	7,4,1	1	1
#2	7,3,4	1	3
#3	6,3	1,2	1
#4	7,3	2	2
#12	6,3,4	2	1
#5	6,1,3,2,4	3	2
#11	2,3,4,1	3	0
#13	2,3,6,4	3	0
#14	3,4,1,7	3	3
#15	2,6,4,3,1	3	0
#9	3,5,1	3,4	4
#10	2,3	3,4	4
#6	2,6,1,4,3	4	0
#7	2,3,4,1	4	2
#8	5,3,7,1	4	4

[a]Site/SN shows site of social networks, listed in order of client's observed interaction propensities: 1 = In around mental health center or other hang-outs of mentally ill in town; 2 = Substance-use hang-outs in city; 3 = Neighborhood; 4 = Site of family, spouse, children, friends; 5 = Case manager's personal world; 6 = In partner's place; 7 = In own dwelling.

[b]SUSN shows substance-use social network, given according to pattern number discussed earlier.

[c]Case Manager shows quality of client's relationship with the case manager: 0 = not engaged with case manager; 1 = reluctantly engaged; 2 = neutrally engaged; 3 = willingly engaged; 4 = closely, personally engaged.

of the larger clinical trial. Sections G and H of that schedule deal with reported family and other social interactions in terms of frequency and emotional quality. By examining client responses to questions on QOLI according to their social pattern of substance-use we may obtain information that neither method alone disclosed. We note the following suggestive trends and regularities. (Small sample size makes impossible the estimation of statistical significance.)

Among the ethnographic subsample, Pattern Four users consistently report in the QOLI interviews the least contact with family members in person or by phone, and the relatively lowest level of satisfaction with activities or relationships that they do have with family members.

Pattern One and Pattern Two users report the fewest phone calls or visits with anyone outside their own dwelling, but report the highest frequency of activity that is planned ahead of time or takes place with some one special friend (partner, lover). Pattern One users most often report having no close friends outside their home or the treatment center, and report having no friends anywhere that are *not* users. Pattern One and Two users report somewhat lower numbers of opportunities to get to know new people. But rather unexpectedly (and for reasons suggested below) clients from Pattern One claim about the same degree of overall satisfaction with the amount of friendship they enjoy in their life as do those found in the other use-patterns.

Pattern Two and Pattern Three users report the highest degree of satisfaction with how they "get along" with people in general.

Pattern Four users report having the most contact with nonusers.

But all clients report on average a similar, moderately high, degree of satisfaction with the activities they engage in with other people.

With one notable exception, there is nothing unexpected or counter-intuitive in these findings. The exception lies with those in Pattern One, who claim about the same degree of satisfaction with their social relationships and activities as do those in the other patterns. In fact the Pattern One clients in the ethnographic subsample surveyed in the QOLI interview were quite isolated. Very likely the "satisfaction" they expressed on the QOLI was based on their lack of any expectation for establishing positive social relationships. Indeed study clients and others in this use-pattern confided to the ethnographer that they despaired of making friends and having a "social life." They had no expectations of meeting and carrying on positive relations with other people. They were resigned at times to their lot, but they weren't satisfied with it. Indeed their drinking—invariably alone and to great excess—is bound up with their general expectation that they were consigned to unremitting isolation.

This information illustrates how valuable it can be to move back and forth between survey-opinion data and ethnographic observation to enable the one to contextualize and interpret the other. The meaning of the responses in this case offered by those in Pattern One can be seen in a light that would not be apparent from the survey data alone. Of course the statistical distribution of these facts would require much further study.

PATTERNS OF USE AND IMPLICATIONS
FOR TREATMENT

Obviously case managers should know what important social consequences a client will face if she/he is persuaded to stop using addictive substances, for, as noted at the outset, to start using is to change one's life and to stop using is to change one's life. Some clients reckon they are never free, always trapped no matter what.

> Whether, like me, you don't stop or whether, like P. you do stop, it's a great monolith. You can't get around it. You are either addicted, craving it, letting it rule your life OR your life purpose is to avoid it, going to meetings, collecting chips.

> If sobriety is a necessary goal to treat mental illness what assurance do I have that attaining sobriety won't lead to another dead-end. You've got to see a way out.

The ethnography discovered that, in general, the mental health service professionals at this Center did not take cognizance of the social matrix of clients' substance-use, despite the fact that for clients themselves, drug or alcohol use for those in Patterns Two, Three, and Four is experienced not simply as a relationship between oneself and an addictive substance but equally as a set of relations to other people via the consumption and sharing of these substances.

> I can't give up friends to be sober. They're talking about my family, my friends, hey, that's everybody I know.

> Cocaine is our way to have a fun time. It's our leisure time.

> I paid for the cocaine with my Friday check, and we had cocaine on the bus to Boston and again on the bus comin' home. We ate out. It was a beautiful day. We had a good time.

Early in the New Hampshire study, though the ethnography was underway, case managers employed a rigid, 12-step approach to substance abuse treatment that neglected social relationships and consequently failed to engage many clients (Noordsy, Schwab, Fox, & Drake, 1996). Only later did case managers shift to a more motivational approach, which takes more specific account of each client's personal resources, social circumstances, and goals (Miller & Rollnick, 1991). The patterns of substance-use identified in this study have several important and fairly obvious consequences for such motivational approaches to treatment.

First, clients in Pattern One are most often solitary in their substance-use and are ill-at-ease in most kinds of social activity, especially if it is forced or contrived. If they have financial means, even episodically, they are at great risk for unobserved, uncontrolled binge drinking that can or will cause serious organic damage and even death. Their aloneness, dejection or depression, difficulty to locate and to engage in therapy—particularly "group therapy"—all put them very much at risk from their substance-use. No one knows what's going on in their lives. The only ethnographic study participant to die during the study was a Pattern One user. She died, alone, drinking. Case managers who believe a client is a Pattern One user must make great efforts to monitor the client's behavior, assertively reach out to gain the client's trust and employ a one-on-one relationship to persuade and support the client in efforts to get sober.

Second, clients in Pattern Two seem to respond relatively well to group therapy. They may seek out and enjoy supportive, patterned social interaction, even that with mental health professionals. They are most at home in small groups and are often good listeners and speakers. It may be that "milieu therapy" approaches, which seek to treat people in the context of natural, already existing groups, would be most effective with those in use-Pattern Two.

Third, Pattern Three users have the most social and economic support for their substance-use and lifestyles in general. The large flexible, multifunctional, permeable network of sometime and full-time substance users permits wide and varied sharing of resources. Pattern Three networks support people who crash and help them get on their feet so they can start using again. Pattern Three networks encapsulate the client, insulating or buffering him or her from case managers' efforts to intervene and help with an addiction problem. Members provide an ideological rationalization for being a user in a using group. Clients in this pattern of use are probably on average the hardest to treat, either individually or in small groups. For one thing they are adept at conning, gaming, and denying, all with social support. Many AA and NA groups will have cynical Pattern Three users in their midst who can ruin the experience for those individuals sincerely trying to kick and stay off drugs or booze. The only Pattern Three users observed to have attained sobriety moved far away from the area where their using network was located.

Pattern Four users are on average—in the short run at least—the most socially adept and street-smart, the biggest social risk takers, those with the most get-up-and-go energy. They are, however, the most likely to get caught using, running, or procuring, and be hospitalized or jailed. Incarceration forces them into periods of sobriety and even at times into a penitent frame of mind. On these occasions they may decide that they really do not want to go back to their old bad habits or haunts. Intervention by case managers when Pattern Four users are discharged, or for other reasons hit bottom and see the light, can be key to supporting them in their vows to go straight, stay clean, or move to a new place to avoid the moral hazard of old user networks. The only participants in the ethnographic study to attain durable sobriety were former Pattern Four users, who had been forced into sobriety, moved away from their old substance-use cliques, were helped to establish themselves in a new community, and were supported in their abstinence from drugs.

CONCLUSIONS

To ask what "motivates" or "causes" an individual, whether mentally ill or not, to use or continue using drugs, or contrariwise, to stop and get a stable, abstinent life, is to ask extremely complicated questions about a person's life as a whole. This ethnography has shown that change in substance-use entails a host of emotion-laden anticipations as well as probable consequences for the material, social conditions of clients' lives. This is in addition to their perceptions of consequent psychological detriment or purely personal well-being such change might bring about.

Effective intervention by case managers to deal with clients' addiction presupposes and necessitates that the social effects and consequences of what case managers entreat clients to do be seen as integral to the process of treatment (Mueser, Drake, & Noordsy, 1998). The four social patterns of use described here are key to different clients' access to alcohol or drugs and reveal clients' predilections for social engagement, which must be satisfied in the sober state. Each pattern entails its own risks and burdens as well as important resources and opportunities for the client and for the case manager in attempting different kinds of substance abuse treatment interventions.

Finally, each social pattern of use appears to be an effective field for finding "how-to" clues on motivating and supporting sobriety. Yet, pattern of use by itself is not predictive of responsiveness to treatment or of sobriety. Although clients in Patterns Two or Four talk of sobriety more often than those in Patterns One or Three, whether they actually become abstinent or sober was observed to depend on other factors having to do with the material and emotional quality of life, which are described in a companion paper (Alverson, Alverson, & Drake, 2000).

ACKNOWLEDGMENTS

This work was supported by U.S. Public Health Service Grants MH-00839, MH-46072, and MH-47567 from the National Institute of Mental Health; by Grant AA-08341 from the National Institutes on Alcohol Abuse and Alcoholism; and also grants from the New Hampshire Division of Behavioral Health and the Mental Health Center of Greater Manchester.

REFERENCES

Alverson, H., Alverson, M., Drake, R. E., & Becker, D. R. (1998). Social correlates of competitive employment among people with severe mental illness. *Psychiatric Rehabilitation Journal, 22*(1), 34–40.

Alverson, H., Alverson, M., & Drake, R. E. (2000). An ethnographic study of the longitudinal course of substance abuse among people with severe mental illness. *Community Mental Health Journal, 36*(6), 557–569.

Alverson, M., Becker, D. R., & Drake, R. E. (1995). An ethnographic study of coping strategies used by persons with severe mental illness participating in supported employment. *Psychosocial Rehabilitation Journal, 18*, 115–128.

American Psychiatric Association. (1994). *Diagnostic and statistical manual of mental disorders.* (4th ed.). Washington, DC: Author.

Bergman, H., & Harris, M. (1985). Substance abuse among young adult chronic patients. *Psychosocial Rehabilitation Journal, 9*(1), 49–54.

Berry, J. (1992). *Cross-cultural psychology: Research and applications.* New York: Cambridge University Press.

Blankertz, L. E., & Cnaan, R. A. (1994). Assessing the impact of two residential programs for dually diagnosed homeless individuals. *Social Service Review, 68*, 536–560.

Caton, C., Shrout, P., Eagle, P., Opler, L., Felix, A., & Dominguez, B. (1994). Risk factors for homelessness among schizophrenic men: A case-control study. *American Journal of Public Health, 84*(2), 265–270.

Clark, R. E. (1996). Family support for persons with dual disorders. In R. E. Drake, & K. T. Mueser (Eds.), *Dual Diagnosis of Major Mental Illness and Substance Abuse Disorder II: Recent Research and Clinical Implications. New Directions for Mental Health Services* (Vol. 70, pp. 65–77). San Francisco: Jossey-Bass.

Clark, R. E., Teague, G. B., Ricketts, S. K., Bush, P. W., Xie, H., McGuire, T. G., Drake, R. E., McHugo, G. J., Keller, A. M., & Zubkoff, M. (1998). Cost-effectiveness of assertive community treatment versus standard case management for persons with co-occurring severe mental illness and substance use disorders. *Health Services Research, 33*(5), 1285–1308.

Cole, M. (1996). *Cultural psychology.* Cambridge: Belknap Press.

Dasen, P. R. (Ed.). (1988). *Health & cross-cultural psychology.* Newbury Park: Sage.

Denzin, N. (1989). *Interpretive interactionism.* Beverly Hills: Sage Press.

Dixon, L., Haas, G., Weiden, P. J., Sweeney, J., & Frances, A. J. (1991). Drug abuse in schizophrenic patients: Clinical correlates and reasons for use. *American Journal of Psychiatry, 143,* 224–230.

Dixon, L., McNary, S., & Lehman, A. (1995). Substance abuse and family relationships of persons with severe mental illness. *American Journal of Psychiatry, 152,* 456–458.

Drake, R. E., McHugo, G. J., Clark, R. E., Teague, G. B., Xie, H., Miles, K., & Ackerson, T. H. (1998). Assertive community treatment for patients with co-occurring severe mental illness and substance use disorder: A clinical trial. *American Journal of Orthopsychiatry, 68*(2), 201–215.

Estroff, S. (1981). *Making it crazy: An ethnography of psychiatric clients in an American community.* Berkley: University of California Press.

Estroff, S. (1991). Everybody's got a little mental illness: Accounts of illness and self among people with severe, persistent mental illnesses. *Medical Anthropology Quarterly, 5*(4), 331–369.

Ferrell, J., & Hamm, M. S. (Eds.). (1998). *Ethnography at the edge: Crime, deviance, and field research.* Boston: Northeastern University Press.

Fetterman, D. (1989). *Ethnography step by step.* Newberry Park: Sage Press.

Geertz, C. (1973). Thick description: Toward an interpretive theory of culture. In C. Geertz (Ed.),

The Interpretation of cultures (pp. 3–32). New York City: Basic Books.

Hekimian, L. J., & Gershon, S. (1968). Characteristics of drug abusers admitted to a psychiatric hospital. *Journal of the American Medical Association, 205,* 125–130.

Jorgensen, D. (1989). *Participant observation.* Beverley Hills: Sage Press.

Judd, C. M., Smith, E. R., & Kidder, L. H. (1991). *Research methods in social relations* (6th ed.). Orlando: Harcourt, Brace, Jovanovich.

Kashner, M., Rader, L., Rodell, D., Beck, C., Rodell, L., & Muller, K. (1991). Family characteristics, substance abuse, and hospitalization patterns of patients with schizophrenia. *Hospital and Community Psychiatry, 42*(2), 195–197.

Kleinman, A. (1980). Major conceptual and research issues for cultural psychiatry. *Culture, Medicine, and Psychiatry, 4*(1), 3–13.

Kleinman, A. (1988). *The illness narratives.* New York City: Basic Books.

McAdams, D. P. (1993). *Personal myths and the making of the self.* New York: Guilford Press.

McHugo, G. J., Paskus, T. S., & Drake, R. E. (1993). Detection of alcoholism in schizophrenia using the MAST. *Alcoholism: Clinical and Experimental Research, 17*(1), 187–191.

Miller, W., & Rollnick, S. (1991). *Motivational interviewing: Preparing people to change addictive behavior.* New York: Guilford Press.

Mueser, K. T., Drake, R. E., & Noordsy, D. L. (1998). Integrated mental health and substance abuse treatment for severe psychiatric disorders. *Journal of Practical Psychiatry and Behavioral Health, 4*(3), 129–139.

Mueser, K. T., Nishith, P., Tracy, J. I., DeGirolamo, J., & Molinaro, M. (1995). Expectations and motives for substance use in schizophrenia. *Schizophrenia Bulletin, 21*(3), 367–378.

Noordsy, D. L., Schwab, B., Fox, L., & Drake, R. E. (1996). The role of self-help programs in the rehabilitation of persons with severe mental illness and substance use disorders. *Community Mental Health Journal, 32,* 71–81.

Romanucci-Ross, L., Moerman, D. E., & Tancredi, L. R. (1997). *The anthropology of medicine: From culture to method* (3rd ed.). Westport, CT: Bergin & Garvey.

Rosenwald, G. G., & Ochberg, R. L. (Eds.). (1992). *Storied lives: The cultural politics of self-understanding.* New Haven: Yale University Press.

Sarbin, T. R. (Ed.). (1986). *Narrative psychology.* New York City: Praeger.

Spradley, J. K. (1980). *Participant observation.* New York City: Holt-Rinehart.

Test, M. A., Wallish, L. S., Allness, D. G., & Ripp, K. (1989). Substance use in young adults with schizophrenic disorders. *Schizophrenia Bulletin, 15*(3), 465–476.

Trumbetta, S. L., Mueser, K., Quimby, E., Bebout, R., & Teague, G. B. (1999). Social networks and clinical outcomes of dually diagnosed homeless persons. *Behavior Therapy, 30,* 407–430.

Verma, G., & Bagley, C. (1988). *Cross-cultural studies of personality.* New York: St. Martins Press.

Warner, R., Taylor, D., Wright, J., Sloat, A., Springett, G., Amold, S., & Weinberg, H. (1994). Substance use among the mentally ill: Prevalence, reasons for use and effects on illness. *American Journal of Orthopsychiatry, 64*(1), 30–39.

Westermeyer, J., & Walzer, V. (1975). Sociopathy and drug use in a young psychiatric population. *Disease of the Nervous System, 36,* 673–677.

COMMENTARY BY: Hoyt Alverson, Marianne Alverson, and Robert E. Drake

PURPOSE

This ethnography of dual diagnoses (Alverson, Alverson, & Drake, 2001) was originally conceived as a qualitative substudy within a larger quantitative study of treatments and outcomes. The ethnography was attached to a multisite randomized controlled trial (RCT) because the RCT researchers (Drake, Teague, & McHugo) believed that studying the treatment of clients with co-occurring disorders was in an exploratory stage, and that the ethnography could help to understand the treatment results and yield important hypotheses concerning phenomenology, social setting, reactions to treatment, course of recovery, nontreatment factors, and so forth. The ethnographic researchers (Alverson, Schwab, & Alverson) had great latitude to pursue emergent issues. From the beginning, they met regularly with the RCT research team to assure cross-fertilization between the two research approaches.

CONCERNS AND TRADE-OFFS IN DESIGN

At the beginning of this project, the quantitative researchers were naïve regarding ethnographic research. The ethnographers slowly educated the rest of the research team, and demonstrated the value and validity of their methods, by revealing important aspects of clients' lives and behavior not addressed in the data collection techniques of the larger quantitative study. Many of the findings, which emerged uniquely in the ethnography, were later incorporated in and corroborated by survey methods—for example, the role of parenting in coping with mental illness or substance use, and documentation of conditions associated with remission and relapse.

An early concern regarding design of the ethnography was how to handle the multisite aspect of the RCT, which was undertaken in seven separate community mental health centers. The ethnographers argued for conducting research in only one site to concentrate resources on a few participants. The quantitative researchers were concerned about the small sample and restriction to one site, which might have precluded learning about a wider range of clients and clients in other locales. The particular site selected for the ethnography had a wide range of clients, in terms of age,

Commentary on article: Alverson, H., Alverson, M., & Drake, R. E. (2001). Social patterns of substance-use among people with dual diagnosis. *Mental Health Services Research, 3,* 3–14.

sex, kinds of places lived, history of involvement with mental health services, illness diagnoses, and economic class background, but not in terms of race or ethnicity, as all were "white" Euro-Americans. The site had a large community mental health center, which welcomed and was hospitable to the study. Its location near many places frequented by clients enabled the ethnographer to efficiently establish her presence and rapport among a large group of clients, some of whom would become study participants.

METHODS

Site, Event, and Person Sampling

Ethnographers use two basic criteria to make sampling decisions. First, the ethnographer needs to get to know an individual client in his/her social world. This means accompanying the client on a daily, weekly, monthly basis. How many individuals can one get to know in this fashion? As a practical matter, one ethnographer could not likely work with more than a dozen or so clients. The principal unit that one is sampling is not only the client as an individual, but also the events and places in the client's life. This is called event and site sampling, respectively, which differ from person sampling. An ethnographer typically experiences dozens of settings, events, and social exchanges, daily, with any one client. The ethnographer is observing and participating in hundreds of events and many settings in a relatively short period of time. This sampling reveals a picture of lives as they are lived with other people, as well as alone.

This sampling approach requires establishing rapport on a community or group basis, not simply one-on-one between ethnographer and individual client. So, before selecting participants for this study, the ethnographer spent several weeks in places where clients "hang out." At first, wearing a winter jacket and old sneakers, she sat in the smoke-filled café where clients socialized, waiting to be called by case managers for groups and appointments. Thus, introductions to clients consisted of a natural "give and take" independent of the proposed research. Once selected, study participants were easy to locate and connect with through the clients' social networks; since much rapport had already been established, no clients refused the invitation to participate in the research project or to give informed consent. Indeed, some of those not selected to participate also asked to be followed. When the ethnographer joined in group activities with study participants, many other clients—not "officially" part of the study—could also feel included.

Though all of the initial client participants were eager to cooperate, the ethnographer decided to drop two of them from the study. One, dropped at the outset, was obsessed by violent fantasies and was subsequently jailed. Another was dropped after a few months, when the client revealed that the ethnographer reminded him of his ex-wife, thus complicating the possibility for a professional relationship. One client was dropped from the larger study because he did not cooperate with interviewers in the quantitative component, but he continued to be followed by the ethnographer.

Clients and the ethnographer met throughout the study period for varying lengths of time and in many places: at a donut shop; in bars; on street corners; in parks; at group meetings; before, after, or during case manager or doctor appointments; and in courts, prisons, or hospitals. In one case, a client-initiated trip to a parent's grave yielded new, valuable information about the client's beliefs concerning the onset of mental illness and recollections of early drug use. While most meetings took place for parts of a day, the ethnographer spent a whole day with each client several times in the course of the study. Meetings might be preplanned, spontaneous, or client-initiated, by appointment or at times by emergency phone calls. All clients were encouraged to telephone the ethnographer (collect) at home to share important news.

Ethnographic sampling usually seeks to include among the small number of study participants one or two important social or cultural characteristics, which might be predicted to be associated in significant ways with variations in clients' life experiences. In this study we were particularly interested that the sample reflect the age and sex distribution found in the larger sample. While there were significantly more men in the quantitative (hence also in the qualitative) study, the ethnographer got to know many more female clients than just the four female study participants. Thus, there was ample opportunity to see how typical of female dually-diagnosed clients in general these four were.

Another important ethnographic sampling consideration is having enough clients in the sample so that the ethnographer can work through her daily schedule efficiently. Since ethnographic research is largely client initiated, directed, and centered, they set the schedule of meetings or other get-togethers. The ethnographer cannot hope to keep a neat appointment book. The time and location of appointments can and do change due to disruptions in clients' often difficult lives. On any given day, the ethnographer may fail to meet a client when previously agreed upon, but may, by happenstance, meet others in the study. One must be prepared to seize the moment, and have a large enough sample to enable such serendipitous encounters to take place. Clearly, the ethnographer must be flexible and patient—able to pick up and go with the flow of clients' sometimes erratic daily rounds. If, for example, a client has been hospitalized, the ethnographer may choose to visit the hospital. But if that client cannot receive visitors, the ethnographer must find other clients to follow. This, in itself, can uncover valuable information, as client companions discuss with each other memories, circumstances, and reasons for hospitalization that pertain not only to the hospitalized client but to their own experiences as well. What people will be attentive to, what they will think to speak about, depends importantly on the "experience-near" events and circumstances. Absent such situational cueing or priming, participants' knowledge remains tacit or quite superficial, and is often inaccessible or unavailable to introspection or even interrogation.

Regarding the number of individuals to include in an ethnographic sample, a rule of thumb is that the sample should be sufficiently large that no one or two individuals appear so different from the others as to suggest there may be segmentations or diversity in the larger population, which the ethnographic sample has failed to include. For example, in the early 1990s there were no Puerto Rican clients of the mental health center in this study, because there was a negligible population of Puerto Ricans in the city. Today there is a large and rapidly growing—but underserved—Puerto Rican population in that city. If, as would be likely today, a very small number of Puerto Ricans showed up in a probability sampling of the service population, the ethnographer may want to either oversample Puerto Ricans (to see how that population fits into the larger picture) or not try to incorporate *any* Puerto Ricans in the ethnographic sample (as just one or two individuals would be too few participants to enable the ethnographer to get to know the Puerto Rican clients well). There should be sufficient commonality among the sample individuals so that when one gets to know a portion of them well, one can predict with some accuracy how the others' lives will appear. If clients' lives do appear markedly different from each other, with no common patterns apparent, then clearly the sample size is too small, it was selected with some bias, or (most likely) there is some segmentation of the population that the sampling has failed to capture. Most ethnographers say that when additional clients present no surprises, one gains confidence that the existing sample is providing an accurate overall picture of cultural patterns and social settings and relationships.

Quality Assurance: Validity and Reliability

The principal technique for establishing validity in ethnography is "triangulation," in which one sees or hears about a given action, event, place, or person from multiple sources and many others' points of view. This tends to yield a high degree of face validity to the overall findings. As an example of triangulation, one female participant in this study readily disclosed childrearing issues and medication use and willingly included the ethnographer in her daily rounds of appointments with case managers and doctors, where she admitted to a few drinks now and then. Her cocaine habit did not come into view or discussion with the ethnographer or mental health staff, however, until her live-in boyfriend openly complained to the ethnographer that he was putting himself at risk more than he'd like by fetching her supply.

In ethnography, one is constantly comparing respondents' personal testimony with the ethnographer's own observations. For example, the ethnographer was present during a meeting with a male client's case manager and doctor, at which the client "swore off" meeting with his drinking buddies on Wednesdays at the local bar. When the ethnographer saw him in his usual place at the bar the following week, she asked him about his recently professed intentions. He replied with a grin that this was not a Wednesday, no drinking buddies were in sight, and he was quite alone with his beer. So, no promise had been broken.

Although participant observation may have revealed disparities between clients' intentions and actual deeds, on numerous occasions it also served to corroborate clients' seemingly outrageous claims regarding treatment by professionals or stigma experienced in their communities. For example, while working alongside clients—who had been asked to wear T-shirts identifying their association with the mental health center, something they refused to do—sweeping sidewalks in a community service program, the ethnographer witnessed the very stigma-laden remarks previously reported by participants: "They're nuts working for the loony bin." Claims about health care professionals could also clearly be corroborated as the ethnographer followed clients on their visits to the mental health center. In one case, a client stated to the ethnographer that an administrator treated her like a number, not a person. This seemed far-fetched. But when this client approached the administrator to request a change of case managers, the administrator never used her name in speaking with her, but commented at some length on how low an identification number she had, how that fact implied she'd been in the system a long time, and therefore a change of case managers would serve no purpose, since she wasn't making any progress.

Validity and reliability of observation is enhanced by frequent participation in a variety of events with study participants. This practice also aids in building the trusting and comfortable relationship between ethnographer and client that is absolutely necessary. For example, once a client reported at an AA meeting that he had not had a beer in three weeks. The ethnographer later observed a friend in conversation with that client referring to "the beers we had last night." This presented a fine opportunity—the client was convinced that the ethnographer would remain nonjudgmental—to open up with the client a discussion of how the client puts his own life experiences into different stories, depending on topic, audience, and setting.

Typically, after the ethnographer has built such a trusting relationship with the client, it can become more difficult to remain neutral as participant-observer. The client may come to think of the ethnographer as a secret sharer from whom one can expect or ask advice. If this happens, the client's request for advice should be turned into a research opportunity, letting the client explore or clarify the issues about which she seeks advice by, for example, asking her to list the pros and cons of the issue at hand.

ORGANIZATION AND ANALYSES
OF THE ETHNOGRAPHIC DATA

While with clients, the ethnographer carried both notepad and analog tape recorder. Clients were comfortable with each; in fact, quite unconcerned about them or their use. Mostly oblivious to notetaking of any sort, occasionally clients wanted to be sure that the information was correct, and checked oral or written records with the ethnographer. Sometimes, too, the ethnographer read over entries or confirmed understandings with the clients. Jottings were often expanded orally on the ride home from the field site by dictating into the recorder. The ethnographer herself then transcribed these oral expansions and written materials within a day into the computer. Notes included records of observations and conversations, as well as questions, hypotheses, and follow-ups for the next visits. Issues regarding the ethnographer's personal feelings were also dutifully noted; often one's feelings can be a guide to further collection of information.

Ethnographic notes were stored as internally uncoded (i.e., thematically uncategorized) documents, by client code name and by date. After all field research had ended, the long process of analyzing the transcribed material began. Some initial analyses of the data were carried out by the field ethnographer alone, with suggestions from members of the RCT team. Later, the senior anthropologist joined in the analysis of the data, which had been collected without his participation. He hypothesized, on the basis of much research conducted elsewhere, that "consumption" of anything—including alcohol or drugs—is in large part a social activity, which sends messages to others and affirms social bonds. While this issue had been one of the foci of the field research from the beginning, and much pertinent data had been collected, it was not apparent until the analysis of the data that these "social relations of consumption" were so clearly patterned.

The senior anthropologist and field ethnographer each read through the several hundred pages of transcribed notes. (The senior anthropologist attempted a lexical item and a thematic sort of the data using qualitative software programs SONAR and NUDIST, but the results were by intuition inadequate and misleading—that is, "garbage.") They then worked collaboratively to extract "by hand" from the notes, for each of the 16 client participants for whom data was complete and commensurate, all textual material relating to the following categories of information: (a) sites of client's engagement with members of his/her documented social network; (b) sites and group characteristics in which client consumed alcohol or street drugs; and (c) quality of client's engagement with the case manager and mental health center.

In each of these three categories of information, the factors found were then given a simple qualitative label—a code number, 1–n. Table 15.1, in the accompanying article "Clients' Social Networks," shows the results of this exercise. As the reader can infer from the table, patterns of substance use became graphically apparent. We then looked for some of the consequences for substance use as a function of site, social network, and substance-use network. Within each of the four discovered patterns, we sought to discover what kind of drugs/alcohol were consumed, how much, and how this was dealt with—if at all—by case managers.

The reliability of the coding and inferences was attested by the fact that there were many additional direct observations (as well as personal testimony of clients) within the notes that supported the initial classifications, which had been made on the basis of those portions of the total corpus of ethnographic descriptions culled on the basis of the initial coding scheme alone. If this task is done by several people, interrater reliabilities of the sorts or selections made using the coding scheme can be computed. But in this case only two people did this, on a consensus basis. When one is focused on site and event sampling, one can use participants' testimony and observed behavior in one sample of occasions, events, or places to make predictions about words and acts from the same individual that one may encounter at other times and places.

RESEARCH SETTINGS

As noted above, ethnography engages numerous research settings and a variety of people, including clients. Each setting has its own demands for accepting the presence of a researcher, and great effort must be made to adjust one's approaches and explanations to the unique characteristics of the different settings. For example, people who are not part of the study might be present, and often the clients have significant interactions with them. Thus, an ethnographer is typically not conducting research one-on-one in complete privacy with clients. In public settings, there is often an audience—people to whom you are directly speaking and others whom you may want to hear a given communication, even if they are not being addressed—in addition to the ethnographer. This nonprivate interaction can be a great source of information (which might never have come out in a one-on-one interview), but it can also be a constraint on what topics the client or ethnographer will comfortably bring up and discuss. Transitions between public and private domains are common: from group meeting, case manager or doctor's appointments, drug sharers, family—back to their own room and private space and thoughts. A male client may talk about his sex life or a female client about sex abuse in a group, and then talk quite differently about that same experience one-on-one with the ethnographer. (See preceding discussion of triangulation.) Both versions singly and together provide the ethnographer with ways to open up further discussion. It is important to observe the client in these groupings and yet be ready to follow the client out of that setting, back into a private conversation, where the client may rehash and comment on what has been discussed publicly.

Clients in their case managers' offices were often observed to agree to accept the goal of sobriety and new medications, but upon leaving the office and walking home, they ruminated not only on their reasons for nonadherence, but also on their strategies for dealing with the case managers themselves, which invariably led them into rich description of their own feelings about themselves and the mental health system. One client, walking out of his third appointment with a new case manager, explained his strategy as follows:

"I'm cooperating with her. We're getting along better. I'm giving her a chance. She was listening to me. I'm being honest with her. I don't wanna sniff cocaine. I just wanna do pot, and that's OK. I don't wanna drink beer, so I won't drink the beers. I don't tell her about the pot. I'll quit the cocaine and beer. She can't have it all. I have to lie a little. They [case managers] all keep secrets." And so, the lies revealed themselves. When this same client was observed drinking beer on his own that same afternoon, he explained it this way.

"It's only a couple to quench my thirst on a hot day, and it feels good, like you watch 'em drink on TV. I don't have a beer problem. I do like pot. The pot helps keep me from the cocaine. So beer and pot help keep me from doin' the worst—cocaine. That's the one I shouldn't use."

When this same client was observed the following week with his girlfriend after a night of cocaine, he explained it this way in her presence:

"We took two pain killers, Norgestic Forte, just two to feel mellow, then cocaine. They [case managers] don't understand. Cocaine is our only way to have a fun time; it's our leisure time. It's not an everyday thing. If drinkin' and druggin' is the only thing that makes you feel better an' you're with your friends an' all. If it gives you somethin' to do, well, what the hell is there if you give it up? But if I told them [case managers] the truth, that I don't wanna dry out, they won't give me meds. And I need my meds. And [pointing to his girlfriend] she could lose her kid."

While the ethnographer did not observe clients getting tired of her presence or conversation, the reverse was common. At times, due to much talking in smoke-filled rooms, the ethnographer needed a break. While clients were pleased to allow the ethnographer into many different arenas of their everyday world, the ethnographer sometimes had to impose limits on clients' entry into her spaces—explaining, for example, that she would not want to be present during illegal activities, and thereby risk arrest. Clients were considerate to warn her of imminent drug deals or shoplifting adventures so she could make a timely exit.

Given the multiple settings required for ethnographic research, the ethnographer must negotiate permission and establish a welcome acceptance not only with the client, but also with numerous others, who are often more skeptical or suspicious of the ethnographer than is the client. Indeed, the client is often the only means by which the ethnographer can establish trust among members of the client's social network, including officials of the mental health system, who generally are not familiar with or accepting of the idea that a client is followed by a participant-observer.

In this particular study, clients' friends and family consistently accepted the ethnographer's presence, but this was not always the case among the mental health professional staff. At the outset the ethnographer was warmly introduced to the case managers and doctors by the director of the mental health center, and the ethnographer, in turn, presented her methodology, stressing the fact that she would keep private and confidential clients' words and deeds observed in their everyday life. In addition, the ethnographer frequented the case managers' lunchroom from time to time to keep communication channels open. Nevertheless, a few case managers were not comfortable with the ethnographer accompanying clients to their appointments, and when one case manager openly protested, the ethnographer withdrew. Most case managers, however, proved very cooperative, understanding that such a study could get a more complete picture of clients' lives than their own caseloads and time/appointment constraints would permit.

Occasionally some case managers deemed the ethnographer's presence to be intrusive and interfering with their own treatment plans for a client:

"Had not Client X been instructed *not* to move from one apartment to another? Had the ethnographer actually let Client X use her vehicle to move a couch?"

Case managers might resent the ethnographer's privileged information, and argue for breach of confidentiality:

"Where did Client X actually move to?" "The ethnographer must divulge the address!"

In cases like this, the ethnographer reviewed once again that strict confidentiality and trust between client and ethnographer are keystones to participant observation, and that, in the end, findings from such a method might benefit mental health services, a hope shared by the director of their center.

FUNDING

We have found it difficult to obtain funding for ethnographic research, which is why we continue to include qualitative studies within our quantitative studies. In the ethnography described here, funding constraints limited the ethnography to one site and to two years of observation. We would have much preferred to conduct the qualitative study in two sites—one urban and one rural—and to conduct longitudinal follow-ups to learn more about the course of disorders.

ETHICAL ISSUES

Several important ethical issues flow from the description of ethnography given above. First, human subjects protection committees, or institutional review boards (IRBs), insist that studies comprise official participants, who give informed consent, and exclude all those who do not give informed consent. In ethnography, the notion of participation in a study is a continuous, fluctuating, and changing social field of the client's and others' actions. It is impossible, categorically, to say who is in the study and who is not. Any potential action or conversation by the client in concert with another can be a rich source of information, yet not all of these coparticipants in the client's social world can be treated as formal participants in a study.

Second, the formalities of informed consent can often sow seeds of mistrust and confusion among clients and/or their associates. This is particularly true when a long, formal document must be signed as part of the informed consent process. The ethnographer must take considerable time to explain a document that clients often find intrusive or even frightening, as it appears to many clients to violate the very idea of privacy and confidentiality.

Waiving of written consent would in many cases be advisable. Many clients do not understand on the basis of one reading or conversation just what "informed consent" means. Keeping participants informed of their consent throughout the study period may be the only way ethically to proceed. No matter how continuous and assiduous one is in orally informing participants of the study's methods and goals, most IRBs remain reluctant to waive the provision of written consent, and an oral recording can be just as off-putting as signing a piece of paper. "Officialese" is not something many clients are comfortable with at all. Trust and confidence in the research process for most client participants are based principally on knowing and trusting the researchers, and not on a firm understanding of the research.

Many state mental health systems have exacting (and, possibly, paternalistic) attitudes and regulations regarding the activities that mental health researchers can engage in with clients. Since ethnography is typically client-directed, the ethnographer makes decisions about what to study based on the client's initiative, which may at times involve the ethnographer in activities that depart from guidelines governing the behavior of mental health professionals. A commonplace example of this is that the ethnographer would observe clients stockpiling pharmaceutical drugs for later trade or barter with others—sometimes other clients—for street drugs or other items. Case managers in their professional roles could not ethically witness this taking place without admonishing the participants, or "turning them in." Naturally, the ethnographer reveals none of this to anyone. If, for some reason, case managers were to become aware of what the ethnographer knew, she would then be in a dilemma and would have to try to negotiate with mental health officials, explaining the rationale for and benefits of client-directed, participant observation, and that the latter requires scrupulous attention to confidentiality and privacy of clients' words and deeds.

One of the most important ethical considerations felt by ethnographers is preparing study participants for the *cessation* of research. The withdrawal of companionship, attention, and exchange can be quite a shock to clients if they are not prepared for it. Clients must be slowly weaned of this interaction, which can be quite empowering. The ethnographer should remain available to visit with clients informally for some time after the research project may be officially completed. Some "transference" is likely to occur, and must be dealt with as part of concluding the research.

INSIGHTS

Unexpected findings from the ethnography are almost too numerous to describe. We will briefly mention three that led to the development of further clinical interventions. The ethnographers noted that clients had often lost custody of their children, and were strongly motivated to increase contacts and regain custody. This led to current work on developing a parental skills training intervention for clients. The ethnography documented the need for several basic supports for stable recovery to occur: safe housing; relationships with non–substance abusers; a regular daily activity such as a job; and a trusting, longitudinal relationship with at least one provider who helps the client to learn how to manage both illnesses. Current dual diagnosis programs in many states now incorporate each of these elements. Finally, ethnographers documented that clients with past histories of trauma had great difficulty sustaining abstinence because of the emergence of untreated symptoms of post-traumatic stress disorder. This insight has led to current development and trials of trauma interventions for similar clients.

STRENGTHS AND LIMITATIONS

A major strength of the ethnography is that it reveals how a client's behavior and thinking is patterned and oriented in relation to specific settings and associations with others. What people say and do, what they think, what they may be conscious of and attend to, vary as a function of specific circumstances. (This is what is meant by "tacit" knowledge becoming explicit and active only in specific contexts.) To gain insight into these thoughts and actions, one must share with clients the circumstances in which these thoughts and actions come to the fore. For example, such simple questions as "What makes you angry?" or "What jobs would you really be good at and enjoy?" are not necessarily questions to which the client can give an adequate (or even accurate) answer. Like the rest of us, clients are often blind to what makes them angry or what jobs they may want to try. By following clients on a daily basis, answers to these questions may easily be obtained. In this particular study, patterns of substance abuse were readily discovered, and yet clients themselves had very little awareness of how their own drug use was socially patterned.

The major limitation of participant observation is that it must deal with a small number of clients intensively, rather than a large number of clients extensively. The sample size is too small to directly generalize or extend to other populations. Results should be used to guide research with other service populations from different sociocultural backgrounds.

ADVICE FOR FUTURE STUDIES

Including an ethnographic substudy within a quantitative study has been an enriching experience for the entire research team. Among the benefits are learning about qualitative methods, helping to understand anomalous findings within the quantitative study, and developing new insights about the clients' worlds that lead to additional or new clinical interventions. Since the study described here was completed, we have used ethnographic methods in two additional mental health studies, with similar positive experiences and successes. In the future, we hope to use ethnographic methods in long-term follow-up investigations of dually diagnosed clients, to learn more about the recovery process over time.

Ethnography as a method is not something one can master with a few days of reading and a weeklong course on techniques; neither, however, is it esoteric. The senior anthropologist has trained and supervised people from various walks of life, of diverse cultural backgrounds, to undertake ethnographic research in a variety of settings on numerous topics. In these cases the apprentice researchers were not functioning as research assistants but as ethnographers. Their basic training in each case required less than two months. However, continuous guidance by an experienced anthropologist will add considerably to the quality of research, especially how effectively it probes and develops serendipitous findings and utilizes the "self-reflexivity" of field ethnographers to pursue leads contained in unlikely or unanticipated observation or discourse.

APPLICATION OF FINDINGS

The findings described in this publication have several implications for social work and for mental health practice. Conditions that are described as psychiatric disorders are often broad difficulties of adjustment and personal suffering, but they have no clear pathophysiology as a singular disease. Substance abuse, as an example, is a highly patterned, dysfunctional behavior that is heavily affected by context, physical setting, interpersonal relationships, and cultural background. The ethnography clarified several of these issues, including a typology of the social contexts of regular substance use. It seems logical that caregivers cannot understand an individual's behavior and help that individual to find a path to better quality of life (i.e., recovery) without being aware of and taking into account contextual factors. For example, clients who drink alone may have poor social skills, lack of employment, or seek isolation because of social phobias or other problems. Each of these possible conditions has obvious implications for intervention. Clients who use alcohol and drugs regularly with other mental health clients tend to be social and quite dependent on their peer group. Interventions might logically be directed to the peer group and their regular activities. Developing a recovery plan with the client must necessarily be informed by detailed information regarding his or her social circumstances and personal proclivities.

Mixed Methods

As presented in this section (and in the last article in Section III), mixed methods—which we define as the use of qualitative and quantitative approaches in the same study—sound very good in theory, but may present problems in implementation. Quantitative and qualitative approaches are based on different epistemologies and methodologies for gathering and analyzing data. Most researchers still have not been fully trained nor do they have equal expertise in both approaches, and so may be likely to prefer one over the other. In the last example in Section III, the authors point out the critical importance of educating researchers performing mixed method research in the purposes and methods of each approach.

The first article in this section presents a situation in which a qualitative, intensive interview component was built on and added to a quantitative panel interview study rather late in the study's history. This was done to understand the inconsistencies in the panel data obtained from the highly structured interview protocol. The researchers involved in the original conceptualization and design of the study were not experienced in qualitative data collection and analysis, which created tensions when the qualitative interview component was added to the study. The second article reflects a different history of merging qualitative and quantitative approaches in the same study. This study was designed from the beginning to include both quantitative and qualitative dimensions, and was carried out by a research team that included individuals primarily trained in either quantitative or qualitative methods.

16

The Bottom Line: Employment and Barriers to Work among Former SSI DA&A Beneficiaries

Kevin Campbell, Jim Baumohl, and Sharon R. Hunt

January 1997 marked the end of the Supplemental Security Income (SSI) program for about 167,000 people with disabilities "materially related" to drug addiction and alcoholism.[1] These "DA&A" beneficiaries (as they were called) did not receive benefits after 1996 unless they had applied to the Social Security Administration for redetermination and been found eligible by virtue of other impairments or a finding that their DA&A classification resulted from administrative error. By the end of 1997, only 35% had requalified (Lewin and Westat, 1998). This was less than half the anticipated requalification rate of 75% (Congressional Budget Office, 1995).

The DA&A program was terminated with little sense of what would happen to those who lost its support. Congress authorized no special effort to promote their employment. Still, Representative E. Clay Shaw, Jr. (R–FL), an architect of the program's demise, told National Public Radio (1999): "I figured some of them would certainly be going to work and have to realize that they'd have to get up in the morning and support themselves." In this paper, we take up how (and if) former DA&A recipients who lost SSI replaced it with employment of some sort in the two years following the program's end. We consider the stability and yield of work, as well as obstacles to getting it and keeping it. In the Results section of the paper, we rely mainly on quantitative findings from our nine-site, two-year panel study. In the Discussion section, we interpret these results with the aid of qualitative data from subsamples interviewed in depth at four sites between the 12- and 18-month follow-ups. The concluding paper in this issue attends to the policy implications of our findings.

From Campbell, K., Baumohl, J., Hunt, S. R. (2003). The bottom line: Employment and barriers to work among former SSI DA&A beneficiaries. *Journal of Contemporary Drug Problems, 30*, 195–240. Reprinted with permission of the publisher.

EMPLOYMENT AND BARRIERS TO EMPLOYMENT
AMONG WELFARE RECIPIENTS

With unemployment rates falling steadily during the course of our study (reaching 4.3% in December 1998), employment prospects for welfare recipients were never better. During 1997 and 1998, the robust American economy contributed mightily to a 30% decline in the average number of families on the rolls of Aid to Families with Dependent Children (AFDC) and its successor, Temporary Assistance for Needy Families (TANF) (U.S. Department of Health and Human Services, 1999).[2]

Unfortunately there is neither a published nor a fugitive literature on the employment experiences of the population of interest to us.[3] Moreover, useful studies of state and local General Assistance (GA) recipients, the welfare population most similar to SSI DA&A beneficiaries,[4] are extremely rare. Henly and Danziger (1996) found that only 31.4% of their sample of Michigan GA recipients found employment (not further defined) in the year following termination of that program in October 1991. These disqualified GA recipients left the rolls in the midst of dull economic times, however, not during the boom that began later in the decade.

Far richer and more temporally relevant data are available on the adult TANF population. A meta-analysis of studies examining employment outcomes among former AFDC and TANF parents whose benefits ended between July 1995 and August 1998 reported point-in-time employment rates ranging from 55% to 71% (Brauner and Loprest, 1999). The same study found that, nationwide, wages for those leaving the rolls typically were less than seven dollars per hour. Most of those employed failed to earn enough to rise above the poverty level; 33%–50% reported a decline in total household income. This was likely due to rapid job loss. A study of AFDC parents found that 45% of those who found work lost their jobs within four months; 75% lost them within one year (Rangarajan et al., 1998).[5]

Such discouraging results in view of the tightening labor market, and the emphasis in most TANF programs on moving recipients rapidly into jobs, suggested to many observers that a sizable welfare residuum is comprised of people facing significant "barriers to employment" (Danziger et al., 1999). In a review of the empirical literature on the impairments of TANF parents, Sweeney (2000) provided a catalogue of health conditions identified as employment barriers by studies in 24 states. A number of these inquiries—in Michigan, Minnesota, Indiana, Kansas, New Jersey, and Utah—demonstrated that various constellations of obstacles are associated with a failure to work. In one of the best-designed studies, Danziger et al. (1999) identified 14 potential employment barriers among single mothers sampled from the TANF rolls in an urban Michigan county in February 1997. Examining the prevalence of these barriers (alone or in combination) and their relationship to subsequent employment, they found problematic transportation to be most common (47%), followed by inadequate education (30%) and the presence of a major depressive disorder (27%). Sparse work experience, few job skills, family health problems, and perceived workplace discrimination (on the basis of race, gender, or welfare status) also were significantly and negatively related to employment. Fully 85% of these TANF mothers reported at least one barrier, 37% reported two or three, and 27% reported four or more. The probability that a respondent worked 20 or more hours a week decreased substantially as the number of obstacles rose: Compared with those with none, women with one barrier were 1.9 times less likely to work 20 or more hours per week, and women reporting four to six barriers were 6.7 times less likely to work that much.

However, former SSI DA&A recipients are quite dissimilar to the TANF group, which is about 90% female and, per eligibility rules, caring for children. TANF parents are also young (largely ages 18–35), and, stereotypes notwithstanding, relatively few seem to be substance abusers. While some studies using less stringent criteria have produced plausible rates as high as 20% (see Sweeney, 2000), using the *DSM-III-R,* Danziger et al. (1999) found that only 6% of their Michigan sample met the standards for drug or alcohol dependence during the previous 12 months. By contrast, most DA&A beneficiaries were 35–50 years old and likely would have met dependence criteria in the relatively recent past.

That our respondents qualified at some point for SSI indicates how different they are from members of other welfare populations. By design, the Social Security Administration's standard of disability is quite strict. SSI eligibility hinges on independent medical evidence of impairment serious enough to prevent for at least a 12-month period the performance of "substantial gainful activity (SGA)," a Social Security term that over the course of this study referred to earnings of merely $500 per month or more.[6] As a San Francisco respondent observed about his ultimately successful redetermination: "I had interviews with physical doctors, two of them, and two mental assessments.... [T]hey want 100% of either mental or physical, but like I got 80% mental and 80% physical.... So to me that adds up to 160% of being 100% fucked up."[7] It is unlikely that the self-reported impairments of TANF parents are comparable to those underlying the certified work disability of SSI beneficiaries.[8]

Former DA&A recipients and TANF parents probably have meager skills and work histories in common, however. A California study of an ill-defined population of "welfare recipients"[9] found that 76% had either "low" or "very low" job skills, meaning they would have difficulty performing the simple arithmetic operations necessary in many clerical and service jobs (Johnson and Tafoya, 1999). In a somewhat more positive vein, Danziger et al. (1999) found that 80% of their TANF mothers (70% of whom were high school graduates) were familiar with at least four of nine basic job skills. A study of Florida TANF mothers interviewed in 1998 reported that 12% had never held a full-time job and that of those who had, 35% had worked full-time for a year or less and 56% for two years or less. Almost two-thirds had no skill or occupation (Merrill et al., undated). We have no comparable data on former DA&A recipients. However, to qualify for SSI, individuals must not only be very poor and disabled by a rigorous standard, they also must not have worked more than 25% of the time after age 21 nor more than five of the previous 10 years (Mashaw and Reno, 1996). Such work histories and the humble educational attainments of former DA&A recipients (in our study, only 55% had completed high school or earned a General Equivalence Diploma) do not suggest the possession of readily marketable skills.

Even the roaring economy of the late 1990s seems not to have produced enough jobs for people with such modest ability. Based on a study of 125 cities, the National Conference of Mayors projected that between 1998 and 2003 there would be two unskilled job seekers for every unskilled job (U.S. Conference of Mayors, 1997). This "job gap" was greatest in the biggest cities, particularly those with the largest concentrations of welfare recipients. The most striking shortfall is anticipated in Detroit, where 24 applicants are expected for each unskilled-job opening. At the other extreme, an unskilled-job surplus is expected in San Francisco, estimated to have four unskilled jobs for every taker in the next few years. Although not selected on this criterion, among the SSI Study sites are cities at each end of the job-gap spectrum. Table 16.1 displays these data for all sites in our study except Stockton, for which they were not available.

Given these conditions and the differences between the SSI and the TANF populations noted above, we would expect DA&A beneficiaries expelled from SSI to do at least as poorly in the job market as adult TANF recipients. That is, we would expect their post-assistance employment to be unskilled, sporadic, and unremunerative.

Table 16.1. Projected Low-Skill Job Gaps for City/County Areas Included in the Five-State Study of Former SSI DA&A Recipients

City	Projected Number of Low-Skill Job Seekers 1998–2003			Projected Number of Low-Skill Jobs 1998–2003	Low-Skill Job Seekers per Job
	Welfare	Other	Total		
Detroit, MI	47,048	8,437	55,485	2,350	23.6
Chicago, IL	92,439	5,437	97,874	20,920	4.7
San Jose, CA	14,386	15,412	29,799	8,650	3.4
Los Angeles and Long Beach, CA	199,184	24,856	224,040	102,000	2.2
Portland, OR	5,046	6,142	11,188	6,850	1.6
Oakland, CA	22,132	3,782	25,194	18,220	1.4
Seattle, WA	12,798	18,709	31,507	28,060	1.1
San Francisco, CA	6,629	1,557	8,186	33,590	0.2

SOURCE: United States Conference of Mayors, November 1997. The "Projected Number of Low-Skill Jobs" reflects projections of employment growth in "low-skill occupations" (i.e., those in the bottom 20% of average pay for all occupations). The projected number of low-skill "welfare" job seekers was estimated at 80% of the 1997 TANF caseload (the minimum percentage required to find work within five years). The projected number of "other" low-skill job seekers (i.e., new low-skill entrants to the labor force not on welfare) was estimated by multiplying the five-year change in the county's labor force by the proportion of new members of the national labor force who were not high school graduates and not on welfare as of the most recent census.

METHODS

Study Sample

The methods of our nine-site, two-year panel study are described in detail in Swartz, Tonkin, and Baumohl (this issue). We will not rehearse them here. Of the 1,764 former SSI DA&A recipients interviewed at baseline, 152 (9%) are not included in the analyses reported in this paper: 71 (4%) died during the study, 68 (4%) were lost to both the 18- and 24-month follow-ups, and 13 cases (1%) lacked data critical to our analyses. Thus a total of 1,612 respondents are included here. Of these, we analyzed employment outcomes only among those who lost SSI and did not replace it with another form of publicly funded income assistance ($n = 611$). Put another way, we did not include respondents in analyses of employment outcomes if they requalified for SSI ($n = 674$) or regularly received benefits from programs like TANF or GA, or collected a veteran's pension ($n = 327$). In the assisted groups, employment rates were low at baseline (generally less than 10%) and remained low throughout the study.[10] Finally, we did not include respondents in analyses of employment rates for any round in which they reported jail or prison as their primary residence. Because of this wave-specific exclusion, the "n" varies slightly across rounds. We excluded 4% of former DA&A beneficiaries without income assistance from the calculation of baseline rates for this reason; we removed 7.2%–8.5% from employment-rate calculations for the six- through 24-month follow-ups.

INDICATOR DEVELOPMENT

Construction of Outcome Indicators

Participation in Publicly Funded Income Assistance Programs. We estimated rates of participation in these programs by classifying individuals according to the regularity with which they received benefits. Table 16.2 details our protocol for identifying Requalified SSI Beneficiaries, Non-SSI Income Assistance Recipients, and Former SSI Beneficiaries without Income Assistance.

Employment Rates. We estimated employment rates based on responses to structured interview questions about income from employment in the 30 days prior to the interview. Respondents were considered employed at a given follow-up if they reported *any* earnings (one dollar or more) from a "legitimate job or business" or "casual work or under-the-table jobs." Similarly, we considered respondents to be "usually" employed during the follow-up period if they reported employment earnings for the majority of interviews completed. To be sure, this is a very generous definition of employment. However, it has a compelling virtue in this case: As no definition could be *more* liberal, we eliminate the possibility that poor employment outcomes are the result of definitional gerrymandering. In this sense, a very liberal definition provides a very conservative test.

Work Retention Rates. By the same logic, we use a very liberal definition of continuous employment. We identified respondents who reported no income from employment in the month prior to the baseline interview but reported employment income at some time during the 24-month follow-up. For present purposes, we take these respondents as those who newly entered the workforce following elimination of the DA&A program, and they form the denominator for calculation of six-month work-retention rates. Treating the follow-up at which these respondents first reported employment income as the "index," we considered them to have retained employment for six months if they reported employment income in the follow-up immediately after this index date. These respondents form the numerator for the calculation. If data were missing on questions about employment in the follow-up immediately after the index date, or if a respondent was not interviewed at the necessary follow-up, we did not calculate a work-retention rate. Overall, we calculated six-month retention rates for 84% of these "new" workers.

Table 16.2. Protocol for Classifying Respondents by Type of Publicly Funded Income Assistance Received in the 24 Months Following Termination of the SSI DA&A Program

Classification	Operational Definition
Requalified SSI Beneficiaries	Respondent usually[a] received SSI benefits during the 24-month follow-up period.
Non-SSI Income Assistance Recipients	Respondent did not usually receive SSI benefits during the 24-month follow-up but usually received some form of publicly funded income assistance that could be used customarily to pay for housing (e.g., General Assistance or TANF, but not food stamps).
Former SSI Beneficiaries w/o Income Assistance	Respondent did not usually receive SSI benefits or non-SSI income assistance during the 24-month follow-up.

[a]"Usually" means that a respondent reported receiving such benefits at the majority of follow-up interviews completed (i.e., two interviews if only two follow-up interviews were completed; at least two interviews if three follow-ups were completed; and at least three interviews if four follow-ups were completed).

Employment Earnings. We calculated employment earnings for each respondent by summing the amount of income reported from a "legitimate job or business" and "casual work or under-the-table jobs" in the 30 days prior to the interview.

Performance of Substantial Gainful Activity. The consistent performance of SGA is taken by the Social Security Administration to indicate the absence of a work-disabling impairment. The SGA level of $500 per month during the study period also corresponded closely to the un-supplemented minimum value of an SSI grant, thus representing a useful surrogate for the amount of SSI income in most states.[11] Setting aside the value of Medicaid benefits, to have earned the SGA level each month during this study was to effectively have replaced the cash value of SSI. For each round of interviews, we classified respondents as achieving SGA if they reported earning $500 or more per month from a "legitimate job or business" and/or "casual work or under-the-table jobs." Respondents were classified as "usually" earning SGA if they reported such income at the majority of follow-ups completed. Note, however, that our definition does not fully capture the meaning of SGA, because the Social Security Administration also counts income from illegal sources when known. We have not included such income here for reasons we take up in the Discussion section, below.

Barriers to Employment

As detailed in Table 16.3, we created indicators to represent whether a respondent experienced each of eight barriers to employment. Table 16.3 also compares the operational definition for each of our barriers with those used by Danziger et al. (1999). Our definitions were similar for obstacles related to education and to domestic abuse, but others differed substantially. Arguably, the Danziger group's constructions of mental-health and substance-abuse barriers are superior to ours because they are based on reasonably precise (or at least accepted) diagnostic criteria. Similarly, to identify physical-health barriers they used a functioning scale with national, age-specific norms, while we did not. We departed deliberately from their construction of a transportation barrier because we did not believe that lack of a car or driver's license constituted *per se* an obstacle to employment in most of our sites. We did not measure equivalents of their barriers related to childcare, under-standing workplace norms, or perceived discrimination at work. Unlike the Danziger group, we included a housing barrier based on indications of literal homelessness. Finally, Danziger and her colleagues included a "work experience" barrier, considering it to be present if a respondent had worked less than 20% of the years since she turned 18. By definition, SSI recipients have little or no recent work experience, and virtually all of our respondents would have met this or a similar criterion.

Given the small sample sizes ($n < 100$) in the sites for which we conducted the barrier analysis, we had to use three categories in order to calculate odds ratios. We created a three-category indi-cator to reflect the number of barriers that each respondent experienced: zero or one; two or three; or four or more.

ANALYTIC METHODS

All analyses described below were conducted with data weighted according to the specifications detailed by Choudhry and Helba (this issue). All sample sizes are expressed in their unweighted forms.

Table 16.3. Barriers to Employment

Type of Barrier	Operational Definition in This Study	Operational Definition in Danziger et al. (1999)
Education	Respondent neither graduated from high school nor received a GED.	Respondent neither graduated from high school nor received a GED.
Job Skills	Respondent reported needing help learning job skills.	Based on assessment of respondent's performance of specific job-related tasks in previous jobs.
Transportation	Respondent reported needing help finding adequate transportation or that, in the 30 days prior to the interview, he/she ran out of money for transportation.	Respondent lacks a car and/or does not have a driver's license.
Domestic Abuse	Respondent reported that in the six months prior to the interview, he/she was physically or emotionally abused by a family member.	Respondent experienced severe physical abuse by a family member (e.g., hit, beaten, choked, threatened with a weapon, forced into sex).
Housing	Respondent reported that in the 30 days prior to the interview, he/she spent time living "on the street," "in a homeless shelter," or in "another type of shelter facility" (e.g., shelter for runaways or battered women).	Not assessed.
Physical Health	We used the Addiction Severity Index (ASI) medical composite (see Guydish et al., this issue) to identify respondents with physical health problems serious enough to constitute a barrier to employment. To determine an appropriate cutpoint, we examined the distribution of these scores among reclassified DA&As who claimed to have been reclassified based solely on physical impairment. As the median medical composite score for this group was .72, we considered the physical health problem serious enough to constitute an employment barrier if the respondent scored .72 or higher.[i]	Used the SF-36 Health Survey—a multi-item physical functioning scale—to identify respondents who scored in the lowest age-specific quartile (based on national norms).
Mental Health	We used the ASI psychiatric composite to identify individuals with mental health problems serious enough to constitute a barrier to employment. To determine the distribution of these scores among reclassified DA&As who claimed to have been reclassified based solely on a psychiatric impairment. As the median psychiatric composite score for this group was .45, we considered the mental health problem serious enough to constitute an employment barrier if the respondent scored .45 or higher.[ii]	Respondents suffered from major depression, post-traumatic stress disorder, or generalized anxiety disorder as measured by the Diagnostic and Statistical Manual, revised third edition (DSM-III-R).
Substance Abuse	A respondent reporting a need for substance abuse treatment was considered to have a substance abuse related employment barrier. Additionally, a respondent reporting no need for substance abuse treatment was considered to have such a barrier if he/she scored .34 or greater on a scale created by summing the ASI's alcohol and drug composites. This value represents the median score for the combined index among those who thought they needed substance abuse treatment but were not in it.[iii]	Respondents suffered from alcohol dependence or drug dependence in the previous 12 months as measured by the DSM-III-R.

[i] At the 12-, 18-, and 24-month follow-ups, median medical composite scores among reclassified DA&A recipients who claimed that they were reclassified based solely on a physical impairment were .72, .71, and .59. We selected the highest median score (.72) as our cutpoint.

[ii] At the 12-, 18-, and 24-month follow-ups, median psychiatric composite scores among reclassified DA&A recipients who claimed to have been reclassified based solely on a psychiatric impairment were .44, .40, and .45. We selected the highest median score (.45) as our cutpoint.

[iii] At the 12-, 18-, and 24-month follow-ups, median scores for the combined alcohol/drug composite among reclassified DA&A recipients who said they needed substance abuse treatment but were not in it were .34, .31, and .32. We selected the highest median score (.34) as our cutpoint.

Statistical Software

We used WesvarPC and SAS's PROC GENMOD to conduct statistical analyses. We did bivariate analyses and logistic regression with Wesvar, using PROC GENMOD for logit analysis of longitudinal data. PROC GENMOD is analogous to logistic regression but allows incorporation of individuals' responses at several points in time by adjusting for autocorrelation (Allison, 1999). Ideally, we would have used Wesvar throughout because, as Choudhry and Helba (this issue) explain, "the complex weighting required to adjust for incomplete frames and nonresponse" render inappropriate "variance estimation techniques typically used by statistical software packages (e.g., SPSS, SAS)." While WesVarPC provides accurate estimates of variance, it does not currently perform longitudinal analyses. Although it is not technically appropriate to use software packages such as SPSS or SAS on our weighted data, results from bivariate analyses and multiple logistic regression using them were—for all practical purposes—identical to WesVarPC's. We therefore have confidence in the results obtained from PROC GENMOD.

Summary of Analyses

We report four sets of site-specific analyses. Recall that our employment analyses include only respondents without income assistance.

First, we estimate SSI requalification rates for each site as well as utilization rates for non-SSI, publicly funded income assistance programs.

Second, we identify population trends in employment rates and earnings. Specifically, we compare employment rates at baseline with those at 24 months and identify sites where the gain was statistically significant.

Third, we estimate rates of "usual" employment (the proportion of respondents employed at the majority of follow-ups). We also identify baseline predictors of usual employment during the follow-up period. To this end, we assessed a variety of baseline indicators as potential predictors: gender, age, education, ethnicity, each of the eight employment barriers, employment status at baseline, and abstinence from alcohol and drugs. We first examined the bivariate relationships between each of the predictors and our indicator of usual employment. We then included significant bivariate predictors in a multivariate logistic regression model to identify independent predictors of usual employment.

Across all sites, only 101 former DA&A recipients without income assistance (17% of that group) were employed at baseline, and 32 of them were in Chicago. In the remaining sites, the number employed at baseline ranged from four to 14. The limited power associated with these small numbers undermines our ability to identify site-specific differences in employment outcomes between those who were employed at baseline and those who were not. Still, we looked for such differences and report them where found. Where we did not find site-specific differences, we combine respondents across sites and compare aggregate outcomes between those employed or not employed at baseline.

Last, we explore the relationship between the types and number of work barriers and performance of SGA. This series of analyses uses PROC GENMOD to model employment at the SGA level as a function of time and of number and types of barriers. Since our concern is with the relationships between the number and types of barriers and SGA, we report only odds ratios associated with these relationships. A graphic representation of changes in employment at the SGA level as a function of time can be found in Figure 16.3. To verify the independence of observed relationships between number and types of barriers and employment at the SGA level, we introduced gender, race/ethnicity, age, receipt of income assistance, and employment status at baseline into the model. As a rule, adding these variables did not affect the statistical significance or magnitude of observed relationships, but on those occasions when it did, inclusion usually strengthened the relationship. (That is, it increased the magnitude of the odds ratio or lowered the p value.) In these analyses, we used data from only six of the nine sites: Seattle, Portland, Chicago, Detroit, Stockton, and Los Angeles. We excluded San Francisco, Oakland, and San Jose because of their extremely small numbers (21–33) of former DA&A recipients without income assistance. Finally, this longitudinal analysis excludes data from the baseline interview because, for the most part, respondents still received SSI at baseline.

Qualitative Analysis of Semistructured Interview Data

To help interpret our findings, we use data from semistructured interviews conducted in Portland, San Francisco, Stockton, and Chicago between late March and late May of 1998; that is, between the one-year and 18-month structured interviews. As Swartz, Tonkin, and Baumohl describe in more detail, we have data from 156 such interviews, but here we rely on the 73 conducted with respondents falling into the "no income assistance" group defined above.

Our lengthy conversations with these respondents yielded detailed work histories and information about current employment and other resource-generating activities. These data are far more detailed than those that could be collected by the structured interviews, and by design they cover periods of time before the study and between interviews that the scripted employment questions do not. The narrative data provide a vivid sense of what we count as work and income in our quantitative analyses, a matter of some importance, as we will see. In the concluding sections of this paper we rely extensively on the narrative data to explore the work our respondents did and their subjective understandings and definitions of it.

We analyzed the voluminous semistructured interview data with the help of software called QSR NUD*IST, version 4 (N4). In its most basic application, N4 is an infinitely flexible electronic filing system that permits multiple-category coding of bits of text that can be viewed categorically and in original context. However, N4 also can execute complicated sequences of logical exercises (called "operators" in N4 lingo) that organize coded text to permit the identification of patterns and the testing of hypotheses with an efficiency that manual qualitative analysis cannot achieve. Further, text in N4 can be linked to quantitative data in spreadsheet format. For the analyses summarized in this paper, we used the unique identification numbers of respondents to connect their structured and semistructured interview data. For each analysis we used the identification numbers to disaggregate the semistructured interview sample by each category of interest (those employed at the level of SGA, for example, or those working at baseline).

RESULTS

Type of Income Assistance Received

The proportion of former DA&A recipients who requalified for SSI and thus received benefits throughout the study ranged from 62% in San Francisco to 25% in Chicago (Figure 16.1). The proportion usually receiving non-SSI income assistance ranged from 8% in Detroit to 29% in Los Angeles, and the proportion receiving no assistance of any kind varied from 17% in San Francisco to 62% in Chicago. These differences reflect local particularities of SSI qualification and requalification (especially the presence of active advocacy organizations) and variations in state and county GA and TANF programs. They are also related to the demographic characteristics of the samples

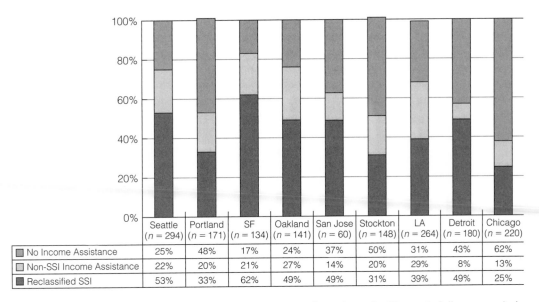

	Seattle (n = 294)	Portland (n = 171)	SF (n = 134)	Oakland (n = 141)	San Jose (n = 60)	Stockton (n = 148)	LA (n = 264)	Detroit (n = 180)	Chicago (n = 220)
■ No Income Assistance	25%	48%	17%	24%	37%	50%	31%	43%	62%
□ Non-SSI Income Assistance	22%	20%	21%	27%	14%	20%	29%	8%	13%
■ Reclassified SSI	53%	33%	62%	49%	49%	31%	39%	49%	25%

FIGURE 16.1. Principal source of income of former SSI DA&As throughout the 24-month follow-up period by site (n = 1,612)

in each site, particularly sex (closely associated with TANF utilization) and age (related to GA and SSI eligibility). Clearly there were large differences among sites in the extent to which public assistance of some kind protected respondents from full exposure to the labor market. For this and other, similar reasons, we report our results by site whenever possible.

Population Trends in Employment Outcomes

Employment Rates.

Rates of Any Employment (monthly earnings of $1 or more): Among those with whom our analysis is concerned, former DA&A recipients without income assistance, employment rates increased significantly in all sites (Figure 16.2). In most places they rose from a 16%–20% level at baseline to 40%–60% at 24 months. As a rule, these increases were realized by six months. In the simplest sense, then, substantially greater numbers of respondents were working at the end of the study than at the beginning.

Rates of Employment at the SGA Level (monthly earnings of $500 or more): When we look at a more meaningful measure of (albeit modest) work, the somewhat encouraging picture changes. While in all sites but Oakland there were significant increases ($p < .10$) in the proportion of respondents with earnings of $500 a month (Figure 16.3), at 24 months rates of employment at SGA were very low: In six of the nine sites, they were less than 25%.

Earned Income. Median monthly earned income among those employed at 24 months ranged from $333 (Portland) to over $1,000 (San Francisco and Stockton). In six of the nine sites (Chicago, Detroit, Seattle, San Jose, Los Angeles, and Oakland), it ranged from $380 to $575. In most places earned income was stable or increased gradually between the six-month and 24-month follow-ups, but there were dramatic increases in Stockton and San Francisco. In Stockton, median earned

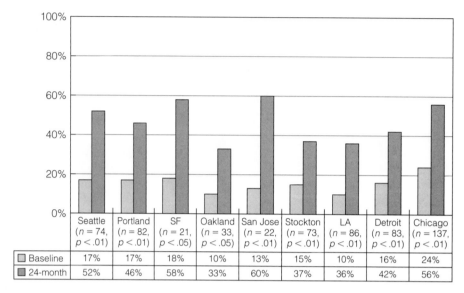

FIGURE 16.2. Employment rates for former SSI DA&As without income assistance: baseline and 24-month follow-up by site (*n* = 611)

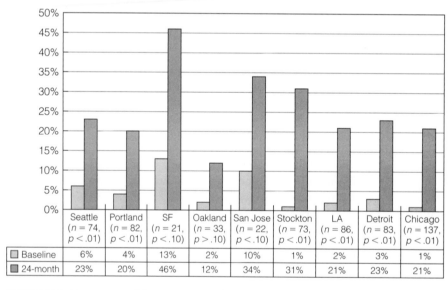

FIGURE 16.3. Percentage of former DA&As without income assistance with earnings of $500 per month or greater: baseline and 24-month follow-up by site (*n* = 611)

income at 24 months was $1,067, a hefty increase from previous waves, for which it ranged from $184 to $584. In San Francisco, earned income was $297 at six months, $1,179 at 12 months, $600 at 18 months, and $1,155 at 24 months. This volatility is an artifact of the small number of employed San Francisco respondents in the no–income-assistance category, which varied from eight at the six-month follow-up to 11 at 24 months.

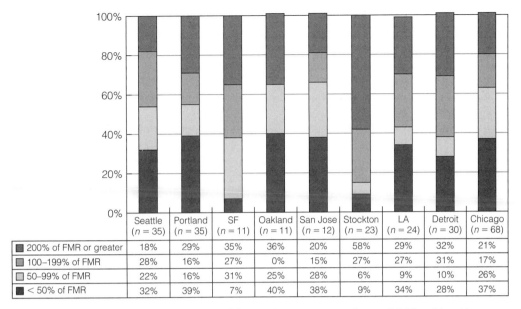

	Seattle (n = 35)	Portland (n = 35)	SF (n = 11)	Oakland (n = 11)	San Jose (n = 12)	Stockton (n = 23)	LA (n = 24)	Detroit (n = 30)	Chicago (n = 68)
■ 200% of FMR or greater	18%	29%	35%	36%	20%	58%	29%	32%	21%
■ 100–199% of FMR	28%	16%	27%	0%	15%	27%	27%	31%	17%
□ 50–99% of FMR	22%	16%	31%	25%	28%	6%	9%	10%	26%
■ < 50% of FMR	32%	39%	7%	40%	38%	9%	34%	28%	37%

FIGURE 16.4. Earned income as percentage of fair market rent among former DA&As without income assistance employed at 24-month follow-up (*n* = 249)

To put such earnings in perspective, it is useful to view them against a measure of the cost of housing. Figure 16.4 shows the 24-month median monthly earned income of former DA&A recipients as a percentage of the 1998 Fair Market Rent (FMR) for a studio ("efficiency") or one-bedroom apartment in each site. These percentages are based on the FMR for a studio except for respondents who reported living with a minor child, in which case we used the one-bedroom FMR.

For their housing to be minimally affordable, our respondents should earn at least 200% of FMR. Even at that level they would spend 50% of gross income on rent, a figure substantially higher than the federal standard of 30% of adjusted income used to set rents in public housing during the study period. They would, in short, remain "shelter poor," having little income left for other needs (see Stone, 1993). As Figure 16.4 illustrates, everywhere but Stockton fewer than 40% (range 18%–36%) earned 200% of FMR. A similar proportion (28%–40% everywhere but Stockton and San Francisco) earned *less than 50% of FMR.* In sum, in most sites few *employed* former DA&A recipients could minimally afford even a tiny apartment, usually of the one-room variety.

Patterns of Employment

Stability of Employment. Everywhere but Oakland and Detroit, at least 30% of former DA&A beneficiaries reported *some* employment earnings at the majority of follow-ups they completed. In our terminology, they were "usually" employed. However, we should not make too much of what we call usual employment, as the case of the Portland woman discussed below will illustrate. The semistructured interviews suggest that among those usually employed, many did only minimum-wage temp work or chased odd jobs cleaning houses and offices, repairing and painting things for neighbors, doing telephone sales once in a while, or, in one case, calling Bingo in a tavern two nights each week.

Among those who became employed after baseline, 59% across sites reported income from work six months after their first such report. Only Detroit's work retention rate (40%) was significantly ($p < .05$) lower than average.[12] Recall, though, that this rate is based on a report of *any* work in the 30 days prior to the index interview and the same kind of report in the following interview. Several sorts of errors involving the structured interviews' temporal blind spots and our definition of employment might cause this indicator to underestimate or overestimate work retention. Using the semistructured interviews to test these, we found no case in which an ill-timed loss of work, for example, resulted in an *underestimate* of job retention. However, we found that of those we call "new" workers, many had only widely spaced odd jobs and yet appeared continuously employed on that basis. A young Portland woman is a good example. She worked a total of 10 hours off-book doing housecleaning and occasional, irregular hours at telephone sales in the month prior to wave 2, and two weeks full-time conducting a house-to-house survey in the month before wave 3. This was the only work she had between July 1996 and March 1998; yet by our definition, she retained employment for six months—in fact, for the whole of 1997. In view of such cases, we think our work retention rates, low as they are, greatly overstate continuity of employment.

Stability of Earnings at the SGA Level. Few former DA&A recipients achieved SGA on a regular basis: Generally, fewer than 20% reported earnings of $500 a month or more at the majority of follow-ups. In six of the nine sites (Seattle, Portland, Oakland, Los Angeles, Detroit, and Chicago), 15% or fewer were "usually" employed at SGA (see Figure 16.5). Even at the level of SGA, however, caveats about the quality of our respondents' work remain in order. In 1998, SGA could be achieved with only 21.5 hours of minimum-wage work each week in Washington, Illinois and Michigan, 19.5 hours in California, and 18.5 hours in Oregon. To be sure, some who regularly earned SGA had good jobs: In the semistructured interviews, we talked with a union shipyard worker in Portland, a union construction worker in San Francisco, an addiction counselor in Stockton, and a welder in Chicago. They made living wages and saw futures for themselves. But they are outliers in the distribution of earned income reported above.

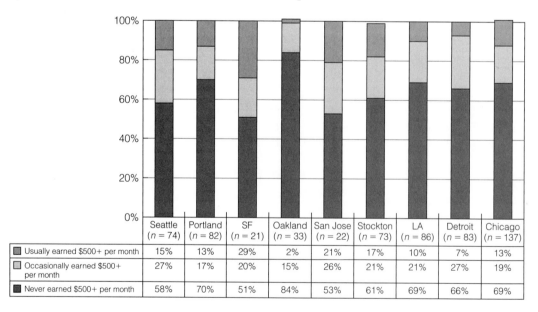

	Seattle (*n* = 74)	Portland (*n* = 82)	SF (*n* = 21)	Oakland (*n* = 33)	San Jose (*n* = 22)	Stockton (*n* = 73)	LA (*n* = 86)	Detroit (*n* = 83)	Chicago (*n* = 137)
■ Usually earned $500+ per month	15%	13%	29%	2%	21%	17%	10%	7%	13%
▫ Occasionally earned $500+ per month	27%	17%	20%	15%	26%	21%	21%	27%	19%
■ Never earned $500+ per month	58%	70%	51%	84%	53%	61%	69%	66%	69%

FIGURE 16.5. Consistency of earnings of $500 or more per month in the 24-month follow-up period among former SSI DA&As without income assistance (*n* = 611)

Independent Predictors of Employment Outcomes. Indicators of employment stability were significantly correlated with employment status at baseline and baseline abstinence from alcohol and illegal drugs. Among the employed, employment status at baseline was correlated with later earned income.

Employment Status at Baseline: In Chicago, among former DA&A recipients not employed at baseline ($n = 103$), only 38% were usually employed during the follow-up period. By contrast, among those already working at baseline ($n = 32$), this figure was 69% ($p < .05$). In Los Angeles, among those unemployed at baseline ($n = 75$), only 21% were usually employed during the follow-up, whereas among those working at baseline ($n = 11$), this figure was 76% ($p < .05$). Across all other sites, these figures were 24% ($n = 329$) and 52% ($n = 58$) ($p < .05$).

Similarly, among those unemployed in Chicago at baseline ($n = 103$), only 7% usually achieved SGA, whereas 30% of those working at baseline ($n = 32$) usually earned $500 per month ($p < .05$). In Los Angeles as well, only 5% of those unemployed at baseline ($n = 75$) usually achieved SGA, whereas 53% of those working at baseline ($n = 11$) usually did so ($p < .05$). Across all other sites, these figures were 9% ($n = 329$) and 23% ($n = 58$) ($p < .05$). We take up employment barriers below; but here we should note that a combined-site analysis revealed, not surprisingly, that at all waves those employed at baseline had fewer barriers to employment than those not working at baseline.

Finally, monthly median earned income was $289 for those in Chicago employed at 24 months but not at baseline ($n = 48$), compared with $497 among those working at both baseline and 24 months ($n = 19$). Across all other sites, these medians were $513 ($n = 138$) and $742 ($n = 43$). In short, while monthly median income rose over time, the value accruing to baseline employment remained.

Substance Use: We found a statistically significant ($p < .05$) relationship between baseline abstinence from alcohol and illegal drugs and the consistent performance of SGA in Chicago and Stockton, where 33% (Chicago, $n = 31$) and 37% (Stockton, $n = 25$) of those abstinent in the six months before baseline "usually" achieved SGA during the study. In comparison, only 6% (Chicago, $n = 106$) and 8% (Stockton, $n = 48$) of those who drank or used in the six months before baseline usually made SGA. We found a similar relationship in Seattle, Portland, and Los Angeles, though it was not statistically significant. We will have more to say about this in the Discussion section, below.

Barriers to SGA

Prevalence of Specific Barriers. Table 16.4 details the prevalence at 24 months of each of the eight barriers to employment for each of the sites included in this analysis. The prevalence of discrete barriers varied widely from place to place. Overall, transportation was the most common obstacle (55%), followed by low levels of education (53%), substance abuse (32%), inadequate job skills (31%), physical health problems (25%), mental health problems (13%), domestic abuse (9%), and unstable housing (8%).

In most sites, the number of barriers was fairly stable over time. In Chicago and Stockton, however, the proportion of respondents experiencing two or more barriers declined slightly between six and 24 months, dropping from 78% to 68% ($p < .05$) in Chicago and 75% to 58% ($p <.05$) in Stockton. With the exception of the job-skills and transportation impediments, the prevalence of specific barriers was similarly stable. The proportion of respondents indicating a need for help with job skills declined in Chicago (48% vs. 33%, $p < .01$), Seattle (52% vs. 35%, $p < .10$), Detroit

Table 16.4. Prevalence of Individual and Multiple Barriers to Performance of SGA at 24-Month Follow-Up Interview by Site

	Chicago (n = 137)	Portland (n = 82)	Detroit (n = 83)	Seattle (n = 74)	Los Angeles (n = 86)	Stockton (n = 73)	Total (n = 535)
	%	%	%	%	%	%	%
Type of Barrier							
Transportation	56	48	66	44	41	37	55
Education	57	32	49	24	47	52	53
Substance Abuse	33	39	29	52	30	32	32
Job Skills	33	52	24	35	30	27	31
Physical Health	20	32	33	35	33	31	25
Mental Health	9	32	18	31	16	19	13
Domestic Abuse	9	20	5	12	5	20	9
Housing	8	17	6	10	9	10	8
Number of Barriers							
0–1 barrier	32	31	33	32	37	42	33
2–3 barriers	48	31	47	39	44	32	46
4 or more barriers	21	38	19	29	18	27	21

(37% vs. 24%, $p < .05$), and Stockton (38% vs. 27%, $p < .10$). The proportion of respondents indicating a need for help with transportation declined in Chicago (73% vs. 56%, $p < .01$), Seattle (61% vs. 44%, $p < .05$), Stockton (63% vs. 37%, $p < .05$), and Los Angeles (60% vs. 41%, $p < .05$).

Our data do not permit us to explain these changes with any confidence. The decline in reported need for job skills may in some part have resulted from training: In all sites but Seattle (where the figure was only 6%), 17%–29% of those reporting a need for training at six months had received some by 24 months. However, the decline may also have been the result of employment, especially at the SGA level: Only 7% of those employed at SGA reaffirmed their need for training at 24 months if they had been unemployed at six months and indicated a need for training but did not get any. In contrast, 50% of those unemployed at 24 months reaffirmed the need for training expressed at six months ($p < .05$).[13]

Similarly, employment at SGA was associated with lower rates of reported transportation problems, but only in some sites. In Portland, 73% of those not earning SGA at 24 months reported transportation problems, whereas no one (0%) earning SGA did so. Findings in Los Angeles (67% vs. 0%) and in Stockton (43% vs. 0%) were similar, though cell sizes were small in all these sites ("ns" ranged from 22 to 24). Earning SGA made no difference in Chicago, Detroit, or Seattle.

Relationship between the Number of Barriers and SGA. In five of the six sites examined (Seattle, Portland, Chicago, Detroit, and Stockton), the likelihood of achieving SGA increased as the number of employment barriers declined (Table 16.5). In Portland, for example, on average across waves, only 2% of respondents who experienced four or more barriers performed SGA. But among those experiencing two to three barriers, 9% reached SGA (OR = 2.1, $p < .01$), and among those with zero or one barrier, 42% did so (OR = 6.1, $p < .05$). We found a similar pattern in Chicago and Stockton, and to a lesser degree in Seattle and Detroit.

Table 16.5. Relationship between the Number of Barriers and Performance of SGA by Site

	% Employed at SGA Level[a]	Odds Ratio[b]	95% CI Low	High	p-Value
Seattle (n = 74)					
4 or more barriers	7	Reference			
2–3 barriers	14	NS			
0–1 barrier	47	8.8	2.3	32.2	< .01
Portland (n = 82)					
4 or more barriers	2	Reference			
2–3 barriers	9	2.1	1.3	3.5	< .01
0–1 barrier	42	6.1	3.1	11.9	< .05
Chicago (n = 137)					
4 or more barriers	3	Reference			
2–3 barriers	10	1.9	1.1	3.1	<.01
0–1 barrier	34	5.8	2.8	11.9	<.05
Detroit (n = 83)					
4 or more barriers	7	Reference			
2–3 barriers	11	NS			
0–1 barrier	21	3.2	1.4	7.4	< .05
Stockton (n = 73)					
4 or more barriers	4	Reference			
2–3 barriers	12	2.5	1.2	5.2	< .01
0–1 barrier	41	7.3	3.2	16.4	< .05
Los Angeles (n = 86)					
4 or more barriers	9	Reference			
2–3 barriers	17	NS			
0–1 barrier	30	NS			

[a]Averaged across all waves of data collection.

[b]From GENMOD analysis.

Individual Barriers Significantly Correlated with SGA. Individual barriers significantly ($p < .05$) correlated with performing SGA are detailed in Table 16.6. *Transportation* problems were significantly correlated with SGA in five of the six sites. Respondents with a transportation barrier were 2.0–4.5 times less likely to be achieving SGA than those without one. Everywhere but in Los Angeles and Detroit, respondents with *more severe substance abuse problems* were 1.8 (Chicago) to 3.4 (Seattle) times less likely to be employed at SGA. In all sites except Los Angeles and Detroit, *low job skills* significantly reduced the likelihood of achieving SGA. Respondents reporting a need for help with job skills were 1.8 (Chicago) to 3.1 (Stockton) times less likely to earn SGA. Respondents with *more severe mental health problems* were less likely to be employed at SGA in Seattle (OR = 2.6), Stockton (OR = 2.9), and Chicago (OR = 2.1). Those with *more severe physical health difficulties* were less likely to earn SGA in Chicago (OR = 2.6) and Detroit (OR = 2.2).

Table 16.6. Barriers Independently Correlated with Non-Performance of Substantial Gainful Activity by Site

Type of Barrier	Seattle (n = 74) Odds Ratio[a]	Portland (n = 82) Odds Ratio	Chicago (n = 137) Odds Ratio	Detroit (n = 83) Odds Ratio	Stockton (n = 73) Odds Ratio	Los Angeles (n = 86) Odds Ratio
Transportation	3.5	4.5	3.4	2.0	3.2	NS
Job Skills	2.7	2.3	1.8	NS	3.1	NS
Substance Abuse	3.4	2.9	1.8	NS	2.6	NS
Mental Health	2.6	NS	2.1	NS	2.9	NS
Physical Health	NS	NS	2.6	2.2	NS	NS

[a]GENMOD analysis. To facilitate interpretation, the odds ratios represent the odds of *not* performing SGA when the barrier is present. Presented this way, the odds are all greater than 1, and the reader is not burdened with interpreting fractions.

DISCUSSION

Summary and Interpretation of the Findings

Our data tell a story about widespread unemployment and sub-employment in the midst of an extraordinarily tight labor market. While rates of any employment (earnings of even one dollar in the previous month) increased substantially after baseline, at the 24-month follow-up fewer than 25% of our respondents earned $500 per month or more. Former DA&A recipients who worked by and large failed to earn their way out of extreme poverty: Across sites, only a small percentage (12%) "usually" earned the $500 per month necessary to replace the cash value of SSI, and most earned far less than required to minimally afford the most modest sort of housing. It should not be surprising, then, that Norris and her colleagues (this issue) found substantially elevated rates of residential doubling-up and literal homelessness among respondents who lost SSI benefits.

Like other analysts of welfare-to-work dynamics, we found that our respondents had a variety of work impediments, and that the more they had, the more poorly they fared in the labor market. Our findings are roughly equivalent to those in the rapidly accumulating literature on TANF, which finds various constellations of work barriers pertaining to both environmental obstacles (notably transportation) and limitations of human capital (particularly education). It would be unwise to go beyond this simple generalization. The characteristics of welfare populations are administrative artifacts in that they derive from the eligibility criteria of specific programs. While welfare populations may share some barriers to work (such as low levels of educational achievement and vocational skills), others are particular to the group assembled under a specific administrative category. For example, child-care problems, which we did not measure, are more likely to constitute a work barrier for TANF parents than for former SSI DA&A beneficiaries. On the other hand, our semistructured interviews suggest that prison experience (unmeasured by the structured interviews) may be a significant work barrier among former DA&A recipients: 30 (41%) of the 73 semistructured interview respondents in the no-income-assistance category spent time in a state or federal prison. Of these 30, six had also been in the California Rehabilitation Center (CRC) for drug offenders, three had been committed to a state forensic psychiatric facility, and one had been in a state prison, a forensic psychiatric hospital, and CRC.[14]

Although our results varied somewhat by place, we found employment barriers related to substance abuse and mental and physical health that would be expected in an impoverished, middle-aged population composed in large part of long-term drug addicts and alcoholics. The prevalence of the substance-abuse barrier was not higher, because, contrary to conventional wisdom, quite a few former DA&A recipients were not drinking or using heavily when the program ended. Indeed, at baseline, across sites, 22% of those without income assistance reported no use of alcohol or illegal drugs during the previous six months.[15]

For all our emphasis on poor employment outcomes, we must also ask why a small percentage of former DA&A recipients did manage to "get up in the morning and support themselves," to invoke Representative Shaw's words once more. There appear to be three related components of what must be a somewhat speculative answer.

The first is economic context. When the demand for labor is sufficiently great and expectations of productivity are sufficiently flexible, people with all sorts of serious impairments can work. During the economic recovery of the Preparedness Era preceding World War I and the subsequent military absorption of tens of thousands of men, admissions to public residential treatment facilities for alcoholism and drug addiction declined dramatically (Baumohl and Tracy, 1994). With the maturation of the Great Depression, admissions rose sharply, only to decline precipitously once more with America's entry into World War II. By late 1942 there was so little slack in employment that the Kaiser Shipyards in Richmond, California, recruited a busload of "winos" from the Los Angeles County Jail to be trained as welders in lieu of their 90-day sentences (Hopper and Baumohl, 1996). Indeed, the necessity to make do with such erratic employees led to the first workplace alcoholism programs during World War II (White, 1998). Our findings probably reflect a similar (if less dramatic) influence: Some former DA&A recipients found regular work because, in the midst of the most sustained economic expansion of the post-war era, some jobs requiring modest skill and experience were available, and some employers, at least, were willing to take on employees with large gaps in their work histories and other significant blemishes.[16] Economic context may also explain why the relationship between the number of employment barriers and the achievement of SGA in Detroit, while significant, is not as strong as in other sites: Where jobs are in short supply and a person has *any* fundamentally discrediting characteristic or environmental obstacle, additional impediments are unlikely to matter.

Second, as we saw in Chicago and Stockton (and perhaps in Seattle, Portland, and Los Angeles—the relationships in these small samples fell short of statistical significance), a period of established sobriety facilitated the regular achievement of SGA. This said, however, we should not expect sobriety and regular SGA to be neatly correlated: Just as sober folks can be chronically unemployed or underemployed, some jobs accommodate heavy drinkers and drug users. A heavy-drinking Stockton native, a man in his mid-40s, described his ideal job as that of "a maintenance man in a large park...keeping the grass clean and green and keeping the roads clean, and working at your own pace, *but no contact with people*." At one time—now at least two generations past—there were many opportunities for the stubbornly dissipated to redeem their time by such isolated labor: Snow, leaves, and garbage long were removed by men (usually) of persistent "unsteady habits," to use an old expression. This Stockton fellow despaired of ever having such a good bad job ("You have to have 20 years of college in order to even apply for them anymore"); but a Portland man a few years older, and no more sober or sociable, fell into one just like it with the ending of the DA&A program. It even came with benefits.

Third, those who regularly achieved SGA reacted to the threat of lost benefits by quickly looking for work even if they pursued an SSI redetermination or appeal at the same time. Significant employment gains typically were realized in the first six months of the study. Across sites, of those already working at baseline, 29% usually achieved SGA over the study's course, as opposed to only 7% of those not working at baseline. Even if their initial employment was modest, some of these respondents were able to increase their hours or get better jobs: Among those working at baseline, only 11% earned SGA at that point; however, two years later 57% of those still employed were making SGA.

But most former DA&A recipients working at baseline did not consistently earn SGA. If the semistructured interviews are reliable guides, most had only occasional work at baseline and had been doing spot jobs during much of their lives and their tenure on SSI. When the program ended, many got along by the haphazard sort of opportunity described by a middle-aged Chicago heroin addict:

> Yeah [I'm using], and I'm really in a pickle barrel, right? I'm busted [broke], I'm getting cut off. I'm living and I gotta spend $250 a month [on rent] that I ain't got. Or soon not to have.... [So I] stretched up until I got cut off. Hammer came down and it was two months I lived free. Told the guy I'm gonna pay him, I'd pay him, I'd pay him. You know how that goes. And stayed there as long as I could. Finally, he threw me out. [So I went to another building.] The guy says, "Danny [not his real name], if you fix my building, you can live free." So he gave me one apartment that was heated and electric. Running water, of course, and everything. But I had to fix the building. Sweep it, clean out the hallways, repair windows. You understand what I'm saying? I was living free on that. He was paying me—like, he'd give me like maybe $50 for the whole week, no money at all.

By contrast, for many of those who consistently earned SGA, looking for work immediately was an extension of their current or recent treatment experience. They defined SSI as a part of the past that needed to be shed, and sometimes they echoed the language of "enabling" frequently used by critics of the DA&A program (see Hunt and Baumohl, *b*, this issue). Listen to a Portland man in his late 30s:

> So they got all these flyers up in the treatment center. If you on SSI and you getting cut off, you can appeal—da-di-da, these numbers, representatives. So they having this big old push, I guess, trying to keep up with everybody now. I guess this about August, September [of 1996]. So I'm in treatment now. I don't want it [SSI] no way. You know what I mean? I'm glad they cutting it off, really, because I've come to the realization that this ain't did nothing but enable me to keep doing what I was doing. It's not they fault, it's mine, you know?... [W]hat did I need a job for? What do people have to work for? They work to pay bills and try to attain something in life, or become a member of society—all the things I never wanted to do anyway.

More typically, those in recovery praised the DA&A program for the material support it offered when they most needed it, but allowed that they became "tired of waiting for the check," or recalled that they were getting restless and it had become "time to move on." Explained a 55-year-old San Francisco man working in human services: "Being in recovery and being, you know, clean, I wanted to try to do something on my own. I wanted to finally start trying to like get a job, become responsible and all that kind of stuff (laughs)."

Others, abstainers and users alike, immediately sought any kind of work because they were afraid and angry. "I was scared," confessed a San Francisco woman in her early 30s who was working several part-time jobs when we spoke with her in April 1998. "I was scared because that money was paying my rent. But I hustled my ass. All my hustling skills came back, and I was like—I was just praying a lot." Said a Portland methadone patient, a man in his 50s who had spent much of his life in prison: "I went to work. I got me a job and quick. I didn't mess around." He found part-time work that provided benefits and some security. He recognized his good fortune and expressed a view common among those who succeeded but felt driven into the labor market: "There's days I wished I was back on SSI. Because my back gives me hell. It does. But I'll never apply for it. I hated President Clinton for what he did, the way he did it so quick, you know. I'm sure a lot of them [former DA&A recipients] do. But, actually, I came out better. I came out better."

Limitations of Work and Income Indicators:
The Problems of Barter and Crime

While our generous indicators substantially overestimate meaningful employment, they allow us to say with confidence that former DA&A recipients had very poor employment outcomes, *even by standards that systematically overestimate success.* But if we have overestimated more or less formal employment, we have underestimated other, employment-like arrangements. Barter and crime are the difficulties here, as the following two cases from the semistructured interviews illustrate.

> A 50-year-old Chicago man explained his current employment this way: "This guy got a, he just opened up a restaurant. He call it a fish house. Okay, I can cook and stuff (chuckles; he's a large man). And then he got this little construction.... [H]e was doing roofing and stuff, too. So he had me cooking and working [and eating] in the restaurant. Now we got it started, me and him, so he tell me, "Well, I can't afford to pay you so and so." Okay, that's cool. But he owns some buildings, so he give me an apartment, a room, in one of the [apartments]."

> A Stockton man of roughly the same age explained that he lived in a trailer on a farm owned by his elderly father. He did substantial chores in lieu of rent. But he also needed cash to pay his utility bill and support his heroin habit. For this, he occasionally worked for a friend who painted houses, and he kept a small heroin trade for "old timers, you know, people who been shooting dope for 20, 30 years...just people I've known forever." He added: "I don't make anything...but it cuts the cost."

The quantitative analyses in this paper treat these men as "usually" employed because each reported income from employment at the various waves. The Chicago man reported the $200 or so he was paid each month for the occasional day spent roofing, framing, or hanging drywall; the Stockton man reported the similar amount of money he earned painting houses with his buddy. But the structured-interview data don't capture the value of the Chicago man's room and board, and they miss the Stockton fellow's chores-for-housing arrangement and his income from drug dealing.

We think such omissions were common. Family relationships, in particular, seriously complicate definitions of work and income. Because exchanges among kin exist outside the market relationships that define terms such as wages, rents, and loans, respondents often struggled to characterize how they made ends meet. Like the Stockton man on his father's farm, respondents who lived continuously with family typically considered doing chores to be courteous "helping out" when they paid rent but as barter or familial duty when they didn't. These are important but subtle distinctions not captured by the structured interviews. Sometimes a family strategy to keep a dependent relative useful, or at least feeling useful, was reported in the structured interviews as employment, sometimes it was called a "gift" or a "loan," and sometimes it simply went unremarked. A 35-year-old woman born and raised in Stockton, and surrounded by her large family, attended elderly kin and cleaned house for other relatives who gave her money "every now and then." This income was not reported in any of the structured interviews. In Chicago, a man in his late 40s was absorbed into a family construction business in such a way that his pay stayed with kin: His son employed him one day a month for a very generous sum so that he could pay rent to the son's aunt (the man's sister). The man wasn't fooled ("The work I do for him ain't worth $200 or $300"), but he appreciated the gesture. In the structured interviews, he reported the money in the spirit in which it was given: as employment earnings. Similarly, in the words of another Chicago man nearing 50, a long-time heroin addict who reported only small amounts of income, mainly from donating blood and scavenging brass and copper fittings from abandoned buildings: "[My family] trusts me, they love me, they have me to their house, I stay over, I watch their kids. They pay me a little money, I clean their yards, I cut their grass. They lend me a little money...knowing I can't pay them back." Finally, a Portland woman indicated at 12 months that she had sold drugs during the previous six months, but she reported no income from it. In the semistructured interview she clarified this response: "I help my sons a lot," she said. "Every day." Her support came in part from such "help," but she would not characterize it as wage earning, nor could she quantify her "draw" on the family drug business.

Because we think that even many of those who reported income from crime gave estimates that were substantially in error (probably on the low side), we did not treat criminal income in a systematic fashion in our quantitative analyses. Prevarication is not the issue, or at least not the main one. Rather, respondents who hustled their livelihoods found it very difficult to specify their income after the fact. In the semistructured interviews, we found that some criminal behavior was sufficiently discrete and infrequent that respondents could report relatively precise amounts of income.[17] The prostitute who worked only occasionally, for example, could often provide a confident estimate.[17] But the hustling poor are a versatile lot, doing a little of this and a little of that in a complicated stream of economic activity not easily reckoned (see Hopper et al., 1985; Snow et al., 1996). A Portland man said: "I might cash [forge] a check, or I might show somebody how to cash a check and get a piece of money or something like that. Or, you know, if somebody wants a certain amount of drugs and I know where to get it, I'll get—like I said, some from both ends." While drug selling among our respondents was most often like that of the Stockton farmer's son— a matter of "dealing for stash," where, if he bothered, a dealer might figure a rough profit as a percentage of his habit subsidized—for some the drug business involved many transactions over a day in which the dealer's capital and the customers' payments were commingled and bookkeeping was further complicated by payments in kind, complimentary "tastes," payments to lookouts and go-betweens, and the dealer's own consumption. "Sometimes I'm out on the street," a 30-year-old Chicago man said, "and the money flows through my hands. I mean, you have to be there to see it. It's hard to explain...I mean, when you're out there money flows through you." He claimed to handle thousands of dollars on a good day. "I can pocket $500, as long as I don't shoot it up or smoke it up," he said—but allowed that this happened rather often.

It is impossible to adjust our quantitative analyses to account for such ambiguous economics.[18] They are an inevitable part of the background noise. It seems certain, though, that if hustling profits were included, many more of our respondents would have reached SGA.[19]

CONCLUSION

Even in the best of times, few former DA&A recipients replaced their lost SSI income with earnings from work. Moreover, the rising rate of meaningful employment in this population stalled a year after baseline, suggesting that outcomes are not likely to improve. While a small number made a successful transition from welfare to work, even their success could be precarious. Shipyard and construction workers face seasonal idleness; none of the public-sector workers with whom we spoke were permanent employees, and thus none had benefits.

Consider the situation of a San Franciscan we'll call John. John collected SSI for less than two years before the DA&A program ended, qualifying shortly after his last parole from prison in 1995. In April 1998, after more than 30 years of heroin addiction and intermittent incarceration, he had been successful with methadone for two years and had a full-time job at nine dollars an hour, grossing over $1,500 monthly. He lived with his girlfriend of 10 years in a hotel room for which they paid only $380 per month. His girlfriend received $370 each month in General Assistance and $81 in food stamps. On the surface, and relative to most former DA&A recipients, John had it made—yet he was a very worried man. His job provided no medical, pension, or vacation benefits. It required him to have a car, which meant paying for insurance, parking, and maintenance. With his girlfriend, a woman in her mid-40s, he had two young children who, because of her drinking and heroin addiction, had been placed by child welfare authorities shortly after John went to prison in 1994. Now that they were both settled in a methadone program, and with John's parole nearing an end, they looked forward to getting their kids back. But this would mean a larger place, requiring probably double their current rent. Moreover, his income would disqualify the family for TANF benefits, although Medicaid (Medi-Cal) would continue for his children. Indeed, now that he was working, his Medi-Cal had been stopped, and the county had sent him a $1,250 bill for his last five months of methadone. "They just got me in one hell of a bind right now," he said angrily. "All of a sudden, bam! I had all my teeth pulled on Medi-Cal. I was gonna get plates and all that. Now this is all out of my pocket. . . . My cholesterol is high. I have high blood pressure. I got blood in my urine. . . . I got hepatitis. . . . I'm gonna be 56. . . . And how much longer can I work? . . . There's gonna be nothing in retirement. So I'm gonna be back on SSI."

Although most former DA&A recipients are younger than John, the majority are in or entering midlife with little education, few skills, and many liabilities. Most who are working have jobs far less remunerative or regular than John's, and they face employment prospects that will not improve with time. Thus a lot of them figure to become reacquainted with SSI, as John foresaw for himself: Many who live long enough and don't spend their golden years in prison will, at 65, qualify for SSI on the basis of impecunious old age rather than disability. When all is said and done, that may be the bottom line.

NOTES

1. The policy change also affected recipients of Social Security Disability Insurance (DI). The figure of 167,000 represents the number of people getting *only* SSI on the basis of an impairment "materially related" to alcoholism or drug addiction (about 120,000) plus "concurrent beneficiaries," those getting *both* SSI and DI on this basis (see Hunt and Baumohl, *a*, this issue, for an explanation of this status). Including those collecting *only* DI, 209,000 recipients were affected.

2. It is tempting to attribute this drop to a tightening labor market, because AFDC rolls had been in decline for several years before TANF was phased in beginning in August 1996. However, during the same time the value of the Earned Income Tax Credit (EITC) for the working poor was rising significantly, and many states already were operating TANF-like programs under federal waivers granting exemptions from AFDC rules. These waiver "experiments," like many subsequent TANF programs, diverted many applicants into job-search activities and eliminated from the rolls families who were not compliant with new administrative

requirements. Thus the decline in the AFDC and TANF rolls represents a complex interaction of labor market conditions, EITC incentives, and welfare-to-work incentives and sanctions. For a detailed consideration of these issues, see Ellwood (2000).

3. An early study of DA&A beneficiaries (SRA Technologies, 1986), conducted before the explosion of the rolls in the 1990s (see Hunt and Baumohl, *a*, this issue), concluded that the population had little employment potential because of its members' poor physical and mental health, limited education, spotty work histories, and advanced age (almost half were 50 or older). This was a younger group by the time the program ended 10 years later, but other significant characteristics seem not to have changed dramatically.

4. Based on data from interviews conducted in 1989, Schmidt et al. (1998) found that GA recipients in a northern California county were about three times as likely to be problem drinkers and heavy drug users, and about four times as likely to have "substance dependencies," as AFDC beneficiaries. AFDC recipients had problem-drinking rates comparable to those of the county's general population, but they were more than three times as likely as general-population members to be heavy drug users or to meet criteria for alcohol or drug dependence.

5. A respondent was considered to have "lost her job" if she lost a job and did not find another within one month.

6. In July 1999, six months after we completed data collection, the SGA level was raised to $700 per month.

7. The quotation is from one of the semistructured interviews that supplemented the scripted interviews. These are described below.

8. Sweeney (2000:14) reached the same conclusion: The "disabilities" that most TANF parents reported "do not meet the stringent tests of the SSI program." Similarly, the Michigan GA data suggest that while many recipients "were not able-bodied," their impairments did not meet SSI standards of disability (Henly and Danziger, 1996:221).

9. "Welfare recipients" were defined as "persons who report living in a household that received AFDC, public assistance, or public welfare in the past 12 months."

10. Under complicated work-incentive rules that do not warrant summary here, SSI beneficiaries may earn over $1,000 per month for 12 months without jeopardizing their eligibility. Thus our finding that a small percentage of requalified former DA&A recipients were working is neither surprising nor evidence of welfare fraud.

11. Because California provides a substantial state supplement to the federal SSI payment, the cash replacement value of SSI in the California counties is actually about $600 per month. To avoid confusion, however, we used the federal minimum for all sites. When we ran analyses at the higher standard for the California counties, our findings were essentially unchanged.

12. In spite of this, the aggregate rates of *any* employment reported above remained relatively unchanged after six months because (1) over 50% of those who lost work between six and 18 months regained some employment by the end of the study and (2) respondents became employed for the first time at different points in the follow-up period: Initial employment came at six months for 55%, at 12 months for 21%, at 18 months for 12%, and at 24 months for 11%. Reemployment and the continuous addition of first-time workers thus stabilized the rates over time.

13. Among those employed at the study's end, income was related to a persistent expression of the need for skills training. Across sites, median income for those restating such a need was $187 per month, compared with $490 for those who reported no need. This trend was most apparent in Chicago ($484 vs. $193), Portland ($627 vs. $98), and Detroit ($593 vs. $236).

14. Overall, 57 (37%) of 156 semistructured-interview respondents spent time in one or another of these institutions.

15. The figures for six-month abstinence among people with no income assistance were highest in San Jose (56%), San Francisco (35%), and Stockton (31%); the lowest rate was in Seattle (14%). Some of the semistructured-interview respondents had been abstinent for several years. In some cases these were people with very serious impairments quite apart from any substance abuse (spinal injuries, for example), and they requalified for SSI as a result. Many of the long abstinent in the no-income-assistance group used SSI to supplement low-wage labor or to support their "recovery work." As Hunt and Baumohl discuss (*a*, this issue), their continuing presence on the rolls was facilitated by the huge backlog of continuing-disability reviews in the DA&A program.

16. These stigmata could be quite literal: Several semistructured-interview respondents discussed the problem of looking for work with gang-related or "politically incorrect" tattoos.

17. One Stockton woman was an especially devout accountant: As technically required, she once reported her sex-work earnings to the Social Security Administration, which dutifully docked her check for the amount over the allowable SSI income limit.

18. By repeatedly interviewing respondents and by encouraging them to save pay stubs and receipts, Edin and Lein (1997) made a heroic effort to document the income and expenditures of 214 welfare mothers in four American cities. Their method was not feasible in this study. Further, drinking and drug use created some reporting problems in their study—problems that likely would have been worse in ours.

19. Some of these criminal enterprises were of long standing. Had the Social Security Administration been aware of them, some of these people would not have qualified for SSI in the first place—at least not by the SGA rules instituted in 1995 (see Hunt and Baumohl, *a*, this issue).

REFERENCES

Allison, Paul, *Logistic Regression Using the SAS System: Theory and Application* (Cary, NC: SAS Institute), 1999.

Baumohl, Jim and Sarah W. Tracy, "Building Systems to Manage Inebriates: The Divergent Paths of California and Massachusetts, 1891–1920," *Contemporary Drug Problems,* 21 (1994), 557–597.

Brauner, Sarah and Pamela Loprest, "Where Are They Now? What States' Studies of People Who Left Welfare Tell Us," The Urban Institute, Series A, #A-32, May 1999.

Choudhry, G. Hussain and Cynthia Helba, "Rationale and Procedures for Weighting the SSI Study Data," *Contemporary Drug Problems,* 30 (2003), 137–146.

Congressional Budget Office [of the United States], *Estimate of HR4, The Family Self-Sufficiency Act of 1995* (Washington, DC: Author), 1995.

Danziger, Sandra, Mary Corcoran, Sheldon Danziger, Colleen Heflin, Ariel Kalil, Judith Levine, Daniel Rosen, Kristin Seefeldt, Kristine Siefert, and Richard Tolman, "Barriers to the Employment of Welfare Recipients," Poverty Research and Training Center, University of Michigan, Revised Version, September 1999.

Edin, Kathryn and Laura Lein, *Making Ends Meet: How Single Mothers Survive Welfare and Low-Wage Work* (New York: Russell Sage Foundation, 1997).

Ellwood, David T., "The Impact of the Earned Income Tax Credit and Social Policy Reforms on Work, Marriage, and Living Arrangements," *National Tax Journal,* 53 (2000), 1063–1105.

Guydish, Joseph, Claudia Ponath, Alan Bostrom, Kevin Campell and Nancy Barron, "Effects of Losing SSI Benefits on Standard Drug and Alcohol Outcome Measures," *Contemporary Drug Problems,* 30 (2003), 169–193.

Henly, Julia R. and Sandra K. Danziger, "Confronting Welfare Stereotypes: Characteristics of General Assistance Recipients and Postassistance Employment," *Social Work Research,* 20 (1996), 217–227.

Hopper, Kim, and Jim Baumohl, "Redefining the Cursed Word: A Historical Interpretation of American Homelessness." In Jim Baumohl (Ed.), *Homelessness in America* (Phoenix, AZ: Oryx Press, 1996), 3–14 (text); 221–224 (notes).

Hopper, Kim, Ezra Susser, and Sarah Conover, "Economies of Makeshift: Deindustrialization and Homelessness in New York City," *Urban Anthropology,* 14 (1985), 183–236.

Hunt, Sharon R. and Jim Baumohl, "Drink, Drugs and Disability: An Introduction to the Controversy," *Contemporary Drug Problems,* 30 (2003), 9–76.

Hunt, Sharon R. and Jim Baumohl, "Now Invited to Testify: Former Beneficiaries Appraise the SSI Drug Addiction and Alcoholism Program," *Contemporary Drug Problems,* 30 (2003), 455–499.

Johnson, Hans and Sonya Tafoya, "The Basic Skills of Welfare Recipients: Implications for Welfare Reform," Public Policy Institute of California, 1999.

The Lewin Group, Inc., and Westat, Inc., *Policy Evaluation of the Effect of Legislation Prohibiting the Payment of Disability Benefits to Individuals Whose Disability is Based on Drug Addiction or Alcoholism: Interim Report Submitted to the Social Security Administration* (Fairfax, VA: Author), July 21, 1998.

Mashaw, Jerry L. and Virginia Reno, *Balancing Security and Opportunity: The Challenge of Disability Income Policy* (Washington, DC: National Academy of Social Insurance), 1996.

Merrill, Jeffrey C., Sarah Ring-Kurtz, Delia Olufokunbi, Sherril Aversa, and Jennifer Sherker, "Women on Welfare: A Study of the Florida WAGES Population." Unpublished manuscript, Treatment Research Institute, University of Pennsylvania School of Medicine, undated (ca. 1999).

National Public Radio, Morning Edition, "Supplemental Security Income," September 15, 1999. Audio stream available at: <http://search.npr.org/cf/cmn/cmnpd01fm.cfm?PrgDate=9%2F15%2F1999&PrgID=3>.

Norris, Jean, Richard Scott, Richard Speiglman, and Rex Green, "Homelessness, Hunger and Material Hardship Among Those Who Lost SSI," *Contemporary Drug Problems,* 30 (2003), 241–273.

Rangarajan, Anu, Peter Schochet, and Dexter Chu, "Employment Experiences of Welfare Recipients Who Find Jobs: Is Targeting Possible?" Mathematica Policy Research, Inc., Reference #8428-600, August 1998.

Schmidt, Laura, Constance Weisner, and James Wiley, "Substance Abuse and the Course of Welfare Dependency," *American Journal of Public Health,* 88 (1998), 1616–22.

Snow, David A., Leon Anderson, Theron Quist, and Daniel Cress, "Material Survival Strategies on the Street: Homeless People as *Bricoleurs.*" In Jim Baumohl (Ed.), *Homelessness in America* (Phoenix, AZ: Oryx Press, 1996), 86–96 (text); 234–236 (notes).

SRA Technologies, Demonstration Project on Intensive Case Management for Drug Addicts and Alcoholics Receiving Supplemental Security Income (Alexandria, VA: Author), 1986.

Stone, Michael E., *Shelter Poverty: New Ideas on Housing Affordability* (Philadelphia: Temple University Press, 1993).

Swartz, James, Peggy Tonkin, and Jim Baumohl, "The Methodology of the Multi-Site Study of the Termination of Supplemental Security Income Benefits for Drug Addicts and Alcoholics," *Contemporary Drug Problems,* 30 (2003), 77–121.

Sweeney, Eileen P., "Recent Studies Indicate that Many Parents Who Are Current or Former Welfare Recipients Have Disabilities or Other Medical Conditions," Center on Budget and Policy Priorities, February 29, 2000.

United States Conference of Mayors, *The Welfare Challenge Facing America's Cities: A 125-City Survey* (Washington, DC: Author), November 1997.

United States Department of Health and Human Services, Administration for Children and Families, Office of Public Affairs, Welfare Caseloads, 1936–1999 (<http://www.acf.dhhs.gov/news/stats/3697.htm>).

White, William L., *Slaying the Dragon: The History of Addiction Treatment and Recovery in America* (Bloomington, IL: Chestnut Health Systems), 1998.

COMMENTARY BY: Jim Baumohl

INTRODUCTION

The distinction between so-called "quantitative" and "qualitative" *studies* is misleading; used this way, the terms conflate the processes of collecting data and analyzing them. Better, I think, to use one vocabulary to characterize the methods by which evidence is gathered and another to talk about how it's treated. We should speak of "qualitative analysis" not "qualitative data," and we should discuss methods of data collection in terms that make clear how the evidence was elicited and with what advantages and disadvantages—regardless of how the data were analyzed subsequently.

By definition, "mixed-methods" research collects and analyzes data in a variety of ways within the same study. This approach is common and has a long history. Ethnography, for example, is closely associated with the data collection methods of observation in natural settings and un-scripted interviewing, and the analytic method of narrative analysis; but classic ethnographies are broad studies of community life that draw on many sources of data and frequently quantify data that are amenable to such treatment even if they are based on narrative.

In what follows I suggest that scripted interviewing of the sort that characterizes large-scale social research in particular can hobble understanding when employed without respondent-guided interviewing. To make my point, I draw on the history of the Supplemental Security Income Study (the "SSI Study") that yielded the paper you've just read ("The Bottom Line"). I begin by considering how the problem was shaped by the common constraint of insufficient time for study design.

THE METHODOLOGICAL IMPACT OF URGENCY

Studies employing more than one method to collect data often were not designed originally to do so. Rather, some initial error of judgment about measurement or the nature of the research questions results in midstream changes. This was the case in the SSI Study.

In March 1996, Congress eliminated disability benefits in the SSI and Social Security Disability Insurance (DI) programs for those whose qualifying impairment was based "materially" on alcoholism and/or other drug addiction. Faced with the unprecedented elimination of an entire impairment category, the Social Security Administration put in place a complex reappraisal process

---

Commentary on article: Campbell, K., Baumohl, J., & Hunt, S. R. (2003). The bottom line: Employment and barriers to work among former SSI DA&A beneficiaries. *Journal of Contemporary Drug Problems, 30,* 195–240.

to requalify or disqualify over 200,000 people within a few months. All "drug addiction and alcoholism" (DA&A) benefits were to end on January 1, 1997 (see Hunt & Baumohl, 2003a).

The SSI Study was cobbled together to take advantage of this "natural experiment." Late in the summer of 1996, the federal Center for Substance Abuse Treatment (CSAT) and two teams of investigators funded by the Robert Wood Johnson Foundation (RWJ) began to organize what became the SSI Study. The details of this process are not important here, but note that fundamental decisions about the study's design were made in a climate of urgency. If the projected two-year, multisite panel study were to capture baseline measurements before or very close to the point of benefit loss, interviews would need to begin in November. In the meantime, sites had to be chosen; an instrument had to be designed, reviewed by several different institutional review boards, and pilot tested; logistics teams had to be put in place; and a workable division of labor and a decision-making process hammered out for the national study team. A startling amount of work was done in about two months.

The speed with which the SSI Study was designed and fielded and the latitude allowed individual sites in order to accommodate disagreements among investigators created a number of subsequent problems in an otherwise quite successful and ambitious project (see Swartz, Tonkin, & Baumohl, 2003). Because the study had to be funded quickly, existing contract mechanisms had to be used. There was no time for the niceties of lengthy peer review or much thoughtful, critical review of any kind. CSAT supplemented the funding of the RWJ projects by employing existing contractors as conduits and brought into the study other sites already funded through its Target Cities Demonstration Program and a demonstration program managed by CSAT but funded by the Social Security Administration (SSA). Target Cities aimed to centralize intake and assessment, allow for treatment matching, and effect a number of treatment system changes in major metropolitan areas. Typically, Target Cities sites enrolled large numbers of DA&A recipients. The SSA-funded project was designed to test the effectiveness of intensive case management for DA&A recipients.

These were treatment demonstration projects and thus most of the original SSI Study team members worked in treatment evaluation. They knew a great deal about alcohol and other drug treatment, evaluation methods, psychometrics, and so forth. Some knew a lot about the criminal justice system. Most knew very little about social benefits, however, or the literature on poverty and welfare. They tended to see the SSI Study in terms of what they knew how to measure: individual outcomes. Moreover, it seemed to me that most were accustomed to using administrative data and packaged instruments and had little experience with the design of interview instruments, especially those for use with a poorly educated respondent group. In my view, as fielded originally the study reflected the psychologism of the majority of the group and its members' lack of awareness of documented problems in getting valid answers to critical questions about such things as income, expenditures, housing stability, and family composition, for example. It struck me as a large "black box" study in which a policy stimulus was specified and individual responses measured, but without any way to understand why the responses were what they were. (Or, as we would discover, whether we really understood what some responses meant!) Put another way, the study seemed to lack a "logic model."

A great deal of research is organized hastily. The lesson here is to beware of using only skills of convenience. As the old saying goes, if your only tool is a hammer, every problem looks like a nail. While the SSI Study Group brought in a range of special skills once data analysis began, the urgency of the design task and the necessity to use researchers who could be paid through existing channels resulted in serious lacunae, less than desirable instrumentation, and perhaps most important, very limited predesign debate about how the study would be focused and related to theory and existing empirical literature. There was no time for thorough pilot-testing of the instruments and data collection procedures, or for study team members to try out potential explanations of hypothetical findings. These design processes prove their value when the time comes to move from summarizing data to achieving a command of their analysis.

In any event, this is how it was and how it had to be under the circumstances. But problems soon became apparent.

INTERROGATING THE SURVEY DATA BY USING NARRATIVE DATA: THE STUDY WITHIN THE STUDY

Preliminary analyses of the second wave of data from the nine study sites revealed some vexing limitations in the survey data. For example, a high percentage of respondents who reported little or no income following the loss of SSI benefits also seemed to report stable housing and consistent sources of food—that is, material circumstances that were not consistent with being broke. It was also obvious that some elements of the instrument were not working well, particularly questions about family composition and respondents' experience with SSI and their attempts to requalify for benefits or their decisions to forgo them.

The problems were twofold. First, the training and instincts of most study team members blinded them to the necessity of understanding outcomes in terms of the social relations that keep poor people afloat. The hasty design by the experts at hand neglected how to measure the existence and dynamics of poverty's makeshifts, most notably the ways people draw on kith and kin. Second, parts of the instrument attempted to reduce to scripted questions (and often precoded answers) a very complicated bureaucratic process (SSI requalification) and ambiguous kinship relations. Respondents answered the questions and the interviewers duly recorded their answers, but on examination, some of the data didn't make sense.

Resources were available to implement a supplemental inquiry to address these and other matters (a remarkable luxury), and so that is what we did. Sharon Hunt and I were its architects. The basic design and logistics of this supplemental study have been described elsewhere (Swartz, Tonkin, & Baumohl, 2003). Some instructive obstacles attended this substudy and I turn to these next.

First of all, the SSI Study was responsible to five different institutional review boards (IRBs). The study's approved design called for five waves of data collection using the instrument submitted originally. An additional interview using a completely different method required full review by all of these IRBs. Thus, during the summer of 1997 we designed an interview format to complement the scripted survey and submitted it for review. Fortunately, we were dealing with responsive IRBs and were able to pilot test the supplemental interview in two sites in the fall of 1997, trying out different interview styles and getting the bugs out of our recording equipment. A lengthy IRB review process would have killed the substudy.

To comply with the terms approved by these various IRBs, we were obliged to seek prior agreement from all potential participants to be contacted about the supplemental study. As the pilot testing needed to occur before wave three, and as wave two had been completed, potential participants were recruited into convenience samples by the logistics teams in the pilot sites during the course of their routine between-wave follow-ups. We administered formal consent at the time of interview. The other four sites required systematic samples, however, and we wanted to draw these on the basis of wave three data, which would not be complete until late in the winter. Thus, at the conclusion of the wave three interviews all respondents at the four supplemental study sites were briefed on the nature of the substudy and asked only to provide permission to be contacted should they be chosen for the sample. Almost everyone agreed.

While cumbersome, this two-stage process of getting permission to contact and then consent at the time of interview (including a separate consent to be recorded) permitted us to approach people in an ethically acceptable way while optimizing the information available for sampling purposes. For each site, we drew equal random samples within strata defined by a respondent's relationship to SSI and employment as reported at wave three (i.e., collecting SSI; not collecting SSI but performing some work for wages; not collecting SSI and not working for wages). We also selected a replacement pool for each site within each stratum.

We conducted 163 semistructured, modified life-history interviews in four sites during the spring of 1998. Limitations of length preclude discussion of the details, but the supplemental study also was designed quickly. The most important drawbacks of haste were insufficient interviewer training and our inability to thoroughly analyze pilot data to be sure that the features of cognitive interviewing that we used in the substudy were implemented consistently and working well, especially the semistructured interview's structure of temporal recall and the event history probes that we employed (for a fine review of these techniques, see Schwarz & Oyserman, 2001).

We did at least one thing very well, however. As our interviews were conducted between the third and fourth waves of the larger study, we had prior access to three waves of data from each respondent. (The response rate for each wave was remarkably high so we had very complete sets of data.) Once we had drawn our samples and replacement pools for the sites and assigned interviewers to respondents, each interviewer carefully compared the existing waves of data from those they were to interview, noting ambiguities and inconsistencies and building into the interview guides clarifying questions and probes about them. Each interview was individualized in this way.

This painstaking preparation allowed us to focus on confusing responses to scripted survey questions, and to individual patterns of change that occurred between survey waves and were therefore undetectable by the survey. (In "The Bottom Line," the paper that accompanies this commentary, you can see how these data permit us to interpret more meaningfully the employment and income data derived from scripted questions.) It also allowed us to flag theretofore-unknown problems. For example, we confirmed that contrary to the SSI Study's intent, some Social Security Disability Insurance (DI) recipients were present in the site samples of the larger study. (We had to eliminate seven substudy respondents for this reason.) The national study team subsequently designed a crosscheck of benefit status in connection with wave four and eliminated DI recipients from future analyses. At wave four, respondents were queried about the day of the month their check arrived and what color it was. This distinguished SSI-only beneficiaries from DI recipients and those who got benefits from both programs. As this status is fixed at the time of benefit approval, we could correct the data retrospectively.

Most of the problems we found were not so easily handled. As you've seen in "The Bottom Line," our qualitative analysis of work and wages engages the complexity of meanings respondents attached to these terms, and uses this to inform the quantitative analyses of survey data. Given the time, we might have done the same with the issue of residential stability (see Norris, Scott, Speiglman, & Green, 2003). For example, a man in Chicago characterized his residence *at the same address* in three different ways: At wave one he claimed to be living in his own apartment; at wave two he was paying rent to stay in his mother's place; and at wave three he was living in his own apartment and information on rent was missing. When queried about this in the supplemental interview he said that he was living the whole time in a basement apartment in a house owned by his mother and was paying rent when he could or serving as janitor or caretaker in lieu of rent. (There is a similar Stockton, California case described in "The Bottom Line.") Another Chicago man appears from the scripted survey data to have moved from his own to someone else's residence at wave two. In fact, he was in the same place, living with his wife and children the whole time, but because he was not contributing to the rent at wave two, he did not regard it as *his* place.

Two particularly interesting problems of scripted language and interpretation concerned alcohol and other drug treatment. We knew going into the supplemental interviews that reports on methadone use at wave one were flawed by the frequent conflation by respondents of prescribed and illicit use. However, most regular users of methadone reported being in drug treatment, and it was reasonable to assume for purposes of analysis that they were enrolled in methadone maintenance, a long-term, drug substitution therapy for opiate addiction. Still, some wave one respondents reported using methadone daily *without* being in treatment. Every one of these respondents we encountered in the supplemental interviews told us that they answered the scripted question this way because they did not believe that methadone maintenance was a form of treatment. Here, the ideology of drug-free recovery, deeply absorbed by many respondents, was at odds with the assumptions of the professional evaluators who framed the treatment questions. Similarly, we found that respondents often confused "outpatient group therapy" with 12-Step participation because the lingo and trappings of the Anonymous fellowships permeated the outpatient groups' processes.

HANDLING DISCREPANCIES IN THE DATA

In July of 1998, less than two months out of the field, Sharon Hunt and I presented to the SSI Study Group a preliminary catalog of apparent problems with the data. We had used only our own notes to create this (between us, we did about 60 percent of the interviews), yet we had numerous examples of interpretive problems, apparent interviewer errors (a woman born in Geneva, Wisconsin was coded as Swiss; a Latina was coded as white; and so forth), respondent mistakes (especially about the ages of their children), confessed misrepresentations (usually due to suspicion of the research intent), and even an apparent joke that was taken seriously (a Stockton woman with a ninth-grade education and a long career as a streetwalker was coded as a college graduate; she claimed to have been "joshing" the interviewer).

Our news was not well received, to say the least. (The universal fate of messengers bearing ill tidings.) It is one thing to identify such problems and quite another to know what to do about them. Changing or discarding data is a controversial matter, and creating alternate fields for analytic purposes is a time-consuming nuisance and of no obvious advantage when considering only a few cases in a study with a large sample. While we were very concerned about the prevalence of such problems in our subsample (about 9 percent of the total SSI Study sample), we had no clear sense of what to do about them, and as per the democratic spirit of the study's management, we put the matter to the group.

The study team was not so concerned. After all, we had spoken with a relatively small number of people and our data offered no way to systematically correct many of the problems we'd found. Who could be sure which responses were "correct"? A couple of team members rather angrily accused us of "dumping on the study" and wanting to use the supplemental interview data as a "gold standard" by which to judge the validity of the survey data.

Our worries about the validity of some of the survey data and the complaint about our "gold standard" reflected divisions in the group about the relative plausibility of different sorts of data. In my view (and some members of the study team agreed), many of the inconsistencies we found were rooted in the differences between tightly scripted instruments with precoded response categories and the semistructured, conversational interviews that we did. In the former, respondents were largely passive, responding to one question after another, many of which sounded alike. With us, after an initial prompt, respondents took the lead on storytelling about a particular subject, and

we interjected questions directly relevant to their tale. To be sure, we recorded a great deal of su-
perfluous material, but we intentionally sacrificed efficiency for engagement. For their part, our
respondents often volunteered that they found the scripted survey interviews "repetitive," "bor-
ing," "confusing," or "much too long" (even though they were much *shorter* than their conversations with us, which often lasted 90 minutes or more). They sometimes found their discussions
with us to be painful, particularly when they talked about their childhood, their parents, their
children, and their own failures as parents. But they were never bored, very rarely hostile, and
given an attentive audience, and they worked hard to reconstruct the chronology of their lives and
the meanings they attached to things. Many of them thanked us for permitting them to tell their
stories this way.

Simply put, the scripted survey and the supplemental interviews created very different contexts
for eliciting data. Short of experimental evidence or a good third-source validity check, there is no
way to know which data were "right." There is good reason to think that our autobiographical
data were distorted in their own ways, and that they represent interpretive truth or in some cases,
elaborate fiction (well-acted, conscious misrepresentation), not factual accuracy. We did not use
data from one Chicago interview because the respondent seemed to be making up a colorful but
wildly inconsistent life story as he went along.

A notable problem with autobiography is not deliberate fabrication, but the tendency of the
storyteller to shape the past in the image of the present; that is, to shape history in ways that make
the present seem like a logical extension of it or a logical break with it. This results in highly
selective recall of events and a tendency to offer interpretations rather than descriptions. The
"temperance tales" of recovering addicts are a very old form of such storytelling: Once sobriety is
stabilized, the past is interpreted through the ideological filter of the recovery process ("I was lost
and now am found"). We heard a fair amount of this and tried to penetrate it by stopping respondents and asking them to focus on how they felt and thought at prior times.

Withal, I believed then and I believe now that substudy respondents did a much better job of
recollecting details and the temporal connections among events than they did in the scripted interviews. I think they provided more accurate (and sometimes more honest) information in several
areas, notably about their drinking and other drug use, their criminal activities (as distinct from
arrests), their involvement with child welfare authorities, and their careers on SSI. But I couldn't
prove these intuitions then and I can't prove them now. Although urinalysis results in several sites
showed that the survey's self-reports greatly (and predictably) underestimated recent drug use (see
Swartz, Hsieh, & Baumohl, 2003), the urinalysis data are not rigorously comparable with the
narrative data. Although they are consistent with the misgivings engendered by the supplemental
interviews, they don't prove anything.

The study team voted to conduct the benefits crosscheck mentioned above and to change the
wording of several questions slightly, but to otherwise leave the data alone. The exiled Wisconsin
woman was not repatriated; the Latina continued to be taken for a WASP; the Stockton prostitute
with the pink hot pants and forward sense of humor retained her college degree.

The ultimate value of our report was its impact on how some of the study's findings were ren-
dered. The problematic items that we identified were not used in analyses, in part because the
wording changes made to mollify us merely introduced a new problem of variable phrasing across
waves. The analysis in "The Bottom Line" reflects a different strategy. It was carefully constructed
to use the narrative data to interrogate systematically the subtler meanings of quantitative findings
derived from survey data. Other papers in the volume could have been written similarly. However,
in spite of its relative wealth of resources, the SSI Study ran afoul of a basic law that governs the
work lives of those who, like most members of the SSI Study Group, make a living from funded

research: The money never covers sufficient writing time. As a result, other papers use only small contributions from the narrative data to qualify or illuminate points derived from analysis of the survey data (for example, Swartz, Campbell, Baumohl, & Tonkin, 2003); Hunt and I wrote a paper based entirely on the supplemental interview data (Hunt & Baumohl, 2003b).

A LESSON IN MIXING METHODS

I now return to the point with which I started. Restated prescriptively, this is: Scripted interviews with precoded responses should be augmented by respondent-guided interviews that produce extensive narrative material. Like items on political opinion polls, scripted survey questions with precoded responses tend to "disarticulate" the views of respondents, who cannot easily qualify, shade, and illustrate meaning by analogy, or explain the logic of seemingly inconsistent responses (see Reinarman, 1987, pp. 203–241). Tight scripting also assumes that the language of questions about fundamentally ambiguous terms like "home," "work," or even "treatment" can be adequately standardized. I think this is a dubious claim.

But let me be clear: I think it's possible to construct good scripted surveys. However, they must be tested carefully for far more than the clarity of skip patterns and other aspects of an instrument's internal logic, or for questions that are obviously too vague or convoluted. Face validity is a complicated issue about which we should not make benign assumptions. There are a number of extremely useful cognitive interviewing techniques that can be used in pilot testing to sort out the tradeoffs involved in alternate wordings, to set reasonable recall periods, to suggest the appropriate level of scripting and the nature of standard probes, and so forth (see Schwarz & Oyserman, 2001). All of these techniques to inform survey construction involve considerable time and money, however, and they are unlikely to be used widely.

If the SSI Study is a helpful guide, under similar circumstances cognitive interviewing techniques can be used to explore face validity even after the commission of original sin. This entails the employment of narrative data to analyze across-wave discrepancies and superficial concordances. It may not be a bad solution to keep in a back pocket for times when things go wrong and we need to amend our mistakes and learn from them.

ACKNOWLEDGMENTS

I am very grateful to my colleagues and coauthors on the SSI Study for helping me think about these matters clearly, even if they disagreed with my views, as many did. In this connection, I am especially indebted to Joe Guydish, Sharon Hunt, Richard Scott, Richard Speiglman, Dick Stephens, and James Swartz. Finally, Julia Littell and Phyllis Solomon made very helpful observations about earlier drafts of this chapter.

REFERENCES

Hunt, S. R., and Baumohl, J. (2003a). Drink, drugs and disability: An introduction to the controversy. *Contemporary Drug Problems, 30,* 9–76.

Hunt, S. R., and Baumohl, J. (2003b). Now invited to testify: Former beneficiaries appraise the SSI Drug Addiction and Alcoholism Program. *Contemporary Drug Problems, 30,* 455–500.

Norris, J., Scott, R., Speiglman, R., and Green, R. (2003). Homelessness, hunger and material hardship among those who lost SSI. *Contemporary Drug Problems, 30,* 241–274.

Reinarman, C. (1987). *American states of mind: Political beliefs and behavior among private and public workers.* New Haven, CT: Yale University Press.

Schwarz, N. and Oyserman, D. (2001). Asking questions about behavior: Cognition, communication, and questionnaire construction. *American Journal of Evaluation, 22,* 127–160.

Swartz, J. A., Campbell, K. M., Baumohl, J., & Tonkin, P. (2003). Drug treatment participation and retention rates among former recipients of Supplemental Security Income for Drug Addiction and Alcoholism. *Contemporary Drug Problems, 30,* 335–364.

Swartz, J. A., Hsieh, C.-M., & Baumohl, J. (2003). Disability payments, drug use, and representative payees: An analysis of the relationships. *Addiction, 98,* 965–975.

Swartz, J. A., Tonkin, P., & Baumohl, J. (2003). The methodology of the multi-site study of the termination of Supplemental Security Income benefits for drug addicts and alcoholics. *Contemporary Drug Problems, 30,* 77–122.

17

Impoverishment and Child Maltreatment in African American and European American Neighborhoods

Jill E. Korbin, Claudia J. Coulton, Sarah Chard, Candis Platt-Houston, and Marilyn Su

Interest in the impact of neighborhood conditions on child development and children's well-being is experiencing a resurgence of interest. Child maltreatment, as a major source of child maladaptation and psychopathology, requires the explanatory power of a complex, ecological-developmental framework (Cicchetti & Lynch, 1993; Cicchetti & Rizley, 1981; Cicchetti & Toth, 1995; National Research Council, 1993). In this paper, we take an ecological approach using social organization theory to examine the relationship of neighborhood structural factors and child maltreatment report rates. Specifically, we investigate this relationship separately for African American versus European American census tracts. We employ a multimethod, quantitative, and qualitative approach to the effort to link neighborhood structural conditions with child maltreatment reports. Aggregate analyses and a focused ethnographic study are used in a complementary fashion to better explain and amplify our findings.

This research was supported by grants from the National Center on Child Abuse and Neglect and the Cleveland and Rockefeller Foundations. The authors thank the Cuyahoga Department of Family and Children's Services for its assistance. The authors also thank the ethnographic team for their contributions to this paper. In addition to authors Chard and Platt-Houston, these individuals include L. Timi Barone, Latina Brooks, Nichelle Dickerson, Jennifer Furin, Mario Houston, Heather Lindstrom-Ufuti, Lisa Reebals, and Sheri Young. The authors also thank the Editors of this Special Issue, Dante Cicchetti and Lawrence Aber, for their comments on an earlier draft of the manuscript.

AN ECOLOGICAL PERSPECTIVE
ON CHILD MALTREATMENT

An ecological model of human development, as conceptualized by Bronfenbrenner (1979), has stimulated theoretical models to explain the complex etiology of child abuse and neglect (e.g., Belsky, 1980; Cicchetti & Lynch, 1993; Garbarino, 1977), and was the orienting framework for the National Research Council's (1993) report on child maltreatment. In these models, child maltreatment is viewed as resulting from complex transactions of factors across multiple ecological levels that encompass individuals, families, communities, and the larger society and culture. Cicchetti and Lynch (1993) conceptualize an ecological-transactional-developmental framework as encompassing both risk and protective factors and a temporal dimension that signifies whether the factor is transient or enduring. Child maltreatment occurs as a result of an imbalance of protective and potentiating factors across ecological levels. Unfortunately, such complex ecological models have too rarely been subjected to empirical test.

Despite long-standing calls for an ecological perspective on child maltreatment (e.g., Belsky, 1980; Cicchetti & Lynch, 1993; Garbarino, 1977; National Research Council, 1993), contextual factors at the neighborhood and community level have received relatively little research attention. Most research has been oriented to explanations at the individual and family level (National Research Council, 1993). The U.S. Advisory Board on Child Abuse and Neglect (1993) identified neighborhood dysfunction as a major cause of child abuse and neglect and called for a reorientation of child protection to neighborhood-based protection and prevention efforts. The impact of neighborhood conditions on children and families more broadly, however, is experiencing a resurgence of interest (e.g., Brooks-Gunn, Duncan, Klebanov, & Sealand, 1993; Brooks-Gunn, Duncan, & Aber, 1997) and stimulating efforts to evaluate the impact of comprehensive community building initiatives on child well-being (e.g., Connell, Kubisch, Schorr, & Weiss, 1995). Our perspective does not seek to discount or minimize individual or family level factors, but to encompass a broader ecological-developmental perspective that includes neighborhood contextual conditions that may contribute to the balance of risk and protective factors implicated in child maltreatment and developmental psychopathology.

CULTURE/RACE/ETHNICITY AND CHILD MALTREATMENT

The literature is somewhat contradictory but has long speculated about differential rates of child maltreatment among cultural or ethnic populations (Korbin, 1997). One of the difficulties with the child maltreatment literature is that race or ethnicity are not consistently disentangled from socioeconomic status. Both official reporting data and self-report data indicate that impoverished families are at increased risk of child maltreatment (e.g., Pelton, 1981; Straus, Gelles, & Steinmetz, 1980). Ethnic groups at greatest risk of poverty, then, also appear to have increased incidence and prevalence of child maltreatment. The ties between socioeconomic status and culture with respect to the occurrence of child maltreatment, however, remain unclear.

None of the three national incidence studies (National Center on Child Abuse and Neglect, 1981, 1988; Sedlack & Broadhurst, 1996) found a significant relationship between race, culture, or ethnicity and the incidence of child maltreatment. However, children and families were classified simply as "Black," "White," or "Other," and these broad classifications do not help in understanding cultural differences (e.g., Korbin, 1997). Some studies using protective services data have found that African Americans are disproportionately reported for abuse (e.g., Jason, Amereuh, Marks, & Tyler, 1982; Lauderdale, Valiunas, & Anderson, 1980), whereas others argue that while Blacks are overrepresented in the abuse and neglect reports, their distribution is equal to their representation on AFDC (Horowitz & Wolock, 1981). Giovannoni and Billingsley (1970) found that it is the poorest of the poor who neglect, regardless of ethnicity. Intragroup variability based on urban versus rural residence and intragroup differences on proportions of types of maltreatment reported also have been documented (Lauderdale et al., 1980). One analysis of central registry data suggested different etiologies by ethnicity, with socioeconomic status of counties the best predictor of increased rates among Whites and urbanization the best predictor of higher rates for Blacks and Hispanics (Spearly & Lauderdale, 1983). Differences in reports by race and ethnicity also may reflect differential availability of services for these populations and whether child maltreatment and family difficulties are managed informally, within kin and community networks, or by recourse to public welfare agencies (Light, 1973).

Self-report data implicates socioeconomic status more clearly than it does ethnicity in the incidence and prevalence of child maltreatment. Self-reports on the Conflict Tactics Scales indicate that lower socioeconomic status is a risk factor for violent behaviors toward children (Gelles & Straus, 1988; Straus et al., 1980). While violence towards children occurs in all social strata, violent behaviors towards children, particularly severe violence, is more likely in poor families. Gelles (1992) further refined the analysis to indicate that a subset of the poor are at increased risk of child abuse. Young parents, particularly mothers, with young children living below the poverty line are at the greatest risk of violent behavior towards children.

The first National Family Violence Study, using self-reports on the Conflict Tactics Scales, did not find a significant difference between Blacks and Whites in reported violent acts towards children (Straus et al., 1980). In the 1975–1985 National Family Violence Restudy, however, the rates of severe violence towards Black children increased, as did the Black–White ratio for severe violence towards children. That Black children did not experience the nearly 50% reduction in severe violence found for the population as a whole (Straus & Gelles, 1986) was explained by self-reports on the CTS that Blacks were more likely to hit a child with an object (Hampton, Gelles, & Harrop, 1989). It should be noted, however, that in Giovannoni and Becerra's (1979) definitional study, ethnic minorities rated maltreatment vignettes more seriously than did Whites.

The disproportionate representation of poor and minority families in child maltreatment report statistics also has been attributed to reporting bias. A reanalysis of the National Incidence Study (National Center on Child Abuse and Neglect, 1981), found that class and race were the best predictors of whether an incident was reported, with impoverished Black families more likely to be reported than affluent White families, even if the severity of the incident was comparable (Hampton & Newberger, 1985). A recent study found that drownings were more likely to be reported to Child Protective Services if, among other variables, the family was non-White and poor (Feldman, Monastersky, & Feldman, 1993). Vignette studies have also suggested reporting bias. Various professionals were more likely to judge an incident as abuse if a lower class caretaker was involved (O'Toole, Turbett, & Nalepka, 1983). Further, child protection workers in socioeconomically disadvantaged areas with more severe abuse and neglect caseloads had a higher threshold while those in socioeconomically advantaged areas had a lower threshold in judging the severity of abuse vignettes (Wolock, 1982). Worker judgments as to whether an incident will be substantiated are also influenced by urban versus rural settings (Craft & Staudt, 1991).

STRUCTURAL FACTORS, COMMUNITY SOCIAL ORGANIZATION, AND CHILD MALTREATMENT

Drawing on community social organization theory (Sampson, 1992), our research in Cuyahoga County (Cleveland), Ohio indicated that community structural factors affected neighborhoods' rates of child maltreatment reports (Coulton, Korbin, Su, & Chow, 1995; Korbin & Coulton, 1997). That study tested a linear model in which the effects of impoverishment, child care burden, instability, and geographic isolation (adjacency to concentrated poverty census tracts) were all found to have a significant effect on child maltreatment rates. The model explained almost half the variance in these rates across census tracts. Furthermore, rates of child maltreatment were correlated with other signs of social organization in a neighborhood such as delinquency, teen pregnancy, and violent crime rates. An ambiguity of the previous analysis, though, was that the racial makeup of census tracts was a variable that was contained within the impoverishment factor because of the high correlation between race and poverty. This made it impossible to explore whether there might be differences in African American and European American neighborhoods in the way structural factors affected maltreatment rates. Therefore, these two types of neighborhoods are contrasted in this analysis.

Prior research has not focused explicitly on whether there are ethnic differences in the impact of structural factors on child maltreatment. Nevertheless, neighborhood poverty rates have been found to respond differently to macrostructural change depending on neighborhood ethnic composition (Galster & Mincy, 1993). Neighborhood structure may have differential effects on ethnic groups because the dynamics of residential choice and location are more constrained for minorities than for Whites of European origin due to housing discrimination and prejudice (Farley & Frey, 1994; Galster, 1992). With respect to African Americans, however, cities seem to differ in the degree to which African Americans with economic resources translate these into neighborhood amenities. Research in Philadelphia found that high status African Americans were much more likely than Whites to live in neighborhoods with generally poor conditions (Massey, Condran, & Denton, 1987). In San Francisco, a city with somewhat lower segregation of African Americans, higher income Blacks were able to achieve somewhat higher neighborhood quality (Massey & Fong, 1990). The degree to which there are differences among ethnic groups in structural effects, therefore, may depend upon the degree of segregation in the metropolitan area. Ethnic differences of greater magnitude would be expected in those regions where residential choice for African Americans is more restricted.

While efforts were made to separate child maltreatment from poverty in public policy (e.g., Nelson, 1984), poverty has been demonstrated to be related to child abuse and neglect at both the individual and aggregate levels (e.g., Coulton et al., 1995; Drake & Pandey, 1996; Pelton, 1981). The association between poverty and child maltreatment has been identified in all three national incidence studies (National Center on Child Abuse and Neglect, 1981, 1988; Sedlack & Broadhurst, 1996). Giovannoni and Billingsley's (1970) classic study of neglect in poor families in San Francisco highlighted differences within a population of mothers in poverty. Regardless of whether families were African American, European American, or Hispanic/Latino, neglect was the most prevalent in the poorest of the poor families. Although impoverishment is linked with child maltreatment at the individual and community levels, the processes by which some communities have an imbalance of risk and protective factors remains elusive.

The possibility that effects of structural factors may differ depending upon the predominant racial and ethnic composition of the neighborhood is suggested by the prolonged and extreme racial segregation that exists, especially in northern industrial cities (Massey & Denton, 1989). The current study was conducted in Cleveland, one of the most segregated cities in the nation (Farley & Frey, 1994). It therefore seemed prudent to investigate differences in the effects of structural factors in predominantly African American and predominantly European American neighborhoods. The effects of impoverishment, child care burden, instability, and geographic isolation on child maltreatment were analyzed separately for the two types of neighborhoods.

METHODOLOGY

The current study was conducted in two phases. The first was an aggregate level analysis of the relationship between macrostructural factors and child maltreatment rates conducted separately for predominantly African American versus predominantly European American census tracts. Second, ethnographic research in a small number of census tracts in the top and bottom quartiles of child maltreatment reports was used to illuminate the findings of the aggregate analysis. This multi-method approach that employs both quantitative and qualitative data to amplify and explain research findings has been found to be a productive strategy (e.g., Korbin & Coulton, 1997; Sullivan, 1996, 1998).

Aggregate Analyses

The aggregate analysis presented in this paper disaggregates neighborhoods into those that are predominantly African American and those that are predominantly European American to compare the impact of community structural factors on child maltreatment rates identified in our previous research (Coulton et al., 1995). The hypothesis that community social organization is related to differences in rates of reported child maltreatment is tested separately for census tracts that are greater than 75% non-Hispanic White ($n = 189$) and greater than 75% non-Hispanic Black ($n = 94$) at the time of the 1990 census. Most tracts in Cuyahoga County fall into one of these classifications because the Hispanic population is small and racial segregation is extreme. The constructs and measures used in the aggregate analysis are explained below.

Child Maltreatment Rates. The aggregate analysis used official reports of child maltreatment. Child abuse and neglect reports are often thought to underestimate the incidence and prevalence of maltreatment and to be biased against poor and ethnic minority families (Newberger, Reed, Daniel, Hyde, & Kotelchuck, 1977; O'Toole et al., 1983). Official reports are frequently considered an imperfect source of data due to variability in definitions and case identification decisions across jurisdictions and within the same agency. Further, official reports reflect child consequences that come to the attention of a child protection agency rather than reflecting all behaviors that pose dangers to children (Barnett, Manly, & Cicchetti, 1993; Straus et al., 1980). However, child abuse and neglect reports are an indicator of the distribution of recognition of and response to child maltreatment and have usefully been applied in past research (Garbarino & Sherman, 1980; National Center on Child Abuse and Neglect, 1988; Pelton, 1981; Zuravin, 1989).

Data on child maltreatment were drawn from the computerized records of the Cuyahoga County Department of Human Services. All "substantiated" and "indicated" reports in 1991 were included in the calculation of rates. In a few cases (9.4%), the same child had multiple reports of maltreatment during the year. In the calculation of rates, these cases were counted only once because we were interested in the proportion of children who were reported as maltreated rather than the number of reports that were made. The rates were calculated by counting the total number of children living in each tract who experienced one or more instances of maltreatment and dividing by the population of the tract ages 0–17.

Cuyahoga County Department of Human Services personnel classify each report as to the type of maltreatment. Cases may be classified as any combination of physical abuse or neglect, emotional-psychological abuse or neglect, and sexual abuse. Because of the considerable comorbidity of types of maltreatment evident in the literature on child maltreatment (e.g., Cicchetti & Rizley, 1981), particularly physical abuse and neglect, we used total maltreatment rates in our analysis.

Indicators of Community Structure. The literature on community social organization suggests economic status, residential mobility, family structure, and race or ethnicity as related macrostructural factors. We also anticipated that the age and gender structure of an area would be important determinants of the available resources for the care and socialization of children and levels of social control. Furthermore, our own work in Cleveland suggested that the actual geographic location of the neighborhoods would be important, especially the degree to which poor neighborhoods are contiguous to other poverty areas and separated from economic opportunities in more affluent neighborhoods (e.g., Brooks-Gunn et al., 1993).

The empirical indicators of community structure are presented in Table 17.1. Because of their high correlations, a principal components analysis was performed and yielded three factors that explained more than 80% of the variance. The first factor was labeled *impoverishment*. It was made up of five variables: female-headed households, poverty rate, unemployment rate, vacant housing, and population loss. This factor represented the overall economic disadvantage experienced in neighborhoods that are disinvested and have high joblessness and one-parent families. The second factor, labeled *instability*, included the proportion of residents who have moved to or from a

Table 17.1. Indicators of Community Structure

Variable	Definition
Impoverishment factors	
Family headship	% Households with children that are female-headed
Poverty rate	% Poor persons, 1990
Unemployment rate	% Residents unemployed
Vacant housing	% Vacant housing units
Population loss	% 1980–1990 population
Instability factors	
Movement, 85–90	% Who moved between 1985 and 1990
Tenure < 10 years	% Households in current residence < 10 years
Recent movement, 89–90	% Households that moved in 1 year
Child care burden factors	
Child/adult ratio	Child (0–12)/adults (21+)
Male/female ratio	Adult male (21–64)/adult female (21–64)
Elderly population	% Population that is over 65 years old
Contiguous to concentrated poverty	Contiguous to poor or nonpoor tracts (0 = borders no poor tracts, 1 = borders one or more poor tracts)

All variables were calculated using the 1990 census data, Summary Tape Files 1 and 3.

different house within the last 5 years, the proportion of the households who have lived in their current home for less than 10 years, as well as the percent of households that have lived in their current home less than 1 year. This factor represents the degree to which the area may be characterized by the movement of residents. The third factor, *child care burden,* included the ratio of children to adults, the ratio of males to females, and the percentage of the population that is elderly. This dimension reflected the amount of adult supervision and resources that may be available for children in the community.

Factor scores were calculated for each census tract for each of the dimensions of community structure. Additionally, a geographic location variable was calculated for each tract because of the recognition that the resources in an area can be affected by resources available in contiguous areas. We restricted our definition to economic resources by taking into account whether each tract was contiguous to areas of highly concentrated poverty. To accomplish this, we first listed the other census tracts that surrounded each of the 177 residential census tracts. The tract was coded as contiguous if any of the surrounding tracts exceeded a threshold of 40% poverty. The choice of the 40% poverty threshold is consistent with the definition of concentrated poverty used in other research and thinking about urban poverty (Jargowsky & Bane, 1991).

Ethnographic Methods

To explore the meaning of the aggregate results, we turned to ethnographic observations and neighborhood resident narratives collected in an earlier phase of our study. In that phase, census tracts ($n = 13$) were selected for ethnographic study to represent neighborhoods with different rates of child maltreatment reports. In that study, we classified census tract child maltreatment report rates as high, low, or medium as determined by whether report rates were a standard deviation above or below the mean. For the current ethnographic analysis, we selected 4 of these original 13 census tracts. These 4 tracts fell within the top and bottom quartiles of child maltreatment report rates for the 177 census tracts in our earlier aggregate analysis (Coulton et al., 1995). One predominantly African American and one predominantly European American census tract were compared and contrasted from the two maltreatment quartiles. We first sought to contrast the ethnographic findings in African American and European American census tracts with similar levels of impoverishment. However, when we examined the impoverishment factor scores in the areas in which we had done ethnographic work, we found that the predominantly European American tracts chosen for their high rates of child maltreatment had much lower impoverishment scores than the African American tracts with the highest rates of child maltreatment. We also saw that several of the predominantly African American tracts in the ethnographies with relatively high impoverishment scores also had quite low rates of child maltreatment.[1] These patterns were consistent with the flatter slope in the African American communities for the effect of the impoverishment factor in predicting child maltreatment rates discussed in the aggregate analysis results section below.

Ethnographies in these four census tracts were used to help illuminate the connection between impoverishment and child maltreatment and to examine why impoverishment and child care burden might be less important correlates of child maltreatment in these predominantly African

---

[1] The only tracts in the original ethnographic study in which predominantly African American and predominantly European American tracts were similar in both their impoverishment scores and their maltreatment rates were middle class tracts with very low rates of child maltreatment in which we did not do ethnographic work.

American communities. It is important to emphasize that four communities cannot capture the full range of types of African American and European American neighborhoods. Rather, these neighborhoods were selected to provide further insight into the aggregate findings because their impoverishment and child maltreatment rates are consistent with the relationships found in the regression analysis reported below in the aggregate results section.

Trained ethnographers matched with the predominant ethnicity of each census tract conducted the research. Ethnographers were kept uninformed as to the child maltreatment report rate in their census tracts. Ethnographers had first explored the census tracts, mapping stores, businesses, churches, day care centers, libraries, schools, recreation centers, and services. They noted the general upkeep of the various blocks in the tract and the amenities such as parks, landscaping, and street repair. Second, they conducted open-ended interviews with key informants, including public officials, ministers, shopkeepers, service providers, and residents regarding their views of neighborhood life with a focus on its effects on families and children. Residents were contacted through churches and community organizations such as block clubs. While this was not a random sample, we sought a population of knowledgeable neighbors who were embedded in their neighborhoods.

RESULTS

Aggregate Analysis

The current analysis tested the effects of the structural factors and the isolation index separately for predominantly African American ($n = 94$) and predominantly European American ($n = 189$) tracts. As anticipated, the distribution of child maltreatment rates was quite different in the two samples (see Figure 17.1). The distribution of the reported maltreatment rate for all tracts is markedly skewed, but the means are quite different depending on the predominant ethnicity of the tract. The mean maltreatment rates are 13.07 per 1,000 children for European American tracts and 42.79 per

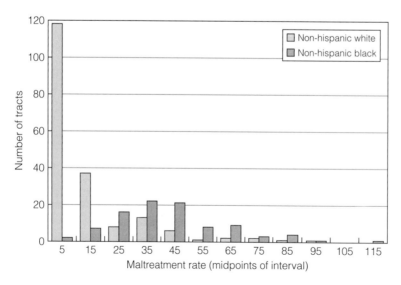

FIGURE 17.1. Histogram of child maltreatment rate by race/ethnicity.

Table 17.2. Means (Standard Deviations) of Variables by Ethnicity

Variables	Census Tracts with > 75% Non-Hispanic White (n = 189)		Census Tracts with > 75% Non-Hispanic Black (n = 94)	
Impoverishment (Factor 1)	−.55	(.58)	.98	(.95)
Instability (Factor 2)	−.03	(.95)	−.34	(.95)
Child care burden (Factor 3)	−.24	(.73)	.55	(1.13)
Contiguous to poverty	.11	(.32)	.64	(.48)
Maltreatment rate	13.07	(16.15)	42.79	(20.23)
Log of maltreatment rate	1.94	(1.17)	3.63	(0.53)

Table 17.3. Comparisons of Regression Coefficients for Community Structural Factors on Log of Child Maltreatment Rate by Ethnicity

Variables	> 75% Non-Hispanic White		> 75% Non-Hispanic Black		T Value for Comparisons Between White and Black Tracts
	Unstandardized Coefficient	Standard Error	Unstandardized Coefficient	Standard Error	
Constant	3.13***	0.11	3.18**	0.08	−0.37
Impoverishment (F1)	1.94***	0.14	0.29**	0.05	11.10
Instability (F2)	.23***	.07	.11	.06	1.30
Child care burden (F3)	.41***	.08	.06	.04	3.91
F1 * F2	−.24**	.08	−.09*	.03	−1.76
Contiguous to poverty	−.16	.20	.26*	.10	−1.88
R^2	.67		.51		

*p < .05.   **p < .01.   ***p < .001.

1,000 children for African American tracts. This is consistent with previous research suggesting high rates of reported maltreatment in low income and minority populations. Because of the skewness of maltreatment rate, the log of the maltreatment rate is used in the regression analyses.

The means and standard deviations for the variables used in the regression analysis are presented in Table 17.2. Only 11% of the predominantly European American tracts were contiguous to other high poverty tracts while 64% of the African American tracts shared a boundary with an extreme poverty tract. Also, the mean factor scores on all three factors were higher for predominantly African American tracts.

The results of the analysis of the structural factors and child maltreatment rates are presented in Table 17.3. The regression coefficient for the impoverishment factor is significantly lower in the predominantly African American than in the predominantly European American tracts. Figure 17.2 illustrates this in a bivariate scatterplot. The slope for African American tracts is much flatter, suggesting a weaker relationship between impoverishment and reported child maltreatment rate. The distribution of the impoverishment factor also differs by ethnicity. In African American tracts it is shifted to the right, as can be seen in Figure 17.3. Most European American tracts have scores on the impoverishment factor that are well below the least impoverished African American tracts. Thus, while more African American tracts have high levels on the impoverishment factor, the strength of

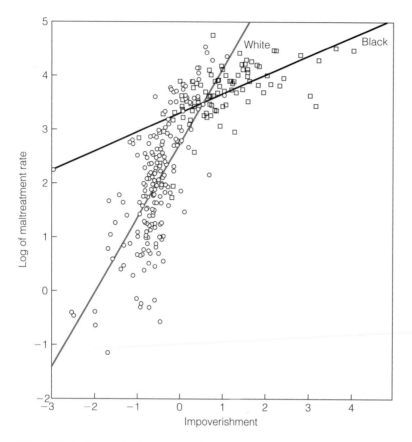

FIGURE 17.2. Scatterplot for log of maltreatment rate on impoverishment by ethnicity.

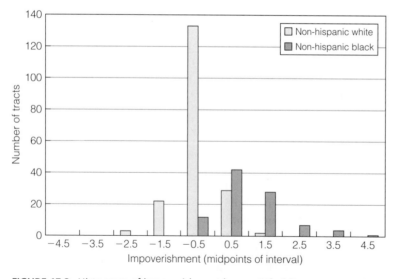

FIGURE 17.3. Histogram of impoverishment by race/ethnicity.

the effect on reported child maltreatment is lower.[2] An analysis of the residuals for both the European American and African American equations revealed that they were normally distributed. An examination of Cook's D revealed no outliers that were having an undue influence on the coefficients. The child care burden factor, although not as strong a predictor of child maltreatment rates in either group as impoverishment, also had a significantly lower regression coefficient in African American tracts. However, unlike the impoverishment factor, the distribution of the child care burden factor is fairly similar in African American and European American tracts. Further, the magnitude of the difference of the coefficients is considerably less. Thus, the rest of this paper uses ethnographic data in an attempt to explain the differential effects of impoverishment.

Ethnographic Findings

Four census tracts will be described using results from the ethnography. Names of the census tract are fictitious. As presented in Table 17.4, the two census tracts selected from the bottom quartile of child maltreatment rates, Burbank, a predominantly European American census tract, and Lennox, a predominantly African American census tract, have comparable scores on the impoverishment factor, percentages of middle class residents, and low rates of child maltreatment reports. The two census tracts selected from the highest quartile of child maltreatment reports, however, are more dissimilar. Dellwood, a predominantly European American neighborhood, is much lower on impoverishment than Gadston, a predominantly African American neighborhood. Dellwood is also lower on the percentage of middle class residents. While both tracts are in the top quartile of child maltreatment reports, Dellwood has much higher rates of child maltreatment reports than Gadston. The descriptions of these four neighborhoods are divided into two basic domains that are not mutually exclusive. First, residential quality, resource availability, and mobility reflect residents' perceptions of their physical environment. The second domain includes both deleterious conditions of crime, danger, and drugs as well as residents' views of the qualities and characteristics

Table 17.4. Ethnography Census Tracts

	Bottom Quartile of Neighborhood Child Maltreatment Report Rates		Top Quartile of Neighborhood Child Maltreatment Report Rates	
	Burbank (European American)	Lennox (African American)	Dellwood (European American)	Gadston (African American)
Impoverishment score	.1	−.07	.59	.88
Reported child maltreatment rate/1000	12	14	92	38
Middle class	48%	38%	11%	23%

[2]We compared unstandardized regression coefficients, which are the slopes of the least squares line. These were chosen over standardized or correlation coefficients due to the different standard deviations in the two types of neighborhoods on the log of maltreatment rate and impoverishment. Restriction of range is known to suppress correlation coefficients. Although unstandardized coefficients are preferred in such instances (Cohen & Cohen, 1983), the slopes in this study are derived from the range that was observed. If the ranges were wider, the results might differ.

of their neighbors. The descriptions and comments below were selected from a larger content analysis to illustrate the views of neighborhood residents.

Residential Quality, Resource Availability, and Mobility

Burbank and Lennox (Bottom Quartile of Neighborhood Child Maltreatment Report Rates). A comparison of the ethnographies from Burbank and Lennox reveals congruence in the appearance of the neighborhood. Ethnographers observed that in both of these census tracts, the homes and yards appeared well-maintained, and the streets were quiet and clean. Residents similarly noted the physical appeal of their neighborhoods. Characterizations of each community as quiet and clean were common themes throughout the ethnographies; residents from both areas describe their communities as quiet, peaceful, and well kept.[3]

> The neighborhood is beautiful with big yards and the houses are different; by that I mean not every house is the same and I like that. And there are lots of trees. I just really like the way it looks around here (Burbank).

> There are big back yards, lawns, and the houses are not too close to the street. [Neighbors] keep the street clean. We don't have junk cars parked on the street all night, and it's a well-lighted neighborhood (Lennox).

Residents in both Burbank and Lennox described good and accessible shopping and service resources, and proximity to family and church. Residents in both communities pointed out the accessibility of the city's downtown area, despite the fact that these two communities are located on opposite sides of the downtown. Residential and business sections were somewhat separate, with businesses on the major streets rather than interspersed with residences.

Residents from both Burbank and Lennox commented on the low transient rate of their neighborhoods and described their neighborhoods as being long-standing and stable places to live. Home ownership and stability of persons living in the neighborhood were regarded as positive attributes of both Burbank and Lennox, as summed up in the following statement:

> We know each other and there are no problems. We own these homes and people keep up their property. People care more about their property when they own it and there's more community interest (Lennox).

> The fact that the community is relatively stable with few transient residents is one of the reasons why the neighborhood is good for raising children (Burbank).

Dellwood and Gadston (Top Quartile of Neighborhood Child Maltreatment Report Rates). As strikingly similar as Burbank and Lennox are in their physical environment, Dellwood and Gadston are strikingly dissimilar. Dellwood, the European American neighborhood, is composed of residential and commercial properties mixed together in a seemingly unpredictable fashion. While the overall appearance of the area is of buildings in poor repair, the properties change in quality of upkeep block by block. Almost all of the houses are relatively small and of wood construction, and there is a striking absence of large, well-kept housing. There are numerous vacant lots, trash in the streets, graffiti, and vandalized buildings and cars. Many commercial

---

[3]All statements are paraphrased from ethnographic fieldnotes. Interviews were not tape recorded for verbatim statements. Comments from residents in the same neighborhood have sometimes been combined for ease of presentation.

properties are vacant or are boarded up, while those remaining often have barred or walled-over windows.

Resource availability in Dellwood is an example of a setting in which objective and subjective impressions may be at odds. Residents gave mixed responses concerning the resources available in the census tract. For example, while a nearby recreation center has among the best facilities in the city, residents hesitate to use it because of fears of gangs that reputedly hang out there. In contrast, many alleyways that could be viewed as eyesores or dangerous by outsiders are considered excellent places for children to play since neighbors can easily keep an eye on them.

In contrast, residents in Gadston, the African American neighborhood, repeatedly mentioned the multiple resources and housing stock of their community as among the best characteristics of their neighborhood. While the housing quality varies in the neighborhood, there are many large, old, well-kept, brick homes in Gadston. In addition to nice homes, residents report on the convenience of resources:

> ... like the barber shop, supermarkets, and the dry cleaners ... it's all right there in Gadston. Another thing is the easy access ... Gadston is right on the bus line. Gadston is in the heart of the city.

Residents in Dellwood report that there is an overabundance of renters who, by definition, are less interested in maintaining property that they do not own or in contributing to a neighborhood in which they are only temporary residents. Many houses have been subdivided into multiple family dwellings, increasing the presence of renters who are viewed by homeowners and longer-term residents as less invested in neighborhood well-being. Ethnographers observed a tension among the homeowners they interviewed who almost invariably blamed renters for neighborhood difficulties. Dellwood residents express distrust and suspicion of their neighbors, particularly renters, who were perceived as coming from more socially and economically impoverished areas, thereby bringing down the neighborhood.

In Gadston, as in Dellwood, residents reported a marked and obvious difference in the upkeep and quality of homes that were owner-occupied versus rented. However, residential mobility, perceived so negatively in Dellwood, was a sign for some optimism in Gadston where some adult children, who years ago moved to the suburbs, were now moving back into the neighborhood, often taking over their parents' homes. One resident described this phenomenon:

> We raised four children in Gadston. Now, my son and his family live there ... in the house in which he was raised. The older people are moving out and their children are moving back. One of my neighbors ... she died about four months ago, her son has moved back into the house to raise his family. The older people who are still there like it ... because they know the background of these young ones ... what kind of people are moving into their neighborhood.

Context for Children: Drugs, Crime, and Neighbors

Burbank and Lennox (Bottom Quartile of Neighborhood Child Maltreatment Report Rates). Residents also commented on the quality of their neighborhoods as a good place to rear children, and spoke of shared concerns for neighborhood children and the connections for meeting other parents of their children's friends, an important component of Coleman's conception of social capital (Coleman, 1987, 1988).

> This is a good place for children ... the boys could play football in the field across the street.... There are lots of people here bringing up children. My boys were in a baseball league here, and we met a lot of nice people that way who became our friends (Burbank).

There are facilities here for children, like the pool at (named recreation center), the playground at (named park) and the one at (named school) (Lennox).

We're all friendly. We look out for everyone, especially us that are home everyday. We look out for the children because there are some "latchkey" kids on the street (Lennox).

Parents and other neighbors in both Burbank and Lennox were depicted quite positively. Respondents from these two low-risk neighborhoods frequently mentioned that the best part of their community was the neighbors themselves, that they were "friendly," "nice," or "willing to get involved."

Neighbors care about neighbors, that's what makes a good neighborhood (Lennox).

The best thing about our neighborhood is the people, our neighbors....Because they are more open and friendly. They are willing to get involved in your life, and willing to let you become involved in theirs (Burbank).

Perceptions in both Burbank and Lennox that their neighborhoods were good places for families and children were tied to views that their neighborhoods were safe and relatively free from crime, drugs, and gangs.

We live in a pocket that criminals tend to forget about. Neighbors also watch out for each other....They watch out formally and informally (Burbank).

It is a quiet and old fashioned neighborhood...there is not much crime (Burbank).

In general I think that this is a good place for kids. I mean there's not any violence, it's a pretty quiet area. Fortunately, there's not too bad a drug problem, I mean I know that some people do have problems like that, but we really don't have such bad problems here (Burbank).

It's quiet, not a lot of crime, no violence (Lennox).

The neighborhood has been relatively safe and relatively quiet. I don't think we have a high rate of crime. I know there is some crime on (named thoroughfare), but it's not a high rate. It's about as safe as any neighborhood in Cleveland (Lennox).

In addition, residents in both Burbank and Lennox expressed optimism about having an ability to have an effect on conditions in their neighborhoods. This is akin to Coleman's (1987, 1988) concept of social capital and Sampson, Raudenbush, and Earl's (1997) concept of community efficacy in that residents believed that they could make a difference in their neighborhoods and viewed one another as a resource for action. Block clubs are active in both communities. In Burbank, several residents recounted the story of the entire neighborhood helping to search for a hit and run driver who killed a young child a few years in the past. Also in Burbank, a grassroots community organization had been successful in closing down a pornographic theater in the neighborhood. Similarly, in Lennox, residents have joined together to limit the establishments that can serve or sell alcohol in their neighborhood.

Dellwood and Gadston (Top Quartile of Neighborhood Child Maltreatment Report Rates). Both Gadston and Dellwood residents described their neighborhoods as having problems with crime, drugs, and violence.

It could be a nice neighborhood if the drugs were gone, if the gangs got pushed out. It's a nice looking street, lots of trees, and the majority of the people living here feel that way, they want the gangs and drugs gone. Right now it's not safe to walk on the street after dark (Dellwood).

There is drug selling on the corners and the people on the corners mess with the kids. People around here even sell drugs right out of their houses (Gadston).

However, Gadston residents reported that these problems were largely, but not exclusively, localized on specific streets. One Gadston resident reported that he drives many blocks out of the way to avoid a major thoroughfare plagued by drugs and violence. Dellwood residents, in contrast, described these problems as more widely dispersed throughout the neighborhood.

It isn't so bad where I live as far as crime, but on (named major street), there is a gang. There is also a gang on (another named major street), but they don't come in my area too much (Gadston).

My block is a good street, but there is a drug dealer on it (Dellwood).

Residents in both Dellwood and Gadston recognize that potential improvements in their neighborhoods are situated in the social capital that can be generated by their neighbors. While there is a community development organization in Dellwood whose mission is to renovate properties, encourage home ownership, and promote the creation of block groups, Dellwood residents described their neighbors as unwilling to become involved in the area or even maintain their homes. When asked what she would change about her neighborhood, one resident responded:

I would get people involved in the neighborhood. I would get them out from behind their curtains and working to make this a better place. We're all here together, so we should act that way (Dellwood).

In contrast, in Gadston there are many active street clubs that work diligently and successfully in maintaining the neighborhood. The councilperson keeps a list of these block clubs and reports that they contact him frequently asking for improvements in their surroundings. The comment of one resident was typical:

The strongest asset about the neighborhood is the people (Gadston).

Finally, Dellwood and Gadston residents differ in the trajectories they see in their neighborhoods. Dellwood has a long history as a transitory neighborhood. Residents of nearby predominantly European American neighborhoods point to Dellwood as an example of what might happen to their own neighborhoods if drugs, crime, undesirable residents (particularly renters), and other social problems are not controlled. Gadston residents, in contrast, expressed both pride and hope in their neighborhood because of its history, housing stock, and current regrowth in housing and shopping development projects. Many believe that Gadston will once again become the prominent neighborhood that it was prior to the riots of the late 1960s.

In summary, we examined three basic domains in the ethnographic descriptions of these four neighborhoods. First, the physical environment and location of the neighborhood was viewed quite similarly by residents of Burbank and Lennox, but as quite dissimilar by the residents of Dellwood and Gadston. This domain centered on aspects of neighborhood life including the quality of housing and surroundings, the balance of renters and homeowners, and the availability of resources. Second, the presence of crime, danger, and drugs in the neighborhood was viewed as a threat in all of the neighborhoods studied. Burbank and Lennox exhibited more of a sense that these problems, while difficult, could be contained. Dellwood and Gadston were similar in perceiving the threat of these problems, and recognizing their existence in their neighborhoods. However, Dellwood residents viewed crime, danger, and drugs as occurring throughout their neighborhood while Gadston residents saw these problems as more localized to specific areas within the neighborhood. And third, the quality of neighbors as contributing to the context for families and children was viewed positively in Burbank and Lennox. Similarly, Gadston residents viewed neighbors as an asset. However, in Dellwood, neighbors were viewed as less likely to be an involved resource for children and families.

DISCUSSION AND CONCLUSIONS

Past research, our own and that of others, has demonstrated that child maltreatment report rates are related to structural factors indicative of neighborhood social organization (Coulton et al., 1995; Drake & Pandey, 1996; Garbarino & Crouter, 1978; Garbarino & Kostelny, 1992; Garbarino & Sherman, 1980; Korbin & Coulton, 1997; Vinson, Baldry, & Hargreaves, 1996; Zuravin, 1989). These findings are consistent with a long-standing research tradition that links social organization to a range of social problems such as crime and juvenile delinquency (e.g., Sampson & Groves, 1989; Shaw & McKay, 1942). These findings are also consistent with an ecological perspective on child maltreatment. Child maltreatment, its etiology, and its impact on child maladaptation and the development of psychopathology must be seen as resulting from the transactions of risk and protective factors at multiple ecological levels (Bergman & Magnusson, 1997; Cicchetti & Lynch, 1993; Cicchetti & Rogosch, 1996; National Research Council, 1993).

This paper also underscores the importance of within group analyses (Duncan & Aber, 1997; Sampson et al., 1997). The aggregate analysis in this paper indicates that impoverishment and child care burden, two structural factors, have less of an impact on child maltreatment rates in predominantly African American than in predominantly European American neighborhoods. The ethnographic analysis suggests that this differential effect is mediated by the perceived quality and social connectedness found in different neighborhoods. Burbank and Lennox had similar child maltreatment report rates and impoverishment scores. In the ethnographies, these two neighborhoods presented a picture of relative similarity in their social fabric. In contrast, Dellwood and Gadston, with child maltreatment reports in the top quartile, presented a picture of dissimilarity. Gadston had a much higher impoverishment score than Dellwood, but Dellwood had higher child maltreatment report rates. Ethnographic data suggest that the higher maltreatment report rates in Dellwood than in Gadston are due to dissimilarity in the social fabric of these two neighborhoods. In addition, Gadston had a higher percentage of middle class residents than did Dellwood. Past research has suggested that the absence of middle class neighbors, more than the presence of poor neighbors, has a detrimental effect on family processes that promote child development (Brooks-Gunn et al., 1993, 1997). Structural factors, then, may be moderated by differences in social fabric at the lower end of the socioeconomic continuum. Garbarino and Ebata (1983) have argued that it is under conditions of socioeconomic deprivation and stress that cultural differences are most important and evident.

In aggregate analyses, measures of social disorganization are typically correlated with ethnic minority status. However, comparative and multimethod analyses such as the one performed here can reveal more subtle effects. Consistent with the literature on the strengths of African American families, social networks, and neighborhoods (e.g., Billingsley, 1992; McAdoo, 1982, 1995; Stack, 1974), this paper suggests that some African American neighborhoods with large numbers of poor, unemployed, and female-headed families retain many signs of strength and solidarity. These noneconomic indicators of community social organization are less apparent in the poorest European American neighborhoods in our study even when their poverty, unemployment, and female-headed family rates would seem to predict that they would be better off. Our aggregate findings on the differential impact of structural conditions and our ethnographic findings on the importance of social fabric also are consistent with calls for broader ecological models to explain developmental processes and competence in minority children (e.g., Garcia Coll et al., 1996).

This study, then, suggests that while African American groups live disproportionately in poor, disinvested areas, when other factors that favor community social organization are in place their neighborhoods can be remarkably supportive of children and families. The fact that some impoverished African American neighborhoods provide a relatively supportive social environment for families should not be taken as an excuse to ignore the serious economic disadvantage within these communities. The loss of industry and public investment in these areas has been devastating and economic opportunity must be restored. The strengths of these neighborhoods can be an important asset in efforts to rebuild the economic base. Unfortunately, business investment and institutional support may not follow, in part, because these areas may be misperceived by outsiders as disorganized due to ethnic stereotyping.

The aggregate and ethnographic analyses in this paper lead us to the conclusion that neighborhood conditions are linked with child maltreatment report rates. Based on the literature, it is a plausible explanation that neighborhood strength contributes in some measure to more positive parenting behaviors and prevention of child maltreatment and that weakness in neighborhood social fabric has the opposite effect. However, based on the data in our study, we cannot explicitly identify the processes that link neighborhood strengths or weaknesses with child maltreatment in families or with the processes that contribute to the development of maladaptation and psychopathology. Our study calls for greater research attention to the precise linkages and processes across ecological levels that contribute to an imbalance of risk and protective factors and that consider the multiple pathways and outcomes possible (Cicchetti & Lynch, 1993; Cicchetti & Rogosch, 1996). One can speculate that those neighborhoods that seem to promote maltreatment would also seem to promote poorer adjustment because "...transactions between people and their environments are thought to direct and redirect the course of their development" (Cicchetti, 1993, p. 480).

We must be cautious in generalizing these findings beyond the areas we have studied for several reasons. First, we were able to conduct ethnographies in only a small number of census tracts. Although they were chosen to represent varying levels of risk and the trend in them mirrors the aggregate findings, some idiosyncrasies are bound to have affected our interpretations. The similarity between Burbank and Lennox, and the dissimilarity between Dellwood and Gadston are not meant to be presented as perfect opposites or to create stereotypes. Second, the forces influencing residential location within ethnic groups are bound to differ across metropolitan areas, thus affecting neighborhood composition. The Cleveland area represents a particular type of region that is extreme in its racial and economic segregation (Coulton et al., 1996; Farley & Frey, 1994). Many metropolitan areas, especially newer cities in the south and west, follow distinctly different patterns. In these locations ethnic differences in structural effects may not be as large.

Third, we have used census tracts and block groups as our units of analyses that may not conform to residents' perceptions of their neighborhood boundaries. And fourth, the aggregate analysis which found weaker effects of impoverishment on maltreatment in African American neighborhoods should be interpreted cautiously because of potential confounding factors. One of these has to do with the differing distribution of impoverishment scores in the two types of neighborhoods. None of the European American neighborhoods had as high levels of impoverishment as the African

American neighborhoods and the distribution of scores in African American neighborhoods was more skewed toward high impoverishment. Although this pattern is common in cities in the United States, it precludes us testing what would have occurred if the two types of neighborhoods had equal distributions representing both the poor and affluent ends of the continuum.

Finally, a measurement artifact that possibly could account for these results is that the direction of reporting bias for maltreatment cases differs by ethnicity. Specifically, if Whites in middle class neighborhoods were underreported for maltreatment while Whites in poor neighborhoods were overreported, the slope for European American neighborhoods could be made steeper by errors in measurement. Similarly, if Blacks in poor neighborhoods were underreported while Blacks in middle class neighborhoods were overreported, this would flatten the slope for impoverishment in African American neighborhoods. Our study did not examine reporting bias, but it cannot be ruled out with the official reporting data available in this study, particularly in light of other research pointing to reporting bias by race and socioeconomic status (e.g., Hampton & Newberger, 1986), and by severity of caseload in different neighborhoods (Wolock, 1982).

In this study, we join those who advocate multiple methods and perspectives on major social problems. We have taken advantage of the complementary nature of qualitative and quantitative methods in understanding both associations among factors and processes underlying those associations (Korbin and Coulton, 1997; Sullivan, 1996, 1998). The aggregate findings would have been difficult to interpret without the ethnographic sources of information. Yet, we would have been hesitant to draw inferences about the effects of community structure from just a few ethnographies. This approach has facilitated consideration of the balance of risk and protective factors (Cicchetti & Lynch, 1993; Garbarino, 1977) as well as incorporating Bronfenbrenner's expansion of an ecological model to encompass neighborhood both as subjectively experienced (1979) and as objectively measured (1988).

We also join those who advocate paying greater attention to within-group differences, especially in research on the poor and disadvantaged (Duncan & Aber, 1997; Sampson et al., 1997). It would be a mistake to think that African American neighborhoods pose greater risk for children merely because they have higher scores on traditional indicators of impoverishment than European American neighborhoods. These primarily economic factors may be only weak proxies for the real conditions in neighborhoods that are salient to families' abilities to care for and nurture their young children. Further, these primarily economic factors may be particularly poor indicators of community capacity when applied to neighborhoods with residents who have been restricted in their economic and social mobility by external forces.

REFERENCES

Barnett, D., Manly, J. T., & Cicchetti, D. (1993). Defining child maltreatment. The interface between policy and research. In D. Cicchetti & S. L. Toth (Eds.) *Child abuse, child development and social policy* (pp. 7–73). Norwood, NJ: Ablex.

Belsky, J. (1980). Child maltreatment: An ecological integration. *American Psychologist, 35,* 320–335.

Bergman, L. R., & Magnusson, D. (1997). A person-oriented approach in research on developmental psychopathology. *Development and Psychopathology, 9,* 291–319.

Billingsley, A. (1992). *Climbing Jacob's ladder. The enduring legacy of African-American families.* New York: Simon & Schuster.

Brooks–Gunn, J., Duncan, G., & Aber, L. (Eds.) (1997). *Neighborhood poverty: Context and consequences for children.* New York: Russell Sage Foundation.

Brooks–Gunn, J., Duncan, G., Klebanov, P., & Sealand, N. (1993). Do neighborhoods influence child and adolescent development? *American Journal of Sociology, 99,* 353–395.

Bronfenbrenner, U. (1979). *The ecology of human development*. Cambridge, MA: Harvard University Press.

Bronfenbrenner, U. (1988). Foreword. In A. Pence (Ed.), *Ecological research with children and families. From concepts to methodology* (pp. ix–xix). New York and London: Teachers College Press.

Cicchetti, D. (1983). Developmental psychopathology: Reactions, reflections, projections. *Developmental Review, 13*, 471–502.

Cicchetti, D., & Lynch, M. (1993). Towards an ecological/transactional model of community violence and child maltreatment. *Psychiatry, 56*, 96–118.

Cicchetti, D., & Rizley, R. (1981). Developmental perspectives on the etiology, intergenerational transmission, and sequelae of child maltreatment. *New Directions for Child Development, 11*, 31–55.

Cicchetti, D., & Rogosch, F. (1996). Equifinality and multifinality in developmental psychopathology. *Development and Psychopathology, 8*, 597–600.

Cicchetti, D., & Toth, S. (1995). A developmental psychopathology perspective on child abuse and neglect. *Journal of the American Academy of Child & Adolescent Psychiatry, 34*, 541–565.

Cohen, J., & Cohen, P. (1983). *Applied multiple regression/correlation analysis for the behavioral sciences*. Hillsdale, NJ: Erlbaum.

Coleman, J. (1987). Families and schools. *Educational Researcher,* August–September, 32–38.

Coleman, J. (1988). Social capital in the creation of human capital. *American Journal of Sociology, 94*(Suppl.), S95–S120.

Connell, J. P., Kubisch, A. C., Schorr, L. B., & Weiss, C. H. (1995). *New approaches to evaluating community initiatives. Concepts, methods, and contexts*. Washington, DC: The Aspen Institute.

Coulton, C., Korbin, J., Su, M., & Chow, J. (1995). Community level factors and child maltreatment rates. *Child Development, 66*, 1262–1276.

Coulton, C., Korbin, J., & Su, M. (1996). Measuring neighborhood context for young children in an urban area. *American Journal of Community Psychology, 24*, 5–32.

Craft, J. L., & Staudt, M. M. (1991). Reporting and founding of child neglect in urban and rural communities. *Child Welfare, 70*, 359–370.

Drake, B., & Pandey, S. (1996). Understanding the relationship between neighborhood poverty and specific types of child maltreatment. *Child Abuse and Neglect: The International Journal, 20*, 1003–1018.

Duncan, G., & Aber, L. (1997). Neighborhood models and measures. In. J. Brooks–Gunn, G. Duncan, & L. Aber (Eds.), *Neighborhood poverty: Context and consequences for children* (pp. 62–78). New York: Russell Sage Foundation.

Farley, R., & Frey, W. (1994). Changes in the segregation of whites from blacks during the 1980s: Small steps toward a more integrated society. *American Sociological Review, 59*, 23–45.

Feldman, K. W., Monastersky, C., & Feldman, G. K. (1993). When is childhood drowning neglect? *Child Abuse and Neglect, 17*, 329–336.

Galster, G. C. (1992). Housing discrimination and urban poverty of African Americans. *Journal of Housing Research, 2*, 87–121.

Galster, G. C., & Mincy, R. B. (1993). Understanding the changing fortunes of metropolitan neighborhoods. *Housing and Policy Debate, 4*, 303–352.

Garbarino, J. (1977). The human ecology of child maltreatment. *Journal of Marriage and the Family, 39*, 721–735.

Garbarino, J., & Crouter, A. (1978). Defining the community context for parent–child relations: The correlates of child maltreatment. *Child Development, 49*, 604–616.

Garbarino, J., & Ebata, A. (1983). The significance of cultural and ethnic factors in child maltreatment. *Journal of Marriage and the Family, 45*, 773–783.

Garbarino, J., & K. Kostelny, K. (1992). Child maltreatment as a community problem. *Child Abuse and Neglect, 16*, 455–464.

Garbarino, J., & Sherman, D. (1980). High-risk neighborhoods and high-risk families: The human ecology of child maltreatment. *Child Development, 51*, 188–198.

Garcia Coll, C., Lamberty, G., Jenkins, R., McAdoo, H. Crnic, K., Wasik, B., & Garcia, H. (1996). An integrative model for the study of developmental competencies in minority children. *Child Development, 67*, 1891–1914.

Gelles, R., & Straus, M. (1988). *Intimate violence*. New York: Simon & Schuster.

Gelles, R. J. (1992). Poverty and violence toward children. *American Behavioral Scientist, 35*, 258–284.

Giovannoni, J., & Becerra, R. (1979). *Defining child abuse*. New York: Free Press.

Giovannoni, J., & Billingsley, A. (1970). Child neglect among the poor: A study of parental adequacy in families of three ethnic groups. *Child Welfare, 49*, 196–204.

Hampton, R., & Newberger, E. (1985). Child abuse incidence and reporting by hospitals: Significance of severity, class, and race. *American Journal of Public Health, 75,* 45–58.

Hampton, R., Gelles, R., & Harrop, J. (1989). Is violence in black families increasing? A comparison of 1975 and 1985 national survey rates. *Journal of Marriage and the Family, 51,* 969–980.

Horowitz, B., & Wolock, I. (1981). Material deprivation, child maltreatment, and agency interventions among poor families. In L. Pelton (Ed.), *The social context of child abuse and neglect* (pp. 137–184). New York: Human Sciences Press.

Jargowsky, P. A., & Bane, M. (1991). Ghetto poverty in the United States, 1970–1980. In C. Jencks & P. E. Peterson (Eds.), *The urban underclass* (pp. 235–273). Washington, DC: The Brookings Institution.

Jason, J., Amereuh, N., Marks, J., & Tyler, C. (1982). Child abuse in Georgia: A method to evaluate risk factors and reporting bias. *American Journal of Public Health, 72,* 1353–1358.

Korbin, J. (1997). Culture and child maltreatment. In M. E. Helfer, R. Kempe, & R. Krugman (Eds.), *The battered child* (5th ed., pp. 29–48). Chicago: University of Chicago Press.

Korbin, J., & Coulton, C. (1996). Neighbors, neighborhood, and child maltreatment. *Journal of Social Issues, 52,* 163–176.

Korbin, J., & Coulton, C. (1997). Understanding the neighborhood context for children and families: Epidemiological and ethnographic approaches. In J. Brooks–Gunn, G. Duncan, & L. Aber (Eds.), *Neighborhood poverty: Context and consequences for children* (pp. 77–91). New York: Russell Sage Foundation.

Lauderdale, M., Valiunas, A., & Anderson, R. (1980). Race, ethnicity, and child maltreatment: An empirical analysis. *Child Abuse and Neglect, 4,* 163–169.

Light, R. (1973). Abused and neglected children in America: A study of alternative policies. *Harvard Educational Review, 43,* 556–598.

Massey, D. S., Condran, G. A., & Denton, N. A. (1987). The effect of residential segregation on black social and economic well-being. *Social Forces, 66,* 29–56.

Massey, D. S., & Denton, N. A. (1989). Hypersegregation in U.S. metropolitan areas: Black and Hispanic segregation along five dimensions. *Demography, 26,* 373–391.

Massey, D. S., & Fong, E. (1990). Segregation and neighborhood quality: Blacks, Hispanics and Asians in the San Francisco metropolitan areas. *Social Forces, 69,* 15–32.

McAdoo, H. P. (1982). Stress absorbing systems in black families. *Family Relations, 31,* 379–488.

McAdoo, H. P. (1995). African-American families: Strengths and realities. In H. I. McCubbin, E. A. Thompson, A. I. Thompson, & J. A. Futrell (Eds.), *Resiliency and ethnic minority families: African-American families* (Vol. 2, pp. 17–30). Madison: University of Wisconsin.

National Center on Child Abuse and Neglect. (1981). *Study findings: National study of the incidence and severity of child abuse and neglect.* Washington, DC: DHEW.

National Center on Child Abuse and Neglect. (1988). *Study findings: Study of national incidence and prevalence of child abuse and neglect: 1988.* Washington, DC: DHEW.

National Research Council (1993). *Understanding child abuse and neglect.* Washington, DC: National Academy Press.

Nelson, B. (1984). *Making an issue of child abuse. Political agenda setting for social problems.* Chicago: University of Chicago Press.

Newberger, E., Reed, R., Daniel, J., Hyde, J., & Kotelchuck, M. (1977). Pediatric social illness: Towards an etiologic classification. *Pediatrics, 60,* 178–185.

O'Toole, R., Turbett, P., & Nalepka, C. (1983). Theories, professional knowledge, and diagnosis of child abuse. In D. Finkelhor, R. Gelles, G. Hotaling, & M. Straus (Eds.), *The dark side of families. Current family violence research.* Beverly Hills: Sage.

Pelton, L. (Ed.). (1981). *The social context of child abuse and neglect.* New York: Human Sciences Press.

Sampson, R. J. (1992). Family management and child development: Insights from social disorganization theory. In J. McCord (Ed.), *Advances in criminological theory* (Vol. 3, pp. 63–93). New Brunswick, NJ: Transaction Press.

Sampson, R. J., & Groves, W. B. (1989). Community structure and crime: Testing social disorganization theory. *American Journal of Sociology, 94,* 775–802.

Sampson, R. J., Raudenbush, S. W., & Earls, F. (1997). Neighborhoods and violent crime: A multilevel study of collective efficacy. *Science, 277,* 918–924.

Sedlack, A., & Broadhurst, D. (1996). *The third national incidence study of child abuse and neglect (NIS-3).* Washington, DC: U.S. Department Health and Human Services.

Shaw, C., & McKay, H. (1942). *Juvenile delinquency in urban areas.* Chicago: University of Chicago Press.

Spearly, J. L., & Lauderdale, M. (1983). Community characteristics and ethnicity in the prediction of child maltreatment rates. *Child Abuse and Neglect: The International Journal, 7,* 91–105.

Stack, C. (1974). *All our kin. Strategies for survival in a Black community.* New York: Harper & Row.

Straus, M., & Gelles, R. (1986). Societal change and change in family violence from 1975–1985 as revealed by two national surveys. *Journal of Marriage and the Family, 48,* 465–479.

Straus, M., Gelles, R., & Steinmetz, S. (1980). *Behind closed doors: Violence in the American family.* New York: Anchor.

Sullivan, M. (1996). Neighborhood social organization. A forgotten object of ethnographic study? In R. Jessor, A. Colby, & R. Shweder (Eds.), *Ethnography and human development. Context and meaning in social inquiry* (pp. 205–224). Chicago: University of Chicago Press.

Sullivan, M. (1998). Integrating qualitative and quantitative methods in the study of developmental psychopathology in context. *Development and Psychopathology, 10*(2), 377–393.

U.S. Advisory Board on Child Abuse and Neglect. (1993). *Neighbors helping neighbors: A new national strategy for the protection of children.* Washington, DC: Administration for Child and Families, U.S. Department of Health and Human Services.

Vinson, T., Baldry, E., & Hargreaves, J. (1996). Neighbourhoods, networks and child abuse. *British Journal of Social Work, 26,* 523–543.

Wolock, I. (1982). Community characteristics and staff judgments in child abuse and neglect cases. *Social Work Research and Abstracts, 18,* 9–15.

Zuravin, S. (1989). The ecology of child abuse and neglect: Review of the literature and presentation of data. *Violence and Victims, 4,* 101–120.

COMMENTARY BY: Claudia Coulton and Jill Korbin

ORIGINS OF THE STUDY

The reprinted article was one in a series of publications coming from our collaborative research on neighborhood factors in child abuse and neglect. We originally came together to do this research from rather different perspectives. Coulton had been studying the economic inequality among urban neighborhoods and had noted that children in persistently poor neighborhoods tended to have significantly higher rates of health and developmental problems. However, she had also observed that not all poor neighborhoods had excessive rates of problems, so she wondered what community processes other than those related to economic status might affect the families and children who lived there. Korbin's long-term interest had been in child abuse and neglect, especially from an ecological perspective. She was curious as to how social and cultural processes within communities might contribute to the risk for child maltreatment. Another aspect of our differing approaches was methodological. Coulton's studies of neighborhoods relied on spatial statistics (i.e., ecological correlations and factor analysis) and multilevel statistical models, whereas Korbin was highly experienced in ethnographic methods. A series of conversations over many months led us to conclude that these two methods could be combined to address our main research question: What aspects of neighborhood social and economic structure and process explain the geographic variation in child abuse and neglect rates?

Our research plan was to begin with the geographic and statistical analysis and then to use focused ethnographies to illuminate the processes behind the statistical associations. We chose this mixed design to overcome the weaknesses inherent in either method alone. The chief advantage of the statistical analysis is that it could include a large sample of neighborhoods and was capable of identifying significant ecological correlations between economic, demographic, social structural, and geographic factors and child abuse and neglect rates. However, it was limited in that these correlations could not necessarily be interpreted as causal, nor could they identify the processes through which children were placed at higher or lower risk. Ethnography, on the other hand, has the advantage of being able to reveal how and why families and children were affected by where they lived. Its main drawback was that it could only be carried out in a few places, and that it is often difficult to know the degree to which generalizations can be made from such findings. By selecting places for ethnography that represented important points on the statistical continuum,

Commentary on article: Korbin, J. E., Coulton, C. E., Chard, S., Platt-Houston, C., & Su, M. (1998). Impoverishment and child maltreatment in African American and European American neighborhoods. *Development and Psychopathology, 10,* 215–233.

we believed that we could apply the deep insight offered by ethnography within the broad parameters of the statistical patterns.

ISSUES IN STUDY IMPLEMENTATION

The study was implemented in two phases: the geo-spatial and statistical analyses were done first, followed by the ethnographic studies and analyses. The phasing was necessary because the ethnography was intended to more deeply investigate the explanations for the patterns revealed in the statistical and spatial analysis. However, we were both closely involved in each phase, attending team meetings and making decisions about details of the data gathering and analysis. This helped to bring the two research approaches together so that they complemented each other.

The statistical portion of the study drew upon available data. The units of analysis were all the census tracts in the county, so limited resources prohibited us from collecting original data in so many places. Many of the study variables could be drawn from neighborhood social and economic data already on hand in the Center on Urban Poverty and Social Change's CAN DO (Cleveland Area Network for Data and Organizing) system. CAN DO is a neighborhood indicators database for the Cleveland region. It contains thousands of measures of the physical, economic, and social conditions in every census tract since 1985. This Web-accessible system (http://povertycenter.case.edu) was put in place in 1992 to enable community planning and action. In many ways, the study would have been prohibitively expensive without the preexistence of this system. However, this study also required obtaining new data on children experiencing maltreatment events for each census tract in Cuyahoga County (Cleveland). For this measure, we planned to use official child abuse and neglect reports made to the Department of Children and Family Services (DCFS). We were aware that maltreatment reports are imperfect measures of the problem, and that there can be both underreporting and unfounded allegations in these reports. However, given the study resources, it was not possible to collect original data on child abuse and neglect in all of the neighborhoods in the region. Moreover, self-report measures of child abuse and neglect also suffer from various biases.

We worked closely with DCFS to obtain and analyze the child abuse and neglect reports. This work was facilitated by a long-standing relationship with agency staff. The first step was to meet with agency officials to describe the study and gain their support for the work. Next, a confidentiality contract was drawn up to cover university personnel acting as agents of the County, following all of the procedures and laws governing the protection of the data. Research staff members were trained in data protection procedures and signed oaths of confidentiality according to County specifications. Secure computer server space was set up to receive the data. Agency staff worked along with the research team to properly interpret the various codes in the data files. The records also had to be geocoded so that they could be aggregated to census tracts for the calculation of rates.

These steps required an unanticipated amount of clerical editing and data cleaning, but were facilitated by strong working relationships between research and agency staff. For example, we defined the child maltreatment rate as the proportion of children in the census tract who were maltreated in a given year. However, many choices had to be made about how to count these children. An important issue was whether to use any report as a sign of maltreatment or to use either those reports that were substantiated or indicated or both. Discussions with agency and research staff and review of the literature led us to the conclusion that we would count children with one or more substantiated or indicated reports in a year as maltreated. Further examination of the data uncovered that some maltreatment reports did not receive their final disposition until the following calendar year. Therefore, we concluded that it was necessary to link data files across multiple years in order to make an accurate count of substantiated or indicated events in each year. An additional ambiguity was what to do with children who moved during the year and were reported for maltreatment in two different neighborhoods. We decided to count the child as a maltreatment victim in the census tract where the first substantiated or indicated report occurred within the calendar year. Geocoding of the addresses of child maltreatment reports also called for conversations between agency and research staff. We wanted the events coded to the residential address of the family at the time of the maltreatment. One illustration of a problem, though, was when numerous reports were found to cluster at one address. A drive-by and conversations led to the conclusion that an agency address, from which several reports were made, had been substituted for the residential addresses in the data file. Such data cleaning problems abound in research that relies on archival or administrative records, and they must be handled with great care. It is important to be able to work closely with the producers of the records to understand the nuances and ambiguities in the data. Researchers often underestimate the time and effort that will be required to accomplish this phase of the research.

After examining the results of the statistical analysis, neighborhoods were selected for the ethnography. An important advantage of selecting neighborhoods based on the statistical analysis was that the ethnography could be targeted at explaining processes associated with neighborhood differences that had been identified in the statistical analysis. The ethnography and the statistical analysis, then, could complement one another. We selected thirteen census tracts to represent high, average, and low child abuse and neglect report rates, with high and low defined as being one standard deviation above or below the mean of 36.3 per 1,000 children. Predominantly African-American and predominantly European-American neighborhoods (>75 percent of the total population) were selected in each of the reporting rate types. Our statistical analyses of neighborhood conditions had found that a factor we termed "impoverishment" explained the greatest amount of variation in child abuse rates across all census tracts. The current paper was stimulated by the finding that the impoverishment factor had a significantly weaker effect on maltreatment rates in African-American than in European-American census tracts. We felt that the ethnography would have something to add to help us interpret this finding. We went back to our thirteen neighborhood ethnographies and selected four census tracts in the highest and lowest quartiles of child maltreatment reports, with one African-American and one European-American census tract in each quartile.

One important decision was the kind of ethnographic approach to take. In this first of our studies, we elected a more traditional ethnographic approach. Our goal was to familiarize ourselves "on the ground" with the neighborhoods we wanted to study. We employed a combination of strategies. Ethnographers conducted unstructured observations and informal interviews at neighborhood facilities such as the local library, the YMCA, and the playground, and participated in activities at neighborhood institutions that were thought to engage the wider neighborhood, such as charity dinners at churches or reading hours at the library. In neighborhoods that had formal organizations, such as block clubs, ethnographers attended meetings and observed and talked informally with residents. Ethnographers kept detailed field notes of all encounters and observations in the neighborhoods; they also used an open-ended interview guide with all neighborhood businesses, religious organizations, and community organizations to get a sense of how the business or organization served the neighborhood and the level of neighborhood residents' engagement with these resources. Finally, in each neighborhood we conducted open-ended ethnographic interviews with residents. Through block clubs and neighborhood resources and organizations, we sought out individuals who were thought by others to be familiar with their neighborhoods, people we referred to as "knowledgeable neighbors." Strict criteria were not applied in identifying these individuals for interviews because we sought a range of residents who might inform us about their neighborhood environment. These people might have lived in the neighborhood for a long time, have been centrally involved in one or more activities in the neighborhood, or be otherwise regarded by others as someone with whom to talk about the neighborhood. In a few cases, these were individuals who might seem to keep to themselves, but others thought that their perspective on the neighborhood would be of value. In a later study (Coulton, Korbin, & Su, 1999), we randomly selected neighborhood residents for a structured interview based, in large part, on what we learned through this first ethnographic study. In addition, ethnographers were blind to the child maltreatment rate of the neighborhoods in which they worked. Because all of the neighborhoods were of low-to-moderate means, the ethnographers had little factual basis to guess rates of child maltreatment reports. Even in the "worst" neighborhoods, ethnographers found strengths and sometimes commented that they hoped that theirs was not a high-maltreatment neighborhood.

An important decision was whether to work with student ethnographers or to hire professionals. We elected to use student ethnographers both because we wished to train students in ethnography in urban settings, and because we had a pool of talented students in anthropology, several of whom had previously worked with Korbin in a course requiring ethnography with inner-city families. We further had to decide if we were going to match ethnographers with the predominant ethnicity of the neighborhood. We decided that matching would increase the comfort level of the participants in the study. While we have no systematic evidence, we do believe that the degree of comfort and the excellence of the team enabled the sharing of sensitive information. For example, a resident's question as to whether "someone white" had made up the questions provided valuable insight for the study. Openness among a mixed-ethnicity research group takes time and trust to achieve but greatly enhances the research.

The assignment of ethnographers to specific neighborhoods also offered insights. Neighborhoods that appeared to be the "worst" assignments—because they seemed to be the most threatening before the ethnographers began work—sometimes ended up being considered good neighborhoods in which to work because of the cohesiveness of the community. Additionally, it was much more difficult to find neighborhood residents at home in the more economically sound neighborhoods because residents were at work during the day. This necessitated more weekend and evening visits, and resulted in greater difficulty identifying a sample and scheduling and completing interviews.

FUNDING

As is often the case, no single funding source supported all of the costs of this research. The study itself received support from the National Center for Child Abuse and Neglect. This funding covered the cost of the statistical analyses and the neighborhood ethnographies. However, the study could not have been done if the neighborhood geographic information system (CAN DO, described earlier) had not already been in place. This database contained boundary files for all census tracts in the county, along with hundreds of social and economic indicators for each tract. Moreover, the geocoding system for county addresses was already in place. These developments had been funded by several private foundations, including the Cleveland Foundation and the Rockefeller Foundation.

Ethnographic work is very expensive because hours of rapport building and preliminary work are often necessary before yielding interesting findings; such work depends on the establishment of relationships, and this is often very time consuming. We could not, for example, track exactly how many hours an ethnographer needed to spend in a neighborhood before identifying appropriate residents for interviews. Also, the nature of ethnographic interviewing is such that interviews using the same interview guide could vary in length by hours, based on the talkativeness of the resident. Some additional graduate student time was donated by the Department of Anthropology. Nevertheless, ethnography is a labor-intensive and costly enterprise.

Keeping a smoothly functioning research team across thirteen neighborhoods required at least weekly team meetings and constant communication. It was important for ethnographers to learn about one another's neighborhoods, both to help interpret the ethnographic findings for the larger study, and also because it might alert them to aspects of their neighborhoods that they might have overlooked.

ETHICAL ISSUES

The two study components involved somewhat different ethical issues. The statistical portion of the study required researchers to use highly confidential child abuse and neglect reports. Each record contained identifying information needed for the study such as the home address of the child and birth date. Even though names were not obtained, address and birth date would be sufficient to identify an individual. Thus, protection of the confidential data was the main ethical concern of this component. Computer security has improved markedly since the early 1990s when this study was initiated but, at that time, we stored the data on the University's mainframe computer due to its high level of security. Analysts geocoded (i.e., attached the latitude and longitude to each record) and aggregated the data to census tract counts before saving data on personal computers. That way, the data on personal computers was not identifiable at the individual level. The raw data came to the university on tapes, which were kept in locked cabinets under the supervision of a programmer fully trained in data security and protection. When the study was over, they were destroyed. We were careful to eliminate from the study any census tracts in which fewer than 30 children lived.

Several ethical issues were involved in the ethnography. Neighborhoods, like individuals, have an identity. Poor African-American neighborhoods, in particular, felt that they had been repeatedly subjected to studies about their pathology and danger. Because child maltreatment is such an emotional issue, no neighborhood wanted to be known as having greater rates of child abuse than another. This called for sensitivity in how these rates were conveyed. While CAN DO includes child maltreatment rates, these rates are but one of hundreds of neighborhood indicators that are available online. In published reports, however, we protected the anonymity of specific neighborhoods, using pseudonyms as in the paper reproduced here.

Ethical issues also arose in considering the implications of our findings. That impoverishment had a significantly weaker effect on child maltreatment rates in predominantly African-American neighborhoods than in predominantly European-American neighborhoods stimulated us to consider aspects of the ethnography that could elaborate on this finding. That the ethnographic data pointed to stronger social fabric in the poor African-American neighborhoods studied created a quandary. On the one hand, we could point to the literature on the strengths of African-American families that our study supported. On the other hand, we were concerned that the finding of a strong social fabric could be interpreted to suggest that these communities can fend for themselves in protecting children.

Because we elected to use student ethnographers, with perhaps less street experience than professional interviewers, the safety of these students had to be addressed not only as a logistical, but also as an ethical issue. This question is often posed to us by others considering research in inner-city neighborhoods. This research was carried out before cell phones were as readily available as they are today. Near the end of the research we secured a few phones to be shared by the ethnographic team. We addressed the problem of safety by having the student ethnographers work in pairs. When this was not possible, we developed a procedure for ethnographers logging the address and time of their appointments in the neighborhood and arranging with another member of the team to track their return. In a subsequent study, in which we sampled door-to-door, ethnographer/interviewers also traveled in pairs, but could be at separate households as long as they were in sight of one another and knew the location of the other. Additionally, as the ethnographers became more familiar with their neighborhoods, they also became better versed in the actual versus supposed dangers of their specific neighborhoods. Residents and others cautioned them about streets to avoid where, for example, there was drug dealing, or times of the day to be out of the neighborhood, such as Friday nights when there was a lot of bar traffic in one neighborhood. Residents were generous in sharing their own strategies with ethnographers.

IDEAS EMERGING AS THE STUDY PROGRESSED

Although this study was exploratory, we were guided in our exploration by theory regarding community social organization. As that theory would predict, we found a relationship between the economic and demographic structure of the community and the rates of child abuse and neglect. However, contrary to our expectations, we found that residential instability was not predictive of high rates of child maltreatment. We had firsthand knowledge of some of the neighborhoods in the region that had experienced high levels of movement in and out, and we used these impressions to generate some hunches about what instability means to a community. We realized that some neighborhoods were experiencing a positive type of movement while in others movement was more disruptive of the social order. For example, one neighborhood that was high on a statistical measure of instability while fairly low on child maltreatment was a place where many offspring of former residents were moving back to the neighborhood. They were not strangers moving in but had a history of social connections to the place. We contrasted that type of instability with another neighborhood where the neighborhood was turning over from middle-class to poor residents, and from home owners to renters. There the maltreatment rates were higher, even though the basic mobility statistics were similar. The article reprinted in this volume came, in part, from that idea, which did not emerge until the study was well underway. We began to realize that measures of community social organization might mean something different in varying contexts, or that they might operate as relative rather than absolute values. Moreover, a community might be more strongly affected based on whether it was improving or getting worse, rather than its level on a measure at a point in time. These hunches could be further tested using the ethnographic data.

It is in the nature of ethnographic work that ideas almost constantly emerge. This is why it is critical to be as systematic as possible with ethnographic data, making sure that one striking anecdote does not lead you down the wrong path. Questions must be continually refined and presented consistently to a wider group of residents.

STRENGTHS AND LIMITATIONS

An important limitation of this study is that it was carried out in one region. Cities differ markedly in the structure and geography of neighborhoods. Cleveland, for example, is an old industrial city in which the central core of neighborhoods grew up around industry. That has served to structure the distribution of the population into sections that are relatively demarcated by race and economics. In fact, Cleveland has one of the highest levels of racial and economic segregation in the nation. The neighborhood effects identified in this research may not be present in other types of cities. Moreover, reports to only one child welfare agency were used in this study. Agencies are known to differ in their policies and practices regarding the investigation of child abuse and neglect reports.

Another shortcoming of this study is that it relied on official maltreatment reports. While official reports are commonly used to study the abuse and neglect that is known to the authorities, there is general agreement that they underrepresent the problem. Surveys that ask parents to self-report behaviors toward their children that are aggressive or violent generally conclude that child abuse occurs much more frequently than official reports suggest (Gallup, Moor, & Schussel, 1997; Straus & Gelles, 1986). Retrospective self-reports by adults on their mistreatment in childhood also confirm higher rates than official reports (Carlin et al., 1994; Fergusson, Horwood, & Woodward, 2000). Moreover, when official reports are combined with counts of children whom professionals believe have been harmed by abuse and neglect but not reported, the rates are measurably higher as well (Sedlak & Broadhurst, 1996). As such, official abuse and neglect reports represent only that portion of maltreated children who are recognized and reported to the public child protection system.

The ethnography also had limitations. The labor-intensive nature of ethnography means that only a few neighborhoods can be studied, and generalizations must be made with caution. An advantage of this ethnography, as noted earlier, is that the selection of neighborhoods for our study was based on a larger analysis of census tracts that guided us toward neighborhoods of interest to the problem at hand. Furthermore, we sought selected residents who were linked to community groups and institutions. In later work we sought to elaborate on these findings in a larger number of neighborhoods, with a more representative sample of residents. Despite these limitations, few studies have systematically coordinated aggregate and ethnographic research, and we believe that this is a promising approach for a better understanding of the findings from both methods.

FUTURE RESEARCH

Following the study described here, we conducted an investigation of child maltreatment in 20 neighborhoods using a structured interview administered in a household survey (Coulton et al., 1999). The survey included the Child Abuse Potential Inventory (CAP), among the most widely used instruments for predicting child abuse potential (Milner, 1994). In part, we elected to use this self-report scale as a measure of maltreatment in order to avoid the limitations of reports to the child welfare agency. As a byproduct of that research, we observed that there was little difference in the mean CAP scores between neighborhoods with high and low reported child maltreatment rates. This more recent study, along with the previous work, has convinced us that future research needs to delve into the process through which child maltreatment is defined, recognized, and reported in communities. We have observed that neighborhood poverty and other signs of economic distress are strong predictors of child maltreatment reports, but they are not highly correlated with the psychological profile of abusive parents that is captured in the CAP. What accounts for these disparities will be the subject of our future studies.

APPLICATION TO POLICY AND PRACTICE

This study suggests that efforts to prevent child abuse and neglect need to be tailored to the conditions in specific communities. Moreover, in addition to providing child welfare services, communities should consider whether fundamental investments in the economic and physical conditions of low-income neighborhoods may have an indirect benefit of lowering child maltreatment rates. It should not be assumed, though, that poor economic status or residential turnover in a neighborhood always portends risk to children. Community strengths and assets are often overlooked by statistics, but they can be revealed through qualitative methods that glimpse the social processes through which neighbors and institutions support children and families.

ACKNOWLEDGMENTS

The research described in this article was in part funded by the National Center for Child Abuse and Neglect (#90CA1494 from 1991–1994 and #90CA1548 from 1994–1998) and by the Foundation for Child Development.

REFERENCES

Carlin, A. S., Kemper, K., Ward, N. G., Sowell, H., Gustafson, B., & Stevens, N. (1994). The effect of differences in objective and subjective definitions of childhood physical abuse on estimates of its incidence and relationship to psychopathology. *Child Abuse and Neglect, 18*(5), 393–399.

Coulton, C. J., Korbin, J., & Su, M. (1999). Neighborhoods and child maltreatment: A multi-level study of resources and controls. *Child Abuse & Neglect, 23*(11), 1019–1040.

Fergusson, D. M., Horwood, L. J., & Woodward, L. J. (2000). The stability of child abuse reports: A longitudinal study of the reporting behaviour of young adults. *Psychological Medicine, 30*(3), 529–544.

Gallup, G. H., Moor, D. W. & Schussel, R. (1997). *Disciplining children in America.* Princeton, NJ: The Gallup Organization.

Korbin, J. E., & Coulton, C. (1997). Understanding the neighborhood context for children and families: Epidemiological and ethnographic approaches.

In J. Brooks-Gunn, L. Aber, & G. Duncan (Eds.), *Neighborhood poverty: Context and consequences for children* (pp. 77–91). New York: Russell Sage Foundation.

Korbin, J., Coulton, C., Chard, S., Platt-Houston, C., & Su, M. (1998). Impoverishment and child maltreatment in African-American and European-American neighborhoods. *Development and Psychopathology, 10*, 215–233.

Milner, J. (1994). Assessing physical child abuse risk: The Child Abuse Potential Inventory. *Child Psychology Review, 14*, 547–583.

Sedlak, A. J., & Broadhurst, D. D. (1996). *Third national incidence study of child abuse and neglect: Final report.* Washington, DC: U.S. Department of Health and Human Services, Administration for Children, Youth, and Families.

Strauss, M. A., & Gelles, R. J. (1986). Societal change and change in family violence from 1975–1985 as revealed by two national surveys. *Journal of Marriage and the Family, 48*(3), 465–479.

SECTION V

Use of Available Data

This section addresses the use of data that have been collected for one purpose, but are being used again as research data for another purpose. "Existing data" refers to a diversity of types of information that are available for others to use, including administrative data collected by human service agencies; large scale government surveys; written documents, such as worker and client interviews, process notes, and legislative hearings; media of all types; and other investigators' research data sets. An important advantage of using existing data in research is that it is generally far less costly than collecting primary data, which is often the most expensive aspect of human service research. However, depending on the form or source of the existing data, obtaining the data can sometimes be quite time consuming (and thus costly). For example, the use of agency case-record data, as discussed in one of the commentaries, can sometimes be a resource-intensive, and consequently expensive, activity.

In this section, researchers discuss issues of locating existing data that address a specific interest of the researcher. Some of the available data sets are far larger, with greater representation of specific groups, than any one researcher could afford to (or be able to) collect alone. A number of the available data sets discussed were collected by government agencies. Accessing these data sets frequently takes a good deal of negotiation with agencies for permission for use, and often requires compromises and contractual agreements. Generally, it is necessary to work with the producers of the data in order to truly understand the meaning of the existing information. In some cases, when the data are in the form of written documents, it is a matter of clearly defining a sampling frame to select the documents to be used, and then applying either an existing coding scheme or one that the researcher develops on his/her own to categorize the data. Available data can provide a clear picture of how clinical service and service system interventions are operating in the real world, thereby providing before-and-after assessment of the impact of evidence-based practices.

18

The Effect of Services on the Recurrence of Child Maltreatment

Diane DePanfilis and Susan J. Zuravin

INTRODUCTION

In 1993, the US Advisory Board on Child Abuse and Neglect (Melton & Barry, 1994) suggested that the current child protection system is fundamentally flawed in its primary emphasis on reporting and investigation in contrast to preventing initial or further harm to children. Based on a national study, McCurdy and Daro (1993) made a similar point by suggesting that nearly half of families in which maltreatment is substantiated do not receive even the pretense of any "service" other than investigation. More recently, it has been suggested that "child welfare analysts, practitioners, and the general public all agree: the child protective services system (CPS) is in crisis and is in urgent need of reform. Children at risk are not being adequately protected, and they and their families are not receiving the services that they need" (Waldfogel, 2000, p. 43). Despite this growing concern, there has been very little research that actually describes what happens to families once CPS has substantiated a report of child abuse and neglect or what effect, if any, service variables have on whether families are identified for future incidents of child maltreatment. This article begins to fill this gap by examining whether services variables predict the recurrence of child maltreatment while child protective services were provided in an urban jurisdiction.

Despite the fact that the *success* of intervention has been suggested to be synonymous with cessation of child maltreatment (Wolfe, 1994) and that the federal government now requires states to report on the degree to which children are safe from recurrences of child maltreatment (US Department of Health and Human Services, Administration for Children and Families, 2000b), there has been little effort to examine how services affect this outcome. Among the 41 states that provided information on services to the National Child Abuse and Neglect Data System (US Department of

The study was funded in part by the National Center on Child Abuse and Neglect, Grant Number 90CA1497. Preparation of this paper was supported by The Lois and Samuel Silberman Fund Faculty Awards Program.

Health and Human Services, Administration for Children and Families, 2001), an average of 55.8% of child victims and their families received services beyond the investigation in 1999. However, there was great variation in the number of child victims who received post-investigative services in 1999 ranging from 15.1% in Illinois to 100% in Arkansas, Mississippi, and Rhode Island. In 1998, the type of service most frequently provided was case management, followed by therapeutic services, such as counseling, mental health and substance abuse treatment, and family-based services, for example, family support, family preservation, and home-based services (US Department of Health and Human Services, Administration for Children and Families, 2000a). In 1999, in an average of 20.7% of the cases, foster care was used to protect the child (US Department of Health and Human Services, Administration for Children and Families, 2001). Again this type of response varied by state ranging from 2.3% to 61.5% of child victims placed in foster care. Most services received by families were on a *semi*-voluntary basis since only about 26.1% involved a juvenile court petition.

A study conducted by Jagannathan and Camasso (1996) suggested that certain types of cases served by CPS agencies generate more work, more unsuccessful contacts, and lead to variations in types of service contacts. If CPS agencies tend to serve many of their cases over and over again because of high levels of recurrences of child maltreatment, it is important that we begin to understand better whether certain CPS responses are more effective than others in reducing the likelihood of future maltreatment.

RELATIONSHIP BETWEEN SERVICES AND CHILD MALTREATMENT RECURRENCES

Prior reviews of child maltreatment recurrence studies (DePanfilis, 1995; Miller, Williams, English, & Olmstead, 1987) have identified a core set of recurrence risk factors related to children, parents, families, index maltreatment, or environment and, to a lesser extent, the intervention. Similarly, comparison of the factors included in risk assessment models (DePanfilis & Scannapieco, 1994; Doueck, English, DePanfilis, & Moote, 1993; Marks, McDonald, & Bessey, 1989; McDonald & Marks, 1991) have identified a rather small set of intervention risk factors included in risk assessment or decision-making models, mostly related to the families' responsiveness to intervention, rather than the availability, accessibility, nature, or extent of intervention that was available or provided by CPS or other service providers.

Intervention Related Risks Found in Recurrence Related Research

Even though the largest body of studies included in this review were treatment outcome studies, most of them were unable to predict that certain types of intervention were more effective than others at reducing the likelihood of future maltreatment. Intervention variables that did predict recurrence (or non-recurrence) fall into one of three types: (1) variables that describe the intervention that was provided previously or in relation to the current incident; (2) types of intervention provided; and (3) variables that describe the level of motivation and cooperation by the family to use services as intended. For the most part, intervention variables were used to predict any recurrence, rather than any specific subtype of recurrence.

Intervention Characteristics

Examples of intervention characteristics that predicted recurrence of any type included variables that increased the likelihood (risk) of recurrence as well as those that decreased the risk of recurrence. Variables that predicted recurrence were: prior CPS case for family (increased risk) (Johnson, 1994; Marks & McDonald, 1989); new to child welfare (decreased risk) (Schuerman, Rzepnicki, & Littell, 1994); prior placements (increased risk) (Baird, 1988); prior inpatient treatment for a family member (increased risk) (Coleman, 1995); child out of home (positive relationship to recurrence) (Browne, 1986); level of training of workers (less increased risk) (Cohn, 1979); length of CPS services (longer services decreased risk) (Berkeley Planning Associates, 1983; Johnson & L'Esperence, 1984); number of in-person casework visits (more decreased risk) (Johnson, 1996); and number of concrete services provided in the first 90 days (positive relationship with recurrence) (Schuerman, Rzepnicki, & Littell, 1994).

More recent analysis of the Schuerman, Rzepnicki, and Littell (1994) study by Littell (1997) suggested that the duration, intensity, and breadth of family preservation services had little overall impact on the recurrence of child maltreatment. In particular, the length of services was not related to recurrence of maltreatment, and the intensity of contact with caseworkers was related to recurrences observed at 3 and 6 months post-termination, but was not significant at 1 year (Littell, 1997). A later analysis conducted by Johnson and Clancy (1990) also contradicted earlier results by Johnson and L'Esperence (1984) with respect to length of services. In the more recent study by Johnson and Clancy (1990), rate of recurrence of maltreatment did not vary as a function of how long cases were served. To some degree, examining the effect of length of services on recurrences is confounded because it is assumed that cases that are considered to be more complex and have a higher risk of maltreatment will likely receive longer services. Thus, the "net" effect of services may not be able to be determined since more serious cases get more and longer services to begin with.

Types of Intervention

Types of intervention that reduced risk of recurrence in the Berkeley Planning Associates (1983) study included: adult client received group counseling (neglect and emotional maltreatment samples); adult client received education or skill development training (neglect sample); adult client received support services (sexual abuse sample); adult client received parent education (sexual abuse sample); child received temporary shelter (adolescent sample); and child received therapeutic daycare (child sample). If a child received medical services, the likelihood of recurrence was increased (likely related to severity of maltreatment, which was also a predictor). Further, if an adolescent received personal skill development classes, increased risk of recurrence was documented. In a study of workload and use of risk assessment, Fluke (1991) found that a local jurisdiction in Maryland, using the Child At Risk Field decision-making system, had a rate of new reports of abuse or neglect lower than the state average. Since a primary goal of using a risk assessment process is to be able to target interventions to reduce the risk of future maltreatment, this could be a promising result that should be examined in other research.

Cooperation of Family

Finally, the last category of intervention variables is extremely interesting and emphasizes the importance of actively engaging families in intervention. The following variables predicted recurrence: motivation of perpetrator of caregiver (Baird, 1988; Baird, Wagner, & Neuenfeldt, 1993; Wagner, 1994); caregiver viewed the current incident as seriously or more seriously than the investigating worker (reduced risk) (Wagner, 1994); and cooperation with agency by non-perpetrator caregiver (more cooperation, less risk) (Baird, 1988; Baird, Wagner, & Neuenfeldt, 1993). In contrast, variables that predicted a higher likelihood of recurrence included: negative attitude toward agency (for sexual abuse sample) (McDonald & Johnson, 1992); family's ability to use agency resources (Johnson & L'Esperance, 1984; Marks & McDonald, 1989); and willingness to use agency resources (Johnson, 1994).

Because of major differences between studies with respect to definitions of the index and recurrence incident, definition of recurrence (report or substantiated report or a specific type of maltreatment or any type of maltreatment), unit of analysis (child, family, perpetrator), follow-up time, and types of data analysis, studies are difficult to compare and therefore draw conclusions.

Risk Factors in Risk Assessment or Decision-Making Systems

Risk assessment models appear to most often use intervention-related factors related to the family's response to treatment, rather than intervention-related characteristics or types. For example, Marks, McDonald, and Bessey (1989) indicated the presence of the following intervention-related factors in risk assessment models: level of cooperation of the child; parental recognition of problems; parental motivation to solve problems (or variations of this construct); and parental cooperation with case planning/services (or variations of this construct). In this same review (Marks, McDonald, & Bessey, 1989), four models were identified as specifically including the availability or accessibility of services as factors that could increase risk of recurrence, and two models considered the impact of intervention as factors that could increase or decrease risk of recurrence.

A separate review of safety decision-making models (DePanfilis & Scannapieco, 1994) identified similar but slightly different intervention-related factors: capacity of parents to change; parents are uncooperative; parents have failed to benefit from past help; previous placements; problem is chronic; refusal to perceive or remedy problems; and unrealistic view of current situation.

Given the preliminary stage of the field, the purpose of this article is to explore what effect service variables have to the epidemiology of child maltreatment recurrences. This study used archival data to explore which services were provided to families and what effect differences in services had to the prediction of child maltreatment recurrence while child protection services were being provided.

METHODS

Study Design and Overview

The design vehicle for achieving the study objective was a nonconcurrent prospective study. To obtain a complete picture of the epidemiology of child maltreatment recurrences, as well as which services followed an index incident, families were followed for 5 years from their first 1988 report (index incident) confirmed by a public CPS agency. Recurrence was defined as any confirmed report of physical abuse, sexual abuse, or neglect of any child in the family that occurred at least 1 day following the index incident report date while the family was receiving CPS intervention. Duplicate reports of the same index incident were not counted as a recurrence. Data were collected and coded from archival sources (management information systems and case records). More detailed discussion about the methods for this study has been previously described (DePanfilis & Zuravin, 1999a; DePanfilis & Zuravin, 1999b; DePanfilis & Zuravin, 2001; Zuravin & DePanfilis, 1996).

Sample

Sampling for this study involved two primary phases: (1) sampling from the population of substantiated CPS reports in 1988 following a set of inclusion and exclusion criteria (Zuravin, DePanfilis, &

Maznyk, 1993), and (2) applying a second set of exclusionary criteria to select a group of CPS families to follow with respect to recurrences (DePanfilis, 1995; DePanfilis & Zuravin, 1999a; DePanfilis & Zuravin, 1999b; Zuravin & DePanfilis, 1996). In the recurrence study, 1167 subject families from a pool of 2902 families who had experienced a substantiated report of child maltreatment during 1988 were followed over 5 years.

Sampling Procedures for This Article

For the purposes of this article, we were interested in looking more carefully at a subset of families in which more in-depth data had been coded from case records. These procedures, which have been previously described (Zuravin, DePanfilis, & Maznyk, 1993; DePanfilis & Zuravin, 1999b), resulted in a sample of 654 families. After excluding families who did not reside together for at least 3 months during the 5 years, 641 families were initially available to examine the effect of services on recurrences. After excluding families whose cases were closed in CPS Intake, had experienced sexual abuse, or multiple types of maltreatment, 446 families were available for estimating a recurrence model that examined the effect of services. Finally, 12 additional families were excluded because service variables were not able to be coded because of missing information in case records. This left 434 families available for examination of the effect of services on the likelihood of recurrences.

Similar to the full population served by CPS in this jurisdiction, the majority (65%) of families were African American and the remaining were White (35%). Mothers were an average of 27 years old at the time of the index report, with 9 years being the average age of the oldest child. Most families received income assistance at the time of the CPS report (62%). Sixty-eight percent of index-substantiated incidents were classified as neglect only, and 32% were classified as physical abuse only.

Data Collection Sources

Data for this study came from two sources, archival records maintained by the Baltimore City Department of Social Services (BCDSS) through information systems and in case records.

Information System

Selected data elements were initially coded on all 1167 families from the statewide Automated Master File Information System (AMF) over a 5 year period to coincide with each family's 5 year anniversary of the 1998 index report. Each case was coded by one person and then edited by a second coder. Staff members (including MSW students) were trained to 95% inter-rater reliability before they were permitted to edit another coder's cases. The project director resolved discrepancies between coders. Double data entry was performed to decrease errors. (Student grades were partially dependent on their accuracy rates for coding and data entry.)

With respect to this article, data were available with respect to the following:

- Child maltreatment reports: dates of all reports of child maltreatment, family members involved in each report, type(s) of maltreatment, and substantiation status;
- Child protective services: types and opening and closing dates (lengths) of child protective services provided to each family member;

- Out-of-home placement services: types and opening and closing dates (lengths) regarding placement of any involved children;

- Other social services: types and opening and closing dates (lengths) of other social services provided to family members, such as daycare, intensive family services, services to families with children, relative placements, services to homeless families, and so forth; and

- Financial services: opening and closing dates (lengths) of AFDC provided to the mother and her children, and opening and closing dates of Food Stamps and Medical Assistance services for families not receiving AFDC.

Case Records

A detailed case record abstraction coding manual specified methods for operationalizing each case record variable and identified primary, secondary, and tertiary sources in case records for information pertinent to each variable. A computer-assisted coding system was developed to eliminate the need for paper coding forms. Each case was coded by one person and then edited by a second coder. Staff members were trained to 95% inter-rater reliability before they were permitted to edit another coder's cases. The project director resolved discrepancies between coders.

Data elements were selected based on an ecological perspective, prior research, and information that was found to be reliably available after pretests of the automated instrument. A summary of data elements coded from case records follows:

- Index incident characteristics: referral source; the type(s) and subtype(s), severity, perpetrator of maltreatment for each victim child; the case active status at the time of the report; the perpetrator's explanation of the incident; the number of physically abused, neglected, and sexually abused children; and the number of prior substantiated reports;

- Descriptive characteristics at index incident: number of biological and other children in the home, and the number of mothers, fathers, and other adult caregivers in the home;

- Situational characteristics at index incident: evidence of financial crisis; environmental stressors; mental health status of mother, father, and other adult caregivers; mental health status of each child in the family, including DSM-III-R diagnoses when applicable; type(s) and frequency of drug use by mother, father, and other adult caregivers; frequency of alcohol use by mother, father, and other adult caregivers; presence of physical health problems of mother, father, and other adult caregivers; physical and developmental status (including disabilities) of all children in the family; family support system characteristics; and indication of criminal involvement of mother, father, and other adult caregivers;

- Service characteristics: case status at the conclusion of the index incident, for example, provided continuing services or closed in intake; service plan characteristics; types of services that have been provided/arranged, offered but refused/not used, or needed but not available to all family members; types of mental health services provided to children identified with mental health problems; number of casework contacts while case was open; motivation of parent during service delivery; number of caseworkers during time case was active; level of improvement for each previously identified problem; and reason for case closing;

- Placement characteristics: placement location for all children placed during intake (including formal and informal placements), reason(s) for placement, and length of out-of-home placement for each child; and

- Juvenile Court status: type of court involvement and disposition of court.

Measures

Selection of predictors was driven by two factors. They included the need to (1) attempt replication of prior studies, and (2) select predictors that were *least* likely to require subjective judgments.

Predictors were obtained from archival sources and measured at the time of the index incident, during the period of continuing service, or at the time of case closing following the index incident. Predictors included in a previously reported recurrence model that predicted recurrence while the family was active in CPS (DePanfilis & Zuravin, 1999b) represented seven constructs: characteristics of the index maltreatment incident, child vulnerability, maternal personal problems, family conflict, family stress, survival stress, and social support deficits. Five out of seven of these constructs were measured by indices, and two were represented by individual items. Because the rationale for selection and the method of measurement has been previously described (DePanfilis & Zuravin, 1999b), only the rationale and methods of measurement of service variables is described here.

Service Variables

Services-related variables represented three constructs: casework services, level of cooperation and motivation, and level of problem resolution. All three constructs were measured by individual variables. Placement status was entered as a control variable.

The predictive models were designed to identify the characteristics about the family and intervention that predict the length of time until recurrence while CPS intervention was being provided.

Casework Services

Theoretically, the risk of recurrence will be at least partially influenced by the nature of CPS intervention. Three variables were selected to represent three dimensions of casework services: (1) the type of continuing service—already active versus opened after the index; (2) the number of in-person casework contacts while the case was active; and (3) the number of caseworkers during CPS continuing services.

The first variable was constructed from information available from the AMF system. If the case was active in CPS when the index report was received, it was coded 0; if the case was opened in CPS following the index, it was coded with a 1. The second variable, number of in-person casework contacts, was constructed by counting the number of actual visits between the caseworker and at least one family member as recorded in the case record. The last variable, number of caseworkers, was a count of how many caseworkers were ever assigned to work with this family during the continuing service period. In addition, another variable meant to reflect the intensity of intervention by dividing the number of casework contacts by the length of service was not selected after initial testing.

Level of Cooperation

There is fairly extensive literature to suggest that motivation and level of cooperation with services will affect treatment outcome. With respect to child maltreatment recurrence research, at least seven separate studies have identified statistically significant predictors (measured differently) in relation to this construct (Baird, 1988; Baird et al., 1993; Johnson, 1994; Johnson & L'Esperance, 1984; Marks & McDonald, 1989; McDonald & Johnson, 1992; Rittner, 1995; Wagner, 1994).

Two individual items were selected to represent this construct: whether any perpetrator admitted to the index maltreatment (yes or no) and whether the family attended services (yes or no). A nine-item index had originally been constructed with these two variables and seven others but was not used because of poor performance. Items not included were: level of cooperation during intake, presence of a signed service agreement, services not used or refused by mother, availability for casework contacts, cooperation of mother during CPS continuing service, resistance of mother during continuing services, and juvenile court used.

Level of Problem Resolution

Conceptually, it was believed that families who were still known to have problems at the time of case closure may have been more likely to experience recurrences. The automated case-coding instrument was programmed to ask a series of questions about the status of client problems at closure based on whether a certain problem was noted to exist at the time of the index incident. For example, if the case was coded as "mother has drug problem" at the time of the index incident, the computer program asked "what is the level of improvement for 'mother has drug problem' at the time of closure?" The coder then entered whether improvement was noted in the record as 0 (no improvement noted in record) or 1 (some improvement noted in record). Using these items, a new variable was constructed to represent percentage of improvement regarding identified problems at intake. This variable was constructed by dividing the number of problems identified at intake by the number of problems that were noted by the caseworker as improved at case closure. One interval level variable was included in the models: percentage of problems with at least some improvement at time of closure (IMPROVE).

Data Analysis

Descriptive analyses were first performed to describe the nature of services provided to families who received continuing protective services because of a substantiated report of child maltreatment. Several questions were used to describe these services: How many families had open case files at the time of the index incident? For how long were families provided continuing services? How many direct casework contacts did families receive? How many families experienced a substantiated report of child maltreatment following the index incident?

The analytic plan for developing the model involved two stages. First, the process used in a previous analysis (DePanfilis & Zuravin, 1999b) was followed for all service-related variables. This involved simultaneously examining the relationship of each variable with the survival function, and testing the proportionality assumption of the Cox model. The Kaplan and Meier (1958) product-limit (PL) method (Norusis, 1994) was used to plot and compare survival curves for each of the possible service-related predictors. Variables with a significant relationship (or trend toward significance) (Wilcoxon text) with survival time (length of time without a recurrence) during the time the case was open or following case closure *and* those that met the proportionality assumption were initially selected.

The models were estimated with the Cox Proportional Hazards Model (Norusis, 1994). Variables were entered in two steps: (1) variables that represented other constructs were entered (DePanfilis & Zuravin, 1999b), and (2) service-related variables were entered to determine whether service variables predicted recurrence while controlling for other variables in the model. Following preliminary analysis which indicated that low power may have influenced results, a reduced model was run selecting only variables that were significant in Block 1 and selecting only one service related variable, that is, attendance (yes or no).

RESULTS

How Many Families Had Open Case Files at Intake?

Of the 434 families selected for this analysis, 51 (11.8%) were already active in CPS when their index incident was substantiated. Therefore, the majority (383 or 88.2%) of families were opened for continuing services following this index incident.

For How Long Were Families Served in Continuing Protective Services?

Length of service ranged from 4 days to 1825 days (5 years), with most families receiving services for 1 year or less (64%) or 2 years or less (85%).

How Many Direct Casework Contacts Did Families Receive?

The average family received 14 face-to-face casework contacts, with a few families receiving as many as 78 face-to-face contacts. In general, there was a relationship between length of services and number of casework contacts since families that were served longer received greater casework contact.

How Many Families Experienced Recurrences?

One hundred fifty-one families (25%) experienced at least one recurrence of child abuse or neglect during the service period.

Cox Proportional Regression Results

For the purposes of comparison of previously presented results, final variables in the first model were: (1) control variable—placement status; (2) maltreatment construct—number of priors (*# of priors*), type of maltreatment (*Index Type*), and severity of maltreatment (*Severity Index*); (3) child vulnerability construct—3-item index (*Child Factors*); (4) maternal problem construct—3-item index (*Mother Factors*); (5) family conflict construct—one individual variable (*partner abuse*); (6) family stress construct—3-item index (*Family Stress*); (7) survival stress construct—4-item index (*Survival Stress*); (8) social support deficits—3-item index (*Social Support*) and service related variables entered in the second block; (9) casework contacts—service status (already opened or opened at index), number of casework contacts, and number of caseworkers; (10) level of cooperation—perpetrator admission and attendance at services; and (11) level of improvement—average percentage of improvement in all problem areas identified at intake.

Table 18.1 presents the results of the first Cox Proportional Hazards Model without the services variables. The analysis tests the global null hypothesis that all parameters = 0. The parameter estimates represent the change in the log odds of the hazard rate, and consequently the length of survival without recurrence. For a dichotomous variable, Cox's proportional hazards model can be used to estimate relative risk when adjustments are made for the other variables in the model. For example, the results for *partner abuse* suggest that the existence of partner abuse in the family at the time of index increases the hazard rate 1.5 times, controlling for other variables in the model. For other variables, relative risk is compared for different values of the independent variable. The results of the *social support* deficit index suggest that for each increase in point on this 3-item index the hazard rate is increased 1.4 times, controlling for other variables in the model.

The test of the null hypothesis that all parameters are equal was made by the likelihood ratio test, that is, comparing the -2LL for a model in which all coefficients are 0 (the initial model) with -2LL

Table 18.1. Proportional Hazards Model for Recurrence while CPS Active (without Service Variables)

Event and censored values

Total: 434   Events: 151   Censored: 283 (65.2%)

Testing Global Null Hypothesis: All Parameters = 0 -Block 1

	Without Covariates	With Covariates	Chi-Square	df.	p
–2 Log Likelihood	1774.662	1696.743	81.506	10	.0000
Change (-2LL)			77.920	10	.0000

Variables in the Equation						
Variable	Parameter Estimate	Stan Error	Wald Chi-Square	Sig	R	Risk Ratio
Placement status	.6776	.1783	14.4492	.0001	.0838	1.9691
# of priors	.0193	.0666	.0832	.77	.0000	1.0195
Index type	−.1117	.1054	1.1239	.28	.0000	.8943
Severity-index	−.0125	.0893	.0196	.88	.0000	.9876
Child factors	.2901	.1329	4.7619	.03	.0394	1.3365
Mother factors	.0725	.1134	.4092	.52	.0000	1.0752
Partner abuse	.3879	.1996	3.7767	.05	.0316	1.4739
Family stress	.2108	.0873	5.8260	.01	.0464	1.2347
Survival stress	.1089	.0832	1.7150	.19	.0000	1.1151
Social support	.3518	.0984	12.7784	.0003	.0780	1.4216

for Model 1. From Table 18.1, we see that –2LL for the initial model is 1774.662. For Model 1, the –2LL is 1696.743. The difference between these two numbers is 77.920. This is the entry labeled "Change (-2LL) from Previous Block." The degrees of freedom are the difference between the number of parameters in the two models (in this case 10 since the model has 10 variables). The observed p-value is small, .0000, so the null hypothesis that all of the coefficients are 0 can be rejected. Another test of the null hypothesis that all parameters are 0 is based on the global chi-square of 81.506, which is very similar to the change in the likelihood statistic. This test also supports rejection of the null hypothesis.

Among the 10 individual variables, five were significant: having a child placed increased the hazard rate by 1.9 times, every one point on the child vulnerability index increased the hazard rate 1.4 times, the presence of partner abuse increased the hazard rate 1.5 times, every point on the family stress index increased the hazard rate 1.2 times, and every point on the social support deficit index increased the hazard rate 1.4 times. The following variables were not significant: three maltreatment variables, mom personal problem index, and survival stress index.

After entering the service variables (see Table 18.2), analysis again tests the global null hypothesis that all parameters = 0. The test of the null hypothesis that all parameters are equal was made by the likelihood ratio test, that is, comparing the –2LL for the first model with the –2LL for Block 2. For Model 1, we see that –2LL for the initial model is 1696.743. After entering Block 2, the –2LL is 1688.285. The difference between these two numbers is only 8.457. This is the entry labeled "Change (-2LL) from Previous Block." The degrees of freedom are the difference between

Table 18.2. Proportional Hazards Model for Recurrence while CPS Active (with Service Variables)

After Block 1 - Model 1, variables not in the equation:
Residual Chi Square = 4.058 with 2 *df*. Sig = .1315
ENTER Block 2-Model with service variables

	Block 1 Covariates	With Block 2	Chi-Square	df.	p
-2 Log Likelihood	1696.743	1688.285	91.467	16	.0000
Change (-2LL)			8.457	1	.2065

Variables in the Equation						
Variable	Parameter Estimate	Stan Error	Wald Chi-Square	Sig	R	Risk Ratio
Placement status	.6382	.1829	12.1720	.0005	.0774	1.8931
# of priors	.0284	.0671	.1787	.67	.0000	1.0288
Index type	−.0738	.1082	.4648	.49	.0000	.9289
Severity-index	−.0441	.0913	.2339	.63	.0000	.9568
Child factors	.3428	.1379	6.1782	.01	.0496	1.4089
Mother factors	.0700	.1166	.3600	.55	.0000	1.0725
Partner abuse	.3573	.2037	3.0749	.08	.0252	1.4294
Family stress	.2190	.0882	6.1678	.01	.0496	1.2448
Survival stress	.1074	.0845	1.6146	.20	.0000	1.1133
Social support	.3657	.0990	13.6442	.0002	.0828	1.4416
Perpetrator admission	.0868	.1705	.2591	.61	.0000	1.0907
Service attendance	−.3783	.1990	3.6141	.05	−.0308	.6850
Service status	−.0614	.1266	.2350	.62	.0000	.9405
Number of contacts	−.1799	.1309	1.8889	.17	.0000	.8354
Number of workers	.2853	.1588	3.2271	.07	.0269	1.3301
% of problems improved	.1378	.2479	.3091	.58	.0000	1.1478

the number of parameters in the final model (in this case 16 since the model has 16 variables). The observed *p*-value is above .05, (i.e., .2065), so the null hypothesis that all of the coefficients are 0 cannot be rejected.

Because it was assumed that these results were influenced by low power (with only 434 subjects and 16 variables), the analysis was repeated by removing the variables in the initial model that were nonsignificant and keeping only one service-related variable, that is, attendance. These results are presented in Tables 18.3 and 18.4.

The results for Block 1 were essentially the same as in the first model. After entering the service variable (see Table 18.4), analysis again tested the global null hypothesis that all parameters = 0. The test of the null hypothesis that all parameters are equal was made by the likelihood ratio test, that is, comparing the -2LL for the first model with the -2LL for Block 2. For Model 1, we see that -2LL for the initial model is 1698.703. After entering Block 2, the -2LL is 1695.013. The difference between these two numbers is 3.690. This is the entry labeled "Change (-2LL) from Previous Block." The degrees of freedom are the difference between the number of parameters in the final model (in this

Table 18.3. Reduced Proportional Hazards Model while CPS Active (without Service Variable)

Event and censored values
Total: 434   Events: 151   Censored: 283 (65.2%)
Testing global null hypothesis: All parameters = 0 -Block 1

	Without Covariates	With Covariates	Chi-Square	df.	p
-2 Log Likelihood	1774.662	1698.703	79.222	6	.0000
Change (-2LL)			75.959	6	.0000

Variables in the Equation						
Variable	Parameter Estimate	Stan Error	Wald Chi-Square	Sig	R	Risk Ratio
Placement status	.6804	.1719	15.6681	.0001	.0838	1.9747
Child factors	.3047	.1303	5.4668	.02	.0442	1.3562
Partner abuse	.3787	.1935	3.8308	.05	.0321	1.4605
Family stress	.2074	.0855	5.8884	.01	.0468	1.2305
Survival stress	.1505	.0750	4.0246	.04	.0338	1.1624
Social support	.3629	.0946	14.7225	.0001	.0847	1.4374

Table 18.4. Reduced Proportional Hazards Model while CPS Active (with Service Variable)

After Block 1 - Model 1, variables not in the equation:
Residual Chi Square = 3.962 with 1 df. Sig = .0465
ENTER Block 2-Model with Service Variable

	Block 1 Covariates	With Block 2	Chi-Square	df.	p
-2 Log likelihood	1698.703	1695.013	82.865	7	.0000
Change (-2LL)			3.690	1	.0547

Variables in the Equation						
Variable	Parameter Estimate	Stan Error	Wald Chi-Square	Sig	R	Risk Ratio
Placement status	.6784	.1719	15.5710	.0001	.0894	1.9707
Child factors	.3328	.1305	6.5056	.01	.0515	1.3949
Partner abuse	.3660	.1941	3.5555	.05	.0303	1.4420
Family stress	.2200	.0849	6.7118	.01	.0527	1.2461
Survival stress	.1454	.0756	3.7029	.05	.0317	1.1565
Social support	.3683	.0946	15.1446	.0001	.0880	1.4453
Service attendance	−.3735	.1887	3.9189	.05	−.0336	.6883

case 7 since the model has 7 variables). The observed p-value is low so the null hypothesis that all of the coefficients are 0 can be rejected. These results suggest that after controlling for other variables in the model, attendance at services decreases the hazard of recurrence by 32%.

CONCLUSIONS

The primary purpose of this article was to assess whether service-related variables would affect the likelihood of recurrence, controlling for other factors that predict recurrence. Limitations of this article are addressed before discussing the implications of findings. There are four design limitations that impede interpretation of findings: measurement problems, threat to construct validity, use of a single sample thereby capitalizing on chance, and threat to external validity. Each limitation is summarized and may be referenced later as specific results are discussed.

Measurement Problems

Although controls were put in place to minimize measurement error associated with coding archival data (careful attention to inter-rater reliability), the study was still limited by the quality of the case record-keeping. Because case record narratives vary by both type of information recorded and degree of detail, the study was limited to what was available and abstracted reliably.

These measurement problems lead to rival explanations. One cannot be assured that findings would be the same if: (1) complete data had been available for all constructs assumed to be related to recurrence, and (2) workers were more thorough and consistent in case recording.

Construct Validity

The study is also limited by the use of only one measure of recurrence, future confirmed child maltreatment reports. Findings could be influenced by differences in levels of surveillance at different points during the case process. Because this study was dependent on the decision-making of caseworkers with respect to confirming future maltreatment incidents, there are rival explanations for the interpretation of findings. In fact, recurrence of maltreatment could have occurred that was either undetected or unreported by the caseworker.

Single Sample

The sample size for model development, while sufficient for developing the initial model, was not large enough when adding the additional service variables. To explore the effect of services, it was necessary to select only one service-related variable for model building. The sample was also not large enough to split into groups. Models developed on single samples capitalize on chance. It is not known whether these results would also be common to the population from which this sample was drawn.

External Validity

Because only one site was used for this study, external validity is limited. Generalization beyond Baltimore City should be approached with caution. Ideally, this study would have been carried out in multiple sites in Maryland to permit comparisons of model performance between sites. However, because of differences in community characteristics, it may be that specific risk models would only be pertinent to a particular jurisdiction. The use of a single site prohibits testing this assumption however.

Implications of Study Findings

There are several important implications from these results. First, the Cox Proportional Regression findings suggest the importance of individual, family, and broader social context-level constructs in a model of child maltreatment recurrence. Many risk assessment models are based on a multi-dimensional model, and these findings identified the relevance of several constructs in a recurrence model. Variables that predicted time until recurrence while CPS was active were factors related to child vulnerability, family stress, partner abuse, social support deficits, and the interaction between stress and social support deficits. The significance of these predictors has been previously discussed (DePanfilis & Zuravin, 1999b).

A second implication can be drawn from the analysis of the impact of services. This exploration suggested that the mere attendance at services (as documented in the case record) might reduce the likelihood of recurrence while the case is open in CPS by 32%. Engagement in treatment and the importance of a helping alliance has been emphasized as an essential ingredient in the risk reduction process (DePanfilis, 2000; Dore & Alexander, 1996; McCurdy, Hurvis, & Clark, 1996). While this variable is not a measure of engagement, it does indicate which families were actively involved in some type of intervention. Families were only identified as attending services if there was evidence in the record that family members were attending services identified in their service plans.

The fact that other service-related variables did not offer insight into their relationship to the likelihood of recurrences was disappointing. No differences were noted based on the admission of the perpetrator, the number of caseworkers or casework contacts, the use of juvenile court, the level of cooperation of the caregiver, the presence of a signed service agreement, or the degree of improvement that was noted by the time the case was closed. Perhaps the sample size was too small to adequately explore the relationship between all of these service variables and recurrence. As indicated in other research (DePanfilis & Zuravin, 2001; Inkelas & Halfon, 1997; US Department of Health and Human Services, Administration for Children and Families, 2000), only a small percentage of families who receive a substantiated report of child maltreatment actually receive any further services by CPS.

Despite the limitations of this exploratory article, the results do suggest the need for further research that examines which families receive intervention following substantiated reports of child maltreatment, describes the nature of services offered and provided to families, and the relationship of service characteristics to the recurrence of child maltreatment.

ACKNOWLEDGMENT

The authors thank the Baltimore City Department of Social Services for their collaboration on this research.

REFERENCES

Baird, S. C. (1988). Development of risk assessment indices for the Alaska Department of Health and Social Services. In T. Tatara (Ed.), *Validation research in CPS risk assessment: three recent studies* (pp. 84–142). Washington, DC: American Public Welfare Association.

Baird, C., Wagner, D., & Neuenfeldt, D. (1993). Actuarial risk assessment and case management in child protective services. In T. Tatara (Ed.), *Sixth national roundtable on CPS risk assessment summary of highlights* (pp. 152–168). Washington, DC: American Public Welfare Association.

Berkeley Planning Associates. (1983). *Evaluation of the clinical demonstrations of the treatment of child abuse and neglect, Volume 2. The exploration of client characteristics, services, and outcomes: final report and summary of findings (HEW 105–78–1108)*. Washington, DC: National Center on Child Abuse and Neglect, Office of Human Development Services, Department of Health and Human Services.

Browne, D. (1986). The role of stress in the commission of subsequent acts of child abuse and neglect. *Journal of Family Violence, 1*(4), 289–297.

Cohn, A. H. (1979). Effective treatment of child abuse and neglect. *Social Work, 24,* 513–519.

Coleman, H. D. J. (1995). *A longitudinal study of a family preservation program*. Doctoral dissertation, University of Utah, School of Social Work.

DePanfilis, D. (1995). *Epidemiology of child maltreatment recurrences*. Doctoral dissertation, University of Maryland at Baltimore.

DePanfilis, D. (2000). How do I develop a helping alliance with the family? In H. Dubowitz & D. DePanfilis (Eds.), *Handbook for child protection practice* (pp. 36–40). Thousand Oaks, CA: Sage.

DePanfilis, D., & Scannapieco, M. (1994). Assessing the safety of children at risk for maltreatment: decision-making models. *Child Welfare, 73,* 229–245.

DePanfilis, D., & Zuravin, S. J. (1999a). Epidemiology of child maltreatment recurrences. *Social Services Review, 73,* 218–239.

DePanfilis, D., & Zuravin, S. J. (1999b). Predicting child maltreatment recurrences during treatment. *Child Abuse & Neglect, 23*(8), 729–743.

DePanfilis, D., & Zuravin, S. J. (2001). Assessing risk to determine the need for services. *Children and Youth Services Review, 23*(1), 3–20.

Dore, M. M., & Alexander, L. B. (1996). Preserving families at risk of child abuse and neglect: the role of the helping alliance. *Child Abuse & Neglect, 20,* 349–361.

Doueck, H. J., English, D. J., DePanfilis, D., & Moote, G. T. (1993). Decision-making in child protective services: a comparison of selected risk-assessment systems. *Child Welfare, 72,* 441–452.

Fluke, J. (1991). Risk assessment and workload characteristics. In T. Tatara (Ed.), *Fourth national roundtable on CPS risk assessment summary of highlights* (pp. 121–143). Washington, DC: American Public Welfare Association.

Inkelas, M., & Halfon, N. (1997). Recidivism in child protective services. *Children and Youth Services Review, 19,* 139–161.

Jagannathan, R., & Camasso, M. J. (1996). Risk assessment in child protective services: a canonical analysis of the case management function. *Child Abuse & Neglect, 20,* 599–612.

Johnson, W. (1994). Maltreatment recurrence as a criterion for validating risk assessment instruments. In T. Tatara (Ed.), *Seventh national roundtable on CPS risk assessment summary of highlights* (pp. 175–182). Washington, DC: American Public Welfare Association.

Johnson, W. (1996). Using risk assessment in the evaluation of public agency child protective services. In T. Tatara (Ed.), *Ninth national roundtable on CPS risk assessment summary of highlights* (pp. 5–20). Washington, DC: American Public Welfare Association.

Johnson, W., & Clancy (1990). Preliminary findings from a study of risk assessment accuracy and service effectiveness in home-based services physical abuse cases. In T. Tatara (Ed.), *Third national roundtable on CPS risk assessment summary of highlights* (pp. 161–171). Washington, DC: American Public Welfare Association.

Johnson, W., & L'Esperance, J. (1984). Predicting the recurrence of child abuse. *Social Work Research and Abstracts, 20*(2), 21–26.

Kaplan, E. L., & Meier, P. (1958). Nonparametric estimation from incomplete observations. *Journal of the American Statistical Association, 53,* 457–481.

Littell, J. H. (1997). Effects of the duration, intensity, and breadth of family preservation services: a new analysis of data from the Illinois Family First experiment. *Children and Youth Services Review, 19*(1/2), 17–39.

Marks, J., & McDonald, T. (1989). *Risk assessment in child protective services: predicting the recurrence of child maltreatment*. Portland, ME: University of Southern Maine, National Child Welfare Resource Center for Management and Administration.

Marks, J., McDonald, T., & Bessey, W. (1989). *Risk factors assessed by instrument-based models*. Portland, ME: National Child Welfare Resource Center for Management and Administration.

McCurdy, K., & Daro, D. (1993). Child maltreatment: a national survey of reports and fatalities. *Journal of Interpersonal Violence, 9,* 75–94.

McCurdy, K., Hurvis, S., & Clark, J. (1996). Engaging and retaining families in child abuse prevention programs. *The APSAC Advisor, 9*(3), 1–9.

McDonald, T., & Johnson, W. (1992). Predicting recurrence of maltreatment for child sexual abuse cases. In T. Tatara (Ed.), *Fifth national roundtable on CPS risk assessment summary of highlights* (pp. 72–89). Washington, DC: American Public Welfare Association.

McDonald, T., & Marks, J. (1991). A review of risk factors assessed in child protection. *Social Services Review, 65,* 112–132.

Melton, G. B., & Barry, F. D. (1994). Neighbors helping neighbors: the vision of the US Advisory Board on Child Abuse and Neglect. In G. B. Melton & F. D. Barry (Eds.), *Protecting children from abuse and neglect* (pp. 1–13). New York: Guilford Press.

Miller, J. S., Williams, K. M., English, D. J., & Olmstead, J. (1987). *Risk assessment child protection: a review of the literature*. Washington, DC: American Public Welfare Association.

Norusis, M. J. (1994). *SPSS advanced statistics 6.1*. Chicago, IL: SPSS.

Rittner, B. A. (1995). Analysis of abuse, neglect and abandonment risk factors in active children's protective services cases as they relate to decision-making processes. *Dissertation Abstracts International, 55*(7), 2548-A.

Schuerman, J. R., Rzepnicki, T. L., & Littell, J. H. (1994). *Putting families first an experiment in family preservation*. New York: Walter de Gruyter, Inc.

US Department of Health and Human Services, Administration for Children and Families. (2000a).

Child maltreatment 1998: reports from the states to the National Child Abuse and Neglect Data System. Washington, DC: Author.

US Department of Health and Human Services, Administration for Children and Families. (January 25, 2000b). Title IV-E foster care eligibility reviews and child and family services state plan reviews; Final Rule. *Federal Register, 65*(16), January 25, 2000b. Available at: http://www.acf.dhhs.gov/programs/cb/laws/fedreg/fr012500.htm.

US Department of Health and Human Services, Administration for Children and Families. (2001). *Child maltreatment 1999: reports from the states to the National Child Abuse and Neglect Data System*. Washington, DC: Author.

Wagner, D. (1994). The use of actuarial risk assessment in criminal justice. What can we learn from the experience? In T. Tatara (Ed.), *Seventh national roundtable on CPS risk assessment summary of highlights* (pp. 211–223). Washington, DC: American Public Welfare Association.

Waldfogel, J. (2000). Reforming child protective services. *Child Welfare, 79,* 43–57.

Wolfe, D. A. (1994). The role of intervention and treatment services in the prevention of child abuse and neglect. In G. B. Melton & F. D. Barry (Eds.), *Protecting children from abuse and neglect* (pp. 224–303). New York: Guilford Press.

Zuravin, S. J., & DePanfilis, D. (1996). *Child maltreatment recurrences among families served by Child Protective Services final report*. Study funded by the US Department of Health and Human Services, National Center on Child Abuse and Neglect 1992–1996 (Grant Number 90CA1497). Baltimore, MD: University of Maryland at Baltimore, School of Social Work.

Zuravin, S. J., DePanfilis, D., & Maznyk, K. (1993). *Teenage motherhood: its relationship to child abuse and neglect, final report*. Study funded by the National Center on Child Abuse and Neglect 1988–1993 (Grant No. 90CA1376). Baltimore, MD: University of Maryland at Baltimore, School of Social Work.

COMMENTARY BY: Diane DePanfilis

This commentary addresses the challenges and benefits of using administrative data to explore what effect, if any, services following a substantiated report of child maltreatment had on the hazard of child maltreatment recurrences. "The effect of services on the recurrence of child maltreatment" (DePanfilis & Zuravin, 2002) was written as secondary analysis of a larger study on the recurrence of child abuse and neglect. The original study, funded by the U.S. Department of Health and Human Services Children's Bureau (Zuravin & DePanfilis, 1996) was funded to identify the patterns and predictors of child maltreatment recurrences. Five prior papers (DePanfilis & Zuravin, 1998; 1999a; 1999b; 2001; Zuravin & DePanfilis, 1997), a book chapter (Zuravin & DePanfilis, 1999), and a doctoral dissertation (DePanfilis, 1995a) had been written using related data to answer questions about child maltreatment recurrences. Support from the Lois and Samuel Silberman Fund presented an opportunity to answer questions about the relationship between services and the recurrence of child maltreatment. The best source of data to answer questions about the services provided following a substantiated report of child maltreatment is the child welfare case record. However, the limitations of using archival data needed to be overcome in order to increase the validity and reliability of data that would be used to draw conclusions.

The paper that is the focus of this commentary is described as secondary analysis. The original study had three levels of data collection: (1) research interviews with the primary caregivers of families involved with Child Protective Services (CPS) because of a substantiated report of child abuse and neglect; (2) case data from statewide child welfare information systems; and (3) data from hard copies of case records. This commentary addresses the key issues to consider after choosing to use archival data for any study. The two primary areas of focus pertain to methods for gaining access to existing data and procedures for coding existing data. Summary points based on experience with the use of archival data are also included.

ACCESS TO EXISTING DATA

To gain access to existing administrative data in information systems and in case records of a local child welfare agency, a number of barriers had to be overcome. Negotiations were necessary between the University of Maryland and the local and state agencies. Procedures had to be followed to protect the rights of human subjects, and options regarding the best methods to obtain the data needed to be considered. Some of the data we sought was already available in statewide information systems. Changes in policies and information systems over time make it difficult to consistently

Commentary on article: DePanfilis, D., & Zuravin, S. J. (2002). The effect of services on the recurrence of child maltreatment. *Child Abuse & Neglect, 26,* 187–205.

obtain longitudinal data in the same format—for example, policy changes (e.g., instead of 2 classifications of a substantiation decision, the state moved to 3 classifications) and the rapid growth in technology (e.g., the file structure and/or codes used to categorize data elements). And most agencies still rely on the hard paper record as the official record of the services delivered to families, making it difficult to answer substantive questions from information system data alone. It is important to remember that while the details of this process may vary due to differences in state laws, gaining access to existing agency data is always a lengthy process. Steps to gain access to existing data are briefly described in the following paragraphs.

1. **Prepare a short prospectus about the proposed study.** This prospectus must detail the scope of the study, what exactly is being requested of the agency, and "what is in it for the agency" to collaborate with the proposed research. In our study, we developed a one-page prospectus that went through several drafts before we presented it to our stakeholders. The time we spent to develop this statement helped us as we entered negotiations with agency personnel.

2. **Schedule face-to-face meetings with agency administrators.** In-person meetings to present the research idea are necessary to describe what is needed from the agency and to present what the agency will get out of the collaboration. The specific persons that must be consulted will vary by state. Regardless of the bureaucratic structure, administrators at state and local levels must approve the study. Approvals must occur prior to submitting a proposal for funding, as a letter that confirms access to the data is required in order to convince a funding source that conducting the study will be feasible in a particular jurisdiction. The researcher is advised to thoroughly understand the state laws about who may have access to existing child welfare data for research purposes *before* developing the prospectus or planning these meetings. If the researcher has a prior relationship with the agency, the likelihood of getting administrators "on board" with the research idea is greater. If no prior relationship exists, it may be possible to gain credibility with the agency by having someone who is known to the agency act as a liaison to introduce the researcher to agency administrators. If these introductions have taken place well in advance of a specific research idea, it may make the process of gaining access much easier. In the study that was the focus of this commentary, both researchers had long-standing relationships with administrators at the local and state levels, so preliminary approval for the research was easily obtained. Because months or years may transpire between when an agency may "approve" of a research idea in principle and when the study is actually implemented; despite preliminary approval, there may be other barriers that arise during the actual implementation of the study.

3. **Gain Human Research Protection Approval for the Use of Archival Records in Research.** Federal policies regarding the protection of human subjects (U.S. Department of Health and Human Services, 1991) must be followed to permit access to archival records for research purposes. A study that involves the review of existing agency records is usually classified as a minimal risk study, and this research may qualify for an exemption from a full protocol under certain circumstances. The researcher is advised to thoroughly study the rules related to the protection of human subjects when using archival data prior to applying for Human Research Protection approval. Institutional procedures may vary depending on the host research institution.

4. **Develop Procedures for Access to Electronic Files.** Once all approvals have been obtained, if data will be used from existing statewide information systems, procedures for

searching and exporting data for the specific subjects under study must be established. In the study referenced in this commentary, we were following specific participants who had previously been randomly sampled from all substantiated reports in a specific year. Procedures for matching data elements must be specified to be certain that the researcher "finds" the correct information for the specific study participants. It is recommended that at least three identifiers be used (e.g., social security number, case number, birth date, name) so that a "correct" matching procedure will occur. While it is much more common for these electronic searches and matches to be worked out today, at the time this study was conducted, the state agency did not have personnel available to assist with this process. Thus, instead of gaining electronic access to search and match and then export a complete data file, we gained access for manual searches of the statewide social services databases. We hired research assistants who already had access to the databases due to their employment or internships within the child welfare agency, and then paid them to search and "print out" all pages from the information system that related to the families and data fields under study (e.g., dates and substantiation status of all child abuse and neglect reports, service codes for case openings and closings). These printouts were then physically transported back to the university-based research office for coding.

5. **Develop Procedures for Access to Case Records.** The specific methods for access to hard copies of case records will vary by jurisdiction. It is likely that the researcher must request office space within the local agency for reviewing and coding case records, as the need to protect the confidentiality of participants' information would usually forbid taking records or copies of records out of the public agency office. In our study, we were provided two different offices within the local Department of Social Services (DSS), in which we housed our computers and other coding materials over three years. We implemented an elaborate case record request and tracking process to obtain sufficient numbers of case records at one time for coding yet not too many records, as our space within the agency was limited. Most often, we were requesting closed case records, which were stored in a location about 50 miles away from the agency. We used normal state procedures for requesting records, and logged them back in against our list when they were obtained. If records were not provided after being requested, we usually did not receive any explanation as to the reason. The records could have been lost or already signed out by someone else, or a clerk may have failed to follow the directions. After trying to solve those glitches, we found that the easiest way to manage this process was to keep missing cases on a list and submit new requests periodically. Records were filed by child abuse or neglect incidents, so case record requests involved multiple records for most families.

6. **Overcome Unanticipated Barriers when Gaining Access to Existing Records.** Because political understanding about the value of social work–related research and legal interpretations of confidentiality laws vary, it is important to remember that changes in administration of agencies may result in differences in opinions. It is not uncommon for the agency administrator who wrote the letter of support at the time a proposal was written to be unavailable at the time a study is implemented. Gaining access to existing data is a labor-intensive process, and sufficient time should be allocated in the implementation plan to solve barriers. About a third of the way into our study, a new administrator at the state level was concerned about the number of research studies being undertaken regarding child welfare policies and practices. This was prompted not by anything specific to our study but by a general protective climate that evolved due to extensive media coverage about child maltreatment–related

fatalities. The administrator asked for a new Attorney General position about the legality of providing access to child welfare data for research purposes. The request for the opinion and the opinion itself resulted in our stopping case-level data collection for nine months. After many negotiations, the problem was solved by developing a subcontract between the university and the local agency that gave the local agency funds to hire our researcher assistants, the data manager, and the project manager as local DSS employees. We also had to request a budget modification from the funding agency in order to permit this subcontract. We submitted biweekly timesheets to the local agency in order to pay research staff. Meanwhile, the agency had taken over our original office space, so we had to find new space within the agency that could accommodate our equipment and personnel. Developing relationships with personnel in charge of the operations of an organization is very important. We went out of our way to give people fruit baskets, to participate in local agency programs, and to touch base with administrators on a regular basis. Anticipating future projects, we wanted to finish the study with positive feelings about our work. We delivered brown bag lectures about the results of the study, and frequently keep in contact with agency administrators about our continued research.

CODING EXISTING DATA

A major concern about using archival data is that it may be incomplete (due to faulty case record-keeping), may not fully represent the actual service delivery process, and may be recorded inconsistently. It is important to develop procedures for determining the best source(s) for data to answer specific questions, and to attempt to increase accuracy by coding data that can be reasonably drawn from archival sources. Based on the research questions under study, planning the implementation of this data collection process took about a year. (Steps for developing coding procedures for the statewide information system and the case record–level data are described separately.)

Coding Data from Statewide Information Systems

Based on the data available in this system (e.g., child abuse and neglect reports, and all service types and service periods), we needed to accurately transform the data from printouts into variables that would be useful to answer our study questions. The key steps in this process are described below.

1. **Develop and Pilot Test Sample Coding Forms and Procedures.** Even if the researcher is fortunate enough to extract data electronically, there is a need to transform the data into variables for analysis. In our case, we were working from printouts for every family and every child. These records were structured for family and child related services, so the first decision was the unit of analysis. Since some of our questions were related to families as the unit of analysis and other questions were related to children as the unit of analysis, we made the decision to develop coding forms (and files) for families and for children. Coding forms were created for transforming data on the printouts (often using state-specific codes) to our own codes. A detailed coding manual was developed, and the process was pilot tested with the first 50 printouts. Based on this pilot, we revised the coding procedures before implementing the actual coding process.

2. **Verify the Accuracy of the Archival Data.** All archival data are not created equal. We knew from experience that data in the statewide information system at the time of this study were not

considered to be accurate portrayals of the real process. Since we had multiple sources of data (information system, case record, client interviews), and because we were asked to present about the challenges of archival data collection by our funding agency (DePanfilis, 1995b), we did a pilot test of the consistency between these multiple data sources. There were numerous discrepancies in basic demographical data between client self-report, state-wide information system, and case record. To reconcile some differences, we asked clients during their research interviews to provide copies of birth certificates and social security cards so that we could match their identifying information with data maintained by the agency. In our pilot (several hundred cases), we found inconsistency in 50 percent of the records that we tried to reconcile. Of most concern were differences with respect to substantiation status of child abuse or neglect reports, and in the number of children in a family that were actually victims of an incident. In most cases, all children in a given family were classified as victims of a substantiated incident in the information system, yet the case record often identified fewer children in a family who were actually involved. Based on these inconsistencies, we made the decision to verify the accuracy of the information system with case record data. This provided support for using family level data to analyze information about child abuse or neglect reports or their recurrences. Using the family as the unit of analysis was consistent with our view of the purposes of CPS. Once a child has been maltreated, the CPS agency provides services to families (DePanfilis & Salus, 2003) to reduce the risk of future child maltreatment and to address the effects of child maltreatment for all children in the family. In our original proposal, we had defined *recurrence* as a new substantiated report on any child in the family. Finding problems with data at the child level confirmed that using the family as the unit of analysis was appropriate.

3. **Develop Procedures for Interrater Reliability.** Regardless of the number of coders, procedures must be implemented to increase the consistency of the coding process. In our study, seven different classes of MSW students (approximately 15 students per class) coded information from data printouts. Our procedures involved initial coding by a student researcher and a second coding by a paid research assistant. Students were informed at the beginning of the semester that part of their grade for participating in this applied research class would be based on their coding accuracy rate. Students were provided with extensive hands-on training, their first sample cases were double coded, and then when they were ready to code "real" cases, each case was checked by a research assistant and accuracy rates were established. Students needed to reach 100 percent accuracy on sample cases before they were permitted to code actual cases. Students who frequently made errors were provided with individual coaching and assistance. Regular memos were provided to all students when "common" mistakes were detected. The project director purposely selected a random number of cases from each student to verify the accuracy of the edits previously performed by research assistants. The project director reconciled differences, and gave advice when decisions about coding a specific data element were questionable due to missing or confusing printout information. In some instances, final decisions about coding a particular case were not made until data could be verified in the case record.

4. **Develop Procedures for Data Entry.** Due to the number of coders and the inaccuracies in the data itself, information was not entered into data files until we were reasonably sure of the accuracy of coded information. Eventually we had family and child level coding forms that needed to be entered into data files. Because of the "era" in which this study was conducted (pre–Windows environment), we used a computer-assisted interviewing program for the data entry process (instead of a typical current environment, e.g., ACCESS). This entry program

was constructed with a screen for each variable. Each screen identified only one variable, as we were not confident that students would work accurately if they were asked to enter data into a table format. The tables created behind the screens did not distract during the data entry process. Using the same MSW classes as described above, students were involved in entering data from the verified forms into data files. We used procedures for double data entry, and then used analytical procedures to match and identify inconsistencies in the entry for each case. When the double data entry did not match, research assistants went back to the original coding form and reconciled these differences in the final data files.

5. **Develop Backup and Documentation Procedures.** To ensure the quality of the data, daily backup procedures and routine data checking are required; these will assure that if there have been problems due to technology or human errors, missing data may be recovered in a timely manner. It is important that these procedures be followed, thoroughly documented, and checked. When numerous individuals are working on the same study, it is easy to get sidetracked and forget the routine rules. The project manager needs to carefully verify that these procedures are actually being implemented. It is also important that routine decisions about coding, data reconciliation, or other data collection procedures are recorded. Otherwise, when the research methods are being described in written reports, it is easy to forget the reasons for specific decisions.

Coding Data from Case Records

Coding data from case records was a more complicated process. We first listed variables that we expected to be available from case records. We then went through numerous pilot tests to verify the best source within the record for each variable. This process also helped us eliminate variables that were inconsistently recorded in the case record. The main steps of this process are described below.

1. **Develop Coding Matrices.** To minimize steps, we designed an automated case coding process and did not use paper coding forms. We had to develop coding specifications for each variable; we started this process by developing matrices with three columns: the variable, the definition and values for the variable, and the best sources for this information in the record. (This process is also referred to as a *data dictionary*.) Each variable had a list of possible sources in the record, with the best source listed first. Over the planning of this coding process, we developed multiple versions of these documents until we were convinced that the procedures would arrive at the greatest consistency in our results.

2. **Pilot Test the Variable List.** Before developing the automated coding files using a computer-assisted interviewing program, we first pilot tested the list of variables. In doing this, we eliminated variables that were inconsistently recorded in records. For example, records usually had extensive detail about a particular incident of child abuse or neglect, the nature of the incident, the severity of the incident, who was identified as responsible, and so on, but provided less detail about the actual services that were provided during home visits. We chose to code variables only if there was a standard format or requirement that certain data be described in the record, and we eliminated variables when they were not routinely recorded in case files. For example, it was not possible to code data about the neighborhoods as sources of stress or support, as this information was usually not available.

3. **Develop Automated Coding Programs.** Computerized coding programs were developed for each of the types of case records we had selected for review. The coding matrices were used as a starting place, and branching variables were added to the matrix to document the

programming steps. This method permitted us to automatically skip from section to section, reducing the likelihood of coding error. For example, we were coding information about each incident of child abuse or neglect over a five-year period. Some families had one incident, but in one case there were as many as 25 incidents over the five years. Branching variables were created to help with programming these skip patterns.

4. **Select Personnel with Advanced Knowledge of Social Work Practice and Research.** As a certain amount of judgment is necessary when coding information from records developed for one purpose (documenting the service activity) into forms for answering research questions about the nature and quality of child welfare decisions and services, we recruited personnel who were likely to stay with the project for at least two years, had some knowledge of child welfare services, and had a higher level of investment in ensuring the quality of the coding process. Most of the research assistants were doctoral students interested in the research, and they participated in making the decisions about the best way to code information from records. We looked for people who were detail-oriented and had good interpersonal skills for communicating with other project staff. It is critical that all members function as a team, and share the responsibility for coding valid and reliable data from records. Staff needed to be extremely flexible about working conditions, as we were borrowing space within the child welfare agency.

5. **Develop and Implement Detailed Coding Procedures.** Detailed coding procedures were developed that paralleled each of the automated coding programs. Each record was coded first by one research assistant; other assistants, designated as supervisors, coded the case a second time. Discrepancies between coders were reconciled by the project director. Weekly memos were generated that reminded coders about proper coding decisions based on unique case examples. To avoid inconsistency with prior coding, we did not change the rules for interpreting data, only clarified the rules with more detailed examples. After coders received extensive training, coding one case took a minimum of two hours, with some cases taking longer than a day to complete.

6. **Develop Sample Case Record Files.** To assist with the coding process, sample case records were constructed that included all forms and the probable location of information for each variable. These sample cases provided concrete examples, so it was easier to locate information in the actual records. Case records in child welfare agencies are notoriously unorganized. Even though most agencies have procedures for where information should be filed within a record, information is frequently not in order, and it is usually necessary to read the file from cover to cover to assure that critical information has not been missed.

7. **Develop Backup and Documentation Procedures.** Procedures similar to those described above were implemented for backing up case record data files and for documenting all steps of the coding process. In addition, because coding records took an extensive period of time, it was not always possible to finish a case before leaving for the day. Detailed documentation about what stage cases were at (e.g., first coding, second coding, edit, final) was maintained in a tracking system. Since we were also using case records to verify information system–level data, sometimes a case was finished for the main coding but still needed to be used to verify information system data about the substantiation status of a report, or to reconcile the correct age of a child. We kept the information system coding forms that needed reconciling at the agency so that they could be corrected and then sent back to the university for data entry. Also, some records may have been coded for a family but other case records for that family

may not have yet arrived. In a few cases, services were still active for a family (or were active again), and records were being used by caseworkers in other buildings. In these situations, we worked out individual procedures for borrowing a record for a few hours and returning it the same day. Every effort was made to assure that we thoroughly documented our work in a timely manner, so that any needed problem solving could also occur at the time. Based on previous experiences, we wanted to avoid finding out later that we were missing data when we no longer had access to the original data sources.

SUMMARY OF THE ADVANTAGES AND CHALLENGES OF USING ARCHIVAL DATA

The use of archival case record data is appropriate to answer questions regarding information that is included in the records on a consistent basis. However, all records are not created and maintained with equal attention to validity and reliability. "The effect of services on the recurrence of child maltreatment" was written specifically to answer questions that could be answered with case record data. The case record is the official source for information about the types and quantities of services that are provided to families served by CPS. Very few papers had previously been written about the kinds of services families receive after a substantiated incident of child abuse or neglect.

Researchers interested in using archival data are wise to realize the limitations of case record data, and to design studies for the greatest chance of yielding data that will be useful for answering specific research questions (and, conversely, to avoid trying to answer questions that cannot be explored with this level of data). Although it is assumed that statewide information system data is now more valid and reliable than it may have been when this study was implemented, we were able to address these limitations because we had multiple sources of data. If a researcher only has access to statewide or national level data that is considerably removed from the actual day-to-day practice, using procedures to explore the quality of the data first may help to avoid lengthy explorations later that may not yield interpretable results.

REFERENCES

DePanfilis, D. E. (1995a). The epidemiology of child maltreatment recurrences. *Dissertation Abstracts International, 56*(12), 1996.

DePanfilis, D. (1995b). *Collecting data from CPS records.* Paper presented at the National Center on Child Abuse and Neglect Research Grantees Meeting, Washington, DC, March 29–30.

DePanfilis, D., & Salus, M. (2003). *Child Protective Services: A guide for caseworkers.* Washington, DC: U.S. Department of Health and Human Services, Administration on Children and Families, Administration for Children, Youth, and Families, Children's Bureau, Office on Child Abuse and Neglect.

DePanfilis, D., & Zuravin, S. J. (1998). Rates, patterns, and frequency of child maltreatment recurrences among public CPS families. *Child Maltreatment, 3,* 27–42.

DePanfilis, D., & Zuravin, S. J. (1999a). Predicting child maltreatment recurrences during treatment. *Child Abuse and Neglect, 23*(8), 729–743.

DePanfilis, D., & Zuravin, S. J. (1999b). Epidemiology of child maltreatment recurrences. *Social Services Review, 73,* 218–239.

DePanfilis, D., & Zuravin, S. J. (2001). Assessing risk to determine the need for services. *Children and Youth Services Review, 23,* 3–20.

DePanfilis, D., & Zuravin, S. J. (2002). The effect of services on the recurrence of child maltreatment. *Child Abuse and Neglect, 26,* 187–205.

U.S. Department of Health and Human Services (1991). *Code of Federal Regulations, Title 45, Public Welfare, Department of Health and Human Services, Part 46—Protection of Human Subjects (45 CFR 46).* Retrieved May 6, 2004 from http://ohrp.osophs. dhhs.gov/humansubjects/guidance/45cfr46.htm

Zuravin, S. J., & DePanfilis, D. (1996). *Child maltreatment recurrences among families served by Child Protective Services final report.* Study funded by the U.S. Department of Health and Human Services, National Center on Child Abuse and Neglect

1992–1996 (Grant Number 90CA1497). Baltimore, MD: University of Maryland School of Social Work.

Zuravin, S. J., & DePanfilis, D. (1997). Factors affecting foster care placement of children receiving child protective services. *Social Work Research, 21,* 34–42.

Zuravin, S. J., & DePanfilis, D. (1999). Predictors of Child Protective Service intake decisions: Case closure, referral to continuing services, or foster care placement. In P. A. Curtis, & G. Dale (Eds.), *The foster care crisis: Translating research into policy and practice* (pp. 63–83). Omaha: The Nebraska Press.

19

Transracial Adoptees
in the Media: 1986–1996

Leslie Doty Hollingsworth, Ph.D.

The adoption of children culturally different from their adoptive parents had its origins among children orphaned by World War II and, later, by the Korean War. Many of these were altruistic adoptions, the aim of which was to provide permanent families to children whose parents died in these wars. However, by the 1950s, the availability of adoptable children in the United States had decreased as artificial birth control measures became available, as society became more tolerant of unwed pregnancies, and as abortion was legalized (McRoy, 1989). Income support programs made it possible for women with limited resources to choose to parent. Adopting internationally and adopting U.S. children of color became a partial solution. In this article, I report the way demographic characteristics and subjective experiences of transracial adoptees are represented in media interviews conducted between 1986 and 1996 (a period of extensive adoption legislation). Results are important as indicators of the media's potential influence on public opinion and public policy, for the information the media provides, and as a guide for future research.

BACKGROUND

Transracial adoptions of African American children reached 2,500 in 1971—35% of the adoptions of African American children that year (McRoy, 1989). In the 5-year period between 1967 and 1971, transracial adoptions of African American children reached 10,000 (McRoy, 1989). The trend evoked the concern of the National Association of Black Social Workers. One concern was about the risk transracial adoption posed to the psychosocial, emotional, and cultural development

I thank Shelley MacDermid, Purdue University Department of Child Development and Family Studies; Professors Paula Allen-Meares, Siri Jayaratne, and Kristine Siefert, University of Michigan, School of Social Work, for their reviews of earlier versions of this article; and Yunju Nam, Betsy Share, and Debra Tucker for assistance with coding.

of African American children. In a resolution introduced in 1972, the Association wrote the following:

> Black children belong physically and psychologically and culturally in black families where they can receive the total sense of themselves and develop a sound projection of their future. Only a black family can transmit the emotional and sensitive subtleties of perceptions and reactions essential for a black child's survival in a racist society. Human beings are products of their environment and develop their sense of values, attitudes, and self-concept within their own family structures. Black children in white homes are cut off from the healthy development of themselves as black people (Simon & Alstein, 1977, p. 50, as cited in McRoy, 1989, p. 150).

The second concern was related to the anticipated loss of transracially adopted children from the social group of African Americans. The Association framed this concern in terms of "the necessity of self-determination from birth to death of all Black people...the need of [young Black people] to begin at birth to identify with Black people in a Black community...[and] the philosophy that we need our own to build a strong nation" (Simon & Alstein, 1977, p. 52).

In an effort to examine these concerns, researchers focused on racial/ethnic identity, self-esteem, psychological adjustment, quality of family life, and intellectual functioning and academic achievement. Results indicate problems with racial/ethnic identity in adolescence (Hollingsworth, 1997; Indigo, 1988; McRoy & Zurcher, 1983) but have not supported the existence of self-esteem problems (Baker, 1992; McRoy & Zurcher, 1983). Higher test scores are found among transracial adoptees compared to biological children of the same group (Scarr & Weinberg, 1976; Weinberg, Scarr, & Waldman, 1992). Adjustment is linked to similarity between adoptive parents and transracial adoptees (Feigelman & Silverman, 1983; for a review, see Hollingsworth, 1998).

METHOD

Procedure

A content analysis was conducted of print-media-reported interviews with adult transracial adoptees. Content analysis uses the characteristics of messages to make inferences (Krippendorff, 1980; Marshall & Rossman, 1989). Of the four potential uses of content analysis identified by Allen-Meares (1985), this study examined media depictions of transracial adoption to evaluate their influences on social welfare policies and to consider new practice developments and trends.

An exhaustive search was conducted of the universe, rather than a representative sample (Allen-Meares, 1985; Krippendorff, 1980; Marshall & Rossman, 1989) of existing media documents containing records of interviews with transracial adoptees. This was because of interest in obtaining all possible information regarding the representation of adoptee experiences. Key words used in the search were *interracial, interethnic, transracial,* and *transethnic* in combination with *adoption*. The search yielded 68 articles, two books containing multiple interviews, and the transcript of an interview from a national television news program, for a total of 120 interviews. Ninety-three met the criteria for an adult age range of 20 years and above.

Krippendorff (1980) described three kinds of units of analysis: sampling units, recording units, and context units. *Sampling units* are "those parts of observed reality or of the stream of source language expressions that are regarded independent of each other" (Krippendorff, 1980, p. 57). In the current analysis, newspaper or magazine articles, book chapters, and printed visual media transcripts of interviews with transracially adopted adults constituted sampling units. *Recording units* refer to the unit of text to be classified (Weber, 1990). These may be words, the sense of words, sentences or phrases, themes, paragraphs, or whole texts. Sentences or complete phrases were coded in this analysis. Finally, *context units* refer to "that portion of the symbolic material that needs to be examined in order to characterize a recording unit" (Krippendorff, 1980, p. 59). Here the context unit was that part of the text that related to the interview itself.

To develop a classification system suggested by Krippendorff (1980), Marshall and Rossman (1989), and Weber (1990), the text was read independently by two researchers, each of whom identified themes. An exhaustive list was developed independently by each reader and the lists were combined. Themes that were identified by one reader but not the other were also retained.

Each theme was classified as a variable and assigned value labels. For example, the adoptee's "childhood experiences with racism" was coded as: 1 = *no childhood racism experiences reported,* 2 = *childhood experiences with racism were reported,* and 99 = *data are unavailable.* Themes (variables) were categorical.

Interview text was entered verbatim into a word processor. Sufficient text was entered from the rest of the article (e.g., historical or political information) to provide sufficient context. Text included quotes by the adoptee and responses attributed to the adoptee by the interviewer. Codes were recorded in the margin of the text unit and numerically on separate data sheets.

A codebook contained descriptions of each variable and its levels, definitions of terms, and instructions for coding the content. Two raters, different from those who initially identified themes, read and discussed codebook content and then coded each transcript.

Interrater reliability was established by calculating the percentage of total agreement and the kappa statistic for the two raters. Hartmann (1977) and Krippendorff's (1980) recommendation of .80 as a minimum standard for reliability was followed. To correct for chance agreement and because most data were nominal, I calculated Cohen's (1960) kappa. Gelfand and Hartmann (1975) recommend that kappa should be greater than .60. Landis and Koch (1977) reported that kappa ranges of .61–.80 indicate substantial strength of association. These standards were followed. When initial reliability fell below the acceptable level, raters were retrained, instructions clarified, and the questionable variable was recoded. In the absence of substantial improvement, the variable was dropped or merged with another, related variable. Percentage agreements for accepted variables ranged from 80–100%, kappa levels from .61 to 1.00.

Method of Analysis

In the final step, all coders collaborated to arrive at a single value for each case on each variable. The *standard of uniform distribution* (developed by Krippendorff, 1980) was used to determine which variables meeting the criteria for reliability were to be admitted into the analysis. This standard is invoked when the frequency in one category is larger or smaller than the average for all categories. Thus, only variables were analyzed whose frequency met the average of all variables in the study originally ($M = 18.28$, $SD = 14.03$). Most variables were collapsed to two levels. Where interviews were reported in more than one source, the interview containing the largest amount of interview data was used. Variables (themes) were categorized conceptually. All variables did not appear in all interviews. Because of the large amount of missing data that resulted, analyses were limited to descriptive statistics.

Limitations of Using Media-Reported Data

Study of media-represented information introduces a number of potential biases. First, interviewees are typically recruited through such convenience methods as contacting an adoption professional who is familiar with a transracial adoptee who meets the criteria sought (e.g., age) or using someone known to the media representative. Persons with highly negative experiences or criticism are not likely to be chosen. Second, interview questions and probes are chosen by the interviewer, who may have a personal opinion about the topic. The interviewer may, albeit inadvertently, select certain questions and omit others. Third, media personnel are faced with strict limitations in the amount of material published or aired. Decisions regarding what is cut are left to the media representative, expanding the potential for bias. Fourth, interviewee responses may be influenced by a social desirability bias. Adoptees seeking to avoid offending their adoptive parents, adoption professionals, or the interviewer may withhold less acceptable responses. Fifth, content analyses cover events that have already occurred. In this analysis, interviews occurred up to 15 years prior (although 98% of interviews were conducted between 1990 and 1996). In many cases, interviewees were reporting childhood experiences. Thus, the potential for historical era bias was introduced. Finally, information provided with regard to value labels of themes is only available for certain variables (themes). The result of all these limitations is that "first-hand" information provided in the media is selective and therefore not generalizable to the population of transracial adoptees. Their benefit is in demonstrating messages the public may have received about this controversial topic and how these messages may influence public opinions and policies.

RESULTS

Demographic Representations

Eight demographic variables were identified from the universe of recorded interviews. The majority of adoptees interviewed were female (63%); African American or biracial (African American and Caucasian; 78%); in college, graduate school, or employed in professional or managerial occupations (88%); between 20 and 29 years (83%); and raised in the East or Midwest (72%), with siblings who were the adoptive parents' biological children, other transracial adoptees, or both (75%). Most interviews were reported in newspapers (75%), and the majority of interviews were published in the period from 1992 to 1996 (85%). Intercoder agreement on demographic items ranged from 82% to 100%, with Cohen's kappa levels of .75–1.00.

Substantive Representations

Forty substantive themes emerging from the analysis were categorized as *adoptive family relationships, direct outcomes, ethnicity and ethnic identification, general adoption issues,* and *racism experiences.* Fifteen met the standard of uniform distribution and had an absolute intercoder agreement of 80% or above and a kappa level of .61 or more (Table 19.1). For some interviews, coders were able to rate an interviewee's specific responses regarding a particular theme, rather than merely coding its presence or absence. Where this occurred, adoptees were presented as being about equally divided on (a) whether or not their parents had provided help with racial/ethnic identity development (51% vs. 49%); (b) the composition of the childhood neighborhood as predominantly Caucasian versus integrated (51% vs. 49%); (c) whether current friendships/affiliations were with the racial/ethnic group versus Caucasians, other, or mixed (48% vs. 52%); and (d) whether they had received criticism versus support or mixed reactions from members of their racial/ethnic group (e.g., for behavior typically associated with Caucasians; 59% vs. 41%). Adoptees were most frequently represented as having positive (95%) versus strained relationships with their adoptive

Table 19.1. Themes Included in Analysis and Intercoder Agreement, by Category (N = 93)

Theme	Frequency	% Agreement	κ
Adoptive family relationships			
Relationship with adoptive parents	39[a]	87[a]	.734**
Parents' help with ethnic identity	27[a]	83[a]	.714**
Parents' help dealing with racism	24[a]	87[a]	.626*
Others' reactions to interracial family	21[a]	95[a]	.831**
Direct outcomes			
Recommendations were made	19[a]	95[a]	.815**
Ethnicity and ethnic identification			
Identification with ethnic group	64[a]	100[a]	1.000**
Attitude toward transracial adoption	50[a]	91[a]	.859**
Ethnic composition of community	49[a]	97[a]	.949**
Relationship with ethnic group	43[a]	85[a]	.610**
Difficulty with ethnic identity	27[a]	89[a]	.762**
Fit in, accepted by transracial group	24[a]	83[a]	.607**
Ethnicity of current friendships	23[a]	86[a]	.629**
Race/ethnic appearance	21[a]	87[a]	.623**
General adoption issues			
Contact with birth parents	21[a]	96[a]	.873**
Racism experiences			
Childhood racism experience	29[a]	87[a]	.678**

[a]Themes met the standard of uniform distribution.

*p < .01.   ** p < .001.

parents; favoring or accepting transracial adoption (70%); having searched for or being interested in their birth parents (81%); having had encounters with racism (97%), not fitting in, or not being accepted by the transracial group (83%); feeling their parents provided none or limited help with racism (75%); having had difficulty with ethnic identity development (82%); and perceiving their physical appearance as most like that of the racial/ethnic group (95%). "Recommendations to parents" and "Outsiders" reactions are examples of a theme being present or absent.

DISCUSSION

The themes appearing with greatest frequency in media interviews were similar to concerns raised by the National Association of Black Social Workers (McRoy, 1989; Simon & Alstein, 1977). The message they convey is that there is partial support among adopted persons interviewed for (a) the expectation that transracially adopted children will be confronted with racism and social exclusion because of their status, (b) the concern that Caucasian parents will be limited in their ability to socialize children of color in developing a racial/ethnic identity and developing skills to success-fully deal with these experiences, and (c) the concern that transracial adoptees will not develop a connectedness with the larger racial/ethnic community. At the same time, interviews conveyed less support for concerns about longer term outcomes since the majority of transracial adoptees were depicted as having a physical and social identification with the ethnic group and as having searched for, being in the process of searching for, or being interested in their birth parents, although they also reported positive feelings toward their adoptive parents.

As noted earlier, the potential bias associated with these data renders them unreliable for generalizing to all transracial adoptees. More rigorous scientific research is needed. In the meantime, however, the potential biases discussed earlier may make the presentation of problematic experiences among media representations more credible. Thus, clinicians may find this information helpful in anticipating what experiences transracial adoptees and their families may have had and in conducting assessments and interventions with those who seek their assistance. Policy advocates may also consider the results of this analysis in addressing future policy needs related to transracial adoption—for example, advocating policies that allow emphasis to be placed on the interconnectedness between transracial adoptees and the racial/ethnic group.

Finally, information in media reports discussed in this article is most likely representative of the messages about transracial adoption received by the public and public policy makers between the mid-1980s and 1990s. It is therefore likely to have influenced public opinion and the direction of such legislation as the Multiethnic Placement Act (1994), the Interethnic Adoption and Adoption Assistance sections of the Small Business Job Protection Act (1996; making it illegal to deny or delay foster or adoptive placement on the basis of race and providing tax credits for adopting), and the Adoption and Safe Families Act of 1997 (that hastened termination of parental rights). This reality emphasizes the need for scholars to conduct rigorous scientific research in areas of controversy and to disseminate results to the public and to public policy makers.

REFERENCES

Adoption and Safe Families Act of 1997, Pub. L. No. 105–189, 111 Stat. 2115 (1997).

Allen-Meares, P. (1985). Content analysis: It does have a place in social work research. *Journal of Social Service Research, 7,* 51–68.

Baker, M. E. (1992). *Psychological adjustment of adopted minority children.* Unpublished master's thesis, University of Houston.

Cohen, J. (1960). A coefficient of agreement for nominal scales. *Education and Psychological Measurement, 20,* 37–46.

Feigelman, W., & Silverman, A. R. (1983). *Chosen children: New patterns of adoptive relationships.* New York: Praeger.

Gelfand, D. M., & Hartmann, D. P. (1975). *Child behavior analysis and therapy.* New York: Persimmon Press.

Hartmann, D. P. (1977). Considerations in the choice of interobserver reliability estimates. *Journal of Applied Behavior Analysis, 10,* 103–116.

Hollingsworth, L. D. (1997). Effect of transracial/transethnic adoption on children's racial identity and self-esteem: A meta-analytic review. *Marriage & Family Review, 25,* 99–130.

Hollingsworth, L. D. (1998). Adoptee dissimilarity from the adoptive family: Clinical practice and research implications. *Child and Adolescent Social Work Journal, 15,* 303–319.

Indigo, E. (1988). Ethnic identity of transethnically-adopted Hispanic adolescents. *Social Work, 33,* 531–535.

Krippendorff, K. (1980). *Content analysis: An introduction to its methodology.* Beverly Hills, CA: Sage.

Landis, J. R., & Koch, G. (1977). The measurement of observer agreement for categorical data. *Biometrics, 33,* 159–174.

Marshall, C., & Rossman, G. B. (1989). *Designing qualitative research.* Newbury Park, CA: Sage.

McRoy, R. G. (1989). An organizational dilemma: The case of transracial adoption. *The Journal of Applied Behavioral Science, 25,* 145–160.

McRoy, R. G., & Zurcher, L. A. (1983). *Transracial and inracial adoptees: The adolescent years.* Springfield, IL: Thomas.

Multiethnic Placement Act of 1994, Pub. L. No. 103–382, §553, 108 Stat. 4057 (1994).

Scarr, S., & Weinberg, R. A. (1976). IQ test performance of black children adopted by white families. *American Psychologist, 76,* 726–739.

Simon, R. J., & Alstein, H. (1977). Transracial adoption. New York: Wiley.

Small Business Job Protection Act of 1996, Pub. L. No. 104–188, §1807 & 1808, 110 Stat. 1755 (1996).

Weber, R. P. (1990). *Basic content analysis* (2nd ed.). Newbury Park, CA: Sage.

Weinberg, R. A., Scarr, S., & Waldman, I. D. (1992). The Minnesota transracial adoption study: A follow-up of IQ test performance at adolescence. *Intelligence, 16,* 117–135.

COMMENTARY BY: Leslie Doty Hollingsworth

M y interest in the controversy surrounding transracial adoption developed rather late in my career. My work as a social worker had always been in the area of direct services at the level of individuals, small groups, and families—which meant that I didn't think a lot about the policy context surrounding the services. During the course of my work training child welfare staff for culturally competent practice with transracial foster and adoptive families, I never questioned whether transracial foster care or adoption should even occur.

This is somewhat surprising because I was a "product" of the civil rights movement of the 1960s. As a freshman student at a historically black women's college in the South, I participated in marches aimed at desegregating public lunch counters, and in other civil rights demonstrations. It was a period of intense activism out of which I, as many other African Americans, began to question, not merely accept, the status quo, particularly regarding race matters. But by the late 1980s, I had moved into an era in which the emphasis was on African American people preparing ourselves to take our places as equals in the marketplace of the United States. Questioning public policies was not part of that.

THE DECISION TO STUDY TRANSRACIAL ADOPTION

In the early 1990s, I enrolled in a doctoral program that exposed me to a class in child and family policy. As a course requirement, I reviewed a C–Span videotaped interview with William Pierce, then President of the National Adoption Committee, an advocacy group for adoptive parents. Much of the interview focused on the controversy surrounding transracial adoption. In addition to reviewing the interview, I researched the policy literature on transracial adoption and interviewed State child welfare administrators. The following semester, as part of a course requirement, I conducted a meta-analysis of comparative studies of transracial adoption, which exposed me to the empirical research in the area.

As I continued my studies, I became more aware of the strong feelings about transracial adoption on both sides of the issue, including the National Association of Black Social Workers' 1972 opposition to the practice (cited in Simon & Alstein, 1977). I became interested in research questions that had not been raised or examined with regard to the plight of transracial adoptees—questions such as what the adoptees' opinions were about whether transracial adoption should occur, and whether they had sought contact with their birthparents.

Commentary on article: Hollingsworth, L. D. (2002). Transracial adoptees in the media: 1986–1996. *American Journal of Orthopsychiatry, 72,* 289–293.

CONDUCTING THE ANALYSIS

Around the time that I was starting my new career as an assistant professor, colleagues and friends, aware of my interest in transracial adoption, were sending me news clippings on the subject. Some contained reports of interviews with adolescent and adult adoptees. Most research up to that time had only involved studies of young children or interviews with their adoptive parents.

Having become familiar with content analysis during my doctoral work, I decided to conduct a content analysis of media reports of these interviews—my first such analysis. My purpose was to hear from transracial adoptees as directly as possible about their experiences; to hear their stories. Quoted material from interviews with them would provide that. In addition, a content analysis could tell me what information the public, including policy makers, was getting about the topic. A deciding factor was time. A content analysis would provide me with desired information without taking the time to conduct primary data collection via a full interview study. The steps followed are discussed below.

1. A research assistant first conducted a search of databases containing published works, particularly media reports of interviews with persons who were transracially adopted. Examples today would include: *LexisNexis Academic, ProQuest Newspapers, WorldCat, Newspaper Abstracts, LegalTrac,* and *FirstSearch.* The research assistant printed out the entire document for each work that contained an interview with a transracially adopted person, and quoted material directly attributable to the adoptee. I remember getting the first stack of printouts and my feeling of anticipation, almost excitement. It was similar to the feeling I'd had when I received the first batch of completed and returned mail surveys in my dissertation study.

   The *Lexis-Nexis* news database yielded the largest number of works and the most useful. Works included articles from local and national news media in the United States and abroad. More traditional searches (such as *PsycINFO, ERIC,* and *Merlyn Catalog*), as opposed to those specifically focusing on media, yielded books containing publications of interviews with transracially-adopted adolescents and young adults; these were also included in the analysis.

2. Works containing 120 different interviews were identified originally. I read each work and identified themes I saw reflected. Variables were mostly those that had been identified and used in previous studies. Examples were what racial group the adoptee identified with, whether the adoptee desired physical features associated with being Caucasian, and whether the neighborhood was integrated or mostly Caucasian. (In this commentary, the terms *theme* and *variable* will be used interchangeably.) As I read, I was aware of a feeling of connection with the adoptees. I felt I knew them and their experiences personally; I felt sad for some of them. When I stopped reading to attend to other demands, I looked forward to returning to the "data."

3. Once we were convinced that searches would yield no further useful databases, the same research assistant, a Caucasian woman in her early twenties, read all works and identified themes independently and with no knowledge of the themes I'd identified. As an African American, this use of an additional person and of a different racial group reduced the possibility that themes identified were only those that were relevant to my own experience.

4. We each listed separately the themes we had identified, then went over them. Since the goal was to obtain all possible themes, we eliminated only obvious duplications, coming up with a "final" list of 30 substantive themes, in addition to 3 demographic themes. At the end of the first project year, the first research assistant graduated and two additional women were hired.

One of the new research assistants was a recently admitted doctoral student in Social Work and Political Science from Korea, who had a Master of Social Work (MSW) degree from a major U.S. university. The other was an African American woman from the west coast, beginning work on her MSW. The ethnicity of these two research assistants, along with the fact that the first had been Caucasian and I was African American, may have helped to strengthen the validity of the study.

5. Using a word processor, the new research assistants typed all direct interview data, including enough contextual material (generally several sentences) so that the question asked or the circumstances surrounding the response were clear. Krippendorff (1980) refers to this surrounding material as "context units." We did not actually analyze whether these context units were sufficient as context or whether the addition of further material would have strengthened coding agreement.

6. The research assistants were each then given the list of themes that the original research assistant and I had identified earlier, and were asked to code all interview data according to these themes. Material identified as quoted in the interview text was coded.

   Variable names were assigned to each variable. Whenever a coder saw evidence of a theme in the text, she wrote the variable name on the document itself. The purpose was to connect the variable with its location in the text, as space had not been provided for writing in the variable names (text typing was single-spaced); the coder wrote wherever she could find space. This resulted in a crowded and somewhat messy document. (I would recommend double-spacing or triple-spacing, with wide margins on all sides; I would also suggest the use of pencils and large erasers, never ink.) Many computer programs now make it possible to insert comments or track changes in the documents themselves.

   A total of 120 interviews were initially coded. This number included 93 adults aged 20 and older and 27 adolescents aged 13–19. (Later, outcome data were separated to permit analysis by age group. The study sample in the accompanying article was the adult sample.)

7. We created a coding sheet to record values assigned to each variable. At the top were lines for coder ID, interview ID, and interviewee's name. The names assigned for each variable were listed in one column and, in the next column, beside each variable name, the coder placed the value of 1 if she saw evidence of the variable being present. Zero was a default value when the variable was not coded as present. All interviews were coded by both coders.

   I then met with the two coders to check intercoder agreement. Based on Hartmann's (1977) and Krippendorff's (1980) recommendations, 80% was chosen as a minimum level of agreement. I recorded the value 1 if both coders agreed on the presence of the variable, 0 if they did not agree. Percentage agreement was then calculated on an aggregate basis for each theme. Thus, if the two coders agreed on a theme (for example, the adopted person's relationship with the adoptive parents) and this agreement was present in 90 of the 120 interviews, we divided 90 by 120, which, in this example, would have yielded an agreement of .75 or 75% for that particular theme.

8. Agreement levels were low initially. (I did not retain the original agreement levels and would suggest that future content analysts do so.) Low agreement between coders generally means that there is a problem with insufficient training of one of the coders, or with the clarity of the code definitions. In our case, the latter seemed to be the problem. We refined some themes. We also went back over the text to identify any themes that had not been identified earlier. Some new themes were added; at this point, the number of themes was 59, with 49 substantive and 10 demographic themes. Coders recoded the material until percentage agreements of at least 80% were obtained.

Double coding of all 120 interviews may not have been necessary. Since completing this analysis, I have come across recommendations that only a representative sample (for example, 20%) needs to be coded (Carey, Morgan, & Oxtoby, 1996). However, we ultimately achieved our goal of 80% intercoder reliability. A potential concern was the large number of variables. We wanted to avoid eliminating useful variables; however, some could probably have been collapsed further.

9. Once 80% intercoder agreement was reached, we calculated kappa statistics to reduce the element of chance agreements. As noted in the accompanying paper, 0.61 was accepted as the minimum kappa level, based on recommendations of Gelfand and Hartmann (1975) and Landis and Koch (1977). Tests for the kappa statistic are accessible through use of the SPSS statistical package. Readers are referred to Allen-Meares (1985) and Bloom, Fischer, & Orme (2003) for methods for reducing chance agreement, using percentages.

10. In deciding what final themes to keep for further analysis, we followed the *standard of uniform distribution* (Krippendorff, 1980). This procedure calls for averaging the frequencies of all themes, and then keeping only those themes whose individual frequency was at or above that average. The average arrived at was 18. Sixteen variables met that criterion (although in a few cases variables meeting the standard of uniform distribution failed to meet standards for both percentage agreement and kappa levels). Of concern here is the possibility that meaningful variables may have been eliminated. For example, the theme of whether or not a *transracial adoptee was able to understand both the transracial and own-race worlds* occurred in 15 of 93 adult interviews (a frequency of 3 lower than the acceptable 18), as well as having intercoder agreement of 89% and a kappa statistic of 0.625 with significance level below .001. Readers interested in this theme for purposes of research planning or assessment planning in direct practice would not have it available. This concern is of particular importance since the standard deviation for the mean frequency of all themes was 14.03. Alternatives would have been to use acceptable percentage agreements or acceptable kappa levels as the standard for keeping variables in. I chose the most conservative of the three approaches.

11. Once coding for the presence of themes was completed, the same research assistants coded the text for themes (variables) that could be dichotomized into a favorable 1 or an unfavorable 0. Here, not only was the theme mentioned in the interview but the interview had provided information on the adopted person's position with regard to the theme. An example was the theme of an adopted person's attitude toward transracial adoption. Codes were 1, 0, and 9. In this example, a code of 1 was assigned if the adopted person's response indicated favoring transracial adoption, 0 if not favoring it, or 9 if insufficient information was available to code this variable. (I was later advised that to insure greater consistency in assigning codes, a preference is to use 1 when the response is consistent with the hypothesis underlying the study and 0 in the case of the opposite response. The hypothesis underlying this analysis was that transracial adoption would be problematic for adoptees. In that case, 1 would be used when the text indicated the adoptee opposed transracial adoption and 0 when the response indicated the adoptee favored the practice.)

12. We refined the definitions of themes once more, this time creating a codebook and providing definitions for each value label in each variable. (Value labels are analogous to attributes or categories of a variable.) We derived the definitions of value labels from the different responses provided in the interview text for a particular variable. The refining process resulted in 40 themes. The following example contains the theme, variable name (in 8 digits), earlier themes that were collapsed into this theme (in parentheses), value labels of 1, 0, and 9, earlier

themes that were collapsed into the value labels (in parentheses), definitions of salient terms, and definitions of value labels.

Example:

Parents' helpfulness to the adoptee in dealing with racism (RACMHELP)
 (Adoptive parenting practices—race issues)
 (Preparing child to deal with racism)

1. Parents were helpful in dealing with racism (Parental guidance—approaches to racism) (White parents providing black culture and tools to deal with racism)

0. Parents were limited in helpfulness in dealing with racism (Parents don't understand the experience of racism) (Consequence of white parents' unfamiliarity with racism)

9. Data unavailable

Definitions of salient terms:

Helpful in dealing with racism: Refers to actions taken or suggested by the adoptive parents that were helpful at times that the adoptee was confronted with an act that most people would consider racially motivated. Examples: telling the adoptee that the person who committed the racist act had problems, not the adoptee, or confronting the person directly; in the case of a child who committed the racist act, confronting the child's parent(s).

Limited in helpfulness in dealing with racism: When told by the adoptee about incidents in which the adoptee was confronted with actions by someone else that most people would consider racially motivated, the adoptive parents were not helpful or were limited in their helpfulness to the adoptee. Examples: taking no action at all or telling the adoptee to ignore the behavior, or being surprised at the intensity of the adopted person's reaction.

Racism is used here to refer to actions, attitudes, and/or behavior that are directed at a person because of his or her color or racial characteristics, by other persons who use the superiority of their race in the social structure as permission to engage in such actions, attitudes, or behavior. Examples: a police officer apprehending someone as a suspect in a crime solely because of color or race; teasing a person about physical characteristics that most people would associate with race or ethnicity; name-calling, where such names are considered by most people to be negatively associated with a particular race or ethnic group; or ignoring or excluding a person from social participation in a group solely on the basis of color, race, or ethnicity.

(Note: The list of themes also contained a separate theme, "childhood racism experiences." For this theme, the focus was on the adoptee's experience with racism rather than the parents' ability to help in coping with racism.)

1. The text contains statements made by or ascribed to the adoptee to the effect that she or he found the adoptive parents helpful in dealing with racist incidents, using the definition of *helpful* and *racist incidents* given above.

0. The text contains statements made by or ascribed to the adoptee to the effect that she or he did not find the adoptive parents helpful in dealing with racist incidents, using the definition of *not helpful* and *racist incidents* given above.

9. The text contains no mention of the adoptive parents in terms of the adopted person's ability to handle racist incidents with which she or he was confronted, using the above definition of racism.

13. Where the two coders agreed, the value agreed on was used for that variable (for example, the adoptee reported never having experienced racism as a child = 0). I coded all variables in all interviews as a third coder. Where there was disagreement between original coders, the two attempted to arrive at agreement. If that was not possible, I broke the tie.

14. An SPSS database containing dichotomized variables was created. To permit analysis, only variables with values of 1 or 0 were used. Frequencies were calculated and cross-tabulations and chi-square analyses were conducted. This was consistent with Marshall and Rossman's (1989) position: "The most common method of summarizing content analytic data is through the use of absolute frequencies. In content analyses exploring relationships, cross-tabulations or chi-square analyses are often used" (p. 100). See the accompanying article for a summary of findings from these calculations.

CHALLENGES AND TRIUMPHS

Coding Challenges

In the process of coding the interview data, several coding challenges were encountered. First, in the initial identification of themes by the first coder and me, we defined themes as narrowly as possible. This was to prevent overlooking themes that were important. This introduced problems with intercoder reliability when subsequent coders began coding the interview data using these themes. In a number of instances, two coders coding the same content would code different themes. An example can be seen in the case of two codes—NONDATES, defined as the race/ethnicity of most of the adopted person's friends, and COMMAFIL, defined in terms of the race or ethnic group of the community with which the adopted person most affiliated. Since community in this case was defined as people with whom the adopted person interacted, it was difficult to distinguish between the two themes. The solution we chose was to create a new variable—NEWCOMM—that combined the two earlier variables, using the definition of "the adopted person's current affiliation with the ethnic community or ethnic friends."

Another challenge was related to our decision to code a number of experiences separately depending on whether they occurred in childhood or adulthood. In some cases, it was difficult to tell. To simplify the coding, we combined the themes that had been separate, regardless of the developmental period they represented. In some instances, however, such as the interviewee's encounters with racism, we kept separate themes for childhood experiences with racism and encounters with racism occurring in adulthood.

A frequent occurrence that helps with coding but can complicate analysis is the presence of multiple categories of a variable. An example is the variable referring to the ethnicity of an adopted person's current friendships. Categories initially were: mostly the ethnic group, mostly the transracial (Caucasian or majority group), about equal, and neither. In these cases, it is helpful to create frequency tables so the numbers of responses in each category can be seen. However, for some analysis purposes, particularly with small samples such as this one, only responses that fit into the first two categories may be used. The downside is that important information may be lost.

In some instances, it was necessary to "break up" a theme according to the research question of interest. The question of whether an adopted person fit in with or felt a sense of belonging in the transracial group was an important one, but so was the question of whether the adopted person had the same feelings of belonging with the ethnic group. We therefore converted an earlier single variable into two variables—one referring to the adopted person's feeling of acceptance by the transracial group, and a separate variable referring to the adopted person's comfort with the ethnic group. Each was coded as a dichotomous variable.

Finally, in spite of these efforts, some overlapping between variables undoubtedly remained. For example, an adopted person's identification with the ethnic group may be related to the ethnicity of one's current friendships and affiliations. This may be an analysis issue rather than a coding issue, but it further demonstrates the challenging nature of coding secondary content.

These challenges call attention to the difficulty often encountered in analyzing secondary data. For example, coders were restricted to what was in the data. They could not ask interviewers for clarification. Our experiences with coding and analysis also called attention to some of the intricacies of working with content related to race and ethnicity. Commonly used terms may present difficulty when efforts are made to arrive at definitions that can be reliably applied.

Other Challenges and Triumphs

There were some additional challenges but also some triumphs in conducting this analysis. An early challenge occurred during the original data-collection phase, when we learned of a university policy that restricted use of the *Lexis-Nexis* database to educational purposes (as opposed to research purposes). Since that database contained the most useful data, we were faced with having to give up conducting the study. A triumph was that the policy was changed by the time we were ready to analyze the data and publish the results, and we were able to move forward with our research.

Another challenge was in getting papers published from the data. Content analysis is both a quantitative and a qualitative method, and both cases allow for quantification. In spite of this, however, and in spite of my following the analysis procedures described by several researchers (see Marshall & Rossman, 1989; Patton, 1990), getting papers accepted for publication was difficult. Most reviewer objections related to methodological concerns, particularly the small sample size and its lack of representativeness with regard to the population of transracial adoptees.

A triumph followed asking a colleague at a peer institution to read my paper and make suggestions regarding its potential for acceptance for publication. It was he who suggested that I frame the paper within the context of the historical era and in terms of reports in the media. (This confirms the helpfulness, throughout one's career, of asking colleagues to read drafts of papers or to look over reviewers' comments and give suggestions. This can be particularly helpful when two reviewers don't agree about the strengths and weaknesses of an article. What one reviewer may see as a strength, another may see as a weakness, and the two opinions have to be reconciled by the author.) The editor of the *American Journal of Orthopsychiatry* expressed interest and willingness to publish the revised paper as a research brief. On that basis, I was able to get it published and therefore to provide potential topics for future research and direct practice assessments. I had begun the content analysis in June, 1996. Manuscripts were written and rewritten and submitted to four different scholarly journals before the current one was accepted as a research brief in April, 2002.

STRENGTHS AND LIMITATIONS

The content analysis had several strengths. First, collecting data helped me to identify large amounts of existing information about transracial adoptees' own stories—as told to the reporters or writers who interviewed them. I did not have the resources to engage in primary data collection at this early point in my academic career; therefore, I would not have had those data otherwise. Second, the content analysis provided an opportunity to systematically analyze what information the public and public policy makers were receiving from the media about transracial adoption. Third, the content analysis was undoubtedly a less expensive process than other methods, since the data were already "collected." This is a big advantage of secondary analyses, of which content analysis is one example. A limitation is that selection bias can occur in the conduct of interviews for media purposes. Readers are directed to the accompanying article for a detailed discussion of this limitation.

Finally, although the data from media reports were immediately available, rigorously conducting the content analysis and getting the results into scholarly journals took a long time. Part of this may have been my lack of experience with getting research reports disseminated. However, content analysis should not be considered a quick research method.

"IF I HAD IT TO DO OVER AGAIN . . . !"

Having said all I have said, I would definitely conduct a content analysis again. As a method that uses both qualitative and quantitative approaches, I found the process rewarding. The experience of reading the narratives of 120 transracial adoptees was an enlightening one. I can't imagine any other source that would have provided that amount of information on transracial adoption, from that number of persons able to speak first-hand about their experience. Looking back, however, there were some things that I might have done differently or additionally. I would have conducted a separate analysis of the proportion of media reports on transracial adoption that mentioned the 1994 Simon, Alstein, and Melli report of a 20-year longitudinal study (summarized in Simon, Alstein, & Melli, 1994). As I conducted the analysis of interviews for the current study, for example, I realized that the report of that study seemed to be referred to frequently in media reports. This book gave a highly positive review of transracial adoption. My view is that it is a much more complex issue than that, yet readers, practitioners, and policy makers could have had their opinions influenced by reports of that study.

Legislative histories related to transracial adoption also seemed to refer frequently to the Simon and Alstein study. A careful review of all legislative histories on the topic would inform us of the extent to which this work was used as empirical support—important in view of the concerns raised about that study.

I would look more closely at the influence of sociohistorical context. Large numbers of interviews with transracial adoptees were reported in the periods prior to and during years when transracial adoption legislation was being considered. For the content analysis, I went back 10 years, beginning in 1987. Only one of the interviews located for the analysis had been published between 1987 and 1988. One other was published in 1989. However, nine were published in 1990, three in 1991, 12 in 1992, 22 in 1993 (the year prior to the passage of the Multi-ethnic Placement Act of 1994), and ten in 1994. Twenty published interviews were found in 1995, and 15 in 1996 (when legislation was passed as part of the Small Business Job Protection Act, strengthening the Multi-ethnic Placement Act). It may be that consideration of legislation on transracial adoption began around 1990—hence, the increase in published interviews during that time. Reviewing legislative histories would provide that information. Collaboration with specialists in communications, particularly journalism, may be useful in this research.

The direction of messages in media reports could also have been analyzed, according to whether the reports were supportive of transracial adoption or in opposition to it. Across all the reports published, this would have alerted us to whether the messages the public received about transracial adoption were favorable or unfavorable, knowledge that may have had implications for understanding attitudes and policies that emerged.

A final "look back" has to do with my purpose in doing the analysis. My original purpose was to learn as much as I could about the experiences of transracial adoptees from as many of them as I could. I wanted to hear their stories and to make their stories available to practitioners, policy makers, and the public at large. In my eventual attempt to get the data disseminated in respected journals, after several rejections, I sacrificed my original purpose. My purpose became simply to disseminate information about themes on transracial adoption that are reflected in the media. Although I included frequency information on themes of interest related to transracial adoption, in the article that was eventually published, those results were not prominently presented.

WHERE DO WE GO FROM HERE?

Writers on qualitative research (for example, see Patton, 1990) stress the importance of triangulated methods; that is, of using several different methods of analysis to address the same research question. The content analysis discussed in this commentary was useful in identifying, and in some cases confirming from earlier research, the themes around which qualitative and quantitative research on transracial adoption may be focused. Future research should be directed first at seeking national samples that are as representative as possible of the population of U.S. transracial adoptees (domestic and international), and at conducting interview studies, using qualitative and quantitative methods. At the same time, I have developed new motivation for moving the content analysis beyond the point that I left it.

REFERENCES

Allen-Meares, P. (1985). Content analysis: It does have a place in social work research. *Journal of Social Service Research, 7,* 51–68.

Bloom, M., Fischer, J., & Orme, J. G. (2003). *Evaluating practice: Guidelines for the accountable professional.* Boston: Allyn and Bacon.

Carey, J. W., Morgan, M., & Oxtoby, M. J. (1996). Intercoder agreement in analysis of responses to open-ended interview questions: Examples from tuberculosis research. *Cultural Anthropology Methods, 8,* 1–5.

Gelfand, D. M., & Hartmann, D. P. (1975). *Child behavior analysis and therapy.* New York: Persimmon Press.

Hartmann, D. P. (1977). Considerations in the choice of interobserver reliability estimates. *Journal of Applied Behavior Analysis, 10,* 103–116.

Hollingsworth, L. D. (1997). Effect of transracial/transethnic adoption on children's racial and ethnic identity and self-esteem: A meta-analytic review. *Marriage & Family Review, 25,* 99–130.

Krippendorff, K. (1980). *Content analysis: An introduction to its methodology.* Beverly Hills, CA: Sage Publications.

Landis, J. R., & Koch, G. (1977). The measurement of observer agreement for categorical data. *Biometrics, 33,* 159–174.

Marshall, C., & Rossman, G. B. (1989). *Designing qualitative research.* Newbury Park, CA: Sage Publications.

Marshall, C., & Rossman, G. B. (1995). *Designing qualitative research* (2nd ed.). Thousand Oaks, CA: Sage Publications.

McRoy, R. G. (1994). Attachment and racial identity issues: Implications for child placement decision-making. *Journal of Multicultural Social Work, 3,* 59–74.

Multi-ethnic Placement Act of 1994. Pub. L. No. 103-382, Section 553, 108 Stat. 4057 (1994).

Padgett, D. K. (1998). *Qualitative methods in social work.* Thousand Oaks, CA: Sage Publications.

Patton, M. Q. (1990). *Qualitative research and evaluation methods.* Newbury Park, CA: Sage Publications.

Simon, R. J., & Alstein, H. (1977). *Transracial adoption.* New York: Wiley.

Simon, R. J., Alstein, H., & Melli, M. S. (1994). *The case for transracial adoption.* Washington, DC: American University Press.

Small Business Job Protection Act of 1996. Pub. L. No. 104-188. Sections 1807 & 1808, 110 Stat. 1755 (1996).

20

Social Embeddedness and Psychological Well-Being among African Americans and Whites

Lonnie R. Snowden

Social and familial ties and community institutions, scholars believe, have played a crucial role in permitting African Americans to adapt socially and psychologically in the face of stigma and social rejection. Family and extended family, neighbors, friends, churches, and civic and fraternal organizations, on this account, have offered sanctuary from a frequently hostile wider society and provided access to needed social, emotional, and material resources (cf. Martin & Martin, 1995).

This view rests on a supportive but limited research base. African Americans have been found to interact with neighbors more frequently than do Whites and in a greater variety of ways (Jackson, 1970; Lee, Campbell, & Miller, 1991), indicating the presence of extensive neighborhood-based and church-based support networks (Jackson, 1970; Stack, 1974; Lee et al., 1991; Walls & Zarut, 1991). The high degree of interdependence believed to occur in such communities has led some scholars (Saegert, 1989) to conceive of a "community household," comprising families and neighbors who share information, coping strategies, advice, and services (e.g., child care and transportation).

The Black church has been regularly identified as central to African American community life (Taylor & Chatters, 1991), serving as a focal point of social involvement, emotional reassurance, and political activism (Taylor & Chatters, 1991). The continuing prominence of the Black church extends a historical legacy begun in the rural South and maintained throughout waves of migration to the urban North. "The church was an agency of moral guidance and social control" (Jaynes & Williams, 1989, p. 173). Religious belief is strong among African Americans: in 1987, 74% of Blacks rated religion as "very important" compared to 55% of Whites. Church attendance on a

This study was supported by Research Award R01 MH52908 from the National Institute of Mental Health.

regular basis is less common (60%) but again more common than that reported by Whites (56%; Jaynes & Williams, 1989).

The close-knit character and cooperative practices described as characterizing African American communities exemplify and enrich a wider concern among social scientists with social ties that furnish emotional and material support. Over the past two decades, many researchers (e.g., Brown & Harris, 1978; Cobb, 1976; Cohen & Wills, 1985; Jackson, 1992; Vaux, 1988) have documented associations of social support with health and well-being. Domains represented in this work include work, school, and family adjustment (Walls & Zarut, 1991; Wilcox, 1981), mental health (Brown & Harris, 1978), and physical health and mortality (Berkman & Syme, 1994; Mor-Barek, Miller, & Syme, 1991; Seeman & Syme, 1987). Social support is thought to enhance well-being and adjustment to stressful life events and conditions through its ameliorative and protective effects, as well as by promoting feelings of belongingness and kinship (Vaux, 1988).

The surge of research on social support was increasingly greeted with expressions of criticism. Social support came to be recognized as vague, expansive, and in need of being disaggregated into components (e.g., Leiberman, 1982). Barrera (1986) distinguished among three aspects of support—social embeddedness, perceived support, and enacted support—and demonstrated that each aspect functions as a distinguishable concept ultimately best understood within complementary theories of support.

One aspect of social support, social embeddedness, refers to ongoing relationships and continuing interaction patterns reflected in social status indicators (e.g., marital status) and social roles. Social embeddedness is comprehensively assessed through social network analysis (Barrera, 1986) and closely resembles social integration, which has been defined as "...the existence and quantity of [social] relationships..." (LaVeist, Sellers, Elliot-Brown, & Nickerson, 1997). In theoretical accounts of support, social embeddedness serves as a background against which support is enacted and might be perceived; although one step removed, social embeddedness has been associated empirically both with enacted and perceived support (Barrera, 1986).

Researchers and theorists have treated social embeddedness as an important concept in its own right. Evidence from a number of studies links embeddedness-related indicators of social status to poor health and shortened life expectancy (Berkman & Syme, 1994). One study of elderly, African American women (LaVeist et al., 1997) found that 5-year death rates of the socially involved and the socially isolated differed by a factor of three. Other theorists have interpreted embeddedness as "social capital" — "...the quantity and quality of interpersonal ties between people" (Aday, 1994, p. 491). Social capital serves not only as a social, health, and psychological resource but also as a form of economic capital, promoting productivity and material well-being (Coleman, 1988; Fukuyama, 1995). Another group of theorists has pointed to embeddedness-related linkages— churches, extended family, friendship and fraternal groups, and other "mediating structures"—in explaining the capacity of African American and other stigmatized communities to overcome sociopolitical oppression (Sonn & Fisher, 1998).

In recent years community psychologists have reported intriguing attempts to use selected features of embeddedness in accounting for African American social support and psychological functioning. Henly (1997) demonstrated that family structure was less important to psychological adjustment and work aspirations among young African American mothers than were emotional and material support. Chen, Telleen, and Chen (1995) found that support from family members predominated, although Miller-Lancar, Erwin, Landry, Smith, and Swank (1998) reported greater conflict in supportive family relationships among African Americans than among other groups and Davis and Rhodes (1994) found that problems in the mother–daughter relationship were associated with psychological well-being to a greater extent than was maternal support. Rhodes, Ebert, and Fisher (1992) discovered the importance of having a mentor: mentored mothers appeared to take better advantage of social support and received greater psychological benefit.

Maton et al. (1996) focused attention on differences in well-being associated with differences in source of support. Among pregnant adolescents, they reported that peer support was more important among African Americans and partner support among Whites. In a second study of college freshmen, Maton et al. found that family support was more important among African Americans and peer support among Whites. In yet another study, Maton (1990) showed that support from friends was associated with greater self-esteem among in-school African American males, but that support from friends was not associated with self-esteem among drop-outs.

Researchers also have studied the adjustment of African American students at major universities. Jay and D'Augelli (1991) reported no difference between African American and White freshmen in support-related network characteristics or in availability or adequacy of support. Among graduate students DeFour and Hirsch (1990) demonstrated the importance of having African American peers and opportunities to interact with African American faculty.

The body of research, when considered as a whole, contains useful insights, but suffers at the same time from important limitations. Even though studies relying on convenience samples and focusing on groups of special concern help to clarify behavior in particular population niches, they cannot address the general African American population or general conditions of living. Nor have these studies focused on embeddedness itself, a concept central to theories of African American community life (cf. Milburn & Bowman, 1991). Studies broader in scope have used convenience samples, or have lacked non–African American samples as a basis for comparison. As a result, investigators have been unable to establish with confidence that observed levels of social interaction generalize widely or apply to African Americans in particular.

In evaluating hypotheses about African American behavior it is sometimes important to adopt a comparative frame of reference. One investigator reported that African Americans facing mental health problems turned frequently to family and friends for help, but did so less frequently than Whites (Snowden, 1998). Another demonstrated that material support available to African Americans was notable, but often proved less than that available to Whites (Roschelle, 1997). Both researchers used probability samples from national surveys.

Another limitation of many previous studies is the relatively small samples they have used. Low statistical power to detect true differences between populations is a pervasive problem in behavioral research, evident in the widespread occurrence of Type II error (improper failure to reject the null hypothesis; Hunter, 1997). The problem is compounded when interaction terms are included in analytic models (McClelland & Judd, 1993). The resulting tendency to draw inappropriate conclusions has inspired a growing movement to ban the practice of testing statistical significance (Hunter, 1997).

The present study examined racial differences in support-related social embeddedness thought to be especially important to African Americans. Women and men were studied separately because of evidence from previous research indicating the frequent occurrence of gender-based interaction in studies of African Americans and Whites, attributable to gender-linked social and cultural patterns of experience (Hines, Snowden, & Graves, 1998; Jones-Webb, Snowden, Herd, Short, & Hannan, 1997; Snowden & Hines, 1998, 1999; Snowden, Libby, & Thomas, 1997).

Social embeddedness was represented following one of two broad approaches identified by Berrera (1986): assessing the frequency of interaction with friends and participation in groups and community organizations. The study addressed two related questions, seeking differences between African Americans and Whites in (1) level of social embeddedness; and (2) the association between social embeddedness and psychological well-being. Avoiding specialized populations and questions, the purpose was to test general hypotheses derived from a literature and pointing toward a social orientation and style of social functioning found especially among African Americans.

The first hypothesis arose from descriptions of African American communities as close-knit and tightly bonded. These characteristics were expected to result in high levels of social embeddedness, higher levels than those found among Whites.

The second hypothesis pertains to the functional and adaptive significance of social integration. Because of a special emphasis placed on interaction and relatedness in African American communities and a tradition of socializing to maintain morale (Dressler, 1985; Martin & Martin, 1995; Milburn & Bowman, 1991), it was expected that, among African Americans more than among Whites, persons who were socially engaged would have better mental health than those who were less engaged. The second hypothesis implies an interaction between African American versus White status and social integration in explaining psychological well-being—that the association between social integration and well-being would be greater among African Americans than among Whites.

METHOD

The data used for the study are from the 1987 National Medical Expenditure Survey (NMES), specifically from the NMES Household Survey. The NMES is a project of the Center for General Health Services Intramural Research of the Agency for Health Care Policy and Research (AHCPR).

The NMES Household Survey drew a national probability sample of the civilian, noninstitutionalized population and included an oversample of population groups of special interest—the poor, the elderly, African Americans, and Latinos. A parallel survey was conducted of American Indian and Alaska Native populations, the Survey of American Indian and Alaskan Natives (SAIAN).

The Household Survey proceeded from a stratified, multistate area probability design with a total sample of roughly 36,400 adults and children (children were excluded from the present analysis). Families participating in the Household Survey were interviewed four times over 16 months beginning in early 1987. Baseline data were collected on household composition, employment, and insurance, and the information was updated at each interview. Additional information was collected on illness, use of health services, and expenditures. The data were collected through face-to-face questions, from calendars/diaries of medical events, and from a self-administered questionnaire including attitude items used in the present study mailed and completed by respondents between Round 1 and Round 2 interviews. Data obtained from the Household Survey were partially corroborated and supplemented with data from the Medical Providers Survey and the Health Insurance Plan Survey that assessed, respectively, respondents' health care utilization as reported by their providers and health insurance benefits as documented by their insurers.

Table 20.1 provides demographic information on the weighted sample. Largely, the sample was composed of married adults living above the poverty line.

Measures

The NMES included five questions on social embeddedness. Three of them were answered on 7-point Likert Scales indicating frequency (over the past 30 days) of visits by friends, visits to friends, and telephone conversations with friends or relatives. Ratings indicated frequencies of contact ranging from *every day* to *not at all in the past month*. A fourth item asked about the frequency respondents attend "church or go to meetings of clubs, lodges, parent groups or other voluntary groups you belong to." Responses were reported on a 6-point Likert Scale indicating frequency of attendance ranging from *every day* to *not at all in the past month*. Responses to this question covered

Table 20.1. National Medical Expenditures Survey: Sample Description

	Percent (*n* = 18,432)[a]
Race/gender	
African American women	6.0
African American men	4.4
White women	43.4
White men	37.0
Other women	4.9
Other men	4.4
Age	
18–39	49.0
40–64	34.4
65 and over	17.7
Region	
Northeast	20.4
Midwest	25.5
South	34.8
West	19.5
Urbanicity	
Large SMSA[b]	26.1
Small SMSA	48.5
Not in SMSA	25.4
Employment	
Employed all year	53.8
Other	46.2
Income	
Lives in poverty	11.3
Other	88.7
Marital status	
Currently married	60.1
Other	39.9

[a]Children under 18 were excluded.

[b]SMSA—Standard Metropolitan Statistical Area: Population center and adjacent communities as defined by Federal Office of Management and Budget.

only six Likert Scale points instead of seven; there was no response indicating a frequency of "twice a week" as was true of the 7-point items. A final question asked whether there was "Any one in your life with whom you can really share your very private feelings and concerns?" Response alternatives were *yes* or *no*.

Psychological symptom distress was assessed via the 5-item version of the Mental Health Inventory (MHI-5), an abbreviated version of the 18-item Mental Health Inventory 18 (MHI-18), itself a shortened version of a 38-item measure used as the principle mental health assessment instrument in the Rand Health Insurance Experiment (Newhouse, 1974). The questionnaire consisted of five questions asking respondents how often during the past 30 days they had been "a very nervous person," "felt downhearted and blue," or "felt so down in the dumps that nothing could cheer you up"; and in a positive vein (scored in the reverse) "were you a happy person?" and felt "calm and peaceful"? All questions are answered on a 6-point scale of frequency ranging from *none of the time* to *all of the time*.

The MHI-5 was carefully investigated and found psychometrically sound. Internal-consistency reliability (alpha) was established at .88. Reliability varied little among subsamples of respondents: elderly versus nonelderly, high school educated versus less than high school educated, physically ill versus healthy (Stewart, Hays, & Ware, 1988). Validity was shown through a strong association with *DSM-III-R* diagnosis as assessed by the Diagnostic Interview Schedule (DIS). The MHI-5 proved as good as the MHI-18 and the General Health Questionnaire-30 at detecting DIS-assessed diagnosis and better than the Somatic Symptom Inventory-28 (Berwick et al., 1991). The method used was ROC analysis (Swets, 1988), which calls for plotting the hit rate (sensitivity) as a function of false alarm rate (1 − specificity) and which thereby evaluates accuracy at all possible cut-points. On an index that is "conceptually the same and numerically virtually identical to the common-language effect size" (Rice, 1997, p. 417), the MHI-5 scored .79 out of 1—widely accepted as indicating a large-size effect (Rice, 1997).

Interaction Terms and Statistical Power

The detection of interactions ("moderator effects") in observational (nonexperimental, field-based) studies has bedeviled researchers for almost 30 years (e.g., Zedeck, 1971). McClelland and Judd (1993) discussed the joint distribution of interacting variables and showed that an optimum joint distribution possible in experimental studies is often approximated only poorly by interaction terms created in observational studies. The result is that in observational studies, residual variance available after accounting for main effects is often highly constrained, leading to weak tests of statistical significance.

Surveys of the literature have indicated the presence of this very kind of limitation. Two reviewers considered "much of the social science literature and reported that field study interactions typically account for about 1%–3% of the variance" (McClelland & Judd, p. 277). Low levels of variance explained are especially likely when differences expected in slopes of regression lines are less than dramatic differences in direction characteristic of "crossover" interactions, where regression lines reverse.

Even when accounting for low percentages of variance, however, interaction remains important to detect. Interaction indicates that a single regression coefficient is inappropriate and separate coefficients are needed—thereby differentiating between competing theoretical accounts and prediction strategies. From statistical simulation, Evans (1985) concluded that as little as 1% of variance (carried by interaction) might have theoretical consequences worthy of note.

Tables of statistical power (Cohen, 1988) indicate that the sample of more than 18,000 respondents analyzed in the present study provided sufficient power for a 99% chance of detecting a 1% increment in variance at the .01 level of significance.

Transformation of Indicators

Social embeddedness was examined at the level of its individual indicators rather than as a composite. For purposes of examining culture-related differences between sociocultural and ethnic groups, investigators have argued (Betancourt & Lopez, 1993) for attention to specific modes of behavior lost in aggregation of individual items (Betancourt & Lopez, 1993).

Items are less reliable than scales according to psychometric theory, and the use of items may result in a loss in reliability. Any such loss must be considered in the context of possible gains in theoretical coherence and cross-cultural validity. In the present analysis, patterns of difference in response between African Americans and Whites ultimately uncovered in the study would have been concealed through mutually canceling effects (African Americans had higher scores on some indicators but lower scores on others) in an analysis of composite scores (see later).

Response scales indicating frequency of interaction were dichotomized to indicate contact of once a week or more frequent contact ("every day," "several days a week," "twice a week") versus less than once a week contact ("2–3 times in the past month," "once in the past month," "not at all in the past month"). The recoding was performed to avoid problems associated with the use of highly skewed response distributions. As a check on any loss of information from use of categories rather than continuous scores, the analysis was repeated using original ratings (see later).

The independent variables described personal and geographical characteristics including race and gender reflected in a four-category nominal variable. Other sets of dummy variables denoted age, using younger adults, age 18–39 as the reference group; region of residence, using the south as the reference group (African Americans remain overrepresented in the south); and size of area of residence, using living in a small Standard Metropolitan Statistical Area as the reference group. In addition, variables were included to measure employment, education, and marital and poverty status.

Analysis

The analysis began by examining bivariate relationships between African American vs. White women and African American vs. White men on the one hand and social embeddedness indicators on the other. Associations were tested via chi-square. Logistic regression was then employed to model the effect of race–gender pairings on each attitude statement recoded to indicate once a week or more frequent contact or having a confidante, after controlling for characteristics confounded with African American vs. White status and gender that might lead respondents to agree with the statement. The resulting five regression equations were weighted to adjust for survey design effects and nonresponse.

A final round of analysis was conducted to determine whether there were differences in the association between social embeddedness indicators of psychological symptom distress. A series of regression equations was estimated using independent variables described previously, along with indicators of social embeddedness taken separately and in turn. The dependent variable was symptom distress, transformed (midpoint dichotomized at the item level) to avoid problems of skew and then summed. Internal consistency reliability (coefficient alpha) of the transformed scale was .78.

This procedure resulted in five regression equations, each of which included social embeddedness indicators (e.g., visits by friends) along with categories reflecting combinations of race and gender (African American females, etc.). Interactions were estimated between social embeddedness indicators and categories of African American vs. White status and gender. The method of regression was ordinary least squares.

As a check on transformations of the dependent variables, multivariate analyses were repeated substituting continuous ratings of social embeddedness indicators for categories using ordinary least squares. There was no difference between procedures in results with respect to which findings proved statistically significant. Logistic regressions are reported because they are free of assumptions about response distributions (i.e., homoscedasticity).

RESULTS

Unadjusted racial differences on indicators of social embeddedness are presented in Table 20.2. African American women were more likely than White women to report visits by friends and about equally likely to report visits to friends. African American women proved more likely than

Table 20.2. Gender Differences in Social Integration: African American vs. White

	% Women ≥ Once per Week		% Men ≥ Once per Week	
	African American	White	African American	White
Visits by friends	46.76	44.33*	51.27	42.32*
Visits to friends	37.43	37.36	50.33	38.89*
Phone close friends or relatives	82.33	89.21*	68.34	75.32*
Church, clubs, lodges, other groups	60.76	53.25*	43.91	43.91
Someone to share private feelings, concerns	82.69	88.23*	81.65	84.96*

Note: Differences tested via chi square: (1) African American women vs. White women; (2) African American men vs. White men.

*p < .05.

Table 20.3. Logistic Regression: Adjusted Black–White Differences in Social Embeddedness

	African American vs. White Women			African American vs. White Men		
% ≥ Once per Week	b	SE	OR	b	SE	OR
Visits by friends	−.11	.07	.90	.19*	.09	1.20
Visits to friends	−.28*	.08	.76	.24*	.10	1.27
Phone close friends or relatives	−.43*	.09	.66	−.24*	.11	.78
Churches, clubs, lodges, other groups	.55*	.07	1.73	.21*	.10	1.24
Someone to share feelings, concerns	−.16*	.07	.85	.01	.02	1.01

Note: Models include age, region, urbanicity, employment, poverty, marital status as covariates.

*p < .05.

White women to indicate attendance at meetings of churches and community groups. On the other hand, White women were more likely than African American women to report making phone calls to close friends or relatives as well as to indicate the presence of someone with whom they might share private feelings and concerns.

Inspection of unadjusted differences among males indicates that African American men were more likely than White men to indicate that they had visited or been visited by friends. White men proved more likely to report having phoned friends or family and to report the existence of a confidante.

Table 20.3 portrays racial differences on variables described in Table 20.2 after adjustment for socioeconomic and geographical differences. African American women were less likely than White women to have made visits to friends, phone calls to close friends and relatives, or to have a relationship where they could share emotions and concerns. On the other hand, African American women once again were more likely than White women to participate more frequently in churches, clubs, lodges, and other groups.

Table 20.4. Social Embeddedness Associated with Psychological Symptom Distress: Ordinary Least Squares

Principle Independent Variable	R^2	Main Effect		Women[a]		Men[a]	
		b	*SE*	*b*	*SE*	*b*	*SE*
Visits by friends	.07*	−.12*	.02	.02	.04	.13*	.06[b]
Visits to friends	.07*	−.25*	.02	.03	.05	.05	.06
Phone close friends or relatives	.07*	−.10*	.02	.06	.04	.00	.04
Churches, clubs, lodges, other groups	.08*	−.38*	.02	.08	.05	−.09	.05
Someone to share private feelings, concerns	.10*	−2.18*	.09	.25	.37	.38	.39

Note: Models include age, region, urbanicity, employment, poverty, marital status as covariates.

[a]Interaction terms: African American-by-White.

[b]Separate regression coefficients indicated by significant interaction: African American men: $b = -.19$; White men: $b = -.06$.

*$p < .05$.

In controlled analysis African American men again proved more likely than White men to indicate being visited by friends and making visits to friends. Unlike in bivariate analysis, they also were more likely to report visiting churches, clubs, lodges, and other groups. White men continued to be more likely to report frequent phone calls to friends and relatives. There was no African American vs. White difference for men in whether or not someone was available to share private feelings and concerns.

Table 20.4 presents main effects and interactions involving embeddedness on the one hand and psychological symptom distress on the other. For all indicators of social embeddedness, main effects were significantly associated with symptom distress, indicating that embeddedness is indeed a protective factor that enhances psychological well-being. The presence of an intimate emotional relationship was especially important; the difference between the presence and absence of such a relationship was, on average, more than two symptoms of distress on the 5-symptom scale.

Only one interaction was significant. Among African American men, visits-by-friends was associated more with symptom distress than it was among White men.

DISCUSSION

Results from the study documented differences between African Americans and Whites in levels of social embeddedness and, to a lesser extent, in the functional significance of social embeddedness. The results also pointed to considerable variation according to gender.

African American men proved more likely than White men to be visited by friends, to make visits to friends, and to attend gatherings of churches, clubs, lodges, and other groups. Perhaps preferring face-to-face contact to interaction by telephone, they were less likely than White men to make phone calls to close friends or relatives. Moreover, African American men who were visited by friends were especially likely to avoid psychological distress; they enjoyed even greater protection from distress than White men did.

Overall, African American men demonstrated a higher degree of social embeddedness than White men did—more involvement on more indicators of embeddedness. Their behavior is consistent with a view of African American social interaction depicted in the literature: relatively frequent contact associated with active peer support networks and high levels of community involvement (Lee et al., 1991).

African American women, on the other hand, were less likely than White women to make visits to friends, as well as to make phone calls to friends or relatives. African American women were also less likely than White women to have a relationship in which they felt able to share private feelings and concerns.

Like their male counterparts, African American women proved more likely to have attended meetings of churches, clubs, lodges, and other groups. Their behavior was striking in this regard; the odds ratio was higher than others. Results from the study thereby confirm the contention that "African Americans participate quite extensively in voluntary associations" including the church (Milburn & Bowman, 1991, p. 31), and an unspoken assumption that they participate more than Whites do. Greater African American social involvement also helps to justify a premise of intervention agents (cf. Sonn & Fisher, 1998); many have predicated their thinking on belief in a cohesive African American community with a vibrant network of mediating structures. The evidence of limited friend involvement among African American women, on the other hand, suggests a need for caution and points to the importance of avoiding overly broad claims.

Results from the study help to clarify and extend findings on patterns of African American embeddedness and support reported in the literature. Thus, while community "...participation is correlated with positive psychological characteristics..." among African Americans (Milburn & Bowman, 1991, p. 32), participation for the most part was equally benificial among Whites. Findings like those indicating a high rate of death among socially isolated African American women (LaVeist et al., 1997) point to an important source of risk, but do not tell us about its unique importance among African Americans. The present study suggests that it cannot be taken for granted that social involvement is particularly important for African Americans.

In another study reported in the literature, Jay and D'Augelli (1991) documented no difference between African Americans and Whites from examining characteristics of their social networks. The present study pointed to differential rates of social interaction, suggesting that equivalence in structural features of networks might not translate into equivalent interaction patterns; or that college freshman represent a special population and that generalization to the larger community is hazardous.

On the other hand, data from the study partially support findings like that of Maton (1990) who indicated that friend-based support was important to psychological well-being among in-school African American males. Maton found no connection between friend support and well-being among drop-outs. Thus, the experience of young African American males who remained in school appears, at least in this instance, to better represent the population at large.

That African American women have relatively low levels of social integration has not been reported elsewhere. Previous research does point to the possibility of problems in the support networks of African American women—especially a greater degree of mother–daughter conflict than among other groups (Davis & Rhodes, 1994). There has been little indication, however, of low involvement with friends.

African American women's lesser involvement with friends was offset partly by a greater involvement in churches, clubs, lodges, and other groups. Conceivably, these social connections serve as a source of mentors who have been shown to assist African American mothers in optimizing access to and use of social support (Rhodes, Ebert, & Fischer, 1992).

This lesser involvement with friends might further be explained by a greater involvement with family and extended family (Wilson, Greene-Bates, McKim, & Simmons, 1995)—social connections barely addressed in the survey. On the other hand, compensatory involvement with family cannot account for the lower percentage of African American than White women who lacked an intimate emotional relationship; the manner in which the question was worded placed no restriction on source and family members were therefore not excluded. Overall, the presence of an intimate emotional relationship proved notably associated with psychological symptom distress.

In view of the protective value of embeddedness demonstrated in the study, relatively low friend involvement and confidanteship place African American women, in comparison with other groups considered, at psychological risk. Evidence from epidemiologic studies is consistent with this contention (Snowden, 1998). For example, reports from successive national surveys (Hines, Snowden, & Graves, 1998; Jones-Webb & Snowden, 1993) documented higher rates of depression symptoms among African American women than among women from other groups. In the more recent survey (Hines, Snowden, & Caetano, 1999) African American women proved 1.5 times more likely than White women or Latinas to report symptoms reaching clinically significant levels.

The differences between African Americans and Whites observed in the study cannot be attributed to methodological factors. The size and representativeness of the sample greatly undermine appeals to statistical power and regional bias as possible weakness. Important demographic differences were controlled. Thus, although African Americans are less likely to be married and employed—both of which might affect levels of social interaction—the differences were controlled. Less telephone contact with friends might be affected by lack of access to the telephone. Control for poverty status helped to reduce, if not eliminate, this bias.

Results from the study suggest the importance of a differentiated view of African American community life and social involvement. The importance of gender stands out especially, and the need for gender-specific accounts of African American social and community participation. Other sources of differences that might be important to consider are urban–rural status, age, socioeconomic standing, and acculturation. More theory and research are needed at an intermediate level. These efforts must seek to describe African American embeddedness and social interaction in more qualified, specific terms than theory and research describing an overarching African American tradition, but with more general application than theory and research on social concerns (e.g., teenage, single parenthood) in special populations.

REFERENCES

Aday, L. A. (1994). Health status of vulnerable populations. *Annual Review of Public Health, 15,* 487–509.

Barrera, M. J. (1986). Distinctions between social support concepts, measures, and models. *American Journal of Community Psychology, 14,* 413–432.

Berkman, L. F., & Syme, L. S. (1994). Social networks, host resistance, and mortality: A nine year follow up study of Alameda County residents. In A. Steptoe & J. Wardle (Eds.), *Psychosocial Processes and Health: A Reader* (pp. 43–67). Cambridge, England: Cambridge University Press.

Berwick, D. M., Murphy, J. M., Goldman, F. A., Ware, J. E., Barsky, A. J., & Weinstein, M. C.

(1991). Performance of a five-item mental health screening test. *Medical Care, 29,* 169–173.

Betancourt, H., & Lopez, S. (1993). The study of culture, ethnicity, and race in American psychology. *American Psychologist, 48,* 629–637.

Chen, S. P. C., Telleen, S., & Chen, E. H. (1995). Family and community support of urban pregnant students: Support person, function, and parity. *Journal of Community Psychology, 23,* 28–33.

Cobb, S. (1976). Social support as a moderator of life stress. *Psychosomatic Medicine, 38,* 300–314.

Cohen, J. (1988). *Statistical power analysis for the behavioral sciences.* Hillsdale, NJ: Erlbaum.

Cohen, S., & Wills, T. A. (1985). Stress, social support, and the buffering hypothesis. *Psychological Bulletin, 5,* 310–357.

Coleman, J. S. (1988). Social capital in the creation of human capital. *American Journal of Sociology, 94*(Suppl.), 95–120.

Davis, A. A., & Rhodes, J. E. (1994). African American teenage mothers and their mothers: An analysis of supportive and problematic interactions. *Journal of Community Psychology, 22,* 12–24.

DeFour, D. C., & Hirsch, B. J. (1990). The adaptation of black graduate students: A social network approach. *American Journal of Community Psychology, 18,* 487–503.

Dressler, W. W. (1985). Extended family relationships, social support, and mental in a southern black community. *Journal of Health and Social Behavior, 26,* 39–48.

Evans, M. G. (1985). A monte carlo study of the effects of correlated method variance in moderated multiple regression analysis. *Organizational Behavior and Human Deviance Processes, 36,* 305–323.

Fukuyama, F. (1995). *Trust: The social virtues and the creation of prosperity.* New York: The Free Press.

Henly, J. (1997). The complexity of support: The impact of family structure and provisional support on African American and white adolescent mothers' well-being. *American Journal of Community Psychology, 25,* 629–655.

Hines, A. M., Snowden, L. R., & Caetano, R. (1999). Depression, alcohol consumption, and AIDS-related sexual behavior among African American, Hispanic, and white women. Manuscript under review.

Hines, A., Snowden, L. R., & Graves, K. L. (1998). Acculturation, alcohol consumption and AIDS-related risky sexual behavior among African American women. *Women and Health, 25,* 125–131.

Hofferth, S. L. (1984). Kin network, race, and family structure. *Journal of Marriage and the Family, 46,* 791–806.

Hunter, J. E. (1997). Needed: A ban on the significance test. *Psychological Science, 8,* 3–7.

Jackson, J. J. (1970). Kinship relations among urban Blacks. *Journal of Social Behavioral Sciences, 16,* 1–13.

Jackson, P. B. (1992). Specifying the buffering hypothesis: Support, strain, and depression. *Social Psychological Quarterly, 55,* 363–378.

Jay, G. M., & D'Augelli, A. R. (1991). Social support and adjustment to university life: A comparison of African American and white freshman. *Journal of Community Psychology, 19,* 95–104.

Jaynes, G. D., & Williams, R. M. (1989). *A common destiny: Blacks and American society.* National Research Council. Washington, DC: National Academy Press.

Jones-Webb, R., & Snowden, L. R. (1993). Symptoms of depression among blacks and whites. *American Journal of Public Health, 83,* 240–244.

Jones-Webb, R., Snowden, L. R., Herd, D., Short, B., & Hannan, P. (1997). Alcohol related problems among Black Hispanic and white men: The contribution of neighborhood poverty. *Journal of Studies on Alcohol, 58,* 539–545.

LaVeist, T. A., Sellers, R. M., Elliot Brown, K. A., & Nickerson, K. J. (1997). Extreme social isolation, use of community-based senior support services, and mortality among African American elderly women. *American Journal of Community Psychology, 25,* 721–731.

Lee, B. A., Campbell, K. E., & Miller, O. (1991). Racial differences in urban neighboring. *Sociological Forum, 6*(3), 525–550.

Leiberman, M. (1982). The effects of social supports on responses to stress. In L. Goldberger & S. Breznitz (Eds.), *Handbook of stress: Theoretical and clinical aspects* (pp. 764–783). New York: The Free Press.

Martin, E., & Martin, J. (1995). *The helping tradition in the black family and community.* Washington, DC: National Association of Social Workers Press.

Maton, K. I. (1990). Meaningful involvement in instrumental activity and well-being: Studies of older adolescents and at risk urban teen-agers. *American Journal of Community Psychology, 18,* 297–320.

Maton, K. I., Teti, D. M., Corns, K. M., Vieria-Baker, C. C., Lavine, J. R., Gouze, K. R., & Keating, D. P. (1996). Cultural specificity of support sources, correlates and contexts: Three studies of African American and Caucasian youth. *American Journal of Community Psychology, 24,* 551–587.

McClelland, G. H., & Judd, C. M. (1993). Statistical difficulties of detecting interactions and moderator effects. *Psychological Bulletin, 114,* 376–390.

Milburn, N. G., & Bowman, C. J. (1991). Neigborhood life. In J. S. Jackson (Ed.), *Life in Black America* (pp. 31–45). Newbury Park, CA: Sage.

Miller-Lancar, C. L., Erwin, C. J., Landry, S. H., Smith, K. E., & Swank, P. R. (1998). Characteristics of social support networks of low socioeconomic status African American, Anglo, and Mexican American mothers of full-term and preterm infants. *Journal of Community Psychology, U26,* 131–143.

Mor-Barek, M. E., Miller, L. S., & Syme, L. S. (1991). Social networks, life events, and health of the poor, frail elderly: A longitudinal study of the buffering versus the direct effect. *Family and Community Health, 14,* 1–13.

Newhouse, J. (1974). A design for a health insurance experiment. *Inquiry, 11,* 5–27.

Rhodes, J. E., Ebert, L., & Fischer, K. (1992). Natural mentors: An overlooked resource in the social networks of young, African American mothers. *American Journal of Community Psychology, 20,* 445–461.

Rice, M. E. (1997). Violent offender research and implications for the criminal justice system. *American Psychologist, 52,* 414–423.

Roschelle, A. R. (1997). *No more kin: Exploring race, class, and gender in family networks.* Thousand Oaks, CA: Sage.

Saegert, S. (1989). Unlikely leaders, extreme circumstances: Older Black women building community households. *American Journal of Community Psychology, 17*(3), 295–316.

Seeman, T. E., & Syme, L. S. (1987). Social networks and coronary artery disease: A comparison of the structure and function of social relations as predictors of disease. *Psychosomatic Medicine, 49*(4), 341–354.

Snowden, L. R. (1998). Racial differences in informal help-seeking for mental health problems. *Journal of Community Psychology, 26,* 429–438.

Snowden, L. R. (1998). Managed care and ethnic minority populations. *Administration and Policy in Mental Health, 25,* 125–131.

Snowden, L. R., & Hines, A. M. (1998). Acculturation, alcohol consumption, and AIDS-related risky sexual behavior among African American men. *Journal of Community Psychology, 26,* 345–359.

Snowden, L. R., & Hines, A. M. (1999). A scale to assess African American acculturation. *Journal of Black Psychology, 25,* 36–47.

Snowden, L. R., Libby, A., & Thomas, K. (1997). Health related and utilization among African American women. *Womens Health:Research on Gender, Behavior, and Policy, 3,* 301–314.

Sonn, C. C., & Fisher, A. T. (1998). Sense of Community: Community resilient responses to oppression and change. *Journal of Community Psychology, 26,* 457–472.

Stack, C. B. (1974). *All our kin: Strategies for survival in a Black community.* New York: Harper & Row.

Stewart, A. L., Hays, R. D., & Ware, J. D. (1988). The MDS short form general health survey. *Medical Care, 26,* 724–732.

Swets, J. A. (1988, June 3). Measuring the accuracy of diagnostic systems. *Science, 240,* 1285–1293.

Taylor, R. J., & Chatters, L. M. (1991). Religious life. In J. S. Jackson (Ed.), *Life in Black America* (pp. 105–123). Newbury Park, CA: Sage.

Vaux, A. (1988). *Social support: Theory, research, and intervention.* New York: Praeger.

Walls, C. T., & Zarut, S. H. (1991). Informal support from Black churches and the well-being of elderly Blacks. *Gerontological, 31,* 490–495.

Wilcox, B. L. (1981). Social support, life stress, and psychological adjustment. *American Journal of Community Psychology, 9,* 371–386.

Wilson, M. N., Greene-Bates, C., McKim, L., & Simmons, F. (1995). African American family life. In M. N. Wilson (Ed.), *African American family life: Its structural and ecological aspects* (pp. 5–21). San Francisco: Jossey-Bass.

Zedeck, S. (1971). Problems with the use of "moderator" variables. *Psychological Bulletin, 76,* 295–310.

COMMENTARY BY: Lonnie R. Snowden

As a mental health services researcher interested in disparities (U.S. Department of Health and Human Services, 2001)—that is, racial, cultural, and ethnic differences in mental health status and treatment—I grapple with several bodies of knowledge, and with formulating and answering questions from several research perspectives. In documenting and explaining disparities I find it necessary to draw from social welfare and social work, ethnomedicine, mental health economics, ethnocultural psychology, and elsewhere.

A crosscutting base of knowledge is needed because disparities occur for many and varied reasons. There are cultural differences in how people express and interpret mental health problems, and in the kinds of help they would prefer to receive; differences in where mental health programs are located and who providers would prefer to treat; differences in organizational mission, staffing, culture, and climate of mental health programs where services are provided; economic and financial differences owing to differences in health insurance coverage; and community-level differences related to tolerance for mental illness and support for persons suffering from mental illness, and norms for recognizing and responding to deviance (e.g., Snowden, 2003b). All bear on disparities.

SECONDARY ANALYSIS AND MINORITY MENTAL HEALTH SERVICES RESEARCH: CREATING NEW OPPORTUNITIES TO GAIN KNOWLEDGE

Because the disparities agenda is broad, no researcher can plan and conduct studies providing more than a narrow band of information. Researchers must take advantage of existing data sources wherever possible to provide greater coverage than would be possible if they were to collect the data entirely on their own. Additional advantage accrues if secondary data provide nationally representative sampling and an oversample of African Americans or other ethnic minority populations.

Researchers often sacrifice a core standard, external validity, because they find it too difficult and expensive to recruit a nationally representative sample, or because they consider national

---

Commentary on article: Snowden, L. R. (2001). Social embeddedness and psychological well-being among African Americans and whites. *American Journal of Community Psychology, 29,* 519–536.

recruitment unnecessary for their purposes. For studying minority populations, however, representativeness is particularly valuable and, if at all possible, should not be sacrificed.

Representativeness is valuable because it permits researchers to provide national estimates of disparities and disparity-related concerns. From national estimates researchers can establish and report the magnitude—and relative importance—of disparities, and compare increases and decreases over time. For example, from national estimates hospitalization itself has declined but, as of 2000, proportional overrepresentation of African Americans has remained surprisingly constant.

Representativeness is especially important as well because estimates of disparities can be biased by differences in the selection of minority and White samples. Many surveys of children are conducted in schools, for example, but because of higher minority drop-out rates, enrolled, school-attending students are less representative of some minority populations than they are of the White population. In a similar fashion, routine omission of homeless and institutionalized persons from household surveys can bias estimates of alcohol, drug, and mental health disparities. African Americans with mental health and substance abuse problems are greatly overrepresented among the homeless and institutionalized persons, and the impact of including homeless and institutionalized persons is negligible for Whites, but is notable for African Americans. As a result, to calculate disparities from samples without homeless and institutionalized persons is to underestimate disparities.

This need to reach beyond my personal capacities to personally collect data increases my awareness of opportunities to address important unanswered or inadequately answered questions from secondary sources. Operating somewhere just below consciousness I am aware of gaps in knowledge, and I scan the research environment for opportunities for accessing existing data to provide needed answers.

These tendencies were reinforced by my experience in contributing to the Surgeon General's Report on Mental Health, and as Co-Scientific Editor of the Supplement on Culture, Race, and Ethnicity. I saw many gaps in knowledge, including an absence of relatively straightforward information about minority populations and their mental health. Often, data were available that would have permitted rigorous estimates, but these data had never been analyzed for that purpose. I was pleased that in several instances, colleagues and I seized opportunities for secondary analysis when they presented themselves, helping to fill in missing pieces of the puzzle (e.g., Zang, Snowden, & Sue, 1998).

My interest in existing data is supported by the existence of many first-rate data sources from federal sources and, increasingly, from foundations. For example, to assess the prevalence of substance abuse and related problems, the federal Substance Abuse and Mental Health Services Administration conducts the National Household Surveys on Drug Use and Health, sampling over 137,000 minority and White children and adults. The National Center for Health Statistics conducts the National Ambulatory Medical Care Survey to report on office-based visits to practicing, nonfederal physicians, permitting assessment of disparities in treatment and quality of care (e.g., Snowden & Pingitore, 2002). Documenting changing trends in the health care infrastructure and health services delivery, the Robert Wood Johnson Foundation's Health Tracking Initiative includes a longitudinal household survey and surveys of employers, physicians, and insurance plans, permitting longitudinal evaluation of disparities. The Urban Institute regularly conducts the National Survey of America's Families on tens of thousands of respondents, with oversamples of minority group persons and the poor. The studies are very expensive and, as one justification for the expense, both federal agencies and foundations sometimes welcome use by outside investigators.

FULFILLING PRIMARY AND SECONDARY RESEARCH AGENDAS: IDENTIFYING AND EVALUATING THE NATIONAL MEDICAL EXPENDITURE SURVEY USED IN THE ACCOMPANYING ARTICLE

The National Center for Health Services Research (NCHSR), now the Agency for Healthcare Research and Quality (AHRQ), encouraged secondary analysis of data from the National Medical Expenditure Survey (NMES). The agency considers its surveys the best source of health care information available because creating and managing such information is central to the agency's mission. I first became aware of the NMES and its predecessor surveys from my service on an NCHSR research review committee, and my general awareness of health-related federal data sources that ask mental-health related questions and have large ethnic minority representations in their samples.

Health services researchers recognize that the NMES presents unique advantages for studying health services. Chief among them is the NMES's approach to assessing insurance status. NMES researchers obtain information, via the Health Insurance Plan Survey, from respondents' insurance companies rather than from respondents themselves. By tracking down insurance policies, the investigators eliminate common, significant errors that occur because many people do not know the terms of their insurance coverage and give inaccurate answers when asked on surveys about their insurance.

Primary Research Agenda

I awaited a chance to use the NMES because it provided an opportunity to address minority–White differences in insurance coverage and to rigorously understand the impact of disparities in insurance coverage on disparities in access. Insurance coverage is a key but largely unexamined explanation for disparities, and I wished to test several explanatory hypotheses about this issue.

In pursuing a disparities agenda, I have been fortunate to be affiliated with a research organization, the Center for Mental Health Services Research, University of California-Berkeley, since 1988. I have had access to an interdisciplinary core of seasoned investigators representing economics, sociology, psychology, psychiatry, social work, and public health. From 1989 to 2000, The National Institute of Mental Health funded the Center.

When projects were programmatic and relevant to the Center's mission, resources could be made available to support identification, screening, and secondary data analysis to address important issues. Recognizing that insurance coverage and disparities are central to the Center for Mental Health Services Research, and that they represented an important extension of ongoing work in mental health economics, my colleagues awarded me a small amount of funding to defray programming costs. They welcomed my suggestion that the proposed analysis of the NMES might provide background for further studies using the NMES's successor, the Medical Expenditure Panel Survey (MEPS).

The work resulted in two published papers demonstrating the impact on access of insurance-related racial and ethnic differences. The papers confirmed results reported previously but only in passing. One paper (Snowden & Thomas, 2000) clarified that the African American–White disparity in outpatient mental health services use exists primarily among the privately insured. When African Americans and Whites are employed and more middle-class in standing, disparities are, paradoxically, greatest.

Access disparities are smallest among poor minority persons and Whites because their mental heath problems are more likely to include the most severe and disabling conditions. For them treatment is often unavoidable and is sometimes coerced. Middle-class minority persons can more readily avoid treatment and, whether from feared loss of precariously held middle-class status or from a lack of welcoming private-sector treatment providers, appear to do so more than Whites. A second paper reported that insurance coverage is less an incentive for minority than for White persons to use mental health services (Thomas & Snowden, 2001). Preferring cultural conceptions of mental illness (e.g., interpreting symptoms as those of spiritual crisis) and avoiding the stigma associated with the label of mental illness, many minority persons never consider treatment in the first place, and thus never contemplate the issue of price. Thus, minority persons respond less to insurance coverage because cultural barriers preempt price as a consideration.

I collaborated on both papers with health economist Kathleen Phillips, then a postdoctoral fellow affiliated with the Center. Kathleen brought two crucial qualifications to the project. First and foremost she is an excellent economist, very strong conceptually and methodologically. Second, Kathleen knew the NMES well because she had been affiliated with AHRQ.

Having as a collaborator someone who is knowledgeable about the problem at hand and experienced with the secondary data source being considered is very desirable indeed. Yet having such a collaborator is not essential to success. I have conducted other projects of secondary analysis working only with a skilled and energetic programmer. Furthermore, programming demands are declining with increasing sophistication of user-friendly computer programs.

Secondary Research Agenda

Having made a commitment to the NMES and become immersed, I began to notice variables apart from those of initial interest, and to consider the data's potential to address questions apart from those for which I originally pursued the NMES. I noticed that, as part of the questionnaire, the investigators had inquired into the social and community engagement of respondents. Although I could identify no established questionnaire as a source, I recognized for two reasons that the questions addressed, at least in part, one of the many facets of social support.

First, an active interest in theories of community functioning and social well-being have led me, for more than 20 years, to teach a course on social networks and social support. From years of reading and thought, I understood social support, social integration, social capital, and related concepts. Conceptually and methodologically, I could interpret the measure presented in the questionnaire provided in the dataset with good understanding of what it included and what it overlooked.

Second, I was interested in depictions of African American life—scholarly, literary, and otherwise. I am interested personally in such characterizations because I am an African American who grew up in an African American community. I am interested professionally because these depictions amount to theories of African American life, theories bearing on the questions I ask in services research and the interpretations I reach in the course of my research.

Scholars and activists have portrayed African American communities as emphasizing a core, supportive orientation. In her classic work, anthropologist Carol Stack (1975) crystallized this view, observing well-functioning kinship networks where others might have seen only poverty and despair.

A belief in strong supportive traditions is justified by appeal to historical experience: slavery, sharecropping, and general societal exclusion forced a turning inward to the African American community, toward mutual assistance and sharing. A tendency to seek help from family and community were reinforced by collectivist values and a communal orientation, perhaps tracing back to the West African origins of many U.S.-born African Americans. To me and to many other African Americans, these characterizations *feel* correct, touching partly on personal experience.

However, there is reason to believe that this picture is exaggerated. Some scholars point to competing African American traditions that interfere with the capacity to provide support (e.g., Patterson, 1998). Demographic data tell of economic, health, and social problems that place an imposing burden on supportive people and institutions, perhaps greater than they can be expected to bear (U.S. Department of Health and Human Services, 2001). Supportive structures and processes may be less than are often presumed (Roschelle, 1997). I came to believe that our conceptions of African American social and community engagement needed to be better explicated and more subject to empirical corroboration.

The issue of support levels available in African American communities is closely linked to subjects of concern to mental health services research. Recovery of persons suffering from mental illness is affected by community support, and support levels in African American communities are often believed to be high.

However, when I had directly investigated the widely accepted hypothesis that African American support from friends, family, and religious figures for mental health problems was greater than that for Whites, results were surprising (Snowden, 1998). The data indicated that African Americans were less likely than Whites to seek help from informal sources. I could no longer take for granted a picture of supportiveness and its favorable mental health–related consequences.

ADDITIONAL REASONS FOR USING THE NMES

A nationally representative sample, survey design and quality, an African American oversample, and the presence of the Mental Health Inventory (MHI-5)—a shortened version of the principal mental health assessment instrument in the Rand Health Insurance Experiment (discussed subsequently)—all recommended the NMES for a test of African American support and mental health. But this contemplated use of the NMES strayed from my earlier uses of the data, which had addressed questions of access and financing. Along with a handful of others, I had previously conducted secondary analysis of the NMES only slightly shifting the focus from its primary purpose, from physical to mental health.

Crucial to success was how well the measure of social and community engagement in the questionnaire might be interpreted in a well-developed theoretical context. How was this measure linked to larger social and community concerns? Was the measure wide enough in scope to justify the considerable effort involved in the full-fledged analysis that would be required to test questions of African American engagement and support?

This domain has been widely studied and interpreted under the rubric of social support. Social support is complex and unwieldy, but I knew that Manuel Barrera had written an important article bringing a measure of order. Barrera (1986) identified "social embeddedness" as one aspect of social support, and linked it clearly to "perceived support" and "enacted support," related but distinguishable aspects, in a comprehensive model. Barrera had shown where embeddness fit into a larger theoretical perspective, and its role in a family of related constructs.

The measure was but one of several I would have included had I designed the survey from the outset as an investigation of social well-being and African American mental health. For comprehensiveness, I would have included indicators of other Barrera-defined constructs, "perceived" and "enacted" support, and would have asked also about family, friends, and others as potential sources of support. On the other hand, the measure was sound, clearly expressed a central construct, and was interpretable (with due attention given to its limited coverage of the domain of interest).

PROCESSES INVOLVED IN DOING SECONDARY ANALYSIS OF LARGE DATA SETS

For anyone contemplating secondary analysis, crucial preliminary steps involve studying not only publications using the data, but also codebooks and data dictionaries obtained from investigators, and actual questionnaires and variables, such as socioeconomic indicators, created through transformation of original questions. Thus, secondary analysts must thoroughly familiarize themselves with materials originally used in the study and any standard transformations of questions, immersing themselves in actual wording of instruments. For it is the questions as actually asked and answered, in relation to theoretical interests, that determine whether the project should continue to be pursued.

Prospective secondary analysts must also consider how long ago data being considered were collected. Aging data is especially a concern because of lags between gathering of data and preparation and release of files for secondary analysis and time for familiarization with the data. With my project the problem was exacerbated by delays in review and an unusually long lag between acceptance and publication.

When viewed in perspective, it can be seen that problems with aging data affect all forms of research. Major studies often require three or four years to conduct, and many more months to prepare data, to complete data analysis, and to report findings in the scholarly literature. Lags from secondary analysis are not unique, but stretch an already lengthy schedule by months or years. Moreover, preparation and release of files has quickened as technology has improved and as acceptance of secondary analysis has grown.

When considering my project, I took note of the fact that African American traditions of engagement and mutual assistance were believed to be enduring. Indeed, a robust quality was often described as a hallmark. Notable changes between 1988 when data were collected and 2001 when the article appeared would have been inconsistent with a core feature of traditions being studied.

Nevertheless, some data are too old for use and *must* be identified as such. In making this determination a key question is whether conditions affecting the research question have changed, rendering results obsolete or affecting them in unknown ways.

In considering the NMES for studying insurance status and minority mental health treatment, I had good reason at the outset to expect an excellent fit between constructs of interest and methods used in data gathering. After all, the NMES was designed with insurance and treatment in mind. Careful inspection of documents bore out this expectation.

Initially, my greatest concern was that the NMES was designed with a primary focus on physical health and thus might not lend itself to addressing mental health questions. I questioned whether procedures for ascertaining mental health services use, and questions to assess mental health-related symptoms and social functioning, were suitable for my purpose. From the study of documents I satisfied myself that I could appropriately assess social functioning and accurately assess mental health services use.

Crucially, I discovered that the NMES had used the MHI-5 as a brief screener to evaluate the need for services from higher or lower levels of access to mental health problems. The MHI-5 has a good pedigree; its origins can be traced to a major policy experiment, the RAND Health Insurance Experiment (Newhouse, 1994). The instrument was backed by extensive psychometric evaluation. Despite its brevity, the MHI-5 promised to provide an excellent assessment of psychological symptoms, comparable to that obtained from lengthier and better-known symptom checklists. Although the study's focus was on physical, not mental, health, the investigators had made a good choice for persons like me with a mental health agenda.

Satisfied that my primary interest in studying insurance and minority access was well served by the NMES, I made a commitment to undertake secondary analysis. This commitment was not made lightly. I knew that activities conducted thus far, including reading existing publications, scrutinizing documents setting forth survey design and procedures, and grappling with codebooks and other materials are only preliminary steps. Acquiring the data and undertaking the analysis is a multistep process demanding technical expertise in data management, programming, and statistical methods, and would require ongoing communication with AHRQ.

Often, even public use data sets from large-scale surveys are works in progress. There can be updates and new releases, reflecting recent availability of data previously not ready for analysis. Existing data are sometimes reorganized and new files created to facilitate widely implemented kinds of analysis. New indices—reflecting, for example, length of insurance coverage—are created, or existing ones updated, in light of user experience and new developments in the field.

Data from any large survey have quirks. For example, there can be recodes for which the attached label gives a misimpression as to how to interpret the recode, or unexpected appearances of many missing values, or variables that do not perform as expected (for no apparent reason) in a wide range of what should be clear-cut situations.

The NMES was especially challenging because it was not one survey but several. It comprises the Household Survey, as well as a Medical Providers Survey asking respondents' health care providers about their health care, and a Health Insurance Plan Survey discussed previously. Files were available combining data from various sources, at family and individual levels. It was important to ascertain where needed variables could be found in a readily usable form.

To learn about updates and ask questions about the data, any secondary analyst should maintain active communication with agencies responsible for the survey. We contacted AHRQ regularly and they provided excellent support. They provided clear and accurate answers to questions in a timely, professional manner.

Ten years ago, when we began to analyze the NMES, secondary analysis was more challenging than it is now. Technical developments alone have brought secondary analysis more within reach. Programming has advanced and computing power has increased—ten years ago we found it necessary to use a mainframe to analyze the NMES. More federal agencies and foundations have made data available for secondary analysis, and everyone's experience base has grown. At the time we conducted the analysis, because of Kathleen's high level of programming and statistical skill and personal relationship with staff at NCHSR, her personal involvement may have been indispensable.

AFRICAN AMERICAN SOCIAL EMBEDDEDNESS AND PSYCHOLOGICAL WELL-BEING: FINDINGS AND NEXT STEPS

I felt justified in beginning the arduous process of testing questions of interest. The process was extensive but not unusual: from preliminary descriptive results to preliminary modeling to final modeling. The process is iterative, and proceeds with checks for integrity. Did our descriptive frequencies contain only values that were allowed by response and coding alternatives specified in supporting documentation? How much missing data were present on variables of interest and what would be its likely impact? Were we able to replicate simple descriptive tables reported by others? Did preliminary regression contain tolerable amounts of missing data? How much collinearity was present and should we implement corrections? Statistics books and software manuals provide guidelines, but there are few hard and fast rules for answering these questions. Answering these and other questions demanded many rounds of analysis, inspection of findings, and reanalysis.

The investment made in the course of earlier work with the NMES yielded dividends in saved time and effort. I went directly to preparation and submission of a manuscript because I had resolved important issues at the outset in deciding whether to embark on this new phase of analysis. The issues had been firmly planted and context well established in the process of justifying the commitment of time and effort.

The accompanying paper contributes a more subtle view of social and community engagement and support in African American communities. It paves the way for further hypothesis formulation and testing from an empirical foundation.

The need for greater complexity is especially evident in findings on levels and types of social and community engagement of African American women. The data revealed African American women to attend church more than others, as hypothesized. They revealed also that African American women are relatively unlikely to report having a confidante and more likely to have less contact with family and friends.

After acceptance of this paper, I followed up this finding with a brief additional analysis of African American women's mental health. I examined individual items from the MHI-5, comparing African American women and men with White women and men as well as Latino women and men from the Latino oversample. By inspecting simple gender by ethnicity tables I discovered an interesting pattern.

Of six groups considered (African Americans vs. Whites vs. Latinos; males vs. females), African American women endorsed two items at higher rates then other groups. One item was having "felt so down in the dumps that nothing could cheer you up." The other was in the past thirty days having felt "calm and peaceful."

I find these data intriguing. They suggest feelings of discouragement, along with a sense of inner peace. One interpretation is that, because of greater burden and lesser social engagement with friends, African American women are sometimes discouraged. However, because of greater participation in church and community groups, at other times African American women experience a sense of well-being more than members of other groups.

The expectation that African American communities are always supportive, then, can give way to a more focused and differentiated form of inquiry. Especially for scholars with applied interests, the issues of greatest concern are less about an all-encompassing African American tradition than about enactment of support under contemporary conditions found in African American communities. The questions apply especially to understanding the circumstances of African American women who, like other women, bear greatest responsibility for provision of support. How much are they themselves supported, and how much support can they provide under adverse conditions facing many African American women? What are the sometimes limited opportunities for them to receive support in return?

CONCLUSION

The accompanying article resulted from simultaneous work on several research agendas, one directly representing mental health services research and the other clarifying a knowledge base from which services-related questions draw. I was attracted to the National Medical Expenditure Survey for its strength in addressing unanswered questions in mental health economics about access and the response of minority persons to mental health insurance coverage.

In the course of this work I discovered that the NMES might serve another purpose. Were African Americans especially socially embedded in supportive communities? While plausible, this claim had been rigorously subjected to few empirical tests. Researchers, policy makers, and practitioners assumed this claim as conventional wisdom, but little data could be adduced in support.

I discovered that with respect to an aspect of support—social and community engagement—questions about African Americans are complex, perhaps more than was previously understood. Answers depend on whether males or females are being considered and on the kind of social and community participation being considered. Results from the study further a process by which sweeping generalizations can give way to more differentiated claims.

As the process of understanding African American life moves forward, secondary analysis can play a vital role by providing a shortcut to avoid the time and expense of large-scale collection of primary data. When presented with national representatives, an African American oversample, and survey purposes central to African American social, psychological, cultural, and community life, secondary analysis should be considered. It should continue to be considered contingent on having programming and statistical support available, having support readily available from the survey research team, and having enough variance on key variables. When these requirements are met, investigators can tackle important questions and further our understanding of African American persons and communities.

REFERENCES

Barrera, M. (1986). Distinctions between social support concepts, measures, and models. *American Journal of Community Psychology, 14*, 413–432.

Cabassa, L. J. (2003). Integrating cross-cultural psychiatry into the study of mental health disparities. *American Journal of Public Health, 93*, 1034.

Newhouse, J. (1994). *Free for all? Lessons from the RAND Health Insurance Experiment.* Cambridge, MA: Harvard University Press.

Patterson, O. (1998). *Rituals of blood: Slavery in two American centuries.* New York: Basic Books.

Roschelle, A. R. (1997). *No more kin.* Thousand Oaks, CA: Sage Publications.

Snowden, L. R. (1998). Racial differences in informal help seeking for mental health problems. *Journal of Community Psychology, 26*, 429–438.

Snowden, L. R. (2003a). Snowden responds. *American Journal of Public Health, 93*, 1034.

Snowden, L. R. (2003b). Bias in mental health assessment and intervention: Theory and evidence. *American Journal of Public Health, 93*, 239–243.

Snowden, L. R., & Pingitore, D. (2002). Frequency and scope of mental health service delivery to African Americans in primary care. *Mental Health Services Research, 4*, 123–130.

Snowden, L. R., & Thomas, K. (2000). Medicaid and African American outpatient treatment. *Mental Health Services Research, 2*, 115–120.

Stack, C. (1975). *All our kin: Strategies for survival in a black community.* New York: Harper & Row.

Thomas, K., & Snowden, L. R. (2001). Minority response to health insurance coverage for mental health services. *Journal of Mental Health Policy and Economics, 4*, 35–41.

U.S. Department of Health and Human Services. (2001). *Mental health: Culture, race, and ethnicity—A supplement to Mental health: A report of the surgeon general.* Rockville, MD: Public Health Service, Office of the Surgeon General.

Zang, A., Snowden, L. R., & Sue, S. (1998). Differences between Asian and white Americans' help-seeking patterns in the Los Angeles area. *Journal of Community Psychology, 26*, 317–326.

Index

Activities of daily living (ADL), 172, 174, 176–182

Addiction Severity Index. *See* ASI

ADL (activities of daily living), 172, 174, 176–182

Adoption, transracial, 443–458

Adoption and Safe Families Act (1997), 448

Adult homelessness
  adverse childhood experiences and, 214–233
  family environment variables and, 234–252

AFDC (Aid to Families with Dependent Children)
  barriers to work, 355, 375*n*–376*n*
  child impoverishment and maltreatment, 389
  income packaging, 282

African Americans
  child impoverishment and maltreatment, 389–391, 393–397, 402–404
  child mental health services experiment, 5
  effectiveness of juvenile justice programs, 123
  homelessness and, 214
  income packaging, 284
  perspectives on residential treatment, 302–325
  schizophrenia study, 42–44, 46–50, 52, 58

social embeddedness and well-being, 459–480

transracial adoption, 443–458

Age
  child mental health services experiment, 5
  homelessness and, 218
  lesbian identity development, 276–277

Aggression, 239–241

AIDS, 251, 266

Aid to Families with Dependent Children. *See* AFDC

Alcohol consumption, 272, 275, 354–386

Alcohol Use Scale, 329

Anger, schizophrenia and, 42

ASI (Addiction Severity Index)
  barriers to work, 360
  methadone patients' employment experiment, 23, 28, 38
  predicting client incarceration, 196–197
  substance abuse and dual diagnoses, 328
  substance abuse treatment for women, 152

Assertive Community Treatment (ACT), 205–206

Attrition of study subjects, 46–47, 187

Available data
  overview, 417
  recurrence of child maltreatment, 418–442
  social embeddedness and well-being, 459–480
  transracial adoption, 443–458

Barriers
  child mental health services experiment, 4, 12
  children's service systems and, 69–70
  methadone patients' employment experiment, 24–26, 28–29
  recurrence of child maltreatment, 434–437
  to work, 354–386
Behavioral family management (BFM), 42
Behavioral problems, 74–75, 240
BFM (behavioral family management), 42
Bias
  adverse childhood experiences and home-lessness, 221–222, 229–230
  child impoverishment and maltreatment, 404
  effectiveness of juvenile justice programs, 141
  against methadone patients, 21
  perspectives on residential treatment, 318
  substance abuse treatment for women, 155
  transracial adoption, 446, 448
Blacks. *See* African Americans
Brief Psychiatric Rating Scale (BPRS), 196–197

Case control designs
  adverse childhood experiences and home-lessness, 214–233
  defined, 150
  homeless adolescents, 234–252
Case managers/counselors
  child impoverishment and maltreatment, 389
  child mental health services experiment, 5–9, 15
  children's service systems and, 69–70, 74, 81–82
  confidentiality intervention and, 98–121
  effectiveness of juvenile justice programs, 142–143
  homeless adolescents, 239, 249
  lesbian identity development, 270
  methadone patients' employment experiment, 22, 28–29, 36, 39–40
  perspectives on residential treatment, 307–308
  predicting client incarceration, 205
  schizophrenia study and, 44, 58

substance abuse and dual diagnoses, 338–339, 343, 347–348
  sufficiency of in-home care, 176, 179–183, 190
Cause and effect
  directionality and, 149
  for homelessness, 215, 221
CBCL (Child Behavioral Checklist), 74–75
CECA (Childhood Experience of Care and Abuse), 227–228
Center for Epidemiologic Studies Depression scale, 218
Centralized intake process, 109–110, 118
Challenges
  barriers to work, 383–385
  child mental health services, 14–16
  recurrence of child maltreatment, 434–441
  sufficiency of in-home care, 188–191
  transracial adoption, 455–456
Child Behavioral Checklist (CBCL), 74–75
Child care burden, 393, 395
Childhood Experience of Care and Abuse (CECA), 227–228
Child maltreatment
  impoverishment and, 387–415
  recurrence of, 418–442
Child mental health services, 3–19
Child protective service system (CPS), 418–442
Children
  adverse experiences and homelessness, 214–233
  effects of organization climate on, 66–97
  homelessness and, 234–252
  impoverishment and maltreatment of, 387–415
  increasing access to mental health services, 3–19
  perspectives on residential treatment, 302–325
  recurrence of maltreatment, 418–442
  women treated for substance abuse and, 151–170
Chronic Conditions Checklist (OARS), 177
Church, social embeddedness and well-being, 459–460, 462, 466–467
CID (community intervention development) models, 14
CMHS (community mental health services), 42
Coming out
  defined, 255
  lesbian identity development, 260–262, 264–266, 269–270, 276

Communities. *See* neighborhoods
Community Adjustment Form (CAF), 45
Community intervention development (CID)
    models, 14
Community mental health services (CMHS), 42
Community Support Programs (CSPs), 50–51
Compensatory equalization, 37
Compensatory rivalry, 37
Confidentiality
    collaboration and, 98–121
    homeless adolescents, 247–248
    lesbian identity development, 276
    predicting client incarceration, 208–209
Conflict Tactics Scales (CTS), 238–239, 389
Correlational designs. *See* observational studies
Cox Proportional Hazards Model, 425–430
CPS (child protective service system), 418–442
Criminal behavior, 374
Cross-sectional designs
    defined, 149
    substance abuse treatment for women,
        151–170
CSPs (Community Support Programs), 50–51
CTS (Conflict Tactics Scales), 238–239, 389
Cultural considerations
    child impoverishment and maltreatment,
        388–389
    perspectives on residential treatment, 307,
        310–311

Daily Contact Log, 58
Data analysis
    adverse childhood experiences and home-
        lessness, 217–220, 228–230
    barriers to work, 361–362, 381–385
    child impoverishment and maltreatment,
        391–397, 402–403
    children's service systems and, 77–81
    confidentiality intervention and, 103–108
    effectiveness of juvenile justice programs,
        130–135, 144–145
    homeless adolescents, 239–240
    income packaging, 297–298
    lesbian identity development, 274–278
    perspectives on residential treatment, 304,
        317–318
    predicting client incarceration, 197–198
    recurrence of child maltreatment, 425–430
    schizophrenia study, 45–46
    social embeddedness and well-being, 465
    substance abuse and dual diagnoses, 346–347

substance abuse treatment for women,
    156–158
sufficiency of in-home care, 176–179,
    192–193
transracial adoption, 445, 453
Data collection
    effectiveness of juvenile justice programs,
        131–133
    lesbian identity development, 256–257, 276
    methadone patients' employment
        experiment, 23
    missing data and, 149
    perspectives on residential treatment, 303,
        316–317
    predicting client incarceration, 196–197, 210
    recurrence of child maltreatment, 422–423
    sufficiency of in-home care, 175, 187
DD&A (drug addiction and alcoholism),
    354–386
Delinquent behavior
    children's service systems and, 66, 74–75
    effectiveness of juvenile justice programs,
        122–147
Delusions, schizophrenia and, 42
Demographic characteristics
    adverse childhood experiences and home-
        lessness, 215–217
    child mental health services experiment, 5
    children's service systems and, 72–74, 76–77
    confidentiality intervention and, 101–102,
        104–107
    effectiveness of juvenile justice programs,
        125–128
    homeless adolescents, 235–237, 245–246
    income packaging, 281, 283–284, 294–295
    lesbian identity development, 255–256, 275
    methadone patients' employment
        experiment, 24
    perspectives on residential treatment, 303,
        319, 321
    predicting client incarceration, 199–200,
        209–210
    recurrence of child maltreatment,
        421–422, 430
    schizophrenia study, 44–45, 57
    substance abuse and dual diagnoses, 343–345
    substance abuse treatment for women,
        152–156
    sufficiency of in-home care, 174–176
Determinants of Outcome of Severe Mental
    Disorders (DOSMD), 41

Diagnostic Interview Schedule (DIS), 464
Diagnostic Interview Schedule for Children
    (DISC), 237
Differential attrition, 37
Diffusion, 37
Directionality, cause and effect and, 149
DIS (Diagnostic Interview Schedule), 464
DISC (Diagnostic Interview Schedule
    for Children), 237
Discussion
    adverse childhood experiences and home-
        lessness, 220–222
    barriers to work, 370–374
    child impoverishment and maltreatment,
        402–404
    child mental health services experiment, 8–9
    children's service systems and, 81–84
    confidentiality intervention and, 107–111
    effectiveness of juvenile justice programs,
        136–138
    homeless adolescents, 240–241
    income packaging, 290–291
    methadone patients' employment experiment,
        28–30
    perspectives on residential treatment, 309–311
    predicting client incarceration, 201–202
    recurrence of child maltreatment, 430–431
    schizophrenia study, 50–53
    social embeddedness and well-being, 467–469
    substance abuse and dual diagnoses, 327–339
    substance abuse treatment for women,
        159–160
    sufficiency of in-home care, 181–183
    transracial adoption, 447–448
Disorientation, schizophrenia and, 42
Displaced workers
    barriers to work, 355–356
    income packaging, 281–301
Domestic abuse, barriers to work, 360, 368
Donations, ethical issues, 247
DOSMD (Determinants of Outcome of Severe
    Mental Disorders), 41
Drug addiction, barriers to work, 354–386
Drug Use Scale, 329
Dual diagnoses, substance abuse and, 326–351

Earned income tax credit (EITC), 283,
    375n–376n
Education
    barriers to work, 355, 360, 368
    Hollingshead Index of Social Class, 177

interorganizational coordination and, 66
    perspectives on residential treatment, 305
    recurrence of child maltreatment, 420
Effect size
    effectiveness of juvenile justice programs, 124,
        129–135
    schizophrenia study, 46
EITC (earned income tax credit), 283,
    375n–376n
Electronic records, child maltreatment and,
    436–437
Emotional abuse, barriers to work, 360
Employment
    barriers to, 354–386
    income packaging, 281–301
    increasing for methadone patients, 20–40
    schizophrenia study and, 44
    social embeddedness and well-being, 463
    substance abuse and dual diagnoses,
        329, 345
"Entrepreneurial Substance Providers" pattern,
    334–338
Ethical issues
    child impoverishment and maltreatment,
        412–413
    child mental health services experiment,
        16–17
    children's service systems and, 92–93
    confidentiality intervention and, 99
    homeless adolescents, 247–248
    income packaging, 299
    methadone patients' employment experiment,
        38–39
    predicting client incarceration, 208–209
    schizophrenia study, 61
    substance abuse and dual diagnoses, 349–350
    substance abuse treatment for women, 165
    sufficiency of in-home care, 191–192
Ethnicity. *See also* minorities
    child impoverishment and maltreatment,
        388–390, 396
    homelessness and, 218
    schizophrenia study, 41–65
    transracial adoption, 444, 455–456
Ethnographic methods
    child impoverishment and maltreatment,
        393–394, 397–402, 410–411
    defined, 253
    substance abuse and dual diagnoses, 326–351
Existing data, 417
Expanded Brief Psychiatric Rating Scale, 328

Exploration, lesbian identity development, 257, 260, 264, 268–269

Externalizing behavioral problems, 74–75

Families
   barriers to work, 355–356, 360, 373–374
   child impoverishment and maltreatment, 389, 392
   confidentiality intervention and, 98–121
   homeless adolescents, 235, 249–250
   homosexuality and, 259, 263, 267
   income packaging and, 286
   perspectives on residential treatment, 302–325
   recurrence of child maltreatment, 418–442
   social embeddedness and well-being, 459–480
   substance abuse and dual diagnoses, 326, 348

Family Environment Scale (FES), 238, 240

Findings. *See* results

Focus groups
   defined, 253
   perspectives on residential treatment, 302–325

Foster care
   child maltreatment and, 419
   child mental health services experiment, 5
   transracial adoption, 448, 450

Funding
   adverse childhood experiences and home-lessness, 223
   child impoverishment and maltreatment, 411–412
   children's service systems and, 91–92
   homeless adolescents, 242, 248–249
   methadone patients' employment experiment, 33, 40
   predicting client incarceration, 202, 205
   schizophrenia study, 60–61
   substance abuse and dual diagnoses, 339, 348–349
   substance abuse treatment for women, 160

GA (general assistance), 355, 357

Gay liberation era, 257–258, 262–266

Gay rights era, 257–258, 266–269

Gender
   homelessness and, 218
   schizophrenia study, 49–50
   social embeddedness and well-being, 461, 463, 465–469

General assistance (GA), 355, 357

Generalizability, 320–321

Generational differences, lesbian identity development, 255–280

Hallucinations, schizophrenia and, 42

Health Insurance Plan Survey, 462, 474

Hierarchical Linear Modeling (HLM), 45–46, 59–60

Hispanics. *See* Latinos

HLM (Hierarchical Linear Modeling), 45–46, 59–60

Hollingshead Index of Social Class, 177

Homelessness
   adult, 214–233
   children and, 234–252
   preventing, 250
   substance abuse and dual diagnoses, 326

Homosexuality
   attitudes toward, 257–258, 262, 269
   lesbian identity development, 255

Hospitalization
   African Americans and, 42
   schizophrenia study, 49

Housing
   barriers to work, 359–360, 368
   child impoverishment and maltreatment, 392–393

IADL (instrumental activities of daily living), 174, 176–182

ICC (intraclass correlation), 45

ICE (Inventory of Childhood Events), 237–238

Identity formation, lesbian identity develop-ment, 255–280

Immersion, lesbian identity development, 257, 260–262, 264–266, 268–269

Impoverishment, child maltreatment and, 387–415

Incarceration
   barriers to work, 370
   predicting, 194–213
   substance abuse and dual diagnoses, 326

Income assistance, barriers to work, 358, 361–366, 376n

Income packaging, 281–301

Indicators. *See* variables

Informed consent
   substance abuse and dual diagnoses, 349
   substance abuse treatment for women, 165

In-home care, sufficiency of, 171–193

Instability, child impoverishment and maltreatment, 392, 395

Institutional review boards. *See* IRBs
Instrumental activities of daily living (IADL),
    174, 176–182
Instrumentation. *See* measurement
Intensive Supervision and Parole
    (ISP), 206
Intent to treat design, 39–40
Internalizing behavioral problems, 74–75
International Pilot Study of Schizophrenia
    (IPSS), 41
Interorganizational coordination, children's
    service systems and, 66–97
Interpersonal Problem-Solving (IPS), 22, 35
Intervention
    child homelessness, 234
    child maltreatment and, 418–420
    child mental health services experiment, 3–4,
        6–9, 12–15
    confidentiality, 104–105
    effectiveness of juvenile justice programs,
        133–135
    homeless adolescents, 249
    methadone patients' employment experiment,
        22, 25, 40
Intraclass correlation (ICC), 45
Inventory of Childhood Events (ICE),
    237–238, 240
IPS (Interpersonal Problem-Solving), 22, 35
IPSS (International Pilot Study of
    Schizophrenia), 41
IRBs (institutional review boards)
    barriers to work, 381
    effectiveness of juvenile justice programs,
        145–146
    qualitative studies and, 254
    schizophrenia study, 61
    substance abuse and dual diagnoses, 349
Irrelevant speech, schizophrenia and, 42
ISP (Intensive Supervision and Parole), 206

Job skills, barriers to work and, 360,
    368–370
Juvenile justice
    interorganizational coordination and, 66
    program effectiveness, 122–147

Lack of care, homelessness and, 217–222,
    228, 235
Latinos
    child impoverishment and maltreatment,
        389–390

child mental health services experiment, 5
effectiveness of juvenile justice programs, 123
perspectives on residential treatment, 307
schizophrenia study, 42–44, 46–50, 52, 58–59
social embeddedness and well-being, 462
Lesbian identity development, 255–280
LISREL (linear structured equation analysis),
    77, 81
Longitudinal designs
    defined, 149
    homeless adolescents, 241
    income packaging, 281–301
    predicting client incarceration, 194–213
    recurrence of child maltreatment, 434–435
    sufficiency of in-home care, 171–193

Marriage, social embeddedness and, 463
Measurement
    adverse childhood experiences and home-
        lessness, 217, 227–228, 230–232
    barriers to work, 358–359
    child mental health services experiment, 8
    children's service systems and, 74–81
    confidentiality intervention and, 102–103,
        120–121
    homeless adolescents, 236–239, 246–247
    methadone patients' employment
        experiment, 38
    recurrence of child maltreatment, 424, 430
    schizophrenia study, 45, 62
    social embeddedness and well-being, 462–464
    substance abuse treatment for women,
        153–155, 165–168
    sufficiency of in-home care, 172
Medicaid, 283, 359
Medical Expenditure Panel Survey (MEPS), 474
Medical-Pharmaceutical (MP) Model, 14
Medication usage
    minorities and, 42
    perspectives on residential treatment,
        306–307, 309–310
    schizophrenia study, 50
Men, social embeddedness and, 461, 463,
    465–469
Mental health
    barriers to work, 356, 368–371
    social embeddedness and well-being, 461–462
Mental Health Inventory (MHI), 463–464,
    477–478
Mental health services
    barriers to work, 370

child, 3–19
interorganizational coordination and, 66
minorities and, 42
predicting client incarceration, 194–213
social embeddedness and well-being, 472–474
Mentors, 461
MEPS (Medical Expenditure Panel Survey), 474
Meta-analysis
defined, 124
effectiveness of juvenile justice programs,
122–147
Methadone maintenance treatment programs
(MMTPs), 20–40, 153
Method
adverse childhood experiences and homelessness, 215–218
barriers to work, 357–362
child impoverishment and maltreatment,
391–394
child mental health services experiment, 4–8
children's service systems and, 72–77
confidentiality intervention and, 101–104
effectiveness of juvenile justice programs,
125–128
homeless adolescents, 235–239
income packaging, 283–284
lesbian identity development, 256–257
methadone patients' employment experiment,
21–23
perspectives on residential treatment, 303–304
predicting client incarceration, 195–197
recurrence of child maltreatment, 421–425
schizophrenia study, 43–46
social embeddedness and well-being, 462–465
substance abuse and dual diagnoses, 327–339,
343–345
substance abuse treatment for women,
154–157
sufficiency of in-home care, 174–179
transracial adoption, 444–446
MHI (Mental Health Inventory), 463–464,
477–478
Minorities. *See also* ethnicity
effectiveness of juvenile justice programs,
122–147
schizophrenia study and, 41–43
Mixed methods
barriers to work, 354–386
child impoverishment and maltreatment,
387–415
overview, 353

MMTPs (methadone maintenance treatment
programs), 20–40, 153
MP (Medical-Pharmaceutical) Model, 14
Multiethnic Placement Act (1994), 448

NASW (National Association of Social
Workers), 98
National Association of Black Social Workers,
443, 450
National Association of Social Workers
(NASW), 98
National Child Abuse and Neglect Data
System, 418
National Family Violence Study, 389
National Institute of Mental Health (NIMH)
children's service systems and, 68, 70–71
FIRST Award, 60–61
social embeddedness and well-being, 474
National Institute on Drug Abuse (NIDA),
33–34
National Medical Expenditure Survey (NMES),
462–463, 474–480
Neighborhoods
child impoverishment and maltreatment,
387–415
social embeddedness and well-being,
459–480
transracial adoption, 444
NIDA (National Institute on Drug Abuse), 33–34
NMES (National Medical Expenditure Survey),
462–463, 474–480

OARS instrument, 176–177
Observational studies
adverse childhood experiences and homelessness, 214–233
homeless adolescents, 234–252
predicting client incarceration, 194–213
substance abuse treatment for women,
151–170
sufficiency of in-home care, 171–193
Organizational climate, effects on children's
service systems, 66–97
Outcome measurement. *See* measurement

Peers
homosexuality and, 259, 263
social embeddedness and well-being, 461
substance abuse and dual diagnoses, 326
Personal Responsibility and Work Opportunity
Reconciliation Act (1996), 281

Physical abuse
    adverse childhood experiences and
        homelessness, 218–221
    barriers to work, 360, 368, 370
Physical health, barriers to work, 360, 368–371
Pilot studies
    child mental health services, 15
    children's service systems, 70–71
    methadone patients' employment experiment,
        33, 39
    perspectives on residential treatment, 319
    schizophrenia study, 56–57
Poverty
    child impoverishment and maltreatment,
        389–390, 392, 395
    social embeddedness and well-being, 463
Pre-Stonewall era, 257–262, 270
Probation, predicting client incarceration study,
    194–213
Problem-solving
    methadone patients' employment experiment,
        20–40
    training in, 15
Prostitution, 234
Protocol deviation, 37
Psychiatric probation and parole service,
    194–213
Psychosocial rehabilitation, 41–65

QDIS (Quick Diagnostic Interview Schedule),
    196, 198, 209
Qualitative methods
    barriers to work, 354–386
    child impoverishment and maltreatment,
        387–415
    income packaging, 281–301
    lesbian identity development, 255–280
    in mixed methods, 353
    overview, 253–254
    perspectives on residential treatment, 302–325
    substance abuse and dual diagnoses, 326–351
Quality of care for in-home care, 171–193
Quality of Life Interview (QOLI), 328,
    335–337
Quantitative methods
    barriers to work, 354–386
    child impoverishment and maltreatment,
        387–415
    in mixed methods, 353
Quasi-experimental designs
    confidentiality intervention, 98–121

effects on children's service systems, 66–97
schizophrenia study, 41–65
Quick Diagnostic Interview Schedule (QDIS),
    196, 198, 209

Race
    child impoverishment and maltreatment,
        388–391, 396
    perspectives on residential treatment, 307
    transracial adoption, 443–458
Rand Health Insurance Experiment, 463
Randomization
    child mental health services experiment, 3–19
    methadone patients' employment experiment,
        41–66
    substance abuse and dual diagnoses, 342
Recruitment
    income packaging, 295
    methadone patients' employment
        experiment, 34
    perspectives on residential treatment,
        315–316, 321
    predicting client incarceration, 195–196, 210
Reflexivity, 319–320
Rehabilitation, schizophrenia study and, 44
Research methods
    challenges with, 15–16
    effectiveness of juvenile justice programs,
        126–127, 140–145
    predicting client incarceration, 205–207
    substance abuse treatment for women,
        163–165
    sufficiency of in-home care, 172–174,
        186–188
"Reservation wage" effect, 282
Residential treatment, perspectives on, 302–325
Responsibility
    children's service systems and, 76
    perspectives on residential treatment,
        308, 311
Responsiveness, children's service systems
    and, 75
Results
    adverse childhood experiences
        and homelessness, 218–220
    barriers to work, 362–370
    child impoverishment and maltreatment,
        394–402
    child mental health services experiment, 8
    children's service systems and, 77–81
    confidentiality intervention and, 104–107

homeless adolescents, 239–240

income packaging, 285–290

lesbian identity development, 257–269

methadone patients' employment experiment, 23–28

perspectives on residential treatment, 304–308

predicting client incarceration, 198–201

recurrence of child maltreatment, 426–430

schizophrenia study, 46–50

social embeddedness and well-being, 465–467, 478–479

substance abuse treatment for women, 157–158, 168–169

transracial adoption, 446–447

Retention of study subjects, 8, 187

Risk assessment, 420–421

Robert Wood Johnson Foundation, 68, 380

Role Functioning Scale (RFS), 45

Safety

homeless adolescents and, 247

perspectives on residential treatment, 309

Sample. See demographic characteristics

Schedule for Affective Disorders and Schizophrenia (SADS), 45

Schizophrenia

family contact and, 99

psychosocial rehabilitation for, 41–65

SCOS (Strauss and Carpenter Outcome Scale), 45, 47

Separation, residential treatment and, 306, 309

Service Utilization Review, 328

Setting. See site selection

Sexual abuse, 218–221, 420

SGA (substantial gainful activity), 359, 361–363, 366–372

Shaw, E. Clay, Jr., 354

Short Blessed Mental Status exam, 177

Site selection

barriers to work, 362

children's service systems and, 72–73

confidentiality intervention and, 101, 116–117

income packaging, 283

lesbian identity development, 256

methadone patients' employment experiment, 34–35

predicting client incarceration, 196, 207

schizophrenia study, 49, 59–61

substance abuse and dual diagnoses, 342–345

Small Business Job Protection Act (1996), 448

SNI (Social Network Interview), 238

Social embeddedness, 459–480

Social functioning

drug use, employment and, 20

schizophrenia study, 48–50

substance abuse and dual diagnoses, 326–351

Social Network Interview (SNI), 238

Social Security Administration (SSA), 359, 377n, 379–380

Social Security Disability Insurance, 375n, 379, 382

Socioeconomic status

child impoverishment and maltreatment, 389

Hollingshead Index of Social Class, 177

homelessness and, 218

social embeddedness and well-being, 460

"Solitary User" pattern, 330–331, 336–338

SSA (Social Security Administration), 359, 377n, 379–380

SSI (Supplemental Security Income), 354–386

State custody, children in, 66, 71

Statistical analyses. See data analysis

Stereotyping, residential treatment and, 307–308, 310–311

Stonewall Riots (1969), 258

Strauss and Carpenter Outcome Scale (SCOS), 45, 47

"Street Corner Clique" pattern, 331–332, 336–338

Structured Clinical Interview, 328

Study process

barriers to work, 381–383

child impoverishment and maltreatment, 408–411

child mental health services experiment, 14–15

children's service systems and, 74–76, 83

homeless adolescents, 244–245

income packaging, 294–299

lesbian identity development, 273–277

methadone patients' employment experiment, 26, 36

perspectives on residential treatment, 303, 314–315

predicting client incarceration, 211–212

recurrence of child maltreatment, 421, 434–441

schizophrenia study, 62

social embeddedness and well-being, 477–478

substance abuse treatment for women, 153

transracial adoption, 451–455

Study strengths/limitations
  adverse childhood experiences and
      homelessness, 221–222
  child impoverishment and maltreatment, 414
  child mental health services experiment, 17
  children's service systems and, 94–95
  effectiveness of juvenile justice programs,
      146–147
  homeless adolescents, 241, 250–251
  lesbian identity development, 279
  methadone patients' employment
      experiment, 39
  perspectives on residential treatment, 311
  schizophrenia study, 63
  social embeddedness and well-being, 461
  substance abuse and dual diagnoses, 350
  sufficiency of in-home care, 193
  transracial adoption, 445–446, 455–457
Substance abuse
  barriers to work, 356, 360, 367–371
  dual diagnoses and, 326–351
  homeless adolescents and, 247
  homelessness and, 234
  women with children and, 151–170
Substance Abuse Treatment Scale, 329
Substantial gainful activity. *See* SGA
Supplemental Security Income (SSI), 354–386
Survey of American Indian and Alaskan Natives
    (SAIAN), 462

TANF (Temporary Assistance for Needy
    Families), 355–357, 370, 375n–376n
Tattoos, 377n
Teacher Report Form (TRF), 74–75
Temporary Assistance for Needy Families
    (TANF), 355–356, 370, 375n–376n
Time-Line Follow-Back, 328
Training
  child mental health services experiment, 15
  confidentiality intervention and, 100–101
  homeless adolescents, 239
  methadone patients' employment experiment,
      21–23, 36
  perspectives on residential treatment, 310–311
  sufficiency of in-home care, 190
Transferability, 320–321
Transportation, barriers to work, 360, 368–370
Transracial adoption, 443–458
Treatment outcomes
  children's service systems, 66–97

  confidentiality intervention and, 120–121
  effectiveness of juvenile justice programs,
      125–128, 130–135
  impact of ethnicity on, 41–65
  schizophrenia study, 47–50, 58–63
  substance abuse treatment for women,
      153–154
Treatment Services Review (TSR), 23
TRF (Teacher Report Form), 74–75
TSR (Treatment Services Review), 23
Type III error, 230–232

Underemployment, 281–301, 355
Unemployment
  barriers to work, 367, 370
  child impoverishment and maltreatment, 392
  income packaging and, 282
Uniform Client Data Inventory, 328
"User Syndicate" pattern, 333–334, 336–338

Validity
  recurrence of child maltreatment, 430–431
  schizophrenia study, 62
  substance abuse and dual diagnoses, 345
Variables
  barriers to work, 361–362, 367, 373–374
  child impoverishment and maltreatment,
      392–397
  children's service systems and, 67, 79
  effectiveness of juvenile justice programs,
      130–135
  homeless adolescents, 234–252
  methadone patients' employment
      experiment, 28
  predicting client incarceration, 197–201, 211
  recurrence of child maltreatment, 419–421,
      424–430
  relationships between, 149
  schizophrenia study, 63
  social embeddedness and well-being, 462–467
  substance abuse treatment for women, 156,
      166–168
  sufficiency of in-home care, 176–178
  transracial adoption, 445–447, 451–452
VEA (Vocational/Educational Assessment), 23
Violence, child impoverishment and
    maltreatment, 389, 400–402
Vocational/Educational Assessment (VEA), 23
VPSS (Vocational Problem-Solving Skills),
    21–22, 28–29, 32, 35–36

Welfare
  barriers to work, 355–357, 370, 376*n*
  income packaging and, 281–301
  interorganizational coordination and, 66
  substance abuse treatment for women, 159
Well-being, social embeddedness and, 459–480
Whites
  child impoverishment and maltreatment,
    389–391, 393–397, 402–404
  child mental health services experiment, 5
  effectiveness of juvenile justice programs, 123,
    136–137

income packaging, 284
social embeddedness and well-being, 459–480
transracial adoption, 446
Women
  physical abuse and, 218–219
  social embeddedness and well-being, 461,
    463, 465–469
  substance abuse treatment for, 151–170
Work-retention rates, barriers to work, 358,
  365–366
World Health Organization (WHO), 41